MOON HANDBOOKS®

FIJI

Rotuma

To Viti Levu
(Approx. 600 km)

SOUTH PACIFIC OCEAN

Kia

Macuata-i-Wai

Yaqaga

Va
Le

Yalewa Kalou

Yasawa
Group

Yasawa

Yadua

▲ Seseleka (421 m)

Navotuvotu
(842 m) ▲

Tavewa

Nacula

Yaduatabu

Bua Bay

Na
Sonisoni

Matacawa Levu

Nabouwalu

Yaqeta

Bligh Water

Viwa

Naviti

Namenala

Nananu-i-Ra

Vatu-i-Cake

Makodroga

Mamanuca
Group

Waya

Malake

Nananu-i-
Cake

Wayasewa

Naigani

Mako

Tomaniivi
(Mt. Victoria)
(1,323 m)

Mt. Tova
(647 m)

Yanuya

Lautoka

Tavua

▲ Koroyanitu
(1,195 m)

Natovi

Wa

Mana

Ovalau

Malolo

Viti Levu

Moturiki

Malololailai

Nadi Bay

Nadi River

Nadi

▲
Koroba
(1,076 m)

Monavatu
(1,131 m) ▲

Tuvutau
(Mt. Gordon)
(933 m) ▲

Mt. Voma
(927 m) ▲

Rewa River

Nausori

Ba

Coral Coast

Navua River

Pacific
Harbor

Suva ✪

Yanuca

Beqa

Vatulele

Kadavu Passage

Solo

Dravuni

Bulia

Ono

Matanuku

Kadavu

0   25 mi

0   25 km

MOON

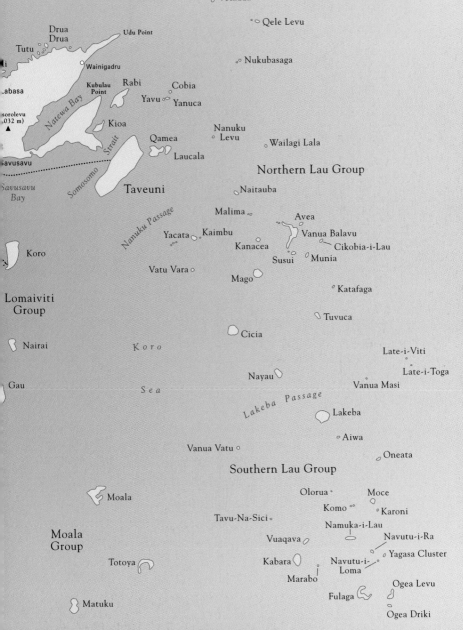

THE FIJI ISLANDS

Cikobia

Vetauua

Qele Levu

Nukubasaga

Drua
Drua
Udu Point
Tutu
Wainigadru
Kubulau
Labasa
Rabi
Point
Cobia
Yavu
Yanuca
Kioa
Nanuku
Qamea
Levu
Wailagi Lala
Laucala
Northern Lau Group
Taveuni
Naitauba
Malima
Avea
Yacata
Kaimbu
Vanua Balavu
Kanacea
Cikobia-i-Lau
Koro
Susui
Munia
Vatu Vara
Mago
Katafaga
Lomaiviti
Group
Tuvuca
Nairai
Koro
Cicia
Late-i-Viti
Sea
Late-i-Toga
Gau
Nayau
Vanua Masi
Lakeba Passage
Lakeba
Aiwa
Vanua Vatu
Oneata
Southern Lau Group
Moala
Olorua
Moce
Komo
Karoni
Tavu-Na-Sici
Namuka-i-Lau
Moala
Vuaqava
Navutu-i-Ra
Group
Kabara
Yagasa Cluster
Navutu-i-
Totoya
Loma
Marabo
Ogea Levu
Fulaga
Matuku
Ogea Driki

Natewa Bay
Somosomo Strait
Savusavu
Savusavu
Bay
Nanuku Passage
sorolevu
.032 m)

VITI LEVU

Bligh *Water*

Waya Island

Wayasewa Island

○ White Rock

Navadra Island

Vomolailai Island

Vomo Island

Nacilau Point

Vatia Point

Tavua

Vatukoula

Nadariv

Ba

Nadariv

★ LOLOLO PINE SCHEME

Yanuya Island

Saweni Beach

Lautoka

Mount Evans Range

Koroyanitu ▲ (1,195 m)

Abaca

Navala

Koro

River

Nac

Mana Island

Beachcomber Island

Treasure Island

Anchorage Beach

Navini Island

Nadi *Bay*

SHERATON HOTEL

Nadi

VATURU DAM

Bukuya

Nanoko

Nubutautau

Na

Castaway Island

Malolo Island

Malololailai Island

Mamanuca Group

Nadi *River*

Nausori Highland

Tubarua

Korolevu

Tavarua Island ○

Koroba (1,076 m)

River

Viti

Levu

Isla

Momi Bay

SEASHELL COVE RESORT ■

○ Tau

Sigatoka *River*

Tuvutau (Mt. Gordon) ▲ (933 m)

Mona (1,13

Lomawai

Robinson Crusoe Island

Natadola Beach

Cuvu

Sigatoka

Korotogo

Navua *River*

Nabukelevu

N

THE FIJIAN HOTEL

QUEENS

Korolevu

TAMBUA SANDS

HIDEAWAY RESORT

RD.

BEACHOUSE

THE NAVITI

THE WARWICK

CRUSOE'S RETREAT

WAIDROKA BAY RESORT

Se Isl

Coral Coast

To Nabouwalu

To Nabouwalu

Nananu-i-Ra Island

Volivoli
Point

Malake Island

Nananu-i-Cake
Island

Vatu Ira
Island

ELLINGTON WHARF

Rakiraki

KINGS RD.

Vaileka

Viti
Levu
Bay

Nanukuloa

Naiserelagi

Barotu

Nakauvadra Range

Dama

Mt. Tova
(647 m)

Rokovuaka

Nataleira

Naigani
Island

Tomaniivi
(Mt. Victoria)
(1,323 m)

Nyavu

Natovi

Ovalau
Island

Levuka

Koro-Ni-O

Wainibuka River

BURETA AIRPORT

MONASAVU
DAM

Wainimala

River

Wailotua

Moturiki
Island

Balea

Naitauvoli

Korovou

Leleuvia
Island

Rewa River

Vunidawa

Waidalice

Nasava

Viwa
Island

Toberua Island

ainikoroiluva
River

vai

Waidina River

Wainimakutu

Baulevu

Bau Island

To Savusavu
and Taveuni

Navunikabi

Namosi

Waimanu River

Nausori

Mt. Voma
(927 m)

Colo-i-Suva

Namuamua

Nasilai
Point

Nabukayesi

Laucala
Bay

Suva

Nua River

Mau

Suva
Harbor

Nukulau
Island

Pacific
Harbor

Navua

Deuba

aloa

0   10 mi

0   10 km

To Kadavu

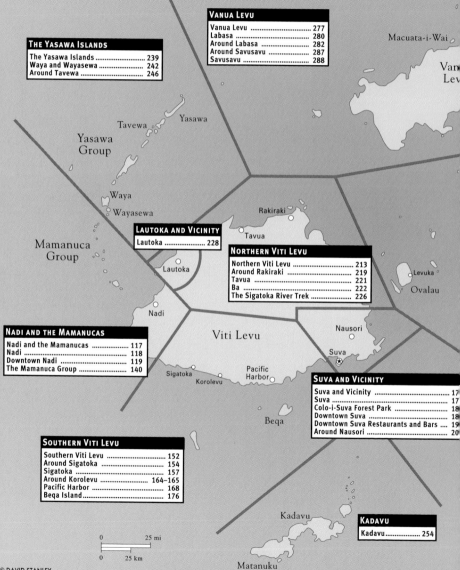

COLOR SECTION

The Fiji Islands
Viti Levu

INTRODUCTION/EXPLORING THE ISLANDS

Western Polynesia 3
Fiji: Political Divisions 31
South Pacific Air Routes 86
Air Pacific Flight Routes 89
Air Routes in Fiji 108

THE YASAWA ISLANDS

The Yasawa Islands 239
Waya and Wayasewa 242
Around Tavewa 246

VANUA LEVU

Vanua Levu 277
Labasa 280
Around Labasa 282
Around Savusavu 287
Savusavu 288

LAUTOKA AND VICINITY
Lautoka 228

NORTHERN VITI LEVU

Northern Viti Levu 213
Around Rakiraki 219
Tavua 221
Ba 222
The Sigatoka River Trek 226

NADI AND THE MAMANUCAS

Nadi and the Mamanucas 117
Nadi 118
Downtown Nadi 119
The Mamanuca Group 140

SUVA AND VICINITY

Suva and Vicinity 17
Suva 17
Colo-i-Suva Forest Park 18
Downtown Suva 18
Downtown Suva Restaurants and Bars 19
Around Nausori 20

SOUTHERN VITI LEVU

Southern Viti Levu 152
Around Sigatoka 154
Sigatoka 157
Around Korolevu 164–165
Pacific Harbor 168
Beqa Island 176

KADAVU
Kadavu 254

Macuata-i-Wai

Van
Lev

Tavewa   Yasawa

Yasawa
Group

Waya
Wayasewa

Mamanuca
Group

Rakiraki

Tavua

Lautoka

Nadi

Levuka

Ovalau

Viti Levu

Nausori

Suva

Pacific
Harbor

Sigatoka
Korolevu

Beqa

Kadavu

Matanuku

0   25 mi

0   25 km

© DAVID STANLEY

MAPS

MAP SYMBOLS

═══	Paved Road	•	Accommodation
═ ═ ═	Unpaved Road	▼	Restaurant/Bar
⊢─⊣─	Railroad	⅃	Golf Course
··········	Ferry	Λ	Campground
─ ─ ─	Trail	▲	Mountain
✕ ✕	Airport/Airstrip	🝆	Reef
⊛	National Capital	〰	Waterfall
○	City/Town	🝆	Marsh
★	Point of Interest	🝆	Mangrove
		■	Other Location

Labasa

Savusavu

Taveuni

Northern Lau Group

TAVEUNI

Taveuni	301
Matei Airport Area	304

Vanua Balavu

Koro

Mago

Lomaiviti Group

Cicia

THE LAU GROUP AND ROTUMA

The Lau Group and Rotuma	318
Vanua Balavu Island	319
Cicia	321
Lakeba Island	323
Moala	324
Rotuma	326

Gau

THE LOMAIVITI GROUP

The Lomaiviti Group	261
Ovalau Island	262
Levuka	263
Gau Island	273
Koro Island	274

Lakeba

Southern Lau Group

Rotuma   PACIFIC

OCEAN

Moala

Moala Group

The Lau Group

MOON HANDBOOKS®

FIJI

SEVENTH EDITION

DAVID STANLEY

AVALON
TRAVEL

Contents

Introduction 1

Fiji is an island escape and more, with a rich mixture of land- and seascapes, diverse cultures, and experiences found nowhere else. Dive beneath serene waters to explore vivid coral reefs. Laze on an isolated beach. Or drink kava at an open-air market. At this crossroads of the South Pacific, all visitors are welcomed with a hearty bula *(hello).*

The Land **2**; Flora and Fauna **11**; History and Government **16**; Economy **33**; The People **39**; Customs **44**

Exploring the Islands 49

Here's everything you'll need to know for the real Fiji experience, including the best diving and surfing sites, local food specialties, village dos and don'ts, booking tips, and island hopping options.

Highlights **49**; Sports and Recreation **52**; Entertainment **56**; Public Holidays and Festivals **57**; Arts and Crafts **57**; Shopping **59**; Accommodations **59**; Food **66**; Tourist Information **68**; Visas and Officialdom **69**; Money **70**; Communications **71**; Media **74**; Health and Safety **75**; What to Take **80**; Time and Measurements **84**; Getting There **85**; Getting Around **107**; Airports **113**

Nadi and the Mamanucas 115

As Fiji's airport town, Nadi is where most visitors hear their first bula. *The colorful marketplace, with its* yaqona *stalls and homemade souvenirs, showcases local culture, and tourist enterprises are everywhere. Nadi is also the gateway for the resort-heavy Mamanuca Group, where sun-soaking options include laid-back surfer camps and exclusive hideaways.*

NADI 116
  Downtown; Wailoaloa Beach; Denarau Marina; Toward the Airport; North of
  Nadi; South of Nadi
THE MAMANUCA GROUP 139
  Malololailai Island; Malolo Island; The Surfing Camps; The Tiny Islands; Mana
  Island; The Outer Islands

Southern Viti Levu 151

Known as the Coral Coast for its fringing reef, southwestern Viti Levu is lined with resorts that offer sun worship and more—hiking and rafting are close by. Farther east, Pacific Harbor offers access to diving, fishing, and kayaking; offshore, serious surfers tackle Frigate Passage's rushing wave.

THE CORAL COAST 152
  Natadola and Robinson Crusoe; The Fijian and Vicinity; Sigatoka Sand Dunes;
  Kulukulu; Sigatoka; Korotogo; Korolevu
PACIFIC HARBOR AND VICINITY 167
  Pacific Harbor; Navua
ISLANDS OFF SOUTHERN VITI LEVU 174
  Vatulele Island; Yanuca Island; Beqa Island

Suva and Vicinity 177

Cosmopolitan Suva is Fiji's pulsing heart. There's no beach, but with hot nightspots, an international dining scene, and the Fiji Museum to explore, you'll hardly need one. Just outside the teeming city, the natural environment persists in Colo-i-Suva Park's pools and green forests.

Central Suva; South Suva; University of the South Pacific; Northwest of Suva;
Colo-i-Suva Forest Park

NAUSORI AND BEYOND 206
Nausori; East of Nausori; Northwest of Nausori; The Trans–Viti Levu Trek

Northern Viti Levu 212

A drive up the Banana Highway offers glimpses of the island's lush interior and stunning "Sunshine Coast." Hop over to Nananu-i-Ra Island for lovely beaches, reefs, and water-kissed moonrises. Or, head to the little-visited Sigatoka River for a spectacular hiking trek.

NORTHEASTERN VITI LEVU 213
Korovou and the Tailevu Coast; Kings Road to Viti Levu Bay; Near Ellington Wharf; Nananu-i-Ra Island; Rakiraki

NORTHWESTERN VITI LEVU 220
Tavua; Vatukoula; Ba

INTO THE INTERIOR 223
Nausori Highlands; Nadarivatu and Beyond; The Sigatoka River Trek

Lautoka and Vicinity 227

Symbols of the area's large Indo-Fijian community— from Jame Mosque to Sri Krishna Kaliya Temple—dot the landscape of Fiji's likeable second city. To the east, Koroyanitu National Heritage Park preserves the islands' only unlogged cloud forest.

Lautoka; Koroyanitu National Heritage Park

The Yasawa Islands 237

Affordable resorts offer basic amenities on Fiji's most magnificent island chain, known for its rough-hewn beauty. Jungle-covered mountains taper down to isolated shores and turquoise water, where mellow travelers sunbathe on white beaches. The more adventurous hike Wayasewa's volcanic peak or snorkel in the Blue Lagoon.

Kuata Island; Wayasewa Island; Waya Island; Naviti Island; Tavewa Island; Nacula Island; Around the Blue Lagoon; Sawa-i-Lau Island; Yasawa Island

Kadavu 253

The underwater caves and abundant marinelife of the Great Astrolabe Reef attract divers from all over the world. On shore, sleepy villages are scattered alongside untouched beaches, and rainforested hilltops come alive with the chatter of musk parrots and the roar of waterfalls.

Vunisea; West of Vunisea; The Great Astrolabe Reef

The Lomaiviti Group 260

On Ovalau Island, Fiji's former capital keeps the country's vivid history alive in its artifact-filled museums, war monuments, and century-old wooden storefronts. The other islands in this volcanic group offer back-packer resorts and coconut tree–lined beaches far from the tourist track.

OVALAU ISLAND 261
Levuka

ISLANDS OFF OVALAU 271
Caqalai Island; Leleuvia Island; Moturiki Island; Naigani Island; Yanuca Lailai Island

OTHER ISLANDS OF THE LOMAIVITI GROUP 272
Batiki Island; Gau Island; Koro Island; Makogai Island; Nairai Island; Wakaya Island

Vanua Levu 276

Experience real Fijian life in the heart of the "friendly north." Two scenic highways sweep across the island: One travels through lush headlands; the other—the Hibiscus Highway—snakes along the verdant coast. To the south, corals and giant clams inhabit the waters off Namenalala, where hawksbill turtles lay their eggs on golden sands.

WESTERN VANUA LEVU 278
Nabouwalu; East of Nabouwalu; The Road to Labasa; Nukubati Island

LABASA AND VICINITY 280
Around Labasa; Natewa Bay and Udu Point

SAVUSAVU AND VICINITY 286
Savusavu; Namenalala Island

BUCA BAY AND RABI 294
Along the Hibiscus Highway; Kioa Island; Rabi Island

Taveuni 300

Considered Fiji's finest island by both locals and in-the-know travelers, Taveuni thrives with colorful plants and wildlife that's near extinction elsewhere. On land, magnificent cascades pour down steep slopes, while at sea, turtles, fish, and soft corals make for world-famous diving sites.

NORTHERN TAVEUNI 303

EASTERN TAVEUNI 308
Bouma National Heritage Park; Lavena

CENTRAL TAVEUNI 310
Around Somosomo

SOUTHERN TAVEUNI 313

ISLANDS OFF TAVEUNI 315
Qamea Island; Matangi Island; Laucala Island

The Lau Group and Rotuma 317

Free from almost all commercial trappings, these most remote islands are the getaway of getaways, where tranquility reigns over undisturbed natural splendor. It's no wonder that legendary deities and chieftains of old chose to spend eternity in these pacific reaches.

NORTHERN LAU 318
Vanua Balavu Island; Other Islands of Northern Lau

SOUTHERN LAU 322
Lakeba Island; Other Islands of Southern Lau

ROTUMA 325

Resources 329

GLOSSARY 330

BASIC FIJIAN 334

BASIC HINDI 335
SUGGESTED READING 336
INTERNET RESOURCES 343
INDEX 345

SPELLING AND PRONUNCIATION

When early British missionaries created a system of written Fijian in the middle of the 19th century, they established a unique set of orthographic rules that are followed to this day. In an attempt to represent the sounds of spoken Fijian more precisely, they rendered "mb" as *b*, "nd" as *d*, "ng" as *g*, "ngg" as *q*, and "th" as *c*. Thus Beqa is pronounced Mbengga, Nadi is Nandi, Sigatoka is Singatoka, Cicia is Thithia, etc. In order to be able pronounce Fijian names and words correctly, visitors must take a few minutes to learn these pronunciation rules. Turn to Basic Fijian in the back of the book for more information.

ABOUT THE AUTHOR
David Stanley

David Stanley has spent much of the past three decades on the road. He has crossed six continents overland and visited 178 of the planet's 245 countries and territories. His travel guidebooks to the South Pacific, Micronesia, Alaska, Eastern Europe, and Cuba opened those areas to independent travelers for the first time.

For his first trip across the Pacific in 1978, Stanley bought the longest ticket ever issued in Canada by Pan American Airways. Since then he has returned many times, visiting and revisiting the islands. His career as a travel writer began with the letters he wrote to Bill Dalton and Tony Wheeler, the pioneers of budget travel to Asia in the 1970s. That feedback soon led to guides of his own. With over a million copies sold, he's still on the road researching guidebooks.

Though Stanley has traveled widely and become a specialist on many parts of the world, he always keeps returning to his favorite area, the South Pacific. One of the biggest treats for a guidebook writer is meeting people who are using the writer's book. Stanley researches his books incognito, and the "Mystery Shopper" approach means he can't always admit who he is, but it's still fun hearing what unsuspecting readers think of his guidebook. Also the author of *Moon Handbooks South Pacific* and *Moon Handbooks Tahiti*, Stanley enjoys receiving mail from those who have used his guides. His website www.southpacific.org provides contact details.

Introduction

Once notorious as the "Cannibal Isles," Fiji is now the colorful crossroads of the South Pacific. Of the 322 islands that make up the Fiji group, more than 100 are inhabited by a rich mixture of exuberant Melanesians, Indo-Fijians, Polynesians, Micronesians, Chinese, and Europeans, each with a cuisine and culture of their own. Here Melanesia mixes with Polynesia, ancient India with the Pacific, and tradition with the modern world in a unique blend.

Fiji preserves an amazing variety of traditional customs and crafts such as kava or *yaqona* drinking,

the presentation of the whale's tooth, firewalking, fish driving, turtle calling, tapa beating, and pottery making. Alongside this fascinating human history is a dramatic diversity of landforms and seascapes, all concentrated in a relatively small area. Fiji's sun-drenched beaches, blue lagoons, panoramic open hillsides, lush rainforests, and dazzling reefs are truly magnificent.

Fiji offers posh resorts, good food and accommodations, nightlife, historic sites, outer-island living, hiking, kayaking, camping, surfing, snorkeling, and scuba diving. Traveling

© DAVID STANLEY

is easy by small plane, interisland catamaran, car ferry, local cargo boat, outboard canoe, open-sided bus, and air-conditioned coach. With even a month at your disposal, you'll barely scratch the surface of all there is to see and do.

Best of all, Fiji is a visitor-friendly country with uncrowded, inexpensive facilities available almost everywhere. You'll love the vibrant, outgoing people whose knowledge of English makes communicating a breeze. In a word, Fiji is a traveler's country *par excellence,* and whatever your budget, Fiji gives you good value for your money and plenty of ways to spend it. *Bula,* welcome to Fiji, everyone's favorite South Pacific country.

The Land

Fiji lies 5,100 kilometers southwest of Hawaii and 3,150 kilometers northeast of Sydney, astride the main air route between North America and Australia. Nadi is the hub of Pacific air routes, while Suva is a regional shipping center. The 180th meridian cuts through Fiji, but the international date line swings east so the entire group can share the same day.

The name Fiji is a Tongan corruption of the indigenous name "Viti." The Fiji Islands are arrayed in a horseshoe configuration with Viti Levu (great Fiji) and adjacent islands on the west, Vanua Levu (great land) and Taveuni to the north, and the Lau Group on the east. This upside-down-U-shaped archipelago encloses the Koro Sea, which is relatively shallow and sprinkled with the Lomaiviti, or central Fiji, group of islands. Together the Fiji Islands are scattered over 1,290,000 square kilometers of the South Pacific Ocean.

If every single island were counted, the isles of the Fiji archipelago would number in the thousands. However, a mere 322 are judged large enough for human habitation, and of those only 106 are inhabited. That leaves 216 uninhabited islands, most of them prohibitively isolated or lacking fresh water.

Most of the Fiji Islands are volcanic oceanic islands. All of Fiji's volcanoes are presently dormant or extinct, although Vuna on Taveuni and Nabukelevu on Kadavu are classified as dormant as they've both erupted within the past 2,000 years. There are as many as 50 groups of hot springs. The two largest islands, Viti Levu and Vanua Levu, together account for 87 percent of Fiji's 18,272 square kilometers of land. Viti Levu has 57 percent of the land area and 75 percent of the people, while Vanua Levu, with 30 percent of the land, has 18 percent of the population. Viti Levu alone is bigger than all five archipelagos of

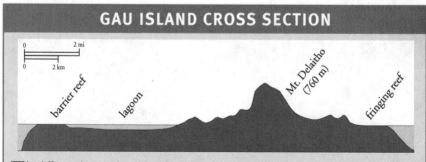

GAU ISLAND CROSS SECTION

The difference between barrier and fringing reefs is illustrated in the southwest-northwest cross section of Gau Island. The vertical scale has been exaggerated. The barrier reef of Gau's southwestern shore is separated from the main island's coast by a deep lagoon, while only a tidal flat lies between Gau's northeastern coast and the edge of the fringing reef.

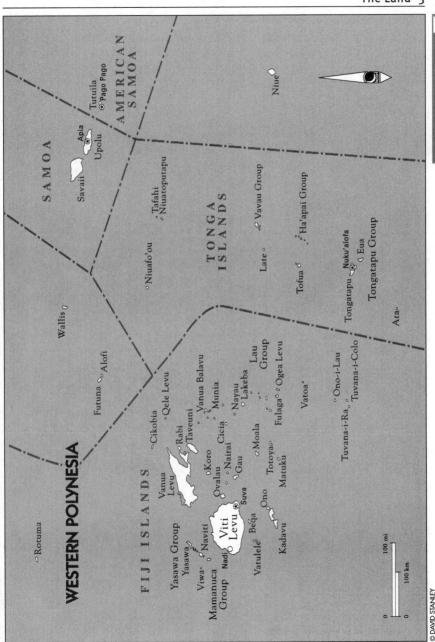

WESTERN POLYNESIA

FIJI ISLANDS

°Rotuma

Yasawa Group
Yasawa°
Mamanuca
Group Nadi ⊙ Naviti
Viwa° Viti
Vatulele° Beqa Levu ⊛
Kadavu Ono° Suva
Vanua
Levu °Koro
Ovalau° ° Nairai
° Gau
Totoya° Cicia
Matuku° °Moala
Rabi°
Taveuni
°Cikobia °Qele Levu
Vanua Balavu
Munia
° Nayau Lau
° Lakeba Group
Fulaga° ° Ogea Levu
Vatoa°
°Ono-i-Lau
Tuvana-i-Ra ° ° Tuvana-i-Colo

Wallis °

Futuna °~ Alofi

°Niuafo'ou

° Tafahi
°° Niuatoputapu

SAMOA
Savaii
Apia ⊛
Upolu

AMERICAN
SAMOA
Tutuila
⊛°Pago Pago

Niue

TONGA
ISLANDS

Late ° ° Vavau Group

Tofua °° °°° Ha'apai Group

Tongatapu ° Nuku'alofa
° Eua
Ata° Tongatapu Group

0   100 mi
0   100 km

© DAVID STANLEY

CORALS OF THE PACIFIC

Acropora

staghorn fire coral
(Millepora accicornis)

table coral

mushroom coral
(Fungia fungites)

elkhorn fire coral
(Millepora platyphylla)

brain coral
(Meandrina)

honeycomb coral (Favia matthaii)

DIANA LASICH HARPER

French Polynesia. In fact, Fiji has more land and people than all of Polynesia combined.

Viti Levu

The 1,000-meter-high Nadrau Plateau in central Viti Levu is cradled between Tomaniivi (1,323 meters) on the north and Monavatu (1,131 meters) on the south. On different sides of this elevated divide are the Colo-East Plateau drained by the Rewa River, the Navosa Plateau drained by the Ba, the Colo-West Plateau drained by the Sigatoka, and the Navua Plateau drained by the Navua. Some 29 well-defined peaks rise above Viti Levu's interior; most of the inhabitants live in the river valleys or along the coast.

The Nadi River slices across the Nausori Highlands, with the Mount Evans Range (1,195 meters) towering above Lautoka. Other highland areas of Viti Levu are cut by great rivers like the Sigatoka, the Navua, the Rewa, and the Ba, navigable far inland by outboard canoe or kayak. Whitewater rafters shoot down the Navua and occasionally the Ba, while the lower Sigatoka flows gently through Fiji's market-garden "salad bowl." Fiji's largest river, the Rewa, pours into the Pacific through a wide delta just below Nausori. After a hurricane the Rewa becomes a dark torrent worth a special visit to Nausori just to see it. Sharks have been known to enter both the Rewa and the Sigatoka and swim far upstream.

Vanua Levu

Vanua Levu has a peculiar shape, with two long peninsulas pointing northeastward. Natewa Bay, the South Pacific's largest bay, almost cuts the island in two. A mountain range between Labasa and Savusavu reaches 1,032 meters at Nasorolevu. Navotuvotu (842 meters), east of Bua Bay, is Fiji's best example of a broad shield volcano, with lava flows built up in layers. The mountains are closer to the southeast coast, and a broad lowland belt runs along the northwest. Of the rivers, the Dreketi is the largest, flowing west across northern Vanua Levu; navigation on the Labasa River is restricted to small boats. The interior of Vanua Levu is lower and drier than Viti Levu, yet scenically superb: The road from Labasa to Savusavu is a visual feast.

Other Islands

Vanua Levu's bullet-shaped neighbor Taveuni soars to 1,241 meters, its rugged southeast coast battered by the trade winds. Taveuni and Kadavu are known as the finest islands in Fiji for their scenic beauty and agricultural potential. Geologically, the uplifted limestone islands of the Lau Group have more in common with Tonga than with the rest of Fiji. Northwest of Viti Levu is the rugged volcanic Yasawa Group.

Coasts and Reefs

More than a quarter of the South Pacific's coral reefs are in Fiji. Fringing reefs are common along most of the coastlines, and is outstanding for its 33 barrier reefs. The Great Sea Reef off the north coast of Vanua Levu is the fourth-longest in the world, and the Great Astrolabe Reef north of Kadavu is one of the most diverse. Countless other unexplored barrier reefs are found off northern Viti Levu and elsewhere. The many cracks, crevices, walls, and caves along Fiji's reefs are guaranteed to delight the scuba diver.

The configuration of the Great Astrolabe Reef off Ono and Kadavu islands confirms Darwin's Theory of Atoll Formation. The famous formulator of the theory of natural selection surmised that atolls form as high volcanic islands subside into lagoons. The original island's fringing reef grows up into a barrier reef as the volcanic portion sinks. When the last volcanic material finally disappears below sea level, the coral rim of the reef/atoll remains as an indicator of how big the island once was.

Of course, all this takes place over millions of years, but deep below every atoll is the old volcanic core. Darwin's theory is well-illustrated here, where Ono and the small volcanic islands to the north remain inside the Great Astrolabe Reef. Return in 25 million years, and all you'll find will be the reef itself.

CORAL REEFS

Coral reefs are the world's oldest ecological system and cover some 200,000 square kilometers worldwide, between 25 degrees north and 25 degrees south latitude. A reef is created by the accumulation of millions of calcareous skeletons left by myriad generations of tiny coral polyps, some no bigger than a pinhead. A small piece of coral is a colony composed of large numbers of polyps. Though the reef's skeleton is usually white, the living polyps are of many different colors. The individual polyps on the surface often live a long time, continuously secreting layers to the skeletal mass beneath the tiny layer of flesh.

Coral polyps thrive in clear salty water where the temperature never drops below 18°C nor goes over 30°C. They require a base not more than 50 meters below the water's surface on which to form. The coral colony grows slowly upward on the consolidated skeletons of its ancestors until it reaches the low-tide mark, after which development extends outward on the edges of the reef. Sunlight is critical for coral growth. Colonies grow quickly on the ocean side, especially the windward side, due to clearer water and a greater abundance of food. A strong, healthy reef can grow four to five centimeters a year. Fresh or cloudy water inhibits coral growth, which is why villages and ports all across the Pacific are located at the reef-free mouths of rivers. Hurricanes can kill coral by covering the reef with sand, which prevents light and nutrients from getting through. Erosion caused by logging or urban development can have the same effect. In Fiji the hard corals have been seriously impacted by coral bleaching related to surges in water temperatures during hurricanes or otherwise; the soft corals are less affected.

Polyps extract calcium carbonate from the water and deposit it in their skeletons. All limy reef-building corals also contain microscopic algae within their cells. The algae, like all green plants, obtain energy from the sun and contribute this energy to the growth of the reef's skeleton. As a result, corals behave (and look) more like plants than animals, competing for sunlight just as terrestrial plants do. Many polyps are also carnivorous; they use their minute, stinging tentacles to capture tiny planktonic animals and organic particles at night.

Coral Types

Corals belong to a broad group of stinging creatures, which includes polyps, soft corals, stony corals, sea anemones, sea fans, and jellyfish. Only those types with hard skeletons and a single hollow cavity within the body are considered true corals. Stony corals such as brain, table, staghorn, and mushroom corals have external skeletons and are important reef builders. Soft corals, black corals, and sea fans have internal skeletons. The fire corals are recognized by their smooth, velvety surface and yellowish brown color. The stinging toxins of this last group can easily penetrate human skin and cause swelling and painful burning that can last up to an hour. The many varieties of soft, colorful anemones gently waving in the current might seem inviting to touch, but beware, because many are also poisonous.

The corals, like most other forms of life in the Pacific, colonized the ocean from the fertile seas of Southeast Asia. Therefore the number of species declines as you move east. More than 800 species of reef-building coral make their home in the Pacific, compared to only 48 in the Caribbean. The diversity of coral colors and forms is endlessly amazing. This is our most unspoiled environment, a world of almost indescribable beauty.

Exploring a Reef

Until you've explored a good coral reef, you haven't experienced one of the greatest joys of nature. While one cannot walk through pristine forests due to a lack of paths, it's quite possible to swim over untouched reefs. Coral reefs are the most densely populated living space on earth—the rainforests of the sea! It's wise to bring along a high-quality mask you've tested thoroughly beforehand as there's nothing more disheartening than a leaky, ill-fitting mask. Also, many dive shops in Fiji rent or sell snorkeling gear.

Conservation

Coral reefs are one of the most fragile and complex ecosystems on earth, providing food and shelter for countless species of fish, crustaceans (shrimps, crabs, and lobsters), mollusks (shells), and other animals. The coral reefs of the South Pacific protect shorelines during storms, supply sand to maintain the islands, furnish food for the local population, form a living laboratory for science, and are major tourist attractions. Reefs worldwide host more than two million species of life. Without coral, the South Pacific would be immeasurably poorer.

Hard corals grow only about 10–25 millimeters a year and it can take 7,000–10,000 years for a coral reef to form. Though corals look solid, they're easily broken. By standing on them, breaking off pieces, or carelessly dropping anchor, you can destroy in a few minutes what took millennia to form. Once a piece of coral breaks off, it dies, and it may be years before the coral reestablishes itself and even longer before the broken piece is replaced. The "wound" may become infected by algae, which can multiply and kill the entire coral colony. When this happens over a wide area, the diversity of marinelife declines dramatically.

We recommend that you not remove seashells, coral, plantlife, or marine animals from the sea. Doing so upsets the delicate balance of nature, and coral is much more beautiful underwater anyway! This is a particular problem along shorelines frequented by large numbers of tourists, who can completely strip a reef in very little time. If you'd like a souvenir, content yourself with what you find on the beach (although even a seemingly empty shell may be inhabited by a hermit crab). Also think twice about purchasing jewelry or souvenirs made from coral or seashells. Genuine traditional handicrafts that incorporate shells are one thing, but by purchasing unmounted seashells or mass-produced coral curios you are contributing to the destruction of the marine environment. The triton shell, for example, helps keep in check the reef-destroying crown-of-thorns starfish.

The anchors and anchor chains of private yachts can do serious damage to coral reefs. Pronged anchors are more environmentally friendly than larger, heavier anchors, and plastic tubing over the end of the anchor chain helps minimize the damage. If at all possible, anchor in sand. A longer anchor chain makes this easier, and a good windlass is essential for larger boats. A recording depth sounder will help locate sandy areas when none are available in shallow water. If you don't have a depth sounder and can't see the bottom, lower the anchor until it just touches the bottom and feel the anchor line as the boat drifts. If it grumbles, lift it up, drift a little, and try again. Later, if you notice your chain grumbling, motor over the anchor, lift it out of the coral, and move. Not only do sand and mud hold better, but your anchor will be less likely to become fouled. Try to arrive before 1500 to be able to see clearly where you're anchoring— Polaroid sunglasses make it easier to distinguish corals.

Stricter government regulation of the marine environment is urgently needed, and in some places coral reefs are already protected. Appeals such as the one above have only limited impact—legislators must write stricter laws and impose fines. If you witness dumping or any other marine-related activity that you think may be illegal, don't become directly involved but do take a few notes and calmly report the incident to the local authorities or police at the first opportunity. You'll learn something about their approach to these matters and make them aware of your concerns.

Resort developers can minimize damage to their valuable reefs by providing public mooring buoys so yachts don't have to drop anchor and pontoons so snorkelers aren't tempted to stand on coral. Licensing authorities can make such amenities mandatory whenever appropriate, and, in extreme cases, endangered coral gardens should be declared off limits to private boats. As consumerism spreads, once-remote areas become subject to the problems of pollution and overexploitation, and the garbage is visibly piling up on many shores. As a guest in Fiji, it's appropriate to take a conservationist approach. For as Marshall McLuhan said, "On Spaceship Earth, there are no passengers, we are all members of the crew."

CLIMATE CHANGE

The gravest danger facing the atolls and reefs of Oceania is the greenhouse effect, a gradual warming of the earth's environment due to fossil fuel combustion and the widespread clearing of forests. By the year 2030, the concentration of carbon dioxide in the atmosphere will have doubled from preindustrial levels. As infrared radiation from the sun is absorbed by the gas, the trapped heat melts mountain glaciers and the polar ice caps. In addition, seawater expands as it warms up, so water levels could rise almost a meter by the year 2100, destroying shorelines created 5,000 years ago.

A 1982 study demonstrated that sea levels had already risen 12 centimeters in the previous century; in 1995, 2,500 scientists from 70 countries involved in the Intergovernmental Panel on Climate Change commissioned by the United Nations completed a two-year study with the warning that during the next century air temperatures may rise as much as 5°C and sea levels could go up 95 centimeters by 2100. Not only will this reduce the growing area for food crops, but rising sea levels will mean saltwater intrusion into groundwater supplies—a troubling prospect if accompanied by the increasing frequency of droughts that have been predicted. Coastal erosion will force governments to spend vast sums on road repairs and coastline stabilization.

Increasing temperatures may already be contributing to the dramatic jump in the number of hurricanes in the South Pacific. For example, Fiji experienced only 12 tropical hurricanes from 1941 to 1980, but 10 from 1981 to 1989, and in the face of devastating hurricanes, insurance companies are withdrawing coverage from some areas. In 1997 and 1998, the El Niño phenomenon brought with it another round of devastating hurricanes. Hurricane Ami in January 2003 was the worst storm to hit Fiji in a decade.

Coral bleaching occurs when the organism's symbiotic algae are expelled in response to environmental stresses, such as when water temperatures rise as little as 1°C above the local maximum for a week or longer. Bleaching is also caused by increased radiation due to ozone degradation, and widespread instances of bleaching and reefs being killed by rising sea temperatures took place in Fiji during the El Niño event of 1998. A "hot spot" over Fiji in early 2000 caused further damage. The earth's surface has warmed 1°C over the past century, and by 2080 water temperatures may have increased 5°C, effectively bleaching and killing all of the region's reefs. In Fiji, coral bleaching will become an annual event by 2050. Reef destruction will reduce coastal fish stocks and impact tourism.

Unfortunately, those most responsible for the problem, especially the United States and Australia, have strongly resisted taking action to significantly cut greenhouse-gas emissions, and new industrial polluters like India and China are sure to make matters much worse. And as if that weren't bad enough, the hydrofluorocarbons (HFCs) presently being developed by corporate giants like DuPont to replace the ozone-destructive chlorofluorocarbons (CFCs) used in cooling systems are far more potent greenhouse gases than carbon dioxide. What to expect? A similar increase in temperature of just 6°C at the end of the Permian period 250 million years ago eventually wiped out 95 percent of species alive on earth at the time, and it took 100 million years for species diversification to return to previous levels.

CLIMATE

Along the coast the weather is warm and pleasant, without great variations in temperature. The southeast trade winds prevail from June to October, the best months to visit. In February and March, the wind often comes directly out of the east. These winds dump 3,000 mm of annual rainfall on the humid southeast coasts of the big islands, increasing to 5,000 mm inland. The drier northwest coasts, in the lee, get only 1,500–2,000 mm.

The official dry season (June–Oct.) is not always dry at Suva, although much of the rain falls at night. In addition, Fiji's winter (May–Nov.) is cooler and less humid, the preferred months for mountain trekking. During the drier season, the reef waters are clearest for the scuba diver. Yet even during the rainy summer months (Dec.–Apr.), bright sun often follows the rains,

and the rain is only a slight inconvenience. The refreshing trade winds relieve the high humidity. Summer is hurricane season, with Fiji, Samoa, and Tonga receiving up to five tropical storms annually.

In Fiji you can obtain prerecorded weather information by dialing 330-1642. The same information is available online at www.met.gov.fj.

Currents and Winds

The Pacific Ocean has a greater impact on the world's climate than any other geographical feature on earth. By moving heat away from the equator and toward the poles, it stretches the bounds of the area in which life can exist. Broad, circular ocean currents flow from east to west across the tropical Pacific, clockwise in the North Pacific, counterclockwise in the South Pacific. North and south of the horse latitudes, just outside the tropics, the currents cool and swing east. The prevailing winds push the same way: the southeast trade winds south of the equator, the northeast trade winds north of the equator, and the low-pressure doldrums in between. Westerlies blow east above the cool currents north and south of the tropics. This natural air-conditioning system brings warm water to Australia and Japan, cooler water to Peru and California.

The climate of the high islands is closely related to these winds. As air is heated near the equator, it rises and flows at high altitudes toward the poles. By the time it reaches about 30 degrees south latitude, it will have cooled enough to cause it to fall and flow back toward the equator near sea level. In the southern hemisphere the rotation of the earth deflects the winds to the left to become the southeast trades. When these cool moist trade winds hit a high island, they are warmed by the sun and forced up. Above 500 meters elevation they begin to cool again and their moisture condenses into clouds. At night the winds do not capture much warmth and are more likely to discharge their moisture as rain. The windward slopes of the high islands catch the trades head-on and are usually wet, while those on the leeward side may be dry.

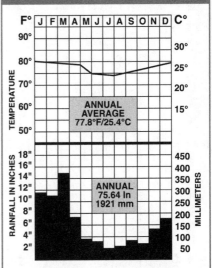

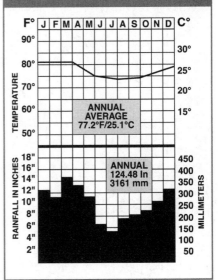

FIJI CLIMATE CHART

LOCATION		JAN.	FEB.	MAR.	APR.	MAY	JUNE	JULY	AUG.	SEPT.	OCT.	NOV.	DEC.	ALL YEAR
Nadi airport,	C	27.0	26.9	26.7	26.2	25.0	24.0	23.3	23.8	24.5	25.2	25.9	26.6	25.4
Viti Levu	mm	294	291	373	195	99	78	51	62	88	73	137	181	1,922
Yasawa Island	C	27.0	26.9	26.6	26.4	26.0	25.3	24.6	24.8	25.1	25.7	26.1	26.7	25.9
	mm	281	287	344	168	110	106	45	68	90	78	187	165	1,929
Ba, Viti Levu	C	27.2	27.1	26.9	26.5	25.3	24.1	23.3	23.8	24.7	25.5	26.1	26.1	25.6
	mm	322	409	387	203	101	67	46	65	72	91	126	228	2,117
Nadarivatu,	C	21.6	22.0	21.5	21.0	20.0	18.9	18.3	18.8	19.0	20.1	20.6	21.1	20.2
Viti Levu	mm	599	668	689	362	181	99	89	125	126	136	220	400	3,694
Rakiraki,	C	27.6	27.6	27.3	26.8	25.9	24.9	24.2	24.6	25.1	25.9	26.6	27.1	26.2
Viti Levu	mm	307	371	372	236	122	66	47	68	74	83	140	221	2,107
Suva, Viti Levu	C	26.8	26.9	26.8	26.1	24.8	23.9	23.1	23.2	23.7	24.4	25.3	26.2	25.1
	mm	314	299	386	343	280	177	148	200	212	218	268	313	3,158
Vunisea,	C	26.4	26.8	26.1	25.4	24.2	23.2	22.4	22.6	23.1	23.9	24.7	26.1	24.6
Kadavu I.	mm	239	225	313	256	208	102	112	121	122	126	151	177	2,152
Nabouwalu,	C	26.9	27.1	26.7	26.3	25.5	24.7	23.9	24.0	24.4	25.2	25.4	26.3	25.6
Vanua Levu	mm	328	354	352	275	198	130	96	114	139	164	208	279	2,637
Labasa,	C	26.8	26.8	26.6	26.2	25.3	24.4	23.8	24.2	24.7	25.4	25.9	26.4	25.6
Vanua Levu	mm	449	457	465	236	97	86	38	60	77	96	210	263	2,534
Vunikodi,	C	26.6	26.7	26.6	26.3	26.0	25.3	24.6	24.7	25.0	25.6	25.9	26.6	25.8
Vanua Levu	mm	302	377	409	225	143	131	92	90	114	132	264	220	2,499
Rotuma Island	C	27.4	27.3	27.2	27.4	27.2	26.8	26.4	26.5	26.7	26.8	27.0	27.2	27.0
	mm	358	390	430	278	262	244	207	230	277	283	327	331	3,617
Matuku,	C	26.8	27.0	26.8	26.3	25.1	24.1	23.1	23.6	24.2	25.0	25.7	26.4	25.3
Lau Group	mm	231	230	265	192	151	116	114	78	110	97	139	152	1,875
Ono-i-Lau,	C	26.3	26.5	26.4	25.7	24.3	23.4	22.4	22.4	22.7	23.6	24.5	25.3	24.4
Lau Group	mm	201	199	266	196	144	109	90	94	106	114	128	145	1,792

HURRICANES IN THE TROPICS

The official hurricane (or cyclone) season south of the equator is November–April, although hurricanes have also occurred in May and October. Since the ocean provides the energy, these low-pressure systems can only form over water with a surface temperature above 27°C; during years when water temperatures are high (such as during an El Niño) their frequency increases. The rotation of the earth must give the storm its initial spin, and this occurs mostly between latitudes 5 and 20 on either side of the equator.

As rainfall increases and the seas rise, the winds are drawn into a spiral that reaches its maximum speed in a ring around the center. In the South Pacific, a cyclone develops as these circular winds, rotating clockwise around a center, increase in velocity: force 8–9 winds blowing at 34–47 knots are called a gale, force 10–11 at 48–63 knots is a storm, force 12 winds revolving at 64 knots or more is a hurricane. Wind speeds can go as high as 100 knots, with gusts to 140 knots on the left side of the storm's path in the direction it's moving.

The eye of the hurricane can be 10–30 kilometers wide and surprisingly clear and calm, although at sea, contradictory wave patterns continue to wreak havoc. In the South Pacific, most hurricanes move south at speeds of 5–20 knots. As water is sucked into the low-pressure eye of the hurricane and waves reach 14 meters in height, coastlines can receive a surge of up to four meters of water, especially if the storm enters a narrowing bay or occurs at high tide.

Flora and Fauna

FLORA

The flora of Fiji originated in the Malaysian region; in the two regions, ecological niches are filled by similar plants. More than 2,000 species of plants grow in Fiji, of which 476 are indigenous to Fiji and 10 percent of those are found only here. Taveuni is known for its rare climbing *tagimaucia* flower. The absence of leaf-eating animals in Fiji allowed the vegetation to develop largely without the protective spines and thorns found elsewhere, and one of the only stinging plants is the *salato*, a shrub or tree bearing large, heart-shaped leaves with purple ribs and ragged edges that inflict painful wounds when touched. Hairs on the leaves break off in the skin, and the intense stinging pain begins half a minute later. This soon diminishes into an itch that becomes painful again if scratched. The itch can recur weeks and even months later.

Patterns of rainfall are in large part responsible for the variety of vegetation here. The wetter sides of the high islands are heavily forested, with occasional thickets of bamboo and scrub. Natural forests cover 40 percent of Fiji's total land area, and about a quarter of these forests are classified as production forest suitable for logging. The towering *dakua* or kauri tree, once carved into massive Fijian war canoes, has already disappeared from Viti Levu, and the last stands are now being logged on Vanua Levu. Since the 1960s, much replanting has been done in mahogany, a hardwood originating in Central America. The native *yaka* is a conifer whose wood has an attractive grain.

Coconut groves fill the coastal plains. On the drier sides, open savanna, or *talasiga*, of coarse saw grasses predominates where the original vegetation has been destroyed by slash-and-burn agriculture. Sugarcane is now cultivated in the lowlands here, and Caribbean pine has been planted in many dry hilly areas, giving them a Scandinavian appearance. Around Christmas, poinciana, or flame trees, along the roads bloom bright red. The islands of the Lau Group are restricted to a few hardy, drought-resistant species such as coconuts and pandanus. Well-drained shorelines often feature ironwood, or *nokonoko*, a casuarina appreciated by woodcarvers.

Mangroves are commonly found along high island coastal lagoons. The cable roots of the saltwater-tolerant red mangrove anchor in the shallow upper layer of oxygenated mud, avoiding the layers of hydrogen sulfide below. The tree provides shade for tiny organisms dwelling in the tidal mudflats—a place for birds to nest and for fish or shellfish to feed and spawn. The mangroves also perform the same task as land-building coral colonies along the reefs. As sediments are trapped between the roots, the trees extend farther into the lagoon, creating a unique natural environment. The past decade has seen widespread destruction of the mangrove forests as land is reclaimed for agricultural use in northwest Viti Levu and around Labasa.

Many of Fiji's forest plants have medicinal applications, which have recently attracted the attention of patent-hungry pharmaceutical giants. The sap of the tree fern *(balabala)* was formerly used as a cure for headaches by Fijians, and its heart was eaten in times of famine.

Though only introduced to Fiji in the late 1860s, sugarcane probably originated in the South Pacific. On New Guinea the islanders have cultivated the plant for thousands of years, selecting vigorous varieties with the most colorful stems. The story goes that two Melanesian fishermen, To-Kabwana and To-Karavuvu, found a piece of sugarcane in their net one day. They threw it away, but, after twice catching it again, they decided to keep it and painted the stalk a bright color. Eventually the cane burst, and a woman came forth. She cooked food for the men but hid herself at night. Finally she was captured and became the wife of one of the men. From their union sprang the whole human race.

FAUNA

Some Fijian clans have totemic relationships with eels, prawns, turtles, and sharks, and are able to summon these creatures with special chants. Red prawns are revered on Vanua Vatu in Southern Lau, on a tiny island off Naweni in southern Vanua Levu, and on Vatulele Island. The Nasaqalau people of Lakeba in southern Lau call sharks, and villagers of Korolevu in central Viti Levu call eels. The women of Namuana on Kadavu summon giant sea turtles with their chants. Turtle calling is also practiced at Nacamaki village, in the northeast corner of Koro. Unfortunately sea turtles are becoming so rare that the turtle callers are having less and less success each year.

Mammals

The first Fijians brought with them pigs, dogs, chickens, and gray rats. The only native mammals are the monkey-faced fruit bat, or flying fox, called *beka* by the Fijians, and the smaller, insect-eating bat.

The Indian mongoose was introduced by planters in the 1880s to combat rats, which were damaging the plantations. Unfortunately, no one realized at the time that the mongoose hunts by day, whereas the rats are nocturnal, so the two seldom meet. Today, the mongoose is the scourge of chickens, native ground birds, iguanas, and other animals, though Kadavu, Koro, Gau, Ovalau, and Taveuni are mongoose-free (and thus the finest islands for bird-watching). Feral cats do the same sort of damage.

Sealife

Fiji's richest store of life is found in the silent underwater world of the pelagic and lagoon fishes. It's estimated that half the fish remaining on our globe are swimming in the Pacific. The Pacific reefs provide a habitat for more than 4,000 fish species, 5–10 times the diversity of temperate oceans.

Coral pinnacles on the lagoon floor provide a safe haven for angelfish, butterfly fish, damselfish, groupers, soldierfish, surgeonfish, triggerfish, trumpet fish, and countless more. These fish seldom venture more than a few meters away from the protective coral, but larger fish such as barracuda, jackfish, parrot fish, pike, stingrays, and small sharks range across lagoon waters that are seldom deeper than 30 meters. The external side of the reef is also home to many of the above, but the open ocean is reserved for bonito, mahimahi, swordfish, tuna, wrasses, and the larger sharks. Passes between ocean and lagoon can be crowded with fish in transit, offering a favorite hunting ground for predators.

In the open sea, the food chain begins with phytoplankton, which flourish wherever ocean upwelling brings nutrients such as nitrates and phosphates to the surface. In the western Pacific this occurs near the equator, where massive currents draw water away toward Japan and Australia. Large schools of fast-moving tuna ply these waters feeding on smaller fish, which consume tiny phytoplankton drifting near the sunlit surface. The phytoplankton also exist in tropical lagoons where mangrove leaves, sea grasses, and other plant material are consumed by far more varied populations of reef fish, mollusks, and crustaceans.

Sharks

Human activities threaten deepwater shark species with extinction. A National Marine Fisheries Service report disclosed that 60,857 sharks were harvested in the central and western Pacific in 1998, a 25-fold increase in just seven years, with the vast majority taken only for their fins. These are used to make soup at Asian restaurants, and the rest of the carcass is dumped back into the sea, a cruel, wasteful practice which is gradually removing this top predator from the ecosystem. The consequences of these depredations are as yet unknown.

In contrast, the danger from sharks to swimmers has been exaggerated. Of some 300 different species, only 28 are known to have attacked humans. Most dangerous are the white, tiger, and blue sharks. Fortunately, all of these inhabit deep water far from the coasts. An average of 70–100 shark attacks a year occur worldwide with 10 fatalities, so considering the number of people who swim in the sea, your chances of being involved are about one in a million. In the South Pacific, shark attacks on snorkelers or scuba divers are extremely rare, and the tiny mosquito is a far more dangerous predator.

Sharks are not aggressive where food is abundant, but they can be very nasty far offshore.

You're always safer if you keep your head underwater (with a mask and snorkel), and don't panic if you see a shark—you might attract it. Even if you do, they're usually only curious, so keep your eye on the shark and slowly back off. The swimming techniques of humans must seem very clumsy to fish, so it's not surprising if they want a closer look.

Sharks are attracted by shiny objects (a knife or jewelry), bright colors (especially yellow and red), urine, blood, spearfishing, and splashing (divers should ease themselves into the water). Sharks normally stay outside the reef, but get local advice. White beaches are safer than dark, and clear water safer than murky. Avoid swimming in places where sewage or edible wastes enter the water, or where fish have just been cleaned. Slaughterhouses sometimes attract sharks to an area by dumping offal into the nearby sea. You should also exercise care in places where local residents have been fishing with spears or even with a hook and line that day.

Never swim alone if you suspect the presence of sharks. If you see one, even a supposedly harmless nurse shark lying on the bottom, get out of the water calmly and quickly, and go elsewhere. Studies indicate that sharks, like most other creatures, have a "personal space" around them that they will defend. Thus an attack could be a shark's way of warning someone to keep his distance, and it's a fact that more than half the victims of these incidents are not eaten but merely bitten. Sharks are less of a problem in the South Pacific than in colder waters, because small marine mammals (commonly hunted by sharks) are rare here, so you won't be mistaken for a seal or an otter.

Let common sense be your guide, not irrational fear or carelessness. Many scuba divers come to actually *look* for sharks, and local divemasters seem able to swim among them with impunity. If you're in the market for some shark action, many dive shops can provide it. Just be aware that getting into the water with feeding sharks always entails some danger, and the divemaster who admits this and lays down some basic safety guidelines (such as keeping your hands clasped or arms folded) is probably a safer bet than the macho man who just says he's been doing it for years without incident. Never snorkel on your own (without an experienced guide) near a spot where sharks are fed regularly, since you never know how the sharks will react to a surface swimmer without any food for them. Like all other wild animals, sharks deserve to be approached with respect.

Sea Urchins

Sea urchins (living pincushions) are common in tropical waters. The black variety is the most dangerous: Their long, sharp quills can go right through a snorkeler's fins. Even the small ones, which you can easily pick up in your hand, can pinch you if you're careless. They're found on rocky shores and reefs, never on clear, sandy beaches where the surf rolls in.

Most sea urchins are not poisonous, though quill punctures are painful and can become infected if not treated. The pain is caused by an injected protein, which you can eliminate by holding the injured area in a pail of very hot water for about 15 minutes. This will coagulate the protein, eliminating the pain for good. If you can't heat water, soak the area in vinegar or urine for a quarter hour. Remove the quills if possible, but as they are made of calcium, they'll decompose in a couple of weeks anyway—not much of a consolation as you limp along in the meantime. In some places sea urchins are considered a delicacy: The orange or yellow urchin gonads are delicious with lemon and salt.

Other Hazardous Creatures

Although jellyfish, stonefish, crown-of-thorns starfish, cone shells, eels, and poisonous sea snakes are dangerous, injuries resulting from any of these are rare. Gently apply methylated spirits, alcohol, or urine (but not water, kerosene, or gasoline) to areas stung by jellyfish. Inoffensive sea cucumbers (bêche-de-mer) punctuate the lagoon shallows, but stonefish also rest on the bottom and are hard to see due to

camouflaging; if you happen to step on one, its dorsal fins inject a painful poison, which burns like fire in the blood. Fortunately, stonefish are not common.

It's worth knowing that the venom produced by most marine animals is destroyed by heat, so your first move should be to soak the injured part in very hot water for 30 minutes. (Also hold an opposite foot or hand in the same water to prevent scalding due to numbness.) Other authorities claim the best first aid is to squeeze blood from a sea cucumber scraped raw on coral directly onto the wound. If a hospital or clinic is nearby, go there immediately.

Never pick up a live cone shell; some varieties have a deadly stinger dart coming out from the pointed end. The tiny blue-ring octopus is only five centimeters long but packs a poison that can kill a human. Eels hide in reef crevices by day; most are harmful only if you inadvertently poke your hand or foot in at them. Of course, never tempt fate by approaching them (fun-loving divemasters sometimes feed the big ones by hand and stroke their backs).

Birds

Of the 70 species of land birds, 37 are endemic, including broadbills, cuckoos, doves, fantails, finches, flycatchers, fruitdoves, hawks, herons, honeyeaters, kingfishers, lorikeets, owls, parrots, pigeons, rails, robins, silktails, swallows, thrushes, warblers, whistlers, and white-eyes. The Fijian names of some of these birds, such as the *kaka* (parrot), *ga* (gray duck), and *kikau* (giant honeyeater), imitate their calls. Red and green *kula* lorikeets are often seen in populated areas collecting nectar and pollen from flowering trees or feeding on fruit. Of the seabirds, boobies, frigate birds, petrels, and tropic birds are present. The best time to observe forest birds is in the very early morning—they move around a lot less in the heat of the day.

More in evidence is the introduced Indian mynah, with its yellow legs and beak, the In-

pink-billed parrot finch

LOUISE FOOTE

dian bulbul, and the Malay turtledove. The hopping common mynah bird (*Acridotheres tristis*) was introduced to many islands from Indonesia at the turn of the century to control insects, which were damaging the citrus and coconut plantations. The mynahs multiplied profusely and have become major pests, inflicting great harm on the very trees they were brought in to protect. Worse still, many indigenous birds are forced out of their habitat by these noisy, aggressive birds. This and rapid deforestation by man have made the South Pacific the region with the highest proportion of endangered endemic bird species on earth.

Reptiles and Amphibians

Three of the world's seven species of sea turtles nest in Fiji: the green, the hawksbill, and the leatherback. Nesting occurs between November and February, at night when there is a full moon and a high tide. Sea turtles lay their eggs on the beach from which they themselves originally hatched. The female struggles up the beach and lays as many as 100 eggs in a hole, which she digs and then covers with her hind flippers. Female turtles don't commence this activity until they are 20 years old, thus a drop in numbers today has irreversible consequences a generation later. It's estimated

tree frog

that breeding females already number in the hundreds or low thousands, and all species of these magnificent creatures (sometimes erroneously referred to as "tortoises") now face extinction due to ruthless hunting, egg harvesting, and beach destruction. Turtles are often choked by floating plastic bags they mistake for food, or they drown in fishing nets. The Fiji Fisheries Department estimates that between 1980 and 1989 more than 10,000 hawksbill turtle shells were exported to Japan. The turtles and their eggs are now protected by law in Fiji (maximum penalty of six months in prison for killing a turtle). Sadly, this law is seldom enforced.

Geckos and skinks are small lizards often seen on the islands. The skink hunts insects by day; its tail breaks off if you catch it, but a new one quickly grows. The gecko is nocturnal and has no eyelids. Adhesive toe pads enable it to pass along vertical surfaces, and it changes color to avoid detection. Unlike the skink, which avoids humans, geckos often live in people's homes, where they eat insects attracted by electric lights. Its loud clicking call may be a territorial warning to other geckos.

One of the more unusual creatures found in Fiji and Tonga is the banded iguana, a lizard that lives in trees and can grow up to 70 centimeters long (two-thirds of which is tail). The iguanas are emerald green, and the male is easily distinguished from the female by his bluish-gray cross stripes. Banded iguanas change color to control their internal temperature, becoming darker when in the direct sun. Their nearest relatives are found in Central America, and how they could have reached Fiji remains a mystery. In 1979 a new species, the crested iguana, was discovered on Yaduataba, a small island off the west coast of Vanua Levu. It's estimated that 6,000 crested iguanas are presently on Yaduataba (www.icffci.com).

Two species of snakes inhabit Fiji: the very rare, poisonous *bolo loa* and the harmless Pacific boa, which can grow up to two meters long. Venomous sea snakes are common on some coasts, but they're docile and easily handled. Fijians call the common banded black-and-white sea snake the *dadakulaci*. The land- and tree-dwelling native frogs are noteworthy for the long suction discs on their fingers and toes. Because they live deep in the rainforests and feed at night, they're seldom seen.

In 1936 the giant toad was introduced from Hawaii to control beetles, slugs, and millipedes. When this food source is exhausted, they tend to eat each other. At night gardens and lawns may be full of them.

Insects and Arachnids

Not to be confused with the inoffensive millipedes are the poisonous centipedes found in Fiji. While the millipede will roll up when touched, the centipede may inflict a painful sting through its front legs. The two types are easily distinguished by the number of pairs of legs per body segment: centipedes one, millipedes two. Fiji's largest centipedes grow up to 18 centimeters long and can have anywhere from 15 to 180 pairs of legs. These nocturnal creatures feed on insects and may be found in houses, while the two species of scorpions dwell only in the forest.

History and Government

HISTORY

The Pre-European Period

The first people to arrive in Fiji were members of a light-skinned Austronesian-speaking race, probably the Polynesians. They originated in Taiwan or insular Southeast Asia and gradually migrated east past the already occupied islands of Melanesia. Distinctive *Lapita* pottery, decorated in horizontal geometric bands and dated from 1290 B.C., has been found in the sand dunes near Sigatoka, indicating they had reached here by 1500 B.C. or earlier. Much later, about 500 B.C., Melanesian people arrived, bringing with them their own distinct pottery traditions. From the fusion of these primordial peoples was the Fijian race born.

The hierarchical social structure of the early Fijians originated with the Polynesians. Status and descent passed through the male line, and power was embodied in the *turaga* (chief). The hereditary chiefs possessed the mana of an ancestral spirit or *vu*. Yet under the *vasu* system, a chiefly woman's son could lay claim to the property of his mother's brothers, and such relationships, combined with polygamy, kept society in a state of constant strife. This feudal aristocracy combined in confederations, or *vanua*, which extended their influence through war. Treachery and cannibalism were an intrinsic part of these struggles; women were taken as prizes or traded to form alliances. For defense, villages were fortified with ring ditches, or built along ridges or terraced hillsides.

The native aristocracy practiced customs that today seem barbarous and particularly cruel. The skull cap of a defeated enemy might be polished and used as a *yaqona* (kava) cup to humiliate a foe. Some chiefs even took delight in cooking and consuming body parts as their agonized victims looked on. Men were buried alive to hold up the posts of new houses, war canoes were launched over the living bodies of young girls, and the widows of chiefs were strangled to keep their husbands company in the spirit world. The farewells of some of these women are remembered today in dances and songs known as *meke.*

These feudal islanders were, on the other hand, guardians of one of the highest material cultures of the Pacific. They built great oceangoing double canoes *(drua)* up to 30 meters long, constructed and adorned large solid thatched houses *(bure),* performed marvelous song-dances called *meke,* made tapa, pottery, and sennit (coconut cordage), and skillfully plaited mats. For centuries the Tongans came to Fiji to obtain great logs for making canoes and sandalwood for carving.

European Exploration

In 1643 Abel Tasman became the European discoverer of Fiji when he sighted Taveuni, although he didn't land. Tasman was searching for *terra australis incognita,* a great southern continent believed to balance the continents of the north. He also hoped to find new markets and trade routes. Unlike earlier Spanish explorers, Tasman entered the Pacific from the west rather than the east. He was the first European to see Tasmania, New Zealand, and Tonga, as well as Fiji. By sailing right around Australia from the Dutch East Indies, he proved New Holland (Australia) was not attached to the elusive southern continent.

In 1774, Captain Cook anchored off Vatoa in southern Lau. Like Tasman he failed to proceed farther or land. It was left to Capt. William

FIJI ISLANDS CHRONOLOGY

1500 B.C. Polynesians reach Fiji
500 B.C. Melanesians reach Fiji
1643 Abel Tasman sights Taveuni
1774 Captain Cook visits southern Lau
1789 Captain Bligh and crew paddle past the Yasawas
1800 sandalwood discovered on Vanua Levu
1820 bêche-de-mer trade begins
1827 Dumont d'Urville visits Bau
1830 Tahitian missionaries arrive in southern Lau
1835 Methodist missionaries arrive at Lakeba
1840 American Exploring Expedition visits Fiji
1847 Tongan invasion of Lau led by Enele Ma'afu
1849 home of John Brown Williams burns
1851 first visit by hostile American gunboats
1854 Chief Cakobau accepts Christianity
1855 Cakobau puts down the Rewa revolt
1858 first British consul arrives in Fiji
1860 founding of the town of Levuka
1862 Britain refuses to annex Fiji
1865 confederacy of Fijian chiefs formed
1867 American warship threatens to shell Levuka
1868 Polynesia Company granted the site of Suva
1871 Cakobau and Thurston form a government
1874 Fiji becomes a British colony
1875 measles epidemic kills a third of Fijians
1879 first indentured Indian laborers arrive
1881 first large sugar mill built at Nausori
1881 Rotuma annexed to Fiji
1882 capital moved from Levuka to Suva
1904 first elected Legislative Council
1916 Indian immigration ends

1920 indenture system terminated
1928 first flight from Hawaii lands at Suva
1939 Nadi Airport built
1940 Native Land Trust Board established
1942 Fijian troops sent to the Solomon Islands
1951 Fiji Airways (later Air Pacific) formed
1953 Queen Elizabeth II visits Fiji
1963 women and Fijians enfranchised
1965 Constitutional Convention held in London
1966 internal self-government achieved
1968 University of the South Pacific established
1970 Fiji's first constitution adopted
1970 Fiji becomes independent
1973 sugar industry nationalized
1977 governor-general overturns election results
1978 Fijian peacekeeping troops sent to Lebanon
1981 Fijian troops sent to the Sinai
1983 Monasavu Hydroelectric Project opens
1987 Labor defeats Alliance Party
1987 two military coups led by Colonel Rabuka
1987 Rabuka declares Fiji a republic
1987 Fiji expelled from British Commonwealth
1990 racially weighted constitution promulgated
1992 Rabuka elected under 1990 constitution
1997 constitution revised to allow common roll voting
1997 Fiji readmitted to the Commonwealth
1998 revised constitution comes into effect
1999 Labor Party under Mahendra Chaudhry elected
2000 civil coup in May topples government
2001 Qarase elected under 1997 constitution
2003 South Pacific Games held in Suva

Bligh to give Europeans an accurate picture of Fiji for the first time. After the *Bounty* mutiny in May 1789, Bligh and his companions were chased by canoe-loads of Fijian warriors just north of the Yasawa Islands as they rowed through on their escape route to Timor. Some serious paddling, a timely squall, and a lucky gap in the Great Sea Reef saved the Englishmen from ending up as the main course at a cannibal feast. The section of sea where this happened is now known as Bligh Water. Bligh cut directly across the center of Fiji between the two main islands, and his careful observations made him the first

real European explorer of Fiji, albeit an unwilling one. Bligh returned to Fiji in 1792, but once again he stayed aboard his ship.

Beachcombers and Chiefs

All of these early explorers stressed the perilous nature of Fiji's reefs. This, combined with tales told by the Tongans of cannibalism and warlike Fijian natives, caused most travelers to shun the area. Then, in 1800, a survivor from the shipwrecked American schooner *Argo* brought word that sandalwood grew in abundance along the Bua coast of Vanua Levu. This precipitated a rush of traders and beach-combers to the islands. A cargo of sandalwood bought from the islanders for $50 worth of trinkets could be sold to the Chinese in Canton for $20,000. By 1814 the forests had been stripped to provide joss sticks and incense, and the trade collapsed.

During this period Fiji was divided among warring chieftains. The first Europeans to actually mix with the Fijians were escaped convicts from Australia, who showed the natives how to use European muskets and were thus well received. White beachcombers such as the Swedish adventurer Charles Savage and the German Martin Bushart acted as middlemen between traders and Fijians and took sides in local conflicts. In one skirmish Savage was separated from his fellows, captured, and eaten. With help from the likes of Savage, Naulivou, the cannibal chief of tiny Bau Island just off eastern Viti Levu, and his brother Tanoa extended their influence over much of western Fiji.

In his book *Following the Equator,* Mark Twain had this to say about the beachcombers:

> *They lived worthless lives of sin and luxury, and died without honor—in most cases by violence. Only one of them had any ambition; he was an Irishman named Connor. He tried to raise a family of fifty children and scored forty-eight. He died lamenting his failure. It was a foolish sort of avarice. Many a father would have been rich enough with forty.*

From 1820 to 1850 European traders collected bêche-de-mer, a sea cucumber which, when smoked and dried, also brought a good price in China. While the sandalwood traders only stayed long enough to take on a load, the bêche-de-mer collectors set up shore facilities where the slugs were processed. Many traders, such as David Whippy, followed the example of the beachcombers and took local wives, establishing the part-Fijian community of today. By monopolizing the bêche-de-mer trade and constantly warring, Chief Tanoa's son and successor, Ratu Seru Cakobau (tha-kom-BAU), became extremely powerful in the 1840s and proclaimed himself Tui Viti, or king of Fiji.

The beginnings of organized trade brought a second wave of official explorers to Fiji. In 1827 Dumont d'Urville, from France, landed on Bau Island and met Tanoa. The Frenchmen caused consternation and confusion by refusing to drink *yaqona* (kava), preferring their own wine. The American Exploring Expedition of 1840, led by Comdr. Charles Wilkes, produced the first recognizable map of Fiji. When two Americans, including a nephew of Wilkes, were speared in a misunderstanding on a beach at Malolo Island, Wilkes ordered the offending fortified village stormed, and 87 Fijians were killed. The survivors were made to water and provision Wilkes's ships as tribute. Capt. H.M. Denham of the HMS *Herald* prepared accurate navigational charts of the island group in 1855–1856, making regular commerce possible.

European and Tongan Penetration

As early as the 1830s, an assortment of European and American beachcombers had formed a small settlement at Levuka on the east coast of Ovalau Island just northeast of Bau, which whalers and traders used as a supply base. In 1846 John Brown Williams was appointed American commercial agent, one step below a consul. On July 4, 1849, Williams's home on Nukulau Island near present-day Suva burned down. Though the conflagration was caused by the explosion of a cannon during Williams's own fervent celebration of his national holiday, he objected to the way Fijian onlookers carried off items that they rescued from the flames. A shameless swindler, Williams had purchased Nukulau for only $30, yet he blamed the Tui Viti for his losses and sent Cakobau a $5,001.38 bill. American claims for damages eventually rose to $45,000, and in 1851 and 1855 American gunboats called and ordered Cakobau to pay up. This threat hung over Cakobau's head for many years, the 19th-century equivalent of 20th-century third world debt. Increasing American involvement in Fiji led the British to appoint a consul, W.T. Pritchard, who arrived in 1858.

CANNIBALISM

I t has been said that the Fijians were extremely hospitable to any strangers they did not wish to eat. Native voyagers who wrecked on their shores, who arrived "with salt water in their eyes," were liable to be killed and eaten, since all shipwrecked persons were believed to have been cursed and abandoned by the gods. Many European sailors from wrecked vessels shared the same fate. Cannibalism was a universal practice, and prisoners taken in war, or even women seized while fishing, were invariably eaten. Most of the early European accounts of Fiji emphasized this trait to the exclusion of almost everything else; at one time, the island group was even referred to as the "Cannibal Isles." By eating the flesh of the conquered enemy, one inflicted the ultimate revenge. One chief on Viti Levu is said to have consumed 872 people and to have made a pile of stones to record his achievement. The leaves of a certain vegetable (*Solanum uporo*) were wrapped around the human meat, and it was cooked in an earthen oven. Wooden forks were employed at cannibal feasts. Men—who usually relied on their fingers to eat other food—used the implements, because it was considered improper to touch human flesh with fingers or lips.

The early 1830s also saw the arrival from Tonga of the first missionaries. Though Tahitian pastors were sent by the London Missionary Society to Oneata in southern Lau as early as 1830, it was the Methodists based at Lakeba after 1835 who made the most lasting impression by rendering the Fijian language into writing. At first Christianity made little headway among these fierce, idolatrous people, and only after converting the powerful chiefs were the missionaries successful. Methodist missionaries David Cargill and William Cross were appalled by what they saw during a visit to Bau in 1838. A white missionary, Rev. Thomas Baker, was clubbed and eaten in central Viti Levu by the *kai colo* (hill people) as late as 1867.

In 1847 Enele Ma'afu, a member of the Tongan royal family, arrived in Lau and began building a personal empire under the pretense of defending Christianity. In 1853 King George of Tonga made Ma'afu governor of all Tongans resident in Lau. Meanwhile, there was continuing resistance from the warlords of the Rewa River area to Cakobau's dominance. In addition, the Europeans at Levuka suspected Cakobau of twice ordering their town set afire and were directing trade away from Bau. With his power in decline, in 1854 Cakobau accepted Christianity in exchange for an alliance with King George, and, in 1855, with the help of 2,000 Tongans led by

King George himself, Cakobau was able to put down the Rewa revolt at the Battle of Kaba. In the process, however, Ma'afu became the dominant force in Lau, Taveuni, and Vanua Levu.

During the early 1860s, as Americans fought their Civil War, the world price of cotton soared, and large numbers of Europeans arrived in Fiji hoping to establish cotton plantations. In 1867 the USS *Tuscarora* called at Levuka and threatened to bombard the town unless the still-outstanding American debt was paid. The next year an enterprising Australian firm, the Polynesia Company, paid off the Americans in exchange for a grant from Cakobau of 80,000 hectares of choice land, including the site of modern Suva. The British government later refused to recognize this grant, though they refunded the money paid to the Americans and accepted the claims of settlers who had purchased land from the company. Settlers soon numbered about 2,000 and Levuka boomed.

It was a lawless era, and a need was felt for a central government. An attempt at national rule by a confederacy of chiefs lasted two years until failing in 1867, then three regional governments were set up in Bau (western), Lau (eastern), and Bua (northern), but these were only partly successful. With prices for Fiji's "Sea Island" cotton collapsing as the American South resumed production, a national administration under

Cakobau and planter John Thurston was established at Levuka in 1871.

However, Cakobau was never strong enough to impose his authority over the whole country, so with growing disorder in western Fiji, infighting between Europeans and Fijian chiefs, and a lack of cooperation from Ma'afu's rival confederation of chiefs in eastern Fiji, Cakobau decided he should cede his kingdom to Great Britain. The British had refused an invitation to annex Fiji in 1862, but this time they accepted, rather than risk seeing the group fall into the hands of another power, and on October 10, 1874, Fiji became a British colony. A punitive expedition into central Viti Levu in 1876 brought the hill tribes *(kai colo)* under British rule. In 1877 the Western Pacific High Commission was set up to protect British interests in the surrounding unclaimed island groups as well. In 1881 Rotuma was annexed to Fiji. At first Levuka was the colony's capital, but in 1882 the government moved to a more spacious site at Suva.

The Making of a Nation

The first British governor, Sir Arthur Gordon, and his colonial secretary and successor, Sir John Thurston, created modern Fiji almost singlehandedly. They realized that the easiest way to rule was indirectly, through the existing Fijian chiefs. To protect the communal lands on which the chieftain system was based, they ordered that native land could not be sold, only leased. Not wishing to disturb native society, Gordon and Thurston ruled that Fijians could not be required to work on European plantations. Meanwhile the blackbirding of Melanesian laborers from the Solomon Islands and New Hebrides had been restricted by the Polynesian Islanders Protection Act of 1872.

By this time sugar had taken the place of cotton and there was a tremendous labor shortage on the plantations. Gordon, who had previously served in Trinidad and Mauritius, saw indentured Indian workers as a solution. The first arrived in 1879, and by 1916, when Indian immigration ended, there were 63,000. To come to Fiji, the Indians had to sign a labor contract *(girmit),* in which they agreed to cut

sugarcane for their masters for five years. During the next five years, they were allowed to lease small plots of their own from the Fijians and plant cane or raise livestock. More than half the Indians decided to remain in Fiji as free settlers after their 10-year contracts expired, and today their descendants form nearly half the population, many of them still working small leased plots.

Though this combination of European capital, Fijian land, and Indian labor did help preserve traditional Fijian culture, it also kept the Fijians backward—envious onlookers passed over by European and (later) Indian prosperity. Installed by the British more than a century ago, the separate administration and special rights for indigenous Fijians continue today.

In early 1875 Cakobau and two of his sons returned from a visit to Australia infected with measles. Though they themselves survived, the resulting epidemic wiped out a third of the Fijian population. As a response to this and other public health problems, the Fiji School of Medicine was founded in 1885. At the beginning of European colonization, there were about 200,000 Fijians, approximately 114,748 in 1881, and just 84,000 by 1921.

The Colonial Period

In 1912 a Gujarati lawyer, D.M. Manilal, arrived in Fiji from Mauritius to fight for Indian rights, just as his contemporary Mohandas Gandhi was doing in South Africa. Several prominent Anglican and Methodist missionaries also lobbied actively against the system. Indentured Indians continued to arrive in Fiji until 1916, but the protests led to the termination of the indenture system throughout the empire in 1920 (Manilal was deported from Fiji after a strike that year).

Although Fiji was a political colony of Britain, it was always an economic colony of Australia: The big Australian trading companies Burns Philp and W.R. Carpenters dominated business. (The ubiquitous Morris Hedstrom is a subsidiary of Carpenters.) Most of the Indians were brought to Fiji to work for the Australian-owned Colonial Sugar Refining Company, which controlled the

A SKELETON IN BRITAIN'S NUCLEAR CLOSET

In 1957 and 1958, some 300 Fijian soldiers and sailors were employed by the British during a hydrogen-bomb testing program in the Line Islands, presently Kiribati (between Hawaii and Tahiti). Three particularly dirty atmospheric tests took place off Malden Island in May and June 1957, and there were another six tests on Christmas Island in November 1957 and September 1958. The troops were exposed to significant levels of radiation, and numerous instances of test-related health problems have been documented among veterans. The most notorious case involves Ratu Penaia Ganilau, later knighted and made president of Fiji, who landed barefoot on Malden immediately after a test in May 1957. Sir Penaia died of leukemia in 1993 after a long illness. Other Fijians were used to clear away thousands of sea birds killed by the blasts, or to dump drums of nuclear waste into the sea. Few protective measures were taken, and there have been accusations that the troops were deliberately exposed to radiation so they could be used as guinea pigs. Litigation against the British government began in 1997, but to date no compensation has been paid by the British to the Fijian victims of their tests.

No representative government existed in Fiji until 1904, when a legislative council was formed with six elected Europeans and two Fijians nominated by the Great Council of Chiefs (Bose Levu Vakaturaga), itself an instrument of colonial rule. In 1916 the governor appointed an Indian member to the council. A 1929 reform granted five seats to each of the three communities: three elected and two appointed Europeans and Indians, and five nominated Fijians. The council was only an advisory body, and the governor remained in complete control. The Europeans generally sided with the Fijians against any demands for equality from the Indians—typical colonial divide and rule.

During World War II, Fijians were outstanding combat troops on the Allied side in the Solomon Islands campaign. In 1952–1956 Fijians helped suppress Malaya's national liberation struggle. So skilled were the Fijians at jungle warfare against the Japanese that it was never appropriate to list a Fijian as "missing in action"— the phrase used was "not yet arrived." The war years saw the development of Nadi Airport. Until 1952, Suva, the present Fijian capital, was headquarters for the entire British Imperial Administration in the South Pacific.

In 1963 the Legislative Council was expanded (though still divided along racial lines), and women and indigenous Fijians got the vote for the first time. Wishing to be rid of the British, whom they blamed for their second-class position, the Indians pushed for independence, but the Fijians had come to view the British as protectors and were somewhat reluctant. A Constitutional Convention was held in London in 1965 to move Fiji toward self-government, and after much discussion a constitution was adopted in 1970. Some legislature members were to be elected from a common roll (voting by all races), as the Indians desired, while other seats remained ethnic (voting in racial constituencies) to protect the Fijians. On October 10, 1970, Fiji became a fully independent nation, and the first Fijian governor-general was appointed in 1973—none other than Ratu Sir George Cakobau, greatgrandson of the chief who had ceded Fiji to Queen Victoria 99 years previously.

sugar industry from 1881 right up until 1973, when it was purchased by the Fiji government for $14 million. After 1935, Fiji's gold fields were also exploited by Australians. Banking, insurance, and tourism are largely controlled by Australian companies today.

Under the British colonial system, the governor of Fiji had far greater decision-making authority than his counterparts in the French Pacific colonies. Whereas the French administrators were required to closely follow policies dictated from Paris, the governors of the British colonies had only to refer to the Colonial Office in London on special matters such as finance and foreign affairs. Otherwise they had great freedom to make policy decisions.

SINCE INDEPENDENCE

Political Development

During the 1940s, Ratu Sir Lala Sukuna, paramount chief of Lau, played a key role in the creation of a separate administration for indigenous Fijians, with native land (83 percent of Fiji) under its jurisdiction. In 1954 he formed the Fijian Association to support the British governor against Indian demands for equal representation. In 1960 the National Federation Party (NFP) was formed to represent Indian cane farmers.

In 1966 the Alliance Party, a coalition of the Fijian Association, the General Electors' Association (representing Europeans, part-Fijians, and Chinese), and the Fiji Indian Alliance (a minority Indian group) won the legislative assembly elections. In 1970 Alliance Party leader Ratu Sir Kamisese Mara led Fiji into independence, and in 1972 his party won Fiji's first post-independence elections. Ratu Mara served as prime minister almost continuously until the 1987 elections.

The formation of the Fiji Labor Party (FLP), headed by Dr. Timoci Bavadra, in July 1985 dramatically altered the political landscape. Fiji's previously nonpolitical trade unions had finally come behind a party that campaigned on bread-and-butter issues rather than race. Late in 1986 Labor and the NFP formed the Coalition with the aim of defeating the Alliance in the next election. In the April 1987 elections, the Coalition won 28 of 52 House of Representatives seats; 19 of the 28 elected Coalition members were Indo-Fijians. What swung the election away from Alliance was not a change in Indo-Fijian voting patterns but support for Labor from urban Fijians and part-Fijians, which cost Alliance four previously "safe" seats around Suva.

The Coalition cabinet had a majority of Indo-Fijian members, but all positions of vital Fijian interest (Lands, Fijian Affairs, Labor and Immigration, Education, Agriculture and Rural Development) went to indigenous Fijian legislators, though none of them was a traditional chief. Coalition's progressive policies marked quite a switch from the conservatism of the Alliance—a new generation of political leadership dedicated to tackling the day-to-day problems of people of all races, rather than dedicated to perpetuating the privileges of the old chiefly oligarchy. Given time, the Coalition might have required the high chiefs to share the rental monies they received for leasing lands to Indo-Fijians more fairly with ordinary Fijians. Most significant of all, the Coalition would have transformed Fiji from a pluralistic society where only indigenous Melanesian Fijians were called Fijians into a truly multiracial society where all citizens would be Fijians.

The First Coup

After the election, the extremist Fiji-for-Fijians Taukei (landowners) movement launched a destabilization campaign by throwing barricades across highways, organizing protest rallies and marches, and carrying out firebombings. On April 24, 1987, Senator Inoke Tabua and former Alliance cabinet minister Apisai Tora organized a march of 5,000 Fijians through Suva to protest "Indian domination" of the new government. Mr. Tora told a preparatory meeting for the demonstration that Fijians must "act now" to avoid ending up as "deprived as Australia's aborigines." (In fact, under the 1970 constitution the Coalition government would have had no way of changing Fiji's land laws without indigenous Fijian consent.)

At 1000 on Thursday, May 14, 1987, Lt. Col. Sitiveni Rabuka (ram-BU-ka), an ambitious officer whose career was stalled at number three in the Fiji army, and 10 heavily armed soldiers dressed in fatigues, their faces covered by gas masks, entered the House of Parliament in Suva. Rabuka ordered Dr. Bavadra and the Coalition members to follow a soldier out of the building, and when Dr. Bavadra hesitated the soldiers raised their guns. The legislators were loaded into army trucks and taken to Royal Fiji Military Forces headquarters. There was no bloodshed, though Rabuka later confirmed that his troops would have opened fire had there been any resistance. At a press conference five hours after the coup, Rabuka claimed he had acted to prevent violence and had no political ambitions of his own.

Australia and New Zealand promptly denounced the region's first military coup. Governor-General Ratu Sir Penaia Ganilau attempted to reverse the situation by declaring a state of emergency and ordering the mutineers to return to their barracks. They refused to obey. The next day Rabuka named a 15-member Council of Ministers, which he chaired, to govern Fiji, with former Alliance Prime Minister Ratu Mara as foreign minister. Significantly, Rabuka was the only military officer on the council; most of the others were members of Ratu Mara's defeated administration. Rabuka claimed he had acted to "safeguard the Fijian land issue and the Fijian way of life."

On May 19, Dr. Bavadra and the other kidnapped members of his government were released after the governor-general announced a deal negotiated with Rabuka to avoid the possibility of foreign intervention. Rabuka's Council of Ministers was replaced by a 19-member caretaker Advisory Council appointed by the Great Council of Chiefs. The council would govern until new elections could take place. Ratu Ganilau would head the council, with Rabuka in charge of Home Affairs and the security forces. Only two seats were offered to Dr. Bavadra's government, and they were refused.

Until the coup, the most important mission of the Royal Fiji Military Forces was service in South Lebanon and the Sinai with peacekeeping operations. Half of the 2,600-member Fiji army was on rotating duty there, the Sinai force financed by the United States, the troops in Lebanon by the United Nations. During World War II, Indo-Fijians refused to join the army unless they received the same pay as European recruits; indigenous Fijians had no such reservations and the force has been 95 percent Fijian ever since. Service in the strife-torn Middle East gave the Fiji military a unique preparation for its often political role in Fiji today. (Not many people outside Fiji realize the fact that, after Australia and New Zealand, Lebanon is the foreign country most familiar to indigenous Fijians.)

The Second Coup

In July and August 1987, a committee set up by Governor-General Ganilau studied proposals for constitutional reform, and, on September 4, talks began at Government House in Suva between Alliance and Coalition leaders under the chairmanship of Ratu Ganilau. With no hope of a consensus on a revised constitution, the talks were aimed at preparing for new elections.

Then, on September 26, 1987, Rabuka struck again, just hours before the governor-general was to announce a government of national unity to rule Fiji until new elections could be held. The plan, arduously developed over four months and finally approved by veteran political leaders on all sides, would probably have resulted in Rabuka being sacked. Rabuka quickly threw out the 1970 constitution and pronounced himself "head of state." Some 300 prominent community leaders were arrested, and Ratu Ganilau was confined to Government House. Newspapers were shut down, trade unions repressed, the judiciary suspended, the public service purged, the activities of political opponents restricted, a curfew imposed, and the first cases of torture reported.

At midnight on October 7, 1987, Rabuka declared Fiji a republic. Rabuka's new Council of Ministers included Taukei extremists Apisai Tora and Filipe Bole, Fijian Nationalist Party leader Sakeasi Butadroka, and other marginal figures. Rabuka appeared to have backing from the Great Council of Chiefs, which wanted a return to the style of customary rule, now threatened by the Indian presence and Western democracy. Regime ideologists trumpeted traditional culture and religious fundamentalism to justify their actions. Ratu Mara himself was annoyed that Rabuka's second coup had destroyed an opportunity to restore the reputations of himself and Ratu Ganilau. On October 16, Ratu Ganilau resigned as governor-general, and two days later Fiji was expelled from the British Commonwealth.

The Republic of Rabuka

Realizing that Taukei/military rule was a recipe for disaster, on December 5, 1987, Rabuka appointed Ratu Ganilau president and Ratu Mara prime minister of the new republic. The 21-member cabinet included 10 members of Rabuka's military regime, four of them army officers. Rabuka himself (now a self-styled brigadier) was once again Minister of Home Affairs. This interim government set itself a deadline of two years to frame a new constitution and return Fiji to freely elected representative government. By mid-1988 the army had been expanded into a highly disciplined 6,000-member force loyal to Brigadier Rabuka, who left no doubt he would intervene a third time if his agenda was not followed. The Great Council of Chiefs was to decide on Fiji's republican constitution.

The coups transformed the Fijian economy. In 1987 Fiji experienced 11 percent negative growth in the gross domestic product. To slow the flight of capital, the Fiji dollar was devalued 33 percent in 1987, and inflation was up to nearly 12 percent by the end of 1988. At the same time, civil servants (half the workforce) had to accept a 25 percent wage cut as government spending was slashed. Food prices skyrocketed, causing serious problems for many families. At the end of 1987, the per capita average income was 11 percent *below* what it had been in 1980. Between 1986 and 1996, some 58,300 Indo-Fijians left Fiji for Australia, Canada, New Zealand, and the United States. Nearly three-quarters of Fiji's administrators and managers, and a quarter of all professional, technical, and clerical workers departed, taking tens of millions of dollars with them, a crippling loss for a country with a total population of less than 750,000.

On the other hand, the devaluations and wage-cutting measures, combined with the creation of a tax-free exporting sector and the encouragement of foreign investment, brought about an economic recovery by 1990. At the expense of democracy, social justice, and racial harmony, Fiji embarked on a standard International Monetary Fund/World Bank-style structural adjustment program. In 1992 the imposition of a 10 percent value-added tax (VAT) shifted the burden of taxation from rich to poor, standard IMF dogma. In effect, Rabuka and the old oligarchs had pushed Fiji squarely back into the third world.

In November 1989, Dr. Bavadra died of spinal cancer at age 55, and 60,000 people attended his funeral at Viseisei; it was the largest funeral in Fijian history. Foreign journalists were prevented from covering the funeral. The nominal head of the unelected interim government, Ratu Mara, considered Rabuka an unpredictable upstart and insisted that he choose between politics or military

service. Thus in late 1989, the general and two army colonels were dropped from the cabinet, though Rabuka kept his post as army commander.

On July 25, 1990, President Ganilau promulgated a new constitution approved by the Great Council of Chiefs, which gave the chiefs the right to appoint the president and 24 of the 34 members of the Senate. The president had executive authority and appointed the prime minister from among the ethnic Fijian members of the House of Representatives. Under this constitution, the 70-member House of Representatives was elected directly, with voting racially segregated. Ethnic Fijians were granted 37 seats from constituencies gerrymandered to ensure the dominance of the eastern chiefs. The constitution explicitly reserved the posts of president, prime minister, and army chief for ethnic Fijians. Christianity was made the official religion, and Rabuka's troops were granted amnesty for any crimes committed during the 1987 coups. The Coalition promptly rejected this supremacist constitution as undemocratic and racist.

Not satisfied with control of the Senate, in early 1991 the Great Council of Chiefs decided to project their power into the lower house through the formation of the Soqosoqo ni Vakavulewa ni Taukei (SVT), commonly called the Fijian Political Party. Meanwhile Fiji's multiethnic unions continued to rebuild their strength by organizing garment workers and leading strikes in the mining and sugar industries.

In June 1991 Major-General Rabuka rejected an offer from Ratu Mara to join the cabinet as Minister of Home Affairs and co-deputy prime minister, since it would have meant giving up his military power base. Instead Rabuka attempted to widen his political appeal by making public statements in support of striking gold miners and cane farmers, and even threatening a third coup.

By now Rabuka's ambition to become prime minister was obvious, and his new role as a populist rabble-rouser seemed designed to outflank both the Labor Party and the chiefs (Rabuka himself is a commoner). President Ganilau (Rabuka's paramount chief) quickly applied pressure, and in July the volatile general reversed himself and accepted the cabinet posts he had so recently refused. As a condition for reentering the government, Rabuka was forced to resign as army commander, and the president's son, Maj. Gen. Epeli Ganilau, was appointed his successor. With Rabuka out of the army, everyone breathed a little easier, and the chiefs decided to co-opt a potential troublemaker by electing Rabuka president of the SVT.

Return to Democracy

The long-awaited parliamentary elections took place in late May 1992, and the SVT captured 30 of the 37 indigenous Fijian seats. Another five went to Fijian nationalists, while the 27 Indian seats were split between the NFP with 14 and the FLP with 13. The five other races' seats went to the General Voters Party (GVP).

Just prior to the election, Ratu Mara retired from party politics and was named vice-president of Fiji by the Great Council of Chiefs. An intense power struggle then developed in the SVT between Ratu Mara's chosen successor as prime minister, former finance minister Josevata Kamikamica, and ex-general Rabuka. Since the SVT lacked a clear majority in the 70-seat house, coalition partners had to be sought, and in a remarkable turn of events populist Rabuka gained the support of the FLP by offering concessions to the trade unions and a promise to review the constitution and land leases. Therefore Rabuka became prime minister thanks to the very party he had ousted from power at gunpoint exactly five years earlier!

The SVT formed a coalition with the GVP, but in November 1993 the Rabuka government was defeated in a parliamentary vote of no confidence over the budget, leading to fresh elections in February 1994. In these elections, Rabuka's SVT increased its representation to 31 seats. Many Indo-Fijians had felt betrayed by FLP's backing of Rabuka's prime ministership in 1992, and FLP representation dropped to seven seats, compared to 20 for the NFP.

Ratu Ganilau died of leukemia in December 1993, and Ratu Mara was sworn in as president in January 1994. Meanwhile, Rabuka cultivated a pragmatic image to facilitate his international ac-

ceptance in the South Pacific, and within Fiji itself he demonstrated his political prowess by holding out a hand of reconciliation to the Indo-Fijian community. The 1990 constitution had called for a constitutional review before 1997, and in 1995 a three-member commission was appointed, led by Sir Paul Reeves, a former governor-general of New Zealand, together with Mr. Tomasi Vakatora, representing the Rabuka government, and Mr. Brij Lal for the opposition.

The report of the commission titled *Towards a United Future* was submitted in September 1996. It recommended a return to the voting system outlined in the 1970 constitution, with some members of parliament elected from racially divided communal constituencies and others from open ridings on a common roll of racially mixed electorates. The commissioners suggested that the post of prime minister no longer be explicitly reserved for an indigenous Fijian but simply for the leader of the largest grouping in parliament of whatever race.

The report was passed to a parliamentary committee for study, and in May 1997 all sides agreed to a power-sharing formula to resolve Fiji's constitutional impasse. The number of guaranteed seats for indigenous Fijians in the lower house was reduced from 37 to 23, and voting across racial lines was instituted in another third of the seats. The prime minister was to be required to form a cabinet comprised of ministers from all parties in proportion to their representation in parliament—a form of power sharing unique in modern democracy. The country's president and nearly half the members of the senate would continue to be appointed by the Great Council of Chiefs. Human rights guarantees were included. The Constitution Amendment Bill passed both houses of parliament unanimously, and was promulgated into law by President Mara on July 25, 1997. In recognition of the rare national consensus that had been achieved, Fiji was welcomed back into the British Commonwealth in October 1997. The new constitution formally took effect in July 1998.

For many years it was unfashionable to look upon Fiji as a part of Melanesia, and the nation's Polynesian links were emphasized. The 1987 coups had a lot to do with rivalry between the eastward-looking chiefs of Bau and Lau and the Melanesian-leaning western Fijians. Ironically, some of the political friction between the dark-skinned commoner Rabuka and the tall aristocrat Ratu Mara can also be seen in this light. The latter was always networking among Fiji's smaller Polynesian neighbors, and it was only in 1996 that Rabuka brought Fiji into the Melanesian Spearhead Group that had existed since 1988. Of course, the pragmatist Rabuka was merely acknowledging the vastly greater economic potential of Melanesia, but he was clearly much more comfortable socializing with the other Melanesian leaders at regional summits than Ratu Mara ever would have been.

People's Coalition Government

In May 1999, Fiji's 419,000 eligible voters participated in the first election under the 1997 constitution. The IMF-style structural adjustment program of the previous government and a strong desire for change were key issues, and although Rabuka himself was elected, his SVT Party took only eight of the 71 parliamentary seats. The NFP allied with Rabuka was wiped out entirely by the Labor Party, which won all 19 Indo-Fijian seats, plus 18 of the 25 common roll seats elected by all voters. Two indigenous Fijian parties, the Fijian Alliance and the Party of National Unity, won a total of 14 seats. They formed an alliance with Labor's 37 members to give "People's Coalition" an overwhelming 51 seats.

Among the seven women elected to parliament were Adi Kuini Vuikaba Speed, widow of former prime minister Timoci Bavadra, and Adi Koila Mara Nailatikau, daughter of President Mara. Labor leader Mahendra Chaudhry was appointed prime minister—the first Indo-Fijian ever to occupy the post. Two-thirds of Chaudhry's cabinet were indigenous Fijians, but it was quite different from the two previous governments, which had included no Indo-Fijians. Rabuka resigned from parliament soon after the election and was made chairman of the Great Council of Chiefs. His departure contributed to a feeling among grassroots Fijians that the Indians had taken over. If Dr. Tupeni Baba, Labor's second-in-

command and an indigenous Fijian, had become prime minister, the situation might have been different, but Chaudhry's struggle had been long, and his victory was so complete that he insisted on getting the top job. Baba became deputy prime minister. NFP leader Jai Ram Reddy issued a portentous warning at the time: "Fiji is not yet ready for an Indian prime minister."

Fiji's first democratic government in a dozen years survived 365 days. Chaudhry vigorously pushed forward his reforms and applied the brakes to privatization, which won him few friends, and his relations with business and the media were antagonistic. In February 2000, the government introduced a "leadership honesty code" bill which would have required politicians to disclose their personal assets in private to the Ombudsman's office. Corruption had been rife during the Rabuka years, culminating in the collapse of the National Bank of Fiji in 1995 after F\$295 million had been siphoned off by politicians and the Fijian chiefs through bad loans and other devices. Mismanagement and cronyism had led to huge losses by the Fiji Development Bank and provincial councils, and kickbacks were routine at Customs & Excise and other government departments. The Chaudhry government's anti-corruption drive was a blast of fresh air.

Reducing poverty was a high priority for the Chaudhry team. People's Coalition attempted to help Fijian villagers through affirmative action programs. The value-added tax and customs duty on basic food items were lowered, utility rates were slashed, and loans were made available for small business.

People's Coalition also bucked the trend toward globalization and lobbied hard for fairer terms of trade. In recognition, Fiji was selected as the venue for the signing of what would have been the Suva Convention, a 20-year successor to the Lomé Agreement governing trade between 77 African, Caribbean, and Pacific (ACP) nations and the 15 European Union states. Dozens of ministers and high officials from these countries were scheduled to be in Suva on June 8, 2000, for the launch of this historic partnership agreement, but it was not to be.

After the May 1999 election, leaders of the

defeated SVT party began working on strategies to bring down the People's Coalition government and return to power. In April 2000, the ultra-nationalist Taukei Movement was revived by Apisai Tora, a fringe politician deeply involved in the 1987 coups. Taukei's declared aim was to revise the 1997 constitution to ensure Fijian political supremacy. The SVT supported Taukei, as did some provincial administrations, but the Fiji army declared that it would not be drawn into any attempt to overthrow the government. Taukei agitators tried to make the future of Indo-Fijian land leases an issue, and demonstrations began in Lautoka and Suva.

The Third Coup

On May 19, 2000, a Taukei protest march wound down Victoria Parade in central Suva. When the thousands of marchers reached the gates of the Presidential Palace, they were told that gunmen had stormed Fiji's parliament, which had been in session, and had taken its members hostage. Many of the marchers rushed to the building, joining terrorists who were only too happy to have willing human shields. In central Suva, gangs of thugs and protesters responded to news of the takeover by looting and burning Indian shops. About 160 shops were emptied or destroyed in the three hours before the police began making arrests.

The initial assault on parliament was led by a failed businessman named George Speight, along with seven renegade members of the army's elite Counter Revolutionary Warfare Unit (also known as the First Meridian Squadron) and 35 ex-soldiers, half of them ex-convicts. The highest-ranking soldier present was retired major Ilisoni Ligairi, a former British Special Air Services warrant officer who had set up the CRW anti-terrorist unit in 1987. Speight had appeared in the Suva High Court on extortion charges five days before the coup, yet he declared he was acting to defend indigenous Fijian rights. In 1997 Speight had been forced to flee Australia after a pyramid scheme he had a hand in collapsed with A$130 million in losses for gullible investors.

Yet to understand what was really happening, we have to back up a bit. In early 1999, a bitter struggle was being waged in government circles over who would gain the right to market Fiji's valuable mahogany forests worldwide. The Rabuka government was known to favor a U.S. company called Timber Resources Management, while the incoming Chaudhry government announced they intended to give the contract to the British-based Commonwealth Development Corporation on the basis of a recommendation from the Australian office of the accountancy firm PricewaterhouseCoopers. Speight had previously worked as a consultant for the Americans, and in June 1999 Chaudhry's Forestry Minister removed him from his position as managing director of the state-owned Fiji Hardwood Corporation and Fiji Pine Limited, because Speight had been a political appointee of the former regime. Chaudhry's surprise election in May 1999 had cost Speight and associates the chance to control the exploitation of mahogany and pine tracts worth hundreds of millions of dollars. Just prior to his assault on parliament, Speight had been trying to foment unrest among landowners by spreading disinformation about the rival bids and the Chaudhry government's intentions. Important figures in the previous Rabuka government were involved in the ongoing mahogany affair, including Rabuka's Minister of Finance and former Speight patron Jim Ah Koy. Speight's coup attempt may have had much more to do with timber rights than indigenous rights.

Among the 45 persons taken hostage by Speight's gang were Prime Minister Chaudhry, and the minister of tourism and transport, President Mara's daughter. Ratu Mara immediately declared a state of emergency, and the Fiji Military Forces commander, Comdr. Voreqe Bainimarama, ordered his men to surround the parliamentary compound. Unlike the situation during the 1987 coups, the army's high command and the bulk of its troops did not support the coup attempt. Bainimarama declined to use force to free the captives for fear of triggering a bloodbath, and many of the hostages were to spend the next 56 days sitting on mattresses with their lives in the hands of heavily armed thugs.

Parliament building, Suva, Viti Levu

On May 27, 80-year-old President Mara officially dismissed the elected Chaudhry government after Speight threatened to kill his daughter. The next day a mob of Speight supporters ransacked the offices of Fiji TV to protest coverage critical of the coup. Soon after, a Fijian policeman was shot dead by gunmen near parliament. On May 29, with the situation deteriorating, the army asked President Mara to "step aside" while it restored order. Mara thereupon withdrew to his power base on remote Lakeba in the Lau Group, the ignominious end of a long and distinguished career. That day Commodore Bainimarama declared martial law, announced the abrogation of the 1997 constitution, and assumed executive authority. Bainimarama ruled out any return to power by Chaudhry.

Meanwhile, as the negotiations continued, Speight was constantly making fresh demands. A struggle for power was underway among the Fijian elite. The Great Council of Chiefs wanted to appoint the vice president, Ratu Josefa Iloilo, to replace Mara, but Speight insisted that Ratu Jope Seniloli, a retired schoolteacher with close ties to the chiefly Cakobau family of Bau but no previous political standing, must become vice president.

Since the death of Ratu Sir George Cakobau in 1989, the once powerful Cakobaus of eastern Viti Levu had been eclipsed by their historic "Tongan" enemies from Lau, led by Ratu Sir Kamisese Mara. Seven weeks into the crisis, Speight moved to have persons with Cakobau connections granted high positions in an interim administration. His choice for prime minister was Adi Samanunu Cakobau, Fiji's high commissioner in Malaysia and Sir George's eldest daughter.

That was the signal for Bainimarama, a longtime Mara ally, to order his army to tighten the noose around Speight by declaring parliament and nearby streets a "military exclusion zone." The next day (July 3) the Great Council of Chiefs named a civilian cabinet led by the former head of the Fiji Development Bank, Laisenia Qarase, another Mara man. This interim government had the army's blessing, and to win acceptance from the international community, high-profile Speight elements were shut out. These developments triggered widespread disturbances by grassroots Speight supporters throughout the country, including the occupation of a few tourist resorts, the blocking of highways, and the burning of the historic Masonic Lodge in Levuka. There was intimidation of Indo-Fijians living in rural areas of northeastern Viti Levu and central Vanua Levu—traditional Cakobau strongholds—with arson, looting, and ethnic cleansing. The military was unable to cope.

Visibly shaken, on July 9 Bainimarama agreed to an amnesty for Speight and the others on the condition that they free the 27 remaining hostages and surrender all arms. The Qarase interim government would be replaced, and Iloilo and Seniloli would become president and vice president. On July 13, the hostage crisis came to a peaceful end at a kava ceremony, when Chaudhry magnanimously said that he harbored no personal animosity toward Speight, though the army noted that not all of the missing weapons were turned in. Upon his release Chaudhry confirmed that he had been beaten by Speight's thugs early on in the hostage crisis.

It's said that only the threat of a military coup from Bainimarama prevented President Iloilo, who was seen as overly sympathetic to Speight's cause, from accepting Adi Samanunu Cakobau as prime minister. Former prime minister Rabuka (who remained on the sidelines during most of the crisis) remarked that Speight was only a puppet, brought in at the last minute by persons unknown.

Speight is only part-Fijian, and the Taukei extremists represent a small minority of opinion in Fiji. The concerns of indigenous Fijians to protect their lands and culture were and are legitimate, but those interests have been enshrined in all three of Fiji's constitutions and no government would have been able to negate them. As previously in recent Fijian history, the race issue was manipulated by defeated politicians and power-hungry individuals, and rural villagers and marginalized urban Fijians proved effective tools in the hands of rabble-rouser George Speight.

Interim Government

After the hostages were freed, Qarase simply stayed on as prime minister. In late July, he appointed a cabinet consisting mostly of indigenous Fijian civil servants and opposition politicians, without any overt Speight insiders. Qarase announced that his military-backed regime would last 18 months, to give time for a new constitution to be drawn up and fresh elections arranged. However, during the week of July 17, Australia, Britain, and New Zealand announced sanctions against Fiji, because the elected government had not been restored.

Speight's agitating continued with Qarase now the target of choice. On July 27, Speight was arrested at an army checkpoint between Suva and Nausori, and the next day the army rounded up 369 of his commoner followers in a forceful manner. Speight and cohorts were charged with carrying arms in contravention of the amnesty deal, and a week later the charge of treason was added. Speight and a dozen key figures in the coup attempt were sent to await trial on tiny Nukulau Island, a former picnic spot off Suva. In protest, pro-Speight soldiers kidnapped 50 Indo-Fijians at Labasa, but released them quickly when the army threatened to intervene.

In September, the interim government set up a 12-member commission to review the 1997 constitution. Asesela Ravuvu, an academic with a long history of advocating hard-line indigenous Fijian positions, was appointed chairman, and among the other members were three Speight supporters. Most Indo-Fijians boycotted the process.

On the afternoon of November 2, 2000, the final act in this tragedy unfolded at Suva's Queen Elizabeth Barracks, as 39 soldiers from the Counter Revolutionary Warfare Unit staged a surprise raid on army headquarters in an attempt to murder Commodore Bainimarama and seize control of Fiji for Speight. Loyal officers helped Bainimarama escape down a gully, and just before dusk the Third Fiji Infantry Regiment launched a fierce counterattack. Five rebels and three government soldiers died in the attempted mutiny, including several rebels who were kicked to death by army troops after being captured. Two dozen soldiers and civilians were wounded, and the army quickly rounded up the remaining mutineers. The nation was shocked by this unprecedented brutality. The plot thickened when it was revealed that ex-general Rabuka had been present at the barracks during the mutiny. Rabuka claimed he had only gone there to mediate, but Bainimarama ordered him not to re-enter the facility.

After the hostages' release, a number of lawsuits were filed before the Fiji High Court claiming that the change in government was unconstitutional. On November 15, 2000, Chief Justice Anthony Gates issued a ruling in response to a plea brought by an ordinary Indo-Fijian farmer, Chandrika Prasad, who claimed that his constitutional rights had been violated by the coup. Gates agreed and declared the Speight coup null and void, the interim government illegal, and the 1997 constitution still the law of the land. Gates ruled that Ratu Mara was still the legal president of Fiji and that he had a duty to appoint a new prime minister from among the parliamentarians elected in 1999. Gates suggested that the interim government resign and allow the formation of a government of national unity comprised of elected members of parliament. That would get Fiji back on track.

A shocked interim Prime Minister Qarase referred the case to the Fiji Court of Appeal, which upheld Chief Justice Gates' ruling in an historic decision on March 1, 2001. Qarase and Iloilo both announced that the court's decision would be respected. Fiji's top judges had suggested that the president recall parliament, and 40 of the 71 parliamentarians deposed by George Speight signed a petition asking that this be done. Yet instead of recalling parliament, President Iloilo dissolved the old parliament and appointed Qarase to run a caretaker government until fresh elections could be held. Qarase quickly brought back his old 30-minister cabinet, and the unelected government the judges had declared illegal just two weeks before was back in business.

As could be expected, the Fiji Crisis had a disastrous impact on the economy. After positive growth of 7.8 percent in 1999, there was 2.8 percent negative growth in 2000. By the end of 2000, more than 7,400 people had lost their jobs. Tourist arrivals for the three months following the coup were only 37,126, compared to 120,156 for the same period in 1999, and the industry was losing US$1 million a day. A US$100 million Hilton hotel project for Nadi was put on hold, and other major resorts at Natadola Beach and elsewhere were canceled. Only in 2001 did the economy again begin to grow. The crisis has seriously widened the gap between the haves and have-nots in Fiji.

New Zealand journalist Michael Field, who was in Fiji throughout the crisis, summed it up thus:

I found it more personal than any other story I've ever covered. People who had long ago stopped just being contacts and stories, but were friends to cherish and love, were hurting so much during those three months. The pain of knowing this was not a pain worth much at all compared to those who were seeing lives and dreams disappear in some indigenous nightmare. In one of the more telling moments, Mara spoke of the way traditional Fiji had a procedure for reconciliation. Like other Polynesian cultures, the business of saying sorry is deeply ingrained and much honored. What he did not say was who was meant to apologize to who. And for what.

Elections and Aftermath

The judges had ruled that the 1997 constitution remained in force, thus attempts by the caretaker government to draft a new constitution weighted toward Fijians were halted. The international sanctions against Fiji continued, and in August 2001 Qarase called early elections to legitimize his rule. Qarase's SDL party won 32 of the 71 parliament seats, Labor 27 seats, and the pro-coup Conservative Alliance six. Despite being imprisoned, George Speight was elected as the Conservative Alliance member from Korovou in northeastern Viti Levu. Qarase formed a government in coalition with the Conservative Alliance after they dropped a demand for an amnesty for Speight, who was formally expelled from parliament in December for failing to attend the sessions.

The 1997 constitution stipulates that any party winning at least 10 percent of the 71 parliamentary seats has a right to be represented in cabinet. This meant Labor was entitled to eight of the 20 cabinet posts, but Qarase claimed that having Labor ministers in his cabinet was "unworkable," and in September 2001 he formed a government without the participation of Labor.

Labor filed suit, and in February 2002 the Fiji Court of Appeal ruled that Qarase had to include Labor in his cabinet. Qarase appealed to Fiji's Supreme Court, which in July 2003 ordered the government to include Labor ministers in the cabinet. In response, Qarase offered to enlarge his cabinet from 22 to 36 ministers, with Labor granted 14 minor portfolios in fields such as libraries and health promotion. All ministers would be required to support government policies or resign. Chaudhry refused to accept this "bloated cabinet" and the matter was referred back to court.

In February 2002, George Speight was sentenced to death for treason, but within hours President Iloilo commuted his sentence to life imprisonment. Speight had entered a guilty plea to avoid a trial which might have revealed the names of those behind the coup. During an April 2001 TV interview, Ratu Mara accused Rabuka and Police Commissioner Isikia Savua of involvement in the coup. Chaudhry also pointed a finger at Savua, who prior to May 2000 had assured him that rumors of a coup were unfounded. During the coup itself, Savua stood by while Suva was sacked, but he was later "cleared" of involvement during a secret inquiry by Chief Justice Sir Timoci Tuivaga, author of the military decrees which attempted to scrap the 1997 constitution. Savua is currently Fiji's ambassador to the United Nations in New York.

In a provocative article in the February 2003 issue of *Pacific Magazine*, Michael Field revealed the existence of a mystery coup conspirator whom Speight had expected to emerge on the day of the coup, but who has still to be identified. In May 2003, Vice President Seniloli, two cabinet ministers, and the deputy speaker of parliament were charged with taking unlawful oaths to commit capital offences during the coup. There has been much speculation about other key figures behind the coup, believed to include several prominent businesspeople, and reports of a cover-up in the investigations and trials continue to emerge.

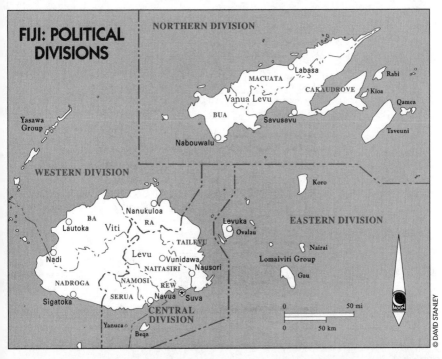

FIJI: POLITICAL DIVISIONS

Both President Iloilo and Prime Minister Qarase owe their positions to the Speight coup, and Qarase's SDL party presently governs in coalition with the pro-Speight Conservative Alliance. Although Qarase's government was elected, the political situation remains shaky, with fresh upheavals to be expected if the agenda of the ultra-nationalists is not followed. It's also quite likely that the last has not been heard from George Speight himself. He's currently being held on Nukulau Island within sight of the parliament building in Suva, a little Napoleon in exile on Elba. It's said that only international opinion and strong objections from Commodore Bainimarama have thus far prevented a pardon for Speight. The shadow of May 19, 2000, continues to hang over Fiji.

GOVERNMENT

The 1997 constitution provides for a parliamentary system of government with a 71-seat House of Representatives, or "lower house," consisting of 46 members from communal ridings and 25 from

FIJI IN A COCONUT SHELL

DIVISION/ PROVINCE	HEADQUARTERS	AREA (SQUARE KM)	POPULATION (1999 EST.)	PERCENT FIJIAN
Central Division	**Suva**	**4,293**	**312,819**	**59.5**
Naitasiri	Vunidawa	1,666	135,220	56.1
Namosi	Navua	570	6,027	91.4
Rewa	Nausori	272	105,458	58.6
Serua	Navua	830	16,125	55.1
Tailevu	Korovou	955	49,989	67.7
Western Division	**Lautoka**	**6,360**	**307,393**	**39.4**
Ba	Lautoka	2,634	220,917	33.2
Nadroga	Sigatoka	2,385	54,859	52.5
Ra	Nanukuloa	1,341	31,617	59.4
Northern Division	**Labasa**	**6,198**	**145,128**	**46.9**
Macuata	Labasa	2,004	83,852	28.2
Bua	Nabouwalu	1,378	15,319	73.6
Cakaudrove	Savusavu	2,816	45,957	72.0
Eastern Division	**Levuka**	**1,422**	**40,928**	**89.4**
Kadavu	Vunisea	478	9,454	99.2
Lau	Lakeba	487	11,700	98.6
Lomaiviti	Levuka	411	16,932	91.2
Rotuma	Ahau	46	2,842	5.8
TOTAL FIJI	**SUVA**	**18,272**	**806,268**	**51.1**

multiracial ridings with elections every five years. Twenty-three communal seats are reserved for indigenous Fijians, 19 for Indo-Fijians, three for general electors (part-Fijians, Europeans, Chinese, etc.), and one for Rotumans. The leader of the largest party or coalition of parties in parliament is the head of government, or prime minister. Voting is compulsory (F$20 fine for failing to vote).

The 32-member "upper house," or Senate, has 14 members appointed by the Great Council of Chiefs, nine by the prime minister, eight by the leader of the opposition, and one by the Council of Rotuma. Any legislation affecting the rights of indigenous Fijians must be approved by nine of the 14 senators appointed by the chiefs. The Great Council of Chiefs also chooses Fiji's head of state, the president, for a five-year term. The three traditional Fijian confederacies are Burebasaga, Kubuna, and Tovata.

Aside from the national government, there's a well-developed system of local government. On the Fijian side, the basic unit is the village (koro) represented by a village herald (turaga-ni-koro), who is chosen by consensus. The 1,169 villages and 483 settlements are grouped into 189 districts (tikina), the districts into 14 provinces (yasana). The executive head of each provincial council is the roko tui, appointed by the Fijian Affairs Board.

The national administration is broken down into four divisions (central, eastern, northern, and western), each headed by a commissioner. These civil servants and the 19 district officers work for the Ministry of Regional Development. The Micronesians of Rabi and Polynesians of Rotuma govern themselves through island councils of their own. Ten city and town councils also function at the local level.

Fiji has a High Court, a Fiji Court of Appeal, and a Supreme Court. The chief justice and eight other judges are appointed by the president after consulting the prime minister. After the collapse of parliament and a change of president in the wake of the Speight coup, the courts emerged as the last bastion of legality in Fiji's national system of government. Criminal and civil cases of lesser importance are handled in magistrates' courts.

Economy

Fiji has a diversified economy based on tourism, garment manufacturing, sugar production, fishing, gold mining, timber, mineral water, vegetables, and coconut products. Although eastern Viti Levu and the Lau Group have long dominated the country politically, western Viti Levu remains Fiji's economic powerhouse, with tourism, sugar, timber, and gold mining all concentrated there.

Aside from the cash economy, subsistence agriculture is important to indigenous Fijians in rural areas, where manioc, taro, yams, sweet potato, and corn are the principal subsistence crops. Coastal subsistence fishing is twice as important as commercial fishing in terms of actual catch.

AGRICULTURE AND INDUSTRY
Sugar

It's estimated that a third of Fiji's population relies on sugar for its livelihood. Although the F$235 million a year Fiji earns from sugar is half of what it makes on tourism, more people rely on sugar than on tourism. Almost all of Fiji's sugarcane is grown by small, independent Indo-Fijian farmers on contract to the government-owned Fiji Sugar Corporation. Some 20,000 farmers cultivate cane on holdings averaging 4.5 hectares and leased from indigenous Fijians, and current problems in renewing these leases could mean that Fiji's sugar industry is ultimately doomed. For many years the corporation has used 595 kilometers of .610-meter narrow-gauge railway to carry the cane to mills at Lautoka, Ba, Rakiraki, and Labasa, and the current shift to truck transport is hurting farmers by increasing costs. Fiji's four aging, inefficient sugar mills are in urgent need of modernization. A distillery at Lautoka produces rum and other liquors from the by-products of sugar.

More than a quarter of a million metric tons of sugar are exported annually to Britain, Japan, and other countries, providing direct or indirect

HOW A SUGAR MILL WORKS

The sugarcane is fed through a shredder toward a row of huge rollers that squeeze out the juice. The crushed fiber (bagasse) is burned to fuel the mill or is processed into paper. Lime is then added to the juice, and the mixture is heated. Impurities settle in the clarifier, and mill mud is filtered out to be used as fertilizer. The clear juice goes through a series of evaporators, in which it is boiled into steam under partial vacuum to remove water and create a syrup. The syrup is boiled again under greater pressure in a vacuum pan, and raw sugar crystals form. The mix then enters a centrifuge, which spins off the remaining syrup (molasses—used for distilling or animal feed). The moist crystals are sent on to a rotating drum, where they are tumble-dried using hot air. Raw sugar comes out in the end.

© DAVID STANLEY

A sugar train crosses the road in downtown Nadi. Sad to say, this means of transport is being phased out in favor of trucks, increasing costs for producers and depriving tourists of a photo op.

employment for 40,000 people. The 14,000 seasonal workers cutting cane earn F$10 a day and two meals. Some 125,000 metric tons of Fiji sugar is sold to the European Union each year at fixed rates four times above world market levels, thanks to import quotas set forth in the Cotonou Agreement. The EU uses this agreement as a way of providing aid to 77 former colonies in Africa, the Caribbean, and the Pacific. Without these subsidies (worth F$100 million a year), Fiji's sugar industry would collapse, as the cost of production is higher than the world market price. Now the World Trade Organization and big producers like Australia and Brazil are putting pres-sure on the EU to phase out the subsidies after the current protocol expires in 2008.

Other Crops and Water

In the past, Fiji has grown almost half its requirements of rice, but the industry has been damaged by competition from imported rice. Much of Fiji's rice is grown around Nausori and Navua, and on Vanua Levu.

Most of Fiji's copra is produced in Lau, Lomaiviti, Taveuni, and Vanua Levu, half by European or part-Fijian planters and the rest by indigenous Fijian villagers. Copra production has slipped from 40,000 tons a year in the 1950s to about 6,000 tons today due to the low prices paid to producers.

In 1998, F$35 million worth of kava root was exported to Germany, the United States, and other countries, where it was used by pharmaceutical firms to make antidepressants and muscle relaxants. In late 2001, kava exports plummeted after the European Union imposed import restrictions on the roots, because of allegations that kava-based medicines might cause liver damage, and in 2002 only F$2 million was exported.

Another unique export is natural artesian water drawn from a well at Yaqara on northwestern Viti Levu and bottled in a modern plant (www.fijiwater.com) set up by Canadian David Gilmour, owner of the Wakaya Club. Gilmour gave the indigenous landowners of the watershed a 25 percent interest in his company, making them the richest clan in Fiji, as sales of Fiji Water in the United States are booming. In 2002, Fiji sold almost F$32 million in water, the sixth largest export.

Timber

Timber is increasingly important as 40,730 hectares of softwood reach maturity, having been planted in western Viti Levu and Vanua Levu by Fiji Pine and private landowners in the late 1970s. Milling and marketing is done by Tropik Timber, a Fiji Pine subsidiary. Processing facilities for the 16,000 hectares of pine on Vanua Levu are inadequate, and round logs must be transported to Viti Levu by truck and ferry at great expense.

In addition to softwood, about 18,000 hectares of hardwood (74 percent of it mahogany) planted by the British after 1952 are mature and ready for harvesting (another 22,000 hectares in southeastern Viti Levu and in central Vanua Levu will be mature in a decade). With buyers in Europe and elsewhere increasingly averse to natural rainforest timber, Fiji is in the enviable position of possessing the world's largest "green" mahogany forest. The government-controlled Fiji Hardwood Corporation was set up in 1997 to manage this asset, which has been valued as high as F$400 million. Thus far, squabbling between the various stakeholders has delayed exploitation of this resource. Fiji already exports about F$42 million a

year in sawed softwood lumber, wood chips, and other wood products (the export of raw logs was banned in 1987).

Yet outside the managed plantations, Fiji's native forests are poorly protected from the greed of foreign logging companies and shortsighted local landowners, and each year large tracts of pristine rainforest are lost. Now that all of the lowland forests have been cleared, attention is turning to the highlands. The planted pine and mahogany have had the corollary benefit of reducing pressure on the natural forests to supply Fiji's timber needs. A factory between Nadi and Sigatoka uses senile coconut trees to make quality furniture, flooring, and panels.

Fishing

Commercial fishing is increasingly important, with a government-owned tuna processing plant at Levuka supplied in part by Fiji's own fleet of longline vessels. Only about 6 percent of the skipjack and albacore tuna is now canned, and most of the rest is chilled and sent to canneries in the United States (see **Ovalau** for more information). Chilled yellowfin tuna is flown to Hawaii and Japan to serve the sashimi (raw fish) market. Fish is now Fiji's third-largest export, and overfishing has resulted from too many fishing licenses being issued to foreign companies by the government.

Related to fishing is the marine-aquarium industry which exports tropical fish and live coral. Walt Smith International (www.waltsmith.com) in Lautoka is a world leader in coral farming, with thousands of living rocks currently growing on iron racks in undersea farms off western Viti Levu.

Mining

Mining activity centers on gold from the Emperor Gold Mine at Vatukoula on northern Viti Levu. Elsewhere on Viti Levu, Emperor controls a rich gold deposit at Tuvatu, unfortunately within the Nadi water-catchment area and thus an environmental hazard. In 1998, the Mount Kasi gold mine on Vanua Levu closed due to low world prices, and the development of other gold fields has been frozen. In 2002, gold exports were worth F$78 million.

Since 1984, Placer Pacific has spent US$10 million exploring the extensive low-grade copper deposits at Namosi, 30 kilometers northwest of Suva, but in 1997, despite offers of near tax-free status from the government, the company put the US$1 billion project on hold saying it was not economical.

Garment Industry

Garments produced by 150 companies that export their clothes mainly to Australia, New Zealand, and the United States are now Fiji's largest export. Some foreign manufacturers have moved their factories to Fiji to take advantage of the low labor costs, and the South Pacific Regional Trade and Economic Cooperation Agreement (SPARTECA) allows Fijian products with at least 50 percent local content partial duty- and quota-free entry into Australia and New Zealand. The value of SPARTECA is gradually eroding and garment exports seem to have peaked.

The garment industry employs 20,000 people, with the mostly female workers earning an average of F$60 a week. At peak periods the factories operate three shifts, seven days a week. Women working in the industry have complained of body searches and sexual harassment; those who protest or organize industrial action are often fired and blacklisted. About 1,000 recently arrived Asian workers are also employed in the factories. In 2002, Fiji exported textiles worth F$245 million.

Other Manufacturing

Companies that process food or make furniture, toys, or shoes are also prominent in the tax-free exporting sector. Until recently, it was believed that manufacturing would eventually overtake both sugar and tourism as the main source of income for the country, but the globalization of trade and the progressive reduction of tariffs worldwide is cutting into Fiji's competitiveness. SPARTECA's local-content rule discourages local companies from reducing costs by introducing labor-saving technology, condemning them to obsolescence in the long term.

ECONOMIC PROBLEMS

In spite of all this potential, unemployment is a major social problem. The economy generates only 2,000 new jobs a year, but 17,000 young people leave school every year, and in 2002 unemployment stood at 14.1 percent. To stimulate industry, firms based in Fiji that export 95 percent of their production are granted 13-year tax holidays, the duty-free import of materials, and the freedom to repatriate capital and profits. An increasing list of incentives is being added to the books.

In 1995, Fiji's financial standing was severely shaken when it was announced that the government-owned National Bank of Fiji was holding hundreds of millions of dollars in bad debts resulting from politically motivated loans to indigenous Fijians and Rotumans. The subsequent run on deposits cost the bank another F$20 million, and the government was forced to step in to save the bank. Vast sums were diverted from development projects to cover the losses, an indication of systemic corruption not usually noticed by visitors. In 1999 Colonial Life Insurance paid F$9.5 million for a 51 percent interest in what was left of the National Bank.

Fiji's government debt is currently F$1.91 billion, 42.8 percent of the gross domestic product. Cronyism and corruption, which the Chaudhry government attempted to control, have returned full force since the May 2000 coup. Bribery by American business interests trying to obtain contracts to harvest Fiji's mahogany reserves may have played a major role in the Speight coup itself, and more recently government officials have been accused of accepting bribes to grant fishing licenses to Asian companies. It's become a standard practice to provide "gifts" to officials when bidding for government contracts. Foreign reserves are falling as the Qarase government borrows tens of millions from the World Bank and Asian Development Bank to cover budget deficits. Debt, deficit spending, and corruption have been identified as major obstacles to aid and investment in Fiji.

TRADE AND AID

Although Fiji imports 39 percent more than it exports, much of the imbalance is resold to tourists and foreign airlines who pay in foreign exchange. Garments are the nation's largest visible export earner, followed by raw sugar, fish, unrefined gold, wood products, mineral water, fruits and vegetables, shoes, fabrics, molasses, coconut oil, and kava, in that order. Large trade imbalances exist with Australia, New Zealand, and most Asian countries.

Mineral fuels used to eat up much of Fiji's import budget, but this has declined since the Monasavu Hydroelectric Project and other self-sufficiency measures came online in the 1980s. Manufactured goods, petroleum products, textiles, food, chemicals, and motor vehicles account for most of the import bill.

Fiji is the least dependent South Pacific nation. Overseas aid totals only F$40 million a year or less than F$50 per capita (as compared to several thousand dollars per capita in French Polynesia). Development aid comes from Australia, the European Union, Japan, New Zealand, and China. North American aid to Fiji is negligible. The New Zealand Government deserves credit for devoting much of its limited aid budget to the creation of national parks and reserves.

Aside from conventional aid, Fiji's army earns money through its participation in multinational forces. The United Nations is currently millions of dollars in arrears in its payments to Fiji for peacekeeping, and in 2002 the last 600 Fiji soldiers returned from service in Lebanon. In late 2003, some 400 Fijian ex-soldiers and police were sent to Iraq by a private British security firm to serve as security guards. The Fiji Army was not involved in this operation, as it was not sanctioned by the United Nations. More than 5,000 people serve in Fiji's armed forces, costing the country F$80 million a year, more than is spent on any other public institution. Many Fijians also enlist in the British Army.

TOURISM

Tourism has been the leading moneymaker since 1989, earning more than F$500 million a year—more than garments and sugar combined. In 2003, some 430,800 tourists visited Fiji—50 percent more than visited Tahiti and more than 10 times as many as visited Tonga. Things appear in better perspective, however,

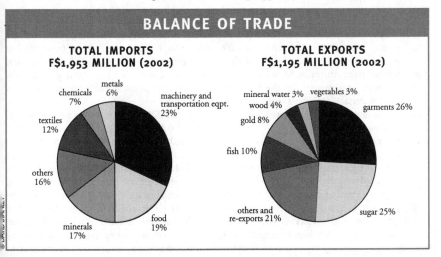

BALANCE OF TRADE

TOTAL IMPORTS
F$1,953 MILLION (2002)

metals 6%
chemicals 7%
textiles 12%
others 16%
minerals 17%
food 19%
machinery and transportation eqpt. 23%

TOTAL EXPORTS
F$1,195 MILLION (2002)

mineral water 3%
vegetables 3%
wood 4%
gold 8%
fish 10%
garments 26%
sugar 25%
others and re-exports 21%

ISLAND ECOTOURISM

Recently ecotourism has become popular, and with increasing concern in Western countries over the damaging effects of solar radiation, more and more people are looking for land-based activities as an alternative to lying on the beach. This trend is being fueled by baby boomers who are eager to spend their disposable income on "soft adventure travel" in exotic locales. In Fiji, the most widespread manifestation of the ecotourism/adventure phenomenon is the current scuba-diving boom, and tours by chartered yacht, ocean kayak, raft, surfboard, bicycle, or on foot are proliferating.

This presents both a danger and an opportunity. Income from visitors wishing to experience nature gives local residents and governments an incentive to preserve the environment, although tourism can quickly degrade that environment through littering, the collection of coral and shells, and the development of roads, docks, and resorts in natural areas. Means of access created for tourists often end up being used by local residents whose priority is not conservation. Perhaps the strongest argument in favor of the creation of national parks and reserves in tropical countries is the ability of such parks to attract visitors from industrialized areas, while at the same time creating a framework for the preservation of nature. For in the final analysis, it is governments that must enact regulations to protect the environment—market forces usually do the opposite.

Too often today, what is called ecotourism is actually packaged consumer tourism with a green coating, or just an excuse for high prices. A genuine ecotourism resort is built of local materials using natural ventilation. That means no air conditioning and only limited use of fans. The buildings fit into the natural landscape and do not restrict access to customary lands or the sea. Local fish and organic vegetables enjoy preference over imported meats on tourist tables, and wastes are minimized and properly treated. The use of motorized transport is kept to an absolute minimum. Cultural sensitivity can be enhanced by profit sharing with the landowning clans and local participation in ownership.

Real ecotourism is a people-oriented form of tourism that benefits the islanders themselves. At smaller, locally owned businesses, visitors get to meet locals on a more personal basis, while contributing to local development. This kind of tourism offers excellent employment opportunities for island women as proprietors, *and* it's exactly what most visitors want. Appropriate tourism requires little investment, there's less disruption, and full control remains with the people themselves.

when Fiji is compared to Hawaii, which is about the same size in surface area. Overpacked Hawaii gets nearly seven million tourists, 20 times as many as Fiji. About 29 percent of Fiji's tourists come from Australia, 18 percent from New Zealand, 15 percent from the U.S., 10 percent from Britain, 9 percent from Japan, 7 percent from continental Europe, and 3 percent from Canada.

Gross receipts figures from tourism are often misleading, as $.56 on every dollar is repatriated overseas by foreign investors or used to pay for tourism-related imports. Because of this, sugar is more profitable for Fiji than tourism. In 2003, the hotel industry employed around 7,000 people with an estimated 40,000 jobs in all sectors related to tourism. Management of the top hotels is usually expatriate, with Indo-Fijians filling technical positions such as maintenance, cooking, accounting, etc., and indigenous Fijians working in more visible positions such as receptionists, waiters, guides, and housekeepers. With an eye to profitability, the resorts try to use as many part-time workers as possible.

Fiji has 220 licensed hotels with a total of around 6,000 rooms, more than a third of the South Pacific's tourism plant. Most of the large resort hotels in Fiji are foreign owned (the Cathay, Hexagon, and Tanoa hotel chains are Fiji-based exceptions). The Fiji government is doing all it can to promote luxury-hotel development by offering 20-year tax holidays on new projects. The May 2000 coup halted resort development and had a heavy impact on upscale ventures dependent on high occupancy levels. Backpacker resorts were far less affected.

Many of the upmarket tourist resorts are centered along the Coral Coast of Viti Levu and in the Mamanuca Islands off Nadi. Backpacker tourism now focuses on the Yasawa Islands. Investment by U.S. hotel chains has increased in recent years as Japanese firms have pulled out. In 1996, ITT-Sheraton bought two luxury hotels on Nadi's Denarau Island from a group of Japanese banks. In 2000, Outrigger Hotels of Hawaii built a major resort on the Coral Coast. Developments by Hilton, Marriott, and Novotel are currently in the works around Nadi.

The People

ETHNIC GROUPS

The Fijians

Fiji is a transitional zone between Polynesia and Melanesia. Indigenous Fijians bear a physical resemblance to the Melanesians, but like the Polynesians, they have hereditary chiefs, patrilineal descent, a love of elaborate ceremonies, and a fairly homogeneous language and culture. Fijians have interbred with Polynesians to the extent that they have lighter skin and larger stature than other Melanesians. In the interior and west of Viti Levu, where there was not as much contact with Polynesians, the people tend to be somewhat darker and smaller than the easterners.

The Fijians live in villages along the rivers or coast, with anywhere from 50 to 400 people led by a hereditary chief. To see a Fijian family living in an isolated house in a rural area is uncommon. The traditional thatched *bure* is fast disappearing from Fiji as villagers rebuild in tin and panel (often following destructive cyclones). Grass is not as accessible as cement, takes more time to repair, and is less permanent.

Away from the three largest islands, the population is almost totally Fijian. *Mataqali* (clans) are grouped into *yavusa* (tribes) of varying rank and function. Several *yavusa* form a *vanua*, a number of which make up a *matanitu*. Chiefs of the most important *vanua* are known as high chiefs. In western Viti Levu, the groups are smaller, and outstanding commoners can always rise to positions of power and prestige reserved for high chiefs in the east.

Fijians work communal land individually, not as a group. Each Fijian is assigned a piece of native land. They grow most of their own food in village gardens, and only a few staples such as tea, sugar, flour, etc., are imported from Suva and sold in local co-op stores. A visit to one of these stores will demonstrate just how little they import and how self-sufficient they are. Fishing, village maintenance work, and ceremonial presentations are done together. While village life provides a form of collective security, individuals are discouraged from rising above the group. Fijians who attempt to set up a business are often stifled by the demands of relatives and friends. The Fijian custom of claiming favors from members of one's own group is known as *kerekere*. This pattern makes it difficult for Fijians to compete with Indo-Fijians, for whom life has always been a struggle. It's estimated that less than 100 of the 5,000 companies operating in Fiji are owned and operated by indigenous Fijians.

The Indo-Fijians

Most of the Indo-Fijians now in Fiji are descended from indentured laborers recruited in Bengal and Bihar a century ago. In the first year of the system (1879), some 450 Indians arrived in Fiji to work in the cane fields. By 1883, the total had risen to 2,300, and in 1916, when the last indentured laborers arrived, 63,000 Indians were present in the colony. In 1920, the indenture system was finally terminated, the cane fields were divided into four-hectare plots, and the Indian workers became tenant farmers on land owned by Fijians. Indians continued to arrive until 1931, though many of these later arrivals were Gujarati or Sikh businesspeople.

In 1940, the Indian population stood at 98,000, still below the Fijian total of 105,000, but by the 1946 census Indians had outstripped

Fijians 120,000 to 117,000—making Fijians a minority in their own homeland. In the wake of the 1987 coups, the relative proportions changed as thousands of Indians emigrated to North America and Australia, and by early 1989 indigenous Fijians once again outnumbered Indo-Fijians. The 1996 census reported that Fiji's total population was 772,655, of which 50.8 percent were Fijian, while 43.7 percent were Indian (at the 1986 census, 46 percent were Fijian and 48.7 percent Indian). Between 1986 and 1996, the number of Indians in Fiji actually decreased by 12,125 with the heaviest falls in rural areas. Since 1987, more than 70,000 people have emigrated from Fiji, 90 percent of them Indians, and more than 5,000 a year continue to leave. Aside from emigration, the more widespread use of contraceptives by Indian women has led to a lower fertility rate. The crude birth rate per 1,000 population is 28.4 for Fijians and 21.0 for Indo-Fijians. It's estimated that by the year 2016, Indo-Fijians will comprise only 30–35 percent of the population while Fijians reach 60–65 percent, largely due to the lower Indo-Fijian birthrate and emigration.

Unlike the village-based Fijians, a majority of Indo-Fijians are concentrated in the cane-growing areas and live in isolated farmhouses, small settlements, or towns. Many Indo-Fijians also live in Suva, as do an increasing number of Fijians. Within the Indo-Fijian community there are divisions of Hindu (80 percent) versus Muslim (20 percent), north Indian versus south Indian, and Gujarati versus the rest. The Sikhs and Gujaratis have always been somewhat of an elite, as they immigrated freely to Fiji outside the indenture system.

The different groups have kept alive their ancient religious beliefs and rituals. Hindus tend to marry within their caste, although the restrictions on behavior, which characterize the caste system in India, have disappeared. Indo-Fijian marriages are often arranged by the parents, while Fijians generally choose their own partners. Rural Indo-Fijians still associate most closely with other members of their extended patrilineal family group, and Hindu and Muslim religious beliefs continue to restrict Indo-Fijian women to a position subservient to men.

It's often said that Indians concentrate on accumulation while Fijians emphasize distribution. Yet Fiji's laws themselves encourage Indians to invest their savings in business by preventing them or anyone else from purchasing native communal land. And it's a fact that Indo-Fijians earn 70 percent of the income and pay 80 percent of the taxes in Fiji, something no government can ignore. Yet high-profile Indian dominance of the retail sector has distorted the picture somewhat, and the reality is that the per capita incomes of ordinary indigenous Fijians and Indo-Fijians are not that different. The Fijians are not poor because they are exploited by Indians; the two groups simply amass their wealth in different ways. In large measure, Fiji's excellent service and retail sectors exist thanks to the thrift and efficiency of the law-abiding Indians. When you consider their position in a land where most have lived four generations, where they form almost half the population, where many laws are slanted against them, and where all natural resources are in the hands of others, their industriousness and patience are admirable.

Other Groups

The 3,000 Fiji-born Europeans, or *kai Vavalagi,* are descendants of Australians and New Zealanders who came to build cotton, sugar, or copra plantations in the 19th century. Many married Fijian women, and the 12,000 part-Fijians, or *Kai loma,* of today are the result. There is almost no intermarriage between Fijians *(kai Viti)* and Indo-Fijians *(kai Idia)* (though Fijians intermarry freely with Chinese and Solomon Islanders). Many other Europeans are present in Fiji on temporary contracts or as tourists.

Most of the 5,000 Chinese in Fiji are descended from free settlers who came to set up small businesses a century ago, although since 1987 there has been an influx of Chinese from mainland China who were originally admitted to operate market gardens, but who have since moved into the towns. Chinese garment workers continue to arrive. Fiji Chinese tend to inter-marry freely with the other racial groups.

The 10,000 Rotumans, a majority of whom now live in Suva, are Polynesians. On neighboring islands off Vanua Levu are the Micronesians of Rabi (from Kiribati) and the Polynesians of Kioa (from Tuvalu). The descendants of Solomon Islanders blackbirded during the 19th century still live in communities near Suva, Levuka, and Labasa. The Tongans in Lau and other Pacific islanders who have immigrated to Fiji make this an ethnic crossroads of the Pacific.

Social Conditions

Some 98 percent of the country's population was born in Fiji. The partial breakdown in race relations since 1987 has been a tragedy for Fiji, though racial antagonism has been exaggerated. At the grassroots level, the different ethnic groups have always gotten along remarkably well, with little animosity. Unfortunately race relations in Fiji have been manipulated by agitators with hidden agendas unrelated to race. As important as race are the variations between rich and poor, or urban (46 percent) and rural (54 percent). Avenues for future economic growth are limited, and unemployment is reflected in an increasing crime rate. Two-thirds of the rural population is without electricity.

Although Fiji's economy grew by 124 percent between 1970 and 2000, the number of people living in poverty increased by two-thirds over the same period. The imposition in 1992 of a 10 percent value-added tax, combined with reductions in income tax and import duties, shifted the burden of taxation from the haves to the have-nots. A third of the population now lives in poverty, and contrary to the myth of Indian economic domination, Indo-Fijians are more likely to be facing abject poverty than members of other groups. Eighty percent of cane farmers now live below the poverty line, and the number of Indo-Fijian beggars on Suva streets has increased in recent years. Single-parent urban families cut off from the extended-family social safety net are the specific group most affected, especially women trying to raise families on their own. As a Fijian woman on Taveuni told us, "Life is easy in Fiji, only money is a problem."

Literacy is high at 87 percent. Although education is not compulsory at any level, 98 percent of children age 6–14 attend school. Many schools are still racially segregated. More than 100 church-operated schools receive government subsidies. The Fiji Institute of Technology was founded at Suva in 1963, followed by the University of the South Pacific in 1968. The university serves the 12 Pacific countries that contribute to its costs. Medical services in Fiji are heavily subsidized. The divisional hospitals are at Labasa, Lautoka, and Suva, and there are also 19 subdivisional or area hospitals, 74 health centers, 100 nursing stations, and 409 village clinics scattered around the country. The most common infectious diseases are influenza, gonorrhea, and syphilis.

LAND RIGHTS

When Fiji became a British colony in 1874, the land was divided between white settlers who had bought plantations and the *taukei ni gele,* the Fijian "owners of the soil." The government assumed title to the balance. Today the alienated (privately owned) plantation lands are known as "freehold" land—about 10 percent of the total. Another seven percent is Crown land, 80 percent of it currently leased for periods of up to 99 years. The remaining 83 percent is inalienable Fijian communal land, which can be leased (about 30 percent is) but may never be sold. Compare this 83 percent (much of it not arable) with only 3 percent Maori land in New Zealand and almost zero native Hawaiian land. Land ownership has provided the Fijians with a security that allows them to preserve their traditional culture, unlike indigenous peoples in most other countries.

Communal land is administered on behalf of some 6,600 clan groups *(mataqali)* by the Native Land Trust Board, an inept government agency established in 1940. The NLTB retains 25 percent of the lease money to cover administration, and a further 10 percent is paid directly to regional hereditary chiefs. In 1966, the British colonial administration established a system which allowed native land to be leased for 10 years, and in 1976 the Agricultural Landlord and Tenants Act (ALTA) increased the period to 30 years. In 1997, the 30-year leases began coming up for renewal, and of the 4,221 which had expired by 2001, only 1,164 were renewed. Thousands of Indo-Fijian farmers have been evicted, and the uncertainty has led to properties being allowed to deteriorate.

Many Fijian clans say they want their land back so they can farm it themselves, and Fiji's remaining 20,000 Indo-Fijian sugarcane farmers are becoming highly apprehensive. If rents are greatly increased or the leases terminated, Fiji's sugar industry will be badly damaged and an explosive social situation created. In the event of a lease not being renewed, the Chaudhry government had been giving farmers the choice of being resettled or of receiving F$28,000 in compensation money for improvements they had made. After the Speight coup, this program was withdrawn. To date, most of the agricultural land taken back by Fijian clans has simply gone out of production.

At the First Constitutional Conference in 1965, Indian rights were promulgated, and the 1970 independence constitution asserted that everyone born in Fiji would be a citizen with equal rights. These rights are reaffirmed in the 1997 constitution. But land laws up to the present have very much favored "Fiji for the Fijians." Indo-Fijians have always accepted Fijian ownership of the land, provided they were granted satisfactory leases. Now that the leases are gradually coming to an end, many Indo-Fijians are being driven from the only land they've ever known. The stifling of land development may keep Fiji quaint for tourists, but it also condemns a large portion of the population of both races to backwardness and poverty.

GENDER ISSUES

Traditionally, indigenous Fijian women were confined to the home, while men handled most matters outside the immediate family. The clear-cut roles of the woman as homemaker and the

man as defender and decision-maker gave stability to village life. Western education has caused many Fijian women to question their subordinate position, and the changing lifestyle has made the old relationship between the sexes outmoded. Women's liberation has arrived as paid employment expands and access to family planning better enables women to hold jobs. Fijian women are more emancipated than their sisters in other Melanesian countries, though men continue to dominate public life throughout the region. Tradition is often manipulated to deny women the right to express themselves publicly on community matters.

Cultural barriers hinder women's access to education and employment, and the proportion of girls in school falls rapidly as the grade level increases. Female students are nudged into low-paying fields such as nursing or secretarial services; in Fiji and elsewhere, export-oriented garment factories exploit women workers, paying low wages amidst poor working conditions. Levels of domestic violence vary greatly, though it's far less accepted among indigenous Fijians than it is among Indo-Fijians, and in Fiji's Macuata Province women have a suicide rate seven times above the world average, with most of the victims being Indo-Fijian. Those little signs on buses reading "real men don't hit women" suggest the problem. Travelers should take an interest in women's issues.

RELIGION

The main religious groups in Fiji are Hindus (290,000), Methodists (265,000), Catholics (70,000), Muslims (62,000), Assemblies of God (33,000), and Seventh-Day Adventists (20,000). About 40 percent of the total population is Hindu or Muslim due to the large Indo-Fijian population, and only 2 percent of Indo-Fijians have converted to Christianity despite Methodist missionary efforts dating back to 1884. About 78 percent of indigenous Fijians are Methodist, and 8.5 percent are Catholic.

Since the 1987 military coups, an avalanche of well-financed American fundamentalist missionary groups has descended on Fiji, and membership in the Assemblies of God and some other new Christian sects has grown at the expense of the Methodists. While the Methodist Church has long been localized, the new evangelical sects are dominated by foreign missionaries, ideas, and money.

The Assemblies of God (AOG) is a Pentecostal denomination founded in Arkansas in 1914 and presently headquartered in Springfield, Missouri. It emphasizes the practice of glossolalia, or "speaking in tongues." Although the AOG carries out some relief work, it doesn't involve itself in social reform in the belief that only God can solve humanity's problems. In Fiji, the number of AOG adherents increased twelve-fold between 1966 and 1992. A large AOG Bible College operates in Suva, and from Fiji the group has spread to other Pacific countries.

The Seventh-Day Adventist Church is a politically ultra-conservative group that grew out of the 19th-century American Baptist movement. The SDA Church teaches the imminent return of Christ, and Saturday (rather than Sunday) is observed as the Lord's day. SDAs regard the human body as the temple of the Holy Spirit, thus much attention is paid to health matters. Members are forbidden to partake of certain foods, alcohol, drugs, and tobacco, and the church expends considerable energy on the provision of medical and dental services. They are also active in education and local economic development.

The ecumenical Pacific Conference of Churches began in 1961 as an association of the mainstream Protestant churches, but since 1976 many Catholic dioceses have been included as well. Both the Pacific Theological College (founded in 1966) and the Pacific Regional Seminary (opened in 1972) are in southern Suva, and the South Pacific is one of the few areas of the world with a large surplus of ministers of religion.

LANGUAGE

Fijian, a member of the Austronesian family of languages, spoken from Easter Island to Madagascar, has more speakers than any other indigenous Pacific language. Fijian vowels are pronounced as in Latin or Spanish, while the consonants are similar to those of English. Syllables end in a vowel, and the next-to-last syllable is usually the one emphasized. Where two vowels appear together they are sounded separately. In 1835, two Methodist missionaries, David Cargill and William Cross, devised the form of written Fijian used in Fiji today. Since all consonants in Fijian are separated by vowels, they spelled "mb" as b, "nd" as d, "ng" as g, "ngg" as q, and "th" as c.

Though Cargill and Cross worked at Lakeba in the Lau Group, the political importance of tiny Bau Island just off Viti Levu caused the Bauan dialect of Fijian to be selected as the "official" version of the language, and in 1850 a dictionary and grammar were published. When the Bible was translated into Bauan, that dialect's dominance was assured, and it is today's spoken and written Fijian. From 1920 to 1970, the use of Fijian was discouraged in favor of English, but since independence there has been a revival.

Hindustani or Hindi is the household tongue of most Indo-Fijians. Fiji Hindi has diverged from that spoken in India, with the adoption of many words from English and other Indian languages such as Urdu. Though a quarter of Indo-Fijians are descended from immigrants from southern India, where Tamil and Telegu are spoken, few use those languages today, even at home. Fiji Muslims speak Hindi out of practical considerations, though they might consider Urdu their mother tongue. In their spoken forms, Hindi and Urdu are very similar.

English is the second official language in Fiji and is understood by almost everyone. All schools teach exclusively in English after the fourth grade. Indo-Fijians and indigenous Fijians usually communicate with one another in English. Gilbertese is spoken by the Banabans of Rabi.

See Basic Fijian and Basic Hindi in Resources for some useful words and phrases.

Customs

Fijians and Indo-Fijians are very tradition-oriented peoples who have retained a surprising number of their ancestral customs, despite the flood of conflicting influences that have swept the Pacific over the past century. Rather than a melting pot where one group assimilated another, Fiji is a patchwork of varied traditions.

The obligations and responsibilities of Fijian village life include not only the construction and upkeep of certain buildings, but personal participation in the many ceremonies that give their lives meaning. Hindu Indians, on the other hand, practice firewalking and observe festivals such as Holi and Diwali, just as their forebears in India did for thousands of years.

Fijian Firewalking

In Fiji, both Fijians and Indo-Fijians practice firewalking, with the difference being that the Fijians walk on heated stones instead of hot embers. Legends tell how the ability to walk on fire was first given to a warrior named Tui-na-viqalita from Beqa Island, just off the south coast of Viti Levu, who had spared the life of a spirit god he caught while fishing for eels. The freed spirit gave to Tui-na-viqalita the gift of immunity to fire. Today his descendants act as *bete* (high priests) of the rite of *vilavilairevo* (jumping into the oven). Only members of his tribe, the Sawau, perform the ceremony. The Tui Sawau lives at Dakuibeqa village on Beqa, but firewalking is now only performed at the resort hotels on Viti Levu.

Fijian firewalkers (men only) are not permitted to have sex or to eat any coconut for two weeks prior to a performance. A man whose wife is pregnant is also barred. In a circular pit about four meters across, hundreds of large stones are first heated by a wood fire until they are white-hot. If you throw a handkerchief on the stones, it will burst into flames. Much ceremony and chanting accompanies certain phases of the ritual, such as the moment when the wood is removed to leave just the white-hot stones. The men psych themselves up in a nearby hut, then emerge, enter the pit, and walk briskly around it once.

Bundles of leaves and grass are then thrown on the stones, and the men stand inside the steaming pit again to chant a final song. They seem to have complete immunity to pain, and there is no trace of injury. The men appear to fortify themselves with the heat, gaining some psychic power from the ritual.

Indian Firewalking

By an extraordinary coincidence, Indo-Fijians brought with them the ancient practice of religious firewalking. In southern India, firewalking occurs in the pre-monsoon season as a call to the goddess Kali (Durga) for rain. Indo-Fijian firewalking is an act of purification, or fulfillment of a vow to thank the god for help in a difficult situation.

In Fiji there is firewalking in most Hindu temples once a year, at full moon sometime between May and September according to the Hindu calendar. The actual event takes place on a Sunday at 1600 on the Suva side of Viti Levu, and at 0400 on the Nadi/Lautoka side. In August, firewalking takes place at the Mahadevi Sangam Temple on Howell Road, Suva. During the 10 festival days preceding the walk, participants remain in isolation, eat only unspiced vegetarian food, and spiritually prepare themselves. There are prayers at the temple in the early morning and a group singing of religious stories evenings from Monday through Thursday. The yellow-clad devotees, their faces painted bright yellow and red, often pierce their cheeks or other body parts with spikes or three-pronged forks as part of the purification rites. Their faith is so strong they feel no pain.

The event is extremely colorful; drumming and chanting accompany the visual spectacle. Visitors are welcome to observe the firewalking, but since the exact date varies from temple to temple according to the phases of the moon (among other factors), you just have to keep asking to find out where and when it will take place. To enter the temple, you must remove your shoes and any leather clothing.

a kava ceremony organized for visitors to Maravu Plantation Resort on Taveuni

The Yaqona Ceremony

Yaqona (yang-GO-na) is a tranquilizing, nonalcoholic drink that numbs the tongue and lips. Better known as kava, it's made from the *waka* (dried root) of the pepper plant *(Macropiper methysticum)*. This ceremonial preparation is the most honored feature of the formal life of Fijians, Tongans, and Samoans. It is performed with the utmost gravity according to a sacramental ritual to mark births, marriages, deaths, official visits, the installation of a new chief, etc.

New mats are first spread on the floor, on which a hand-carved *tanoa* (a wooden bowl nearly a meter wide) is placed. A long fiber cord decorated with cowrie shells leads from the bowl to the guests of honor. At the end of the cord is a white cowrie, which symbolizes a link to ancestral spirits. As many as 70 men take their places before the bowl. The officiants are adorned with tapa, fiber, and croton leaves, their torsos smeared with glistening coconut oil, their faces usually blackened.

The guests present a bundle of *waka* to the hosts, along with a short speech explaining their visit, a custom known as a *sevusevu*. The *sevusevu* is received by the hosts and acknowledged with a short speech of acceptance. The

waka are then scraped clean and pounded in a *tabili* (mortar). Formerly they were chewed. Nowadays the pulp is put in a cloth sack and mixed with water in the *tanoa*. In the ceremony the *yaqona* is kneaded and strained through *vau* (hibiscus) fibers.

The mixer displays the strength of the grog (kava) to the *mata ni vanua* (master of ceremonies) by pouring out a cupful into the *tanoa*. If the *mata ni vanua* considers the mix too strong, he calls for *wai* (water), then says *lose* (mix), and the mixer proceeds. Again he shows the consistency to the *mata ni vanua* by pouring out a cupful. If it appears right, the *mata ni vanua* says *loba* (squeeze). The mixer squeezes the remaining juice out of the pulp, puts it aside, and announces, *sa lose oti saka na yaqona, vaka turaga* (the kava is ready, my chief). He runs both hands around the rim of the *tanoa* and claps three times.

The *mata ni vanua* then says *talo* (serve). The cupbearer squats in front of the *tanoa* with a *bilo* (half coconut shell), which the mixer fills. The cupbearer then presents the first cup to the guest of honor, who claps once and drains it, and everyone claps three times. The second cup goes to the guests' *mata ni vanua,* who claps once and drinks. The man sitting next to the mixer says *aa*, and everyone answers *maca* (empty). The third cup is for the first local chief, who claps once before drinking, and everyone claps three times after. Then the *mata ni vanua* of the first local chief claps once and drinks, and everyone says *maca*. The same occurs for the second local chief and his *mata ni vanua*.

After these six men have finished their cups, the mixer announces, *sa maca saka tu na yaqona, vaka turaga* (the bowl is empty, my chief), and the *mata ni vanua* says *cobo* (clap). The mixer then runs both hands around the rim of the *tanoa* and claps three times. This terminates the full ceremony, but then a second bowl is prepared and everyone drinks. During the drinking of the first bowl, complete silence must be maintained.

Social Kava Drinking

While the passage above describes one of several forms of the full *yaqona* ceremony, which is performed only for high chiefs, abbreviated versions are put on for tourists at the hotels. However, the village people have simplified grog sessions almost daily. Kava drinking is an important form of Fijian entertainment and a way of structuring friendships and community relations. Even in government offices, a bowl of grog is kept for the staff to take as a refreshment at *yaqona* breaks. Some say the Fijians have *yaqona* rather than

blood in their veins. Excessive kava drinking over a long period can make the skin scaly and rough, a condition known as *kanikani*.

Individual visitors to villages are invariably invited to participate in informal kava ceremonies, in which case it's customary to present a bunch of kava roots to the group. Do this at the beginning, before anybody starts drinking, and make a short speech explaining the purpose of your visit (be it a desire to meet the people and learn about their way of life, an interest in seeing or doing something in particular on their island, or just a holiday from work). Don't hand the roots to anyone, just place them on the mat in the center of the circle. The bigger the bundle of roots, the bigger the smiles. (The roots are easily purchased at any town market for about F$15 a half kilo.)

Clap once when the cupbearer offers you the *bilo*, then take it in both hands and say *"bula"* just before the cup meets your lips. Clap three times after you drink. Remember, you're a participant, not an onlooking tourist, so don't take photos if the ceremony is formal. Even though you may not like the appearance or taste of the drink, do try to finish at least the first cup. Tip the cup to show you are done.

It's considered extremely bad manners to turn your back on a chief during a kava ceremony, to walk in front of the circle of people when entering or leaving, or to step over the long cord attached

---

TABUA

The Fijians share *yaqona* (or kava) with the Polynesians, but the *tabua*, or whale's tooth, is significant only in Fiji. The *tabua*, obtained from the sperm whale, have always played an important part in Fijian ceremonies. In the 19th century, they were hung around the necks of warriors and chiefs during festivals. Even today they are presented to distinguished guests and are exchanged at weddings, births, deaths, reconciliations, and also when personal or communal contracts or agreements are entered into. *Tabua*, contrary to popular belief, have never been used as a currency and can not be used to purchase goods or services. It is a great honor to be presented with *tabua*.

to the *tanoa*. During a semi-formal ceremony, you should remain silent until the opening ritual is complete, signaled by a round of clapping.

Presentation of the Tabua

The *tabua* is a tooth of the sperm whale. It was once presented when chiefs exchanged delegates at confederacy meetings and before conferences on peace or war. In recent times, the *tabua* is presented during chiefly *yaqona* ceremonies as a symbolic welcome for a respected visitor or guest or as a prelude to public business or modern-day official functions. On the village level, *tabuas* are still commonly presented to arrange marriages, to show sympathy at funerals, to request favors, to settle disputes, or simply to show respect.

Old *tabuas* are highly polished from continuous handling. The larger the tooth, the greater its ceremonial value. *Tabuas* are prized cultural property and may not be exported from Fiji. Endangered-species laws prohibit their entry into the United States, Australia, and many other countries.

Stingray Spearing and Fish Drives

Stingrays are lethal-looking creatures with caudal spines up to 18 centimeters long. To catch them, eight or nine punts are drawn up in a line about a kilometer long beside the reef. As soon as a stingray is sighted, a punt is paddled forward with great speed until close enough to hurl a spear.

Another time-honored sport and source of food is the fish drive or *yavirau*, in which an entire village participates. Around the flat surface of a reef at rising tide, sometimes as many as 70 men and women group themselves in a circle a kilometer or more in circumference. All grip a ring of connected liana vines with leaves attached. While shouting, singing, and beating long poles on the seabed, the group slowly contracts the ring as the tide comes in. The shadow of the ring alone is enough to keep the fish within the circle. The fish are finally directed landward into a net or stone fish trap.

The Rising of the Balolo

This event takes place only in Samoa and Fiji. The *balolo (Eunice viridis)* is a thin, segmented worm of the Coelomate order, considered a culinary delicacy throughout these islands—the caviar of the Pacific. It's about 45 centimeters long and lives deep in the fissures of coral reefs. Twice a year it releases an unusual "tail" that contains its eggs or sperm. The worm itself returns to the coral to regenerate a new reproductive tail. The rising of the *balolo* is a natural almanac that keeps both lunar and solar times, and has a fixed day of appearance—even if a hurricane is raging—one night in the last quarter of the moon in October, and the corresponding night in November. It has never failed to appear on time for more than 100 years now, and you can even check your calendar by it.

Because this rising occurs with such mathematical certainty, Fijians are waiting in their boats to scoop the millions of writhing, reddish brown (male) and moss-green (female) spawn from the water when they rise to the surface before dawn. Within an hour after the rising, the eggs and sperm are released to spawn the next generation of *balolo*. The free-swimming larvae seek a suitable coral patch to begin the cycle again. This is one of the most bizarre curiosities in the natural history of the South Pacific, and the southeast coast of Ovalau is a good place to observe it.

CONDUCT

Foreign travel is an exceptional experience enjoyed by a privileged few. Too often, tourists try to transfer their lifestyles to tropical islands, thereby missing out on what is unique to the region. Travel can be a learning experience if approached openly and with a positive attitude. So read up on the local culture before you arrive and become aware of the social and environmental problems of the area. A wise traveler soon graduates from hearing and seeing to listening and observing. Speaking is good for the ego and listening is good for the soul.

The path is primed with packaged pleasures, but pierce the bubble of tourism and you'll encounter something far from the schedules and organized efficiency: a time to learn how other people live. Walk gently, for human qualities are as fragile and responsive to abuse as the brilliant reefs. The islanders are by nature soft-spoken and reserved. Often they won't show open disapproval if their social codes are broken, but don't underestimate them. Consider that you're only one of thousands of visitors to their country, so don't expect to be treated better than anyone else. Respect is one of the most important aspects of Pacific life, and humility is also greatly appreciated.

If you're alone, you're lucky, for the single traveler is everyone's friend. Get away from other tourists and meet the people. There aren't many places on earth where you can still do this meaningfully, but Fiji is one of them. If you do meet people with similar interests, keep in touch by writing. This is no tourist's paradise, though, and local residents are not exhibits or paid performers. They have as many or more problems as you, and if you see them as real people, you are less likely to be viewed as a stereotypical tourist. You may have come to escape civilization, but keep in mind that you're just a guest.

Most important of all, try to see things their way. Take an interest in local customs, values, languages, challenges, and successes. If things work differently than they do back home, give thanks that you are experiencing this different culture. Reflect on what you've experienced, and you'll return home with a better understanding of how much we all have in common, outwardly different as we may seem.

Dress

It's important to know that the dress code in Fiji is strict. Wearing short shorts, halter tops, and bathing costumes in public shows a lack of respect. In Fijian villages, it's considered offensive to reveal too much skin. Wrap a *sulu* around you to cover up. Men should always wear a shirt in town, and women should wear dresses that adequately cover their legs while seated. Nothing will mark you so quickly as a tourist, nor make you more popular with street vendors, than scanty dress. Of course, it is permissible to wear skimpy clothing on the beach in front of a resort hotel. Yet in a society where even bathing suits are considered extremely risqué for local women, public nudity is unthinkable, and topless sun-bathing by women is also banned in Fiji (except at isolated island resorts).

Questions

The islanders are eager to please, so phrase your questions carefully. They'll answer yes or no according to what they think you want to hear—don't suggest the answer in your question. Test this by asking your informant to confirm something you know to be incorrect. Also don't ask negative questions, such as "you're not going to Suva, are you?" Invariably the answer will be "yes," meaning "yes, I'm not going to Suva." It also could work like this: "Don't you have anything cheaper?" "Yes." "What do you have that is cheaper?" "Nothing." Yes, he doesn't have anything cheaper. If you want to be sure of something, ask several people the same question in different ways.

Dangers and Annoyances

Littering is punished by a minimum F$40 fine, and breaking bottles in public can earn six months in jail (unfortunately seldom enforced).

In Suva, beware of the seemingly friendly Fijian men (usually with a small package or canvas bag in their hands) who will greet you on the street with a hearty *Bula!* These are "sword sellers" who will ask your name, quickly carve it on a mask, and then demand F$20 for a set that you could buy at a Nadi curio shop for F$5. Other times they'll try to engage you in conversation and may offer a "gift." Just say "thank you very much" and walk away from them quickly without accepting anything, as they can suddenly become unpleasant and aggressive. Their grotesque swords and masks themselves have nothing to do with Fiji.

Similarly, overly sociable people at bars may expect you to buy them drinks and snacks. This may not be a problem in the beginning but know when to disengage. In the main tourist centers such as Nadi and Suva, take care if a local invites you to visit his home, as you may be seen mainly as a source of beer and other goods. Also, don't be fooled by anyone on the street who claims to work at your resort and offers to show you around. They only want to sell you something.

Exploring the Islands

Highlights

Fiji is brimming with colorful attractions, splendid scenery, friendly people, and exciting things to do. From the gateway city **Nadi** with its numerous shopping and dining possibilities, it's only a quick commuter hop to the enticing **Mamanuca Group** with about half of Fiji's island resorts. The clear waters, golden sands, dazzling reefs, and good facilities have made this a popular vacation destination for Australians and New Zealanders, but islands like Malololailai, Malolo, and Mana also attract scuba divers and yachting enthusiasts. The long, narrow **Yasawa Group** off the sugar city Lautoka is wilder, mightier, and less developed than the Mamanucas: The beaches are longer, the jungle-clad mountains higher, and the accommodations rougher. It's Fiji's most magnificent island chain.

Fiji's mainland, **Viti Levu,** is the "real" Fiji, where much of the country's history has unfolded

and the bulk of the Fijian people live out their lives. The 486-kilometer highway around the island passes a series of appealing towns and cities with bustling markets, bus stations, shops, cafés, clubs, monuments, and facilities of every kind. The **Coral Coast** in the south is the country's second resort area, with a series of large hotels nicely spaced between Nadi and Pacific Harbor. Visitors looking for more than only beach life often pick these resorts for the numerous tours and sporting activities available. **Pacific Harbor** itself offers access to some of the best diving, fishing, kayaking, white-water rafting, and golfing in the South Pacific, and **Nananu-i-Ra Island** off Viti Levu's north coast is a favorite of divers, windsurfers, and backpackers.

Fiji's contemporary capital, **Suva,** has the country's finest cinemas, monuments, museums, nightclubs, restaurants, stores, and all of the excitement of the South Pacific's biggest town. Ships, buses, and planes depart Suva for every corner of the republic. The campus of the region's main university, the headquarters of international organizations, government ministries, embassies, libraries, and the large trading companies are all here. It's a fascinating place to explore.

Several adjacent islands allow one to escape from Suva. **Kadavu** to the south is a characteristic Fijian island of small villages strewn between beaches and hills, but it's also a mecca for scuba divers who come for the Great Astrolabe Reef, and for surfers who have discovered Kadavu's waves. Several well-established backpacker camps and upscale resorts make visiting Kadavu easy. Back toward Viti Levu are **Beqa,** with several upscale scuba resorts, and **Yanuca,** with inexpensive beach camps full of enthusiastic surfers.

Anyone with even the slightest interest in Fiji's vivid history won't want to miss **Ovalau Island** and the timeworn old capital, **Levuka.** The town's long row of wooden storefronts looks like the set of a Wild West film, and there are abundant monuments, museums, and historic buildings to discover, all of it set below towering volcanic peaks. Despite these attractions, Levuka remains remarkably unvisited by

10 TOP SIGHTS OF FIJI

- **Sigatoka Sand Dunes, Viti Levu:** coastal scenery, archaeology, exhibits, hiking (p. 155)
- **Frigate Passage, Beqa Barrier Reef:** top surfing venue, scuba diving (p. 169, 175)
- **Fiji Museum, Suva:** unique historical exhibits, botanical garden, library, bookshop (p. 181)
- **Colo-i-Suva Forest Park, Suva:** nature walks, natural history, cool climate (p. 184)
- **Koroyanitu National Heritage Park, Lautoka:** waterfall, mountains, hiking, culture (p. 234)
- **Wayasewa and Waya Islands, Yasawas:** snorkeling, diving, hiking, Fijian culture (p. 242, 243)
- **Tavewa and the Blue Lagoon, Yasawas:** beaches, reefs, scenery, snorkeling, hiking (p. 246)
- **Levuka, Ovalau:** historic monuments, scenery, laid-back atmosphere, budget hotels (p. 261)
- **Savusavu, Vanua Levu:** yachting, scuba diving, colorful town, excellent facilities (p. 286)
- **Bouma National Heritage Park, Taveuni:** hiking, swimming, culture, natural beauty (p. 308)

most tourists, largely thanks to the absence of a good beach. It's the best-preserved relic of the old South Seas anywhere between San Francisco and Sydney.

Across the Koro Sea from Ovalau is Fiji's second island, **Vanua Levu,** heart of the "friendly north." Because a slight effort is required to get there, far fewer tourists ply these exotic shores. Yet **Savusavu** is Fiji's most picturesque town after Levuka, set along a splendid wide bay with an attractive waterfront promenade. Long a center of the Fiji copra trade, planters from the surrounding farms still congregate at the town's colonial-style club on Sundays. Two spectacular highways sweep away from Savusavu: One travels through the mountains to the mill town of Labasa, and another snakes east along the verdant coast to Buca Bay.

Repeat visitors and local Fijians often assert that **Taveuni** is Fiji's finest island, a claim which is difficult to deny. The island's high spine is draped in impenetrable rainforest, with huge coconut plantations tumbling to the coast. Magnificent waterfalls pour down the steep slopes, and the scuba diving is world famous. Yet Fiji doesn't end here: There are many little-known isles in the Lau and Lomaiviti groups, including some like **Vanua Balavu** with satisfactory facilities for visitors.

Budget travelers often appreciate Tavewa, Nacula, and adjacent islands of the Yasawas, which rank high for their spellbinding environment, stimulating activities, and agreeable company. Waya and Wayasewa are similar. City slickers won't bore easily in Suva, and it's *the* place to be if you like studying. The city's excellent libraries and museums are meant to be savored slowly. Kadavu and Ono both have backpacker camps offering unlimited swimming, snorkeling, scuba, and exploring. Leleuvia just south of Ovalau is also great for a relaxing holiday with abundant diving. Two weeks is the absolute minimum required to get a feel for Fiji, and after a month you'll be in a position to begin planning your next visit.

Suggested Itineraries

Most visitors arrive in Nadi, with a large percentage immediately transferring to resorts in the Mamanucas and Yasawas or along the Coral Coast. Overland travelers intent on seeing Fiji on their own, should start moving the morning after they arrive. Save your sightseeing around Nadi until the end of your trip.

Those with **one week** in Fiji can easily circumnavigate Viti Levu by public bus, and since there are far fewer places to stop along Kings Road, it's best to cover the north side of the island first. Starting from Nadi or Lautoka, you can easily make it through to Suva in a day. After a night or two there, fly to Levuka for two nights. Return to Suva on the early morning Patterson Brothers bus (daily except Sunday), then catch a connecting bus to somewhere on the Coral Coast. The next day you can head back to Nadi with time for a stop at the Sigatoka Sand Dunes. However, if beaches and natural beauty mean more to you than history and culture, consider spending your entire week in the Yasawa Islands.

Visitors with **two weeks** at their disposal can also visit "the friendly north." The most practical way to get started is to fly directly from Nadi to Taveuni, then work your way back overland. Depending on your schedule, there are ferries from Taveuni straight to Savusavu and Suva, or you can fly to Savusavu and catch a ferry from there. Then follow the Levuka-Coral Coast route described above. Otherwise spend your first week in the Yasawas and the second circling Viti Levu.

Visitors with **three weeks** can see a lot of Fiji. Begin with a one-week trip to the glorious Yasawa Islands, then either fly directly to Taveuni or begin working your way around Viti Levu. You could stop at Nananu-i-Ra Island off northern Viti Levu for two nights, from whence there are ferries to Vanua Levu. Or continue to Suva and catch a ferry to Savusavu or Taveuni from there. Otherwise, make a side-trip to Levuka from Suva and return to Nadi via the Coral Coast. If you still have ample time after Levuka, fly from Suva to Kadavu, where you'll want to spend three or four nights. From Kadavu, you can fly directly to Nadi or return to Suva and be bused along the Coral Coast. Toward the end of your trip, a few nights on one of the Mamanuca Islands is an appropriate choice. For ecotourists, Koroyanitu National Heritage Park is nearby.

Parks and Reserves

The **National Trust of Fiji** (tel. 330-1807, fax 330-5092) administers several nature reserves and historic sites. Of these, the Sigatoka Sand Dunes National Park between Nadi and Sigatoka has a visitor center easily accessible by public bus. The Momi Bay Gun Site south of Nadi and the Waisali Nature Reserve near Savusavu are also accessible, but advance clearance is required to visit the iguana sanctuary on Yaduatabu Island off Vanua Levu.

Koroyanitu National Heritage Park, inland from Lautoka, is easily reached and has accommodations for hikers. Although not an official reserve, the forested area around Nadarivatu in central Viti Levu is similar. Bouma National Heritage Park around Bouma and Lavena on the northeastern side of Taveuni features unspoiled rainforests and waterfalls reachable along hiking trails. Colo-i-Suva Forest Park behind

Suva also beckons the nature lover with quiet walks through a mahogany forest.

Fiji's only official marine conservation areas are a stretch of fringing reef off Ono Island near Kadavu, and the Waitabu Marine Park, part of the Bouma National Heritage Park project off northeastern Taveuni. Some resorts such as Beachcomber, Navini, and Namenalala Islands have banned fishing on their fringing reefs. These places are ideal for beach-based snorkeling, but many other easily accessible areas have been fished out by locals with spearguns and most scuba diving is done from boats.

Sports and Recreation

Scuba Diving

Fiji has been called "the soft coral capital of the world," and seasoned divers know well that Fiji has some of the finest diving in the South Pacific, with top facilities at the best prices. You won't go wrong choosing Fiji. The worst underwater visibility conditions here are the equivalent of the finest off the Florida coast. In the Gulf of Mexico, you've about reached the limit if you can see for 15 meters; in Fiji the visibility begins at 15 meters and increases to 45 meters in some places. Many fantastic dives are just 10 or 15 minutes away from the resorts by boat (whereas at Australia's Great Barrier Reef, the speedboats often have to travel more than 60 kilometers to get to the dive sites). Here are some of Fiji's most popular diving locations:

- The Great Astrolabe Reef, Kadavu: caves, marinelife (p. 255)
- Namena Barrier Reef, south of Savusavu: giant clams (p. 293)
- Rainbow Reef, west of Taveuni: crevices, soft coral (p. 303)
- Sidestreets, Beqa Lagoon: soft corals, sea fans (p. 169)
- Supermarket, west of Mana Island: shark feeding (p. 139)
- Wakaya Passage, east of Levuka: rays, hammerheads (p. 275)

Diving is possible year-round, with the marinelife most bountiful July–November. The best diving conditions are March–December, the calmest seas in April and May. Visibility is tops June–October, then slightly worse November–February due to rainfall and plankton growth. Water temperatures vary from 24°C in June, July, and August to 30°C in December, January, and February. Wetsuits are recommended during the winter months.

Facilities for scuba diving exist at most of the resorts in the Mamanuca Group, along Viti Levu's Coral Coast and at Pacific Harbor, on Kadavu, Leleuvia, Beqa, Nananu-i-Ra, Naviti, Tavewa, and Wayasewa, at Levuka, Nadi, and Savusavu, and on Taveuni and adjacent islands. Low-budget divers should turn to the Kadavu, Leleuvia, Nadi, Tavewa, and Wayasewa sections in this book and read. Specialized non-hotel dive shops are found at Levuka, Nadi, Pacific Harbor, Savusavu, and on Taveuni. When choosing a place to stay, pick somewhere as close as possible to the sites you wish to dive, as scuba operators generally resist spending a lot of money on fuel to commute to distant reefs.

Serious divers will bring along their own mask, buoyancy compensator, and regulator. If you've never dived before, Fiji is an excellent place to learn, and the Kadavu, Leleuvia, Levuka, Musket Cove, Nadi, Nananu-i-Ra, Pacific Harbor, Taveuni, Tavewa, and Wayasewa scuba operators offer open-water certification courses lasting four or five days. The best course prices are usually offered by the Nadi-area dive shops, which can afford to charge less due to their high volume of customers. Leleuvia is also good. Learning to dive on Taveuni is more than a hundred dollars more expensive. If you have children, Subsurface Fiji at Musket Cove Resort and on Beachcomber Island specializes in teaching diving to kids as young as 12! Many of the scuba oper-

10 SAFETY RULES OF DIVING

1. The most important rule in scuba diving is to BREATHE CONTINUOUSLY. If you establish this rule, you won't forget and hold your breath, and overexpansion will never occur.

2. COME UP AT A RATE OF 18 METERS PER MINUTE OR LESS. This allows the gas dissolved in your body under pressure to come out of solution safely and also prevents vertigo from fast ascents. Always make a precautionary decompression stop at a depth of five meters.

3. NEVER ESCAPE TO THE SURFACE. Panic is the diver's worst enemy.

4. STOP, THINK, THEN ACT. Always Maintain control.

5. PACE YOURSELF. KNOW YOUR LIMITATIONS. A DIVER SHOULD ALWAYS BE ABLE TO REST AND RELAX IN THE WATER. Proper use of the buoyancy vest allows you to rest on the surface and maintain control under water. A diver who becomes fatigued in the water is a danger to himself and his buddy.

6. NEVER DIVE WITH A COLD. Avoid alcoholic beverages but drink plenty of water. Get a good night's sleep and refrain from strenuous physical activities on the day you dive. Dive conservatively if you are overweight or more than 45 years of age. Make fewer dives the last two days before flying and no dives at all during the final 24 hours.

7. PLAN YOUR DIVE. Know your starting point, your diving area, and your exit areas. DIVE YOUR PLAN.

8. NEVER EXCEED THE SAFE SPORT-DIVING LIMIT OF 30 METERS. Make your first dive the deepest of the day.

9. All equipment must be equipped with QUICK RELEASES.

10. WEAR ADEQUATE PROTECTIVE CLOTHING AGAINST SUN AND CORAL.

ators listed in this book also offer introductory "resort courses" for those who want only a taste of scuba diving. For information about liveaboard dive boats, see Scuba Cruises in the Getting There section.

Snorkeling

Even if you aren't willing to put the necessary money and effort into scuba diving, you will want to investigate the many snorkeling possibilities. Some dive shops take snorkelers out in their boats for a nominal fee, but there are countless places around Fiji where you can snorkel straight out to the reef for free, mostly on smaller outer islands. The beach snorkeling off Viti Levu and Vanua Levu is usually poor, and it's a complete waste of time around Nadi, Lautoka, Pacific Harbor, Suva, and Labasa. The snorkeling along the Coral Coast is fair, but only at high tide, and even then you must take care with currents in the channels. Around Savusavu, sharp rocks make it hard to get into the water at all (and the top beaches are private). On the other hand, you'll have no trouble finding glorious reefs in the Mamanuca Group, the Yasawas, off Nananu-i-Ra, Kadavu, Ono, and Taveuni, and at the small resort islands near Ovalau.

Be careful, however, and know the dangers. Practice snorkeling in the shallow water; don't head into deep water until you're sure you've got the hang of it. Breathe easily; don't hyperventilate. When snorkeling on a fringing reef, beware of deadly currents and undertows in channels that drain tidal flows. Observe the direction the water is moving before you swim into it. If you feel yourself being dragged out to sea through a reef passage, try swimming across the current rather than against it. If you can't resist the pull at all, it may be better to let yourself be carried out. Wait until the current diminishes, then swim along the outer reef face until you find somewhere to come back in. Or use your energy to attract the attention of someone onshore.

Snorkeling along the outer edge of a reef at the drop-off is thrilling for the variety of fish and corals, but attempt it only on a very calm day. Even then, it's wise to have someone stand onshore or paddle behind you in a canoe to watch for occasional big waves, which can take you by surprise and smash you into the rocks. Also, beware of unperceived currents outside the reef—you may not get a second chance.

A far better idea is to limit your snorkeling to the protected inner reef and leave the open waters to the scuba diver. Yet while scuba diving quickly absorbs large amounts of money, snorkeling is free and you can do it as often as you like. You'll encounter the brightest colors in shallow waters anyway, as lower than six meters the colors all turn blue as short wavelengths are lost. By diving with a scuba tank, you trade off the chance to observe shallow water species in order to gain access to the often larger deep-water species. The best solution is to do a bit of both. In any case, avoid touching the reef or any of its creatures, as the contact can be very harmful to both you and the reef. Take only pictures and leave only bubbles.

Excellent snorkeling awaits you just off Nananu-i-Ra Island near Rakiraki, Viti Levu.

Surfing

A growing number of surfing camps are off southern and western Viti Levu. The most famous is Tavarua Island in the Mamanuca Group, accessible only to American surfers on prepackaged tours from the States. Other mortals can also use speedboats from Seashell Cove and Rendezvous resorts to surf nearby reef breaks at far less expense, or try to get a booking at the top-end surf resort on Namotu Island right next to Tavarua. Beach break surfing (as opposed to more challenging reef break surfing) is possible at Club Masa near Sigatoka, and budget surfing camps have been built on Yanuca and Kadavu islands. In 2000, a surfing resort opened at Nagigia Island just off west Kadavu, and the Batiluva Beach Resort on Yanuca is very accessible. Surfing is the main activity at the Waidroka Bay Resort on the Coral Coast. Few of Fiji's waves are for the beginner, especially the reef breaks, and of course, you must bring your own board(s). One of the few companies actively renting surfboards is Viti Surf Legend in Nadi. There's surf throughout the year, with the best swells out of the south March–October.

Fijian clans control the traditional fishing rights *(qoli qoli)* on their reefs, and on many islands they also claim to own the surfing rights. This can also apply at breaks off uninhabited islands and even ocean reefs. In the past, upscale surfing camps like Tavarua, Marlin Bay, and Namotu have paid big bucks to try to corner the right to surf famous waves like Cloudbreak and Frigate, and they often attempt to keep surfers from rival resorts away. Although none of this is enshrined in law, it's wise to keep abreast of the situation. When surfing in a remote area without facilities, it's essential to present a *sevusevu* (a formal presentation of *yaqona*) to the local chief and to be on your best behavior.

Windsurfing

Windsurfing is possible at a much wider range of locales than surfing, and many upmarket beach hotels off southern and western Viti Levu include equipment in their rates. Windsurfing is possible at most of the Mamanuca resorts, including Castaway, Musket Cove, Malolo Island, Plantation Island, Tokoriki, and Treasure Island. Other offshore resorts around Fiji offering windsurfing are Matana Resort, Naigani Island, Qamea Beach, Toberua Island, Turtle Island, and Vatulele. Windsurfing tours to Nananu-i-Ra are well promoted. Almost all of the surfing camps also offer windsurfing.

Boating

Exciting **white-water rafting** on the cliff-hugging rapids of the Upper Navua River is offered by Rivers Fiji at Pacific Harbor. More white-water rafting is available on the Ba River below Navala. In central Viti Levu, villagers will pole you through the Waiqa Gorge on a bamboo raft from Naitauvoli to Naivucini villages, or down the Navua or Wainibuka rivers.

In the past, organized **ocean kayaking** expeditions have been offered among the Yasawa Islands, around Beqa and Kadavu, in Vanua Levu's Natewa Bay, and off Taveuni and Vanua Balavu (see Getting There, below, for details of sea-kayaking tours). Those who only want to dabble can hire kayaks at Kadavu, Taveuni, Savusavu, and a number of other places. Several upmarket Mamanuca Resorts loan kayaks to their guests.

Get in some **sailing** by taking one of the day cruises by yacht offered from Nadi. Yacht charters are available at Musket Cove Resort in the Mamanuca Group.

Hiking

All of the high islands offer hiking possibilities, and many remote villages are linked by well-used trails. The most important hike described in this book is the two-day Sigatoka River Trek down the Sigatoka River from Nadarivatu. Fiji's highest mountain, Tomaniivi, can be climbed in the same area. Levuka makes an excellent base, with the trail to The Peak beginning right behind the town, and a challenging cross-island trail to Lovoni is nearby. Easy day hikes are found in Colo-i-Suva Forest Park near Suva, and the waterfall and coastal hikes in Bouma National Heritage Park on Tave-

uni. More arduous is the all-day climb to Lake Tagimaucia on Taveuni. Koroyanitu National Heritage Park near Lautoka offers many hiking possibilities, including the famous Mount Batilamu Trek. The cane railway lines of western Viti Levu provide excellent hiking routes, such as from Sigatoka to the Tavuni Hill Fort and from Shangri-La's Fijian Resort to Natadola Beach. For some outer-island hiking, you can walk right around Nananu-i-Ra in less than a day, or across Waya or Wayasewa. Kadavu provides more of the same.

Bicycling

If you brought along a bicycle, you'll have several possibilities. Queens Road around the southern side of Viti Levu is favored by kamikaze drivers, so you're better off following the northerly Kings Road from Nadi Airport. At Ellington Wharf near Rakiraki, you can board the Vanua Levu ferry. The Hibiscus Highway east from Savusavu to Buca Bay is undulating and picturesque. At Natuvu, you can connect with the boat to Taveuni, one of Fiji's finest islands for cycling. From Taveuni, catch a ship to Suva and return to Nadi via Kings Road. A sidetrip to Ovalau on the Natovi ferry is highly recommended, if you have the time.

Golf

Golfers are well catered for in Fiji. The two most famous courses are the fantastic Denarau Golf Club, next to the Sheraton hotels at Nadi, and the renowned Pacific Harbor Country Club, one of the finest courses in the Pacific. Many tourist hotels have golf courses, including the Mocambo at Nadi; Shangri-La's Fijian Resort and Naviti Beach Resort on the south side of Viti Levu; Naigani Island Resort and The Wakaya Club in Lomaiviti; and Taveuni Estates on Taveuni. More locally oriented are the city golf courses at Nadi Airport, Lautoka, and in Suva, and the company-run courses near Rakiraki and Labasa sugar mills and at the Vatukoula gold mine, all built to serve former expatriate staffs. All are open to the public, and only the Sheraton course could be considered expensive.

Team Sports

The soccer season in Fiji is February–November (www.fijifootball.com), while rugby is played almost year-round. The main rugby season is June–November, when there are 15 players on each side. From November–March, rugby is played as "sevens," with seven team members to a side. (The Fijians are champion sevens players—"wild, intuitive, and artistic"—and in 1997 they defeated South Africa to take the Rugby World Cup Sevens in Hong Kong.) Rugby is played only by Fijians, while soccer teams are both Fijian and Indo-Fijian. Cricket is played November–March, mostly in rural areas. Lawn bowling is also popular. Saturday is the big day for team sports (only soccer and lawn bowling are practiced on Sunday).

Entertainment

It's cheap to go to the movies in towns such as Ba, Labasa, Lautoka, Nadi, Nausori, and Suva, if a repertoire of romance, horror, and adventure is to your liking (only in Suva can you see the latest Hollywood films). Most Indian films are in Hindi, sometimes with English subtitles. These same towns have local nightclubs where you can enjoy as much drinking and dancing as you like without spending an arm and a leg. When there's live music, a cover charge is collected.

A South Pacific institution widespread in Fiji is the old colonial clubs that offer inexpensive beer in safe, friendly surroundings. Such clubs are found in Labasa, Lautoka, Levuka, Nadi, Savusavu, Sigatoka, Suva, and Tavua, and although they're all private clubs with Members Only signs on the door, foreign visitors are allowed entry (except at the pretentious Union Club in Suva). Many of these are male domains, although women are not refused entry. The yacht clubs in Savusavu and Suva also have good bars. Many bars and clubs in Fiji refuse entry to persons dressed in flip-flops, boots, rugby jerseys, shorts, tank tops, or T-shirts, and one must remove one's hat at the door.

Fiji's unique spectacle is the **Fijian firewalking** performed several times a week at the large hotels along the southwest side of Viti Levu: Sheraton-Fiji (Wed.), Shangri-La's Fijian Resort (Fri.), Outrigger Reef Resort (Fri.), Hideaway Resort (Thurs.), The Naviti (Wed.), the Warwick (Mon. and Fri.), and the Pacific Harbor Cultural Center (Thurs.). A fixed admission price is charged, but it's well worth going at least once. For more information on firewalking, see Customs earlier in this Introduction. The same hotels that present

seated hand dancers performing a *meke* in a village on northern Taveuni

firewalking usually stage a Fijian *meke* (described below) on an alternate night.

Fijian Dancing (Meke)

The term *meke* describes the combination of dance, song, and theater performed at feasts and on special occasions. Brandishing spears, their faces painted with charcoal, the men wear frangipani leis and skirts of shredded leaves. The war-club dance reenacts heroic events of the past.

Both men and women perform the *vakamalolo,* a sitting dance, while the *seasea* is danced by women flourishing fans. The *tralala,* in which visitors may be asked to join, is a simple two-step shuffle danced side-by-side (early missionaries forbade the Fijians from dancing face-to-face). As elsewhere in the Pacific, the dances tell a story, though the music now is strongly influenced by Christian hymns and contemporary pop. Less sensual than Polynesian dancing, the rousing Fijian dancing evokes the country's violent past. Fijian *meke* are often part of a *magiti,* or feast, performed at hotels.

Public Holidays and Festivals

Public holidays in Fiji include New Year's Day (January 1), National Youth Day (variable), Good Friday and Easter Monday (March/April), Ratu Sukuna Day (a Monday around May 29), Queen Elizabeth's Birthday (a Monday around June 14), Prophet Mohammed's Birthday (variable), Fiji Day (a Monday or Friday around October 10), Diwali (October or November), and Christmas Days (December 25 and 26).

Check with the Fiji Visitors Bureau to see if any festivals are scheduled during your visit. The best known are the Bula Festival in Nadi (July), the Hibiscus Festival in Suva (August), the Sugar Festival in Lautoka (September), and the Back to Levuka Festival (early October). Around the end of June there's the President's Cup Yacht Series at Nadi. Before Diwali, the Hindu festival of lights, Hindus clean their homes, then they light lamps or candles to mark the arrival of spring. Fruit and sweets are offered to Lakshmi, goddess of wealth. Holi is an Indian spring festival in February or March. The Third Melanesian Arts Festival will be held in Fiji in 2006.

The International Triathlon at Nadi is in May.

One of the main sporting events of the year is the **International Bula Marathon** held in June. The main event involves a 42-kilometer run from Lautoka to the Sheraton at Nadi.

When to Go

Compared to parts of North America and Europe, the seasonal climatic variations in Fiji are not extreme. There's a hotter, more humid season November–April, and a cooler, drier time May–October. Hurricanes can occur during the "rainy" season but they only last a few days a year. The sun sets around 1800 year-round, and there aren't periods when the days are shorter or longer.

Seasonal differences in airfares are often more influential in deciding when to go. On Air New Zealand flights from North America, the low season is mid-April to August, the prime time in Fiji. Christmas is busy, but in February and March, many hotels stand half empty and special discount rates are on offer. In short, there isn't really any one season which is the "best" time to go, and every season has its advantages.

Arts and Crafts

The traditional art of Fiji is closely related to that of Tonga. Fijian canoes, too, were patterned after the more-advanced Polynesian type, although the Fijians were timid sailors. War clubs, food bowls, *tanoas* (kava bowls), eating utensils, clay pots, and tapa cloth *(masi)* are considered Fiji's finest artifacts.

There are two kinds of wood carvings: the ones made from *vesi (Intsia bijuga)*—ironwood in English—or *nawanawa (Cordia subcordata)* wood are superior to those of the lighter, highly breakable *vau (Hibiscus tiliaceus).* In times past, it often took years to make a Fijian war club, as the carving was done in the living tree and left to grow into the desired shape. The finest *tanoas* are carved in the Lau Group.

Although many crafts are alive and well, some Fijians have taken to carving "tikis" or mock New Guinea masks smeared with black shoe polish to look like ebony for sale to tourists. Also avoid crafts made from endangered species such as sea turtles (tortoiseshell) and marine mammals (whales' teeth, etc.). Prohibited entry into most countries, these will be confiscated by customs if found.

Pottery Making

Fijian pottery making is unique in that it's a Melanesian art form. The Polynesians forgot how to make pottery thousands of years ago. Today the main center for pottery making in Fiji is the Sigatoka Valley on Viti Levu. Here, the women shape clay by pressing a wooden paddle against a rounded stone held inside the future pot. The potter's wheel was unknown in the Pacific.

A saucerlike section forms the bottom; the sides are built up using slabs of clay, or coils and strips. These are welded and battered to shape. When the form is ready, the pot is dried inside the house for a few days, then heated over an open fire for about an hour. Resin from the gum of the *dakua* (kauri) tree is rubbed on the outside while the pot is still hot. This adds a varnish that brings out the color of the clay and improves the pot's water-holding ability.

This pottery is extremely fragile, which accounts for the quantity of potsherds found on ancient village sites. Smaller, less breakable pottery products such as ashtrays are now made for sale to visitors.

Weaving

Woven articles are the most widespread handicrafts. Pandanus fiber is the most common, but coconut leaf and husk, vine tendril, banana stem, tree and shrub bark, the stems and leaves of water weeds, and the skin of the sago palm leaf are all used. On some islands the fibers are passed through a fire, boiled, then bleached in the sun. Vegetable dyes of very lovely mellow tones are sometimes used, but gaudier store dyes are much more prevalent. Shells are occasionally utilized to cut, curl, or make the fibers pliable.

Tapa Cloth

This is Fiji's most characteristic traditional product. Tapa is light, portable, and inexpensive, and a piece makes an excellent souvenir to brighten up a room back home. It's made by the women on Vatulele Island off Viti Levu and on certain islands of the Lau Group.

To produce tapa, the inner, water-soaked bark of the paper mulberry *(Broussonetia papyrifera)* is stripped from the tree and steeped in water. Then it's scraped with shells and pounded into a thin sheet with wooden mallets. Four of these sheets are applied one over another and pounded together, then left to dry in the sun.

While Tongan tapa is decorated by holding a relief pattern under the tapa and overpainting the lines, Fijian tapa *(masi kesa)* is distinctive for its rhythmic geometric designs applied with stencils made from green pandanus and banana leaves. The stain is rubbed on in the same manner in which temple rubbings are made from a stone inscription.

The only colors used are red, from red clay, and a black pigment obtained by burning candlenuts. Both powders are mixed with boiled gums made from scraped roots. Sunlight deepens and sets the colors. Each island group had its characteristic colors and patterns, ranging from plantlike paintings to geometric designs. Sheets of tapa feel like felt when finished. On some islands, tapa is still used for clothing, bedding, and room dividers, and as ceremonial red carpets. Tablecloths, bedcovers, place mats, and wall hangings of tapa make handsome souvenirs.

Shopping

Most large shops in Fiji close at 1300 on Saturday, but smaller grocery stores are often open on Sunday. After the 1987 military coups, most commercial business was suspended on Sunday, but these restrictions were dropped in 1996, and you'll find many restaurants and bars now open on Sunday. Indo-Fijians dominate the retail trade. If you're buying from an Indo-Fijian merchant, always bargain hard and consider all sales final. Indigenous Fijians usually begin by asking a much lower starting price, in which case bargaining isn't so important.

Fiji's "duty-free" shops such as Prouds or Tappoo are not really duty-free, as all goods are subject to various fiscal duties, plus the 12.5 percent value-added tax. Bargaining is the order of the day, but to be frank, Americans can usually buy most of the Japanese electronics sold "duty-free" in Fiji cheaper in the States, where more recent models are available. If you do buy something, get an itemized receipt and international guarantee, and watch that they don't switch packages and unload a demo on you. Once purchased, items cannot be returned, so don't let yourself be talked into anything. Camera film is inexpensive, however, and the selection is good—stock up.

If you'd like to do some shopping in Fiji, locally made handicrafts such as tapa cloth, mats, kava bowls, war clubs, wood carvings, etc., are a much better investment (see Arts and Crafts). The four-pronged cannibal forks available in most souvenir stores make unique gifts, but avoid the masks, which are made only for sale to tourists and have nothing to do with Fiji. If you're spending serious money for top-quality work, visit the Fiji Museum or the Government Handicraft Center in Suva beforehand to see what is authentic.

To learn what's available on the tourist market and to become familiar with prices, browse one of the half-dozen outlets of **Jack's Handicrafts** around Viti Levu. You'll find them in downtown Nadi, Sigatoka, and Suva. If the salesperson is overenthusiastic and begins following you around too closely, just stop and say you're only looking today, and they'll probably leave you alone.

You can often purchase your souvenirs directly from the Fijian producers at markets, etc. Just beware of aggressive indigenous Fijian "sword sellers" on the streets of Suva, Nadi, and Lautoka who peddle fake handicrafts at high prices, or high-pressure duty-free touts who may try to pull you into their shops, or self-appointed guides who offer to help you find the "best price." If you get the feeling you're being hustled, walk away.

Accommodations

With *Moon Handbooks Fiji* you're guaranteed a good, inexpensive place to stay on almost every island. Nearly every hotel in the country is included herein, not just a selection. We consistently do this to give you a solid second reference in case your travel agent or someone else recommends a certain place. To allow you the widest possible choice, all price categories are included, and throughout we've tried to spotlight properties that offer value for money. If you think we're wrong or you were badly treated, be sure to send us a written complaint. Equally important, let us know when you agree with what's here, or

if you think a place deserves a better review. Your letter will be taken seriously! You can contact the author directly through his website.

We don't solicit freebies from the hotel chains; our only income derives from the price you paid for this book. So we don't mind telling you that, as usual, some of the luxury hotels are just not worth the exorbitant prices they charge. Many simply re-create Hawaii at twice the cost. Even worse, they tend to isolate you in an American/Australian environment, away from the Fiji you came to experience. Most are worth visiting as sightseeing attractions, watering holes, or

Backpackers traveling to outer islands of the Yasawa Group usually stay in thatched *bure* such as this.

sources of entertainment, but unless you're a millionaire, sleep elsewhere. Plenty of middle-level hotels charge about half of what the top-end places ask, while providing adequate comfort.

Dormitory or other backpacker accommodations are available on all of the main islands, with communal cooking facilities often provided. If you're traveling alone, these are excellent, since they're just the place to meet other travelers. Couples can usually get a double room at a hostel for a price only slightly above two dorm beds. Many outer-island resorts also rent dorm beds, but they're more expensive as compulsory meals are included. For the most part, the dormitories are safe and congenial for those who don't mind sacrificing their privacy to save money.

Be aware that some of the low-budget places included in this book are a lot more basic than what is sometimes referred to as "budget" accommodations in the United States. The standards of cleanliness in the common bathrooms may be lower than you expected, the furnishings very basic, the beds uncomfortable, linens and towels skimpy, housekeeping nonexistent, and window screens lacking, but ask yourself,

where in the U.S. are you going to find a room for a similar price? Luckily, good medium-priced accommodations are usually available for those unwilling to put up with Spartan conditions.

When picking a hotel, keep in mind that although a thatched bungalow is cooler and infinitely more aesthetic than a concrete box, it's also more likely to have insect problems. If in doubt, check the window screens and carry mosquito coils and repellent. Hopefully there'll be a resident lizard or two to feed on the bugs. Always turn on a light before getting out of bed to use the facilities at night, as even the finest hotels in the tropics have cockroaches.

A room with cooking facilities can save you a lot on restaurant meals, and some moderately priced establishments have weekly rates. If you have to choose a meal plan, take only breakfast and dinner (Modified American Plan or MAP) and have fruit for lunch. As you check into your room, note the nearest fire exits. And don't automatically accept the first room offered; if you're paying good money look at several, then choose.

Needless to say, always ask the price of your accommodations before accepting them. In cases where there's a local and a tourist price, you'll always pay the higher tariff if you don't check beforehand. Asking first gives you the opportunity to bargain if someone quotes an absurdly high starting price.

When things are slow, specials are offered and some prices become negotiable, and occasionally you'll pay a third less than the prices quoted in this book. This is most likely to happen in February and March, the lowest tourist season. Otherwise, prices are usually the same year-round without seasonal variations. Many medium-priced hotels and resorts around Fiji have reduced "local rates," which are usually also available to foreign tourists who are already in Fiji and book direct. Always ask for it if you haven't made reservations. In this handbook, we quote the published "rack rates," which can be as much as 50 percent higher than the "local rate" or the specials.

A 12.5 percent government tax is added to all accommodations prices. Most hotels include the tax in their quoted rates, but some don't. If this might have a bearing on your choice, ask beforehand.

RESERVING AHEAD

Booking accommodations in advance usually works to your disadvantage as overseas travel agents will begin by trying to sell you their most expensive properties (which pay them the highest commissions) and work down from there. The quite adequate middle and budget places included in this handbook often aren't on their screens, or are sold at highly inflated prices. Few hotels charging less than US$80 have the accounting wherewithal to process agency commissions. Herein we provide the rates for direct bookings, and if you book through a travel agent abroad, you could end up paying considerably more as multiple commissions are tacked on. Thus we suggest you avoid making any hotel reservations at all before arriving in Fiji (unless you're coming for a major event). Specials and local rate discounts are never available to people who book by email or through travel agents.

There aren't many islands where it's to your ad-

ACCOMMODATION PRICE RANGES

Throughout this handbook, accommodations are grouped in the price categories that follow, based on the price of a double room. The two-for-one conversion rate used is indicated below, and of course, currency fluctuations and inflation can lead to slight variations.

Under US$25	(Under F$50)
US$25–50	(F$50–100)
US$50–100	(F$100–200)
US$100–150	(F$200–300)
US$150 and up	(F$300 and up)

EXPLORING THE ISLANDS

vantage to book ahead in the medium to lower price range, but you can often obtain substantial discounts at the upscale hotels by including them as part of a package tour. If you intend to spend most of your time at a specific first-class hotel, you'll benefit from bulk rates by taking a package tour instead of paying the higher "rack rate" the hotels charge to individuals who walk in off the street. Call up some of the agents listed herein in Getting There and check their websites.

FijiBedBank.com (www.fijibedbank.com) and **Fijiagent.com** (www.fijiagent.com) book rooms online via a secure server, though only wholesalers and travel agents can use these services. **TravelMaxia.com** (www.travelmaxia.com) provides information that allows you to make direct contact with the resorts.

ACCOMMODATION CATEGORIES

Fiji offers a wide variety of places to stay, from low-budget to world-class. Standard international hotels are found in Nadi and Suva, while many of the upmarket beach resorts are on small islands in the Mamanuca Group off Nadi or along the Coral Coast on Viti Levu's sunny south side. The Mamanuca resorts are secluded, with fan-cooled *bure* accommodations, while at the Coral Coast hotels you often get an air-conditioned room in a main building. The Coral Coast has more to offer in the way of land tours, shopping, and entertainment/eating options, while the offshore resorts are preferable if you want a rest or are into water sports. The Coral Coast beaches are only good at high tide and the reefs are degraded, while on the outer islands the reefs are usually pristine. Some resorts cater almost exclusively to scuba divers or surfers, and these may not be the best places to stay if you aren't interested in those activities.

In recent years, smaller luxury resorts have multiplied in remote locations, from former plantations near Savusavu and on Taveuni to isolated beach resorts on outlying islands such as Beqa, Kadavu, Matangi, Naigani, Namenalala, Nukubati, Qamea, Toberua, Turtle, Vatulele, Wakaya, and Yasawa. Prices at the "boutique" resorts begin at several hundred dollars a day and rise to four figures, so some care should be taken in selecting the right one. A few such as Beqa, Kadavu, and Taveuni are marketed almost exclusively to scuba divers, and Namenalala is a good ecotourism choice. If you delight in glamorous socializing with other upscale couples, Turtle and Vatulele are for you. Families are most welcome at Beachcomber, Castaway, Cousteau, Koro Sun, Malolo, Maravu, Matangi, Naigani, Naviti, Outrigger Reef, Plantation, Shangri-La's Fijian, Sonaisali, Toberua, Treasure, and Warwick, but children are generally not accepted at all at Katafaga, Lomalagi, Matamanoa, Matana, Namale, Namotu, Natadola, Nukubati, Qamea, Taveuni, Tokoriki, Turtle, Vatulele, Wadigi, Wakaya, and Yasawa. The very wealthy will feel at home on Katafaga, Turtle, and Wakaya, whereas Mamanuca resorts like Castaway, Mana, and Plantation are designed for larger numbers of guests interested in intensive sporting and social activities.

The low-budget accommodations are spread out, with concentrations in Korotogo, Nadi, Lautoka, Levuka, Suva, and Savusavu, and on Taveuni. Low-cost outer-island beach resorts exist on Caqalai, Kadavu, Kuata, Leleuvia, Mana, Nacula, Nananu-i-Ra, Nanuya Lailai, Naviti, Ono, Tavewa, Waya, Wayasewa, and Yanuca. The largest budget chain in Fiji is Cathay Hotels with properties in Suva, Lautoka, and on the Coral Coast (visit their Fiji For Less website at www.fiji4less.com). Since September 2000, several dozen new backpacker resorts have appeared in the Yasawa Islands under the auspices of the Nacula Tikina Tourism Association (www.fijibudget.com), with the support of millionaire environmentalist Richard Evanson. Most of these cater to a younger crowd who decide where they'll stay as they go, and the easiest way to book rooms is to call them up after you get to Fiji or to work through an agent in Nadi.

A few of the cheap hotels in Suva, Nadi, and Lautoka double as whorehouses, making them cheap in both senses of the word. At all of the low-budget hostels, women should exercise care in the way they deal with the male staff as we've received complaints about harassment. Many hotels, both in cities and at the beach, offer dormitory beds as well as individual rooms. Most of the dorms are mixed. Women can sometimes request a women-only dorm when things are slow, but it's usually not guaranteed. Some budget-priced city hotels lock their front doors at 2300 (or at 2200 in Labasa), so ask first if you're planning a night on the town. Several islands with air service from Suva, including Moala, Gau, and Cicia, have no regular accommodations for visitors at all, so it's best to know someone who lives there before heading to those islands.

CAMPING

Camping facilities (bring your own tent) are found at backpacker resorts on Caqalai, Kadavu, Kuata, Leleuvia, Mana, Nacula, Nanua Lailai, Naviti, Ono, Ovalau, Taveuni, Tavewa, Waya, Wayasewa, and Yanuca Lailai Islands. A few shoestring hostels in Nadi and Suva also allow it, as do Viti Levu beach resorts like Seashell Cove, The Beachouse, and the Coral Coast Christian Camp. On Vanua Levu, you can camp at Mumu Resort.

Elsewhere, get permission before pitching your tent, as all land is owned by someone, and land rights are sensitive issues in Fiji. Some freelance campers on beaches, such as Natadola near Nadi and around Pacific Harbor, have had their possessions stolen, so take care.

In Fijian villages, don't ask a Fijian friend for permission to camp beside his house. Although he may feel obligated to grant the request of a guest, you'll be proclaiming to everyone that his home isn't completely to your liking. If all you really want is to camp, make that clear from the start and get approval to do so on a beach or by a river, but *not* in the village. A *sevusevu* should always be presented in this case. There's really nowhere to camp totally for free. Never camp under a coconut tree, as falling coconuts can harm or kill you (actually, coconuts have two eyes so they only strike the wicked).

STAYING IN VILLAGES

The most direct way to meet the Fijian people and learn a little about their culture is to stay in a village for a couple of nights. A number of hiking tours offer overnight stays in remote villages, and it's also possible to arrange it for yourself. **Fijibure.com** (www.fijibure.com) organizes stays at Namatukula, Namuamua, and Navutulevu villages in southern Viti Levu at F$50 pp a night. If you befriend someone from an outlying island, ask them to write you a letter of introduction to their relatives back in the village. Mail a copy of it ahead with a polite letter introducing yourself, then slowly start heading that way.

In places well off the beaten track where there are no regular tourist accommodations, you could just show up in a village and ask permission of the *turaga-ni-koro* (village herald) to spend the night. Both Indo-Fijians and native Fijians will probably spontaneously invite you in to their homes. The Fijians' innate dignity and kindness should not be taken for granted, however.

All across the Pacific, it's customary to reciprocate when someone gives you a gift—if not now, then sometime in the future. In Fiji, this type of back and forth is called *kerekere*. Visitors who accept gifts (such as meals and accommodations) from islanders and do not reciprocate are undermining traditional culture and causing resentment, often without realizing it. It's sometimes hard to know how to repay hospitality, but Fijian culture has a solution: the *sevusevu*. This can be money, but it's usually a 500-gram "pyramid" of kava roots *(waka)*, which can be easily purchased at any Fijian market for about F$15. *Sevusevu* are more often performed between families or couples about to be married, or at births or christenings, but the custom is a perfectly acceptable way for visitors to show their appreciation.

We suggest travelers donate at least F$20 pp per night to village hosts (carry sufficient cash in small denominations). The *waka* bundle is additional, and anyone traveling in remote areas of Fiji should pack some (take whole roots, not powdered kava). If you give the money up front together with the *waka* as a *sevusevu*, they'll know you're not a freeloader, and you'll get VIP treatment, though in all cases it's absolutely essential to contribute something.

The *sevusevu* should be placed before (not handed to) the *turaga-ni-koro*, or village herald, so he can accept or refuse. If he accepts (by touching the package), your welcome is confirmed and you may spend the night in the village. It's also nice to give some money to the lady of the house upon departure, with your thanks. Just say it's your goodbye *sevusevu* and watch the smile. A Fijian may refuse the money, but he or she will not be offended by the offer if it is done properly. Of course, developing interpersonal relationships with your hosts is more important than money, and mere cash or gifts is no substitute for making friends.

If you're headed for a remote outer island without hotels or resorts, you could also take some gifts along, such as lengths of material, T-shirts, badges, pins, knitting needles, hats, acoustic guitar strings, school books, colored pens, toys, playing cards, fishhooks, line, or lures, or a big jar of instant coffee. Keep in mind, however, that Seventh-Day Adventists are forbidden to have coffee, cigarettes, or kava, so you might ask if there are any SDAs around in order to avoid embarrassment. Uncontroversial food items to donate include sugar, flour, rice, corned beef, matches, chewing gum, peanuts, and biscuits. One thing *not* to take is alcohol, which is always sure to offend somebody.

Once you're staying with one family, avoid moving to the home of another family in the same village, as this would probably be seen as a slight to the first. Be wary of readily accepting invitations to meals with villagers other than your hosts, as the offer may only be meant as a courtesy.

EXPLORING THE ISLANDS

VILLAGE ETIQUETTE IN FIJI

- It's a Fijian custom to smile when you meet a stranger and say something like "Good morning," "Bula," or at least "Hello." Of course, you needn't do this in large towns, but you should do so almost everywhere else. If you meet someone you know, stop for a moment to exchange a few words. As you shake hands, tell the person your name.

- Fijian villages are private property and you should only enter after you've been welcomed. Of course it's okay to continue along a road that passes through a village, but make contact before leaving the road. Wait until someone greets you, then say you wish to be taken to the *turaga-ni-koro* (village herald). This village spokesperson will accept your *sevusevu* of kava roots and grant you permission to look around, unless something important is happening, such as a funeral, celebration, feast, or church service (avoid arriving on a Sunday). A villager will be assigned to act as your guide and host. Yet even after this, you should still ask before taking pictures of individuals or inside buildings.

- If you wish to surf off the coast of a village, picnic on a village beach, or fish in the lagoon near to a village, you should also ask permission. You'll almost always be made most welcome and granted any favors you request if you present a *sevusevu* to the village herald or chief. If you approach the Fijians with respect, you're sure to be treated the same way in return.

- Take off your footwear before entering a *bure*, and stoop as you walk around inside. Fijian villagers consider it offensive to walk in front of a person seated on the floor (pass behind) or to fail to say *tulou* (excuse me) as you go by. Clap three times when you join people already seated on mats on the floor. Shake hands with your hosts.

- In a *bure*, men should sit cross-legged, women with their legs to the side. Sitting with your legs stretched out in front or with your knees up during presentations is disrespectful. After a meal or dur-

ing informal kava drinking, you can stretch your legs out, but never point them at the chief or the kava bowl. Don't sit in doorways or put your hand on another's head.

- If offered kava *(yaqona)*, clap once with cupped hands, take the bowl, say *bula*, and drink it all in one gulp. Then hand the bowl back to the same person and clap three times saying *vinaka* (thanks). Don't stand up during a *sevusevu* to village elders—remain seated. When you give a gift hold it out with both hands, not one hand. Otherwise just place the bundle on the floor before them.

- It's good manners to take off your hat while walking through a village, where only the chief is permitted to wear a hat. Some villagers also object to sunglasses. Objects such as backpacks, handbags, and cameras should be carried in your hands rather than slung over your shoulders.

- Dress modestly in the village, which basically means a shirt for men and covered shoulders and thighs for women. Short shorts are not the best attire for men or women (long shorts okay), and bikinis are analogous to nudity (this also applies when swimming in a village river, pool, or beach). Wrapping a *sulu* around you will suffice.

- Don't point at people in villages. Do you notice how the Fijians rarely shout? In Fiji, raising your voice is a sign of anger. Don't openly admire a possession of someone, as he or she may feel obligated to give it to you. If sharing a meal, wait until grace has been said before eating. Alcohol is usually forbidden in villages.

- Fijian children are very well behaved, and there's no running or shouting as you arrive in a village, and they'll leave you alone if you wish. The Fijians love children, so don't hesitate to bring your own. You'll never have to worry about finding a baby-sitter. Just make sure your children understand the importance of being on their best behavior in the village.

Don't overly admire any of the possessions of your hosts, or they may feel obligated to give them to you. If you're forced to accept a family heirloom or other item you know you cannot take, ask them to keep it there for you in trust.

When choosing your traveling companions for a trip that involves staying in Fijian villages, make sure you agree on these things before you set out. Otherwise you could end up subsidizing somebody else's trip, or worse, have to stand by and watch the Fijian villagers subsidize it. Never arrive in a village on a Sunday, and don't overstay your welcome.

We received this comment from a Norwegian reader:

We were invited to the chiefly village of Nukubalavu, where we were introduced to the big chief of Savusavu and we had to do the kava offering, keeping our heads low. I read about this in your book and thought it was an out of date fashion to bring kava around to give the chiefs when you travel, but the forms here are quite serious, as we also experienced at a ceremony in town today when the president of Fiji was visiting on Coconut Day. No joke! He got a whole kava bush!

Village Life

As you approach a Fijian village, people will usually want to be helpful and will direct or accompany you to the person or place you seek. It's customary to present a *sevusevu* to the *turaga-ni-koro* if you'd like to be shown around. If you show genuine interest in something and ask to see how it is done, you'll usually be treated with respect and asked if there's anything else you'd like to know. Initially, Fijians may hesitate to welcome you into their homes, because they may fear you will not wish to sit on a mat and eat native foods with your fingers. Once you show them this isn't true, you'll receive the full hospitality treatment.

Consider participating in the daily activities of the family, such as weaving, cooking, gardening, and fishing. Your hosts will probably try to dissuade you from "working," but if you persist you'll become accepted. Staying in a village is definitely not for everyone. Many houses contain no electricity, running water, toilet, furniture, etc., and only native food will be available. Water and your left hand serve as toilet paper.

You should also expect to sacrifice most of your privacy, to stay up late drinking grog, and to sit in the house and socialize when you could be out exploring. On Sunday, you'll have to stay put the whole day. The constant attention and lack of sanitary conditions may become tiresome, but it would be considered rude to attempt to be alone or refuse the food or grog.

With the proliferation of backpacker resorts, staying in villages has become far less a part of visits to the remoter parts of Fiji than it was a decade ago, and relatively few travelers do it today. The Australian mass-market guidebooks also discourage travelers from going off the beaten track. However, so long as you're prepared to accept all of the above and know beforehand that this is not a cheap (or easy) way to travel, a couple of nights in an outlying village could well be the highlight of your trip.

EXPLORING THE ISLANDS

Food

Unlike some other South Pacific destinations, Fiji has many good, inexpensive eateries. The ubiquitous Chinese restaurants are probably your best bet for dinner, and you can almost always get alcohol with the meal. At lunchtime, look for an Indian place. The Indian restaurants are life-savers for vegetarians, as all too often a vegetarian meal elsewhere is just the same thing, but with the meat removed.

Many restaurants are closed on Sunday, and a 12.5 percent tax is added to the bill at some up-market restaurants, although it's usually included in the menu price. The service at restaurants is occasionally slow. Fijians have their own pace, and trying to make them do things more quickly is often counterproductive. Their charm and the friendly personal attention you receive more than compensate.

The Hot Bread Kitchen chain of bakeries around Fiji serves fresh fruit loaves, cheese and onion loaves, muffins, and other assorted breads. The Morris Hedstrom supermarket chain is about the cheapest, and many have milk bars with ice cream and sweets.

The famous Fiji Bitter beer is brewed in Suva by Australian-owned Carlton Brewery Ltd., part of the famous Fosters Brewing Group. The 750-milliliter beer bottle is called a "long neck," while the smaller "stubbie" is a "short neck." Another Carlton-owned company, South Pacific Distilleries Ltd., produces Bounty Rum, Regal Whisky, Czarina Vodka, and eight other alcoholic beverages at their plant in Lautoka. Beer and other alcohol is only available at supermarkets in Fiji on weekdays 0800–1800, Saturday 0800–1300. By law, licensed restaurants can only serve alcohol to

FIJIAN AND INDIAN SPECIALTIES

Traditional Fijian food is usually steamed or boiled, instead of fried, and dishes such as baked fish (ika) in coconut cream (lolo) with cassava (tavioka), taro (dalo), breadfruit (uto), and sweet potato (kumala) take a long time to prepare and must be served fresh, which makes it difficult to offer them in restaurants. Many resorts bake fish, pork, and root vegetables wrapped in banana leaves in a lovo (earth oven) at least once a week. Don't pass up an opportunity to try duruka (young sugar cane) or vakalolo (fish and prawns), both baked in lolo. Kokoda is an appetizing dish made of diced raw fish marinated in coconut cream and lime juice, while smoked octopus is kuita. Taro leaves are used to make a spinach called palusami (often stuffed with corned beef), which is known as rourou when soaked in coconut cream. Taro stems are cut into a marinated salad called baba. Seasoned chicken (toa) is wrapped and steamed in banana leaves to produce kovu. Miti is a sauce made of coconut cream, oranges, and chilies.

Indian dishes are spicy, often curries with rice and dhal (lentil soup), but practicing Hindus don't consume beef and Muslims forgo pork. Instead of bread Indians eat roti, a flat, tortilla-like pancake also called a chapati. Puri are small, deep-fried rotis. Baked in a stone oven roti becomes naan, a Punjabi specialty similar to pita bread. Papadam is a crispy version of the same. Palau is a main plate of rice and vegetables always including peas. Samosas are lumps of potato and other vegetables wrapped in dough and deep-fried. Pakoras are deep-fried chunks of dough spiced with chili and often served with a pickle chutney. A set meal consisting of dhal, roti, rice, one or two curries, and chutney, served on a metal plate, is called a thali. If meat is included, it's called simply a non-vegetarian thali. Yogurt mixed with water makes a refreshing drink called lassi. If you have the chance, try South Indian vegetarian dishes like iddili (little white rice cakes served with dhal) and masala dosai (a potato-filled rice pancake served with a watery curry sauce called sambar).

THE COCONUT PALM

Human life would not be possible on most of the Pacific's far-flung atolls without this all-purpose tree. It reaches maturity in eight years, then produces about 50 nuts a year for 60 years. Aside from the tree's aesthetic value and usefulness in providing shade, the water of the green coconut provides a refreshing drink, and the white meat of the young nut is a delicious food. The harder meat of more mature nuts is grated and squeezed, which creates a coconut cream that is eaten alone or used in cooking. The oldest nuts are cracked open and the hard meat removed then dried to be sold as copra. It takes about 6,000 coconuts to make a ton of copra. Copra is pressed to extract the oil, which in turn is made into candles, cosmetics, and soap. Scented with flowers, the oil nurtures the skin.

The juice or sap from the cut flower spathes of the palm provides toddy, a popular drink; the toddy is distilled into a spirit called arrack, the whiskey of the Pacific. Otherwise the sap can be boiled to make candy. Millionaire's salad is made by shredding the growth cut from the heart of the tree. For each salad, a fully mature tree must be sacrificed.

The nut's hard inner shell can be used as a cup and makes excellent firewood. Rope, cordage, brushes, and heavy matting are produced from the coir fiber of the husk. The smoke from burning husks is an effective mosquito repellent. The leaves of the coconut tree are used to thatch the roofs of the islanders' cottages or are woven into baskets, mats, and fans. The trunk provides timber for building and furniture. Actually, these are only the common uses; there are many others as well.

EXPLORING THE ISLANDS

those who order meals. Drinking alcoholic beverages on the street is prohibited. Unlike Australia and New Zealand, it's not customary to bring your own (BYO) booze into restaurants.

Traditional Foods

The traditional diet of the Fijians consists of root crops and fruit, plus lagoon fish and the occasional pig. The vegetables include taro, yams, cassava (manioc), breadfruit, and sweet potatoes. The sweet potato *(kumala)* is something of an anomaly—it's the only Pacific food plant with a South American origin. How it got to the islands is not known.

Taro is an elephant-eared plant cultivated in freshwater swamps. Although yams are considered a prestige food, they're not as nutritious as breadfruit and taro. Yams can grow up to three meters long and weigh hundreds of kilograms. Papaya (pawpaw) is nourishing: A third of a cup contains as much vitamin C as 18 apples. To ripen a green papaya overnight, puncture it a few times with a knife. Don't overeat papaya—unless you *need* an effective laxative.

The ancient Pacific islanders stopped making pottery more than a millennium ago and instead developed an ingenious way of cooking in an underground earth oven known as a *lovo*. First a stack of dry coconut husks is burned in a pit. Once the fire is going well, coral stones are heaped on top, and when most of the husks have burnt away, the food is wrapped in banana leaves and placed on the hot stones—fish and meat below, vegetables above. A whole pig may be cleaned, then stuffed with banana leaves and hot stones. This cooks the beast from inside out as well as outside in, and the leaves create steam. The food is then covered with more leaves and stones, and after about two and a half hours everything is cooked.

The *lovo* feasts staged weekly at many large hotels around Nadi or on the Coral Coast offer a good opportunity to taste authentic Fijian food and see traditional dancing. These feasts are usually accompanied by a Fijian *meke,* or song-and-dance performance, in which legends, love stories, and historical events are told in song and gesture. Alternatively, firewalking may be presented.

Tourist Information

Information

The government-funded **Fiji Visitors Bureau** (tel. 330-2433, fax 330-0970, www.bulafiji.com) mails out general brochures, free upon request. In Fiji, they have walk-in offices at Nadi Airport and in Suva. Their overseas offices are listed on www.southpacific.org/info.html.

The Fiji Visitors Bureau sends out a useful tourism newsletter called *Bula News Update* via email twice a month. To subscribe, simply send a blank email to bulanews@fijifvb.gov.fj with "Subscribe" in the subject heading, and your email address will be automatically added to the distribution list. To be removed from the list, repeat the process with "Unsubscribe" in the subject heading.

Book buyers should browse the two book centers at the University of the South Pacific in Suva, as only these have a wide selection of titles.

Travel Agencies

If you like the security of advance reservations but aren't interested in joining a regular packaged tour, several local companies specialize in booking cruises, hotel rooms, airport transfers, sightseeing tours, rental cars, etc. Only the Blue Lagoon and Captain Cook mini-cruises mentioned in Getting There really need to be booked well in advance from abroad; upon arrival you'll have dozens of hotels and resorts competing for your business at prices much lower than what your travel agent back home will charge. So rather than risk being exiled to one of Fiji's most expensive resorts by some agent only thinking of his/her commission, wait to make most of your ground arrangements upon arrival at Nadi Airport.

Fiji's largest in-bound tour operator is **Rosie The Travel Service** (tel. 672-2935, fax 672-2607), with a 24-hour office in the arrivals arcade at Nadi Airport and 16 branches around Viti Levu. This handbook will give you an idea of what's out there, and upon arrival in Fiji, Rosie can make your accommodations bookings for you on the spot and at rates far lower than you'll pay working through travel agents overseas. Of course, you run the risk of finding that your place of choice is

TOURIST OFFICES

Fiji Visitors Bureau: GPO P.O. Box 92, Suva, Fiji Islands; tel. 679/330-2433, fax 679/330-0970, www.bulafiji.com

Fiji Visitors Bureau: Suite 220, 5777 West Century Blvd., Los Angeles, CA 90045, U.S.A.; tel. 310/568-1616 or 800/932-3454, fax 310/670-2318, www.bulafijiislands.com

Fiji Visitors Bureau: Level 12, St. Martin's Tower, 31 Market St., Sydney, NSW 2000, Australia; tel. 61-2/9264-3399, fax 61-2/9264-3060, www.bulafiji-au.com

Fiji Visitors Bureau: P.O. Box 1179, Auckland, New Zealand; tel. 64-9/376-2533, fax 64-9/376-4720, www.bulafiji.co.nz

Fiji Visitors Bureau: 14th floor, NOA Bldg., 3–5, 2-Chome, Azabudai, Minato-ku, Tokyo 106, Japan; tel. 81-3/3587-2561, fax 81-3/3587-2563, www.bulafiji-jp.com

South Pacific Tourism Organization: 48 Glentham Rd., Barnes, London SW13 9JJ, United Kingdom; tel. 44-20/8741-6082, fax 44-20/8741-6107, www.spto.org

South Pacific Tourism Organization: Petersburger Str. 94, D-10247 Berlin, Germany; tel. 49-30/4225-6026, fax 49-30/4225-6287, www.spto.org

fully booked. This locally owned business has provided efficient, personalized service since 1974.

Rosie's main competitor is the **United Touring Company** (tel. 672-2811) with an office at Nadi Airport and tour desks at many Nadi and Coral Coast hotels. **Coral Sun Fiji** (tel. 672-2268) is also very reliable. Numerous other private travel agencies have offices at Nadi Airport and in town, many of them oriented toward backpackers or budget travelers. These are discussed in this book's Nadi chapter.

Visas and Officialdom

Everyone needs a passport that is valid at least three months beyond the date of entry. No visa is required of visitors from 101 countries (including Western Europe, North America, Japan, Israel, and most Commonwealth countries) for stays of up to four months. A complete list of exempt nationalities is on www.bulafiji.com. Tickets to leave Fiji are officially required but usually not checked. The obligatory vaccination against yellow fever or cholera only applies if you're arriving directly from an infected area, such as the Amazon jungles or the banks of the Ganges River (no vaccinations necessary if you're arriving from North America, New Zealand, or Australia).

Extensions of stay are given out by the immigration offices at Lautoka, Nadi Airport, Savusavu, and Suva. You must apply before your current permit expires. After the first four months, you can obtain another two months to increase your total stay to six months by paying a F$82.50 fee. Bring your passport, onward or return ticket, and proof of sufficient funds. After six months, you must leave and stay away at least four days, after which you can return and start on another four months. An exception is made for yachties who can obtain extensions for up to one year.

Residence permits are difficult to obtain, and the fastest means of obtaining one is to invest F$200,000 or more in the country. For information on business opportunities in your field of expertise, contact the **Fiji Trade and Investment Bureau** (tel. 331-5988, fax 330-1783, www.ftib.org.fj), Civic Tower, Level 6, directly behind the Suva City Library on Victoria Parade. Foreigners holding professional or technical qualifications in fields required by Fiji also receive preference. Fiji's trade commissioners in Los Angeles, Taiwan, and Australia should be able to assist with the process.

Fiji has four ports of entry for yachts: Lautoka, Levuka, Savusavu, and Suva. The Ports Authority can be contacted over VHF channel 16. Calling at an outer island before clearing customs is prohibited. Levuka is the easiest place to check in or out, as all of the officials have offices right on the main wharf, and Savusavu is also convenient. Lautoka is

DIPLOMATIC OFFICES

Permanent Mission to the United Nations: 630 Third Ave., 7th floor, New York, NY 10017, U.S.A.; tel. 212/687-4130, fax 212/687-3963

Embassy of Fiji: 2233 Wisconsin Ave. N.W., Suite 240, Washington, DC 20007, U.S.A.; tel. 202/337-8320, fax 202/337-1996

High Commission of Fiji: 19 Beale Cres., Deakin, ACT 2600, Australia; tel. 61-2/6260-5115, fax 61-2/6260-5105

High Commission of Fiji: 31 Pipitea St., Thorndon, Wellington, New Zealand; tel. 64-4/473-5401, fax 64-4/499-1011, www.fiji.org.nz

High Commission of Fiji: Defense House, 4th floor, Champion Parade, Port Moresby NCD, Papua New Guinea; tel. 675/321-1914, fax 675/321-7220

High Commission of Fiji: 34 Hyde Park Gate, London SW7 5DN, United Kingdom; tel. 44-20/7584-3661, fax 44-20/7584-2838

Embassy of Fiji: 92–94 Square Plasky, 1030 Brussels, Belgium; tel. 32-2/736-9050, fax 32-2/736-1458

Embassy of Fiji: Noa Building, 14th floor, 3–5, 2-Chome, Azabudai, Minato-Ku, Tokyo 106, Japan; tel. 81-3/3587-2038, fax 81-3/3587-2563

High Commission of Fiji: Level 2, Menara Chan, 138 Jalan Ampang, 50450 Kuala Lumpur, Malaysia; tel. 60-3/2732-3335, fax 60-3/2732-7555

the most inconvenient as the popular yacht anchorages off western Viti Levu are far from Lautoka. To visit the outer islands, yachts require a letter of authorization from the Ministry of Foreign Affairs in Suva, or the commissioner (at Labasa, Lautoka, or Nausori) of the division they wish to visit. Yacht clubs in Fiji can advise on how to obtain permission. Yacht Help (www.yachthelp.com) also has useful information for yachties.

Money

The currency is the Fiji dollar, which is about two to one to the U.S. dollar in value. To obtain the current rate, visit www.xe.com/ucc. The Fiji dollar is a stable currency, pegged to a basket of the U.S., New Zealand, and Australian dollars, the yen, and the pound.

The first Fijian coins were minted in London in 1934, but Fiji continued to deal in British currency until 1969, when dollars and cents were introduced (at the rate of two Fiji dollars to one pound). There are coins of F$.01, F$.02, F$.05, F$.10, F$.20, and F$.50 and F$1, and bills of F$2, F$5, F$10, F$20, and F$50 (be careful as the F$5 and F$50 notes, as well as the F$2 and F$20 notes, are confusingly similar.

Banking hours are Monday–Thursday 0930–1500, Friday 0930–1600. A 24-hour bank is at Nadi Airport. Commercial banks operating in Fiji include the ANZ Bank, Indian-owned Bank of Baroda, Pakistani-owned Habib Bank, Colonial National Bank, Merchant Bank, and Westpac Banking Corporation. There are bank branches in all the main towns, but it's usually not possible to change traveler's checks or foreign banknotes in rural areas or on the outer islands. Avoid the ANZ Bank which charges a F$5 commission on traveler's checks (but not on cash exchanges). At last report, the Westpac Bank and Colonial National Bank charged no commission. Also take care when changing at the luxury hotels, as they often give a rate much lower than the banks. Recent cases of stolen traveler's checks being changed in Fiji has caused many hotels and restaurants to refuse them. It's a good idea to plan ahead and change enough money at a bank to get you through the weekends. Always have an ample supply of small notes to pay small bills and carry cash to the outer islands.

Credit cards are strictly for the cities and resorts (the most useful cards to bring are American Express, Diners Club, JCB International, MasterCard, and Visa). The ANZ Bank gives cash advances on MasterCard and Visa, but remember that cash advances are con-

sidered personal loans and accrue interest from the moment they are paid. If you're forced to get a cash advance through a large supermarket or resort, they'll probably take 10 percent commission for the favor. Many tourist facilities levy a 5 percent surcharge on credit card payments.

Both the ANZ Bank and Westpac Bank now have automated teller machines (ATMs) outside their branches, and these provide local currency at good rates against most debit cards. The charges can be deducted from your checking account automatically so you avoid interest charges. Be aware, however, that both your bank and the one providing the ATM may charge a fee for each transaction. Ask your bank how much they'll charge if you use an ATM in Fiji, what your daily limit will be, and if you'll need a special personal identification number (PIN). Occasionally the machines don't work due to problems with the software, and to avoid emergencies (such as if a machine were to "eat" your card), it's better not to be too dependent on ATMs. Some ATMs at Westpac Bank and Colonial National Bank branches still accept only local debit cards.

The import of foreign currency is unrestricted, but only F$500 in Fiji banknotes may be imported or exported. Avoid taking any Fiji banknotes out of the country at all, as Fiji dollars are difficult to change and heavily discounted outside Fiji. The Thomas Cook offices in Suva and Nadi will change whatever you have left into the currency of the next country on your itinerary (don't forget to keep enough local

currency to pay your airport departure tax at the check-in counter). Officially you're only allowed to export a maximum of F$5,000 in foreign cash, although this will only become an issue if they catch you for something else, such as narcotics, pornography, firearms, or immigration offenses.

For security the bulk of your travel funds should be in traveler's checks. American Express is probably the best kind to have, as they're represented by Tapa International in Suva (Level 4, Downtown Boulevard Plaza, Ellery St.; tel. 330-2333, fax 330-2048). If your American Express checks or card are lost or stolen, contact them. Thomas Cook has offices of their own in Suva (30 Thomson St.; tel. 330-1603, fax 330-0304) and in Nadi (tel. 670-3110).

If you need money sent in an emergency, Western Union can receive fast transfers from anywhere in the world at their offices in Suva (tel. 331-4812) and Lautoka (tel. 665-2509) or most post offices in Fiji. The sender pays the fee. Many banks will hold a sealed envelope for you in their vault for a nominal fee—a good way to avoid carrying unneeded valuables with you all around Fiji on an extended visit.

In 1992, Fiji introduced a value-added tax (VAT), currently 12.5 percent, which is usually (but not always) included in quoted prices. Among the few items exempt from the tax are unprocessed local foods, books printed in Fiji, and bus fares. Despite VAT, Fiji is still one of the least expensive countries in the South Pacific, although costs have been creeping up in recent years (inflation was 4.7 percent in 2003). Tipping isn't customary in Fiji, although some visitors are working hard to change this. A few resorts have a staff Christmas fund to which contributions are always welcome. Maybe have a quality baseball cap or a small bottle of nice perfume in your bag to give to anyone who has really gone out of their way for you.

Communications

Post

Post offices are generally open weekdays 0800–1600 and they hold general delivery mail two months. Postcard postage is inexpensive, so mail lots of them from here! Consider using air mail for parcels, since surface mail takes up to six months. The weight limit for overseas parcels is 10 kilograms. Post Fiji's *fast* POST service guarantees that your letter or parcel will get on the first international airline connection to your destination for a small surcharge. Express mail service (EMS) is more expensive but faster, and up to 20 kilograms may be sent. Main post offices around Fiji accept EMS mail.

When writing to Fiji, use the words "Fiji Islands" in the address (otherwise the letter might go to Fuji, Japan) and underline Fiji (so it doesn't end up in Iceland). Also include the post office box number, as there's no residential mail delivery in Fiji. If it's a remote island or small village you're writing to, the person's name will be sufficient. Sending a picture postcard to an islander is a very nice way of saying thank you.

Aside from EMS, the other major courier services active in Fiji are **CDP** (tel. 331-3077) at Ba, Labasa, Lautoka, Levuka, Nadi, Savusavu, Sigatoka, and Suva, **DHL** (tel. 331-3166) with offices at Levuka, Nadi, Savusavu, and Suva, **TNT** (tel. 330-8677) at Nadi and Suva, and **UPS** (tel. 331-2697) at Lautoka, Nadi, and Suva. To Europe or North America, DHL charges F$175 for a small box up to 10 kilograms or F$290 for a big box up to 25 kilograms.

Telecommunications

Card telephones (www.payphones.com.fj) are very handy, and if you're staying in Fiji more than a few days and intend to make your own arrangements, it's wise to purchase a local telephone card upon arrival, as coin telephones don't exist. In this handbook we provide all the numbers you'll need to make hotel reservations, check restaurant hours, find out about cultural shows, and compare car rental rates, saving you a lot of time and inconvenience.

By using a telephone card to call long distance, you limit the amount the call can possibly cost and won't end up overspending should you forget to keep track of the time. On short calls, you avoid three-minute minimum charges. International telephone calls placed from hotel rooms are always more expensive than the same calls made from public phones using telephone cards (ask the receptionist for the location of the nearest public phone). What you sacrifice is your privacy, as anyone can stand around and listen to your call, which often happens. Public phones are usually found outside post offices or large stores. Check that the phone actually works before bothering to arrange your numbers and notes, as it seems like quite a few of the public phones in Fiji are out of order at any given time.

Tele Cards (www.telecard.com.fj) are sold at all post offices and many shops in denominations of F$3, F$5, F$10, F$20, and F$50 (foreign phone cards cannot be used in Fiji). It's wiser to get a F$3 or F$5 card rather than one of the higher values in case you happen to lose it. With a Tele Card, you scratch off a strip on the back of the card to reveal a code number. On hearing a dial tone, dial 101 and follow the voice prompts. The Tele Card can be used from all types of phones, but you must enter the code numbers slowly, one by one, otherwise you'll get message telling you the code is invalid.

As far as telephone charges go, Fiji is divided into three regions. Western includes all of Viti Levu west of Rakiraki and Sigatoka, plus the Yasawas. Eastern is all of Viti Levu east of Korolevu, plus Ovalau and Kadavu. Northern is Vanua Levu and Taveuni. Calls within a region are F$.20 per 45 seconds, while inter-regional calls are F$.20 per 15 seconds. Thus you can call anywhere in the country for a mere F$.20, though you get more time if the call is within the same region. On local calls, you get 10 minutes for your F$.20.

Trunk Radio System (TRS) calls can be direct-dialed from inside Fiji, but must go through an operator from overseas. All such seven-digit numbers have 11 in the first three numbers and many are only answered at certain times of day (usually 0800–1000 and 1400–1600). Many resorts in the Yasawa Islands or the interior of Viti Levu have very high frequency (VHF) radio-telephone connections. In these cases, dial the

number provided in this book, wait for two beeps, then key in the extension number. Be aware that only one person at a time can speak over radio-telephone hookups.

Because rural telephone services in Fiji are poor, many people carry mobile phones supplied by Vodafone. These numbers begin with a nine, and you should avoid using them, as such calls cost a minimum of F$.80 a minute and your phone card will soon be devoured.

You can search for any telephone number in Fiji at www.whitepages.com.fj and www.yellowpages.com.fj. Within Fiji, domestic directory assistance is 011, international directory assistance 022, the domestic operator 011, the international operator 022. In emergencies, dial 911.

Fiji's international access code from public telephones is 00, so insert your card, dial 00, the country code, the area code, and the number (to Canada and the United States, the country code is always 1). To call overseas collect (billed to your party at the higher person-to-person rate), dial 031, the country code, the area code, and the number. If calling Fiji from abroad, dial your own international access code, Fiji's telephone code **679**. There are no area codes in Fiji. If the line is inaudible, hang up immediately and try again later.

The basic long-distance charge for three minutes is F$4.26 to Australia or New Zealand, F$7.20 to North America, Europe, or Japan. All operator-assisted international calls have a three-minute minimum charge and additional time is charged per minute, whereas international calls made using telephone cards have no minimum and the charges are broken down into flat six-second units (telephone cards with less than F$3 credit on them cannot be used for international calls).

If you have a calling card or phone pass issued by your own telephone company, you can access an operator or automated voice prompt in your home country by dialing a "country direct" number from any touch-tone phone in Fiji. Such calls are billed to your home telephone number at the full non-discounted rate that an operator-assisted call to Fiji would cost from your country, which in Fiji works out to about 50 percent more than using a local telephone card for international calls, as described above. (Don't be fooled by misleading advertisements implying that "direct" calls are cheaper.) Still, if you don't mind paying extra for the convenience, the "country direct" numbers to dial include:

- TNZ New Zealand 004/890-6401
- Telstra Australia 004/890-6101
- Optus Australia 004/890-6102
- AT&T United States 004/890-1001
- MCI United States 004/890-1002
- Sprint United States 004/890-1003
- Telecom Hawaii 004/890-1004
- Teleglobe Canada 004/890-1005
- BT United Kingdom 004/890-4401

The service is also available for calls to France, Hong Kong, Japan, Korea, Singapore, Switzerland, and Taiwan. Even though the phone companies have the cheek to suggest it, never use a "direct" number to place a domestic call within a single foreign country or an international call to a country other than your own. The call will be routed through your home country, and you'll be shocked when you see the bill.

Fax

Faxes can be sent from the post offices in Labasa, Lautoka, Ba, Nadi, Sigatoka, and Suva. Outgoing faxes cost F$9.65/12.15 for the first page to regional/other countries, additional pages F$6/9. You can also receive faxes at these post offices for F$1.65 a page. The numbers you'll probably use are fax 670-2467 at Nadi Airport Post Office, fax 670-2166 at Nadi Town Post Office, fax 666-4666 at Lautoka Post Office, and fax 330-2666 at Suva General Post Office.

If a fax you are trying to send to Fiji from abroad doesn't go through smoothly on the first or second try, wait and try again at another time of day. If it doesn't work then, stop trying as the fax machine at the other end may not be able to read your signal, and your telephone company will levy a minimum charge for each attempt. Call the international operator to ask what is wrong.

The Internet

Fiji is the most advanced country in the South Pacific as far as the Internet goes. Most tourism-related businesses in Fiji now have email addresses and websites, making communication from abroad a lot cheaper and easier. In this handbook, we've embedded the website addresses in the listings whenever possible, but we only list an email address if a website is not currently available. Email addresses tend to change over time, whereas Web addresses are semi-permanent. Most websites list the current email address of the company, and it's a good idea to check the site beforehand anyway, as your question may be answered there.

The electronic listings herein have been carefully researched and tested. For updates, check www.bulafiji.com, and visit www.southpacific.org for additional links and information.

In 2002, Connect Internet Services (www.connect.com.fj) changed all Fiji email addresses ending with @is.com.fj to @connect.com.fj. This change is reflected in this handbook, but older brochures (and many websites!) may still list the original form. If you come across an address ending with ending @is.com.fj, just substitute @connect.com.fj and it should work. (Also in 2002, Telecom Fiji increased all Fiji telephone numbers from six to seven digits. We've updated all the phone numbers in this book but you'll still see six-digit numbers in older brochures.)

When sending email to Fiji, never include an attachment such as Excel or Word files or photos with your message unless it has been specifically requested, as the recipient may be forced to pay stiff long-distance telephone charges to download it. Many people delete such files unopened for security reasons.

In Fiji, public Internet access is available in Nadi, Lautoka, Sigatoka, Pacific Harbor, Suva, Savusavu, and a few other places. Some resorts also provide computers at slightly higher rates than the public Internet cafés. If your Internet service provider doesn't have an electronic mailbox you can use on the road, you should open a free online email account at www.yahoo.com or www.hotmail.com before leaving home.

Media

Print Media

The Fiji Times (tel. 330-4111, fax 330-2011), "the first newspaper published in the world today," was founded at Levuka in 1869 but is currently owned by the Rupert Murdoch News Ltd. group. The Fiji government has a controlling 44 percent interest in the *Daily Post* (tel. 331-3342, fax 331-3320), which is also partly owned by Colonial Mutual Insurance. The *Daily Post* appeared just after the Rabuka coups in 1987. The more critical *Fiji Sun* (tel. 330-7555, fax 331-1455, www.sun.com.fj) was established in 1999.

The region's leading newsmagazines are *Islands Business* (tel. 330-3108, fax 330-1423), published monthly in Suva, and Hawaii-based *Pacific Magazine* (www.pacificislands.cc). There's also a fortnightly Fijian news and business magazine called *The Review* (tel. 330-0591, fax 330-2852, www.fijilive.com). Turn to Resources at the end of this book for more Pacific-oriented publications.

TV

Television broadcasting began in Fiji in 1991. Fiji 1 (www.fijitv.com.fj) is on the air daily 1600–midnight, with Australian programming rebroadcast at other hours. Fiji 1 gives the Fiji news at 1800 and 2155 daily, the BBC world news at 1830 weekdays. Government-owned Yasana Holdings has a majority interest in the station. In addition to this free station, there's a paid service for which a decoder must be rented. The three paid channels are Sky Plus (English-language programming), Sky Entertainment (Hindi programming from India), and Star Sports. The daily papers provide program guides, or call tel. 186-0100.

Radio

A great way to keep in touch with world and local affairs is to take along a portable radio. Your only expense will be the radio itself and batteries. Below, we provide the names and frequencies of the local stations, so set your tuning buttons as soon as you arrive.

Fiji doesn't have a shortwave broadcaster, but privately owned **Communications Fiji Ltd.** (tel. 331-4766, www.fijivillage.com) rebroadcasts the BBC World Service over 88.2 MHz FM and Radio Australia at 92.6 MHz FM 24 hours a day (available around Suva only). Communications Fiji Ltd. also operates four lively commercial FM stations, which broadcast around the clock throughout the country: **FM 96** (www.fm96.com.fj) and **Legend** in English, Viti FM in Fijian, and Radio Navtarang in Hindi. FM 96 caters to the under-30 age group, while Legend is aimed at a more mature audience.

In addition, the public **Fiji Broadcasting Corporation** (tel. 331-4333, fax 330-1643, www.radiofiji.org) operates five AM/FM radio stations: **Bula 100 FM** in English, Radio Fiji One (RF1) in Fijian for older listeners, Bula 102 FM in Fijian for younger listeners, Radio Fiji Two (RF2) in Hindi for older listeners, and Bula 98 FM in Hindi for younger listeners. The Bula stations (or "Bula Network") are funded by commercial advertising, while the public-service Radio Fiji stations are supported by a government grant.

In Suva, you can pick up the local stations at the following frequencies: FM 96 at 96.0 MHz, Bula 98 FM at 98.0 MHz, Navtarang at 98.8 MHz, Bula 100 FM at 100.4 MHz, Bula 102 FM at 102.0 MHz, Viti FM at 102.8 MHz, RF2 at 105.2 MHz FM, Legend at 106.8 MHz, and RF1 at 558 kHz AM.

At Nadi and Lautoka, check the following frequencies: FM 96 at 95.4 MHz, Navtarang at 97.4 MHz, Bula 98 FM at 98.2 MHz, Viti FM at 99.6 MHz, Bula 102 FM at 102.4 MHz, RF2 at 105.4 MHz, and Legend at 106.4 MHz. At Lautoka, you'll also get Bula 100 FM at 94.6 and 100.0 MHz. Privately-run ZFM Classic at 101.0 MHz is based in Lautoka.

On the Coral Coast, it's Bula 98 FM at 98.2 MHz, FM 96 at 99.0 MHz, Bula 100 FM at 100.6 MHz, Navtarang at 102.2 MHz, Bula 102 FM at 103.0 MHz, Legend at 107.2 MHz, Viti FM at 107.8 MHz, RF1 at 927 kHz, and RF2 at 1206 kHz.

Around Rakiraki, look for Bula 98 at 93.0 MHz, Navtarang at 97.0 MHz, Bula 100 FM at 100.0 MHz, Viti FM at 104.8 MHz, RF1 at 1152 kHz, and RF2 at 1467 kHz. At Ba, you can get ZFM Classic at 88.8 MHz, Bula 100 FM at 94.6 MHz, FM 96 at 99.2 MHz, Navtarang at 101.6 MHz, and Viti FM at 103.8 MHz.

On Vanua Levu, check the following frequencies at Labasa: FM 96 at 95.4 MHz, Navtarang at 97.4 MHz, Bula 98 FM at 98.2 MHz, Viti FM at 99.6 MHz, Bula 100 FM at 100.0 MHz, Bula 102 FM at 102.4 MHz, RF1 at 684 kHz, and RF2 at 810 kHz. At Savusavu, it's Bula 98 FM at 98.4 MHz, Bula 100 FM at 100.0 MHz, Bula 102 FM at 102.4 MHz, and RF2 at 1152 kHz.

On Taveuni, you may hear Bula 100 FM at 100.6 MHz and Bula 102 FM at 103.0 MHz.

The local stations broadcast mostly pop music and repetitive advertising with very little news or commentary (the presenters sometimes get things hilariously mixed up). Bula 100 FM broadcasts local news and a weather report on the hour weekdays 0600–2200 (weekends every other hour) with a special news-of-the-day report at 1745, followed by the BBC world news just after 1800. The BBC news is also broadcast on Bula 100 FM at 1900 and 2100. Radio FM 96 broadcasts news and weather on the hour weekdays 0600–1800, Saturday and Sunday at 0800, 0900, 1000, 1200, 1300, 1700, and 1800.

Health and Safety

Fiji's climate is a healthy one, and the main causes of death are non-communicable diseases such as heart disease, diabetes, and cancer. The sea and air are clear and usually pollution-free. The humidity nourishes the skin, and the local fruit is brimming with vitamins. If you take a few precautions, you'll never have a sick day. The information provided below is intended to make you knowledgeable, not fearful. If you have access to the Internet, check www.cdc.gov/travel/austspac.htm for up-to-the-minute information.

Health care is good, with an abundance of hospitals, health centers, and nursing stations scattered around the country. The largest hospitals are in Labasa, Lautoka, Levuka, Ba, Savusavu, Sigatoka, Suva, and Taveuni. The crowded government-run medical facilities provide free medical treatment to local residents but have special rates for foreigners. It's usually no more expensive to visit a private doctor or clinic, where you'll receive much faster service since everyone is paying. We've tried to list private doctors and dentists throughout the handbook, but in emergencies and outside clinic hours, you can always turn to the government-run hospitals. Unfortunately, very few facilities are provided for travelers with disabilities.

To call an ambulance dial 911. In case of scuba-diving accidents, a dive recompression chamber is available at the excellent Suva Private Hospital (tel. 330-5154 in Suva, or 885-0630 in Savusavu). The 24-hour recompression emergency numbers are tel. 999-3506 and 999-5500.

Travel Insurance

The sale of travel insurance is a big business, but the value of the policies themselves is often questionable. If your regular group health insurance also covers you while you're traveling abroad, it's probably enough, as medical costs are generally low in Fiji. Most policies only pay the amount above and beyond what your national or group health insurance will pay and are invalid if you don't have any health insurance at all. You may also be covered by your credit card company if you paid for your plane ticket with the card. Buying extra travel insurance is about the same as buying a lottery ticket: There's always the chance it will pay off, but it's usually money down the drain.

If you do opt for the security of travel insurance, make sure emergency medical evacuations are covered. Some policies are invalid if you engage in "dangerous activities," such as scuba diving, parasailing, surfing, or even riding a motor scooter, so be sure to read the fine print. Some companies will pay your bills directly, while others require you to pay and collect receipts, which may be reimbursed later.

EXPLORING THE ISLANDS

Some policies also cover travel delays, lost baggage, and theft. In practice, your airline probably already covers the first two adequately, and claiming something extra from your insurance company could be more trouble than it's worth. Theft insurance never covers items left on the beach while you're swimming. All said, you should weigh the advantages and decide for yourself if you want a policy. Just don't be too influenced by what your travel agent says, as they'll only want to sell you coverage to earn another commission.

Acclimatizing

Don't go from winter weather into the steaming tropics without a rest before and after. Minimize jet lag by setting your watch to local time at your destination as soon as you board the flight. Westbound flights to Fiji from North America or Europe are less jolting, since you follow the sun and your body gets a few hours extra sleep. On the way home, you're moving against the sun, and the hours of sleep your body loses cause jet lag. Airplane cabins have low humidity, so drink lots of juice or water instead of carbonated drinks, and don't overeat in-flight. It's also wise to forgo coffee, as it will only keep you awake, and alcohol, which will dehydrate you.

Scuba diving on departure day can give you a severe case of the bends. Before flying, there should be a minimum of 12 hours surface interval after a nondecompression dive and a minimum of 24 hours after a decompression dive. Factors contributing to decompression sickness include a lack of sleep and/or the excessive consumption of alcohol before diving.

If you start feeling seasick on board a ship, stare at the horizon, which is always steady, and try to stop thinking about it. Anti-motion-sickness pills are useful to have along; otherwise, ginger helps alleviate seasickness. Travel stores sell

A TRAVELER'S NOTES ON AIDS AND HIV

In 1981, scientists in the United States and France first recognized the Acquired Immune Deficiency Syndrome (AIDS), which was later discovered to be caused by a virus called the Human Immunodeficiency Virus (HIV). HIV breaks down the body's immunity to infections leading to AIDS. The virus can lie hidden in the body for up to 10 years without producing any obvious symptoms or before developing into the AIDS disease, and in the meantime the person can unknowingly infect others.

HIV lives in white blood cells and is present in the sexual fluids of humans. It's difficult to catch and is spread mostly through sexual intercourse, by needle or syringe sharing among intravenous drug users, in blood transfusions, and during pregnancy and birth (if the mother is infected). Using another person's razor blade or having your body pierced or tattooed are also risky, but the HIV virus cannot be transmitted by shaking hands, kissing, cuddling, fondling, sneezing, cooking food, or sharing eating or drinking utensils. One cannot be infected by saliva, sweat, tears, urine, or feces; toilet seats, telephones, swimming pools, or mosquito bites do not cause AIDS. Ostracizing a known AIDS victim is not only immoral but also absurd.

Most blood banks now screen their products for HIV, and you can protect yourself against dirty needles by only allowing an injection if you see the syringe taken out of a fresh unopened pack. The simplest safeguard during sex is the proper use of a latex condom. Unroll the condom onto the erect penis; while withdrawing after ejaculation, hold onto the condom as you come out. Never try to recycle a condom, and pack a supply with you, as it's a nuisance trying to buy them locally.

HIV is spread more often through anal than vaginal sex, because the lining of the rectum is much weaker than that of the vagina, and ordinary condoms sometimes tear when used in anal sex. If you have anal sex, only use extrastrong condoms and special water-based lubricants, since oil, Vaseline, and cream weaken the rubber. During oral sex you must make sure you don't get any semen or menstrual blood in your mouth. A woman runs 10 times the risk of contracting AIDS from a man than the other way around, and the threat is always greater when another sexually transmitted disease (STD) is present.

AcuBands that find a pressure point on the wrist and create a stable flow of blood to the head, thus miraculously preventing seasickness!

Frequently the feeling of thirst is false and only due to mucous-membrane dryness. Gargling or taking two or three gulps of warm water should be enough. Keep moisture in your body by having a hot drink like tea or black coffee, or any kind of slightly salted or sour drink in small quantities. Salt in fresh lime juice is remarkably refreshing.

The tap water in Fiji is usually drinkable, except immediately after a cyclone or during droughts, when care should be taken. If in doubt, boil it or use purification pills. Natural artesian water in plastic bottles is widely available. Tap water that is uncomfortably hot to touch is usually safe. Allow it to cool in a clean container. Don't forget that if the tap water is contaminated, the local ice will be too. Avoid brushing your teeth with water unfit to drink, and wash or peel fruit and vegetables if you can. Cooked food is less subject to contamination than raw.

Sunburn

Though you may think a tan will make you look healthier and more attractive, it's actually very damaging to the skin, which becomes dry, rigid, and prematurely old and wrinkled, especially on the face. Begin with short exposures to the sun, perhaps a half-hour at a time, followed by an equal time in the shade. Avoid the sun from 1000 to 1500, the most dangerous time. Clouds and beach umbrellas will not protect you fully. Wear a T-shirt while snorkeling to protect your back. Drink plenty of liquids to keep your pores open. Sunbathing is the main cause of cataracts to the eyes, so wear sunglasses and a wide-brimmed hat, and beware of reflected sunlight.

EXPLORING THE ISLANDS

The very existence of AIDS calls for a basic change in human behavior. No vaccine or drug exists that can prevent or cure AIDS, and because the virus mutates frequently, no remedy may ever be totally effective. Other STDs such as syphilis, gonorrhea, chlamydia, hepatitis B, and herpes are far more common than AIDS and can lead to serious complications such as infertility, but at least they can usually be cured.

The euphoria of travel can make it easier to fall in love or have sex with a stranger, so travelers must be informed of these dangers. As a tourist, you should always practice safe sex to prevent AIDS and other STDs. You never know who is infected or even if you yourself have become infected. It's important to bring the subject up *before* you start to make love. Make a joke out of it by pulling out a condom and asking your new partner, "Say, do you know what this is?" Or perhaps, "Your condom or mine?" Far from being unromantic or embarrassing, you'll both feel more relaxed with the subject off your minds, and it's much better than worrying afterwards if you might have been infected. The golden rule is safe sex or no sex.

Currently, an estimated 40 million people worldwide are HIV carriers, and three million a year are dying of AIDS. In the South Pacific, the number of cases is still extremely small compared to the hundreds of thousands of confirmed HIV infections in the United States. Yet it's worth noting that other STDs have already reached epidemic proportions in the urban areas of Fiji, demonstrating that the type of behavior leading to the rapid spread of AIDS is present.

An HIV infection can be detected through a blood test, because the antibodies created by the body to fight off the virus can be seen under a microscope. It takes at least three weeks for the antibodies to be produced and in some cases as long as six months before they can be picked up during a screening test. If you think you may have run a risk, you should discuss the appropriateness of a test with your doctor. It's always better to know if you are infected so as to be able to avoid infecting others, to obtain early treatment of symptoms, and to make realistic plans. If you know someone with AIDS, you should give them all the support you can (there's no danger in such contact unless blood is present).

Use a sunscreen lotion containing PABA rather than oil, and don't forget to apply it to your nose, lips, forehead, neck, hands, and feet. Sunscreens protect you from ultraviolet rays (a leading cause of cancer), while oils magnify the sun's effect. A 15-factor sunscreen provides 93 percent protection (a more expensive 30-factor sunscreen is only slightly better at 97 percent protection). Apply the lotion *before* going to the beach to avoid being burned on the way, and reapply every couple of hours to replace sunscreen washed away by perspiration. Swimming also washes away your protection. After sunbathing, take a tepid shower rather than a hot one, which would wash away your natural skin oils. Stay moist, and use a vitamin E evening cream to preserve the youth of your skin. Calamine ointment soothes skin already burned, as does coconut oil. Pharmacists recommend Solarcaine to soothe burned skin. Rinsing off with a vinegar solution reduces peeling, and aspirin relieves some of the pain and irritation. Vitamin A and calcium counteract overdoses of vitamin D received from the sun. The fairer your skin, the more essential it is to take care.

As Earth's ozone layer is depleted due to the commercial use of chlorofluorocarbons (CFCs) and other factors, the need to protect oneself from ultraviolet radiation is becoming more urgent. Previously the cancers didn't develop until age 50 or 60, but now much younger people are affected.

Ailments

Cuts and scratches become infected easily in the tropics and take a long time to heal. Prevent infection from coral cuts by immediately washing wounds with soap and fresh water, then rubbing in vinegar or alcohol (whiskey will do)—painful but effective. Use an antiseptic like hydrogen peroxide and an antibacterial ointment such as Neosporin, if you have them. Islanders usually dab coral cuts with lime juice. All cuts turn septic quickly in the tropics, so try to keep them clean and covered.

For bites, burns, and cuts, an antiseptic such as Solarcaine speeds healing and helps prevent infection. Pure aloe vera is good for sunburn,

scratches, and even coral cuts. Bites by sand flies itch for days and can become infected. Not everyone is affected by insect bites in the same way. Some people are practically immune to insects, while traveling companions experiencing exactly the same conditions are soon covered with bites. You'll soon know which type you are.

Prickly heat, an intensely irritating rash, is caused by wearing heavy clothing that is inappropriate for the climate. When sweat glands are blocked and the sweat is unable to evaporate, the skin becomes soggy, and small red blisters appear. Synthetic fabrics like nylon are especially bad in this regard. Take a cold shower, apply calamine lotion, dust with talcum powder, and take off those clothes! Until things improve, avoid alcohol, tea, coffee, and any physical activity that makes you sweat. If you're sweating profusely, increase your intake of salt slightly to avoid fatigue, but not without concurrently drinking more water.

Use antidiarrheal medications such as Lomotil or Imodium sparingly. Rather than take drugs to plug yourself up, drink plenty of unsweetened liquids like green coconut or fresh fruit juice to help flush yourself out. Egg yolk mixed with nutmeg helps diarrhea, or eat rice and drink tea for the day. Avoid dairy products. Most cases of diarrhea are self-limiting and require only simple replacement of the fluids and salts lost in diarrheal stools. If the diarrhea is persistent or you experience high fever, drowsiness, or blood in the stool, stop traveling, rest, and consider seeing a doctor. For constipation, eat pineapple or any peeled fruit.

Other Diseases

Infectious hepatitis A (jaundice) is a liver ailment transmitted person to person or through unboiled water, uncooked vegetables, or other foods contaminated during handling. The risk of infection is highest among those who eat village food, so if you'll be spending much time in rural areas, consider getting an immune globulin shot, which provides six months of protection. Better is a vaccine called Havrix, which provides up to 10 years of protection (given in two doses two weeks apart, then a third dose six months later). If you've ever had hepatitis A in your life, you are already immune. Otherwise, you'll know you've got the hep when your eyeballs and urine turn yellow. Time and rest are the only cure. Viral hepatitis B is spread through sexual or blood contact.

There's no malaria here, but a mosquito-transmitted disease known as dengue fever is endemic. In early 1998, a major outbreak in Fiji resulted in an estimated 25,000 cases and 14 deaths. Signs are headaches, sore throat, pain in the joints, fever, chills, nausea, and rash. This painful illness, also known as "breakbone fever," can last anywhere from five to 15 days. Although you can relieve the symptoms somewhat, the only real cure is to stay in bed, drink lots of water, and wait it out. Avoid aspirin, as this can lead to complications. No vaccine exists, so just try to avoid getting bitten (the *Aedes aegypti,* or black-and-white-striped mosquito, bites only during the day). Dengue fever can kill infants, so extra care must be taken to protect them if an outbreak is in progress.

Vaccinations

Most visitors are not required to get any vaccinations at all before coming to Fiji. Tetanus, diphtheria, and typhoid-fever shots are not required and only worth considering if you're going far off the beaten track. Tetanus and diphtheria shots are given together, and a booster is required every 10 years. The oral typhoid-fever vaccine is administered every seven years, if necessary. Polio is believed to have been eradicated from the South Pacific, and no cases of tetanus or diphtheria have been reported in Fiji in recent years.

The cholera vaccine is only 50 percent effective and valid for just six months, and bad reactions are common, which explains why most doctors in developed countries won't administer it. Just forget it, unless you're sure you're headed for an infected area (which is unlikely).

A yellow-fever vaccination is required if you've been in an infected area within the six days prior to arrival. Yellow fever is a mosquito-borne disease that occurs only in Central Africa and northern South America (excluding Chile), places you're not likely to have been just before arriving in Fiji. Since the vaccination is valid for 10 years, get one if you're an inveterate globe-trotter.

Immune globulin (IG) and the Havrix vaccine aren't 100 percent effective against hepatitis A, but they do increase your general resistance to infections. IG prophylaxis must be repeated every five months. Hepatitis B vaccination involves three doses over a six-month period (duration of protection unknown) and is recommended mostly for people planning extended stays in the region.

Safety

Although *The Fiji Times* is often full of stories of violent crimes, including assaults, robberies, and burglaries, it's partly the novelty of these events that makes them worth reporting. Fiji is still a much safer country than the United States, and tourists are not specifically targeted for attack, but normal precautions should still be taken. Keep to well-lit streets at night, take a taxi if you've had more than one drink, and steer clear of poorly dressed Fijian men who may accost you on the street for no reason. Don't react if offered drugs. It's wise to lock your valuables in your bag in your hotel room before going out on the town.

Women should have few real problems traveling around Fiji on their own, so long as they're prepared to cope with frequent offers of marriage. Although a female tourist has less chance of facing sexist violence than a local woman does, it's smart to be defensive and to lie about where you're staying. If you want to be left alone, conservative dress and purposeful behavior will work to your advantage. In village situations, seek the company of local women.

EXPLORING THE ISLANDS

What to Take

Packing

Assemble everything you simply must take and cannot live without—then cut the pile in half. If you're still left with more than will fit into a medium-size suitcase or backpack, continue eliminating. You've got to be tough on yourself and just limit what you take. Now put it all into your bag. If the total (bag and contents) weighs more than 16 kilograms, you'll sacrifice much of your mobility. If you can keep it down to 10 kilograms, you're traveling *light.* Categorize, separate, and pack all your things into clear plastic freezer bags or stuff sacks for convenience and protection from moisture. Items that might leak should be in resealable bags. In addition to your principal bag, you'll want a day pack or flight bag. When checking in for flights, carry anything that cannot be replaced in your hand luggage. *The biggest mistake of first-time travelers to Fiji is bringing too much baggage.*

Your Luggage

Veteran travelers often recommend a small suitcase with wheels and a retractable handle that you can sometimes take aboard flights as carry-on luggage. Officially, economy passengers are only allowed one item of cabin baggage with overall dimensions no greater than 115 centimeters. The bag must be able to fit under the seat in front of you, and must not weigh more than five kilograms. In first and business classes you may carry two bags aboard, which when added together do not exceed 115 centimeters or seven kilograms in weight. Larger bags must usually be checked in at the airline counter.

Also ideal is a soft medium-size backpack with a lightweight internal frame. Big external-frame packs are fine for mountain climbing but get caught in airport conveyor belts and are very inconvenient on public transport. The best packs have a zippered compartment in back where you can tuck in the hip belt and straps before turning your pack over to an airline or bus. This type of pack has the flexibility of allowing you to simply walk when motorized transport is unavailable or

unacceptable, and with the straps zipped in, it resembles a regular suitcase, should you wish to go upmarket for a while.

Make sure your pack allows you to carry the weight on your hips, has a cushion for spine support, and doesn't pull backwards. The pack should strap snugly to your body but also allow ventilation for your back. It should be made of a water-resistant material such as nylon and have a Fastex buckle.

Look for a pack with double, two-way zipper compartments and pockets you can lock with miniature padlocks. They might not *stop* a thief, but they will deter the casual pilferer. A 60-centimeter length of lightweight chain and another padlock will allow you to fasten your pack to something. Keep valuables locked in your bag, out of sight, as even upscale hotel rooms aren't 100 percent safe.

Clothing and Camping Equipment

For clothes, take loose-fitting cotton washables, light in color and weight. Synthetic fabrics are hot and sticky, and most of the things you wear at home are too heavy for the tropics—be prepared for the humidity. Dress is casual, with slacks and a sports shirt okay for men, even at dinner parties. Local women often wear long colorful dresses in the evening, but respectable shorts are okay in daytime. If in doubt, bring the minimum with you, and buy tropical garb upon arrival. Stick to clothes you can rinse in your room sink, and don't bring more than two outfits. In midwinter (July and August), it can be cool at night, so a light sweater or windbreaker may come in handy.

The *sulu* is a bright two-meter piece of cloth that both men and women wrap about themselves as an all-purpose garment. Any islander can show you how to wear it.

Take comfortable shoes that have been broken in. Running shoes and rubber thongs (flip-flops) are handy for day use but will bar you from nightspots with strict dress codes. Scuba divers' wetsuit booties are lightweight and perfect for both crossing rivers and lagoon walking, though an old pair of sneakers may be just as good (never use the booties to walk on breakable coral). A disposable pair of shoes is also essential if you plan to do any serious interior hiking, as quality hiking boots would be ruined during the many river crossings.

You'll seldom need a sleeping bag in the tropics, so that's one item you can easily cut. A youth-hostel sleeping sheet is ideal—all HI handbooks give instructions on how to make your own or buy one at your local hostel. If you bring a tent, don't bother bringing a foam pad, as the ground is seldom cold here.

Below, we've provided a few checklists to help you assemble your gear. The listed items combined weigh well more than 16 kilograms, so eliminate what doesn't suit you:

- pack with internal frame
- day pack or airline bag
- sun hat or visor
- essential clothing
- modest bathing suit
- sturdy walking shoes
- rubber thongs (flip-flops)
- rubber booties
- sleeping sheet

Accessories

Bring some reading material, as good books can be hard to find in resort areas. A mask and snorkel are essential equipment—you'll be missing half of Fiji's beauty without them. Scuba divers will bring their own regulator, buoyancy compensator, and gauges to avoid gear fees and to eliminate the possibility of catching a transmissible disease from rental equipment. This is most important if you plan to dive with backpacker dive shops, which can't always afford the best equipment. A lightweight three-millimeter Lycra wetsuit will provide protection against marine stings, coral, and cold.

Neutral gray eyeglasses protect your eyes from the sun and give the least color distortion. Take an extra pair (if you wear them).

Also take along postcards of your hometown and snapshots of your house, family, work-place, etc; islanders love to see these. Always keep a promise to mail islanders the photos you take of them.

- portable shortwave radio
- camera and 10 rolls of film
- compass
- pocket flashlight
- extra batteries
- candle
- pocket calculator
- travel alarm clock
- extra pair of eyeglasses
- sunglasses
- mask and snorkel
- padlock and lightweight chain
- collapsible umbrella
- string for a clothesline
- powdered laundry soap
- universal sink plug
- mini-towel
- silicon glue
- sewing kit
- mini-scissors
- nail clippers
- fishing line for sewing gear
- plastic cup and plate
- can and bottle opener
- corkscrew
- penknife
- spoon
- water bottle
- matches
- tea bags

Toiletries and Medical Kit

Since everyone has his or her own medical requirements, and brand names vary from country to country, there's no point going into detail here. Note, however, that even the basics (such as aspirin) are unavailable on some outer islands, so be prepared. Bring medicated powder for prickly heat rash. Charcoal tablets are useful for diarrhea and poisoning (they absorb the irritants). Bring an adequate supply of any personal medications, plus your prescriptions (in generic terminology), as American-made medications may be unobtainable in the islands.

EXPLORING THE ISLANDS

Antibiotics should only be used to treat serious wounds, and only after medical advice dictates their use.

High humidity causes curly hair to swell, straight hair to droop. If it's curly, have it cut short, or keep it long in a ponytail or bun. Water-based makeup is preferable, as the heat and humidity cause oil glands to work overtime. High-quality, locally made shampoo, body oils, and insect repellent are sold on all the islands, and the bottles are conveniently smaller than those sold in Western countries. See Health, above, for more ideas.

- wax earplugs
- soap in plastic container
- soft toothbrush
- toothpaste
- roll-on deodorant
- shampoo
- comb and brush
- skin creams
- makeup
- tampons or napkins
- white toilet paper
- vitamin/mineral supplement
- insect repellent
- PABA sunscreen
- lip balm
- a motion-sickness remedy
- contraceptives
- iodine
- water-purification pills
- a diarrhea remedy
- Tiger Balm
- a cold remedy
- Alka-Seltzer
- aspirin
- antihistamine
- antifungal
- Calmitol ointment
- antibacterial ointment
- antiseptic cream
- disinfectant
- simple dressings
- adhesive bandages (like Band-Aids)
- painkiller
- prescription medicines

Money and Documents

All post offices have passport applications. If you lose your passport, you should report the matter to the local police at once, obtain a certificate or receipt, then proceed to your embassy for a replacement. If you have your birth certificate with you, it expedites the process considerably. Don't bother getting an international driver's license, as your regular license is all you need to drive here.

Traveler's checks are recommended, and in Fiji, American Express is the most efficient company when it comes to providing refunds for lost checks. Thomas Cook also has offices in Fiji. If you're from the States, bring along a small supply of US$1 and US$5 bills to use if you run out of local currency and can't get to a bank.

Carry your valuables in a money belt worn around your waist or neck under your clothing; most camping stores have these. Make several photocopies of the information page of your passport, personal identification, driver's license, scuba certification card, credit cards, airline tickets, receipts for purchase of traveler's checks, etc.—you should be able to get them all on both sides of one page. On the side of the photocopy, write the phone numbers you'd need to call to report lost documents. A brief medical history with your blood type, allergies, chronic or special health problems, eyeglass and medical prescriptions, etc., might also come in handy. Put these inside plastic bags to protect them from moisture, then carry the lists in different places, and leave one at home.

- passport
- airline tickets
- scuba certification card
- driver's license
- traveler's checks
- some U.S. cash
- credit card
- photocopies of documents
- money belt
- address book
- notebook
- envelopes
- extra ballpoints

Film and Photography

The type of camera you choose could depend on the way you travel. If you'll be staying mostly in one place, a heavy single-lens reflex (SLR) camera with spare lenses and other equipment won't trouble you. If you'll be moving around a lot for a considerable length of time, a 35mm automatic compact camera will be better. The compacts are mostly useful for close-up shots; landscapes will seem spread out and far away. A wide-angle lens gives excellent depth of field, but hold the camera upright to avoid converging verticals. A polarizing filter prevents reflections from glass windows and water, and it makes the sky bluer. These days, however, digital cameras are more popular.

Although film is cheap and readily available in Fiji, you never know if it's been spoiled by an airport X-ray on the way there. On a long trip, mailers are essential, as exposed film shouldn't be held for long periods. Choose 36-exposure film over 24-exposure to reduce the number of rolls you have to carry. When purchasing film in the islands, take care to check the expiration date.

Films are rated by their speed and sensitivity to light, using ISO numbers from 25 to 1600. The higher the number, the greater the film's sensitivity to light. Slower films with lower ISOs (like 100–200) produce sharp images in bright sunlight. Faster films with higher ISOs (like 400) stop action and work well in low-light situations, such as in dark rainforests or at sunset. If you have a manual SLR you can avoid overexposure at midday by reducing the exposure half a stop, but *do* overexpose when photographing dark-skinned Fijians. From 1000 to 1600 the light is often too bright to take good photos, and panoramas usually come out best early or late in the day.

Keep your photos simple, with one main subject and an uncomplicated background. Get as close to your subjects as you can, and lower or raise the camera to their level. Include people in the foreground of scenic shots to add interest and perspective. Outdoors, a flash can fill in unflattering facial shadows caused by high sun or backlit conditions. Most of all, be creative. Look for interesting details, and compose the photo before you push the trigger. Instead of taking a head-on photo of a group of people, step to one side and ask them to face you. The angle improves the photo. Photograph subjects coming toward you rather than passing by. Get consent before photographing people. If you're asked for money (rare), you can always walk away—give your subjects the same choice. There is probably no country in the world where the photographer will have as interesting and willing subjects as in Fiji.

When packing, protect your camera against vibration. Checked baggage is scanned by powerful airport X-ray monitors, so carry both camera and film aboard the plane in a clear plastic bag, and ask security for a visual inspection. Some airports will refuse to do this, however. A good alternative is to use a lead-laminated pouch. The old high-dose X-ray units are seldom seen these days, but even low-dose inspection units can ruin fast film (400 ISO and above). Beware of the cumulative effect of X-ray machines. Digital-camera images are not affected by X-rays.

Store your camera in a plastic bag during rain and while traveling in motorized canoes, etc. In the tropics, the humidity can cause film to stick to itself; silica-gel crystals in the bag will protect film from humidity and mold growth. Protect camera and film from direct sunlight, and load the film in the shade. When loading, check that the take-up spool revolves. Never leave camera or film in a hot place like a car floor, glove compartment, or trunk.

Time and Measurements

Time

The international date line generally follows 180 degrees longitude and creates a difference of 24 hours in time between the two sides. It swings east at Tuvalu to avoid slicing Fiji in two. Everything in the Eastern Hemisphere west of the date line is a day later, while everything in the Western Hemisphere east of the line is a day earlier (or behind). Air travelers lose a day when they fly west across the date line and gain it back when they return. Keep track of things by repeating to yourself, *If it's Sunday in Seattle, it's Monday in Manila.*

Fiji time is Greenwich Mean Time (GMT) plus 12 hours. When it's noon in Fiji, it will be 1000 in Sydney, 1200 in Auckland (same time), 1300 in Tonga, 1400 the day before in Hawaii, 1600 the day before in Los Angeles, 1900 the day before in Toronto, and midnight in London, England. To look at it another way, Fiji is 20 hours ahead of California and also two hours ahead of Sydney, Australia! You can check the exact time locally in Fiji by dialing 014.

You're better telephoning Fiji from North America in the evening, as it will be mid-afternoon in the islands (plus you'll probably benefit from off-peak telephone rates). From Europe, call very late at night. In the other direction, if you're calling from Fiji to North America or Europe, do so in the early morning, as it will already be afternoon in North America and evening in Europe.

In this book, all clock times are rendered according to the 24-hour system, i.e. 0100 is 1:00 A.M., 1300 is 1:00 P.M., 2330 is 11:30 P.M. There isn't much twilight in the tropics, and when the sun begins to go down, you've got less than half an hour before nightfall. The islanders operate on "coconut time"—the nut will fall when it is ripe. In the languid air of the South Seas, punctuality takes on a new meaning. Appointments are approximate and service casual. Even the seasons are fuzzy: sometimes wetter, sometimes drier, but almost always hot. Slow down to the island pace, and get in step with where you are.

Measurements

The metric system is used in Fiji. Study the conversion table at the back of this handbook if you're not used to thinking metric. Most distances herein are quoted in kilometers—they become easy to comprehend when you know than one kilometer is the distance that a normal person walks in 10 minutes. A meter is slightly more than a yard, and a liter is just more than a quart.

Electric Currents

If you're taking along a plug-in razor, radio, computer, electric immersion coil, or other electrical appliance, be aware that Fiji uses 240 AC voltage, 50 cycles. Most appliances require a converter to change from one voltage to another. You'll also need an adapter to cope with the three-pronged socket plugs (with the two top prongs at angles). Pick up both items before you leave home, as they can be hard to find here. Remember voltages if you buy duty-free appliances: Dual voltage (110/220 V) items are best.

Videos

Commercial travel videotapes make nice souvenirs, but always keep in mind that there are three incompatible video formats in the world: NTSC (used in North America), PAL (used in Britain, Germany, Japan, Australia, New Zealand, and Fiji), and SECAM (used in France and Russia). Don't buy prerecorded tapes abroad unless they're the same kind used in your country.

Getting There

Fiji's geographic position makes it the hub of transport for the entire South Pacific, and Nadi is the region's most important international airport, with long-haul services to points all around the Pacific Rim. Thirteen international airlines fly into Nadi: Aircalin, Air Fiji, Air Nauru, Air New Zealand, Air Pacific, Air Vanuatu, Freedom Air, Korean Air, Pacific Blue, Polynesian Airlines, Qantas Airways, Royal Tongan Airlines, and Solomon Airlines. Air Pacific and Air Fiji also use Suva's Nausori Airport. The websites of all these carriers are linked to www.southpacific .org/air.html.

Fiji's national airline, **Air Pacific,** was founded in 1951 as Fiji Airways by Harold Gatty, a famous Australian aviator who had set a record with American Willy Post in 1931 by flying around the world in eight days. In 1972, the airline was reorganized as a regional carrier and the name changed to Air Pacific. The carrier flies from Nadi to Apia, Auckland, Brisbane, Honiara, Honolulu, Los Angeles, Melbourne, Port Vila, Sydney, Tokyo, Tongatapu, and Vancouver, and from Suva to Auckland and Sydney.

Qantas owns 46.5 percent of Air Pacific (the Fiji government owns the rest), and all Qantas flights to Fiji are actually code shares with the Fijian carrier. Qantas is Air Pacific's general sales agent in Europe, and you'll fly Air Pacific to Fiji if you booked with Qantas. Air Pacific codeshares with Solomon Airlines when going to Honiara and Port Vila.

BOOKING TIPS

Preparations

First decide when you're going and how long you wish to stay away. Your plane ticket will be your biggest single expense, so spend some time considering the options. Read this entire chapter right through before going any further. If you're online, check the Internet sites of the airlines, then call the airlines on their toll-free 800 numbers to hear the sort of fare information they're providing. The following airlines have flights to Fiji from North America:

Air New Zealand: tel. 800/262-1234, www.air newzealand.com

Air Pacific: tel. 800/227-4446, www.air pacific.com

Sometimes Canada and parts of the United States have different toll-free numbers, so if a number given in this chapter doesn't work, dial toll-free information at 800/555-1212 (all 800, 866, and 888 numbers are free). In Canada, Air New Zealand's toll-free number is tel. 800/663-5494.

Call both Air New Zealand and Air Pacific and say you want the *lowest possible fare.* Cheapest are the excursion fares, but these usually have limitations and restrictions, so be sure to ask. Some have an advance-purchase deadline, which means it's wise to begin shopping early. If you're not happy with the answers you get, call back later and try again. Many different operators take calls on these lines, and some are more knowledgeable than others. The numbers are often busy during peak business hours, so call first thing in the morning, after dinner, or on the weekend. *Be persistent.*

Cheaper Fares

In recent years, South Pacific airfares have been deregulated, and companies like Air New Zealand no longer publish fare-price lists. Their Internet websites are also evasive, usually with tariff information undisclosed (they might have prices on the Web for their all-inclusive package tours but not air prices alone). Finding your way through this minefield can be the least enjoyable part of your pre-trip planning, but you'll definitely pay a premium if you take the easy route and accept the first or second fare you're offered.

With fares in flux, the airline employees you'll get at the numbers listed above aren't likely to quote you the lowest fare on the market, but at least you'll have their official price to use as a

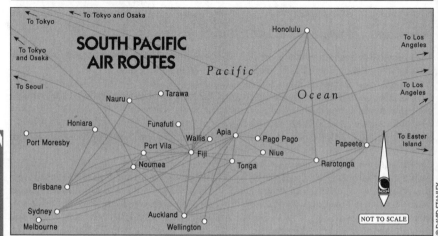

benchmark. After you're heard what they have to say, turn to a "consolidator," a specialist travel agency that deals in bulk and sells seats and rooms at wholesale prices. Many airlines have more seats than they can market through normal channels, so they sell their unused long-haul capacity to "discounters" or "bucket shops" at discounts of 40–50 percent off the official tariffs. The discounters buy tickets on this gray market and pass the savings along to you. Many such companies run ads in the Sunday travel sections of newspapers like the *San Francisco Chronicle, The New York Times,* and *Toronto Star,* or in major entertainment weeklies.

Despite their occasionally shady appearance, most discounters and consolidators are perfectly legitimate, and your ticket will probably be issued by the airline itself. Most discounted tickets look and are exactly the same as regular full-fare tickets, but they're usually nonrefundable. There may also be other restrictions not associated with the more expensive tickets, as well as penalties if you wish to change your routing or reservations. Such tickets may not qualify for frequent-flier miles. Rates are competitive, so allow yourself time to shop around. A few hours spent on the phone, asking questions and doing time on hold, could save you hundreds of dollars.

Once you've done a deal with an agent and

have your ticket in hand, call the airline again using their toll-free reservations number to check that your flight bookings and seat reservations are okay. If your agent said it was possible to freely change your reservations, verify that this is so. Considerable consumer protection is obtained by paying by credit card.

Seasons

The date of outbound travel from North America determines which seasonal fare you'll pay, and proper advance planning could allow you to reschedule your vacation slightly to take advantage of a lower fare. The following is Air New Zealand and Air Pacific's fare season schedule for flights to Fiji from North America:

Dec. 29–Feb. 22—high season
Feb. 23–Apr. 25—shoulder season
Apr. 26–June 17—low season
June 18–July 18—shoulder season
July 19–Aug. 26—low season
Aug. 27–Dec. 4—shoulder season
Dec. 5–Dec. 11—high season
Dec. 12–Dec. 28—peak season

Air New Zealand and Air Pacific have made March–November—the top months in Fiji—their off-season, because that's winter in Australia and New Zealand. If you're only going to

Fiji and can make it at this time, it certainly works to your advantage.

For travel to Fiji originating in New Zealand, the fare seasons are as follows:

Jan. 1–Jan. 20—shoulder season
Jan. 21–Mar. 9—low season
Mar. 10–May 31—shoulder season
June 1–Sept. 30—high season
Oct. 1–Oct. 31—shoulder season
Nov. 1–Nov. 30—low season
Dec. 1–Dec. 17—shoulder season
Dec. 18–Dec. 24—high season
Dec. 25–Dec. 31—shoulder season

In Canada and Australia, the fare seasons are different again. Call the airlines to verify these dates, as they vary slightly from year to year.

Internet Bookings

For an exact fare quote you can book instantly online, simply access an online travel agency. You type in your destination and travel dates, then watch as the site's system searches its database for the lowest fare. You may be offered complicated routings at odd hours, but you'll certainly get useful information. You can also sign up to be notified by email when a special deal to your destination becomes available.

Try a couple of sites for comparison, such as **Cheap Tickets** (www.cheaptickets.com), **Lowestfare.com** (www.lowestfare.com), **Microsoft Expedia** (www.expedia.com), **OneTravel.com** (http://air.onetravel.com), **Orbitz** (www.orbitz.com), and **Sabre Travelocity** (www.travelocity.com). **Priceline.com** (www.priceline.com) is unique in that it allows you to name your own price for your ticket! If your bid is accepted by an airline, your credit card will be charged immediately, and the ticket cannot be changed, transferred, or canceled. Priceline promises an answer within 15 minutes.

All these companies are aimed at the U.S. market, and a credit card with a billing address outside the United States may not be accepted. For the South Pacific, you'll need a paper ticket, and it's unlikely the agency will agree to send it to an address that is different from the one on your card. So despite the global reach of the Internet, you'll probably have to use a site based in your own country.

If you live in Europe, turn to **Flightbookers** (www.ebookers.com) in the United Kingdom and 11 other European countries. **Flights.com** (www.flights.com) is in Frankfurt, Germany, while **Travel Overland** (www.travel-overland.de) is in Munich. **Sabre Travelocity.ca** (www.travelocity.ca) is based in Canada, and there are branches in Germany and the United Kingdom. **Expedia.ca** (www.expedia.ca) is in Canada, and **Expedia.co.uk** (www.expedia.co.uk) is in the United Kingdom. **Cheap Flights Canada** (www.cheapflights.ca) allows you to search for specials online. In Australia, it's **Travel.com.au** (www.travel.com.au) and **Flightcentre.com** (www.flightcentre.com.au). Flightcentre.com links to similar sites in Canada, New Zealand, South Africa, and the United Kingdom.

Many more online agencies are listed on www.etn.nl. When comparing prices, note whether taxes, processing fees, airline surcharges, and shipping are charged extra. Check beforehand if you're allowed to change your reservations or refund the ticket. After booking, print out your confirmation. If you're reluctant to place an order on an unfamiliar site, look for their contact telephone number and give them a call to hear how they sound (a listing here is not a recommendation). At all of these sites, you'll be asked to pay by credit card over their secure server. If that idea worries you, look for a local packager willing to order online on your behalf. Since you'll have already checked the price yourself, you'll know if you're getting a good deal. Let your agent surprise you by finding an even lower online fare. After all, they should know this business better than you.

Student Fares

Students and people under 26 years old can sometimes benefit from lower student fares by booking through **STA Travel** (www.statravel.com) with branches around the world. In the United States, call their toll-free number (tel. 800/781-4040) for information. **Student Universe** (100 Talcott Ave. East, Watertown, MA

02472, U.S.A.; tel. 617/321-3100 or 800/272-9676, www.studentuniverse.com) allows you to get quotes and purchase student tickets online. Canada's largest student travel organization is **Travel Cuts** (www.travelcuts.com).

Current Trends

High operating costs have caused the larger airlines to switch to wide-bodied aircraft and long-haul routes with less frequent service and fewer stops. In the South Pacific, this works to your disadvantage, as even major destinations like Fiji get bypassed. Most airlines now charge extra for stopovers that once were free, or simply refuse to grant any stopovers at all on the cheapest fares.

Increasingly, airlines are combining in global alliances to compete internationally. Thus Qantas is part of the "Oneworld" family (www.oneworldalliance.com), comprising Aer Lingus, American Airlines, British Airways, Cathay Pacific, Finnair, Iberia, and LanChile, while Air New Zealand is a member of the "Star Alliance" (www.star-alliance.com) of United Airlines, Air Canada, Lufthansa, SAS, Singapore Airlines, Thai, All Nippon, and others. This is to your advantage, as frequent-flier programs are usually interchangeable within the blocks, booking becomes easier, flight schedules are coordinated, and through fares exist.

It's now possible to design some extremely wide-ranging trips by accessing the network of one of the two competing groups. For example, Oneworld's **Oneworld Explorer** allows six stops selected from more than 570 destinations worldwide.

Similar is the Star Alliance's **Round-the-World Ticket** valid on flights operated by the 15 members of the Star Alliance. You're allowed 29,000, 34,000, or 39,000 miles with a minimum of three and a maximum of 15 stops. One transatlantic and one transpacific journey must be included, but the ticket is valid for one year, and backtracking is allowed. Fiji, Tahiti, and Rarotonga can be visited on this fare. Air New Zealand offices in North America sell these round-the-world tickets, starting at US$3,530. In Britain, you can buy the same thing for about half of what it costs in North America.

Air New Zealand's **Circle-Pacific Fare** provides a trip around the Pacific (including Asia) on Air New Zealand and other Star Alliance carriers. With this one you get 22,000 or 26,000 miles, starting at US$2,688 with all the stops you want (minimum of three). Travel must begin in either Los Angeles or Vancouver (no add-ons). It's valid for six months, but you must travel in a continuous circle without any backtracking. No date changes are allowed for the outbound sector, but subsequent changes are free. To reissue the ticket (for example, to add additional stops after departure) costs US$75, so plan your trip carefully.

In conjunction with Qantas, Northwest Airlines offers a Circle-Pacific Fare of US$3,277 from Los Angeles with add-on airfares available from other North American cities. This ticket allows four free stopovers in Asia and the South Pacific, additional stops US$75 each. Qantas and Air Pacific also have Circle-Pacific fares, so compare.

From Australia, the Circle South West Pacific pass allows stops of two or more at Fiji, Samoa, Tonga, Solomon Islands, Vanuatu, and New Caledonia, beginning at A$780. The maximum stay is 28 days, and travel must begin and end at Sydney, Melbourne or Brisbane.

AIR SERVICES
From North America

Air New Zealand and Air Pacific are the major carriers serving Fiji out of Los Angeles. Air Pacific flies nonstop from Los Angeles to Nadi four times a week (10.5 hours) and from Honolulu three times a week (six hours).

Air Pacific also flies to Fiji from Vancouver, Canada, via Honolulu twice a week—convenient as no transfers from one aircraft to another are required. Air New Zealand passengers originating in Canada must change planes in either Honolulu or Los Angeles.

From Los Angeles, a seven to 30-day round-trip ticket to Fiji on Air Pacific is US$1,088/1,328/1,608/1,688 low/shoulder/high/peak season. From Honolulu, it's about US$200 cheaper. These are the midweek fares—weekend departures are US$70 more expensive—and some restrictions apply.

Air New Zealand

Air New Zealand offers more direct flights to the South Pacific than any other airline. In the 1950s, the carrier pioneered its "Coral Route" using Solent flying boats, and it still dominates long-haul air routes into the region by allowing stopovers in Tahiti, Cook Islands, and Fiji as part of through services between North America and New Zealand. Air New Zealand operates three nonstop flights from Los Angeles to Nadi every week, plus one Coral Route island hopper via Tahiti and Rarotonga.

Air New Zealand's first priority is to fly people to Auckland, and it's sometimes cheaper to buy a return ticket to Auckland with a couple of free stops in the islands than a roundtrip ticket from Los Angeles only as far as Tahiti-Rarotonga-Fiji. If you don't wish to visit New Zealand, you can transfer at Auckland airport the same day. Despite Air New Zealand's frequent services, travelers in Europe and North America sometimes have difficulty booking seats, and it's advisable to reserve well ahead.

Return tickets to Fiji on Air New Zealand usually cost exactly the same as on Air Pacific. Ask for the "No Stop Apex," which is US$1,088/1,328/1,608/1,688 if you leave Los Angeles at the beginning of the week. To set out on Thursday, Friday, Saturday, or Sunday costs US$80 more. The maximum stay is one month, and you must pay at least 21 days before departure (50 percent cancellation penalty). If you book on shorter notice, the fare is almost 50 percent higher.

It's not that much more expensive to add a couple of other islands. Air New Zealand allows one stop plus your destination, with additional stops available at US$150 each. Thus you can fly Los Angeles-Tahiti-Rarotonga-Fiji-Los Angeles for US$1,248/1,478/1,758/1,838 low/shoulder/high/peak season if you leave at the beginning of the week for a trip of three months maximum. Add US$150 if you wish to extend your period of stay to six months, plus another US$80 if you'd like to set out on Thursday, Friday, Saturday, or Sunday. Drop either Tahiti or Rarotonga from your itinerary, and you'll save US$160. Remember that this fare must be purchased 14 days in advance, and there's a US$125 penalty to change your flight dates. A 35 percent cancellation fee also applies after the 14-day ticket deadline.

For a more wide-ranging trip with fewer restrictions, ask for Air New Zealand's "12-month Excursion Pass," which costs US$2,098/2,388/2,668/2,748 low/shoulder/high/peak season. This worthwhile ticket allows you to fly Los Angeles-Tahiti-

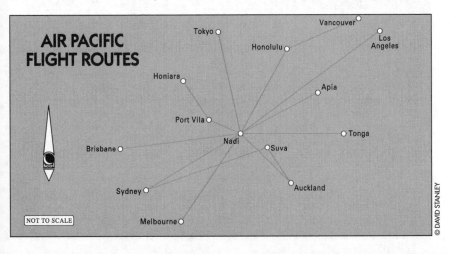

AIR PACIFIC FLIGHT ROUTES

Rarotonga-Fiji-Auckland-Tongatapu-Los Angeles or vice versa. Extend the ticket to Australia for US$100 more. You can stay up to one year, but rerouting costs US$125 (date changes are free). There's no advance purchase requirement, and you can go any day.

In Canada, Air New Zealand offers similar fares called the "Explorer fare, 12 months multi stop," the "Stopover fare one month with no stops," and the "Bungy one and 12-month fare with one free stop." On most tickets special "add-on" fares to Los Angeles or Vancouver are available from cities right across the U.S. and Canada—be sure to ask about them.

Air New Zealand's cabin service is professional, and you'll like the champagne breakfasts and outstanding food with complimentary beer and wine. Another plus are the relaxing seats with adjustable head rests and lots of leg room. The *Life in Pacifica* videos about their destinations are entertaining the first time you see them, but after a while you get bored. The only reading material provided is the *Panorama* in-flight magazine, the *Skyshop* duty-free catalog, and the *Primetime* entertainment magazine. These are unlikely to hold your attention for long, so bring along a book or magazine of your own (the daily newspaper is provided only to passengers in first class).

North American Ticket Agents

South Pacific Direct (8345 Kittyhawk Ave., Los Angeles, CA 90045-4226, U.S.A.; fax 310/568-8294, www.southpacificdirect.com) offers the same tour packages featured in glossy brochures and on fancy websites at a considerable savings to you. Its personalized service is available only by email, and the lower operating costs mean you get high quality hotel arrangements at the best possible price.

A wider selection of Fiji travel arrangements is available through **South Pacific Holidays** (10906 NE 39th St., Suite A-1, Vancouver, WA 98682-6789, U.S.A.; tel. 877/733-3454 or 360/944-1712, fax 360/253-3934, www.tropicalfiji.com).

Some of the cheapest round-trip tickets to Fiji are sold by **Fiji Travel** (8885 Venice Blvd., Suite 202, Los Angeles, CA 90034, U.S.A.; tel. 310/202-4220 or 800/500-3454, fax 310/202-8233, www.fijitravel.com). It makes its money through high volume, and to attract customers it keeps its profit margins as low as possible. Thus you should absorb the airline's time with questions

AIRPORT CODES

AKL—Auckland	LEV—Levuka	SEA—Seattle
APW—Apia/Faleolo	LKB—Lakeba	SFO—San Francisco
BNE—Brisbane	MEL—Melbourne	SIN—Singapore
CHC—Christchurch	MFJ—Moala	SUV—Suva
FGI—Apia/Fagalii	MNF—Mana	SVU—Savusavu
FUN—Funafuti	NAN—Nadi	SYD—Sydney
HIR—Honiara	NGI—Gau	TBU—Tongatapu
HNL—Honolulu	NOU—Nouméa	TRW—Tarawa
ICI—Cicia	OSA—Osaka	TVU—Taveuni
INU—Nauru	POM—Port Moresby	TYO—Tokyo
IPC—Easter Island	PPG—Pago Pago	VBV—Vanua Balavu
IUE—Niue	PPT—Papeete	VLI—Port Vila
KDV—Kadavu	PTF—Malololailai	WLG—Wellington
KXF—Koro	RAR—Rarotonga	WLS—Wallis
LAX—Los Angeles	RTA—Rotuma	YVR—Vancouver
LBS—Labasa	SCL—Santiago	YYZ—Toronto

M

EXPLORING THE ISLANDS

about fare seasons, schedules, etc., and only call companies like Fiji Travel when you know exactly what you want and how much everyone else is charging.

Goway Travel (86751 Lincoln Blvd., Los Angeles, CA 90045, U.S.A.; tel. 800/387-8850, www.goway.com), with additional offices in Sydney, Toronto, and Vancouver, offers competitive fares to Fiji. A leading Canadian specialist travel agency is **Pacesetter Travel** (3284 Yonge St., Suite 301, Toronto, ON M4N 3M7, Canada; tel. 416/322-1031 or 800/387-8827, fax 416/322-7086, www.pacesettertravel.com), with offices in Calgary, Ottawa, Toronto, Vancouver, and Victoria.

For circle-Pacific or round-the-world fares, try **Airtreks** (tel. 877/247-8735, www.airtreks.com) and **Air Brokers International** (tel. 415/397-1383 or 800/883-3273, www.airbrokers.com), both based in San Francisco. In Canada, there's **Long Haul Travel** (www.longhaultravel.ca) in Toronto.

From Australia

Air Pacific offers nonstop flights to Nadi from Brisbane, Melbourne, and Sydney (all Qantas flights to Fiji are now operated by Air Pacific planes). From Sydney, Air Pacific also has direct flights to Suva. Air New Zealand is competing fiercely in the Australian market, and they offer competitive fares to many South Pacific points via Auckland.

You can usually get a better price by working through an agent specializing in bargain airfares rather than buying at the airline office itself. The airlines sometimes offer specials during the off months, so check the travel sections in the weekend papers and call Flight Centres International. Also call **Trailfinders** (8 Spring St., Sydney, NSW 2000, Australia; tel. 02/9247-7666, www.trailfinders.com.au), with additional offices in Brisbane, Cairns, Melbourne, and Perth. The website of **Hideaway Holidays** (www.hideawayholidays.com.au) carries abundant information on air passes to the South Pacific.

Apex (advance-purchase excursion) tickets must be bought 14 days in advance, and heavy cancellation penalties apply. The low season ex-Australia is generally mid-January–June and October–November. Shop around, as you can often find much better deals than the published Apex fares, especially during the off months.

From New Zealand

Both Air New Zealand and Air Pacific fly from Auckland to Nadi daily, and Air Pacific also flies from Auckland to Suva twice a week. Unrestricted low airfares to Fiji can be hard to come by, and some tickets have advance-purchase requirements, so start shopping well ahead. Ask at a number of different travel agencies for special unadvertised or under-the-counter fares. Agents to call include STA Travel and Flight Centre International (www.flightcentre.co.nz). The website of **Travel Online** (www.travelonline.co.nz) provides specific quotes on flights to Fiji.

Air New Zealand offers reduced excursion fares from Auckland to Fiji with a maximum stay of 90 days at NZ$963/1,057/1,151 low/shoulder/high season (see Seasons above for the applicable dates). Seasonal "specials" are regularly available. It's sometimes cheaper to buy a package tour to the islands with airfare, accommodations, and transfers all included, but these are usually limited to seven nights on one island, and you're stuck in a boring tourist-oriented environment. Ask if you can extend your return date and still get the tour price.

In early 2004 the New Zealand-based discount carrier Freedom Air (www.freedomair.co.nz) began weekly service from Hamilton and Palmerston North in New Zealand to Nadi. Their super-low discount fares are designed to cut into Air Pacific's market, and Air New Zealand has also begun offering cheaper "Express" fares to Fiji. To boot, Pacific Blue (www.flypacificblue.com), part of the Virgin airline empire of Sir Richard Branston, has announced its intention of launching budget-priced flights to Fiji from Australia. With all this competition, companies like Flight Centre International have been selling one-week packages from New Zealand to Fiji for as little as NZ$500.

EXPLORING THE ISLANDS

EXPLORING THE ISLANDS

From Europe

Since no European carriers reach Fiji, you'll have to use a gateway city such as Los Angeles, Honolulu, or Sydney. Air New Zealand offers daily nonstop flights London-Los Angeles, with connections in Los Angeles direct to Fiji two or three times a week. Similarly, Lufthansa's Frankfurt-Los Angeles and Munich-Los Angeles flights code-share with Air New Zealand's nonstop flights between Los Angeles and Nadi. This means that European passengers can fly to Fiji from London or Germany with only one change of aircraft (at Los Angeles). It may be cheaper to travel via Seoul on Korean Air.

Air New Zealand reservations numbers around Europe are tel. 03/202-1355 (Belgium), tel. 0800/907-712 (France), tel. 0800/181-7778 (Germany), tel. 800/876-126 (Italy), tel. 0800-2527 (Luxembourg), tel. 0800/022-1016 (Netherlands), tel. 900/993241 (Spain), tel. 020/792-939 (Sweden), tel. 0800/557-778 (Switzerland), and tel. 0800/0284149 (United Kingdom). Call them up and ask about their Coral Route fares. Be aware that Air New Zealand flights from Europe are heavily booked and reservations should be made far in advance.

Also call your local British Airways or Qantas office and ask what connections they're offering to Fiji on Air Pacific. It's possible that the disadvantage of having to change airlines halfway around the world may be compensated for by a lower fare.

The British specialist in South Pacific itineraries is **Trailfinders** (1 Threadneedle St., London EC2R 8JX, United Kingdom; tel. 020/7628-7628, www.trailfinder.com), in business since 1970. Its 13 offices around the United Kingdom and Ireland offer a variety of discounted round-the-world tickets through Fiji, which are often much cheaper than the published fares. If you're in the U.K., it's easy to order a free copy of their magazine *Trailfinder* and brochures online.

Bridge the World (45–47 Chalk Farm Rd., Camden Town, London NW1 8AJ, United Kingdom; tel. 0870/443-2399, www.bridgethe world.com) sells discounted round-the-world

tickets which include Fiji, Rarotonga, Tahiti, and a variety of stops in Asia. **Western Air Travel** (Bickham, Totnes, Devon TQ9 7NJ, United Kingdom; tel. 0800/330-1100, fax 44-870/330-1133, www.westernair.co.uk) is also good on round-the-world tickets. Check the ads in the London entertainment magazines for other such companies.

Barron & De Keijzer Travel (Noordermarkt 16, 1015 MX Amsterdam, the Netherlands; tel. 020/625-8600, www.barron.nl) with additional offices in Antwerp, Den Bosch, and Rotterdam, specializes in the Pacific islands. In Sweden, there's **Tour Pacific** (Sundstorget 3, SE-25110 Helsingborg, Sweden; tel. 042/179500, fax 042/143055, www.tourpacific.se).

In Switzerland, try **Globetrotter Travel Service** (Rennweg 35, CH-8023 Zürich, Switzerland; tel. 01/213-8080, www.globetrotter.ch), with offices in Baden, Basel, Bern, Biel, Fribourg, Lucerne, Olten, St. Gallen, Thun, Winterthur, Zug, and Zürich. You can order a free copy of their magazine, *Globetrotter,* through their website.

Bucket shops in Germany sell a "Pacific Airpass" on Air New Zealand from Frankfurt to the South Pacific that allows all the usual Coral Route stops and is valid six months. All flights must be booked prior to leaving Europe, and there's a charge to change the dates once the ticket has been issued. One of the most efficient agencies selling such tickets is **Jet-Travel** (Buchholzstr. 35, D-53127 Bonn, Germany; tel. 0228/284315, www.jet-travel.de). The websites of **Travel Overland** (Barerstr. 73, D-80799 Munich, Germany; tel. 089/2727-6300, www.travel-overland.de) and **Adventure Holidays** (Wacholderbergstr. 29, D-90587 Veitsbronn, Germany; tel. 0911/979-9555, fax 0911/979-9588, www.adventure-holidays.com) quote exact fares on flights to Nadi.

REGIONAL AIRLINES

Aside from Air New Zealand, Air Pacific, Qantas, and Korean Air, a number of regional carriers fly to and from Fiji. Samoa's **Polynesian Airlines** (tel. 800/264-0823) arrives from Apia twice a week. **Aircalin** (tel. 800/237-2747) flies to Fiji from Nouméa and Wallis. From Suva, **Air Fiji** (www.airfiji.net) flies north to Funafuti in Tuvalu and east to Tongatapu. **Air Nauru** (tel. 800/677-4277) flies to Nadi from Nauru and Tarawa twice a week. **Royal Tongan Airlines** has flights to Nadi from Tongatapu twice a week. **Air Vanuatu** (tel. 800/ 677-4277) arrives from Port Vila. **Solomon Airlines** (tel. 800/677-4277) links Fiji to Honiara and Port Vila. Keep in mind that few regional flights operate daily, and many are only once or twice a week.

Regional Air Passes

The **Visit South Pacific Pass** allows travelers to include the services of nine regional carriers in a single ticket valid for six months. You have to buy the initial two-leg airpass in conjunction with an international ticket into the region, but you can buy additional legs up to a maximum of eight after arrival. Only the first sector has to be booked ahead.

The flights are priced at three different levels. For US$190 per sector, you can go Fiji-Apia/ Tongatapu/Port Vila, Tongatapu-Apia/Niue, or Nouméa-Port Vila. For US$240, you have a choice of Honiara-Nadi/Port Vila/Port Moresby, Fiji-Nauru/Tarawa/Nouméa, or a variety of flights from Australia and New Zealand to the islands. For US$340, there's Tahiti-Nouméa, Sydney-Tongatapu/Apia, or Fiji-Port Moresby. It's a great way of getting around the South Pacific.

Airlines which should know about this ticket include Air Pacific, Polynesian Airlines, Qantas, Royal Tongan Airlines, and Solomon Airlines, so call them up on the toll-free 800 numbers provided earlier. Also try **Air Promotion Systems** (5757 West Century Blvd., Suite 660, Los Angeles, CA 90045-6407, U.S.A.; tel. 310/670-7302 or 800/677-4277, fax 310/338-0708, www.pacificislands.com).

Air New Zealand's **South Pacific Airpass** is valid on their flights between Tahiti, Rarotonga, and Fiji from NZ$400 a hop. It can also be used to travel to/from Australia and New Zealand. The Airpass can be purchased together with an international ticket to the region or within 30 days of arrival in the South Pacific. There are two fare options, standard and supersaver, based on availability. It's not available to residents of Australasia, and at least two flights must be booked. It's an inexpensive way of extending your trip.

For more information on these, click "Air Passes" at www.southpacific.org/air.html and follow the links.

Air Pacific

Air Pacific has two different **Pacific Triangle Fares,** good ways to experience the region's variety of cultures: Fiji-Apia-Tongatapu-Fiji (US$484), Fiji-Nouméa-Port Vila-Fiji (F$850), Fiji-Honiara-Port Vila-Fiji (US$648). All three are valid for one year and can be purchased at any travel agency in Fiji or direct from the airline. Flight dates can be changed at no charge, but they're usually valid only for journeys commencing in Fiji. When booking these circular tickets, be aware that it's much better to go Fiji-Apia-Tongatapu-Fiji than vice versa, because the flights between Apia and Fiji are often fully booked while it's easy to get on between Tonga and Fiji. Also obtainable locally are Air Pacific's special 28-day round-trip excursion fares from Fiji to Apia (F$706), Tongatapu (F$714), Port Vila (F$649), and Honiara (F$1,176). Some of these fares have seasonal variations.

Polynesian Airlines

Polynesian Airlines (www.polynesianairlines .com) offers a **Polypass** valid for 45 days unlimited travel between Fiji, Tonga, Samoa, and Pago Pago, plus one round-trip from Sydney, Melbourne, Auckland, or Wellington for US$1,099. From Honolulu, the pass costs US$1,349, from any one of six U.S. west coast airports US$1,699. Restrictions are that your itinerary must be worked out in advance and can only be changed once for free (subsequent changes US$50 each). Thus it's important to book all flights well ahead. A 20 percent penalty is charged to refund an unused ticket (no refund after one year). Also known as the

"Pacific Explorer Airpass," the Polypass is not available in December and January.

Air Nauru

Air Nauru, flag carrier of the tiny Republic of Nauru in Micronesia, has flights from Nadi to Tarawa twice a week. An Air Nauru 30-day round-trip excursion fare from Nadi to Tarawa costs F$1,445 February–November, F$1,630 December–January. If you just want to say you've been to Kiribati, a "weekend special" fare leaving Fiji on Friday and returning on Monday is F$890 roundtrip. Kiribati visas can be obtained at the consulate in Suva.

Important Note

Airfares, rules, and regulations tend to fluctuate a lot, so some of the information above may have changed. This is only a guide; we've included a range of fares to give you a rough idea how much things might cost. Your travel agent will know what's available at the time you're ready to travel, but if you're not satisfied with his/her advice, keep shopping around. The biggest step is deciding to go—once you're over that, the rest is easy!

PROBLEMS

When planning your trip allow a minimum two-hour stopover between connecting flights at U.S. airports, although with airport delays on the increase, even this may not be enough. In the islands, allow at least a day between flights. Try to avoid flying on weekends and holidays when the congestion is at its worst. In some airports, flights are not called over the public address system, so keep your eyes open. Whenever traveling, always have a paperback or two, some toiletries, and a change of underwear in your hand luggage.

If your flight is canceled due to mechanical problems with the aircraft, the airline will cover your hotel bill and meals. If they reschedule the flight on short notice for reasons of their own or you're bumped off an overbooked flight, they should also pay. They may not feel obligated to pay, however, if the delay is due to

weather conditions, a strike by another company, national emergencies, etc., although the best airlines still pick up the tab in these cases.

It's an established practice among airlines to provide light refreshments to passengers delayed two hours after the scheduled departure time and a meal after four hours. Don't expect to get this from Air Fiji or Sun Air at some outer-island airport, but politely request it if you're at a gateway airport.

Overbooking

To compensate for no-shows, most airlines overbook their flights. To avoid being bumped, ask for your seat assignment when booking, check in early, and go to the departure area well before flight time. Of course, if you *are* bumped by a reputable international airline at a major airport, you'll be regaled with free meals and lodging and sometimes even free flight vouchers or cash payments (don't expect anything like this from Air Fiji or Sun Air).

Whenever you break your journey for more than 72 hours, reconfirm your onward reservations and check your seat assignment at the same time. Get the name of the person who takes your reconfirmation so they cannot deny it later. Failure to reconfirm could result in the cancellation of your complete remaining itinerary. This could also happen if you miss a flight for any reason. If you want special vegetarian food in-flight, request it when buying your ticket, booking, and reconfirming.

When you try to reconfirm your Air New Zealand flight, the agent will tell you that this formality is no longer required. Theoretically this is true, but unless you request your seat assignment in advance, either at an Air New Zealand office or over the phone, you could be "bumped" from a full flight, reservation or no reservation. Air New Zealand's ticket cover bears this surprising message:

> *. . . no guarantee of a seat on a particular flight is indicated by the terms "reservation," "booking," "O.K." status, or the times associated therewith.*

It does admit in the same notice that confirmed passengers denied seats are eligible for compensation, so if you're not in a hurry, a night or two at an upmarket hotel with all meals courtesy of Air New Zealand may not be a hardship. Your best insurance if you don't want to get "bumped" is to request seat assignments for your entire itinerary before you leave home, or at least at the Air New Zealand office in Nadi or Suva. Any good travel agent selling tickets on Air New Zealand should know enough to automatically request your seat assignments as they make your bookings. In the islands, Air New Zealand offices will still accept a local contact telephone number from you, thereby confirming that your booking is in their system. Check Air New Zealand's reconfirmation policy as it could change.

Baggage

International airlines generally allow economy-class passengers 20 kilograms of baggage. However, if any U.S. or Canadian airport is included in your ticket, the allowance is two pieces not more than 32 kilograms each for all of your flights on that carrier. Under the piece system, neither bag must have a combined length, width, and height of more than 158 centimeters (62 inches), and the two pieces together must not exceed 272 centimeters (107 inches). On most long-haul tickets to/from North America or Europe, the piece system should apply to all sectors, but check this with the airline and look on your ticket. The frequent-flier programs of some airlines allow participants to carry up to 10 kilograms of excess baggage free of charge. Both commuter carriers in Fiji restrict you to 20 kilograms total, so pack according to the lowest common denominator. Overweight luggage costs 1 percent of the full first-class fare per kilogram—watch out, this can be a lot!

Bicycles, folding kayaks, and surfboards can usually be checked as baggage (sometimes for an additional US$60 "oversize" charge), but sailboards may have to be shipped airfreight. If you do travel with a sailboard, be sure to call it a surfboard at check-in.

Tag your bag with name, address, and phone number inside and out. Stow anything that could conceivably be considered a weapon (scissors, sewing needles, razor blades, nail clippers, etc.) in your checked luggage. Metal objects, such as flashlights and umbrellas, which might require a security inspection should also be packed away. One reason for lost baggage is that some people fail to remove used baggage tags after they claim their luggage. Get into the habit of tearing off old baggage tags, unless you want your luggage to travel in the opposite direction! As you're checking in, look to see if the three-letter city codes on your baggage tag receipt and boarding pass are the same. If you're headed to Nadi, the tag should read NAN (Suva is SUV).

Check your bag straight through to your final destination, otherwise the airline staff may disclaim responsibility if it's lost or delayed at an intermediate stop. If your baggage is damaged or doesn't arrive at your destination, inform the airline officials *immediately* and have them fill out a written report; otherwise future claims for compensation will be compromised. Keep receipts for any money you're forced to spend to replace missing items. If you notice that a bag has been mysteriously patched up with tape since you last saw it, carefully examine the contents right away. This could be a sign that baggage handlers have pilfered items from inside, and you must report the theft before leaving the customs hall in order to be eligible for compensation.

Claims for lost luggage can take weeks to process. Keep in touch with the airline to show your concern, and hang on to your baggage tag until the matter is resolved. If you feel you did not receive the attention you deserved, write the airline an objective letter outlining the case. Get the names of the employees you're dealing with, so you can mention them in the letter. Of course, don't expect any pocket money or compensation on a remote outer island. Report the loss, then wait until you get back to their main office.

ORGANIZED TOURS

Packaged Holidays

Any travel agent worth their commission would rather sell you a package tour instead of only a plane ticket, and it's a fact that some vacation packages actually cost less than regular round-

EXPLORING THE ISLANDS

trip airfare! While packaged travel certainly isn't for everyone, reduced group airfares and discounted hotel rates make some tours an excellent value. For two people with limited time and a desire to stay at first-class hotels, this is the cheapest way to go.

The "wholesalers" who put these packages together get their rooms at bulk rates far lower than what individuals pay, and the airlines also give them deals. If they'll let you extend your return date to give you some time to yourself, this can be a great deal, especially with the hotel thrown in for "free." Special-interest tours are very popular among sportspeople who want to be sure they'll get to participate in the various activities they enjoy.

The main drawback to the tours is that you're on a fixed itinerary in a tourist-oriented environment, out of touch with local life. You may not like the hotel or meals you get, and singles pay a healthy supplement. You'll probably get prepaid vouchers to turn in as you go along and won't be escorted by a tour conductor. Some tour companies do not accept consumer inquiries and require you to work through a travel agent. Do check all the restrictions.

What follows is a list of North American companies which make individualized travel arrangements and offer package tours to Fiji. Spend some time surfing through their websites, and crosscheck the resorts they offer using the listings in this handbook.

All Inclusive Fiji, 1505 S.W. Broadway, Portland, OR 97201, U.S.A.; tel. 503/224-6659 or 866/444-8518, fax 503/224-6216, www.allinclusivefiji.com

Destination World, P.O. Box 1077, Santa Barbara, CA 93102, U.S.A.; tel. 888/345-4669 or 800/536-0022, www.southpacificgateway.com

eTravelBound, 2312 Ryan Way, Bullhead City, AZ 86442, U.S.A.; tel. 888/540-8445, www.etravelbound.com

Fiji Fantasy Holidays, 207 E. Hwy. 260, Payson, AZ 85541, U.S.A.; tel. 877/727-3454, fax 520/472-2580, www.fijifantasyholidays.com

Fiji Travel, 8885 Venice Blvd., Suite 202, Los Angeles, CA 90034, U.S.A.; tel. 310/202-4220 or 800/500-3454, fax 310/202-8233, www.fijitravel.com

Goway Travel, 86751 Lincoln Blvd., Los Angeles, CA 90045, U.S.A.; tel. 800/387-8850; 3284 Yonge St., Suite 300, Toronto, Ontario M4N 3M7, Canada; tel. 416/322-1034; 1200 W. 73rd Ave., Suite 1050, Vancouver, BC V6P 6G5, Canada; tel. 604/264-8088, www.goway.com

Islands in the Sun, 2381 Rosecrans Ave., Suite 325, El Segundo, CA 90245, U.S.A.; tel. 310/536-0051, fax 310/536-6266, www.islandsinthesun.com

McCoy Travel, 355 Hukilike St., Suite 207, Kahului, Maui, HI 96732, U.S.A.; tel. 808/893-0388 or 800/588-3454, fax 808/893-0138, www.mccoytravel.com

Pacific Destination Center, 18685 Main St., Suite 622, Huntington Beach, CA 92648, U.S.A.; tel. 714/960-4011 or 800/227-5317, www.pacific-destinations.com

Pacific Escapes, 1605 N.W. Sammamish Rd., Suite 310, Issaquah, WA 98027, U.S.A.; tel. 425/657-1900 or 800/777-7992, www.pacificescapes.com

Pacific for Less, 1993 S. Kihei Rd. #21-130, Kihei, HI 96753, U.S.A.; tel. 808/249-6490, fax 808/875-7414, www.pacific-for-less.com

Quiksilver Travel, 15202 Graham St., Huntington Beach, CA 92649, U.S.A.; tel. 877/217-1091, fax 714/889-2250, www.quiksilvertravel.com

Solace Destinations, 10625 N. 25th Ave., Suite 200, Phoenix, AZ 85029, U.S.A.; tel. 800/548-5331, www.solace1.com

South Pacific Direct, 8345 Kittyhawk Ave., Los Angeles, CA 90045-4226, U.S.A.; fax 310/568-8294, www.southpacificdirect.com

South Pacific Getaways, 4885 Mt. Elbrus Dr., San Diego, CA 92117, U.S.A.; tel. 858/560-6154 or 800/458-2499, www.southpacificgetaways.com

South Pacific Holidays, 10906 N.E. 39th St., Suite A-1, Vancouver, WA 98682-6789, U.S.A.; tel. 360/944-1712 or 877/733-3454, fax 360/253-3934, www.tropicalfiji.com

Sunspots International, 1918 N.E. 181st, Portland, OR 97230, U.S.A.; tel. 503/666-3893 or 800/334-5623, fax 503/661-7771, www.sunspotsintl.com

Rob Jenneve of **Island Adventures** (225 C North Fairway, Goleta, CA 93117, U.S.A.; tel. 805/685-9230 or 800/289-4957) puts together customized flight and accommodation packages, which are only slightly more expensive than regular round-trip airfare. Rob can steer you toward deluxe resorts, which offer value for money, and he's willing to spend the time to help you plan your trip. According to him, "It's no problem to vary your nights, extend your return, or leave some free time in the middle for spontaneous adventure."

Rascals in Paradise (Theresa Detchemendy and Deborah Baratta, 1 Daniel Burnham Ct., Suite 105-C, San Francisco, CA 94109, U.S.A.; tel. 415/921-7000, www.rascalsinparadise.com) has been organizing personalized tours to Fiji for families since 1987. Since then, they have been instrumental in initiating numerous children's programs.

Margi Arnold's **Creative Travel Adventures** (8500 E. Jefferson Ave., Unit 5H, Denver, CO 80237, U.S.A.: tel. 303/694-8786 or 888/568-4432, www.honeymoonfiji.com) specializes in honeymoon travel.

From Australia

Hideaway Holidays (Val Gavriloff, P.O. Box 121, West Ryde, NSW 2114, Australia; tel. 02/9743-0253, fax 02/9743-3568, www.hideawayholidays.com.au) specializes in packages to Fiji and the South Pacific. It's been in the business since 1977.

Other Australian wholesalers and tour operators involved in Fiji include:

Adventure World, 73 Walker St., 3rd Fl., North Sydney, NSW 2060, Australia; tel. 02/8913-0755, fax 02/9956-7707, www.adventureworld.com.au

ATS Pacific Ltd, P.O. Box A2494, Sydney South, NSW 2000, Australia; tel. 02/9268-2111, fax 02/9267-9733, www.atspacific.com

Coral Seas Travel, 92 Pitt St., Suite 502, Sydney, NSW 2000, Australia; tel. 02/9231-2944, fax 02/9231-2029, www.coralseas.com.au

Essence Tours, 1666 Old Cleveland Rd., Chandler, QLD 4155, Australia; tel. 07/3245-7815, fax 07/3245-6372, www.essencetours.com.au

Executive Destinations, 38–40 Garden St., South Yarra, VIC 3141, Australia; tel. 03/9823-8300, fax 03/9823-8383, www.edfiji.com

Goway Travel, 350 Kent St., 8th Fl., Sydney, NSW 2000, Australia; tel. 02/9262-4755, fax 02/9290-1905, www.goway.com

Orient Pacific Holidays, 14A Sandilands St., South Melbourne, VIC 3205, Australia; tel. 03/9690-1500, fax 03/9690-1942, www.orientpacific.com.au

Talpacific Holidays, 91 York St., Level 1, Sydney, NSW 2000, Australia; tel. 02/9244-1850, fax 02/9262-6318, www.talpacific.com

Venture Holidays, 234 Sussex St., Sydney, NSW 2000, Australia; tel. 02/9236-5222, fax 02/9221-5394, www.ventureholidays.com

From New Zealand

Fathom South Pacific Travel (P.O. Box 2557, Shortland St., Auckland, New Zealand; www.fathomtravel.com) is a packager oriented toward adventure travel. It books rooms at all the top resorts, but also has numerous options for scuba diving and kayaking.

Ninety-five percent of its bookings are via the Internet.

Ginz Travel (183 Victoria St., Christchurch, New Zealand; tel. 03/366-4486, www.ginz.com) arranges flights, accommodations, rental cars, and package deals to Fiji.

Talpacific Holidays (P.O. Box 297, Auckland, New Zealand; tel. 09/914-8728, www.talpacific.com) also offers package tours throughout Fiji.

From Europe

Austravel (17 Blomfield St., London EC2M 7AJ, United Kingdom; tel. 0870/166-2130, www.austravel.com), with nine locations in the United Kingdom, is a South Pacific-oriented tour company owned by the Thomson Travel Group. **Tailor Made Travel** (18 Port St., Evesham, Worchestershire, WR11 6AN, United Kingdom; tel. 01386/712-005, www.tailor-made.co.uk) specializes in upscale South Pacific tours.

All Ways Pacific Travel (7 Whielden St., Old Amersham, Bucks HP7 0HT, United Kingdom; tel. 01494/432747, www.all-ways.co.uk) sells packages to Fiji for senior or retired travelers.

In Germany, the **Pacific Travel House** (Bayerstr. 95, D-80335 München; tel. 089/543-2180, www.pacific-travel-house.com) offers a variety of package tours.

In Austria, the South Pacific specialist is **Coco Weltweit Reisen** (Eduard-Bodem-Gasse 8, A-6020 Innsbruck; tel. 0512/365-791, www.coco-tours.at).

Scuba Tours

Fiji is one of the world's prime scuba locales, and most of the islands have excellent facilities for divers. Although it's not that difficult to make your own arrangements as you go, you should consider joining an organized scuba tour if you want to cram in as much diving as possible. To stay in business, the dive-travel specialists mentioned below are forced to charge prices comparable to what you'd pay on the beach, and the convenience of having everything prearranged is often worth it. Before booking, find out exactly where you'll be staying, and ask if daily trans-

CORAL REEF ADVENTURE

Since 1993, the live-aboard *Nai'a* has been the flagship of Fiji's diving industry, discovering and naming many remote sites now regularly visited by other boats. In addition to *Nai'a's* regular cruises around Fiji, humpback whale tours to Tonga, and scientific expeditions to the shark-rich waters of Kiribati are annual events. During late 2000 and early 2001, the MacGillivray Freeman Films IMAX production *Coral Reef Adventure* was filmed in Fiji by Howard Hall, who selected *Nai'a's* Cat Holloway and Rob Barrel as his guides, both topside and underwater. And *Nai'a* divemaster Rusi Vulakoro has one of the starring roles in the film. *Nai'a* passengers will recognize their favorite dive sites on the giant screen, as well as the sharks, turtles, manta rays, sea snakes, gobies, and shrimp that they have come to love. One of the highlights of every *Nai'a* voyage is an afternoon spent in a village on the island of Gau. So impressed were Howard and Michelle Hall when they first visited Gau as *Nai'a* passengers that the whole village visit is captured in *Coral Reef Adventure.*

fers and meals are provided. Of course, diver certification is mandatory.

Before deciding, carefully consider booking a cabin on a "live-aboard" dive boat discussed in the Cruises and Charters section which follows. They're a bit more expensive than hotel-based diving, but you're offered up to five dives a day and a total experience. Some repeat divers won't go any other way.

Companies specializing in dive tours to Fiji include:

Dive Discovery, 77 Mark Dr., Suite 18, San Rafael, CA 94903, U.S.A.; tel. 415/444-5100 or 800/886-7321, fax 415/444-5560, www.divediscovery.com

Island Dreams, 1309 Antoine Dr., Houston, TX 77055, U.S.A.; tel. 713/973-9300 or 800/346-6116, fax 713/973-8585, www.islandream.com

Poseidon Ventures Tours, 359 San Miguel Dr., Newport Beach, CA 92660, U.S.A.; tel. 800/854-9334, fax 949/644-5392, www.posei dontours.com

South Pacific Island Travel, 537 N. 137th St., Seattle, WA 98133, U.S.A.; tel. 206/367-0956 or 877/773-4846, fax 206/306-9288, www.spis landtravel.com

Trip-N-Tour, 131 E. Fig St., Ste 4, Fallbrook, CA 92028, U.S.A.; tel. 760/451-1001 or 800/348-0842, www.trip-n-tour.com

World of Diving, 301 Main St., El Segundo, CA 90245, U.S.A.; tel. 800/463-4846, www.worldofdiving.com

Aqua-Trek (601 Montgomery St., Suite 650, San Francisco, CA 94111, U.S.A.; tel. 800/541-4334, www.aquatrek.com) is unique in that they operate their own dive shops in Fiji at Matamanoa, Mana, Robinson Crusoe Island, Pacific Harbor, and Taveuni.

In Australia try Dive Adventures (Level 9, 32 York St., Sydney, NSW 2000, Australia; tel. 02/9299-4633, fax 02/9299-4644, www.divead ventures.com), a scuba wholesaler with packages to Fiji. They also have an office in Melbourne. All-ways Dive Expeditions (168 High St., Ashburton, Melbourne, VIC 3147, Australia; tel. 03/9885-8863, fax 03/9885-1164, www.allwaysdive .com.au) organizes dive expeditions to Fiji.

Dive, Fish, n' Snow Travel (15e Vega Pl., Mairangi Bay, Auckland 10, New Zealand; tel. 09/479-2210, www.divefishsnow.co.nz) arranges scuba and game-fishing tours to Fiji at competitive rates.

In Europe, Schöner Tauchen (Hastedter Heerstr. 211, D-28207 Bremen, Germany; tel. 0421/450-010, fax 0421/450-080, www.schoener-tauchen.com) specializes in dive tours to Fiji.

Alternatively, you can make your own arrangements directly with island dive shops. Information about these operators is included under the heading Sports and Recreation in the respective chapters of this handbook.

Kayak Tours

Among the most exciting tours to Fiji are the nine-day kayaking expeditions offered May–October by Southern Sea Ventures (Al Bakker, P.O. Box 781, Newport, NSW 2106, Australia; tel. 02/9999-0541, fax 02/9999-1357, www.southernseaventures.com). Their groups (limited to 12 people) paddle stable expedition sea kayaks through the sheltered tropical waters of the northern Yasawa chain. Accommodations are tents on the beach, and participants must be in reasonable physical shape, as three or four hours a day are spent on the water. The A$1,920 price doesn't include airfare. Southern Sea Ventures also operates kayak tours to Vanua Balavu in Fiji's Lau Group.

Tamarillo Tropical Expeditions (Anthony Norris, P.O. Box 9869, Wellington, New Zealand; tel. 04/239-9885, fax 04/239-9895, www.tamarillo.co.nz) organizes one-week kayaking trips to Ono and Kadavu year-round at NZ$2,150 all inclusive from Nadi. Two support boats carry the luggage and food. Nights are spent at small island resorts and in local villages, not in tents. Every third or fourth trip, Tamarillo offers a more rigorous "classic extreme" expedition (same price) for experienced kayakers who want to push the envelope a little further.

Sailboarding Safari Holidays (Warren Francis, P.O. Box 454, Collaroy Beach, NSW 2097, Australia; tel. 02/9971-2211, fax 02/9971-2211, www.sailboardingsafaris.com) runs windsurfing and sea-kayaking tours to Nananu-i-Ra Island off northern Viti Levu.

Surfing Tours

The largest operator of surfing tours to the South Pacific is The Surf Travel Company (P.O. Box 446, Cronulla, NSW 2230, Australia; tel. 02/9527-4722, fax 02/9527-4522, www.surf travel.com.au) with packages to Waidroka Bay, Nagigia Island, and Seashell Cove. Also check Go Tours Travel (www.surftheearth.com.au).

For information on tours to Tavarua Island and the famous Cloudbreak, contact Tavarua Island Tours (P.O. Box 60159, Santa Barbara, CA 93160, U.S.A.; tel. 805/686-4551, fax 805/683-6696, www.tavarua.com). A one-week

EXPLORING THE ISLANDS

package will run US$2,631. Tavarua is often sold out six months in advance, but check with **Global Surf Trips** (2033 B San Elijo Ave., Suite 322, Cardiff By the Sea, CA 92007, U.S.A.; www.globalsurftravel.com) for "last minute opportunities."

Waterways Surf Adventures (22611 Pacific Coast Hwy., Malibu, CA 90265, U.S.A.; tel. 310/456-7744, www.waterwaystravel.com) handles bookings for Tavarua's neighbor, Namotu Island Resort. Seven-night package tours from Los Angeles with airfare, meals, and boat transfers included are US$2,598 pp. Only group bookings for 20 or more persons are accepted March–December (individual bookings accepted Jan.–Feb.). However they do keep a waiting list of people who wish to be informed of vacancies at any time of year. Additional information on both Tavarua and Namotu is provided in the Nadi and the Mamanucas chapter.

Quiksilver Travel (15202 Graham St., Huntington Beach, CA 92649, U.S.A.; tel. 877/217-1091, fax 714/889-2250, www.quiksilver travel.com) and **Wavehunters Surf Travel** (2424 Vista Way, Suite 203, Oceanside, CA 92054, U.S.A.; tel. 888/899-8823, fax 760/433-4476, www.wavehunters.com) also has surfing tours to Fiji.

Tours for Naturalists

Perhaps the most rewarding way to visit Fiji is with **Coral Cay Conservation** (The Tower, 13th Floor, 125 High St., Colliers Wood, London SW19 2JG, United Kingdom; tel. 0870/750-0668, fax 0870/750-0667, www.coralcay.org). Its Fiji Reef Conservation Project helps protect vulnerable coral reefs and islands by gathering information urgently needed for new marine reserves and forest sanctuaries. Non-divers must first take a scuba certification course in Fiji, followed by a two-week training program. The length of time actually spent as a volunteer working in Fiji is optional. For dates and costs, check their website.

Reef and Rainforest Adventure Travel (400 Harbor Dr., Suite D, Sausalito, CA 94965, U.S.A.: tel. 415/289-1760 or 800/794-9767, fax 415/289-1763, www.reefrainforest.com)

books diving, kayaking, cruises, and other adventure tours to Fiji.

Outdoor Travel Adventures (2927-A Canon St., San Diego, CA 92106, U.S.A.; tel. 619/523-2137 or 877/682-5433, www.otadventures.com) offers a 10-day adventure tour to Fiji which combines kayaking, hiking, cycling, rafting, and snorkeling. Offered May–October, it's US$2,295, excluding airfare.

BWT Travel Office (P.O. Box 444, Pacific Harbor, Fiji; tel. 345-0444, www.cycle-fiji.com) operates 10-night bicycle tours across central Viti Levu at US$849 pp from Nadi.

Hiking Tours

Yearround **Adventure Fiji,** a division of Rosie The Travel Service (P.O. Box 9268, Nadi Airport; tel. 672-2755, fax 672-2607, www .rosiefiji.com) at Nadi Airport, runs adventuresome hiking trips in the upper Wainibuka River area of central Viti Levu, south of Rakiraki. Horses carry trekkers' backpacks, so the trips are feasible for almost anyone in good condition. Accommodation is in actual Fijian villages. The F$542/726 pp price for three/five-night includes transport to the trailhead, food and accommodations at a few of the 11 Fijian villages along the way, guides, and a bamboo raft ride on the Wainibuka River. Trekkers only hike about five hours a day, allowing lots of time to get to know the village people. You'll probably be required to ford rivers along the way, so have along a pair of cheap canvas shoes to avoid ruining your expensive hiking boots.

Bus Tours

Feejee Experience (tel. 672-0097, www.feejee experience.com) at Nadi Airport offers organized backpacker bus tours around Fiji. The "Hula Loop" travel pass around Viti Levu is F$269 (food and accommodations extra). For F$425, you can extend the pass to Vanua Levu. Activities such as rafting, hiking, kayaking, village visits, and beach stops are included. The minimum time required to do such a trip is four days, but the passes are valid for one year of continuous travel (without backtracking). Although some people like the organized program and party atmosphere

Feejee Experience provides, you can do about the same thing on your own for less than half the price and decide for yourself where you stay.

Tours for Seniors

Since 1989, the **Pacific Islands Institute** (354 Uluniu St., Suite 408, Kailua, HI 96734, U.S.A.; tel. 808/262-8942, www.pac-island.com) has operated educational tours to most of the South Pacific countries in cooperation with Hawaii Pacific University. Their **Elderhostel** people-to-people study programs, designed for those aged 55 or over (younger spouses welcome), are offered between four and six times a year. These culturally responsible trips are highly recommended.

CRUISES AND CHARTERS

Tourist Cruises

Blue Lagoon Cruises Ltd. (P.O. Box 130, Lautoka, Fiji; tel. 666-3938, fax 666-4098, www.bluelagooncruises.com) has been offering upscale minicruises from Lautoka to the Yasawa Islands since its founding by Capt. Trevor Withers in 1950. The two-night trips (from F$1,609) and three-night trips (from F$2,419) leave twice a week, while the six-night cruise (from F$4,354) is weekly. Prices are per cabin (two persons) and include meals (but not alcohol), entertainment, shore excursions, and tax (no additional "port charges" and no tipping). We quote the high-season fares charged April–December (low season Jan.–Mar. is 30 percent cheaper). Single occupancy is F$248–619 less. "A" deck is about 15 percent more expensive than the main deck, but you have the railing right outside your cabin door, instead of a locked porthole window. On the shorter cruises, Blue Lagoon uses older three-deck, 40-passenger vessels, while larger four-deck, 60-passenger mini–cruise ships are used on the longer voyages. Since 1996, the 72-passenger luxury cruiser *Mystique Princess* has operated three-night "gold club" cruises from F$3,150 double. The meals are often beach-barbecue affairs, with Fijian dancing. You'll have plenty of opportunities to snorkel in the calm, crystal-clear waters (bring your own gear). A special scuba-diving cruise leaves on the first Saturday of each month. Though a bit expensive, Blue Lagoon Cruises has an excellent reputation. There are almost daily departures year-round, but reservations are essential.

Captain Cook Cruises (P.O. Box 23, Nadi, Fiji; tel. 670-1823, fax 670-2045, www.captaincook.com.fj) operates out of Nadi's Denarau Marina, rather than Lautoka, and it's also recommended. Like Blue Lagoon Cruises they offer three/four-night cruises to the Yasawa Islands aboard the 63-meter MV *Reef Escape,* departing Nadi Tuesday and Saturday. The 60 double-occupancy cabins begin at F$1,270/1,694 pp twin with bunk beds. The two itineraries vary considerably, and there's a discount if you do both in succession. The *Reef Escape* was formerly used for cruises along Australia's Great Barrier Reef, and it's considerably larger than the Blue Lagoon vessels. The food is good, cabins bright, activities and entertainment fun, and there's even a miniature swimming pool and spa! Most of your fellow passengers will be Australians, which can be stimulating, and the Fijian staff will spoil you silly.

In addition, Captain Cook Cruises operates two/three-night cruises to the southern Yasawas on the 33-meter topsail schooner *Spirit of the Pacific*—a more romantic choice than the minicruise ships. These trips depart Nadi every Monday and Thursday morning and cost F$540/684 pp for two/three nights (children under 12 not accepted). You sleep ashore in a double *bure,* the food is good with lots of fresh vegetables and salads, and the staff is friendly and well organized. Captain Cook Cruises also sometimes uses the 34-meter square-rigged brigantine *Ra Marama* on these trips. It's a fine vessel built of teak planks in Singapore in 1957 for a former governor-general of Fiji. These trips can be booked through most travel agents in Fiji or via the website; readers who've gone report having a great time.

Awesome Adventures (P.O. Box 718, Nadi, Fiji; tel. 675-0499, www.awesomefiji.com) at the Denarau Marina offers two-night "Wanna Taki" cruises around the tiny islands off the south end of Naviti in the Yasawa Group aboard the 27-meter catamaran *Taralala*. Everyone sleeps in an air-conditioned dormitory or under the stars on the upper deck at F$350 pp (extra nights F$99 each). Meals, kayaks, swimming with manta rays (maybe), and transfers from Nadi on the *Yasawa Flyer* are included.

The 39-meter three-masted schooner *Tui Tai* of **Tui Tai Adventure Cruises** (P.O. Box 474, Savusavu, Fiji; tel. 885-3032 or 999-6375, www.tuitai.com), based at Savusavu, also caters to younger travelers. The four-night cruise departing Savusavu on Tuesday is F$1,700/2,250 single/double in the six double cabins with shared bath, or F$915 per bunk in an air-conditioned 28-bed dorm or on deck. If you board at Taveuni for a three-night cruise, it's F$1,350/1,800 or F$733. Both trips tour Koro or the Lau Group and end at Savusavu on Saturday. Meals and activities (bicycling, snorkeling, kayaking) are included, but scuba diving is extra.

Scuba Cruises

Several **live-aboard dive boats** ply Fiji waters. A seven-night stay aboard one of these vessels could run as high as F$6,500 pp (airfare, alcohol, and tax extra), but the boat anchors right above the dive sites, so no time is wasted commuting back and forth. All meals are included, and the diving is unlimited. Singles are usually allowed to share a cabin with another diver to avoid a single supplement. Bookings can be made through any of the scuba wholesalers previously mentioned under Scuba Tours.

The five-stateroom *Sere Ni Wai* (or "song of the sea") is a 30-meter boat based at the Raffles Tradewinds Hotel in Suva and operating around Beqa, Kadavu, Lomaiviti, and northern Lau. Capt. Greg Lawlor's family has been in Fiji for four generations, but his boat is relatively new, launched in 1995. If you're already in Fiji, try calling **Mollie Dean Cruises** (P.O. Box 3256, Lami, Fiji; tel. 336-1174, www.sere.com.fj), which books divers on the *Sere Ni Wai* locally. In the U.S., the *Sere Ni Wai* is marketed as the *Fiji Aggressor II* (www.pac-aggressor.com).

Another famous boat is the 34-meter, eight-cabin *Nai'a* which does seven-day scuba cruises

to Lomaiviti and northern Lau at US$2,700, or 10 days for US$3,850, excluding airfare. Capt. Rob Barrel and Dive Director Cat Holloway have a longstanding interest in dolphins and whales, and whale-watching expeditions to Tonga are organized annually. Long exploratory voyages are occasionally made to places as far afield as Vanuatu and the Phoenix Islands of Kiribati (in June). Local bookings are accepted when space is available, and you might even be able to swing a discount. **Nai'a Cruises** (P.O. Box 332, Deuba, Fiji; tel. 345-0382, fax 345-0566, www.naia.com.fj) has an office in the Cultural Center complex at Pacific Harbor, though the *Nai'a* itself is based at Lautoka. In North America call tel. 866/776-5572.

Also based at Pacific Harbor is the 18-meter live-aboard *Beqa Princess,* operated by **Tropical Expeditions** (Charles Wakeham, P.O. Box 129, Deuba, Fiji; tel. 345-0666, fax 330-9551). The three spacious air-conditioned cabins accommodate six divers on three-night cruises to the Beqa Lagoon for about F$500 pp a day. Get a half dozen friends together and charter this boat for an unforgettable trip at F$3,600 daily.

Yacht Tours and Charters

Due to the risks involved in navigating Fiji's poorly marked reefs, yacht charters aren't at all as common in Fiji as they are in Tonga or Tahiti. "Bareboat" charters (where you're given a yacht to sail around on your own) aren't available, and all charter boats are required by law to carry a local skipper or guide.

Musket Cove Yacht Charters (Private Mail Bag NAP 0352, Nadi Airport, Fiji; tel. 672-2488, fax 672-3773, www.musketcovefiji.com) offers crewed yacht charters among the Mamanuca and Yasawa islands from their base at the Musket Cove Marina on Malololailai Island in the Mamanuca Group. Surfing and diving charters are available. For example, the ketch *Hobo* can be chartered for Yasawa cruises at F$950/1,100 a day for two/four people, provisions and crew included. The 14-meter catamaran *Take a Break* is also available at F$1,200/1,600 for two/four passengers.

Valentino Sailing Safaris (P.O.Box 10562, Nadi Airport, Fiji; tel. 672-4428 or 992-9182, www.sailsafari.com.fj) offers Mamanuca and Yasawa charters on the crewed 11-meter catamaran *Moana Uli Uli* based at Nadi. It's F$750 for up to four guests, meals and drinks included (minimum of two nights).

Sailing Adventures Ltd. (Peter Kinsey, P.O. Box 7531, Lautoka, Fiji; tel. 666-5244, fax 666-5335, www.fijisail.com), based at the Vuda Point Marina between Nadi and Lautoka, offers charters on the three-cabin, 15.5-meter yacht *Tavake*. A one-week cruise around the Mamanuca and Yasawa groups will cost F$12,600 for two people or F$18,522 for six persons including meals, taxes, crew, guides, and most activities. Scuba diving can be arranged at additional cost. You're promised a cultural experience!

Larger groups could consider the 27-meter ketch *Tau* at the Raffles Tradewinds Hotel, Suva, which costs US$1,800/12,000 a day/week for up to four persons, including all meals, drinks, and an experienced crew (scuba diving is extra). It's available year-round. For full information contact Tau Charter Yacht (Tony Philp, tel. 336-2128).

Many overseas yacht brokers arrange charters in Fiji. The American veteran of custom chartering is Ocean Voyages Inc. (1709 Bridgeway, Sausalito, CA 94965, U.S.A.; tel. 415/332-4681 or 800/299-4444, fax 415/332-7460, www.ocean voyages.com). Trips of a week or more can be arranged in the Yasawas, Mamanucas, Taveuni, and out of Suva. Longer Fiji/Tonga or Fiji/Vanuatu charters of two or three weeks are also possible. In all, Ocean Voyages has nearly a half dozen vessels in the area, and scuba diving is possible at extra cost on some boats.

In Australia, Paradise Adventures & Cruises (Heidi Gavriloff, P.O. Box 121, West Ryde, NSW 2114; tel. 02/9743-0253, fax 02/9743-3568, www.paradiseadventures.com.au) specializes in privately crewed sailing trips in the Mamanuca and Yasawa groups. Paradise Adventures also has all-inclusive packages in conjunction with Blue Lagoon Cruises.

A few other private brokers arranging yacht charters in Fiji are:

Charter World Pty. Ltd., 23 Passchendaele St., Hampton, Melbourne, VIC 3188, Australia; tel. 03/9521-0033 or 800/335-039, www.charter world.com.au

Crestar Yacht Charters, 16/17 Pall Mall, London SW1Y 5LU, United Kingdom; tel. 020/7766-4329, www.crestaryachts.com

Sail Connections Ltd., P.O. Box 90961, 8 Madden St., Auckland 1, New Zealand; tel. 09/358-0556, www.sailconnections.co.nz

Yachting Partners International, 28–29 Richmond Pl., Brighton, East Sussex, BN2 9NA, United Kingdom; tel. 800/626-0019 or 01273/571-722, www.ypi.co.uk

One of the classic "tall ships" cruising the South Pacific is the classic two-masted brigantine *Soren Larsen,* built in 1949. From May–November, this 42-square-meter rig vessel operates 10–17 day voyages to Tahiti, Cook Islands, Tonga, Fiji, Vanuatu, and New Caledonia costing US$1,500–2,550. The 12-member professional crew is actively assisted by 22 voyage participants. For information, contact Square Sail Pacific (P.O. Box 310, Kumeu, Auckland 1250, New Zealand; tel. 09/411-8755, fax 09/411-8484, www.sorenlarsen.co.nz). Their U.K. agent is Explore Worldwide (1 Frederick St., Aldershot, Hants GU11 1LQ, United Kingdom; tel. 01252/760-000, fax 01252/760-001, www.ex ploreworldwide.com). Ocean Voyages Inc. handles bookings in North America.

The Oceanic Schooner Co. (www.fijiis landvoyager.com) proposes Mamanuca or Yasawa charters on the 25-meter motor vessel *Island Voyager.* The six-cabin, 12-passenger ship can be chartered at F$3,500 a day, plus F$100 pp per day for meals. Four kayaks and fishing gear are available on board.

If price is no obstacle, you can also charter the 35-meter superyacht *Surprise* (P.O. Box 1874, Auckland, New Zealand; tel. 09/302-0178, www.surpriseshipping.com), based at Nadi. A minimum five-day charter for up to nine guests will run about F$75,000 all-inclusive.

EXPLORING THE ISLANDS

MARITIME COORDINATES

ISLAND GROUP/ ISLAND	LAND AREA (SQUARE KM)	HIGHEST POINT (METERS)	LATITUDE	LONGITUDE
Viti Levu Group				
Beqa	36.0	439	18.40°S	178.13°E
Vatulele	31.6	34	18.50°S	177.63°E
Viti Levu	10,531.0	1,323	17.80°S	178.00°E
Yasawa Group				
Naviti	34.0	388	17.13°S	177.25°E
Yasawa	32.0	244	16.80°S	177.50°E
Kadavu Group				
Dravuni	0.8	40	18.78°S	178.53°E
Kadavu	450.0	838	19.05°S	178.25°E
Ono	30.0	354	18.88°S	178.50°E
Lomaiviti Group				
Gau	140.0	747	18.00°S	179.30°E
Koro	104.0	522	17.30°S	179.40°E
Makogai	8.4	267	17.43°S	178.98°E
Ovalau	101.0	626	17.70°S	178.80°E
Wakaya	8.0	152	17.65°S	179.02°E
Vanua Levu Group				
Namenalala	0.4	105	17.11°S	179.10°E
Qamea	34.0	304	16.77°S	179.77°W
Rabi	69.0	463	16.50°S	180.00°E
Taveuni	442.0	1,241	16.85°S	179.95°E
Vanua Levu	5,587.0	1,032	16.60°S	179.20°E
Yaduatabu	0.7	100	16.84°S	178.28°E

BY SHIP

Even as much Pacific shipping was being sunk during World War II, airstrips were springing up on the main islands. This hastened the inevitable replacement of the old steamships with modern aircraft, and it's now extremely rare to arrive in Fiji by boat (private yachts excepted). Most islands export similar products and there's little interregional trade; large container ships headed for Australia, New Zealand, Japan, and the United States usually don't accept passengers. Arriving by cruise ship here is also far less common than it is in places like Vanuatu or French Polynesia.

Those bitten by nostalgia for the slower prewar ways may like to know that a couple of passenger-carrying freighters do still call at the islands, though their fares are much higher than those charged by the airlines. A specialized agency booking such passages is **TravLtips** (P.O. Box 580188, Flushing, NY 11358, U.S.A.; tel. 800/872-8584, www.travltips.com). Also try **Freighter World Cruises** (180 South Lake Ave., Suite 335, Pasadena, CA 91101, U.S.A.; tel. 626/449-3106 or 800/531-7774, www.freighterworld.com).

These companies can place you aboard a British-registered **Bank Line** container ship on its

ISLAND GROUP/ ISLAND	LAND AREA (SQUARE KM)	HIGHEST POINT (METERS)	LATITUDE	LONGITUDE
Lau Group				
Cicia	34.0	165	17.75°S	179.33°W
Fulaga	18.5	79	19.17°S	178.65°W
Kabara	31.0	143	18.95°S	178.97°W
Kanacea	13.0	259	17.25°S	179.17°W
Lakeba	54.0	215	18.20°S	178.80°W
Ogea Levu	13.3	82	19.18°S	178.47°W
Ono-i-Lau	7.9	113	20.80°S	178.75°W
Vanua Balavu	53.0	283	17.25°S	178.92°W
Vuaqava	7.7	107	18.83°S	178.92°W
Wailagi Lala	0.3	5	16.75°S	179.18°W
Moala Group				
Matuku	57.0	385	19.18°S	179.75°E
Moala	62.5	468	18.60°S	179.90°E
Totoya	28.0	366	18.93°S	179.83°W
Ringgold Isles				
Qelelevu	1.5	12	16.09°S	179.26°W
Rotuma Group				
Conway Reef	0.1	2	21.77°S	174.52°E
Rotuma	47.0	256	12.50°S	177.13°E

way around the world from Europe via the Panama Canal, Papeete, Nouméa, Suva, Lautoka, Port Vila, Santo, Honiara, and Papua New Guinea. A round-the-world ticket for the four-month journey is US$12,725, but segments are sold if space is available 30 days before sailing. These ships can accommodate only about a dozen passengers, so inquire well in advance.

BY SAILING YACHT
Getting Aboard

It's possible to hitch rides into the Pacific on yachts from California, Panama, New Zealand, and Australia, or around the yachting triangle of Papeete-Suva-Honolulu. If you've never crewed before, consider looking for a yacht already in the islands. In Fiji, the best places to look for a

boat are the Royal Suva Yacht Club and Tradewinds Hotel Marina in Suva, the Vuda Point Marina, Port Denarau Marina, and Musket Cove Resort, all near Nadi, and the Copra Shed Marina at Savusavu. Cruising yachts are recognizable by their foreign flags, wind-vane steering gear, sturdy appearance, and laundry hung out to dry. Good captains evaluate crew on personality, attitude, and willingness to learn more than experience, so don't lie. Be honest and open when interviewing with a skipper—a deception will soon become apparent.

It's also good to know what a captain's *really* like before you commit yourself to an isolated week or two with her/him. To determine what might happen should the electronic gadgetry break down, find out if there's a sextant aboard and whether he/she knows how to use it. A boat that looks run-down may often be mechanically unsound too. Also be concerned about a skipper who doesn't do a careful safety briefing early on, or who seems to have a hard time hanging onto crew. If the previous crew has left the boat at an unlikely place, there must have been a reason. Once you're on a boat and part of the yachtie community, things are easy.

Time of Year

The weather and seasons play a deciding role in any South Pacific trip by sailboat, and you'll have to pull out of many beautiful places, or be unable to stop there, because of bad weather. The prime season for rides in the South Pacific is May–October; sometimes you'll even have to turn one down. Be aware of the hurricane season (November to March in the South Pacific) as few yachts will be cruising at that time.

Also, know which way the winds are blowing; the prevailing trade winds in the tropics are from the northeast north of the equator and from the southeast south of the equator. North of the tropic of Cancer and south of the tropic of Capricorn, the winds are out of the west. Due to the action of prevailing southeast trade winds, boat trips are smoother from east to west than west to east throughout the South Pacific, so that's the way to go.

Yachting Routes

The common yachting route, or "Coconut Milk Run," across the South Pacific utilizes the northeast and southeast trade winds: from California to Tahiti via the Marquesas or Hawaii, then Rarotonga, Vava'u, Fiji, and New Zealand. Some yachts continue west from Fiji to Port Vila. Cruising yachts average about 150 kilometers a day, so it takes about a month to get from the west coast of the United States to Hawaii, then another month from Hawaii to Tahiti.

To enjoy the finest weather conditions, many yachts clear the Panama Canal or depart California in February to arrive in the Marquesas in March. From Hawaii, yachts often leave for Tahiti in April or May. Many stay on for the *Heiva i Tahiti* festival, which ends on July 14, at which time they sail west to Vava'u or Suva, where you'll

find them in July and August. From New Zealand, the Auckland-to-Fiji yacht race in June brings many boats north. In mid-September, the yachting season culminates with a race by about 40 boats from Musket Cove on Fiji's Malololailai Island to Port Vila (it's very easy to find a ride at this time).

By late October, the bulk of the yachting community is sailing south via New Caledonia to New Zealand or Australia to spend the southern summer there. In April or May on alternate years (2005, 2007, etc.), there's a yacht race from Auckland and Sydney to Suva, timed to coincide with the cruisers' return after the hurricane season. Jimmy Cornell's website, www.noonsite.com, provides lots of valuable information for cruising yachties.

Life Aboard

To crew on a yacht, you must be willing to wash and iron clothes, cook, steer, keep watch at night, and help with engine work. Other jobs might include changing and resetting sails, cleaning the boat, scraping the bottom, pulling up the anchor, and climbing the main mast to watch for reefs. Do more than is expected of you. As a guest in someone else's home, you'll want to wash your dishes promptly after use and put them, and all other gear, back where you found them. Tampons must not be thrown in the toilet bowl. Smoking is usually prohibited as a safety hazard.

Anybody who wants to get on well under sail must be flexible and tolerant, both physically and emotionally. Expense-sharing crew members pay US$50 a week or more per person. After 30 days, you'll be happy to hit land for a freshwater shower. Give adequate notice when you're ready to leave the boat, but *do* disembark when your journey's up. Boat people have few enough opportunities for privacy as it is. If you've had a good trip, ask the captain to write you a letter of recommendation; it'll help you hitch another ride.

Food for Thought

When you consider the big investment, depreciation, cost of maintenance, operating expenses, and considerable risk (most cruising yachts are not insured), travel by sailing yacht is quite a luxury. The huge cost can be surmised from charter fees (US$600 a day and up for a 10-m yacht). International law makes a clear distinction between passengers and crew. Crew members paying only for their own food, cooking gas, and part of the diesel are very different from those who charter, who do nothing and pay full costs. The crew is there to help operate the boat, adding safety, but like passengers, they're very much under the control of the captain. Crew has no say in where the yacht will go.

The skipper is personally responsible for crew coming into foreign ports: He's entitled to hold their passports and to see that they have onward tickets and sufficient funds for further traveling. Otherwise the skipper might have to pay their hotel bills and even return airfares to the crew's country of origin. Crew may be asked to pay a share of third-party liability insurance. Possession of drugs can result in seizure of the yacht. Because of such considerations, skippers often hesitate to accept crew. Crew members should remember that at no cost to themselves they can learn a bit of sailing and visit places nearly inaccessible by other means. Although not for everyone, it's *the* way to see the real South Pacific, and folks who arrive by yacht are treated differently from other tourists.

Getting Around

BY AIR

While most international flights are focused on Nadi, Fiji's domestic air service radiates from Suva and two local airlines compete fiercely. **Air Fiji** (tel. 331-3666, fax 330-0771, www.airfiji.net) flies Brazilian-made Embraer Brasilias (30 seats), fast Embraer Bandeirantes (18 seats), sturdy Canadian-made Twin Otters (18 seats), efficient TriIslanders (16 seats), and pocket-sized Britten-Norman Islanders (nine seats). From Suva's Nausori Airport, flights operate six times a day to Nadi (F$104), five times a day to Labasa (F$139), twice a day to Levuka (F$52), Savusavu (F$111), and Taveuni (F$138), daily except Sunday to Kadavu (F$81), three times a week to Gau (F$64), and weekly to Cicia (F$121), Koro (F$92), Lakeba (F$131), Moala (F$118), Vanua Balavu (F$130), and Rotuma (F$339). Savusavu to Taveuni (F$74) is twice daily (all quoted fares are one-way). From Nadi, they fly to Labasa (F$163), Savusavu (F$148), and Taveuni (F$183) twice a day. Air Fiji's 30-day "Discover Fiji Air Pass" (US$270) is valid on any four flights between Kadavu, Nadi, Savusavu, Suva, and Taveuni, but it must be purchased prior to arrival in Fiji. Buying tickets as you go is a better value than this pass.

Sun Air (tel. 672-3016, fax 672-0085, www.fiji.to) bases much of its domestic network at Nadi, with three flights a day to Labasa (F$175), twice daily to Suva (F$104), Savusavu (F$159), and Taveuni (F$183), and daily to Kadavu (F$104). Also from Nadi, the resort island of Malololailai (F$48) gets four to eight flights a day, while Mana Island (F$58) is visited five times a day. From Suva, Sun Air has flights to Labasa (twice daily, F$147) and Nadi (two daily, F$104). From Taveuni, they go to Savusavu (twice daily, F$75) and Labasa (three times a week, F$75). Flying in their nine-passenger Britten-Norman Islanders, speedy eight-passenger Beechcraft, and versatile 19-passenger Twin Otters is sort of fun.

Turtle Airways Ltd. (tel. 672-1888, fax 672-0095, www.turtleairways.com), owned by Richard Evanson of Turtle Island Resort, flies their five four-seat Cessna 206 floatplanes and one seven-seat DeHaviland Beaver three times a day from Nadi to Castaway and Mana Islands (F$134/268 one-way/round-trip). Turtle Airways also services the Yasawas. The Beaver is a classic aircraft, performing remarkable whitewater takeoffs and landings.

Because only Nadi and Nausori airports have electric lighting on their runways, all flights are during daylight hours. The gravel runways and vintage planes are part of the fun of flying here. Those unaccustomed to island flying should prepare themselves for abrupt landings on short

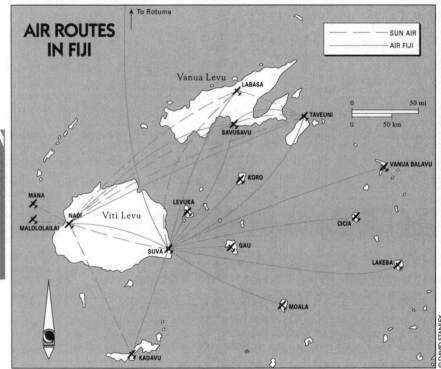

AIR ROUTES
IN FIJI

To Rotuma

SUN AIR
AIR FIJI

Vanua Levu   LABASA

TAVEUNI

SAVUSAVU

0   50 mi
0   50 km

VANUA BALAVU

KORO

MANA

LEVUKA

MALOLOLAILAI   NADI   Viti Levu   CICIA

SUVA   GAU

LAKEBA

MOALA

KADAVU

EXPLORING THE ISLANDS

© DAVID STANLEY

airstrips cut out of the bush or aircraft carrier–style takeoffs over the sea. The views from these low flying planes can be exceptional. Don't be surprised if one of the pilots opens his window during the flight to get a bit of air. What may seem scary to you is just routine for them. Always reconfirm your return flight immediately upon arrival at an outer island, as the reservation lists are sometimes not sent out from Suva. Failure to do so could mean you'll be bumped without compensation.

Be aware that flights on the domestic carriers booked from abroad or over the Internet are 25 percent more expensive than the same tickets purchased in Fiji. In this book, we quote the reduced local fare, though you won't always be able to get it (the staff at the check-in counters at Nadi Airport usually charge foreigners full fare). The big advantage to booking ahead from overseas is that you'll be guaranteed a seat on these heavily booked flights and will be first in line if

the carrier decides to downsize the plane and bump a few passengers.

Add a F$3.50 insurance surcharge to the cost of each flight. Student discounts are for local students only, and there are no standby fares. Children aged 12 and under pay 50 percent, infants aged two and under carried in arms pay 10 percent. Both Sun Air and Air Fiji allow passengers with full-fare international tickets to carry 20 kilograms of baggage, while tickets issued in Fiji at the reduced local residents rate cover only 15 kilograms. The allowance on Turtle Airways is always 15 kilograms.

BY BOAT

Since most shipping operates out of Suva, passenger services by sea both within Fiji and to neighboring countries are listed in the Suva section. Ferries to the Mamanuca and Yasawa groups are covered under Nadi and Yasawa Islands, while those between Vanua Levu and Taveuni are under Buca Bay and Taveuni.

The largest local company is **Patterson Brothers Shipping,** set up by Levuka copra planter Reg Patterson and his brother just after World War I. Patterson's Japanese-built car ferry, the *Princess Ashika,* is usually used on the Buresala-Natovi-Nabouwalu-Ellington Wharf run. (In August 2003, a sister ship, the MV *Ovalau,* sank two kilometers off Nananu-i-Ra Island after springing a leak the pumps could not control. Passengers and crew were rescued by the *Princess Ashika* before the ship went down. A replacement, the **Ovalau III,** may enter service soon.) Patterson's other ferry, the *Island Navigator,* does trips to Lau and Rotuma. Delays or reduced schedules due to mechanical failures are routine.

Consort Shipping Line runs the large car ferry *Spirit of Fiji Islands* from Suva to Koro, Savusavu, and Taveuni twice a week. The car ferry *Adi Savusavu* of **Beachcomber Cruises** (www.beachcomberfiji.com) also visits Savusavu and Taveuni from Suva three times a week.

Other regular boat trips originating in Suva include the Patterson Brothers "Sea Road" shuttle to Levuka, and the weekly ferries to Kadavu. From Nadi, **South Sea Cruises** operates fast catamaran shuttles to the Mamanuca Group on the *Tiger IV* and to the Yasawas on the *Yasawa Flyer.* A sea voyage is an essential part of any authentic Fiji experience.

By Ocean Kayak

Ocean kayaking is experiencing a boom in Fiji with kayaking tours now offered in the Yasawas, Kadavu, Taveuni, Van Balavu, and Vanua Levu. Most islands have a sheltered lagoon ready-made for the excitement of kayak touring, and this effortless transportation mode can make you a real independent 21st-century explorer! Many international airlines accept folding kayaks as checked baggage at no additional charge.

For a better introduction to ocean kayaking than is possible here, check at your local public library for sea-kayaking manuals. Noted author Paul Theroux toured the entire South Pacific by kayak, and his experiences are recounted in *The Happy Isles of Oceania: Paddling the Pacific.*

The Patterson Brothers car ferry *Princess Ashika* sails regularly between Ovalau, Viti Levu, and Vanua Levu.

BY BUS

Scheduled bus service is available all over Fiji, and the fares are low. If you're from North America, you'll be amazed how accessible, inexpensive, and convenient the bus service really is. Most long-distance bus services operate several times a day, and bus stations are usually adjacent to local markets. Buses with a signboard in the window reading Via Highway are local "stage" buses that will stop anywhere along their routes and can be excruciatingly slow on a long trip. Express buses are faster, but they'll only stop in a few towns, and some won't let you off at resorts along the way. Strangely, the times of local buses are not posted at the bus stations, and it's often hard to find anyone to ask about buses to remote locations. The people most likely to know are the bus drivers themselves, but you'll often receive misleading or incorrect information about local buses. Express bus times *are* posted at some stations, and it's sometimes possible to pick up printed express bus timetables at tourist offices.

On Viti Levu, the most important routes are between Lautoka and Suva, the biggest cities. If you follow the southern route via Sigatoka, you'll be on Queens Road, the smoother and faster of the two. Kings Road via Tavua is longer, and it can be rough and dusty, but you get to see a bit of the interior. Fares from Suva are F$2.95 to Pacific Harbor, F$6.95 to Sigatoka, F$10.10 to Nadi, F$10.55 to Nadi Airport, F$11.60 to Lautoka, and F$13.35 to Ba. Fares average just more than F$2 for each hour of travel.

Pacific Transport Ltd. (tel. 330-4366) has 11 buses a day along Queens Road, with expresses leaving from across the street from the Flea Market in Suva for Lautoka at 0645, 0830, 0930, 1210, 1500, and 1730 (221 km, five hours). Eastbound, the expresses leave Lautoka for Suva at 0630, 0700, 1210, 1550, and 1730. An additional Suva-bound express leaves Nadi at 0900. These buses stop at Navua, Pacific Harbor, Sigatoka (coffee break), Nadi, and Nadi Airport, plus a few major resorts upon request (ask). The 1500 bus from Suva continues to Ba. If you want off at a smaller place, you might have to take one of the five local "stage" buses, which

take six hours to reach Lautoka via Queens Road. Sunbeam Transport operates five daily express buses between Sigatoka and Suva, stopping at many resorts along the way.

The daily **Sunset Express** (Island Buses Ltd., tel. 331-2504) leaves Suva for Sigatoka, Nadi, and Lautoka at 0845 and 1600 (four hours, F$10). From the Lautoka end, it leaves at 0930 and 1515, passing Nadi Airport at 1000 and 1545. The Sunset Express is faster than the Pacific Transport expresses, as it makes fewer and shorter stops.

Sunbeam Transport Ltd. (tel. 338-2704) services the northern Kings Road from Suva to Lautoka five times a day, with expresses leaving Suva at 0600, 0645, 0815, 1200, 1330, and 1715 (265 km, six hours, F$13.90). From Lautoka, they depart at 0615, 0630, 0815, 1215, and 1630. A Sunbeam express bus along Kings Road is a comfortable way to see Viti Levu's picturesque back side, though some of their buses play insipid videos. The expresses stop only at Nausori, Korovou, Ellington, Vaileka (Rakiraki), Tavua, Ba, and a few other places. If time doesn't matter, there's also a "stage" bus which leaves Suva at 0750 and Lautoka at 0835, spending nine fun-filled hours on Kings Road.

Coral Sun Fiji (tel. 672-2268) operates daily air-conditioned tourist expresses called the "Fiji Express" and "Queens Express" between Nadi and Suva via the Coral Coast resorts. These cost twice as much as the regular expresses.

There are many local buses, especially closer to Suva or Lautoka, some with big open windows with roll-down canvas covers which give you a panoramic view of Viti Levu. The local buses often show up late, but the long-distance buses are usually right on time. Bus service on Vanua Levu and Taveuni is also good, but there are no buses on Kadavu and most outer islands. In rural areas, passenger trucks called "carriers" charge set rates to and from interior villages.

Running Taxis

Shared "running" taxis and minibuses also shuttle back and forth between Suva, Nadi, and Lautoka, leaving when full and charging only a few dollars more than the bus. Look for them in the markets around the bus stations. They'll often drop you exactly where you want to go; drawbacks include the less-than-safe driving style and lack of insurance coverage. In a speeding minibus, you miss out on much of the scenery, and tourists have been killed in collisions. It's possible to hire a complete taxi from Nadi Airport to Suva for about F$90 for the car, with brief stops along the way for photos, resort visits, etc.

Often the drivers of private or company cars and vans try to earn a little extra money by stopping to offer lifts to persons waiting for buses beside the highway. They ask the same as you'd pay on the bus but are much faster and you'll probably be dropped off exactly where you want to go. Many locals don't understand hitchhiking, and it's probably only worth doing on remote roads where bus service is inadequate. In such places, almost everyone will stop. Be aware that truck drivers who give you a lift may also expect the equivalent of bus fare; locals pay this without question. It's always appropriate to offer the bus fare.

TAXIS

Fiji's taxis are plentiful and among the cheapest in the South Pacific, affordable even for low-budget backpackers. Only in Suva do the taxis have meters, and even there it's sometimes easier to ask the driver for a flat rate before you get in. If the first price you're quoted is too high, you can often bargain (although bargaining is much more accepted by Indo-Fijian than by indigenous Fijian drivers). A short ride across town might cost F$2, a longer trip into a nearby suburb about F$3. Taxis parked in front of luxury hotels will expect much more than this, and it may be worth walking a short distance and flagging one down on the street. Taxis returning to their stand after dropping off other passengers will often pick up people waiting at bus stops and charge the regular bus fare (ask if it's the "returning fare"). All taxis have their home base painted on their bumpers, so it's easy to tell if it's a returning car.

Don't tip your driver; tips are neither expected nor necessary. And don't invite your driver for a drink or become overly familiar with him, as he may abuse your trust. If you're a woman taking a cab alone in the Nadi area, don't let your driver think there is any "hope" for him, or you could have problems (videos often portray Western women as promiscuous, which leads to mistaken expectations).

CAR RENTALS

Rental cars are expensive in Fiji, due in part to high import duties on cars and the 12.5 percent value-added tax, so with public transportation as good as it is here, you should think twice before renting a car. By law, third-party public-liability insurance is compulsory for rental vehicles and is included in the basic rate, but collision damage waiver (CDW) insurance is F$12–22 per day extra. Even with CDW, you're still responsible for a "nonwaivable excess," which can be as high as the first F$500–5,000 in damage to the car! Many cars on the road have no insurance, so you could end up paying for damage, even if you're not responsible for the accident.

Your home driver's license is recognized for your first three months in Fiji, provided it's readable in English. Driving is on the left (as in Britain and Australia), and you should request an automatic if you might be uncomfortable shifting gears with your left hand. Seat belts must be worn in the front seat, and the police are empowered to give roadside breath-analyzer tests. Around Viti Levu, they occasionally employ handheld radar. Speed limits are 50 kph in towns, 80 kph on the highway. Pedestrians have the right-of-way at crosswalks.

Unpaved roads can be very slippery, especially on inclines. Fast-moving vehicles on the gravel roads throw up small stones, which can smash your front window (and you'll have to pay the damages). As you pass oncoming cars, hold your hand against the windshield just in case. When approaching a Fijian village, slow right down, as poorly marked speed bumps usually cross the road. Also beware of narrow bridges, and take care with local motorists, who sometimes stop in the middle of the road, pass on blind curves, and drive at high speeds. Cane-hauling trains have the right of way at level crossings. Driving can be an especially risky business at night. Many of the roads are atrocious (check the spare tire), although the 486-kilometer road around Viti Levu is now fully paved except for a 62-kilometer stretch on the northeast side, which is easily passable if you go slowly. Luckily, there isn't a lot of traffic.

If you plan on using a rental car to explore the rough country roads of Viti Levu's mountainous interior, think twice before announcing your plans to the agency, as they may suddenly decline your business. The rental contracts all contain clauses stating that the insurance coverage is not valid under such conditions. Budget and a few others have 4WD vehicles that may be driven into the interior. You're usually not allowed to take the car to another island by ferry. Tank up on Saturday, as many gas stations are closed on Sunday, and always keep the tank more than half full. If you run out of gas in a rural area, small village stores sometimes sell fuel from drums. At regular gas stations, expect to pay about F$1.21 a liter (or F$4.58 per US gallon).

Several international car rental chains are represented in Fiji, including Avis (www.avis.com.fj), Budget (www.budget.com.fj), Hertz, and Thrifty (www.rosiefiji.com). Local companies like Central Rent-a-Car (www.central-rent-car.com.fj), Dove Rent-a-Car, Kenns Rent-a-Car, Khan's Rental Cars (www.khansrental.com.fj), Quality Rent-a-Car, Satellite Rentals, Sharmas Rental Cars (www.sharmasrental.com), and Tanoa Rent-a-Car are often cheaper, but check around as prices vary. The international companies rent only new cars, while the less expensive local companies may offer secondhand vehicles. If in doubt, check the vehicle carefully before driving off. The international franchises generally provide better support should anything go wrong. Budget, Central, Kenns, and Khan's won't rent to persons under age 25, while most of the others will, as long as you're over 21.

The main companies have offices in the arrivals concourse at Nadi Airport, and three are also at Nausori Airport. Agencies with town offices in Suva include Avis, Budget, Central,

Dove, and Thrifty. In Lautoka, you'll find Central. Avis and Thrifty also have desks at or near many resort hotels on Viti Levu. In northern Fiji, Budget has offices at Labasa and Savusavu and on Taveuni, but rental cars are not available on the other islands.

Both unlimited-kilometer and per-kilometer rates are offered. **Thrifty** (tel. 672-2935), run by Rosie The Travel Service, has unlimited-kilometer prices from F$128/691 daily/weekly, which include CDW (F$700 nonwaivable) and tax. **Budget** (tel. 672-2735) charges F$141/696 for their cheapest mini including insurance (F$500 nonwaivable). **Avis** (tel. 672-2233) begins at F$125/735 including insurance (F$2,000 nonwaivable). Prices with Avis and Budget may be lower if you book ahead from abroad. Though more expensive, the international chains are more likely to deliver what they promise.

The insurance plans used by all of the local companies have high nonwaivable excess fees, which makes renting from them more risky. Also beware of companies like Satellite and Tanoa which add the 12.5 percent tax later (most of the others include it in the quoted price). Of the local companies, **Sharmas Rental Cars** (tel. 672-1908), next to the ANZ Bank in Nadi town, offers unlimited-kilometer rates starting at F$55 (three-day minimum), plus F$12.50 a day insurance. **Khan's Rental Cars** (tel. 672-3506), in office No. 10 upstairs from arrivals at Nadi Airport, charges F$420 a week plus F$10 a day insurance (F$2,000 nonwaivable) for their cheapest car. **Central** (tel. 331-1866, fax 330-5072) in Nadi, Suva, and Lautoka charges F$105/450 a day/week including insurance (F$1,500 nonwaivable) for their cheapest car.

Many of the local car rental agencies offer substantial discounts on their brochure prices for weekly rentals, and you shouldn't hesitate to bargain as there's lots of competition. Some companies advertise low prices with the qualification in fine print that these apply only to rentals of three days or more. Ask how many kilometers are on the odometer, and beware of vehicles above 50,000 kilometers as they may be unreliable. On a per-kilometer basis, you'll only want to use the car in the local area. Most companies charge a F$15–40 delivery fee if you don't return the vehicle to the office where you rented it, although Thrifty allows you to drop the car off at any of their numerous offices around Viti Levu at no additional charge. If you want the cheapest economy sub-compact, reserve ahead. Also be prepared to put up a cash deposit on the car.

If you rent a car, remember those sudden tropical downpours, and don't leave the windows open. Also avoid parking under coconut trees (a falling nut might break the window), and never go off and leave the keys in the ignition.

Airports

Nadi International Airport

Nadi Airport (NAN) is between Lautoka and Nadi, 22 kilometers south of the former and eight kilometers north of the latter. There are frequent buses to these towns until about 2200. To catch a bus to Nadi (F$.65), cross the highway; buses to Lautoka (F$1.30) stop on the airport side of the road. A few express buses drop passengers right outside the international departures hall. A taxi from the airport should be F$7 to downtown Nadi or F$25 to Lautoka.

An ANZ Bank "Currency Express" window in the baggage-claim area opens for all international flights. Two ATMs are there, and another is next to the 24-hour ANZ Bank branch just beyond the customs controls (Visa and MasterCard accepted). These banks deduct a F$5 commission on exchanges but give rates similar to those of other banks in Fiji. A third banking counter (for changing leftover Fiji dollars back into other currencies) is in the departure lounge.

As you come out of customs, uniformed tour guides will ask you where you intend to stay, in order to direct you to a driver from that hotel. Most Nadi hotels offer free transfers (ask), but you ought to change money before going. Agents of other hotels will try to sign you up for the commission they'll earn, so be polite but defensive in dealing with them. The people selling stays at the outer-island backpacker resorts can be persistent. Many of the Yasawas and Mamanuca resorts have offices in the airport concourse in front of you—the upmarket places downstairs, the backpacker resorts upstairs. The office of the Fiji Visitors Bureau (tel. 672-2433) is hidden away in office No. 20, upstairs in a back corner of the arrivals terminal.

Many travel agencies and car rental companies are also located in the arrivals arcade. The rent-a-car companies you'll find here are Avis, Budget, Europcar, Hertz, Khan's, Sharmas, Tanoa, and Thrifty. Most of the international airlines flying into Nadi have offices upstairs from this same arcade (Air Fiji represents Air Vanuatu and Polynesian Airlines).

The airport post office is across the parking lot from the arrivals terminal (ask). If you'd like to use a public telephone at the airport to check reservations, you can buy a phone card at the gift shop near the international departures gate in the departures terminal.

The left-luggage service in the domestic departures area opposite the Sun Air check-in counter is open 24 hours (bicycles or surfboards F$6.15 a day, suitcases and backpacks F$4.10 a day, other smaller luggage F$3.10 a day). Most hotels around Nadi will also store luggage, often for free. A three-dog sniffer unit checks all baggage passing through NAN for drugs.

Several places to eat are in the departures terminal, including an overpriced snack bar (daily 0500–2230) near the domestic check-in counters and the air-conditioned Café International just before the international departures gate. The best coffee is served at the Republic of Cappuccino on the right near the departures gate, and they also offer Internet access at F$.25 per minute. To save money, visit the open-air food market between the guard post at the entrance to the airport compound and the bus stop on the main highway. The women there sell excellent potato rotis for only a dollar.

Duty-free shops (www.dutyfreefiji.com.fj) are found in both the departure lounge and in the arrivals area next to the baggage-claim area. If you're arriving for a prebooked stay at a deluxe resort, grab two bottles of cheap Fiji rum, as drinks at the resort bars are expensive (you can usually get mix at the hotel shops). You can spend leftover Fijian currency on duty-free items just before you leave Fiji (the famous Bounty Rum brewed in Lautoka costs around F$18). For security reasons, souvenir cannibal forks are not sold at the departure lounge shops, so purchase these beforehand and pack them in your suitcase.

A departure tax of F$30 in cash (in Fijian currency) is payable on all international flights, but transit passengers connecting within 12 hours and children under the age of 12 are exempt (no airport tax on domestic flights). The international departure tax is sometimes included in the ticket price, so ask your airline if you've already paid. The international departures gates are upstairs, but the nicest seating area is hidden downstairs in front of the VIP lounges below the escalator. You can stretch out and sleep on the comfortable long padded benches there if you happen to get stuck in the departure lounge overnight (but you can't see the departure gates from here, so beware of missing your flight). Nadi Airport never closes. NAN's 24-hour flight arrival and departure information number is tel. 672-2777 (www.ats.com.fj).

Nausori Airport

Nausori Airport (SUV) is on the plain of the Rewa River delta, 23 kilometers northeast of downtown Suva. Air Fiji runs an aviation academy at the airport. After Hurricane Kina in January 1993, the whole terminal was flooded by Rewa water for several days.

There's no special airport bus, and a taxi direct to/from Suva will run about F$18. You can save money by taking a taxi from the airport only as far as Nausori (four km, F$3), then a local bus to Suva from there (19 km, with services every 10 minutes until 2100 for F$1.40). When going to the airport, catch a local bus from Suva to Nausori, then a taxi to the airport. It's also possible to catch a local bus to Nausori on the highway opposite the airport about every 15 minutes for F$.50.

The ANZ Bank branch opens for most international flights (except those to/from Tuvalu). They charge F$5 commission. Avis and Budget have car rental offices in the terminal, and a lunch counter provides light snacks. You're not allowed to sleep overnight at this airport. The departure tax is F$30 on all international flights, but no tax is levied on domestic flights. The Air Fiji information number at Nausori Airport is tel. 347-8077.

Nadi and the Mamanucas

At 10,531 square kilometers, Viti Levu is the second largest island in the South Pacific, about the same size as the Big Island of Hawaii. This 1,323-meter-high island accounts for more than half of Fiji's land area, and Nadi itself is a main gateway to the entire South Pacific region.

Nadi International Airport faces Nadi Bay in the center of an ancient volcano the west side of which has fallen away. A small airstrip existed at Nadi even before World War II, and after Pearl Harbor the Royal New Zealand Air Force began converting it into a fighter strip. The U.S. military soon arrived to construct a major air base with paved runways for transport aircraft supplying Australia and New Zealand. In the early 1960s, Nadi Airport was expanded to accommodate jet aircraft, and today the largest

jumbo jets can land here. This activity has made Nadi what it is.

The area's predominantly Indo-Fijian population works the cane fields surrounding Nadi. There aren't many sandy, palm-fringed beaches on this western side of Viti Levu—for that you have to go to the nearby Mamanuca and Yasawa groups where a string of sun-drenched resorts soak up vacationers in search of a place to relax. The long gray mainland beaches near Nadi face shallow murky waters devoid of snorkeling possibilities, but okay for windsurfing and water-skiing. Fiji's tropical rainforests are on the other side of Viti Levu, not on this dry side of the island.

Nadi

In recent years, Nadi (NAN-di) has grown into Fiji's third-largest town, with a population of 32,000. The town center's main feature is a long stretch of restaurants and shops with high-pressure sales staffs peddling luxury goods and mass-produced souvenirs. It's easily the most tourist-oriented place in Fiji, yet there's also a surprisingly colorful market, and the road out to the airport is flanked by an excellent choice of places to stay. Nadi is Fiji's "border town," and to experience "real Fijian life" you have to get beyond it. Nearby Lautoka (see the separate Lautoka chapter later in this handbook) is far less foreigner-oriented, though it doesn't have as wide a choice of activities and places to stay.

SIGHTS

To get a glimpse of the "real Fiji," visit **Nadi Market,** off Hospital Road between the bus station and downtown Nadi. It's open daily, except Sunday, but busiest on Saturday when city folk and villagers mix to buy and sell the week's produce. One corner of the market is assigned to *yaqona* (kava) vendors, and it's possible to order a whole bowl of the rooty drink for about a dollar (the locals will gladly help you finish the bowl, so don't worry about having to drink more than you want). Some market stalls also sell a few homemade souvenirs, and there are lots of cheap places to eat in the surrounding streets (observe what others are having and order the same). It's all quite a contrast to the tourist scene along Main Street!

Nadi's only other substantial sight is the **Sri Siva Subrahmaniya Swami Temple,** off Queens Road at the south entrance to town,

Sri Siva Subrahmaniya Swami Temple, Nadi

erected by local Hindus in 1994 after the lease on their former temple property expired. This colorful South Indian-style temple, built by craftspeople flown in from India itself, is the largest and finest of its kind in the South Pacific. Visitors may enter this consecrated place of worship, but shoes must be removed at the entrance, and you must cover bare shoulders or legs with a *sulu.* Smoking and photography are prohibited inside the compound (open daily 0500–2000, admission free).

SPORTS AND RECREATION

Scuba Diving and Snorkeling

Aqua-Trek (tel. 670-2413, fax 670-2412, www.aquatrekdiving.com), on Main Street opposite Prouds in downtown Nadi, is a commercial diving contractor and diving-equipment retailer that doesn't offer diving from Nadi itself. You can get information here on Aqua-Trek's resort dive centers at Mana Island, Matamanoa Island, Robinson Crusoe Island, Pacific Harbor, and Taveuni.

Aqua Blue Dive & Snorkel (Carol Douglas, tel./fax 672-6111, www.aquabluefiji.com) is a new dive operation unconnected to Aqua-Trek, despite the name. Their shop is next to the pool at the Aquarius Fiji Resort on Wailoaloa Beach. Diving from their nine-meter aluminum boat, *Aquarium,* is F$95/135 with one/two tanks, and snorkelers can go for F$30. Aqua Blue's open-water certification course is F$425, a resort course F$110.

Inexpensive diving is offered by **Inner Space Adventures** (Frank Wright, tel./fax 672-3883), opposite Horizon Beach Resort at Wailoaloa Beach. They go out daily at 0900, charging F$80/110 for one/two tanks, equip-

ment and a pickup anywhere around Nadi included. Snorkelers are welcome to tag along at F$30 pp, gear included. Frank's four-day open-water certification course costs F$380—one of the least expensive PADI courses in Fiji. Not only that, but after finishing the course, you'll pay only F$40 a dive for subsequent dives!

Dive Tropex (Eddie Jennings, tel. 675-0944, fax 675-0955, www.divetropex.com), at the Sheraton Royal and Trendwest resorts, offers scuba diving at F$115/180/610 one/two/eight tanks including all gear. When space is available, snorkelers can go along for F$55. A four-day PADI certification course is F$650. For an introductory dive, it's F$170. Several Japanese instructors are on the staff.

Air Snorkel (tel. 672-5909 or 992-5909, www.airsnorkel.com) uses the "hookah system" which allows you to snorkel up to 12 meters below the surface while attached to a tube that supplies air from a device floating on the surface. No experience is required. A half-day reef trip with pickups around Nadi is F$80 pp.

Surfing

Viti Surf Legend (tel. 670-5960, www.vitisurflegend.com), above Victory Tours at the corner of Hospital Road and Main Street in downtown Nadi, organizes three-hour surfing lessons and surf trips to the coast at F$100 for the first person, then F$50 pp to a maximum of five people. Board rentals cost F$35 for a longboard, F$30 for a shortboard, or F$25 for a bodyboard.

NADI AND THE MAMANUCAS

PACIFIC OCEAN

Nadi

NADI AND THE MAMANUCAS

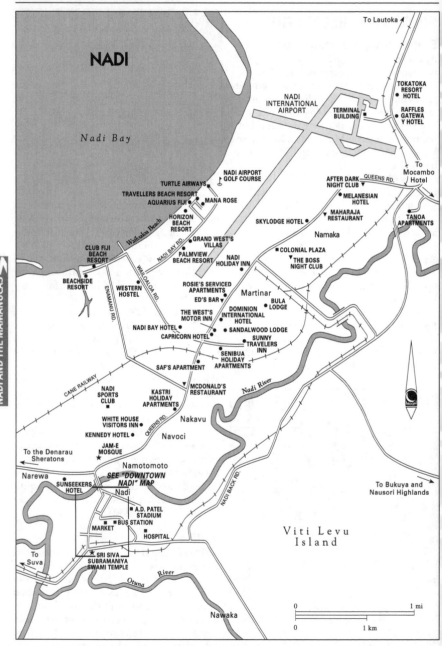

NADI AND THE MAMANUCAS

NADI

Nadi Bay

To Lautoka

NADI
INTERNATIONAL
AIRPORT

TERMINAL
BUILDING

TOKATOKA
RESORT
HOTEL

RAFFLES
GATEWA
Y HOTEL

To
Mocambo
Hotel

NADI AIRPORT
GOLF COURSE

TURTLE AIRWAYS

AFTER DARK
NIGHT CLUB

QUEENS RD.

MELANESIAN
HOTEL

TRAVELLERS BEACH RESORT
AQUARIUS FIJI

MANA ROSE

MAHARAJA
RESTAURANT

TANOA
APARTMENTS

HORIZON
BEACH
RESORT

SKYLODGE HOTEL

Waikalou Beach

Namaka

GRAND WEST'S
VILLAS

CLUB FIJI
BEACH
RESORT

NADI BAY RD.

PALMVIEW
BEACH RESORT

NADI
HOLIDAY INN

COLONIAL PLAZA

THE BOSS
NIGHT CLUB

BEACHSIDE
RESORT

WAILOALOA RD.

ROSIE'S SERVICED
APARTMENTS

Martinar

ENAMANU RD.

WESTERN
HOSTEL

ED'S BAR

BULA
LODGE

THE WEST'S
MOTOR INN

DOMINION
INTERNATIONAL
HOTEL

NADI BAY HOTEL

SANDALWOOD LODGE

CAPRICORN HOTEL

SUNNY
TRAVELERS
INN

SENIBUA
HOLIDAY
APARTMENTS

SAF'S APARTMENT

Nadi River

CANE RAILWAY

NADI
SPORTS
CLUB

KASTRI
HOLIDAY
APARTMENTS

MCDONALD'S
RESTAURANT

Nakavu

WHITE HOUSE
VISITORS INN

KENNEDY HOTEL

Navoci

QUEENS RD.

JAM-E
MOSQUE

To the Denarau
Sheratons

Namotomoto

**SEE "DOWNTOWN
NADI" MAP**

Narewa

SUNSEEKERS
HOTEL

Nadi

A.D. PATEL
STADIUM

NADI BACK RD.

To Bukuya and
Nausori Highlands

BUS STATION

MARKET

HOSPITAL

*Viti Levu
Island*

To
Suva

SRI SIVA
SUBRAMANIYA
SWAMI TEMPLE

Otuna *River*

Nawaka

0   1 mi

0   1 km

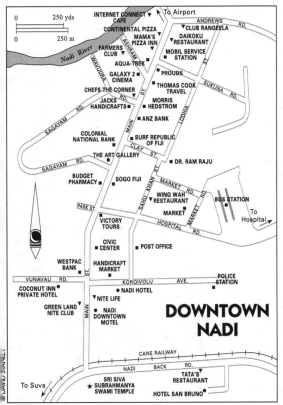

staying at one of the Sheratons or F$100 for other mortals. Golfers are not allowed to walk around the course, but a shared electric cart is included. Clubs can be rented at F$30 a set. Call ahead for a starting time, and be aware of the dress code: collared shirt and dress shorts for men, smart casual for women, and golf shoes for all (no jeans, bathing suits, or metal spiked shoes). Ten tennis courts (four floodlit) are available here at F$15/20 day/night per hour. Rackets and shoes can be rented at F$8 each, and a can of balls is F$5.

Other Recreation

Skydive Fiji (tel. 672-1415, fax 672-1451, www.skydivefiji.com.fj) offers tandem skydiving jumps from their base at Plantation Island Resort on Malololailai. It's F$385 pp including catamaran transfers from Nadi to Malololailai, plus F$175 for photos and videos, if desired.

Babba's Horse-Riding (tel. 672-4449 or 670-3652) at Wailoaloa Beach offers one-hour beach rides at F$20, 1.5 hours cross-country at F$25, or a two-hour combination at F$30. Longer rides can be arranged. Ask for Baba at Travelers Beach Resort.

See rugby or soccer on Saturdays at the A. D. Patel Stadium, near Nadi Bus Station. You might also see soccer on Sundays.

ACCOMMODATIONS

Most of the hotels offer free transport from the airport, which is lucky because only a couple are within walking distance of the terminal itself. In front of you as you leave customs, you'll see a group of people representing the hotels. If you know which hotel you want, tell them the name, and if a driver from that hotel is present, you should get a free ride (ask). (Be aware that the

Golf

The 18-hole, par-70 **Nadi Airport Golf Club** (tel. 672-2148) is pleasantly situated between the airport runways and the sea at Wailoaloa Beach. Greens fees are F$15, plus F$20 for clubs and F$10 for a caddy. There's a bar and billiard table in the clubhouse (tourists are welcome). The course is busy with local players on Saturday but quiet during the week.

The 18-hole, par-72 course at the **Denarau Golf & Racquet Club** (tel. 675-9710 or 675-9711, fax 675-0484) opposite the Sheratons was designed by Eiichi Motohashi. This fabulous course features bunkers shaped like a marlin, crab, starfish, and octopus, and water shots across all four par-three holes (the average golfer loses four balls per round). Greens fees are F$95 for those road from the north side of Nadi town across the bridge to the Sunseekers, White House, and Kennedy hotels, and the isolated roads around Wailoaloa Beach, may be unsafe, and a bus or taxi is recommended in those areas after dark, especially if you'll be carrying a backpack.)

Most repeat visitors know that many Nadi hotels, including the Raffles Gateway, Rosie's Serviced Apartments, Sandalwood Lodge, and the West's Motor Inn, regularly discount their official "rack rates" for walk-in bookings, and you could pay considerably less than the full undiscounted prices quoted herein (in this book, we provide the published rates). Rosie The Travel Service at the airport sometimes arranges specials at the Dominion International and other hotels.

Under US$25

There are three budget choices in the downtown area, two with confusingly similar names but under separate management. The seedy **Nadi Downtown Motel** (tel. 670-0600, fax 670-1541, www.pacificvalley.com.fj), also known as the "Backpackers Inn," occupies the top floor of an office building opposite the BP service station in the center of Nadi. Its main attraction is the price: F$25/30 single/double with fan, F$35/40 with air-conditioning, both with private bath. The five-bed dormitory is F$8 pp, and basic rooms with shared bath are F$20. This place looks sleazy from the outside, but some of the rooms upstairs are okay. The adjacent Nite Life Night Club projects a steady disco beat toward the north side of the motel well into the morning. PVV Tours below the motel arranges transport to Nananu-i-Ra Island at F$25/35/45 pp for four/three/two people.

Around the corner on Koroivolu Street is the two-story, 31-room **Nadi Hotel** (tel. 670-0000, fax 670-0280, www.nadi-hotel.com). Spacious rooms with private bath begin at F$48 twin standard with fan, F$58 superior with air-conditioning, or F$15 pp in a basic 12-bed dorm. Deluxe rooms with fridge are F$68 single/double. Baggage storage is F$1. The neat courtyard with a swimming pool out back can make this a pleasant, convenient place to stay, provided there aren't a lot of rowdy local guests in the house.

The standard and deluxe rooms are subjected to the same nightclub noise, so ask for a superior room in the block at the back beyond the pool. The hotel restaurant is okay for breakfast, but skip the dinner.

The two-story **Coconut Inn Private Hotel** (37 Vunavau St.; tel. 670-1169, fax 670-0616, coconutinn2000@yahoo.com) is around the corner from the Westpac Bank. The 22 upstairs rooms with private bath begin at F$30/40 single/double (plus F$10 for air-conditioning), and downstairs is an F$11 dorm (three beds). Beware of dirty rooms without windows.

The two-story **Hotel San Bruno** (tel. 670-0444, fax 670-3067, sanbruno@connect.com.fj) is on Nadi Back Road east of the Sri Siva Subrahmaniya Swami Temple. The 13 fan-cooled rooms are F$40/50 single/double, while the seven with air-conditioning are F$50/60. The one/two-bedroom family "villas" are F$70/100 each. Dormitory accommodations are F$12 pp. A miniature swimming pool is in front of the billiard room, but the San Bruno doesn't have much atmosphere.

On Narewa Road at the north edge of Nadi town is the **Sunseekers Hotel** (tel. 670-1655). The 24 rooms here are F$33/38 single/double with fan but shared bath, F$39/44 with air-conditioning and private bath, or F$9 for a bunk in the six or 10-bed dorms. There's a bar on the large deck out back, which overlooks the swimming pool (often dry) and surrounding countryside. Despite the sign, this is not an approved Hostelling International associate, but it's quite popular among backpackers. Airport pickups are free, but to return to the airport you must take a taxi (F$7).

The two-story **White House Visitors Inn** (40 Kennedy Ave.; tel. 670-0022, fax 670-2822), is behind Dainty Restaurant just off Queens Road, a 10-minute walk north of central Nadi. The 12 fan-equipped rooms are F$30 double with shared bath, F$33/44 single/double with private bath, or F$11 pp in the dorm. Rooms with air-conditioning cost F$5.50 extra. The beds are comfortable, and a weight-watchers' toast-and-coffee breakfast is included in the price. You can cook your own meals in the communal kitchen, and there's a tiny grocery store across the street. You'll probably find the small swimming pool too dirty to use. Baggage storage is F$1 per day (but only if you make your outer-island bookings through them). Houseguests get a 15 percent discount at the adjacent Dainty Chinese Restaurant.

Half a block up Kennedy Avenue from the White House is the three-story **Kennedy Hotel** (tel. 670-2360, fax 670-2218). The 16 air-conditioned rooms with private bath, TV, and coffee-making facilities are F$60 single or double without fridge, F$70 with fridge, tax included. Deluxe two-bedroom apartments with cooking facilities are F$109. Rooms with shared bath are F$25. Beds in the four fan-cooled, 10-bed dormitory blocks cost F$10 pp, or F$15 for a bed in the four-bed air-conditioned dorm. The Kennedy is quite popular but the cheaper rooms are small and shabby, so have a look before committing yourself. A plus are the spacious grounds with a large swimming pool, and there's a large restaurant/bar on the premises.

The following listings are arranged by location along Queens Road from the airport into town. The **Kon Tiki Private Hotel** (tel. 672-2836) is in a quiet if isolated location, a 15-minute walk inland from Queens Road past the Fiji Mocambo Hotel (Votualevu bus). The 18 rooms go for F$25/35 single/double with private bath and fan, F$45 with air-conditioning, F$11 pp dormitory (four beds), plus tax. Avoid the noisy rooms near the television and bar. Camping is F$8 pp. Breakfast is included with the rooms, and you can use their kitchen. Several small stores are nearby. There's a nice swimming pool in the back yard. Call for a free airport pickup (taxi F$4).

The **Melanesian Hotel** (Hexagon Group of Hotels, tel. 672-2438, fax 672-0425, melnesian hotl@connect.com.fj), at Namaka, has two wings separated by a swimming pool, bar, and restaurant. The 16 rooms with bath in the old wing begin at F$45/50 single/double, or F$55/60 with air-conditioning. Six five-bed dorms (F$18 pp) are also available. The new **Grand Melanesian Apartment Hotel** wing, which is right on the highway, has 22 deluxe air-conditioned rooms with fridge and TV at F$78 for up to three people.

The single-story **Nadi Holiday Inn** (tel. 672-5076, www.pacificvalley.com.fj), on Queens road

just north of Martintar, has a dubious reputation (no connection with the famous Holiday Inn chain). Rooms with private facilities are F$35 single or double (plus F$10 for air-conditioning). A bar is on the premises, and there's a lot of in/out action late at night.

Across the street from the Shell service station in Martintar and above the Bounty Restaurant is **Mountainview Apartments** (tel. 672-1880, fax 672-1800) with six fan-cooled rooms with bath at F$35/40 single/double. The two air-conditioned rooms are F$45/50. It's also questionable and is overpriced to boot.

The **Hotel Martintar** (22 Kennedy Street; tel. 651-1777, fax 672-0807, hotelmartin tar@connect.com.fj), around the corner from Ed's Bar in Martintar, has three rooms with bath and fan at F$44 single or double, four air-conditioned rooms at F$55, and an air-conditioned two-bedroom flat at F$88. Fully renovated in 2002, it's a good value at these prices.

The **Sunview Motel & Hostel** (tel. 672-4994) is 300 meters down Gray Road behind the Bounty Restaurant. The seven rooms in their new two-story building are F$30/35 single/double, or F$15 pp in a six-bed dorm, with toast, coffee, and juice in the morning included. Cooking facilities are available, and it's clean, quiet, and friendly.

A new place to stay in Martintar is **Senibua Holiday Apts** (tel. 672-2574), near Wearsmart Textiles on Northern Press Road. The three units with double bed are F$40, while the four with one double and one single are F$60. All units are in a long single-story block and have air-conditioning and cooking facilities.

The 14-room **Sunny Travelers Inn** (67 Northern Press Rd.; tel. 672-5883) is F$28 single or double with shared bath, F$35 with private bath, or F$10 in the five-bed dorm. Self-contained apartments with cooking facilities are F$45. It's a little noisy from the nocturnal comings and goings of certain guests and cannot be recommended.

Three-story **Saf's Apartment** (tel. 672-3988), on Queens Road just south of Martintar, has 17 rooms with bath at F$35/45 with fan/air-conditioned single or double. It's also pretty sleazy and not suitable for respectable travelers.

Kastri Holiday Apartment (tel. 672-5056), on Queens Road not far from McDonald's, only opened in 2003. The 14 air-conditioned rooms with fridge, basic cooking facilities, and bathroom are F$35 single or double. Noise levels in this prefabricated building would depend on who else is staying there.

Wailoaloa Beach (also known as New Town Beach) is for backpackers what Denarau Island is for tourists on upscale package tours. A half dozen inexpensive places to stay are near the seaplane base and golf club on the opposite side of the airport runway from the main highway, a three-kilometer hike from the Nadi Bay Hotel. Ask for their free shuttle buses at the airport or take a taxi (F$6 from the airport, or F$3 from the junction at Martintar). The Shahabud Transport bus (F$.55) to Wailoaloa New Town leaves Nadi Bus Station Monday to Saturday at 0615, 0815, 1115, 1510, and 1700 (no service on Sunday). It leaves the beach to return to town about 20 minutes after these times.

Wailoaloa is probably your best bet on the weekend, and sporting types can play a round of golf on the public course or go jogging along the beach (the swimming in the knee-deep, murky water is poor). Inner Space Adventures and Aqua Blue Dive & Snorkel are here, and horseback riding is also on offer. Remain aware of your surroundings if you stroll far down the lonely beach, as assaults on tourists have occurred.

On your way to the beach, you'll pass the **Western Hostel** (tel. 672-4440) on Wailoaloa Road. Rooms with shared bath here are F$45 single or double, or F$12 pp in the nine-bed dorm, continental breakfast included. The rooms are overpriced, although the dorm is okay. This hostel provides communal cooking, laundry, and TV facilities. It's a little far from everything, and few people stay here.

The **Horizon Beach Resort** (10 Wasawasa Rd.; tel. 672-2832, fax 672-0662, www.horizonbeachfiji.com), is a large wooden two-story building just across a field from the beach. The 14 rooms with bath begin at F$35/40 single/double with fan, F$55/70 with air-conditioning. Horizon's 10-bed dormitory is F$10 pp (F$18 pp with air-conditioning) including a cup of tea and a piece of toast for breakfast. No cooking facilities are provided, but there's a medium-priced restaurant/bar and a tiny swimming pool. To use the washer/drier is F$10 a full load.

The **Tropic of Capricorn Backpackers Retreat** (11 Wasawasa Rd.; tel. 672-3089, fax 672-3050, chopkins@bigpond.net.au), right next to Horizon Beach Resort, faces the sea. There's a 12-bed dorm at F$15 pp including breakfast, one four-bed room next to the swimming pool at F$60, and five self-catering rooms upstairs at F$30/50 single/double. This smart new place run by Mama Selena opened in 2001.

A hundred meters inland from Horizon is the friendly two-story **New Town Beach Motel** (5 Wasawasa Rd.; tel. 672-3339 or 672-3420, fax 672-0087). The seven clean rooms with fan are F$39 single or double, $50 triple (or F$14 pp in the five-bed dorm), plus tax. There's no cooking, but a huge dinner can be ordered at F$8. A nice protected swimming pool is in the back yard.

Edgewater Backpackers Accommodation (33 Wasawasa Rd.; tel. 672-5868, edgewater@connect.com.fj), on the opposite side of Inner Space Adventures from Horizon, is an older wooden building with an eight-bed dorm at F$12 pp, one single at F$25, and a family room for F$40. Camping space in their fenced yard is F$6 pp—one of the only places around Nadi where you can camp!

A few minutes' walk north along the beach from the Aquarius Fiji Resort is **Travelers Beach Resort** (tel. 672-3322, fax 672-0026, beachvilla @connect.com.fj). The 12 fan-cooled standard rooms with private bath are F$33/40 single/double, the eight air-conditioned rooms F$40/55, the two air-conditioned beachfront rooms F$70 single or double, and the 13 villas with kitchenette F$66/77 fan/air-conditioned double (or F$99 for up to four). Four four-bed dorms are available at F$11 pp. The villas are tightly packed in a compound a block back from the beach. There's an overpriced restaurant/bar and a swimming pool, but many of the other facilities listed in their brochure seem to have vanished. Somehow this place has an unpleasant air, and you're better off staying elsewhere.

Opposite the Travelers Beach Resort villas is a large modern house called **Mana Rose Apartments** (tel. 672-3333, fax 672-0552). Ratu Kini Bokoniqiwa uses this place to accommodate backpackers on their way to his hostel on Mana Island. The three six-bed air-conditioned dorms are F$15 pp including breakfast, private rooms F$40/45 single/double, and there's a plush lounge downstairs. If you're not on your way to Mana, you'll probably find the transient atmosphere unappealing.

US$25–50

The medium-priced selections that follow are highly competitive and most offer walk-in specials that reduce the quoted rack rates by a third. **Rosie's Deluxe Serviced Apartments** (tel. 672-2755, fax 672-2607, www.rosiefiji.com), in Martintar near Ed's Bar, offers studio apartments accommodating four at F$45/69 walk-in/rack rate, one-bedrooms for up to five at F$68/92, and two-bedrooms for up to eight at F$80/123. All eight air-conditioned units have cooking facilities, fridge, and private balcony. You may use the communal washer and drier for free. Martintar Bakery next door sells bread, muffins, and newspapers. Rosie's is used mostly by people in transit, and there's no swimming pool. The Rosie The Travel Service office at the airport books this place and arranges free airport transfers in both directions at any time of night or day.

Bula Lodge (49 McElrath Cres.; Karl Hofman, tel. 672-5909, info@bulalodge.com), off Gray Road behind the Bounty Restaurant in Martintar (ask directions), has four double rooms with shared bath at F$50 pp. This upscale homestay has a lounge where you can listen to music in the evening or chat with other visiting couples. It's not your usual backpacker hangout.

Sandalwood Lodge (Ana and John Birch, tel. 672-2044, fax 672-0103, sandalwood@connect.com.fj), 250 meters inland on Ragg Street behind the Dominion International Hotel, has 33 air-conditioned rooms with bath, Sky TV, fridge, and cooking facilities at F$66/74/82 single/double/triple, plus tax. Two of the two-story blocks were built in 1992, and a third was added in 2001 (all rooms face the swimming pool). Sandalwood caters to those in search of a quiet, safe, thoroughly respectable place to stay.

The West's Motor Inn (tel. 672-0044, fax 672-0071), also near the Dominion International, is another good choice. The 62 air-conditioned rooms with private bath and fridge begin at F$60 single or double standard (or F$75 for a larger deluxe room). The name really doesn't do justice to this pleasant two-story resort hotel with its courtyard swimming pool, piano bar, restaurant, conference room, secretarial services, and United Touring Company desk. The West's Motor Inn is considered Nadi's most gay-friendly hotel, although you probably wouldn't have noticed if you weren't told. It's owned by Hexagon Hotels.

The **Capricorn International Hotel** (tel. 672-0088, fax 672-0522, www.capricorn-hotels-fiji.com), beside The West's Motor Inn, consists of two-story blocks surrounding a swimming pool. The 62 small air-conditioned rooms with fridge begin at F$85 single or double. The 17-bed dorm here is F$20 pp. Cooking facilities are not provided, but there's a restaurant/bar on the premises. UTC has a tour desk here.

Next door to the Capricorn is **Traveler's Holiday Apartments** (tel. 672-4675), a new three-story hotel containing 14 rooms with bath, starting at F$50 double (F$10 extra for air-conditioning). Beware of a misleading sign outside that advertises supercheap rooms which have yet to be built!

A few hundred meters down Wailoaloa Road off the main highway is the **Nadi Bay Hotel** (tel. 672-3599, fax 672-0092, www.fijinadibayhotel.com), a two-story concrete edifice enclosing a swimming pool. The 25 rooms are F$48/56 single/double with fan, F$72/88 with private bath and air-conditioning. An air-conditioned apartment with cooking facilities is F$85/110 single/double. Beds in the 10/four-bed dorms are F$18/22 pp. Other features include a congenial bar and an inexpensive restaurant. Breakfast is included with the rooms but not in the dorm. The Nadi Bay is run by an old Fiji hand named Errol Fifer, who built upscale resorts on Mana and Malolo islands—an interesting person to meet. The Nadi Bay Hotel is something of a staging point for young tourists on "Feejee Experience" packages or headed for the low-budget beach resorts in the Yasawas. It's the sort of place where you're likely to see bored backpackers lounging by the pool reading Lonely Planet, or posing in the restaurant and bar. The airport flight path passes right above the Nadi Bay.

Right on Wailoaloa Beach between the Tropic of Capricorn Backpackers Retreat and Travelers Beach Resort is the new **Aquarius Fiji Resort** (Louise and Terry Buckley, tel. 672-6000, tblpfiji@connect.com.fj). This large mansion contains four garden-view rooms at F$75 double, and four oceanview rooms at F$85. Third persons pay F$23. Otherwise there are two two-bed dorms at F$26 pp, plus six- and 10-bed dorms at F$23 pp. Aquarius has a swimming pool right on the beach with the Aqua Blue dive shop to one side. It's a trendy place to stay at the moment.

On Wailoaloa Beach, a kilometer southwest of the places near the golf course, is **Club Fiji Beach Resort** (tel. 670-2189, fax 672-2324, www.clubfiji-resort.com). It's three kilometers off Queens Road from McDonald's (F$3 one way by taxi). The 24 thatched duplex bungalows, all with veranda, private bath, solar hot water, and fridge, are priced according to location: F$68 single or double for a garden unit, F$90 ocean view, or F$124 on the beach. The eight air-conditioned so-called "beachfront villas" in a two-story building are strangely overpriced at F$152/167 double/triple. One duplex has been converted into a pair of 12-bunk dormitories at F$14 pp. The atmosphere is friendly and relaxed, and you'll meet other travelers at the bar. Tea- and coffee-making facilities are provided, but there's no cooking, and main plates at the Club's restaurant are overpriced at F$15–24. Special evening events include the *lovo* on Thursday (F$25) and the beach barbecue on Sunday night (F$15–22). Horseback riding is F$20 an hour, the Hobie cat is F$40 an hour, and windsurfing and paddle boats are complimentary. The day tour to Natadola Beach costs F$45 with lunch. At low tide, the beach resembles a tidal flat, but there's a small, clean swimming pool, and the location is lovely.

Also very good is the **Beachside Resort** (tel. 670-3488, fax 670-3688, www.beachsideresort fiji.com), next to Club Fiji at Wailoaloa. The 15 clean air-conditioned rooms in the main building are F$70/90 double or triple downstairs/upstairs. The rooms have a fridge and tea/coffee, but no cooking facilities. Adjacent to the main building are two smaller studios at F$45 double and four mountainview rooms with fan at F$55 single or double. These units are duplexes with connecting doors—convenient for families and small groups. There's an attractive dining room that serves breakfast at F$12.50, while the blackboard menu lists dinner dishes priced F$15–18. Despite the name, the Beachside isn't right on the beach, although it does have a pleasant swimming pool.

US$50–100

Once again, the listings that follow are arranged starting from the airport and heading south toward town. The **Tokatoka Resort Hotel** (Hexagon Group of Hotels, tel. 672-0222, fax 672-0400, www.tokatoka.com.fj), a short walk north on Queens Road from the airport terminal, caters to families with young children by offering 116 air-conditioned villas and rooms with cooking facilities, mini-fridge, and video beginning at F$144/159 single/double. Eight rooms for guests with disabilities are available. The restaurant serves a buffet dinner Sunday (F$20) and a buffet lunch Saturday and Sunday (F$15). Happy hour by the swimming pool is from 1700–1900 daily. The large designer swimming pool with a water slide is usually full of noisy kids. A Jack's Handicrafts outlet is on the premises.

The two-story, colonial-style **Raffles Gateway Hotel** (tel. 672-2444, fax 672-0620, www.rafflesgateway.com), just across the highway from the airport, is within easy walking distance of the terminal. Its 92 air-conditioned rooms are officially F$117 single or double (though 22 standard rooms without TVs are offered at a discount). The Gateway's poolside bar is worth checking out if you're stuck at the airport waiting for a flight. A Rosie Travel desk is here.

People on brief prepaid stopovers in Fiji are often accommodated at one of three hotels off Votualevu Road, a couple of kilometers inland from the airport (take a taxi). The closest to the terminal is **Tanoa Apartments** (tel. 672-3685, fax

672-1193, www.tanoahotels.com), on a hilltop overlooking the surrounding countryside. The 20 self-catering apartments begin at F$169 (weekly and monthly rates available). Local rate reductions are possible for walk-in bookings. Facilities include a swimming pool, tennis courts, hot tub, and sauna. First opened in 1965, this property was the forerunner of today's locally-owned Tanoa hotel chain.

A few hundred meters inland from Tanoa Apartments is the Malaysian-owned **Fiji Mocambo Hotel** (tel. 672-2000, fax 672-0324, www.shangri-la.com), a sprawling two-story hotel with mountain views from the spacious grounds on Namaka Hill. The 127 air-conditioned rooms with patio or balcony and fridge begin at F$180/203 single/double including breakfast. It's overpriced unless you get a discount. A swimming pool is available, and there's a par-27, nine-hole executive golf course on the adjacent slope (free/F$11 for guests/non-guests). Lots of in-house entertainment is offered, including a *meke* on Mondays. A live band plays in the Marau Lounge Friday and Saturday from 2030. A Rosie Travel desk is here.

Across the street from the Fiji Mocambo is the two-story **Tanoa International Hotel** (tel. 672-0277, fax 672-0191, www.tanoahotels.com), formerly the Nadi Travelodge Hotel. It's now the flagship of the Tanoa hotel chain, owned by local businessman Yanktesh Permal Reddy. The 133 superior air-conditioned rooms with fridge start at F$190 single or double and children under 16 may stay free. Walk-in local rate discounts are possible. They also have a half-price day-use rate, which gives you a room from noon until midnight if you're leaving in the middle of the night (airport transfers are free). A swimming pool, fitness center, floodlit tennis courts, and a UTC tour desk are on the premises. The Tanoa International is a cut above the Fiji Mocambo, but no nonhotel shops or restaurants are within walking distance of either hotel.

Several kilometers southwest of the airport on Queens Road is the **Skylodge Hotel** (tel. 672-2200, fax 672-4330, www.tanoahotels.com), which was constructed in the early 1960s while Nadi Airport was being expanded to take jet aircraft. Airline crews on layovers originally stayed here, and business travelers still make up 50 percent of the clientele. The 53 air-conditioned units begin at F$121 single or double; children under 16 are free, provided the bed configurations aren't changed. It's better to pay F$11 more here and get a room with cooking facilities in one of the four-unit clusters well-spaced among the greenery, rather than a smaller room in the main building or near the busy highway. If you're catching a flight in the middle of the night, there's a F$55 "day use" rate valid noon–2000. The rooms are fine but avoid the restaurant. A swimming pool and UTC tour desk are on the grounds. Airport transfers are free.

The **Dominion International Hotel** (tel. 672-2255, fax 672-0187, www.dominion-international.com), at Martintar on Queens Road halfway between the airport and town, is one of Nadi's nicest large hotels. This appealing three-story building was built in 1973, and they've done their best to keep the place up. The 85 air-conditioned rooms with balcony or terrace are F$125/130/140 single/double/triple, plus F$22 extra if you want a "deluxe" with a TV and a bathtub instead of a shower. The 40 percent discount late check-out rate allows you to keep your room until 2200. If you stay six nights, the seventh is free. Lots of well-shaded tables and chairs surround the swimming pool, and the nearby hotel bar has a happy hour 1700–1900 daily. On Saturday night you'll be treated to a *meke* (F$22). There's a Rosie Travel desk at the Dominion, a barber shop/beauty salon, and a taxi stand. The hotel bottle shop facing the highway is open Monday–Friday 1100–2100, Saturday 1100–1400 and 1600–2100, should you wish to stock your fridge. The tennis court is free for guests (day use only).

Grand West's Villas (tel. 672-4833, fax 672-5015, grandwestvillas@connect.com.fj), near Wailoaloa Beach between Nadi Bay Road and the airport runway, was built by the Hexagon Group of Hotels in 2001. The 20 luxurious, two-story townhouses in several long blocks are F$125/145 double/triple. These spacious, self-catering apartments are good value for the money and a small grocery store is on the premises, but unfortunately the location is poor as the beach is some distance away. The new **Palmview Beach Resort** next door shares the same disadvantage.

Ocean's Edge (Penny and Steve Ellis, tel. 651-1560, fax 670-7222, www.oceansedge.org) is beside the river at Fantasy Estates, just beyond the Beachside Resort at Wailoaloa. The four duplex rooms are F$99 single or double, continental breakfast included. Lunch and dinner can be ordered at around F$10 for lunch or F$12–20 for dinner mains. What is special here is the fitness and health spa with a studio providing skin and body treatments beginning at F$9.50 (F$97 for the three-hour pamper package). Steam and sauna rooms, a 20-meter exercise pool, and a gym are on the premises.

US$150 and up

Nadi's big transnational resorts, the Sheraton Royal and the Sheraton Fiji, are on Denarau Island (www.denarau.com) opposite Yakuilau Island, seven kilometers west of the bridge on the north side of Nadi town. It's a 15-minute drive from the airport. The murky waters lapping the gray sands of Sheraton shores aren't the best for swimming, but two pontoons have been anchored in deeper water. There'd be no point in snorkeling here, and windsurfing, water-skiing, and sailing are better choices as activities. If you came to Fiji mainly for the beach, you should skip Denarau entirely and head for a resort in the Mamanuca Islands.

Sidestepping the Waikiki syndrome, neither Sheraton is taller than the surrounding palms, though the manicured affluence has a dull Hawaiian neighbor-island feel. In 1993, a F$15-million championship golf course opened on the site of a former mangrove swamp adjacent to the resort, and in 1996, ITT-Sheraton bought both resorts from Japanese interests that had controlled them since 1988. Two-thirds of the hotel staff and all of the taxi drivers based here belong to the landowning clan. Plans for additional resort development in this area by Hilton and Accor/Novotel were put on hold after the May 2000 coup but are now being revived.

Almost all of the tourists staying at the Denarau resorts arrive on package tours, and they pay less than the rack rates quoted below. These hotels are rather isolated, and the hotel restaurants are pricey, so you should take the meal package if you intend to spend most of your time here. Bring insect repellent, unless you want to be on the menu yourself, and have something warm to wear in your room, as the air-conditioning is strong enough to give you pneumonia in this climate.

The **Sheraton Royal Denarau Resort** (tel. 675-0000, fax 675-0259, www.sheraton.com /denarauresort) opened in 1975 as The Regent of Fiji. This sprawling series of two-story clusters with traditional Fijian touches contains 273 spacious rooms (from F$415 single or double, plus tax and including breakfast) between the golf course and beach. Facilities include an impressive lobby with shops to one side, a thatched pool bar you can swim right up to, and 10 floodlit tennis courts.

The Sheraton Royal's neighbor to the south, the modern-style **Sheraton Fiji Resort** (tel. 675-0777, fax 675-0818, www.sheraton.com/fiji), has 292 rooms that begin at F$575 single or double, plus tax but including a buffet breakfast and nonmotorized sports. For the presidential suite it's F$1,145. This US$60-million, two-story hotel opened in 1987, complete with a 16-shop arcade and an 800-seat ballroom. Outstanding among the hotel boutiques is Michoutouchkine Creations with hand-decorated clothing by two of the Pacific's most famous artists, and the Pacific Art Shop (www.pacific art.com.fj) with local paintings. Avis Rent-a-Car, United Touring Company, and the Westpac Bank all have counters at the Sheraton Fiji.

Between the two Sheratons and opposite the golf club is a cluster of two-story buildings called the **Sheraton Denarau Villas** (tel. 675-0777, fax 675-0818, www.sheraton.com/denarauvil las), which opened in 1999. The 82 condos with one, two, or three bedrooms have kitchenettes, washer/drier, TV, and lounge, starting at F$781 plus tax for a family of two adults and two children, breakfast included. The swimming pool and bar face the beach.

Another new development, a bit south of the Sheraton Fiji Resort, is the **Trendwest Resort** (tel.

675-0442, fax 675-0441, www.trendwest.com). It features as series of two- and three-story blocks between the reception and a large beachside pool (which compensates for the lousy beach). Most of the 138 spacious self-catering apartments in this "vacation ownership resort" have been sold to individual buyers under a timeshare arrangement with WorldMark. All stays are prebooked and walk-in guests are not accepted. The Seafront Restaurant near the pool is part of the Chefs chain. There's a Rosie Travel desk at the reception. Dive Tropex runs the scuba concession here.

A local bus marked "Westbus" operates between Nadi and the Sheratons about every hour (F$.55). It leaves Nadi Bus Station Monday–Saturday at 0700, 0800, 0830, 0930, 1015, 1100, 1215, 1300, 1430, 1545, 1700, and 1800, Sunday at 0700, 0830, 0930, 1300, 1430, and 1700. For the departure times from the Sheratons, add about 25 minutes to these times (which could change). Resort receptionists sometimes pretend not to know about this bus.

The taxis parked in front of the hotels ask a firm F$10 to/from Nadi town or F$22 to the airport. Walk down the road a short distance and stop any returning taxi headed for Nadi—most will take you for F$3. If your travel agent booked you into any of these resorts, you'll be wrapped in North American security and sheltered from the real Fiji.

FOOD
Downtown
Several places along Sahu Khan Street near the market serve a good cheap breakfast of coffee and egg sandwiches. The **Wing Wah Restaurant** is typical of these.

A real find if you like Indian food is **Tata's Restaurant** (tel. 670-0502; weekdays 0900–2100, Sat. 0900–1700), on Nadi Back Road between the Siva Temple and the Hotel San Bruno. The vegetable curries are great value at F$3, and other inexpensive dishes are listed on a blackboard. Though this place is surrounded by automotive workshops, the seating is pleasantly outside on a terrace.

papaya, pineapples, and root vegetables for sale at a Nadi street market

Chopsticks Restaurant (tel. 670-0178; daily 0900–1500, 1800–2200), upstairs from the Bank of Baroda on Main Street, offers a large selection of Chinese dishes, curries, and seafood at excellent prices (entrées F$6–11). A second Chopsticks location (tel. 672-1788) is near Morris Hedstrom at Namaka toward the airport. Plenty of local Asians eat here—a recommendation.

Package tour buses often park in front of **Chefs The Corner** (Mon.–Sat. 0900–2130), at Sagayam Road and Main Street opposite Morris Hedstrom. This rather expensive self-service restaurant (entrées F$6–7) does have some of the best-selling ice cream in town (F$2–4). Just down Sangayam Road are **Chefs The Edge** (Mon.–Sat. 0900–2200) and **Chefs The Restaurant** (tel. 670-3131; Mon–Sat. 1100–1400, 1800–2200, www.chefs .com.fj), both run by former Sheraton chef Eugene Gomes (and owned by Jack's Handicrafts). At dinner the seafood and meat entrées average F$38, or you can order something from the grill. It's international dining at its finest.

Two pizza places are opposite the Mobil service station on Main Street at the north end of

Nadi town. **Mama's Pizza Inn** (tel. 670-0221; daily 1000–2300) serves pizzas at F$6–23. Mama's has a second location in Colonial Plaza halfway out toward the airport. A better bet is **Continental Cakes & Pizza** (tel. 670-3595; daily 0900 until late), just down from Mama's, which has three sizes of pizza from F$7–22, plus deli rolls for F$3.50, and delicious cakes for F$2.50 and up. Their coffee is about the best in town, and the clean washrooms are a relief. The German owner Dietmar Luecke makes sure everything is just right.

The **Daikoku Japanese Restaurant** (tel. 670-3622; Mon.–Sat. 1130–1400, 1800–2200, Sun. 1800–2100), facing the bridge at the north end of Nadi, is the place to splurge on *teppan-yaki* dishes (F$20–48) cooked right at your table. Ask for the special seafood sauce.

Denarau Marina

Cardo's Steakhouse & Bar (tel. 675-0900; daily 1000–2300), at the Denarau Marina, offers charbroiled steaks of 250, 300, or 400 grams for F$19–35. Other meals from prawns to pizza cost F$9–29. You'll have a good view of Nadi's bustling tourist port from their terrace. It's an okay place to eat out if you're staying at the Sheratons, a 15-minute walk away.

Toward the Airport

Poon's Restaurant (tel. 672-5396), also called the Jun Sang Seafood Restaurant, beside a textile factory on Northern Press Road just east off Queens Road in Martintar, offers filling meals at reasonable prices. Ordinary Chinese dishes are F$3–10, special Chinese dishes F$7–14, and European dishes F$5–11. Complete Cantonese meals are F$35/62 for two/four people.

RJ's for Ribs (Hans Kehrli, tel. 672-2900; Tues.–Sun. 1800–2300), in the Millennium Center opposite the Dominion International Hotel, has a sister establishment in Beverly Hills, California. Pork barbecue ribs run F$19, cordon bleu F$27, and a skewer of garlic prawns F$29 (all meals include the salad bar). The Skytop Bar on the roof prepares a Mongolian barbecue for F$6.

The **Bounty Restaurant** (Veronika and Brian Smith, tel. 672-0840), a bit north and across the highway from RJ's, has Chinese or Fijian dishes and hamburgers for lunch, steaks and seafood for dinner. Lunch specials here average F$8, while dinner plates are F$16–28. There's also a popular tourist bar (happy hour 1700–1900).

Rik's Café (tel. 672-2110; daily 0700–2200), across the street from the Bounty Restaurant, offers things like breakfast (F$6.50), sandwiches (F$4), fish burgers (F$4.50), and fish and chips (F$6). Beer is not sold.

The **Masala Restaurant** (tel. 672-2275; Mon.–Sat. 0730–2030), opposite Rik's Café, serves Indian dishes from the warmer at F$6–7.

The **Ed's Bar** complex, located a little north of the Dominion International Hotel in Martintar, is probably the top place to eat out in Nadi. It's fun to dine on appetizers at the bar, such as a plate of six big, spicy barbecued chicken wings for F$6. Otherwise, go through the connecting door into the adjacent **West Coast Café** (Mon.–Sat. 1730–2300) for fried fish or steak and eggs at F$12. The upscale dining room called the **Seafood Grill** (tel. 672-4650; daily 1730–2300) beyond the bar serves dishes like *kokoda* (F$7), grilled fish (F$19), pork chops (F$20), seafood hot combo (F$28), steaks, and lobster tails in a gentile setting.

The cheapest place to eat in Martintar is **Millennium Fast Food** (tel. 672-5548; daily 0700–1800), at the Shell service station across the street from the Bounty Restaurant. Taxi drivers often drop in here and order meals from what's in the warmer on the counter.

The **Maharaja Restaurant** (tel. 672-2962; Mon.–Sat. 0900–2200, Sun. 1700–2200), out near the Skylodge Hotel, is popular with flight crews who come for the spicy Indian curries, tandoori dishes, and local seafood (main dishes F$10–18). It's one of Fiji's finest Indian restaurants (dinner is generally better than lunch here).

ENTERTAINMENT

Nadi has two movie houses: **Galaxy 2 Cinema** (tel. 670-0176), on Ashram Road between Tappoo and the Farmers Club; and **Novelty Cinema** (tel. 670-0155), upstairs from the mall at the

Nadi Civic Center, not far from the post office. They usually show Indian films in Hindi.

Bars and Clubs

The **Nadi Farmers Club** (tel. 670-0415; Mon.–Thurs. 1000–2200, Fri. and Sat. 1000–2300, Sun. 0900–2100), just up Ashram Road from the Mobil station in Nadi town, is a male drinking place where tourists are welcome. The club's restaurant at the back of the building serves Indian curries in the F$4–7 price range.

Nite Life (tel. 670-0000), next to the Nadi Hotel, has a live rock band 2100–0100 on Friday and Saturday nights (Tues.–Thurs. recorded music). It's not a tourist scene, so be prepared. Locals call it "the zoo."

Another rough place is **Green Land Nite Club** (38 Main St.; Aiyaz Khan, tel. 670-7449; Mon.–Sat. 1800–0100, admission free), opposite the Nadi Downtown Motel.

Club Rangeela (Moh'd Kaiyum, tel. 670-7171; Thurs.–Sat. 2030–0100, admission F$5), on Andrews Road at the north end of town, caters mostly to Indo-Fijians.

Better than any of the above is **Ed's Bar** (tel. 672-4650), a little north of the Dominion International Hotel in Martintar. You'll enjoy chatting with the friendly staff and meeting the trendy locals and surfers who hang out here. Happy hour is 1730–2000 daily. It's a colorful spot that you'll want to visit again.

The Boss Night Club (Wed.–Sat. 1830–0100, admission F$5), in an industrial area behind Colonial Plaza off the road to the airport, is popular among Nadi's Indo-Fijian population. When guest acts like Black Rose appear here, the house is really packed. Drinks are expensive.

After Dark Night Club (daily 2000–0100), above Chopsticks Restaurant at Namaka, just northeast of Morris Hedstrom and not far from the Melanesian Hotel, hosts a mostly indigenous Fijian crowd. They play recorded newly released music. You may be viewed as a source of beer by some of the other clients here.

Cultural Shows for Visitors

The **Sheraton Fiji** (tel. 675-0777) has a *meke*

and *magiti* (feast) Saturday at 1800 (F$49). Wednesday at 2000, Fijian firewalking comes with the *meke*, and a F$12 fee is charged.

You can also enjoy a barbecue and *meke* at the **Dominion International Hotel** (tel. 672-2255) on Saturday (F$22). On Mondays, the **Fiji Mocambo Hotel** (tel. 672-2000) has a *lovo* feast (F$35).

Shopping

Most shops in Nadi are closed on Sunday. The **Nadi Handicraft Market,** opposite the Nadi Hotel just off Main Street, provides you with the opportunity to buy directly from the handicraft's producers. Several large curio emporia are along Main Street, including **Jack's Handicrafts** (tel. 670-0744, www.jacksfiji.com), opposite Morris Hedstrom. Visit a few of these before going to the market, to get an idea of what's available and how much your preferred items should cost.

The Art Gallery (220 Main St. at Sagayam Rd.; Yogesh Gokal, tel. 670-0722; weekdays 0900–1730, Sat. 0900–1500), has ties with the Oceania Center for Art and Culture at the University of the South Pacific in Suva. Its shows change monthly. Check out the compact discs (F$40) of panpipe music here.

The **Surf Republic of Fiji** (tel. 670-5666), Main and Clay Streets, sells trendy resort and swim wear. Don't miss the small art gallery with carefully selected artworks from Fiji, Indonesia, and Papua New Guinea at one side of the shop. The upscale coffee and ice cream bar here is also nice.

Prouds and Tappoo on Main Street sell the type of shiny luxury goods usually seen in airport duty-free shops. **Sogo Fiji** (tel. 670-1614) nearby is the place to pick up tropical clothing and beachwear. Just beware of the friendly handshake in Nadi, for you may find yourself buying something you neither care for nor desire. Lots of visitors get conned in Nadi.

If you have an interest in world literature, you can purchase books on yoga and Indian classics at the **Sri Ramakrishna Ashram** (tel. 670-2786; Mon.–Fri. 0800–1300 and 1400–1700, Sat. 0800–1230), across the street from the Farmers

Club. There's a prayer session in the Ashram on Sunday morning, followed by a vegetarian feast.

INFORMATION

The **Fiji Visitors Bureau** office (tel. 672-2433, fax 672-0141) is well hidden in office No. 20 upstairs in the arrivals concourse at the airport. There's no official tourist information office in downtown Nadi, and the travel agencies masquerading as such give biased information.

The **Nadi Town Council Library** (tel. 670-0133, ext. 126; Mon.–Fri. 0900–1700, Sat. 0900–1300) is upstairs in the mall at the Nadi Civic Center on Main Street.

Travel Agents

Rosie The Travel Service (tel. 672-2935, www.rosiefiji.com), at Nadi Airport and opposite the Nadi Handicraft Market in town, is an inbound tour operator that books somewhat upmarket tours, activities, and accommodations. They'll often give you a discount on their day tours and trekking if you book directly with them. **Adventure Fiji** (tel. 672-5598), two offices down from Rosie at the airport, is a branch of the same company specifically oriented toward backpackers.

The **United Touring Company** (tel. 672-2811), at the airport and at several hotels, and Coral Sun Fiji (tel. 672-2268, reservations@csf .com.fj) at the airport are similar to Rosie and quite reliable.

Tourist Transport Fiji (tel. 672-0455, fax 672-0184), next to the washrooms in the arrivals area at Nadi Airport, handles the "Feejee Experience" backpacker bus tours around Viti Levu. They should have information on the Mount Batilamu Trek in Koroyanitu National Heritage Park and on the Abaca day tours.

Many smaller travel agencies upstairs from the arrivals concourse at Nadi Airport book budget resorts in the Yasawa Islands and elsewhere around Fiji. For example, there's **Rabua's Travel Agency** (tel. 672-1377 or 672-3234) in office No. 23. The friendly manager, Ulaiasi "Rambo" Rabua, represents Wayalailai Resort on Wayasewa (his home island) and most other offshore backpacker resorts. Louise Blake and Loma at **Island**

Travel Tours (tel. 672-4033 or 672-5930, fax 672-5753, www.travellingfiji.com), in office No. 14 upstairs, **Sunset Tours** (Poni Natadra, tel. 672-0266), and **Western Travel Services** (tel. 672-4440), in office No. 4, do the same. Among the backpacker resorts with offices of their own upstairs at the airport are Ratu Kini of Mana Island in office No. 26, David's Place of Tavewa Island in office No. 31, and Dive Trek Wayasewa in office No. 23. The Turtle Island office (tel. 672-2921), downstairs in the arrivals terminal, handles Oarsman's and Safe Landing resorts.

The largest backpacker-oriented travel agency is **Victory Tours** (tel. 670-0243, fax 670-2746; daily 0730–2000, www.victory.com.fj) with an office at the corner of Main Street and Hospital Road in downtown Nadi. Their signpost reads Tourist Information Center, but this is a purely commercial operation. Victory sells a variety of 4WD and trekking "inland safari" excursions into the Nausori Highlands, as well as booking low-budget beach resorts on Mana, Malolo, Tavewa, and Waya islands. Their prices are not fixed, and you may feel hustled here.

Pacific Valley View Tours (tel. 670-0600), at the Nadi Downtown Motel, is similar. Better known as PVV Tours, their specialty is Nananu-i-Ra and Mana Island bookings and transfers. Prices vary here as well, and bargaining might work.

You can often get a better deal by booking direct with a resort over the phone. The Nadi agents collect commissions as high as 30 percent, and the resort owners are often willing to pass along some of their savings to those who call. Always keep in mind that the Nadi travel agents only promote properties that pay them commissions. If they warn you not to go somewhere, it may only be because they don't get an adequate commission from the place.

Airline Offices

Reconfirm your flight, request a seat assignment, or check the departure time by calling your airline: Aircalin (tel. 672-2145), Air Nauru (tel. 672-2795), Air New Zealand (tel. 672-2955), Air Pacific (tel. 672-0888), Air Vanuatu (tel. 672-2521), Korean Air (tel. 672-1043), Polynesian Airlines (tel. 672-2521), Qantas

Nadi is a convenient, inexpensive place to check email.

Airways (tel. 672-2880), Royal Tongan Airlines (tel. 672-4355), and Solomon Airlines (tel. 672-2831). Most of these offices are at the airport (Air Fiji represents Air Vanuatu and Polynesian Airlines).

SERVICES

Money

The Westpac Bank opposite the Nadi Handicraft Market, the ANZ Bank near Morris Hedstrom, and the Colonial National Bank between these, are open Monday–Thursday 0930–1500, Friday 0930–1600. The ANZ Bank charges F$5 commission whereas the others do not. If you need a Visa/MasterCard ATM, go to the ANZ Bank branches in downtown Nadi, at Namaka toward the airport, and at the airport itself. McDonald's also has an ATM!

Money Exchange (tel. 670-3366; Mon.–Fri. 0830–1700, Sat. 0830–1300), between the ANZ Bank and Morris Hedstrom, changes cash and traveler's checks without commission at a rate comparable to the banks (and without the line).

Thomas Cook Travel (tel. 670-3110; Mon.–Fri. 0830–1700, Sat. 0830–1200), beside Prouds on Main Street, is a good source of the banknotes of other Pacific countries—convenient if you'll be flying to Australia, New Caledonia, New Zealand, Samoa, Solomon Islands, Tonga, or Vanuatu and don't want the hassle of having to change money at a strange airport upon arrival. They'll also change leftover banknotes of these countries into Fiji dollars.

Post

There are two large post offices, one next to the market in central Nadi, and another between the cargo warehouses directly across the park in front of the arrivals hall at Nadi Airport. Check both if you're expecting general-delivery mail. Nadi Town Post Office near the market receives faxes sent to 670-2166. At the Nadi Airport Post Office, the public fax number is 672-0467. Both post offices are open Monday–Friday 0800–1600, Saturday 0800–1200.

Internet Access

If you're headed for the Yasawa resorts, Nadi offers your last chance to check email and prices are competitive. **Cybercafé** (501 Main St.; tel. 670-2226; Mon.–Fri. 0800–1730, Sat. 0800–1500), between Mama's Pizza Inn and Continental Pizza in downtown Nadi, charges F$.10 a minute or F$4 an hour for Internet access in private cubicles.

The **Internet Connect Café** (tel. 670-3562; weekdays 0800–2000, Sat. 0800–2200, Sun. 1000–1800, www.connect.com.fj), on Main Street beside the bridge at the north end of town, charges F$5 an hour.

Noveix Microsystems (tel. 670-5100; Mon.–Sat. 0800–1830), across the street from the Nadi Civic Center, offers fast Internet access at F$.10 a minute or F$5 for two hours.

Internet service is available in room 201 at the **Capricorn International Hotel** (tel. 672-0088) in Martintar at F$3 for 30 minutes.

The **Internet Café** (tel. 672-3758; Mon.–Sat. 0800–2000, Sun. 0800–1300), opposite Rik's Café at Martintar, charges F$.10 a minute.

The Bottle Shop (tel. 672-4650; weekdays 0800–1700, Sat. 0800–1300), next to Ed's Bar in Martintar, provides Internet access at F$2 for 10 minutes.

Immigration Office

Visa extensions can be arranged at the Immigration office (tel. 672-2263; Mon.–Fri. 0900–1300 and 1400–1430), upstairs from near the Sun Air check-in counter at Nadi Airport.

Consulates

The **Canadian Consulate** (tel./fax 672-1936) is at Nadi. For the **Italian Honorary Consul,** call Mediterranean Villas (tel. 666-4011).

Launderettes

Self-Service Launderette (tel. 670-5155; Mon.–Sat. 0900–1700), in a two-story building on Queens Road just north of the Bounty Restaurant at Martintar, charges F$6.50 to wash and dry (soap F$.50).

Prabhat Steam Laundry (tel. 672-3061; Mon.–Sat. 0800–1300 and 1400–1600), at the end of Northern Press Road beside Sunny Travelers Inn, charges F$3.50 a kilogram to wash, dry, and fold your laundry. Ironing is F$2–3 a piece.

Toilets

Free public toilets are at the corner of Nadi Market closest to the post office, at the bus station, and in the Nadi Civic Center.

HEALTH

The outpatient department at **Nadi District Hospital** (tel. 670-1128), inland from Nadi Bus Station, is open Monday to Thursday 0800–1630, Friday 0800–1600, and Saturday 0800–1200.

You'll save time by visiting Dr. Ram Raju (tel. 670-1375; Mon.–Fri. 0830–1630, Sat. and Sun. 0900–1230), Lodhia and Clay Streets, a family doctor specializing in travel health.

Dr. Abdul Gani (tel. 670-3776; Mon.–Fri. 0800–1700, Sat. 0800–1300) has his dental surgery downstairs in the mall at the Nadi Civic Center near the post office. (Dr. Gani is also the mayor of Nadi.)

Dr. Shyamendra Sharma (tel. 672-2288) runs the Namaka Medical Center on Queens Road near the Melanesian Hotel. After hours, press the bell for service.

Budget Pharmacy (tel. 670-0064) is opposite Sogo Fiji on Main Street in town.

TRANSPORTATION

See the Getting Around section in the Exploring the Islands chapter for information on regular Air Fiji and Sun Air flights to Malololailai and Mana islands and other parts of Fiji.

Turtle Airways (tel. 672-1888, fax 672-0095, www.turtleairways.com), next to the golf course at Wailoaloa Beach, runs a seaplane shuttle to the main Mamanuca resorts at F$134 one-way, F$268 round-trip (minimum of two passengers, baggage limited to one 15-kg suitcase plus one carry-on). Special backpacker fares to the Yasawa Islands are available at F$119 one-way (minimum of four passengers).

South Sea Cruises (tel. 675-0500, fax 675-0501, southsea@connect.com.fj), owned by Fullers of New Zealand, operates a high-speed catamaran shuttle to the offshore island resorts on the 27-meter, 213-passenger *Tiger IV.* The boat leaves from Nadi's Port Denarau daily at 0900, 1215, and 1515 for Treasure (F$46 each way), Malolo (F$56), Castaway (F$56), and Mana (F$56). Connections to Matamanoa or Tokoriki via Mana are available (F$97). Interisland hops between the resorts themselves are F$41 each. Children under 16 are half price on all trips (under five free). Be prepared to wade on and off the boat in ankle deep water at all islands except Mana. If all you want is a glimpse of the lovely Mamanuca Group, a four-island, three-hour, nonstop round-trip cruise is F$56. South Sea Cruises also sends the 25-meter catamaran *Yasawa Flyer* from Nadi to the Yasawa islands daily at 0915 (turn to the Yasawa Islands chapter for details). Catamaran bookings can be made at any travel agency around Nadi, and bus transfers to the wharf from the main Nadi hotels are included.

Highway Transport

Nadi's bus station adjoining the market is an active place. **Pacific Transport** (tel. 670-0044) has express buses to Suva via Queens Road daily at 0720, 0750, 0900, 1300, 1640, and 1820 (188 km, four hours, F$10). The 0900 bus is the most convenient, as it begins its run at Nadi (all the others arrive from Lautoka). Five other Pacific Transport "stage" buses also operate daily to Suva (five hours). The **Sunbeam Transport** express buses to Suva at 1100 and 1200 make resort stops along the way. Collective taxis and minibuses parked in a corner of Nadi Bus Station take passengers nonstop from Nadi to Suva in three hours for F$15 pp.

Coral Sun Fiji (tel. 672-3105, reservations@csf.com.fj) at Nadi Airport operates the air-conditioned "Fiji Express" luxury coach to Suva via the Coral Coast resorts, departing Nadi Airport at 1300 daily (F$31 to Suva). The "Queens Deluxe Coach" leaves the airport for Suva at 0730 daily (F$19), calling at all of the Coral Coast resorts.

Local buses to Lautoka (33 km), the airport, and anywhere in between pick up passengers at a bus stop on Main Street opposite Morris Hedstrom.

Unmarked white "Viti Mini" minibuses shuttle frequently between the bus stop on the highway outside Nadi Airport and Nadi town at F$.50 a ride. Collective taxis cruising the highway between the airport and Nadi do the same, taking about what you'd pay on a bus, but ask first.

For information on car rentals, turn to the Getting Around section in the Exploring the Islands chapter.

Local Tours

Numerous day cruises and bus tours operating in the Nadi area are advertised in free tourist brochures. Reservations can be made through Rosie The Travel Service or UTC, with several offices around Nadi. Bus transfers to/from your hotel are included in the price, though some trips are arbitrarily canceled when not enough people sign up.

The "road tours" offered by **Rosie The Travel Service** (tel. 672-2935, www.rosiefiji.com), at Nadi Airport and opposite the Nadi Handicraft Market in town, are cheaper than those of other companies because lunch isn't included (lunch is included on all the cruises and river trips). Rosie's day trips to Suva (F$49) involve too much time on the bus, so instead go for the Sigatoka Valley/Tavuni Hill Fort (F$63 including entry fees) or Emperor Gold Mine (F$55) full-day tours. If you're looking for a half-day tour around Nadi, sign up for the four-hour Vuda Lookout/Viseisei Village/Garden of the Sleeping Giant tour, which costs F$50, including admission to the garden (the lookout and garden are not accessible on public transport). These trips only operate Monday–Saturday, but on Sunday morning Rosie offers a half-day drive to the Vuda Lookout and the Garden of the Sleeping Giant at F$44 pp. On Thursdays there's a tour to Pacific Harbor (F$92) which includes firewalking and a *meke*. Also ask about the full-day hiking tours to the Nausori Highlands (daily except Sunday, F$69), the easiest way to see this beautiful area.

The **United Touring Company** (tel. 672-2811, fax 672-0389, www.utcfiji.com), or UTC, is in the office marked "accommodation information" near the public toilets in the airport's arrivals terminal, to the left as you come out of customs. They offer the same kind of day tours as Rosie, such as a half-day Orchid Tour to Viseisei and the Garden of the Sleeping Giant at F$50. UTC can also book budget-priced beach resorts on Viti Levu, such as Saweni and Tubakula, with air-conditioned bus transfers.

Victory Tours (tel. 670-0243), also known as the "Tourist Information Center," offers "Adventure Jungle Treks" with stays in different Fijian villages at F$199/230 for one/two nights. The hiking trips offered by **Adventure Fiji**, a division of Rosie The Travel Service, are more expensive than these, but the quality is more consistent (see the Hiking Tours section in the Exploring the Islands chapter).

Wacking Stick Adventure Tours (tel. 672-4673, www.wackingstickadventures.com) operates quality mountain-bike tours to Natadola Beach (F$95) and the Sleeping Giant Mountain Range (F$125). Bikes, lunch, admissions, and Nadi hotel transfers are included.

Day tours are easily arranged with taxi drivers around Nadi, costing about F$70 as far as Lautoka or Korotogo (three hours) or F$120 to

South Sea Cruises runs the fast catamaran *Tiger IV* from Nadi to the main Mamanuca resorts three times a day.

Pacific Harbor (five hours)—worth considering if there are a few of you. The collective taxis at Nadi Bus Station can be hired for leisurely one-way tours to Suva (offer around F$100 for a five-hour ride with lots of stops). Write out a list of everything you want to see and agree on the price and time length beforehand.

Should you not wish to join an organized bus tour from Nadi, you can easily organize your own **self-guided day tour** by taking a local bus (not an express) to the Sigatoka Sand Dunes National Park visitor center on Queens Road. After a hike over the dunes, catch another bus on to Sigatoka town for lunch, some shopping and sightseeing, and perhaps a taxi visit to the Tavuni Hill Fort. Plenty of buses cover the 61 kilometers from Sigatoka back to Nadi until late. All of this will cost you far less than the cheapest half-day tour and you'll be able to mix freely with the locals.

Day Cruises

Food and accommodations at the Mamanuca island resorts are expensive, and a cheaper way to enjoy the islands—for a day at least—is by booking a day cruise to Castaway (F$99), Malolo (F$99), or Mana (F$99) on the fast catamaran *Tiger IV,* operated by **South Sea Cruises** (tel. 675-0500, southsea@connect.com.fj) and departing from Port Denarau. The price includes transfers from most Nadi hotels, the boat trip, a buffet lunch on the island of your choice, nonmotorized sporting activities, and a day at the beach (children under 16 are half price). South Sea Cruises also has day trips to the outer Mamanuca islands (including Monuriki from the Tom Hanks movie *Castaway)* on the two-masted schooner *Seaspray* (F$165 with lunch and drinks).

Several companies offer day cruises to imaginatively named specks of sand such as Daydream Island (tel. 670-2774), Malamala Island (tel. 670-2443), Bounty Island (tel. 672-2852 or 672-2869), and South Sea Island (tel. 675-0500) costing F$69–89, always including lunch and Nadi hotel pickups, and usually drinks and nonmotorized sporting activities as well. Children under 16 are usually half price. These trips are fine if all you want is a day at the beach, otherwise you'll find them a colossal bore. Any hotel tour desk can book them. Ask about reduced "early bird" prices, if you're willing to arrive and leave early.

Youthful travelers will enjoy a day cruise to **Beachcomber Island** (tel. 672-3828, www .beachcomberfiji.com), Fiji's unofficial Club Med for the under-35 set. Operating daily, the F$69 pp fare includes bus transfers from Nadi hotels, the return boat ride via Lautoka, and a buffet lunch. Families should consider Beachcomber because children under 16 are half price and infants under two are free. Beachcomber has an office downstairs in the arrivals terminal at Nadi Airport, or book through any Rosie The Travel Service or UTC desk.

Captain Cook Cruises (tel. 670-1823) runs day cruises to tiny Tivua Island on the sailing vessel *Ra Marama* for F$89 including a picnic lunch, four drinks, and non-motorized water sports. Two bungalows on Tivua host those who'd like to stay overnight at F$353/520 single/double all-inclusive. Three-hour starlight dinner cruises on the ship *City of Nadi* are F$85.

The **Oceanic Schooner Co.** (tel. 672-2455 or 672-3590, funcruises@connect.com.fj) does upscale "fun cruises" on the 30-meter schooner *Whale's Tale,* built at Suva's Whippy Shipyard in 1985. You get a champagne breakfast and gourmet lunch served aboard ship, an open bar, and sunset cocktails in the company of a limited number of fellow passengers at F$165 pp. *Whale's Tale* is a nicer vessel than the *Seaspray* mentioned above, but both cruises are good.

Several other companies run Mamanuca charters and cruises, often with the promise of dolphin encounters. Hotel receptions often display brochures from **Coral Cats** (tel. 672-5961), **Crystal Blue** (tel. 675-0950), and **Sea Fiji** (tel. 672-5961). Some of the same companies offer deep-sea fishing at about F$700/1,050 a half/full day (six anglers maximum).

The most ambitious day cruise from Nadi is aboard the 20-meter catamaran *Tamusua Explorer* to the Sawa-i-Lau Cave in the Yasawa Islands, departing Lautoka every Tuesday, Thursday, and Saturday at 0800. It's F$189 roundtrip including a buffet lunch and Nadi hotel pickups. Contact **Yasawa Island Eco Tours** (tel. 672-1658, fax 672-5208, yiet@connect.com.fj) next to Rik's Café in Martintar or any hotel tour desk.

Thirty-minute jet-boat rides around the mouth of the Nadi River are offered by **Shotover Jet** (tel. 675-0400, fax 675-0666) about every half hour daily 0800–1600 from Port Denarau (adults F$75, children under 15 years F$35, hotel transfers included). It's fairly certain the birds and fish of this mangrove area are less thrilled by these gas-guzzling, high-impact craft than the tourists seated therein.

Flightseeing

Turtle Airways (tel. 672-1888) offers scenic flights in their Cessna floatplanes at F$190 pp for 30 minutes (minimum of two persons). **Coral Air** (tel. 672-4490, www.coralair.com) has an amphibious seaplane used mostly for flightseeing around Nadi (F$239 pp for 30 minutes, minimum of two), but also available for trips to the Sawa-i-Lau Caves and the Blue Lagoon (F$645 pp, minimum of two). **Island Hoppers** (tel. 672-0410, www.helicopters.com.fj), in a separate terminal behind the airport post office, proposes helicopter tours around Nadi and the Mamanucas starting at F$144 pp (minimum of two).

NORTH OF NADI

A popular legend invented in 1893 holds that **Viseisei village,** on the old road between Lautoka and Nadi, was the first settlement in Fiji. It's told how the early Fijians, led by Chiefs Lutunasobasoba and Degei, came from the west, landing their great canoe, the *Kaunitoni,* at Vuda Point, where the oil tanks are now. A Centennial Memorial (1835–1935) in front of the church commemorates the arrival of the first Methodist missionaries in Fiji, and opposite the memorial is a traditional Fijian *bure*—the official residence of Tui Vuda. Fiji's current president, Ratu Josefa Iloilo, holder of the Tui Vuda title, lives in the green-roofed house behind this central *bure.*

Near the back of the church is another monument, topped by a giant war club, the burial place of the village's chiefly family. The late Dr. Timoci Bavadra, the prime minister of Fiji deposed during the Rabuka coup in 1987, hailed

the guns of Lomolomo on a hilltop between Lautoka and Nadi

from Viseisei and is interred here. Dr. Bavadra's traditional-style home faces the main road near the church. His son presently lives there, and with his permission you'll be allowed to enter to see the photos hanging on the walls.

All of the above is only a few minutes' walk from the bus stop, but you're expected to have someone accompany you through the village. Most visitors arrive on sightseeing tours, and if you come on your own, you should ask permission to visit of anyone you meet at the bus stop. They'll probably send a child along with you, and as you part, give the child a pack of chewing gum or a similar item (give something else if your escort is an adult). There's a fine view of Nadi Bay from Viseisei, and the bus tours often stop here, as the souvenir vendors in the village indicate. In any case, don't come on a Sunday. A bypass on Queens Road avoids Viseisei, and only local buses between Lautoka and Nadi take the back road past the village.

A couple of kilometers from the village on the airport side of Viseisei, just above Lomolomo Public School, are two **British six-inch guns** set up here during World War II to defend the north side of Nadi Bay. Between 1939 and 1941, coastal defense batteries were established at five points around Viti Levu. It's a fairly easy climb from the main highway, and you'll get an excellent view from the top.

Many tours visit **Perry Mason's Orchid Garden** (Mon.–Sat. 0900–1700, Sun. 0900–1200, admission F$10), also known as the Garden of the Sleeping Giant, 2.5 kilometers down Wailoka Road off Queens Road north of the airport. The brochure claims 2,000 kinds of orchids are kept in these gardens at the foot of the hills, though they're slightly overrated.

Accommodations

The **Stoney Creek Resort** (Gary and Michelle Jones, tel. 672-2206, www.stoneycreekfiji.com) is on Sabeto Road six kilometers east of Queens Road, about 11 kilometers northeast of Nadi Airport. There are two *bure* at F$55/75 double/triple, plus a beautifully designed hilltop dormitory with a splendid mountain view at F$20 pp. A deluxe room behind the restaurant is F$120 double. The 16 dorm beds are divided among four separate cubicles, and there are hammocks from which to take in the scene. The restaurant and bar serves lunch at F$7.50–8.50, dinner F$17.50–18.50, and a Sunday buffet dinner (F$16). There's a swimming pool. Half-day hiking and kayaking tours are F$25 pp, horseback riding F$20 a half day, bicycle rentals F$10 a day (guests only). Situated above the Sabeto River and below scenic mountains, this is an excellent ecotourism alternative to the Nadi hotels. The Sabeto bus runs to Stoney Creek five times a day, or hire a carrier from Queens Road for F$5.

Mediterranean Villas (tel. 666-4011, fax 666-1773, medvillas@connect.com.fj), on Vuda Hill overlooking Viseisei village just off Viseisei Back Road, has six individually decorated self-catering villas with fridge priced F$110–260 single or double. There's a pool, but the beach is far from here. This hotel acts as the honorary Italian consulate in Fiji. Local buses between Lautoka and Nadi stop nearby.

Two kilometers down Vuda Road from Mediterranean Villas is the **Anchorage Beach Resort** (tel. 666-2099, fax 666-5571, www.tanoa hotels.com), which was taken over by the Tanoa hotel chain in 1996. It's on a hilltop just before the descent to First Landing Resort, a 15-minute walk along the cane railway line or beach from Viseisei. The eight garden-view rooms are F$132 single or double, the four oceanview rooms F$143, and the two panoramic rooms F$154. The only two rooms with cooking facilities are also F$143 (other guests must use the restaurant). All units are air-conditioned, and each has a fridge and balcony. A swimming pool is on the premises. The shoreline below Anchorage isn't as good for swimming as the beach at nearby First Landing Resort, but the views across Nadi Bay are nice.

First Landing Resort (tel. 666-6171, fax 666-8882, www.firstlandingfiji.com) is next to the Vuda Point Yacht Marina, three kilometers down Vuda Road from Mediterranean Villas. The beach here is much better than those in and around Nadi, but you'd only call it good at high tide. The 14 deluxe/superior duplex units facing the swimming pool are F$195/255 single or double, while the 18 duplex beachfront units go for F$325 (extra persons F$35). All units have fully screened porches and are equipped with a fridge and coffee-making facilities (but no cooking facilities). Connecting doors make the

units ideal for large families or small groups. Three units are wheelchair accessible. One beach villa opposite the reception has its own kitchen and pool at F$650. A continental breakfast is included in all rates. The large garden restaurant on the premises bakes pizza (F$10–26), seafood (including lobster), and bread in a wood-fired stone oven. Menu items average F$17–31. The cafe in the adjacent Vuda Point Marina (daily 0700–1500, also Tues., Thurs., and Sat. until 2100) is far less expensive and recommended. Stephen and Julie Lynn of Aquacadabra Diving (tel./fax 664-5911, www.aqua cadabradiving.com) organize scuba diving from First Landing Resort using the dive boat *Mer-lynn's Magic*. The places just mentioned are okay for a night or two, but you'd be making a mistake to plan your whole vacation around them.

SOUTH OF NADI
Sonaisali Island Resort

Opened in 1992, this upscale resort (tel. 670-6011, fax 670-6092, www.sonaisali.com) is on Naisali, a long, low island surrounded by mangrove flats in Momi Bay, just 300 meters off the coast of Viti Levu. The turnoff is 10 kilometers south of Nadi, then it's three kilometers down Nacobi Road (paved) to the landing. The 32 air-conditioned rooms with fridge in the two main two-story buildings are F$335 single or double, and there are 49 thatched *bure* at F$405–550 including tax (no cooking facilities). It's necessary to make dinner reservations, and you may have difficulty arranging a convenient time (the food and drink itself is overpriced and the dining room service poor). The water pressure at Sonaisali is low, and it takes ages to fill the spa baths built into some of the units. The resort features a marina, large swimming pool (which could use a cleaning), tennis courts, a children's program, and free nonmotorized water sports, but the snorkeling off their artificial beach is nothing. Scuba diving is available, and Rosie The Travel Service has a desk at Sonaisali. A taxi from the airport might cost F$25. Non-guests wishing to take the "free" shuttle boat across to the island must first pay F$25/12.50 per adult/child for a non-refundable food-and-beverage credit. Frankly, this place is not recommended.

Surf & Dive Rendezvous

In 2001, Ben and Naoko Seduadua established a backpacker camp called **Surf & Dive Rendezvous** (tel. 651-0571, www.infofiji.com/rendezvous) on Uciwai Beach north of Nabila village, right next to the landing for Tavarua and Namotu islands. Accommodations include one room with private bath (F$75 pp), a Fijian *bure* with private bath (F$70 pp), four rooms with shared bath (F$65/130 single/double), a 20-bed dorm (F$55 pp), and camping space (F$45 pp), all with three meals included in the rates. Scuba diving is F$140 for two tanks, plus F$30 for gear. Ben's three- to four-day open-water certification course is F$500. Surfing trips to the reefs off Namotu and Malolo islands are F$55 pp (to Cloudbreak Sat. mornings only). Surfboard rental, sale, and repair is available. Other activities include surfing lessons, fishing, and horseback riding. The beach is okay for Viti Levu. Internet access is F$.20 a minute. The turnoff to Rendezvous is at Uciwai Junction, 15 kilometers south of Nadi town on Queens Road, then it's another six kilometers west on a gravel road. Get there on the Uciwai bus from Nadi at 0800, 1300, and 1700 daily except Sunday (or pay F$25 for a taxi).

Momi Battery Historic Park

On a hilltop overlooking Momi Bay, 28 kilometers from Nadi, are two **British six-inch guns** named Queen Victoria (1900) and Edward VII (1901). Both were recycled from the Boer War and set up here by the New Zealand Army's 30th Battalion in 1941 to defend the southern approach to Nadi Bay. The only shots fired in anger during the war were across the bow of a Royal New Zealand Navy ship that forgot to make the correct signals as it entered the passage. It quickly turned around, made the proper signals, and reentered quietly. You get a great view of the Mamanuca Group, reefs, and surrounding countryside from the guns. This historic site is managed by the National Trust for Fiji (tel. 997-1508, daily 0900–1700, admission F$3). To reach the battery, catch the Nabila Bus Station at

0900, 1600, and 1715 (only the 0900 bus returns to town the same day). The turnoff from Queens Road is at Nawai Junction, 17 kilometers south of Nadi town, then it's another nine kilometers along a gravel road to the guns. Seashell Cove Resort is nine kilometers south.

Seashell Cove

Seashell Cove Resort (Virginia Smith, tel. 670-6100, fax 670-6094, www.seashellresort.com), on Momi Bay, 29 kilometers southwest of Nadi, has been around since the 1980s. They have six duplex *bure* with fans, fridge, and cooking facilities at F$150 for up to three, and 17 lodge rooms with lumpy beds and shared bath at F$60 single or double, F$70 triple. Six larger units near the restaurant are available for families at F$195 for up to six, and baby-sitters are provided. The two honeymoon suites attached to a lodge are also F$195. Not all of the rooms face the water. The dormitory above the bar includes three six-bed rooms at F$55 per bed including three meals. Otherwise, pitch your own tent beside the volleyball court for F$10. Everything other than the dormitory is a bit overpriced.

Cooking facilities are not provided for campers or lodge guests, although the good-value meal plan is F$35 pp, and there's a small grocery store just outside the resort. A *meke* and Fijian feast (F$20) occurs on Friday. Some surfers stay up all night drinking kava with the friendly staff, a great opportunity to get to know them. Baggage storage is available free of charge. Internet access at the office is F$6 for 15 minutes.

A small saltwater swimming pool is near the shore, but there's no beach here, only a concrete seawall. At low tide, it's a 10-minute trudge across the mudflats to the water. Amenities and activities include a swimming pool, day trips to Natadola Beach (F$35 including lunch), tennis, and volleyball. There's a horse used to walk kids under 10 around the resort, but the free kayaks leak and become unstable after 20 minutes. A two-island, three-resort day cruise from here costs F$65.

Daily at 0700, the Seashell boat shuttles surfers out to the reliable left at Namotu Island breakers or long hollow right at Wilkes Passage (F$30 pp). The boat also goes to Swimming Pools, Desperations, and Mini Cloudbreak, staying with the surfers while they surf. The famous Cloudbreak lefthander at Navula Reef between Wilkes and Seashell is visited only on Saturday (F$40 pp), provided the Tavarua people aren't using it. Even then, expect crowds of 25 guys in the water—all other spots are less crowded. There's also an offshore break near the Momi Bay Lighthouse. This type of reef break surfing can be dangerous for the inexperienced.

Seashell Cove's scuba-diving operation, **Scuba Bula** (www.scubabula.com), can handle to up to 24 divers at a time from beginners to advanced. The cost is F$75/110 for two tanks plus F$20 for gear and F$440 for a PADI certification course (minimum of two). Seashell divers experience lots of fish/shark action at Navula

Lighthouse, and there's great drift diving at Canyons (the guides really know their spots). When there's space, snorkelers are welcome to go along at F$20 pp.

The turnoff to Seashell Cove is at Nawai Junction, 17 kilometers south of Nadi town on Queens Road, then it's another 12 kilometers to the resort on a rough gravel road. Airport transfers arranged through the resort are F$15 pp each way. A taxi from Nadi Airport will cost F$40, from Nadi town F$30, from Sigatoka F$50. Dominion Transport (tel. 670-1505) or Ram Dayal Transport (tel. 670-0236) has buses direct to Seashell from Nadi Bus Station Monday–Saturday at 0830, 1430, and 1600 (F$1.70). From Sigatoka Bus Station, buses to Seashell leave Monday–Saturday at 1030 (F$2.65).

The Mamanuca Group

The Mamanuca Group is a paradise of eye-popping reefs and sand-fringed isles shared by traditional Fijian villages and jet-age resorts. The white coral beaches and super snorkeling grounds attract visitors aplenty; boats and planes arrive constantly, bringing folks in from nearby Nadi. These islands are in the lee of big Viti Levu, which means you'll get about as much sun here as anywhere in Fiji. Some of the South Pacific's finest scuba diving, surfing, game fishing, and yachting await you, and many nautical activities are included in the basic resort rates.

The Mamanucas are fine for a little time in the sun, though much of it is a tourist scene irrelevant to Fiji life. The only resort islands also inhabited by Fijian villagers are Mana and Malolo, and the Mana people have established low-budget backpacker accommodations in their village to make a little money on the side. If the beach is your main focus, you won't mind staying on a tiny coral speck like Beachcomber, Bounty, Matamanoa, Namotu, Navini, Tavarua, and Treasure, but if hiking and land-based exploring are also on your agenda, you'll do better on the larger Yasawa Islands.

Dive Sites

Some of Fiji's most exhilarating scuba diving is on the Malolo Barrier Reef and the passages around tiny **Namotu** or "Magic Island" where nutrients are swept in by strong currents. Both pelagic and reef fish abound in the canyons, caves, and coral heads around Namotu, but in some places the action has been distorted by scuba operators who regularly feed the fish. The outer slopes of Namotu, where the reef plunges 1,000 meters into the Pacific abyss, feature turtles, reef sharks, and vast schools of barracuda, with visibility up to 50 meters. Dolphins also frequent this area.

Bigger fish, manta rays, and ocean-going sharks are often seen at **The Big W** on the outer edge of the Malolo Barrier Reef. Susie, the friendly bronze whale shark, happens by from time to time. Vertical walls drop 70 meters at this spectacular site.

In another passage in the outer barrier reef are the pinnacles of **Gotham City,** so called for the batfish seen here, along with brilliantly colored soft corals and vast schools of tropical fish.

One of the world's most famous reef shark encounter venues is **Supermarket,** a 30-meter wall just west of Mana Island. Grays, white tips, and black tips are always present, and you might even see a tiger shark. Divemasters hand-feed

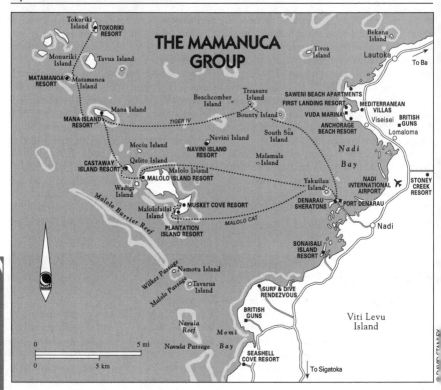

sharks more than two meters long on this exciting dive.

Shallow Kaka Reef north of Mana Island is known as **The Circus** for the myriad clown fish and colorful corals. Eagle rays sometimes frequent the **South Mana Reef** straight out from the island's wharf. Other well-known Mamanuca dive sites include Japanese Gardens, Lobster Caves, the Pinnacles (near Malolo), Sunflower Reef, The Barrel Head, The Fingers, Jockie's Point, a B-26 bomber dating from World War II, and the wreck of the *Salamanda,* a decommissioned Blue Lagoon cruise ship.

MALOLOLAILAI ISLAND

Malololailai, or "Little Malolo," 22 kilometers west of Nadi, is a 216-hectare island eight kilometers around (an interesting walk). In 1880, an American sailor named Louis Armstrong purchased Malololailai from the Fijians for one musket; in 1964, Dick Smith bought it for many muskets. You can still be alone at the beaches on the far side of the island, but with two growing resorts, a marina, a nine-hole golf course, and projects for lots more time-share condominiums in the pipeline, it's becoming overdeveloped. An airstrip across the island's waist separates its two resorts; inland are rounded, grassy hills.

Plantation Island

Plantation Island Resort (tel. 666-9333, fax 672-0620, www.plantation-island.com), on the southwest side of Malololailai, is one of the largest resorts off Nadi. It belongs to the Raffles Group, which has other large hotels in Nadi and Suva. The 142 rooms are divided between 41 air-conditioned hotel rooms in a two-story building and 101 individual or duplex *bure*. Rates start at F$209 single or double plus tax for one of the 26 garden rooms and increase to F$462 for a beachfront *bure*. The rooms have a fridge but no cooking facilities, so add F$55 pp for all meals. A supermarket is at the airport end of the resort. Plantation Island Resort tries hard to cater to families, with two children under 16 accommodated free when sharing with their parents and a children's meal plan at F$33. Crèche and baby-sitting services (F$3 an hour) are available, and there's a 20-meter waterslide and two pools.

Free activities here include snorkeling gear, windsurfing, paddle boats, and Hobie cat sailing, and daily snorkeling and fishing trips are offered at no charge. Scuba diving with Snuba Reef Tours is F$77/132 for one/two tanks, while a scuba certification course is F$570/470 pp for one/two students. Snuba will give you a sample lesson in the resort's pool for only F$5. Plantation Island's golf course toward the airport offers a F$40/50 single/double package which includes greens fees, clubs, and cart. When things are slow, they'll probably allow you to go around the nine holes twice during the same session at no additional cost; just don't drive their golf cart anywhere other than on the course, unless you're looking for trouble. Plantation Island has a better beach than neighboring Musket Cove and is much more of an integrated resort. Musket Cove is a funky do-it-yourself kind of place.

A budget section of Plantation Island Resort called **Lailai Lodge** or "Dive Lodge" (www.lailailodge.com) is along the road behind the tennis courts. The two 12-bed dormitories are F$54 pp, and kitchens and bathrooms are shared. Guests have access to most resort facilities. Reservations must be made in advance through the Raffles Gateway Hotel (tel. 672-2444) in Nadi.

Musket Cove

Also on Malololailai Island is **Musket Cove Resort** (Dick and Carol Smith, tel. 666-2215, fax 666-2633, VHF 68, www.musketcovefiji.com), which opened in 1977. This is one of the few Mamanuca resorts that provides cooking facilities for its guests, but these vary according to the class of accommodations. Full facilities are pro-

vided in the six two-bedroom villas, costing F$530 for four persons, plus F$25 per extra adult to a maximum of six. The eight seaview and four garden *bure* also have kitchenettes at F$375 single or double. However, only breakfast bars are provided in the 18 beachfront and lagoon *bure* (from F$410 single or double). The six air-conditioned rooms (F$240 single or double) upstairs in the resort's administration building have no cooking facilities at all. You can tell that Musket Cove has been patched together over time, as the accommodations are so dissimilar.

Musket Cove's well-stocked grocery store sells fresh fruit and vegetables, and a coin laundry is near the store. A F$50/62 pp two/three meal plan is available at Dick's Place Restaurant by the pool. Otherwise lunch/dinner entrées average F$13/24. Entertainment is provided every night, except Sunday. The bar on Ratu Nemani Island, a tiny coral islet connected to the marina by a floating bridge, is popular among yachties off the many boats anchored here.

Activities such as snorkeling, windsurfing, canoeing, kayaking, line fishing, and taking village boat trips are free for Musket Cove guests. Paid activities include the Hobie cats (F$12.50 an hour) and waterskiing (F$12.50). Four-seat golf carts are for rent at F$60 a day. The launch *Anthony Star* is available for deep-sea game-fishing charters at F$75 pp for four hours with a four-person minimum. The 10-meter cruiser *Dolphin Star* can be chartered for longer fishing trips at F$130 an hour (maximum four people). The 17-meter ketch *Dulcinea* does cruises to Castaway Island (F$50 pp without lunch), dolphin-watching trips (F$45 pp), and sunset viewing (F$30 pp). Unfortunately some of the Musket Cove staff seem rather jaded and not entirely happy with their jobs.

Subsurface Fiji (www.fijidiving.com) runs the scuba-diving concession at the Musket Cove marina, and many famous dive sites are less than 15 minutes away. It's F$84/164 for one/two tanks including equipment, or pay F$570 for the four-day PADI certification course (minimum of two persons). Children 12 years and up are accepted at their scuba school. **Musket Cove Yacht Charters** has a small fleet of charter yachts stationed

NADI AND THE MAMANUCAS

here. The ketch *Hobo* can do a five-day crewed cruise to the Yasawas.

Malololailai is a favorite stopover for cruising yachts with water and clean showers provided at the marina (mooring is F$8/46/172 a day/week/month). Fuel and groceries are also available. The marked anchorage is protected and 15 meters deep, with good holding. Most of the boats in the Auckland-to-Fiji yacht race in June end up here just in time for the President's Cup, Fiji's prestige yachting event. In mid-September, there's a yachting regatta week at Musket Cove, culminating in a 965-kilometer yacht race from Fiji to Port Vila timed for the boats' annual departure, prior to the onset of the hurricane season. If you're on a boat in Fiji at this time, Musket Cove is *the* place to be, and if you're trying to hitch a ride as crew, you won't go wrong. There are even stories of people being *paid* to serve as crew for the race!

Getting There

Malololailai's grass-and-gravel airstrip is the busiest in the Mamanuca Group and serves as a distribution point for the other resorts. Sun Air has flights from Nadi four to eight times a day between 0730–1730. The one-way fare is F$48. Otherwise, take the catamaran *Malolo Cat* from Nadi's Port Denarau at 1030, 1400, or 1700 (50 minutes, F$40 one way). A F$49 same-day return fare is also offered. From Malololailai, the *Cat* departs at 0900, 1230, and 1530. Call 672-2444 or 666-2215 for a free pickup at any Nadi area hotel.

MALOLO ISLAND

At low tide you can wade from Malololailai to nearby Malolo Island, largest of the Mamanuca Group. Yaro, one of two Fijian villages on Malolo, is known to tourists as "shell village" for what the locals offer for sale. In 2003, a New Zealand television company called Touchdown took over the former Lako Mai Resort near Yaro with the intention of producing a series of reality TV programs there.

Malolo Island Resort (tel. 666-9192, fax 666-9197, www.maloloisland.com), formerly Naitasi Resort, is at Malolo's western tip. The resort is owned by the Whitton family of Nadi, which also runs Rosie The Travel Service. Malolo Island Resort offers 30 oceanview bungalows at F$487 double, 18 deluxe oceanview bungalows at F$568, and one family bungalow at F$1,013 for up to eight persons. All but the family bungalow are duplexes. Up to two children under 12 can stay with their parents free. The meal plan costs F$72 pp (half price for children under 12). The Rosie office at Nadi Airport sometimes offers walk-in specials here. Malolo Island Resort has a two-tier freshwater swimming pool, and most nonmotorized water sports are free. Scuba diving with Subsurface Fiji costs extra.

The *Tiger IV* catamaran arrives from Nadi's Port Denarau three times a day at F$56 each way. South Sea Cruises offers a day trip to Malolo Island Resort at F$99 including lunch and snorkeling gear (children half price). Otherwise fly Sun Air to Malololailai (F$48), then catch a connecting speedboat straight to the resort at F$90 one-way for the boat. The Turtle Airways seaplane from Nadi is F$134 pp one-way.

THE SURFING CAMPS

Tavarua Island

Tavarua Island Resort (Jon Roseman, tel. 670-6513, fax 670-6395, www.tavarua.com), just south of Malololailai, is the South Pacific's most famous surfing resort. It caters to more affluent and mature surfers than the places on Viti Levu, Yanuca, and Kadavu. Although you can sometimes surf the same waves as the Tavarua crowd from budget resorts like Seashell Cove and Rendezvous on the mainland, you won't have the constant immediate access you have here.

Guests are accommodated in 12 newly renovated beach *bure* with hot showers and private bath, plus two larger family *bure*. A one-week package from Los Angeles will cost US$2,631 including airfare. The facilities have been upgraded, with a lagoon-style swimming pool and a large hot tub.

Amenities aside, it's the exclusivity you pay for here, as Tavarua has negotiated sole access to some of Fiji's finest waves. There are both lefts and rights in Malolo Passage at Tavarua, although the emphasis is usually on the lefts. When the swell is high enough, you'll have some of the best surfing anywhere in the world. On the off days you can get in some deep-sea fishing, windsurfing, snorkeling, or scuba diving (extra charge). Surfing guests are expected to have had at least three years experience in a variety of conditions.

Bookings must be made six months in advance through Tavarua Island Tours in Santa Barbara, California. See the Getting There section in the Exploring the Islands chapter for details. Local bookings from within Fiji are not accepted, and they're usually sold out anyway, as Tavarua has become *the* place to go for top U.S. surfers.

Namotu Island

Just across Malolo Passage from Tavarua Island on tiny Namotu Island is **Namotu Island Resort** (Scott and Amanda O'Connor, tel. 670-6439, fax 670-6039, namotu@connect.com.fj), a "Blue Water Sports Camp" for surfers. It's similar to Tavarua but slightly more accessible. They have one double *bure,* three triple *bure,* one villa with two double rooms, and two "VIP" dorm-style *bure* with six single beds in each. Children under 12 are not generally accepted.

All guests arrive on seven-night package tours from Los Angeles, costing US$2,700 pp including airfare, accommodations, meals, and unlimited access to the local surf breaks. The price is same regardless of how many people are in the room. All reservations must go through Waterways Travel in Malibu, California (www.waterwaystravel.com). Local bookings from within Fiji are only possible in January and February, if space happens to be available. However, Namotu is usually sold out.

You must bring your own surfboards, sailboards, and kite sails as none are available on the island. Snorkeling gear, kayaks, outrigger canoes, and wakeboards are loaned free of charge. Fishing is also included, although lost lures must be paid for. Scuba diving is arranged with Subsurface Fiji at F$95 per dive including gear. Massage also costs extra.

As at Tavarua, Namotu's market is mostly American water-sports enthusiasts who fly down from the United States to ride Fiji's spectacular waves. Namotu Left is a world-class reef break that's more forgiving than its fearsome, famous neighbor Cloudbreak. At five meters, **Cloudbreak** is the thrill of a lifetime; at two meters, it's a longboarder's paradise. The powerful right barrels of Wilkes Passage are good anywhere from one to three meters. Rounding out the scene is Swimming Pools, a playful, full wraparound right break on the leeward side of Namotu that, with its crystal-blue water and sheltered position, has to be one of the world's most remarkable breaks.

THE TINY ISLANDS
Beachcomber Island

Beachcomber Island (Dan Costello, tel. 666-1500, fax 666-4496, www.beachcomberfiji.com), 18 kilometers west of Lautoka, is Club Med at a bargain price. Since the 1960s, this famous resort has received many thousands of young travelers, and it's still a super place to meet the opposite sex. You'll like the informal atmosphere and late-night parties; there's a sand-floor bar, dancing, and floor shows four nights a week. The island is so small that you can stroll around it in 10 minutes, but there's a white sandy beach and buildings nestled among coconut trees and tropical vegetation. This is one of the few places in Fiji where both sexes might be able to sunbathe topless. A beautiful coral reef with numerous well-fed fish extends far out on all sides, and scuba diving is available with Subsurface Fiji (F$84/164 for one/two tanks, PADI open-water certification F$570). A full range of other sporting activities is available at an additional charge (parasailing F$60, windsurfing F$22 an hour, waterskiing F$32, Jet Skis F$60 for 15 minutes).

Accommodations include all meals served buffet style. Most backpackers opt for the big, open mixed dormitory where the 42 double-decker bunks (84 beds) cost F$75 each a night. Secure lockers are provided. The 14 simple lodge rooms at F$179/238 single/double (fridge and fan provided) are a good compromise for budget-conscious couples. You can also get one of 22 thatched beachfront *bure* with ceiling fan, fridge, and private facilities for F$270/320/395

Beachcomber Island, Fiji's Club Med for the under-30 set

single/double/triple. The *bure* are ideal for young families as children under 16 enjoy reduced rates. The resorts' former water problems have been solved by laying pipes from the mainland and installing solar water heating. Drinks at the bar are pricey, and a duty-free bottle purchased upon arrival at the airport will come in handy here.

Of course, there's also the F$69 round-trip boat ride from Nadi or Lautoka to consider, but that includes lunch on arrival day. You can make a day trip to Beachcomber for the same price if you only want a few hours in the sun. There's a free shuttle bus from all Nadi hotels to the wharf; the connecting catamaran *Drodrolagi* leaves from Port Denarau daily at 0900. From Lautoka, the pickup is at 1030 daily except Tuesday and Thursday. The *Yasawa Flyer* picks up passengers for the Yasawas every morning at 1000, and it can also drop you off here on the way back to Nadi (but it can't carry you between Beachcomber and Nadi).

Beachcomber has been doing it right for decades, and the biggest drawback is its very popularity, which makes it crowded and busy. Reserve well ahead at their Nadi Airport or Lautoka offices, or at any travel agency.

Bounty Island

Bounty Island Sanctuary Resort (tel. 651-1271, fax 651-1390, www.fiji-bounty.com), run by the same company as nearby Treasure Island Resort, imitates the Beachcomber Island formula with 28 bunks in two dorms at F$71 pp. Otherwise the eight set tents are F$140 for up to four persons, plus F$25 pp a day for meals. The eight fan-cooled rooms with shared bath are F$140 for up to five persons, plus F$25 pp (children under 12 half price). The included food is great. At 20 hectares, Bounty is much larger than Beachcomber with more nature to explore; otherwise, most of the information above also applies here. Choose Bounty over Beachcomber if you like to party now and then, but don't wish to be part of a 24-hour circus. Transfers are via the Vuda Point Marina and cost F$40 pp each way including hotel pickups. The South Sea Cruises catamaran from the Denarau Marina will drop you here for F$46, and you can also transfer to the *Yasawa Flyer* at South Sea Island. Bounty Island reservations are handled by Hunts of the Pacific (tel. 672-2852, fax 672-0397) at Nadi Airport.

Castaway Island

Castaway Island Resort (tel. 666-1233, fax 666-5753, www.castawayfiji.com), on 174-hectare Qalito Island just west of Malolo, was built by Dick Smith in 1966 as Fiji's first outer-island resort. Today it's owned by Geoff Shaw, who also owns the Outrigger Reef Resort on the Coral Coast. It has always been one of Fiji's most popular resorts. The 66 closely-packed thatched *bure* sleep four—F$583 and up. No cooking facilities are provided but the all-meal plan is F$70 pp. The *lovo* and *meke* are on Wednesday night, the beach barbecue on Saturday.

Among the free water sports are sailing, windsurfing, paddleboats, tennis, and snorkeling, but sportfishing and scuba diving (with Geof and Trudy Loe) are extra. Diving is F$90/180 for one/two tank dives with shark feeding. Otherwise pay F$565 for three tanks a day for the duration of your stay! The PADI certification course is F$710 for one, or F$560 pp for two or more, and several other courses are also available. There's a swimming pool. Many Australian holidaymakers return to Castaway year after year; families with small children are welcome. A free "kids club" operates from 0900–1600 and 1900–2100 daily with lots of fun activities for those aged three and over, while Mom and Dad have some time to themselves.

There's the catamaran *Tiger IV* three times a day from Nadi's Port Denarau (F$56 each way), and Turtle Airways has three seaplane flights a day from Nadi for F$134. Castaway Island Resort's own boat, the 10-meter *Teivovo*, takes only 30 minutes to travel between Nadi and the island at speeds exceeding 100 kph. South Sea Cruises offers day trips to Castaway at F$99 including lunch and snorkeling gear (children half price). Only 10 persons a day are allowed to book the day cruises, so inquire early.

Navini Island

Navini Island Resort (Arthur, Helen, and Simone Reed, tel. 666-2188, fax 666-5566, www.navinifiji.com.fj) is a secluded ecoresort on a 2.5-hectare coral isle with just 10 beachfront *bure* nicely ensconced in the low island's shrubbery. Rates vary from F$470 double for a fan-cooled unit with a motel-like bathroom and small beds to F$650 for the deluxe honeymoon *bure* with a bathtub and enclosed courtyard. Discounts are available for stays of more than a week and for children. The compulsory two/three meal package is F$80/87 pp a day—excellent food, and you have a choice. Everyone gets to know one another during pre-dinner cocktails and by eating together at long tables at fixed times. Navini is ideal for couples and families looking for a quiet holiday—those interested in an intense social life or lots of organized activities might get bored. Complimentary morning boat trips are offered, as are snorkeling gear, paddleboats, sailboats, and kayaks. Scuba diving with Subsurface Fiji can be arranged, and the snorkeling right off their beach is good (abundant marinelife as fishing has been banned here for many years). Massage is F$50 an hour. Car/boat transfers from Nadi via the Vuda Point Marina are arranged anytime upon request (F$180 pp return, or free if you stay a week). Only overnight guests are accepted (no day-trippers).

South Sea Island

This is one of the smallest Mamanuca islands, a sandbank reminiscent of the shipwreck cartoons. Thirty people are packed into a thatched dormitory upstairs in a two-story building at F$70 pp, or sleep in a hut at F$170 double, good buffet meals and lots of water sports included. Even though the beach is fine, the developers have constructed a tacky little swimming pool in the center of the island. Boat transfers from Nadi are F$40 each way, but most guests use the free stopover here allowed on *Yasawa Flyer* tickets to the Yasawa Islands. Awesome Adventures and South Sea Cruises deliver as many day-trippers to this tiny island as they possibly can. It's overcrowded and not as clean as it could be, but fine if swimming and socializing are the things you like most to do. In short, South Sea (tel. 651-0506) is a party island for young backpackers.

Treasure Island

Beachcomber's little neighbor, **Treasure Island**

NADI AND THE MAMANUCAS

Resort (tel. 666-1599, fax 666-3577, www.fiji -treasure.com), caters to couples and families. It's extremely popular among packaged New Zealand and Australian vacationers, and occupancy levels seldom drop below 80 percent. The resort is half owned by the Tokatoka Nakelo landowning clan, which also supplies most of the workers, although the management is European. The 67 air-conditioned units, each with three single beds (F$495 single or double), are contained in 34 functional duplex bungalows packed into the greenery behind the island's white sands. Cooking facilities are not provided, so add F$68 pp daily for the meal plan. Special dinners and evening entertainment are scheduled every other night. Some nautical activities such as windsurfing, sailing, canoes, and spy board, which cost extra on Beachcomber, are free on Treasure Island. Scuba diving with Subsurface Fiji (www.fijidiving.com) is F$99/150 including gear for one/two-tank boat dives. Unlike Beachcomber, Treasure doesn't accept any day-trippers. Guests arrive on the shuttle boat *Tiger IV*, which departs Nadi's Port Denarau three times a day (F$40 each way, half price under age 16).

Wadigi Island

In 1998, a tiny resort called **Wadigi Island** (Ross and Jeni Allen, tel. 672-0901, www.wadigi.com) opened on the isle of the same name off the west end of Malolo. Each group of visitors gets exclusive use of the entire three-suite resort, costing F$2,310 for a couple, plus F$880 pp for the first two additional persons and F$770 pp for the next two up to six maximum (children under 12 not accepted). Included in the tariff are all meals, drinks, and sporting equipment such as kayaks, windsurfers, spy boards, fishing rods, and snorkeling gear. Only deep-sea fishing, surfing trips, and scuba diving (with Subsurface Fiji) cost extra. Transfers to the island from Nadi are also not included.

MANA ISLAND

Mana Island, 32 kilometers northwest of Nadi, is well known for its scuba diving and luxury resort,

Mana Island's South Beach is shared by a Fijian village, backpacker camps, and an upscale resort. The ferry from Nadi ties up to a wharf here.

but in recent years a whole slew of backpacker hostels have sprouted in the Fijian village on the eastern side of the island. There's much bad blood between the Japanese investors who run the resort and the Fijian villagers who accommodate the backpackers, and a high fence has been erected down the middle of the island to separate the two ends of the market. Uniformed security guards patrol the perimeter and shoestring travelers are most unwelcome anywhere in the resort, including the restaurants, shop, bars, and dive shop. In contrast, tourists from the resort are quite welcome to order drinks or meals at the backpacker camps.

Although this situation does poison the atmosphere on Mana Island slightly, there are lots of lovely beaches all around the island, most of them empty because the packaged tourists seldom stray far from their resort. The long white beach on the northeast side of the island is deserted. At the resort, the snorkeling is better off South Beach at low tide, off North Beach at high tide, but the nicest beach is Sunset Beach at the western end of the island. There's a great view of the Mamanucas and southern Yasawas from the highest point on Mana, a 10-minute hike from the backpacker camps, and splendid snorkeling on the reef. The Mana Main Reef is famous for its drop-offs with visibility never less than 25 meters, and you'll see turtles, fish of all descriptions, and the occasional crayfish.

The presence of the resort supports the frequent air and sea connections from Nadi, and the budget places allow you to enjoy Mana's stunning beauty at a fraction of the price tourists at the Japanese resort are paying. But to be frank, both of the main backpacker camps on Mana are rather squalid, and the places in the Yasawa Islands offer better accommodations for only a bit more money.

Sports and Recreation

Resort guests may patronize **Aqua-Trek** (tel. 666-9309, www.aquatrekdiving.com), which offers boat dives at F$83 for one tank plus F$11 for equipment, or F$462 for a six-dive package. Night dives are F$99. They run a variety of dive courses, beginning with a four-day PADI open-

water certification course (F$660). Underwater shark feeding is Aqua-Trek Mana's specialty, usually every Wednesday and Saturday at 0830.

Aqua Trek doesn't accept divers from the backpacker camps, who must dive with Ratu Kini's dive operation **Mana Pacific Divers** (tel. 666-9143), on the beach adjacent to Mereani's Inn. It charges F$80 for a one-tank lagoon dive, F$150 for a two-tank outer-reef dive, or F$100 for a night dive. Snorkeling gear is rented out at F$10, while guided snorkeling trips are F$20 pp.

Awesome Adventures operates the watersports concession on South Beach at the resort, offering waterskiing, Jet Skiing, water scooters, knee boarding, wakeboarding, sky riding, banana riding, and parasailing. Unlike Aqua-Trek, it doesn't discriminate against backpackers, and everyone is welcome (this could change).

The Backpacker Camps

Right up against the security fence near an enclosed sentry box is **Mereani's Backpackers Inn** (Mereani Ratunavu, tel. 666-3099, fax 670-3466), a large house with two five-bunk dormitories at F$45 pp and four double rooms at F$80 double. When the dorms in the main hostel fill up, they open a 19-bed dorm in the village. A separate "beach house" unit has one double at F$95 and a five-bed family room at F$130. If you have your own tent, you can camp at F$25 pp. All rates include three generous meals served to your table (breakfast is a buffet). You can get drinks at their bar all day. Activities include deep-sea fishing trips and four-island boat excursions (F$35 pp). Those staying a week get an extra night free and several complimentary trips.

Ratu Kini's Resort or "Mana Backpackers" (tel. 672-9143, fax 672-1959, rtkinihostel@connect.com.fj) has their reception and dining areas alongside the resort's security fence right next to Mereani's Inn, but the large accommodations building is 100 meters back in the village. The concrete main house has a 22-bunk dorm downstairs and a 26-bunk dorm upstairs, plus another four-bunk dorm in the corridor. Nearby are two thatched dormitory *bure* with seven and 14 bunks, all costing F$45 pp. The main house also contains three double rooms with shared bath at F$65/85 single/double, and six better rooms with private bath at F$75/95. A thatched four-bed *bure* in the backyard is F$130 double, plus F$25 per additional person. Have a look around before committing yourself, as all of the rooms are different. Camping is F$35 pp. Buffet-style meals are included in all rates (on Thursdays, they prepare a *lovo* and non-guests are welcome at F$10 pp). Reader reviews of the food vary from "awful" to "outstanding." A full-day boat trip to Malololailai Island is F$35 pp with lunch. A two-hour snorkeling trip is F$20 pp for the boat (minimum of four). Ratu Kini works out of office No. 26, upstairs from arrivals at Nadi Airport. People on their way to Ratu Kini's often stay at Mana Rose Apartments near Travelers Beach Resort at Wailoaloa Beach in Nadi. Both Ratu Kini's and Mereani's have electricity generators. Expect water shortages, occasional overcrowding, nocturnal animal sounds, a party atmosphere, and a lack of privacy in the mixed dorms of both hostels. Unattended gear may disappear from the beach.

Rara Cava's **Mana Lodge** (no phone) is a new place on the beach near Mereani's. There are four rooms with bath in one house at F$120 double, plus a separate beach *bure* at F$200, meals included. Mana Lodge has a large beach bar.

Another backpacker resort called **Dream Beach** (no phone) is run by Jerry and Kelera on a splendid beach on the north side of Mana Island, across the hill from Ratu Kini's. Since a fire destroyed one of the houses in 2001, there's only an eight-bunk dorm here. The owners say they intend to build five bungalows, but they'll need to solve their water problems first. For now, it's just a basic place to crash. Dream Beach is nicely secluded from the village and resort, so it's always worth asking about.

Accommodations

Juxtaposed against the backpacker camps is **Mana Island Resort** (tel. 666-1455, fax 666-1562, www.manafiji.com), by far the biggest of the tourist resorts off Nadi, with numerous tin-roofed bungalows clustered between the island's grassy rounded hilltops, white sandy beaches, and crystal-clear waters. The 40 "garden bungalows" are F$338 single or double, while the 20 "deluxe oceanview bungalows" and 32 hotel rooms are F$400. The 12 "executive oceanview bungalows" are F$500. Then there are the six "beachfront bungalows" with Jacuzzi at F$800 and seven "honeymoon bungalows" west of the airstrip at F$900. In 2003, 30 "oceanfront suites" were added in a hotel section near the wharf at F$731. Yuppie backpackers who find Mereani's and Ratu Kini's too basic can get a third off these rates by requesting the "walk-in special." Mana Island Resort caters to guests of all ages and has a daily "Kids Club" program. Children under 12 sleep free if sharing with one or two adults. All prices include a buffet breakfast and some nonmotorized water sports, but add 12.5 percent tax. Cooking facilities are not provided, so you'll need to patronize their restaurants (entrées F$20 and up). Live entertainment is presented nightly, and there's a Fijian *meke* on Tuesday and Saturday and a Polynesian show on Friday.

Getting There

The airstrip on Mana receives five Sun Air flights a day from Nadi (F$58 each way). The terminal is a seven-minute walk west of the resort (to get to the backpacker camps, head for the wharf from which the security fence will be visible).

If you're already staying in Nadi, it's just as easy to arrive on the *Tiger IV* catamaran, which runs three times a day from Port Denarau (F$56 each way including Nadi hotel pickups). Otherwise, South Sea Cruises runs a day trip from Nadi, including lunch at Mana Island Resort for F$99 (children under 16 half price). The ferry ties up to a wharf at South Beach, in fact, Mana is the only Mamanuca island with a wharf, so you don't need to take off your shoes.

Ratu Kini's own shuttle boat leaves Wailoaloa Beach at 1100 daily, costing F$40/70 one way/return including bus transfers from Nadi hotels. Mereani's guests must use the safer *Tiger IV*. Any Nadi travel agency or hotel can book these transfers.

THE OUTER ISLANDS

Matamanoa Island

Matamanoa Island Resort (tel. 666-0511 or 672-3620, fax 666-1069 or 672-0282, www.matamanoa.com), to the northwest of Mana Island, is the closest resort to **Monuriki Island,** the uninhabited island seen in the Tom Hanks film *Castaway.* It has 13 air-conditioned motel-style rooms at F$291 single or double, and 20 fan-cooled *bure* at F$470, tax included. Children under 12 are not accepted. The full American breakfast included in the basic price is good, but the same cannot be said of the lunch and dinner (limited choice, same all the time, too much deep-frying). Even so, the meal plan costs F$68 pp extra. Complimentary afternoon tea is served at the bar, followed by snacks during happy hour 1730–1830. Bring along a few packets of instant soup and some freeze-dried food, so you can spare yourself the meals! Loud cruise-ship-style entertainment is laid on at meal times and during the evening. The tiny island's beach is complemented by a small swimming pool. Scuba diving is with Aqua-Trek.

Boat transfers from Nadi on the *Tiger IV* cost F$97 pp each way, with a change of boats at Mana Island. If you fly to Mana, it's F$45 each way for the boat between Mana and Matamanoa. The schooner *Seaspray* operates all-inclusive day cruises from Matamanoa for F$125.

Tokoriki Island

Tokoriki Island Resort (tel. 666-1999 or 672-5926, fax 666-5295 or 672-5928, www.tokoriki.com) is the farthest Mamanuca resort from Nadi and the most private and secluded. There are 29 spacious fan-cooled *bure* from F$690 double (no cooking facilities). The three-meal plan is F$94 pp. To enhance the attraction for honeymooners and romantic couples, children under 12 are not accepted. The resort faces west on a kilometer-long beach, and water sports such as reef fishing, windsurfing, and Hobie cats are free

CASTAWAY, THE MOVIE

In early 2001, moviegoers worldwide got a taste of the savage beauty of Fiji's westernmost islands from Robert Zemeckis' film *Castaway.* The story revolves around a Federal Express employee (Tom Hanks) who becomes stranded on an uninhabited tropical isle after his plane goes down in the Pacific. The plane-wrecked air courier eventually spends four years on the island, and to achieve the desperate look needed to play his role, Hanks had to lose 40 pounds and grow a ragged beard. Thus *Castaway* was filmed in two stages eight months apart, with the second portion shot on location in the western Mamanucas in early 2000. For this event, about 100 members of the film crew descended on tiny **Monuriki Island**, between Matamanoa and Tokoriki.

At the time, concerns were raised that there might be a repeat of the damaging controversy surrounding the filming of *The Beach* in Thailand, when the producers were accused of inflicting environmental damage on Maya Beach in Krabi's Phi Phi Islands National Park. To avoid this, Zemeckis was careful to have veteran naturalist and author Dick Watling do an environmental-impact assessment before the filming, and the film crew followed Watling's recommendations carefully. Later, when naturalists from the World Wide Fund for Nature in Suva investigated the affair, they gave Zemeckis and his team high marks.

Ironically, 50-odd feral goats have long ravaged the vegetation on Monuriki, threatening the island's rare crested iguanas with extinction. The filmmakers offered to pay the Fijian landowners a bounty of F$100 per goat to remove the beasts, but their offer was refused. To Monuriki's customary owners on nearby Yanuya Island, a steady supply of goat meat is worth more than money or iguanas. Although no Fijians appear in *Castaway,* it conveys well the spellbinding scenery of this exotic region. To see the island off-screen, day cruises to Monuriki, such as the one offered by **South Sea Cruises** (tel. 675-0500, southsea@connect.com.fj) on the two-masted schooner *Seaspray* (F$165 with lunch and drinks), can be booked through hotel tour desks in Nadi.

(sportfishing available at additional charge). Scuba diving with Dive Tropex (www.toko rikidiving.com) also costs extra. At the center of the island is a 94-meter-high hill offering good views of the Yasawa and Mamanuca groups.

As on Matamanoa, you must take the fast catamaran *Tiger IV* to Mana, then a launch to Tokoriki (F$97 pp each way). If you fly to Mana, you can catch this launch straight to Tokoriki for F$45 one way. Turtle Airways charges F$154 pp to fly from Nadi to either Matamanoa or Tokoriki (Pacific Island Seaplanes charges F$193 pp). Island Hoppers (tel. 672-0410) at Nadi Airport offers direct helicopter transfers to either Tokoriki or Matamanoa at F$98 pp (minimum of two persons).

Vomo Island

Standing alone midway between Lautoka and Wayasewa Island (see the Yasawa Islands map), 91-hectare Vomo is a high volcanic island with a white beach around its west side. Since 1993, the coral terrace and slopes behind this beach have been the site of the luxurious **Vomo Island Resort** (tel. 666-7955 or 666-8122, fax 666-7997 or 666-8500, www.vomofiji.com). The 28 large air-conditioned villas with individual hot tubs run F$770 pp double occupancy, including all meals and nonmotorized activities, plus 12.5 percent tax (minimum stay three nights). Once part of the Sheraton chain, Vomo Island Resort offers swimming and snorkeling infinitely better than anything at Denarau. Scuba diving is with Aquacadabra Diving. The nine-hole pitch-and-putt golf course is free to guests. Pacific Island Seaplanes (tel. 672-5644) charges F$135 pp each way for transfers, while Turtle Airways is F$148 pp.

Southern Viti Levu

The southwest side of Viti Levu along the Queens Road is known as the Coral Coast for its fringing reef. Sigatoka and Navua are the main towns in this area, with most accommodations at Korotogo, Korolevu, and Pacific Harbor. This shoreline is heavily promoted as one of the top resort areas in Fiji, probably because of its convenient location along the busy highway between Nadi and Suva, but to be honest, the beaches here are second rate, with good swimming and snorkeling conditions only at high tide. Much of the coral has been destroyed by hurricanes, and beaches have been washed away. To compensate, most of the hotels have swimming pools, and in some places you can go reef walking at low tide. Top sights include the Sigatoka Sand Dunes and the impressive Navua River Gorge. The possibility of rainfall and the lushness of the vegetation increase as you move east.

Getting Around

An easy way to get between the Coral Coast resorts and Nadi/Suva is on the air-conditioned **Fiji Express** shuttle bus run by Coral Sun Fiji

(tel. 672-3105). The bus leaves the Holiday Inn, Tanoa Plaza, and other top hotels in Suva (F$31) at 0730 and calls at the Pacific Harbor International Hotel (F$27), The Warwick Hotel (F$22), Naviti Resort, Hideaway, Tambua Sands, Outrigger Reef Resort (F$20), Fijian Hotel (F$18), most Nadi hotels, and the Sheratons (F$7), arriving at Nadi Airport at noon (quoted fares are to the airport). It leaves Nadi Airport at 1300 and returns along the same route, reaching Suva at 1730. Bookings can be made at hotel tour desks. At Nadi Airport, contact Coral Sun Fiji (tel. 672-2268) in the arrivals area.

Coral Sun Fiji also books the air-conditioned **Queens Coach,** which runs in the opposite direction, leaving Nadi Airport for Suva at 0730, The Fijian Hotel at 0910, the Warwick and Naviti at 1010, and Pacific Harbor at 1110. The return trip departs the Holiday Inn around 1615, arriving at the airport at 2040. It's cheaper at F$19 between Nadi and Suva.

Many less expensive non-air-conditioned express buses pass on the highway, but make sure you're waiting somewhere they'll stop (any local will know). Pacific Transport's "stage" or "highway" buses between Lautoka/Nadi and Suva will stop anywhere along their routes, but the express buses call only at Sigatoka, Pacific Harbor, Navua, and some Coral Coast resorts.

The Coral Coast

NATADOLA AND ROBINSON CRUSOE

Natadola Beach

The long, white sandy beach here is easily the best on Viti Levu and a popular picnic spot with day-trippers arriving on the sugar train from The Fijian Hotel on the Coral Coast. Care should be taken while swimming in the ocean, as the waves can be unexpectedly strong. The small left point break at Natadola is good for beginning surfers, but one must always be aware of the currents and undertow. The left-hand breaks outside the reef are only for the experienced.

Plans to erect three or four luxury hotels on Natadola have been stalled by limited water supplies at the site. In 1999, it was announced that a 500-room resort to be managed by the Four Seasons chain would be erected here after the Fiji Government agreed to spend millions on infrastructure. Unfortunately, the project was scrapped after the May 2000 coup, but the Natadola Marine Resort Company (www.natadolafiji.com) is getting ready to try again. Shangri-La Hotels also has property here. A modern highway has been built from Queens Road directly to the beach at government expense.

At the moment, very few facilities are available, although the local villagers offer horseback riding to a cave at F$10. It's possible to rent a *bure* in Sanasana village at the south end of the beach at F$25 pp including meals. In the past, travelers have camped on Natadola Beach, but theft is a real problem here. Don't leave valuables unattended on this beach.

The dusty, Santa Fe–style **Natadola Beach Resort** (Thomas Hovelle, tel. 672-1001, fax 672-1000, www.natadola.com), across the road

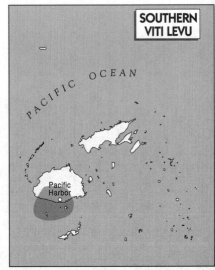

SOUTHERN VITI LEVU HIGHLIGHTS

Natadola Beach: white sands, clear water, horseback riding (p. 152)

Sigatoka Sand Dunes: visitor center, trails, accessible scenery (p. 155)

Tavuni Hill Fort: archaeological site, views, stories (p. 156)

Fijian firewalking: an unforgettable spectacle (p. 163)

Frigate Passage: a super scuba-diving and surfing venue (p. 169, 175)

Navua River Gorge: white-water and bamboo rafting, village tours (p. 172)

from the public beach, offers one block of six suites, plus another block of four suites, at F$308 single or double including continental breakfast. The luxurious "sandcastle" villa is F$369. Honeymooners are the target clientele, and children under 16 are not accepted. Each of the 10 fan-cooled units has a fridge, but no cooking facilities are provided. The resort's restaurant serves sandwiches (F$11), salads (F$11), and hamburgers (F$12.50) at lunch, while dinner mains cost F$27–42. A long swimming pool meanders between huge native trees in a garden setting. Unfortunately, shell peddlers and horseback riders waiting outside the resort gate can be a nuisance.

Paradise Transport (tel. 650-0028) has buses on weekdays from Sigatoka to Vusama village about four kilometers from the beach at 0900, 1130, 1300, and 1500 (ask the driver if the bus is going on to Sanasana). Otherwise, get off any Nadi bus at the Tuva Indian School stop on Queens Road, and hitch the eight kilometers straight to the beach. It's also possible to hike to Natadola in three hours along the coastal railway line from opposite Shangri-La's Fijian Resort.

Robinson Crusoe Island

The most popular offshore resort in this area is Robinson Crusoe Island (tel. 670-0026, fax 651-0100, www.robinsoncrusoeislandfiji.com), on Likuri Island, a small coral isle just north of Natadola. Not to be confused with Crusoe's Retreat on the Coral Coast toward Pacific Harbor, Robinson Crusoe caters to a more active crowd. The 11 simple *bure* with shared bath are F$79 pp, while the dorm *bure* with 20 beds upstairs and 38 downstairs is F$65 pp. Prices include three good meals, fishing, and snorkeling. Aqua-Trek has a dive shop on the island, charging F$80/120 for one/two tanks or F$450 for an open-water certification course (minimum of two persons). **Tropical Fishing and Watersports** (Bret Roberts, tel. 992-3233, www.sportfishingfiji.com) offers game fishing from the island at F$485/800 a half/full day (five anglers). Boat transfers at 1000 and 1630 from the Tuva River Jetty near Natadola are F$49 pp roundtrip, bus transfers from Nadi included. Day tours to Robinson Crusoe Island are offered on Tuesday, Thursday, and Sunday, costing F$79 pp including Nadi hotel transfers and a *lovo* lunch. The beach here is great, and this is a good alternative to the better-known Mamanuca resorts for the young at heart.

THE FIJIAN AND VICINITY

Shangri-La's Fijian Resort (tel. 652-0155, fax 650-0402, www.shangri-la.com) occupies all 40 hectares of Yanuca Island (not to be confused with another island of the same name west of Beqa). "The Fijian" (as it's often called) is connected to Viti Levu by a causeway 10 kilometers west of Sigatoka and 61 kilometers southeast of Nadi Airport. Opened in 1967, this Malaysian-owned complex of three-story Hawaiian-style buildings was Fiji's first large resort, and it's still Fiji's biggest hotel, catering to a predominantly Japanese clientele. The 436 air-conditioned rooms are F$370 single or double in the "lagoon wings," F$405 in the "ocean wings," F$505 for a family room, F$680 for a suite, or F$950 for one of the four beach *bure,* plus 12.5 percent tax. Included is a buffet breakfast for two people per room. A third adult is F$55, but two children 18 or under who share their parents' room stay free (kids 12 and under also eat for free). This makes Shangri-La's Fijian an ideal choice for families. The resort offers a nine-hole

AROUND SIGATOKA

To Suva →

NALIKO RD.

NATIVAKABUTA RD.

Natawarau Reef

TUBAKULA RESORT

KULA ECO PARK

Korokune (210 m)

OUTRIGGER REEF RESORT

VALAVA RD.

KAVANAGASAU RD.

MARAU MOTEL

VAKAVITI MOTEL

CROW'S NEST

WARATAH LODGE

Korotogo

TAVUNI HILL FORT

Naroro

Sigatoka River

KAVANAGASAU RD.

V i t i   L e v u   I s l a n d

To Tubarua →

Muasara Point

QUEENS   ROAD

CANE RAILWAY

Nakabuta

Lawai

Laselase

Maunivanua Point

Nayawa

Sigatoka River

Butoni (274 m)

SIGATOKA VALLEY RD.

SEE "SIGATOKA" MAP

Sigatoka

Nukunuku Island

CLUB MASA

Kulukulu

Koroua Island

Valeta Creek

To Vunatovau →

SIGATOKA WATER SUPPLY RD.

RD.

Lawaqa

KULUKULU RD.

Rakirakilevu Settlement

HOSPITAL

Sigatoka Sand Dunes National Park

1.5 mi

1.5 km

VISITOR CENTER

0

0

QUEENS RD.

To Nadi →

S O U T H   P A C I F I C   O C E A N

Rova Reef

© DAVID STANLEY

golf course (par 31), five tennis courts, numerous restaurants and bars, three swimming pools, and a white sandy beach. Every Friday night, there's firewalking, a *meke,* and a *lovo* (F$57). Avis Rent A Car has a desk in The Fijian, and an ANZ Bank ATM is available.

John Anthony's **Coral Coast Scuba Ventures** (tel. 652-8793, fax 652-0356, www.coral coastscuba.com) has the diving concession at Shangri-La's Fijian Resort. There are morning and afternoon dives, costing F$117/195 for one/two tanks including gear. Night diving (on Tuesday and Thursday) is F$145. Daily at 1300, there's a free scuba lesson in the resort's pool. Dive sites such as Nabaibai Passage, Barracuda Drift, The Wall, Golden Reef, and The Pinnacles are within a few minutes of the resort jetty.

Attractions Near the Fijian

Train buffs won't want to miss the *Fijian Princess,* a restored narrow-gauge railway originally built to haul sugarcane. It now runs 16-kilometer day trips along the coast to Natadola Beach daily at 1000. The station is on the highway opposite the access road to Shangri-La's Fijian Resort, and the ride costs F$79 pp including a picnic lunch. Another train tour goes to Sigatoka and the Tavuni Hill Fort. Otherwise there's a trip which combines Natadola with Robinson Crusoe Island. For information about hotel pickups, call the **Coral Coast Railway Co.** (tel. 652-0434 or 652-8731).

Across the road from the train station is the **Kalevu Cultural Center** (tel. 652-0200, fax 652-0322; Tues.–Sun. 0900–1700, www.fijicul turalcentre.com), a re-created Fijian village dispensing instant Fijian culture to tourists. The basic one-hour tour is F$20, while a full day at the center costs F$79 including tours of the Fiji, Samoa, Tonga, Rotuma, New Zealand, and Kiribati villages, a dance show, hotel transfers, and a *lovo* lunch. This tour is offered Tuesday, Thursday, and Saturday from 1000–1600, and if you can make your own way to the Center and don't require a hotel pickup, the price drops to F$49. The Ka Levu Cultural Center also provides accommodations with three large dormitories at F$55 pp and double rooms at F$65 pp. Both options include all meals and a guided tour.

Pacific Green Fiji (tel. 650-0055, www.paci ficgreenfiji.com), on Queens Road 3.5 kilometers east of the Ka Levu Cultural Center, manufactures stylish tropical furniture from coconut-tree logs. Visitors are welcome.

Malaqereqere Villas

Malaqereqere Villas (tel. 652-0704, fax 652-0708), 500 meters off Queens Road, 2.5 kilometers east of Shangri-La's Fijian Resort, stands on a hill overlooking Cuvu Bay. The four deluxe villas, each with three bedrooms, kitchen, fridge, and lounge are F$394 single or double, F$475 for three to six persons (minimum stay three nights). The local walk-in rate is about 40 percent lower than this. There's a swimming pool.

SIGATOKA SAND DUNES

From the mouth of the Sigatoka River westward, five kilometers of incredible 20-meter-high sand dunes separate the cane fields from the beach. These dunes were formed over millennia as sediments brought down by the river were blown back up onto the shore by the southeast trade winds. The winds sometimes uncover human bones from old burials, and potsherds lie scattered along the seashore—these fragments have been carbon-dated at up to 3,000 years old. Now and then, giant sea turtles come ashore here to lay their eggs.

It's a fascinating, evocative place, protected as a national park since 1989 through the efforts of the National Trust for Fiji. The **Visitors Center** (tel. 652-0243; daily 0800–1800, admission F$5, persons 18 and under F$2) is on Queens Road, about seven kilometers east of Shangri-La's Fijian Resort and four kilometers west of Sigatoka. Exhibits outline the ecology of the park, and you can hike along trails over dunes that reach as high as 50 meters in one area. For an extra F$3, a park ranger will give you a personal guided tour. It's well worth a visit to experience this unique environment. (Sandboarding down the side of the dunes is not allowed.) Most buses between Nadi and Sigatoka will drop you right in front of the Sand Dunes Visitors Center on the main highway (though some express buses won't stop here).

KULUKULU

Fiji's superlative surfing beach is near Kulukulu village, five kilometers south of Sigatoka, where the Sigatoka River breaks through Viti Levu's fringing reef to form the Sigatoka Sand Dunes. The surf is primarily a river-mouth point break with numerous breaks down the beach. It's one of the only places for beach-break surfing on Viti Levu, and unlike most other surfing locales around Fiji, no boat is required here. The windsurfing in this area is fantastic, as you can either sail "flat water" across the river mouth or do "wave jumping" in the sea (all-sand bottom and big rollers with high wind). The surfing is good all the time, but if you want to combine it with windsurfing, it's good planning to surf in the morning and windsurf in the afternoon when the wind comes up. You can also bodysurf here. Be prepared, however, as these waters are treacherous for novices. There's a nice place nearby where you can swim in the river and avoid the ocean's currents. The beach itself looks like an elephant graveyard, covered with huge pieces of driftwood.

American surfer Marcus Oliver runs a small budget resort behind the dunes called **Club Masa** (tel. 650-1282), also known as Oasis Budget Lodge, three kilometers off Queens Road. The rates, including two good meals, are F$28 pp in the 10-bed dormitory or F$50 pp in the two double rooms and a four-bed room. Camping is F$22 pp. There's no electricity, but the layout is attractive and the location excellent. Have a beer on their pleasant open porch. Food and drinks are not available during the day, but you can use their kitchen to prepare lunch (bring snack foods). Leave your valuables behind before going out for an evening stroll, however, as this is an isolated area. Snorkeling trips are F$10 including gear, horseback riding F$20, and fishing F$10–30 pp. Surfboard rentals are F$30 a day. When Marcus is away, his father Gordon Oliver manages the property. It's a good base from which to surf this coast.

Sunbeam Transport (tel. 650-0168) has buses (F$.60) from Sigatoka to Kulukulu village nine or 10 times a day Monday–Saturday, but none on Sunday and holidays. Taxi fare to Club Masa should be around F$5, and later you may have to pay only F$1 for a seat in an empty taxi returning to Sigatoka. Due to a land dispute with the local village, taxis cannot drive right up to Club Masa, and you must walk the last ten minutes from a reception building.

SIGATOKA

Sigatoka (sing-a-TO-ka) is the main business center for the Coral Coast and headquarters of Nadroga/Navosa Province. The racially mixed population numbers about 8,000. A new bridge over the Sigatoka River opened here in 1997, replacing an older bridge damaged during a 1994 hurricane but still used by pedestrians and the cane railway. The town has a picturesque riverside setting and is pleasant to stroll around. The pink-and-white fantasy mansion up on the hill above Sigatoka and visible from afar is owned by local businessman Bal Krishna Naidu.

Upriver from Sigatoka is a wide valley known as Fiji's "salad bowl" for its rich market gardens beside Fiji's second-largest river. Vegetables are grown in farms on the west side of the valley, while the lands on the east bank are planted with sugar cane. Small trucks use the good dirt road up the west side of the river to take the produce to market, while a network of narrow-gauge railways collects the cane from the east side. You can drive right up the valley in a normal car. The locals believe that Dakuwaqa, shark god of the Fijians, dwells in the river.

The valley also supplies South Pacific Foods Ltd., an organic food producer owned by the French transnational entrepreneur Pernod Ricard. The company's Sigatoka cannery produces juices from bananas, mangoes, guava, papayas, and tomatoes purchased from villagers who harvest fruit growing wild on their land. Large plantations have never flourished here due to the threat of hurricanes.

Near Sigatoka, five kilometers up the left (east) bank of the river from the bridge, is the **Tavuni Hill Fort** on a bluff at Naroro village. The fort was established by the 18th-century

Tongan chief Maile Latemai and destroyed by native troops under British control in 1876. The nearby village is still inhabited by persons of Tongan descent. An interpretive center and walkways have been established here, and admission is F$6 for adults or F$3 for children (closed Sun.). There's a good view of the river and surrounding countryside from this site. Those without transport can take a taxi from Sigatoka to the reception area (about F$15 return including a one-hour wait). Otherwise, the Mavua bus will bring you here from Sigatoka at 0830 or 1030. To hike there from Sigatoka takes about an hour or so each way, and it's more pleasant to walk along the cane railway line than on the dusty road.

Accommodations

The **Riverview Hotel** (tel. 652-0544), above Melrose Restaurant facing the new bridge in town, has six rooms with bath and balcony at F$35/45 single/double. A large public bar is downstairs, so be prepared for noise.

The **Sigatoka Club** (tel. 650-0026), across the traffic circle from the Riverview, has four fan-cooled rooms with private bath at F$35/45 single/double. Check that there's water before checking in, and bring mosquito coils. The rooms are often full, but the Club's bar is always good for a beer or a game of pool (three tables). The bar is open Monday–Saturday 1000–2200, Sunday 1000–2100.

SIGATOKA

Viti Levu Island

To Sigatoka Valley
To Tavuni Hill Fort

Qereqere Creek
River
Laselase

T. WICKS LTD.
ONE STOP RESTAURANT
TAPPOO
MISSION RD.
PEDESTRIAN BRIDGE
SIGATOKA VALLEY RD.
NAVUA ST.

SINGH'S COMFORT
MARKET
BUS STATION
MARKET RD.
WESTPAC BANK
ANZ BANK
MORRIS HEDSTROM
TAXI STAND
LE CAFÉ
RIVERVIEW HOTEL
VILISITE'S SEAFOOD RESTAURANT
RAJ'S CURRY HOUSE
QUEENS RD.
SIGATOKA CLUB
BOUNTY TOURS

Lawaqa Creek
POLICE STATION
LAWAQA
LAWAQA STADIUM PARK
RD.
POST OFFICE
TOWN COUNCIL
NADROGO NAVOSA PROVINCIAL COUNCIL
KHANS RENTAL CARS
MOSQUE
SOUTH PACIFIC FOODS CANNERY
QUEENS RD.

0   100 yds
0   100 m

CANE RAILWAY
BUDGET RENT-A-CAR
Yavulo Creek
Yavulo
Sigatoka
Nayawa

To Nadi and Sand Dunes
To Suva

© DAVID STANLEY

SOUTHERN VITI LEVU

Singh's Travelers Comfort (tel. 650-0514), also known as "Singh's Millennium Backpackers Motel," upstairs in a gloomy two-story building behind The Chemists facing Sigatoka market, has a few rooms at F$20/30 single/double. Ask at Singh's Chinese Restaurant in the arcade of the same building.

Food

A number of basic restaurants around the bus station and market dispense greasy fast food to bus passengers during their 15-minute stop here. Some of the worst food in Fiji is served here.

If you don't have to catch a bus, it's worth the short stroll to **One Stop Restaurant** (tel. 652-0602; Mon.–Sat. 0700–1700), near Tappoo on Sigatoka Valley Road. Don't take the fast food in the warmer on the counter—ask for the hot Indian curries made to order at about F$4 a plate. The same family operates another restaurant of the same name a bit farther along the same way, and you should check both (the duplication in names is to avoid buying another business license).

Le Café (tel. 652-0877; Mon.–Sat. 0900–1700), next to Jack's Handicrafts, offers a choice of nine set lunches for F$6.50 (pizzas F$7–16). Connect to the Internet at Le Surf Café here for F$.20 a minute. Le Café is sort of touristy and always full of day-trippers from the resorts.

Sigatoka's top Indian restaurant is **Raj's Curry House** (tel. 650-1470; daily 0800–2300), on Queens Road next to the Riverview Hotel. The curries listed on their printed menu are priced F$5.50–9.50, including five vegetarian dishes at around F$5. It's always full of savvy locals.

The chef at Raj's used to cook for the **Sigatoka Club** (tel. 650-0026) across the street where meals cost F$7.50–15.50 (printed menu). You're better off eating at Raj's, then crossing the street for a beer.

Vilisite's Seafood Restaurant (tel. 650-1030; daily 0800–2130), on Queens Road, has sandwiches (F$3), curries, fried rice, chop suey (F$5–8), and fish and chips (F$6–12) for lunch. At dinner from 1900–2130 you have a choice of six complete meals priced F$20–45. Taxi dri-

vegetable vendors outside the main market in Sigatoka

vers get a commission to bring tourists here, but it's still good value compared to the resorts.

Shopping

Sigatoka has ubiquitous souvenir shops and a colorful local market with a large handicraft section (especially on Wednesday and Saturday). **Jack's Handicrafts** (tel. 650-0810, www.jacks fiji.com) facing the river sells the traditional handmade **Fijian pottery** made in Nakabuta and Lawai villages near Sigatoka.

For quality snorkeling gear, try **Nats** (tel. 650-0064), upstairs between the Colonial National Bank and Big Bear on the street facing the river.

Services

There are four banks in Sigatoka. The ANZ Bank opposite the bus station and the Westpac Bank have Visa/MasterCard ATMs outside their offices.

Sigatoka Money Exchange (tel. 652-0422; weekdays 0830–1700, Sat. 0830–1300), between Jack's Handicrafts and the Riverview Hotel, changes money at rates similar to the banks, without commission.

T-Wicks Ltd. (tel. 652-0505), on Sigatoka Valley Road, offers Internet access at F$.20 a minute.

Health

The District Hospital (tel. 650-0455) is 1.5 kilometers southwest of Sigatoka, out on the road to Nadi.

Dr. Gurusmarna D. Dasi (tel. 650-0369) and Dr. Rudy Gerona and Dr. (Mrs.) Aida Gerona (tel. 652-0128) all work out of offices on Sigatoka Valley Road, facing the river a bit north of the old bridge. They're open weekdays 0730–1600, Saturday 0730–1300.

Patel Chemist (tel. 650-0213) is behind the market.

Transportation

Pacific Transport (tel. 650-0088) express buses leave Sigatoka for Suva at 0845, 0910, 1010, 1425, 1800, and 1945 (127 km, 3.5 hours, F$7.45), and for Nadi Airport at 0935, 1115, 1220, 1500, 1800, and 2020 (70 km, 1.5 hours, F$4.05). **Sunbeam Transport** has express buses

to Suva at 0640, 0800, 1220, 1320, and 1500. Many additional local services also operate to/from Nadi (61 km). Beware of taxi drivers hustling for fares at the bus station who may claim untruthfully that there's no bus going where you want to go.

Weekdays you can arrange your own 4.5-hour, F$6 tour by taking the 0900 **Paradise Transport** (tel. 650-0028) bus up the west side of the Sigatoka Valley to Tubarua and back. Other buses to Tubarua leave at 1130, 1430, 1730, and 1900. Carriers to places farther up the valley like Korolevu (F$7) and Namoli (F$7) leave weekdays just after noon, returning the next day. They park beside a mango tree at the market, just around the corner from Sigatoka Bus Station.

Budget Rent-a-Car (tel. 650-0986) is at Niranjan's, opposite the Mobil service station at the west entrance to town. **Khan's Rental Cars** (tel. 650-1229) has an office at Midas Automotive next to the mosque in Sigatoka.

KOROTOGO

A cluster of budget places to stay and one large American-run resort are at Korotogo, eight kilometers east of Sigatoka, with only the Outrigger Reef Resort, Sandy Point Beach Cottages, and Tubakula Beach Resort right on the beach itself. Most of the places to stay farther east at Korolevu are more upmarket. East of Korotogo, the sugar fields of western Viti Levu are replaced by coconut plantations with rainforests creeping up the green slopes behind.

A road almost opposite the Outrigger Reef Resort leads to a bird park called **Kula Eco Park** (tel. 650-0505, fax 652-0202; daily 1000–1630, admission F$15, children under 12 half price, www.fijiwild.com). It's your only chance to get a close look at the *kula* lorikeet, the Kadavu musk parrot, the goshawk, flying fox fruit bats, and others in near-natural settings. The park has a captive breeding program for the endangered crested iguana and peregrine falcon. Displays explain it all.

Sports and Recreation

Aqua Safari (Kaylee Birch, tel. 652-0901, fax

652-0907, aquasafari@connect.com.fj), on the traffic circle at Korotogo, does two-tank dives each morning at F$140. In the afternoon, there's a snorkeling trip costing F$30 pp including gear. Their PADI certification course is F$575.

Mountain View Horse Riding (tel. 923-4783), on the beach opposite The Crow's Nest, charges F$10/20 for a short/long ride.

Accommodations

Under US$25: Just west of the Outrigger Reef Resort at Korotogo is **Waratah Lodge** (tel. 650-0278), with three large A-frame bungalows at F$45 double, plus F$10 per additional person up to six maximum. The two rooms below the reception in the main building are F$39 single or double. Cooking facilities are provided. The swimming pool and charming management add to the allure. It's good value and recommended.

A bit east of the Outrigger and right on the beach, **Tubakula Beach Resort** (tel. 650-0097, fax 650-0201, www.fiji4less.com) offers a holiday atmosphere at bargain rates. The 22 pleasant A-frame bungalows with fan, cooking facilities, and private bath—each capable of sleeping three or four—vary in price from F$66 triple near the highway or F$73 in the garden (F$13.50 extra for a fourth person). Renovated bungalows are F$85 double poolside, F$90 garden, or F$96 beachfront (third persons F$17.50). One self-catering house has three rooms with shared bath at F$39/43 single/double. Their "Beach Club" dormitory consists of eight rooms, each with four or five beds at F$17.50 a bed. Tubakula caters to independent travelers rather than people on "Feejee Experience" type of packages. Prices have remained relatively low because the owners don't pay commissions to Nadi travel agents, which works to your advantage. Instead, small discounts are available to youth hostel, VIP, and Nomads cardholders, and if you stay a week, it's 10 percent off. A communal kitchen is available to all, plus a swimming pool, restaurant, game room, nightly videos, and minimarket. Late readers will like the good lighting. Tubakula's conference building can host conferences, meetings, and seminars for up to 250 people (it's often used by NGOs). Several sightseeing attractions and local cafes are within

walking distance. Ask about the Thursday-night *lovo* (underground-oven feast) at Malevu village, 500 meters east of Tubakula. The snorkeling here is good, there's surfing and scuba diving nearby, and bus or taxi excursions are available. What more do you want? Basically, Tubakula is a quiet, do-your-own-thing kind of place for people who don't need lots of organized activities. Seated on your terrace, watching the sky turn orange and purple behind the black silhouettes of the palms along the beach, a bucket of cold Fiji Bitter stubbies close at hand, you'd swear this was paradise! It's one of the most popular backpacker resorts in Fiji and well worth a couple of nights.

US$25–50: Grayelen Lodge (Graham and Helen Mulligan, tel./fax 652-0677), off Queens Road, four kilometers east of Sigatoka and two kilometers west of the Korotogo traffic circle, has three self-catering units with fridge at F$50 for up to four persons. There's a swimming pool and a large porch with a deck, though it's on a hill rather than the beach. It's still good value.

The **Marau Motel** (tel. 652-0807, fax 652-0829, maraumotel@connect.com.fj), 19 Queens Road north of the traffic circle in Korotogo, has four self-catering apartments at F$35/55/70 single/double/triple including a light breakfast. A backpacker dorm upstairs with five beds and its own kitchen is F$18 pp. It's some distance from the beach.

Uncle T's Lodge (tel./fax 652-0235), on Queens Road a bit closer to the traffic circle, has a self-catering, two-bedroom flat on the back side of the owner's home at F$100. Taken separately, the two doubles and one single room are F$40/50 single/double with breakfast, or F$20 pp in a four-bed dorm.

The **Crow's Nest Resort** (tel. 650-0230, fax 652-0354, www.crowsnestfiji.com), on Sunset Strip a few hundred meters southeast of the traffic circle, offers 18 split-level duplex bungalows with cooking facilities and veranda at F$88 single or double, plus F$20 pp to four maximum. The Crow's Nest Dormitory behind the reception is F$20 pp for the eight beds. The restaurant facing the swimming pool often has inexpensive curry specials. The nicely landscaped grounds are just across the road from the beach, and good views over the lagoon are obtained from the Crow's Nest's elevated perch. "Feejee Experience" groups often stay here.

The **Vakaviti Motel and Dorm** (tel. 650-0526, fax 652-0424, www.vakaviti.com), next to the Crow's Nest, has four self-catering units facing the pool at F$65 single or double, and a five-bed family *bure* with one double and three single beds at F$75 double. Children under 12 are free. The six-bed dormitory is F$15 pp. Stay a week, and the eighth night is free. Facilities include a swimming pool and a large lending library/book exchange at the reception. Day trips to Natadola Beach are F$15 pp.

The **Casablanca Hotel** (tel. 652-0600), next door to Vakaviti, is a two-story hillside building on the inland side of Sunset Strip. Its eight rooms with cooking facilities and arched balconies begin at F$45/60 single/double.

Sandy Point Beach Cottages (Bob Kennedy, tel. 650-0125, fax 652-0147, cbcom@con nect.com.fj) shares the same beach with the adjacent Outrigger Reef Resort. Three fan-cooled beachfront units with full cooking facilities are offered at F$75 single, F$85 double or triple, one garden bungalow is F$75 double, and a five-bed cottage is F$135. Set in spacious grounds right by the sea, Sandy Point has its own freshwater swimming pool. The eight huge satellite dishes you see on their lawn allow you to pick up 10 channels on the TV in your room. It's a good choice for families or small groups, but it's often full, so you must reserve well ahead.

US$50–100: The **Bedarra Inn** (77 Sunset Strip; tel. 650-0476, fax 652-0116, www.bedar rafiji.com) a bit west of the Outrigger, has 21 air-conditioned rooms with fridge in a two-story block at F$125/145/165 double/triple/quad. It's all tastefully decorated but only four rooms have microwaves. A swimming pool, video room, and lounge round out the facilities.

US$150 and up: The 254-room **Outrigger Reef Resort** (tel. 650-0044, fax 652-0074, www.outrigger.com/fiji) plunges down the hillside from Queens Road to a sandy beach. A great view of this Fijian village-style complex can be had from the reception. In 2000, this property underwent a US$23.3 million redevelopment,

and to provide more building space the main highway was rerouted away from the coast. The new hotel is owned by Australians Geoff Shaw and Bob Cliff, who also run Castaway Island Resort in the Mamanucas, and it's managed by Outrigger Hotels of Hawaii. The Outrigger Reef caters to the middle market, providing comfortable, unpretentious facilities at affordable package prices. The four-story main building on the hill has 167 air-conditioned rooms with ocean views and balconies, beginning at F$410 for up to four people. Down near the huge million-liter swimming pool by the beach is a three-story block remaining from the old Reef Resort with 40 air-conditioned rooms starting at F$440. Scattered around the grounds are 47 regular thatched *bure* with fan from F$475, and five big duplex *bure* at F$1,150 for a family of up to six. Rates include tax and a buffet breakfast, and a reduced local walk-in rate is often offered. Wheelchair-accessible rooms are available. A free "kids club" operates from 0900–2100. Even if you're not staying here, it's worth coming for the Fijian firewalking Friday at 1830 (F$15), followed by *meke* and buffet (F$45) in the restaurant. There's a small shopping mall, and Thrifty Car Rental and Rosie The Travel Service have desks just off the lobby. A tunnel under the highway near the tennis courts leads to the Kula Eco Park. Internet access is F$5 for 15 minutes.

Food

Facing the beach just west of the Outrigger Reef Resort is the **Beach Side Restaurant** (tel. 652-0584; daily 0800–2130) with chicken, meat, and seafood dishes for F$5–14, vegetarian food at F$5.50–7. Pizza is F$7–15 (dinner only). A minimarket and handicraft shop adjoin the restaurant. To get there from the Outrigger, go down onto the beach and walk west.

Le Café Garden Restaurant (tel. 652-0877; daily 1000–2300) is between the Beach Side Restaurant and Waratah Lodge. Pizzas are F$7–16, specials F$6.50 (choice of six). Happy hour is 1700–1900, and there's disco dancing after 2200 Friday and Saturday. Under Swiss management, this place has class, although the food receives varied reviews.

Another evening you could walk 800 meters west to the **Crow's Nest Restaurant** (tel. 650-0230; daily 0700–1500 and 1800–2130) with dinner mains at F$10. The nicest place for a meal out along this way is the **Bedarra Inn** (tel. 650-0476; daily 0700–1500 and 1800–2200), with main dishes ranging from pasta Bedarra at F$15 to lobster for F$38. Their specialty is seafood curry (F$23). The **Sinbad Pizza Restaurant** (tel. 652-0600) at the Casablanca Hotel isn't as nice as these (pizza F$8–22).

Getting There

Local buses on Queens Road stop at the doors of the Outrigger Reef Resort and Tubakula Beach Resort. For the Crow's Nest, Vakaviti, Casablanca, Bedarra, and Waratah, get off the bus at the traffic circle on the coast, just where the highway turns inland and heads east toward the Outrigger. From there, follow the old highway (Sunset Strip) south along the beach to your hotel.

Car Rentals and Tours

Thrifty Car Rental (tel. 652-0242) has a desk in the lobby of the Outrigger Reef Resort. The **Avis** office (tel. 652-0144) is on the beach opposite Waratah Lodge just west of the resort.

Coastal Rental Cars (tel. 652-0228, fax 652-0888, coastalrentalcar@connect.com.fj), on Korotogo Back Road near the traffic circle at Korotogo, rents cars at F$115/500 for one/six days including tax and insurance.

The **Beach Side Restaurant** (tel. 652-0584), across the street from Avis, rents cars at F$100 a day all inclusive. They also offer taxi tours to Natadola (F$80) and Pacific Harbor (F$80) or a full day of sightseeing at F$100—all prices are for the car. Jiten Kumar of **Sunstrip Tours** (tel. 924-7161) offers the same and is very accommodating.

Adventures in Paradise (tel. 652-0833, fax 652-0848, wfall@connect.com.fj) operates tours to Biausevu Falls (F$89 including lunch, drinks, and guides) and the Naihehe Cave (F$99). For pick-ups around Nadi, add F$20 to these prices. Book through your hotel tour desk (and wear disposable shoes on the falls hike). These trips are highly rated.

Vatukarasa

This small village between Korotogo and Korolevu is notable for its quaint appearance and **Baravi Handicrafts** (tel. 652-0364), 7.5 kilometers east of the Outrigger Reef Resort. Baravi carries a wide selection of Fijian handicrafts at fixed prices, and it's worth an outing if you're staying at one of the Coral Coast resorts. If you swim here, beware of dangerous currents.

KOROLEVU

At Korolevu, east of Korotogo, the accommodations tend to cater to a more upscale crowd, and cooking facilities are usually not provided for guests. These places are intended primarily for people on packaged beach holidays who intend to spend most of their time unwinding. Distances between the resorts are great, so for sightseeing you'll be dependent on your hotel's tour desk. An exception is The Beachouse, which opened in 1996. The Coral Village Resort and Waidroka Bay Resort farther east also accommodate budget travelers, but they're both far off the highway.

Sports and Recreation

Mike's Divers (Mike and Phylis Jaureguy, tel./fax 653-0222, www.dive-fiji.com), at Votua village near Korolevu, offers diving at F$75/125/350/500 for one/two/six/10 tanks, plus F$20 for gear. Night diving is F$95. Non-divers can snorkel from the boat for F$20 (or free from their beach). All the usual courses are offered, including open-water certification at F$450. Drift diving along Morgan's Wall is Mike's specialty (giant sea fans, soft corals, lionfish). Or ask to go to Turtle Town where all good turtles sleep.

South Pacific Adventure Divers (tel. 653-0055, fax 672-0719, www.divetravelfiji.com), based next to the pool at The Warwick Resort, also handles diving at The Naviti, Hideaway Resort, and Tambua Sands (free pick-ups). They frequent the top dive sites in the Beqa Lagoon, 40 minutes away by boat, as well as colorful sites closer to home. For Coral Coast dives, it's F$75/140 for one/two tanks including gear and lunch. Dive excursions to the Beqa Lagoon or

FIREWALKING VENUES

Fijian firewalking over hot stones originated on Beqa and Yanuca Islands off southern Viti Levu, but it's now performed exclusively at resort hotels around Nadi and along the Coral Coast. **Shangri-La's Fijian Resort** west of Sigatoka presents firewalking together with a *meke* (traditional Fijian dance show) on Friday nights. The F$57 package also includes a *lovo* (underground oven) meal. The other resorts all charge a flat F$15 admission fee to witness their firewalking performances, which generally begin around 1830. It happens at **The Warwick Fiji** on Mondays and Fridays, at **The Naviti Resort** on Wednesdays, at **Hideaway Resort** on Thursdays, and at the **Outrigger Reef Resort** on Fridays. Another great place to witness firewalking is at **Pacific Harbor's Cultural Center** where you get handicraft demonstrations and a tour of a re-created Fijian village for your F$18 admission. The Pacific Harbor shows only occur on Thursday afternoons, but firewalking alternates with performances by the Dance Theater of Fiji on different weeks, so call ahead to verify the program. Also check the dates at the hotels as these things do change.

Vatulele are F$255 for two tanks including gear (six-person minimum). SPAD's PADI four-day, open-water course is F$580.

Air Snorkel (tel. 672-5909, www.airsnorkel .com) offers an underwater snorkeling experience using a line attached to a floating device on the surface. Snorkeling this way from a pontoon anchored near The Warwick costs F$49 pp.

Several companies offer tours to **Biausevu Falls,** a 25-minute hike from Biausevu village, itself just less than three kilometers inland from Queens Road between The Warwick and Vilisite's Restaurant. The trail to the falls zigzags across the river a half dozen times (expect to get your feet wet), but you'll enjoy a refreshing swim in the pool at the foot of the cascading waterfall. The village charges F$10 pp admission (children F$3) to the area. Call Adventures in Paradise (tel. 652-0833) in Korotogo for information on tours.

Accommodations

US$25–50: Vilisite's Restaurant (tel./fax 653-0054; daily 0800–2200), by the lagoon between The Warwick and The Naviti resorts at Korolevu, has four spacious air-conditioned rooms with bath and fridge at F$55/66 single/double, plus one four-person family room at F$75. Though the accommodations are good value, "Felicity's Place" is better known for its restaurant, as this is *the* place to stop for food between Nadi and Suva. You might bump into your country's ambassador on their beachside terrace. The favorite lunch dish is fish and chips at F$6/12 for a small/large portion. Otherwise there's chop suey or curries from F$5–8. Dinner consists of a choice of six set seafood menus costing F$20–45. The champagne sunsets here from 1800–1900 are unforgettable. Vilisite's gift shop has good prices on handicrafts. It's worth the taxi ride if you're staying at The Warwick or The Naviti.

One of the South Pacific's best budget resorts, **The Beachouse** (tel. 653-0500 or 653-0530, www.fijibeachouse.com), is on a palm-fringed white beach just off Queens Road, between Navola and Namatakula villages, five kilometers east of The Warwick. It's 35 kilometers east of Sigatoka and 43 kilometers west of Pacific Harbor. Their slogan is "low-cost luxury on the beach" and the whole project was painstakingly designed to serve the needs of backpackers (and not as a dormitory tacked onto an upmarket resort as an afterthought). The two wooden accommodation blocks each have four five-bunk dorms downstairs (F$19 pp) and four fan-cooled loft rooms upstairs (F$22/25 pp in a three/two-bed dorm). In addition, 12 neat little units in a quadrangle at the heart of the property are F$60 single or double. Campers are allowed to pitch their tents on the wide lawn between the rooms and the beach at F$12 pp. Tax is included. Stay six nights and the seventh night is free. Separate toilet/shower facilities for men and women are just behind the main buildings, and nearby is a communal kitchen and dining area. It's all very clean and pleasant. Daily afternoon tea and scones are free for guests (a beach-volleyball game usually follows). Meals in their beachfront Coconut Cafe consist of fish and chips, steak burgers, and vegetarian fare, costing F$9 or less (open until midnight). The closest grocery store is in Korolevu (there's only a tiny cooperative store in Namatakula). Not only is the ocean swimming good at high tide (unlike the situation at many other Coral Coast hotels where you may end up using the pool), but they'll take you out to the nearby reef in their launch for snorkeling (F$8 for a mask and fins, if required). However, do ask about the currents before going far off on your own—tourists have drowned after being swept out through the reef passage here. A shopping shuttle to Suva can be arranged (F$14 pp return, minimum of five). A vigorous four-hour round-trip hike to Navola Falls is possible. Sea kayaks (F$3 an hour) and bicycles (F$3 for two hours) are available, and there's a bush track up into the hills behind the resort. The lending library serves those who only came to relax. Check your email for F$.20 a minute. The Beachouse does get crowded whenever the "Feejee Experience" groups arrive, so call ahead for reservations.

Coral Village Resort (tel. 650-0807, corvill@connect.com.fj) is just beyond Namaqumaqua village, 4.5 kilometers off Queens Road down the same difficult access road as Crusoe's Retreat (see below). Coral Village is set in a narrow valley that opens onto a lovely white beach (one of the Coral Coast's best) facing a protected lagoon. The eight large rooms with fan and fridge are F$60 pp including two meals. There's also a five-bed dorm at F$30 pp including two meals. Cooking your own food is not possible and lunch is extra (sandwiches F$5). Massage is F$30 an hour. Diving and other sporting activities must be arranged through Crusoe's Retreat. Unfortunately, Coral Village has gone downhill in recent years and now has a rundown, abandoned air.

The **Waidroka Bay Resort** (Michael Kaz, tel. 330-4605, fax 330-4383, www.waidroka.com) is up the steep, rough gravel road leading to the Dogowale Radio Tower between Korovisilou and Talenaua, four miles off Queens Road. Operating since 1995, Waidroka has earned a reputation as one of Fiji's top surfing resorts. Accommodations include a 12-bed dormitory at F$18 pp, and three lodge rooms with shared

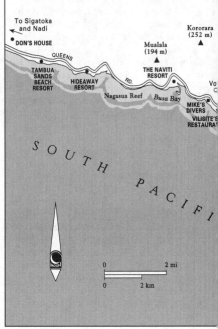

AROUND KOROLEVU

bath at F$54 triple. The five neat little oceanfront bungalows with private bath, fan, bamboo walls, and covered deck are F$99/134 double/triple. The two superior bungalows are F$139/174/209 double/triple/quad, while five terrace rooms in a long building on the hillside are F$89 single or double, F$124 triple. The optional meal plan is F$38 pp a day (cooking facilities are not provided), otherwise dinner entrées in the restaurant are F$12–23. Videos are shown in the jungle bar at night. The surfing crowd loves this place, and it's the only "mainland" resort surfing Frigate Passage and six other local breaks. Three breaks are just a five-minute boat ride from the resort, and they'll ferry you out there at F$20 pp for two hours. Snorkeling trips, which cost the same, are necessary, because Waidroka's beach is mediocre. Waidroka's 10-meter dive boat *Fiji Explorer* has two 200-horsepower engines, which enables it to reach Frigate Passage in

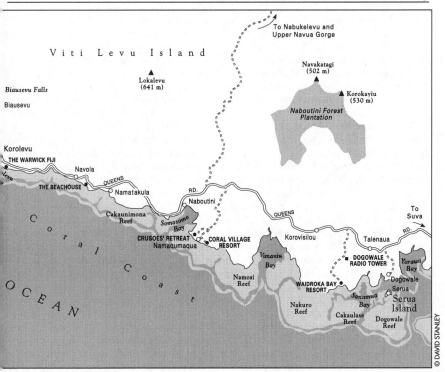

© DAVID STANLEY

just 20 minutes (surfers pay F$45 pp including lunch, with a F$180 minimum charge for the boat). Scuba diving is F$70/130 for one/two tanks, plus F$25 for equipment. Open-water certification is F$499 (advanced courses available). Sportfishing aboard *Fishing Machine* is F$600/1,000 a half/full day for four persons. All this is fine, but you should be aware that the Waidroka Bay Resort is only of interest to those intending to participate in the various sporting activities. Those more interested in a relaxing seaside vacation probably won't like the fishing-camp atmosphere. Call ahead, and they'll pick you up at Korovisilou village on Queens Road at F$10 for the car. Reservations are necessary, as the Waidroka Bay Resort is often full.

US$50–100: Two self-catering flats are for rent at **Don's House** (no phone, http://members.optusnet.com.au/~jflight), a duplex building above Queens Road just west of Namada vil-

lage, between the Baravi Handicraft Boutique and the Tambua Sands Beach Resort. Each air-conditioned unit has a full kitchen, lounge, floor-to-ceiling windows, and laundry facilities, and there's a small saltwater pool on the large covered deck out front. A sandy beach is across the highway. The price for up to five persons is F$140 for one unit and F$160 for the other or F$270 for both. Discounts are offered for stays of more than four nights. Reservations must be made through James and Lyndae Flight (tel. 61-2-9546-6256, fax 61-2-9594-1217, jflight@optusnet.com.au) in Sydney, Australia, as the on-site caretaker is unable to rent the units. Visiting celebrities in need of privacy often book this place.

The good-value **Tambua Sands Beach Resort** (tel. 650-0399, fax 652-0265, www.tambuasandsfiji.com), in an attractive location facing the sea about 10 kilometers east of the Outrigger Reef Resort, conveys a feeling of calm and peace.

The 31 beach bungalows are F$125 double garden or F$135 beachfront (third persons F$30), continental breakfast included. No cooking facilities are provided. Though the restaurant is nothing special, there's a swimming pool, excellent live music most evenings, and a *meke* on Saturday night if enough guests are present. UTC has a tour desk at this hotel.

US$100–150: The 100-room **Hideaway Resort** (tel. 650-0177, fax 652-0025, www.hideawayfiji.com) at Korolevu, is three kilometers east of Tambua Sands and 20 kilometers east of Sigatoka. Set on a palm-fringed beach before a verdant valley, the 30 fan-cooled *bure* are F$280 triple, while the 58 *bure* with air-conditioning go for F$305. The 10 air-conditioned villas are F$364. Four larger family units suitable for up to six people go for F$482. Some rooms get a lot of disco noise from the bar or traffic noise from the adjacent highway. A full buffet breakfast is included in all rates (no cooking facilities). The lunch-and-dinner plan is F$40 pp a day (minimum of three days). This big resort provides entertainment nightly, including a *meke* on Tuesday and Friday (free), firewalking on Thursday (F$15), and an all-you-can-eat Fijian feast Sunday night (F$26.50). The resort's oceanside pool is one of the largest on the Coral Coast. Surfing is possible on a very hollow right in the pass here (not for beginners), and scuba diving can be arranged. Beware of unperceived currents, and expect dead coral if you snorkel here (possible at high tide only). The Rosie Travel Service desk arranges other trips and Thrifty Car Rental bookings.

Crusoe's Retreat (Liam and Cathie Costello, tel. 650-0185, fax 652-0666, www.crusoesretreat.com), by the beach four kilometers off Queens Road from Naboutini, was formerly called the Man Friday Resort. It's the most isolated place to stay on the Coral Coast. The 28 large *bure* each have two double beds, a fridge, and a porch. The 11 "seaside" *bure* are F$236 double, while the 17 "seaview" bungalows on the hillside are F$195. Only units Nos. 1–6 have thatched roofs (No. 1 is the closest to the beach). Readers have complained about salty, damp rooms and low water pressure here. Children under 12 sleep free. Prices include a buffet breakfast, afternoon

tea, and nonmotorized sports such as kayaks, sailboards, and paddleboards. The mangrove-jungle tour is free, and a daily activity program is prepared. The lunch-and-dinner plan is F$45 pp. Don Wood runs the on-site dive shop (www.divecrusoes.com), charging F$92/169 for one/two tanks including gear. The resort's name alludes to Daniel Defoe's novel *Robinson Crusoe,* and the footprint-shaped freshwater swimming pool symbolizes Man Friday. This resort is much more upscale than nearby Coral Village Resort, although the beach isn't as nice. If you call ahead, they'll pick you up from the bus stop on the main highway at F$5 per carload.

US$150 and up: The **Naviti Resort** (tel. 653-0444, fax 653-0099, www.navitiresort.com.fj), five kilomters east of Hideaway Resort and 100 kilometers from Nadi Airport, has 140 spacious air-conditioned rooms and suites in a series of two-story blocks beginning at F$364/472 single/double. The price includes all meals with unlimited wine or beer plus many activities. Breakfast is the best meal of the day. The all-inclusive price allows you to enjoy your holiday without mounting bills (a room alone is F$282 single or double). Kids under 16 stay and eat free when sharing with parents on the Naviti's comprehensive all-inclusive plan. The Naviti is also one of the more wheelchair-accessible resorts on this coast. There's firewalking on Wednesday (F$15) and a *lovo* on Friday (F$30). The five tennis courts are floodlit at night. Nonguests may use the nine-hole golf course for F$20, and scuba diving is offered. Other facilities include a swimming pool, mini fitness center, beauty center, Internet access (F$.30 a minute), ATM in the lobby, and a boutique. Rosie The Travel Service has a desk at The Naviti. Scuba diving is with South Pacific Adventure Divers. This spacious resort shares its beach with a Fijian village.

The Warwick Fiji (tel. 653-0555, fax 653-0010, www.warwickfiji.com), on the Queens Road six kilometers east of The Naviti, is the third-largest hotel on the Coral Coast (after The Fijian and the Outrigger Reef). Erected in 1979 and part of the Hyatt Regency chain until 1991, it's now owned by the same Singapore-controlled company as The Naviti, and there's a shuttle bus between the two. The 250

The Wicked Walu restaurant is on a point just off the main beach at The Warwick Fiji resort.

air-conditioned rooms are in three-story wings running east and west from the soaring Hyatt-style lobby. It's F$332 double for the 51 rooms with mountain views, F$371 for the 166 with ocean views, F$523 for the 23 club rooms, and F$697 for the 10 suites, buffet breakfast included. Two children 12 and under sleep and eat free when sharing with their parents. The Wicked Walu seafood restaurant, on a small offshore islet connected to the main beach by a causeway, serves large portions but is expensive (dinner only). The other hotel restaurants can be crowded with Australian families and you might even end up waiting in line (F$53 meal plan). There's live music in the Hibiscus Lounge Wednesday–Saturday until 0100 and nightly disco dancing. The firewalking is on Monday and Friday at 1830 (F$15). This plush resort is very much oriented toward organized activities and has a complete sports and fitness center. South Pacific Adventure Divers' dive shop is next to the pool. Thrifty Car Rental and Uunited Touring Company have desks at The Warwick. The Avis Rent A Car office (tel. 653-0833) is 1.5 kilometers west at the BP service station in Korolevu. If you enjoy the excitement of large resorts full of guests, The Warwick may be for you.

Pacific Harbor and Vicinity

Southeastern Viti Levu from Deuba to Suva is wetter and greener than the coast to the west, and the emphasis changes from beach life to cultural and natural attractions. Pacific Harbor satisfies sporting types, while Fiji's finest river trips begin at Navua. In this area, scattered Indo-Fijian dwellings join the Fijian villages that predominate farther west. All of the places listed below are easily accessible on the fairly frequent Galoa bus from Suva market.

Pacific Harbor is a sprawling South Florida-style condo development and instant culture village, 148 kilometers east of Nadi Airport and 49 kilometers west of Suva. It was begun in the early 1970s by Canadian developer David Gilmour (the current owner of Wakaya Island) and his father Peter Munk, and good paved roads meander between the landscaped lots with curving canals to drain what was once a swamp. Many residents have boats tied up in their backyards, and if it weren't for the backdrop of deep green hills you'd almost think you were in some Fort Lauderdale suburb. Many of the 180 individual villas are owned by Australian or Hong Kong investors.

In recent years, Pacific Harbor has been eclipsed by the sunnier Denarau area near Nadi, and after the May 2000 coup, tourism to Pacific Harbor dropped to nearly nothing. Some relief came in mid-2003 when Columbia Pictures filmed *Anacondas: The Hunt for the Blood Orchid* around Pacific Harbor, injecting millions of dollars into the local economy. Where Pacific Harbor sparkles is in the excellent scuba diving in the Beqa Lagoon to the south and the river trips into the interior to the north. The beach here is the last reasonable beach before Suva.

SIGHTS

At last report, Pacific Harbor's imposing **Cultural Center** (tel. 345-0095, www.pacific-har bour.com) presented shows only on Thursdays. For their F$18 admission, visitors are shown around a re-created Fijian village, featuring a small "sacred island" dominated by a 20-meter-tall Bure Kalau (Spirit House). A tour guide "warrior" carrying a spear gives a spiel to visitors seated in a double-hulled *drua,* and Fijians attired in jungle garb demonstrate traditional canoe making, weaving, tapa, and pottery at stops along the route. Performances by the Dance Theater of Fiji or Fijian firewalking end the program. The Center's Waikiki-style **Marketplace of Fiji,** made up of mock-colonial boutiques and assorted historical displays, is open daily and accessible free of charge. It's always worth a stop, as you'll be able to see quite a bit of the Cultural Center from the catwalk and there are a few tourist shops and restaurants (but no bank). The main Pacific Harbor post office (with two card phones) is next to the Cultural Center.

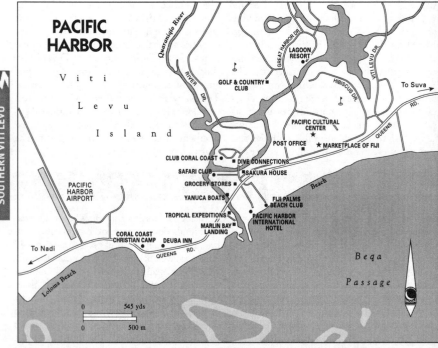

SPORTS AND RECREATION

The 65 kilometers of barrier reef around the 390-square-kilometer Beqa Lagoon south of Pacific Harbor features multicolored soft corals and fabulous sea fans at **Sidestreets**, and an exciting wall and big fish at Cutter Passage. Aside from its surfing potential, **Frigate Passage** on the west side of the Beqa barrier reef is one of the top scuba-diving sites near Suva. A vigorous tidal flow washes in and out of the passage, which attracts big schools of fish, and there are large coral heads. **Sulfur Passage** on the east side of Beqa is equally good. The top dive sites just north of Yanuca Island, such as Sidestreets, Soft Coral Grotto, Caesar's Rocks, and Coral Gardens, are easily accessible from Pacific Harbor.

Scuba Diving

Dive Connections (16 River Dr.; tel. 345-0541, fax 345-0539, diveconn@connect .com.fj), just across the bridge from the Sakura Japanese Restaurant, visits all the best dive sites off Yanuca Island on their spacious 12-meter dive boat, *Scuba Queen*. They charge F$90/110 for one/two tank dives. Night dives are F$80. You can rent gear at F$30 a day, but it's better to bring your own. Four-day PADI open-water certification is F$450 (medical examination not required), otherwise there's an introductory two-dive package for F$150. Snorkelers are welcome to go along on their daily dive trips at F$50 pp including a nice lunch and snorkeling gear (they'll drop you off on Yanuca for snorkeling). The dive boat is also available for fishing charters. Dive Connections is run by a kai Vavalagi couple, Leyh and Edward Harness, descendents of European settlers who arrived in Fiji a century and a half ago. Ask about the self-catering flat next to their office which they rent at F$50 double. They'll pick up anywhere within eight kilometers of the Pacific Harbor bridge.

Aqua-Trek Beqa (Brandon Paige, tel./fax 345-0324, www.aquatrekdiving.com) at the Pacific Harbor International Hotel's marina is an efficient operation with good rental equipment. They send their 11-meter boat, the *Aqua-Sport,* to the Beqa Lagoon twice daily. A two-dive excursion costs F$165, plus F$15 for gear. You may be offered a discount if you just walk in and book direct. If the boat isn't crowded, they'll take along non-divers for snorkeling at about F$40 pp. Some of Fiji's top shark diving is on offer here: You may see several three-meter bull sharks, plus gray reef, black-tip, white-tip, and nurse sharks. They only do the shark dive a couple of times a week, so call ahead.

Tropical Expeditions (tel. 345-0666), run by personable Charles Wakeham, operates the 18-meter live-aboard *Beqa Princess,* based near the bridge across the river from the Pacific Harbor International Hotel. This relatively small live-aboard carries only six divers on three-night scuba cruises to the islands south of Viti Levu, or on day trips to the Beqa Lagoon. Two-tank day trips are F$140 including lunch, or the boat may be chartered. A compressor is on board.

Fishing

Baywater Charters (Steven Hay, tel. 345-0573), near the bridge at Pacific Harbor, operates the 18-meter *Turaga Levu* for fishing charters at F$1,500 a full day including lunch for six to eight anglers. They'll also rent the six-berth boat as a live-aboard fishing boat at F$1,800 for 24 hours all inclusive.

Xtasea Charters (Rob Krause, tel. 345-0280, www.xtaseacharters.com) at Pacific Harbor offers game fishing from the 10-meter aluminum boat *Xtasea* at F$700/1,200 a half/full day (six anglers).

Golf

Pacific Harbor's focal point is the soggy 18-hole, par-72 championship course at the **Pacific Harbor Golf and Country Club** (tel. 345-0048, fax 345-0262), designed by Robert Trent Jones Jr. The big event here is the Pacific Harbor Open in September. Greens fees are F$15/30 for nine/18 holes; electric-cart rental is F$20/35 for nine/18 holes, and club hire is a further F$20. The clubhouse is a couple of kilometers inland off Queens Road. Unfortunately the greens and fairways aren't being maintained as well as previously.

SOUTHERN VITI LEVU

ACCOMMODATIONS

Under US$25

The 10-room **Pacific Safari Club** (tel. 345-0498, fax 345-0499, www.pacificsafari.com) is just down Atoll Place from Sakura House Restaurant. A bed in a clean, modern four-bed dorm here is F$20, otherwise it's F$40/45 single/double with bath, fan, TV, and full cooking facilities (use of the air-conditioning is F$5 extra). The manager can organize scuba-diving discounts for you.

Club Coral Coast (12 Belo Cir.; Tak Hasegawa, tel. 345-0421, fax 345-0900, clubcoralcoast@connect.com.fj) is near Dive Connections. There are four air-conditioned rooms with bath in a self-catering villa at F$90/110 double/triple, plus three non-air-conditioned rooms in another building with a larger kitchen and terrace at F$80/90. In addition, three budget rooms with shared facilities go for F$20 pp. Amenities include a 20-meter swimming pool, tennis, and a gym.

For a cheaper room, you must travel one kilometer west from the bridge at Pacific Harbor. In 1994, the **Deuba Inn** (tel. 345-0544, fax 345-0818, theislander@connect.com.fj) opened at Deuba, 13 kilometers west of Navua. They have eight small rooms with shared bath at F$17/27 single/double and five self-catering units at F$50/60 double/triple. The five-bed dorm and camping space are both F$10 pp. The Inn's restaurant serves excellent meals and their Sand Bar is handy if you're staying at the "dry" Christian Camp next door. Email access is F$.25 a minute.

Adjacent to the Deuba Inn is the friendly **Coral Coast Christian Camp** (tel. 345-0178, coralcoastcc@connect.com.fj). They offer four five-bed Kozy Korner rooms with a good communal kitchen and cold showers at F$12/21/30 single/double/triple (the warm shower in the ladies bathroom takes a F$.50 token). The five adjoining motel units go for F$21/34/43, complete with private bath, kitchen, fridge, and fan. Camping costs F$6 pp. A small selection of snack foods is sold at the office. No alcoholic beverages are permitted on the premises. The Camp is just across the highway from long golden Loloma Beach, the closest public beach to Suva. Watch your valuables if you swim

there (place everything in the trunk if you have a rental car). The snorkeling is good in calm, dry weather. This beach may soon be redeveloped as the five-star Taunovo Bay Resort (www.taunovobay.com). The CCCC is a good place to spend the night while arranging to get out to the surfers' camps on Yanuca Island. Just avoid arriving on a weekend, as it's often fully booked by church groups from Friday afternoon until Sunday afternoon.

US$25–50

Harbor Property Services Ltd. (tel./fax 345-0959, www.fijirealty.com), with an office at the Marketplace of Fiji, rents out five of the Pacific Harbor villas at F$95–110 for up to eight persons. All villas have kitchens, lounge, and washing machine, and some also have a pool. The minimum stay is three nights, and there's a reduction after a week. A onetime cleaning fee of F$25 is charged, and F$5 a day for electricity is extra. It's good value and well worth considering for a longer stay.

US$50–100

The 84 air-conditioned rooms at the three-story **Pacific Harbor International Hotel** (tel. 345-0022, fax 345-0262) are F$158 single or double plus tax. Specials are often available for a few musty, non-air-conditioned rooms. Formerly known as the Centra Resort, the Pacific Harbor International Hotel dates back to 1972 and has undergone several changes of ownership in recent years. It's at the mouth of the Qaraniqio River, between Queens Road and a long sandy beach, on attractive grounds and with a nice deep swimming pool. Unfortunately, an unpleasant sharp smell from the nearby mangroves can engulf the rooms after heavy rains.

The **Fiji Palms Beach Club and Resort** (Wendy Montgomery, tel. 345-0050, fax 345-0025, fijipalms@connect.com.fj), right next to the Pacific Harbor International Hotel, has 14 two-bedroom apartments with cooking facilities. Although most of the units have been sold as part of a timeshare scheme, they're sometimes available on a casual basis at F$165/990 a day/week (Sat.–Sat.) for up to six people.

The **Lagoon Resort** (Heather and Jim Sherlock, tel. 345-0100, fax 345-0270, www.lagoonresort.com), inland a couple of kilometers behind the Cultural Center, is beautifully set on Fairway Place between the river and the golf course, a 10-minute walk from the clubhouse. The 22 plush rooms with marble bathrooms and TV start at F$130 double. This hotel started out in 1988 as the Atholl Hotel, an upscale brothel for Middle Eastern potentates. It's a little secluded, and VIP parties often stay here. In 2003, the Hollywood crew filming *Anaconda 2* spent 24 weeks here, and a few props from the film are on the resort grounds.

FOOD

Kumarans Restaurant (tel. 345-0294; daily 0800–2000), across the highway from the Pacific Harbor International Hotel, has curry specials at lunchtime (F$4–5), but the dinner menu is pricey (F$8–12).

Curry House Fast Food (daily 0800–1700), at the back of the Shell service station opposite the Pacific Harbor International Hotel, serves tasty curries in the F$4–5 range.

Et's Eatery (Mon.–Sat. 0700–1800, Sun. 0900–1800), at the Pic'n Pac Supermarket in the Marketplace of Fiji, serves sandwiches at F$2.50, hamburgers or fish and chips F$4.

The **Oasis Restaurant** (tel. 345-0617; daily 0930–1430 and 1800–2200), in the Marketplace of Fiji, has a sandwich (F$5), salad, and burger (F$7.50) menu at lunchtime, and more substantial main courses for dinner (F$15–30). A pot of tea is F$2.50. Internet access here is F$.30 a minute, and a large selection of paperbacks is for sale at F$2.50 a book.

There are five small grocery stores beside Kumarans near the bridge at Pacific Harbor and a supermarket in the Marketplace of Fiji. For fruit and vegetables, you must go to Navua.

TRANSPORTATION

Only group charter flights from Nadi Airport land at Pacific Harbor's airstrip, but all of the Queens Road express buses stop here. The express bus to Pacific Harbor from Suva stops next to the highway near the Pacific Harbor International Hotel, a kilometer from the Cultural Center. The slower Galoa buses will stop right in front of the Cultural Center itself (advise the driver beforehand).

The air-conditioned Queens Coach leaves from the front door of the Pacific Harbor International Hotel for Suva at 1110 (F$12) and for Nadi at 1715 (F$15). The air-conditioned Fiji Express leaves the hotel for Nadi at 0830 (F$27) and for Suva at 1630 (F$16). Much cheaper and just as fast are the regular Pacific Transport express buses, which stop on the highway: to Nadi Airport at 0750, 0930, 1035, 1315, 1605, and 1835 (148 km, three hours, F$8); to Suva at 1015, 1100, 1155, 1555, 1930, 2115 (49 km, one hour, F$2.95). Sunbeam Transport buses to Lautoka stop here at 1100, 1210, and 1415.

Rosie The Travel Service (tel. 345-0655) in the Marketplace of Fiji can make any required hotel or tour bookings, and they also represent Thrifty Car Rental. Call ahead if you want to pick up a car here.

NAVUA

The bustling riverside town of Navua (pop. 4,500), 39 kilometers west of Suva, is the market center of the mostly Indian-inhabited rice-growing delta area near the mouth of the Navua River. It's also the headquarters of Serua and Namosi provinces. If low-grade copper deposits totaling 900 million metric tons located just inland at Namosi are ever developed, Navua will become a major mining port, passed by four-lane highways, ore conveyors, and a huge drain pipe for copper tailings. For at least 30 years, millions of tons of waste material will be dumped into the ocean every year by an operation consuming more fossil-fuel energy than the rest of the country combined. The present quiet road between Navua and Suva will bustle with new housing estates and heavy traffic, Fiji's social and environmental balance will be turned on its head, and the change from today will be total!

For visitors, Navua town is important as the gateway to the fabulous Navua River. The lower Navua below Namuamua is navigable in large outboard motorboats, while rubber rafts are used on the much faster upper Navua through the narrow **Navua River Gorge.** Either way, a river trip will give you a memorable glimpse of central Viti Levu.

Transportation

All buses between Suva and Nadi stop at Navua. Large village boats leave from the wharf beside Navua market for Beqa Island south of Viti Levu daily except Sunday, but more depart on Saturday (F$15 pp one-way). Be aware that safety equipment is usually absent on such boats. Regular flat-bottomed punts carry local villagers 25 kilometers up the Navua River to Namuamua village on Thursday, Friday, and Saturday afternoons, and they'll probably agree to take you along for about F$7. You can charter an outboard from Navua wharf to Namuamua almost anytime at F$70 for the boat round-trip. The hour-long ride takes you between high canyon walls and over boiling rapids with waterfalls on each side. Above Namuamua is the fabulous **Upper Navua,** accessible only to intrepid river-runners in rubber rafts. It's also possible to reach the river by road at Nabukelevu.

River Tours

An easy way to experience the picturesque lower Navua is with **Discover Fiji Tours** (Lionel Danford, tel. 345-0180 or 346-0480, fax 345-0549, discoverfiji@connect.com.fj), which has an office on the riverside in Navua. They offer a "Jewel of Fiji Day Tour" up the Navua River by motorized canoe, leaving Navua at 1030 daily and returning at 1630. You then have a choice of any two of three activities: a swim at a waterfall, a visit to a Fijian village with a welcoming kava ceremony, or a float down the river on a bamboo raft (no village visits on Sunday). The cost is F$90 pp from Suva (minimum of two), lunch included. Call to arrange a pick-up, or meet them at their river base office in Navua (open 0930–1130 and 1530–1700).

Wilderness Ethnic Adventure Fiji (Donald Mani, tel. 331-5730, fax 330-5450, www.wildernessfiji.com.fj) also runs full-day motorized boat trips 20 kilometers up the river from Navua to

Village boats from Beqa Island collect passengers near Navua market.

Nukusere village, where lunch is served and visitors get an introduction to Fijian culture. Any travel agent in Suva can make the bookings (adults F$79, children F$44, minimum of 10). Wilderness also has canoe and rubber-raft trips down the Navua River (F$89, minimum of four). You must call ahead, as they don't hang around in Navua waiting for customers to appear.

In addition, **Mr. Sakiusa Naivalu** (tel. 346-0641) of Navua organizes upriver boat trips to Namuamua village at F$80 pp (minimum of three) with the possibility of spending the night there. These trips depart Navua at 1000, returning at 1600. Readers found Sakiusa's tour "enjoyable."

The brochures of some of the Navua River tour companies promise a kava ceremony and other events, but these are only organized for groups. If only a couple of you are going that day, nothing much of the kind is going to happen. Ask when booking, otherwise just relax and enjoy the boat ride and scenery, and wait to see dancing elsewhere. And even if there is a ceremony, you may find sitting on the hard floor uncomfortable. The bamboo-raft trip may also be shorter

THE LEGEND OF MAU

Long ago, a group of mountain warriors moved down to a coastal flatland. They built *bure* and called their new home Mau. The warriors brought with them many things, such as mountains, birds, springs, prawns, and a natural pool with a waterfall. Blessed by Mother Nature, they developed their culture. Today, Mau is still set amidst tall mountains and thick jungles. The forests are full of tropical birds and beautiful flowers. A river flows to mangroves by the sea. The people of Mau reveal their ancient totems to guests, and take them fishing and snorkeling on the coral reefs. Visits that begin with a kava ceremony always end with a heartfelt farewell.

than you expected, and the climb to the highest waterfall could be a strenuous. At some point, you may be asked to make a "contribution" to the village, and the ladies will display their handicrafts in a manner that makes it difficult to refuse to buy. Although this visit isn't for everyone, it could also be the highlight of your trip. (If saving money is a priority and you can get a small group together, it's much cheaper to go to Navua by public bus and hire a market boat from there.)

White-Water Rafting

Exciting white-water rafting trips on the Upper Navua River west of Namuamua are offered by **Rivers Fiji** (tel. 345-0147, fax 345-0148, www.riversfiji.com), with an office on the grounds of the Pacific Harbor International Hotel. You're driven over the mountains to a remote spot near Nabukelevu where you get in a rubber raft and shoot through the fantastic Upper Navua Gorge (inaccessible by motorized boat).

Experienced paddlers can do the same on their own in an inflatable kayak, upon request. Due to the Class III rapids involved, children under 12 are not accepted, but for others it's F$180 including lunch.

Rivers Fiji also does a less strenuous run down the Wainikoroiluva River north of Namuamua, on which it's possible to paddle your own inflatable kayak. This costs F$160 for adults, or F$80 for children under the age of 12 who are floating with a paying adult. Two days of kayaking on the Wainikoroiluva is F$430. If you're really keen, ask about overnight camping expeditions on the Upper Wainikoroiluva. These trips conclude with a motorized punt ride down the Lower Navua Gorge from Namuamua to Nakavu village, where you reboard the van to your hotel.

Rivers Fiji also offers one-day sea-kayaking trips to Beqa Island (F$150 pp, minimum of eight). You cross to Beqa by catamaran, then explore a tiny uninhabited island and paddle into Malumu Bay. Deep inside this cliff-lined bay, hundreds of fruit bats are seen clinging to the trees. A secret mangrove tunnel provides an escape south to the great blue beyond. A different trip takes you along the coast of Viti Levu from Pacific Harbor in a two-person sea kayak at F$65 pp. It's a great way to explore the mangroves or glide across the reefs. All prices above include pick-ups around Pacific Harbor. Transfers from other Coral Coast and Suva hotels are F$30 pp extra, from Nadi F$45 extra.

Discover Fiji Tours (tel. 346-0480, discoverfiji@connect.com.fj) also does a Wainikoroiluva River trip between Naqarawai and Navunikabi villages, with white-water rafting, swimming at a waterfall, and a long boat ride down the river. It's F$145/165 pp from Navua/Nadi (two-person minimum).

Islands off Southern Viti Levu

VATULELE ISLAND

This small island, 32 kilometers south of Viti Levu, reaches a height of only 34 meters at its north end; there are steep bluffs on the west coast and gentle slopes facing a wide lagoon on the east. Both passes into the lagoon are from its north end. Five different levels of erosion are visible on the cliffs from which the uplifted limestone was undercut. There are also rock paintings, but no one knows when they were executed. Vatulele today is famous for its tapa cloth *(masi)*.

Other unique features of 31-square-kilometer Vatulele are the sacred **red prawns,** which are found in tidal pools at Korolamalama Cave at the foot of a cliff near the island's rocky north coast. These scarlet prawns with remarkably long antennae are called *ura buta,* or cooked prawns, for their color. The red color probably comes from iron oxide in the limestone of their abode. It's strictly *tabu* to eat them or remove them from the pools. If you do, it will bring ill luck or even shipwreck. The story goes that a princess of yesteryear rejected a gift of cooked prawns from a suitor and threw them in the pools, where the boiled-red creatures were restored to life.

In 1990, Vatulele got its own luxury resort, the **Vatulele Island Resort** (tel. 672-0300, fax 672-0062, www.vatulele.com) on the island's west side. The 18 futuristic villas in a hybrid Fijian/New Mexico style sit about 50 meters apart on a magnificent white-sand beach facing a protected lagoon. The emphasis is on luxurious exclusivity: Villas cost F$2,700 per couple a night, including meals, alcohol, and tax. "The Point," a two-story unit on a low cliff over the ocean, is F$5,850 with private pool. The minimum stay is four nights, and to make the resort more attractive to couples, children under 12 are not accepted. To preserve the natural environment, motorized water sports and a swimming pool are not offered, but there's lots to do, including sailing, snorkeling, windsurfing, paddling, fishing, tennis, and hiking, with guides and gear provided at no additional cost. Other than airfare to the island (see below), about the only things you'll be charged extra for are scuba diving (F$130/220 for one/two tanks) and massage (F$100 an hour). Vatulele's desalination plant ensures abundant fresh water. This world-class resort is a creation of Australian film producer Henry Crawford and thus appeals to the show-business set, as well as upscale honeymooners (weddings arranged, bring your own partner). At Nadi Airport, you'll find them in office No. 15, upstairs from arrivals.

The 990 inhabitants live in four villages on the east side of Vatulele. Village boats from Viti Levu leave Paradise Point near Korolevu Post Office on Tuesday, Thursday, and Saturday if the weather is good. Resort guests arrive on a daily charter flight from Nadi, which costs F$792 pp round-trip (or F$1,620 one-way for a special four-person flight). The charters are operated by **Pacific Island Seaplanes** (tel. 672-5644, fax 672-5641), which uses a four-seat Beaver seaplane able to land on the lagoon near the resort. If weather conditions prevent use of the seaplane, a Twin Otter aircraft is sent. It lands on the island's small private airstrip near the villages, six kilometers from Vatulele Island Resort.

YANUCA ISLAND

This island west of Beqa should not to be confused with the Yanuca Island on which Shangri-La's Fijian Resort is found. In a coconut grove tucked below the jungly green peaks on the northwest side of the island is the **Batiluva Beach Resort** (tel. 992-0019, tel./fax 345-1019, www.batiluva.com). Batiluva is one of Fiji's top surf resorts, and since its opening in 1998, Americans Sharon Todd and Dan Thorn have had to pay a high premium to the landowners to be able to operate here. The single 12-bed dorm is F$100 pp and a double "honeymoon" *bure* is available at F$120 pp—excellent value compared to places like Namotu and Tavarua. There's only kerosene lighting here, but the grounds are nicely landscaped with lots of places

Hamburgers are served for lunch at Batiluva Beach Resort on Yanuca Island. Lighting after dark is by romantic kerosene lamp.

also known as Frigate Surfriders or Pena's Resort. It offers bunks in a 12-bunk dormitory *bure* at F$120 pp, plus tax. Private *bure* are F$180/290/420 single/double/triple. Included are accommodations and meals, surf transfers, and sportfishing. Boat transfers from the mainland are F$40 pp return. In 2004, this resort was completely rebuilt, so check their website for the latest details.

The left-hander in **Frigate Passage** southwest of Yanuca has been called the most underrated wave in Fiji: "fast, hollow, consistent, and deserted." Pena's leaflet describes it thus:

> *Frigate Passage, out on the western edge of the Beqa Barrier Reef, is a sucking, often barreling photocopy of Cloudbreak near Nadi. The wave comprises three sections that often join up. The outside section presents a very steep take-off as the swell begins to draw over the reef. The wave then starts to bend, and you enter a long walled speed section with stand-up tubes. This leads to a pitching inside section that breaks onto the reef, and if your timing is right you can backdoor this part and kick out safely in deep water.*

to sit and hammocks under the trees. Included are gourmet meals, appetizers, kayaks, paddleboats, surfing, snorkeling, village tours, and transfers. Fishing and scuba diving are available at additional cost. This is the closest resort to Frigate Passage and Batiluva's surfing boats go there every day (30–40 minutes away). This resort is on the leeward side of the island, so it's usually calm, and you can snorkel among the colorful fish right off their excellent white beach. Several top dive sites, including Three Nuns, Sidestreets, Soft Coral Grotto, and Gilligan's Tower, visited daily by the dive boats from Pacific Harbor, are only a kilometer straight out from this beach. During the sailing season, yachts rock offshore.

A 10-minute walk east of Batiluva over a rocky headland is a second surfing camp called the **Yanuca Island Resort** (Ratu Penaia Drekeni, tel. 345-0801 or 996-5937, www.frigatesreef.com),

All surfing is banned on Sunday. Yet even without the surfing, Yanuca is still well worth a visit (great beach-based snorkeling). The resorts are across the island from Yanuca's single Fijian village, a 30-minute walk. Shells, mats, and necklaces can be purchased from the locals. And as on neighboring Beqa, Fijian firewalking is a tradition here. Village boats to the one Fijian village on Yanuca depart on Monday and Saturday afternoons from the bridge near the Pacific Harbor International Hotel. Call Batiluva or Pena's for direct transfers.

BEQA ISLAND

Beqa (MBENG-ga) is the home of the famous Fijian firewalkers; Rukua, Naceva, and Dakuibeqa are firewalking villages. Nowadays, they perform mostly at the hotels on Viti Levu, although the local resorts ocasionally stage a show. At low tide, you can hike part of the 27 kilometers around the island: Rukua to Waisomo and Dakuni to Naceva are not hard, but the section through Lalati can be difficult. Malumu Bay, between the two branches of the island, is thought to be a drowned crater. Climb Korolevu (439 m), the highest peak, from Waisomo or Lalati. Kadavu Island is visible to the south of Beqa.

The **Lawaki Beach House** (Sam and Christine Tawake-Bachofner, tel. 992-1621 or 338-1273, fax 330-7386, www.lawakibeachhouse.com) faces the golden sands of Lawaki Beach west of Naceva village. This resort has two double *bure* at F$80/140 single/double and one six-bed family *bure* or dormitory at F$60 pp, all meals included (reduced rates for children under 12). To camp (own tent) is F$40 pp including meals (no self-catering facilities provided). There's a spacious lounge in the main house and good snorkeling right offshore. Boat transfers from Navua are F$140 round-trip for the first person, then F$20 per additional person. You can also get there on village boats departing the wharf beside Navua market around noon daily, except Sundays (F$12–15 pp one-way). Ask for the Naceva boat (Sam or Christine can arrange this for you).

Beqa's newest top-end place is the **Kulu Bay Resort** (tel. 331-6444, www.kulubay.com) which opened on the south side of Beqa a bit closer to Naceva in 2003. The seven spacious *bure* are F$2,000 pp all inclusive. Scuba diving is available at an additional charge.

The **Marlin Bay Resort** (tel. 330-4042, fax 330-4028, www.marlinbay.com), on the west side of Beqa between Raviravi and Rukua villages, dates back to 1991. The 25 *bure* start at F$370 single or double. The meal plan is F$110 pp a day (no cooking facilities). In practice, almost everyone arrives on a prearranged package tour, so these prices are only indicative. Most guests are scuba divers who come to dive

the Beqa Lagoon, and it's worth noting that the famous dive sites like Golden Arch and Sidestreets are almost as far from Marlin Bay as they are from Pacific Harbor (where diving costs a lot less). It's F$160 for a two-tank boat dive (plus F$50 for equipment, if required). Surfing runs to Frigate Pass are arranged at F$160/320 pp a half/full day. The Marlin Bay boat picks up guests at Pacific Harbor for F$100 pp round-trip. Add 12.5 percent tax to all rates.

The more upscale **Lalati Resort** (tel. 347-2033, fax 347-2034, www.lalati-fiji.com), at the north opening of Malamu Bay, has six two-bedroom *bure* at F$660/860/1,110 single/double/triple including meals, kayaking, and windsurfing. A two-tank dive is F$180, plus F$60 for gear. Lalati has cast itself as an upscale sports resort with gourmet meals and spacious accommodations. There's a swimming pool and spa. Compulsory bus/boat transfers from Suva or Nadi are F$190 pp round-trip.

Suva and Vicinity

The pulsing heart of the South Pacific, Suva is the largest and most cosmopolitan city in Oceania. The port is always jammed with ships bringing goods and passengers from afar, and busloads of commuters and enthusiastic visitors stream constantly through the busy market bus station. In the business center, there are Indo-Fijian women in saris, expatriate Australians and New Zealanders in shorts, indigenous Fijians, industrious Asians, and wavy-haired Polynesians from Rotuma and Tonga.

Suva squats on a hilly peninsula between Laucala Bay and Suva Harbor in the southeast corner of Viti Levu. The verdant mountains north and west catch the southeast trade winds, producing damp conditions year-round. Visitors sporting sunburns from Fiji's western sunbelt resorts may appreciate Suva's warm tropical rains (which fall

mostly at night). In 1870, the Polynesia Company sent Australian settlers to camp along mosquito-infested Nubukalou Creek on land obtained from High Chief Cakobau. When efforts to grow sugar cane in the area failed, the company convinced the British to move their headquarters here, and since 1882 Suva has been the capital of Fiji.

Today this exciting multiracial city of 170,000—a fifth of Fiji's total population and half the urban population—is also about the only place in Fiji where you'll see a building taller than a palm tree. Growing numbers of high-rise office buildings and hotels overlook the compact downtown area. The British left behind imposing colonial buildings, wide avenues, and manicured parks as evidence of their rule. The Fiji School of Medicine, the University of the South Pacific, the Fiji Institute of Technology, the Pacific Theological College, the Pacific Regional Seminary, and the headquarters of many regional organizations and diplomatic missions have been established here. In addition, the city offers some of the hottest nightlife between Kings Cross (Sydney) and North Beach (San Francisco), plus shopping, sightseeing, and many good-value places to stay and eat. About the only thing Suva lacks is a beach.

Keep in mind that on Sunday the shops may be closed, restaurants keep reduced hours, and fewer taxis or buses are on the road. In short, the city is very quiet—a good time to wander around in relative peace. If you decide to catch a

boat or flight to Levuka and spend the weekend there, you should book your ticket a couple of days in advance. Otherwise, it's worth dressing up and attending church to hear the marvelous choral singing. Most churches have services in English, but none compare with the 1000 Fijian service at Centenary Methodist Church on Stewart Street.

The lovely "Isa Lei," a Fijian song of farewell, tells of a youth whose love sails off and leaves him alone in Suva, smitten with longing.

Sights

Central Suva

The largest retail produce market in the Pacific, Suva's colorful **municipal market,** off Rodwell Road next to the bus station, is a good place to dabble. If you're a yachtie or backpacker, you'll be happy to hear that the market overflows with fresh produce of every kind. Bundles of kava roots are sold, and liquid kava is consumed, at *yaqona* dens upstairs in the market. On the street outside, Fijian women sell fresh pineapple and guava juice from glass "fish tank" containers.

From the market, walk south on Scott Street to the **Fiji Visitors Bureau** in a former customs house (1912) opposite Suva's General Post Office. At the corner of Thomson and Pier Streets opposite the Visitors Bureau is the onetime **Garrick Hotel** (1914), with a Szechuan Chinese restaurant behind the wrought-iron balconies upstairs. Go east on Thomson to the picturesque colonial-style arcade (1919) along **Nubukalou Creek,** a campsite of Suva's first European settlers. The block behind the arcade is the site of a former Morris Hedstrom store, which burned in late

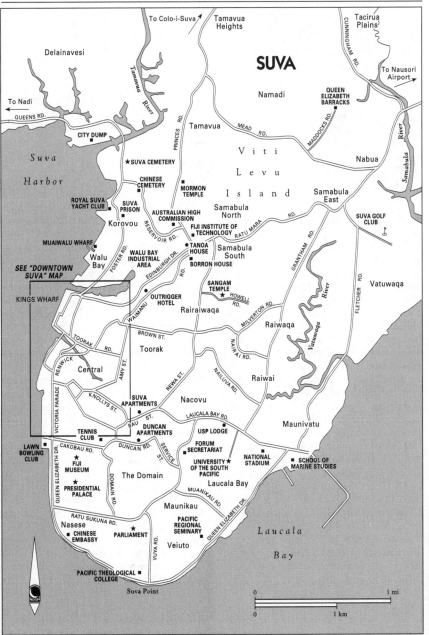

© DAVID STANLEY

SUVA AND VICINITY HIGHLIGHTS

Suva Municipal Market: food, kava, shopping, excitement (p. 178)

Fiji Museum: lovely garden, outstanding exhibits (p. 181)

University of the South Pacific: art gallery, bookstore, library (p. 183)

Colo-i-Suva Forest Park: rainforest hikes, birds, pools (p. 184)

Rewa River Bridge: colorful local scene, off the beaten track (p. 206)

1998. Carpenters Fiji Ltd. is now redeveloping the property.

Cumming Street, Suva's main shopping area, runs east from the park by the bridge over the creek. Suva's original vegetable market was here until it moved to its present location just prior to World War II. During the war, Cumming Street became a market of a different sort as Allied troops flocked here in search of evening entertainment, and since the early 1960s, Cumming has served tourist and local shoppers alike in its present form. To continue your walk, turn right on Renwick Road and head back into town.

At the junction of Renwick Road, Thomson Street, and Victoria Parade is a small park known as **The Triangle** with five concrete benches and a white obelisk bearing four inscriptions: "Cross and Cargill first missionaries arrived 14th October 1835; Fiji British Crown Colony 10th October 1874; Public Land Sales on this spot 1880; Suva proclaimed capital 1882." Inland a block on Pratt Street is the **Catholic cathedral** (1902), built of sandstone imported from Sydney, Australia. Between The Triangle and the cathedral is the towering **Reserve Bank of Fiji** (1984), which is worth entering to see the currency exhibition (Mon.–Fri. 0900–1600, www.rbf.gov.fj).

Return to Suva's main avenue, Victoria Parade, and walk south past **Sukuna Park,** the site of pro-democracy demonstrations in 1990 and occasional political protests even today. Farther along are the colonial-style **Fintel Building**

(1926), nerve center of Fiji's international telecommunications links, the picturesque **Queen Victoria Memorial Hall** (1904), later Suva Town Hall and now the Ming Palace Restaurant, and the **City Library** (1909), which opened in 1909, thanks to a grant from American philanthropist Andrew Carnegie (one of 2,509 public library buildings Carnegie gave to communities in the English-speaking world). All of these sights are on your right.

South Suva

Continue south on Victoria Parade past the headquarters of the **Native Land Trust Board,** which administers much of Fiji's land on behalf of indigenous landowners. Just beyond and across the street from the Holiday Inn is Suva's largest edifice, the imposing **Government Buildings** (1939), once the headquarters of the British colonial establishment in the South Pacific. A statue of Chief Cakobau stares thoughtfully at the building. Here on May 14, 1987, Col. Sitiveni Rabuka carried out the South Pacific's first military coup, and for the next five years, Fiji had no representative government. The chamber from which armed soldiers abducted the parliamentarians is now used by Fiji's high court, accessible from the parking lot behind the building. Prime Minister Timoci Bavadra and the others were led out through the doors below the building's clock tower (now closed) and forced into the back of army trucks waiting on Gladstone Road.

The main facade of the Government Buildings faces **Albert Park,** where aviator Charles Kingsford Smith landed his trimotor Fokker VII-3M on June 6, 1928, after arriving from Hawaii on the first-ever flight from California to Australia. (The first commercial flight to Fiji was a Pan Am flying boat, which landed in Suva Harbor in October 1941.) Facing the west side of the park is the elegant, Edwardian-style **Grand Pacific Hotel,** built by the Union Steamship Company in 1914 to accommodate its transpacific passengers. The 75 rooms were designed to appear as shipboard staterooms, with upstairs passageways surveying the harbor, like the promenade deck of a ship. For

HANNAH DUDLEY'S LEGACY

One of the few Methodist missionaries to achieve lasting success proselytizing among Fiji's Indian community was an Englishwoman named Hannah Dudley, who had previously worked in India, where she learned Hindustani. An individualist unwilling to follow the usual rules for white evangelists laid down by the male-managed mission of her day, "our Miss Dudley" (as her fellow missionaries called her) arrived in Suva in 1903 to work among the indentured Indian laborers. Hannah adopted vegetarianism as a step toward godliness, and she visited the Hindu and Muslim women in their own homes, as only a woman could. Through the woman and men she made contact with, and her Bible classes, she soon created a circle of Indian converts in Suva.

Although conditions for the Indians of her day were harsh, Hannah didn't protest to the colonial authorities, as some other Methodist missionaries had, but gathered the needy and lost around her. Her own home became an orphanage, and her Indian contacts and converts soon came to know her as *mataji*, the little mother. When Hannah returned to Calcutta in 1905 to work with the Bengali Mission, she took her orphans along. In 1934, members of the Indian Methodist congregation in Suva erected the Dudley Memorial Church on the spot where Hannah first preached. The cream building, strongly influenced by Hindu architecture with its domes and central Moorish arch, can still be seen at the corner of Toorak Road and Amy Street, just up the hill from downtown Suva.

Dudley Memorial Church's South Asian architectural touches suggest the building's role as the main place of worship for Suva's Indo-Fijian Methodists.

decades, the Grand Pacific was the social center of the city, but it has been closed since 1992. In 2002, the Government of Fiji purchased the building for F$4.7 million from the Republic of Nauru which had been doing nothing with it. Hopefully a suitable partner willing to renovate the property will appear and the Grand Pacific will again be grand.

South of Albert Park are the pleasant **Thurston Botanical Gardens,** opened in 1913, where tropical flowers such as cannas and plumbagos blossom. The original Fijian village of Suva once stood on this site. On the grounds of the gardens is a clock tower dating from 1918, and the **Fiji Museum** (tel. 331-5944, fax 330-5143; Mon.–Sat. 0930–1600, admission F$7, children under 13 F$5, www.fijimuseum.org.fj), founded in 1904 and the oldest in the South Pacific. The

first hall deals in archaeology, with much information about Fiji's unique pottery. The centerpiece is a double-hulled canoe made in 1913, plus five huge *drua* steering oars each originally held by four men, several large sail booms, and a bamboo house raft *(bilibili)*. The cannibal forks near the entrance are fascinating, as are the whale-tooth necklaces and the large collection of Fijian war clubs and spears. The history gallery beyond the museum shop has a rich collection of 19th-century exhibits, featuring items connected with the many peoples who have come to Fiji, including Tongans, Europeans, and Solomon Islanders. Notice the rudder from HMS *Bounty.* An air-conditioned room upstairs contains an exhibition of tapa cloth and displays on Indo-Fijians. The museum shop sells copies of the museum journal, *Domodomo,* plus other interesting books.

The imposing Presidential Palace behind the Fiji Museum was once the seat of British governors.

South of the gardens is the **Presidential Palace,** formerly called Government House, the residence of the British governors of Fiji. The original building, erected in 1882, burned after being hit by lightning in 1921. The present edifice, which dates from 1928, is a replica of the former British governor's residence in Colombo, Sri Lanka. The grounds cannot be visited.

From the seawall south of the palace, you get a good view across Suva Harbor to Beqa Island (to the left) and the dark, green mountains of eastern Viti Levu punctuated by Joske's Thumb, a high volcanic plug (to the right). Follow the seawall south past a few old colonial buildings, and turn left onto Ratu Sukuna Road, the first street after the Police Academy.

About a kilometer up this road is the 1992 **Parliament of Fiji** (www.parliament.gov.fj), an impressive, traditional-style building with an orange pyramid-shaped roof. From May 19 to July 13, 2000, Fiji's prime minister and several dozen members of parliament were held hostage in the parliamentary complex by a gang of rebel soldiers and assorted thugs led by bankrupt businessman George Speight, who claimed his coup attempt was in defense of indigenous Fijian rights. Thankfully, things are almost back to normal now, and the gatekeeper at the main entrance around the corner off Vuna Road will give you a Visitors Pass to go inside. Huge tapa banners hang from the parliament's walls, and skillfully plaited coconut-fiber ropes from the Lau Group highlight the decor. The parliamentary mace is Chief Cakobau's historic war club, originally presented to Queen Victoria and later returned to Fiji by Britain. It's only brought out when Parliament is in session. The location is spectacular with scenic sea and mountain views.

Both Protestants and Catholics have their most important regional training facilities for ministers and priests in South Suva, and the **Pacific Theological College** is just down Vuna Road from Parliament. From **Suva Point** nearby, you get a good view of **Nukulau,** a tiny reef island southeast of Suva. This was the site of the residence of the first U.S. consul to Fiji, John Brown Williams, and the burning of Williams's house on July 4, 1849, set in motion a chain of events that led to Fiji becoming a British colony.

Later, Nukulau was used as the government quarantine station, and most indentured Indian laborers spent their first two weeks in Fiji here. Until recently, it was a public park, but coup master George Speight is now serving a life sentence in jail on Nukulau.

From Suva Point, it's a good idea to catch a taxi to the University of the South Pacific (F$2.50). The Nasese bus does a scenic loop through the beautiful garden suburbs of South Suva: Just flag it down if you need a ride back to the market. In the other direction, catch it from the southwest corner of the bus station.

University of the South Pacific

A frequent bus from in front of the Vanua Arcade opposite Sukuna Park on Victoria Parade brings you directly to the University of the South Pacific (get off when you see a McDonald's on the left). Founded in 1968, this beautiful 72.8-hectare campus on a hilltop overlooking Laucala Bay is jointly owned by 12 Pacific countries. Although more than 70 percent of the 3,750 full-time and 4,750 part-time students here are from Fiji, the rest are on scholarships from every corner of the Pacific. The site of the USP's Laucala Campus was a Royal New Zealand Air Force seaplane base before the land was turned over to the USP.

From Laucala Bay Road, follow the main walkway to the **University Library,** erected in 1988 with Australian aid. Across a wooden bridge behind the library, past the ANZ Bank and university bookstore, is a traditional Fijian *bure* called the Vale ni Bose, which is used for workshops and seminars. To the left of the *bure* is the **Oceania Center for Arts and Culture,** the university's art gallery (free), with a curvilinear mosaic floor. The center's director is the famous Tongan novelist Epeli Hau'ofa. To the right of (and behind) the *bure* is the **Institute of Pacific Studies,** housed in the former RNZAF officers' mess. This Institute is a leading publisher of insightful books written by Pacific islanders; these books may be perused and purchased at their book room inside the building.

Students from outside the Pacific islands pay F$1,390 tuition for each undergraduate course they take at the USP. Room and board are available at F$4,580 a year, and books will run another F$780. There are academic minimum-entry requirements, and applications must be received by December 31 for the following term. The two semesters are late February to the end of June, and late July until the end of November. Many courses in the social sciences have a high level of content pertaining to Pacific culture, and postgraduate studies in a growing number of areas are available. Check the university's website (www.usp.ac.fj) for more information.

The USP is always in need of qualified staff, so if you're from a university milieu and looking for a chance to live in the South Seas, this could be it. If your credentials are impeccable, you should write to the registrar from home. On the spot, it's better to talk to a department head about his/her needs before going to see the registrar.

Northwest of Suva

The part of Suva north of Walu Bay accommodates much of Suva's shipping and industry. Carlton Brewery on Foster Road cannot be visited. About 600 meters beyond the brewery is the vintage **Suva Prison** (1913), a sinister colonial structure with high walls and barbed wire. Plans to replace this anachronism with a more modern facility have been on the back burner for years. Despite the colorful murals along Foster Road, one look at this place and you'll be a law-abiding citizen for the rest of your stay in Fiji! Opposite the prison is the **Royal Suva Yacht Club,** where you can sign in and buy a drink, meet some yachties, and maybe find a boat to crew on. In the picturesque **Suva Cemetery,** just north, the Fijian graves are wrapped in colorful *sulus* and tapa cloth, and make good subjects for photographers. Gangs of inmates from the nearby jail are often assigned to dig the graves, a common practice in Fiji.

Catch one of the frequent Shore, Lami, or Galoa buses west on Queens Road, past the city dump and **Suvavou** village, home of the Suva area's original Fijian inhabitants, to the **Raffles Tradewinds Hotel** beyond Lami town, seven kilometers from the market. Many cruising yachts tie up at the marina here, and the view of the Bay of Islands from the hotel is good.

Colo-i-Suva Forest Park

This lovely park, at an altitude of 122–183 meters, offers 6.5 kilometers of trails through the lush forest flanking the upper drainage area of Waisila Creek. The mahogany trees you see here are natives of Central America and were planted after the area was logged in the 1950s. The park first opened in 1973. Enter from the Forestry Station along the Falls Trail. A half-kilometer nature trail begins near the Upper Pools, and aside from waterfalls and natural swimming pools, there are thatched pavilions with tables at which to picnic. With the lovely green forests behind Suva in full view, this is one of the most breathtaking places in all of Fiji, and you may spot a few native butterflies, birds, reptiles, and frogs. The park is so unspoiled, it's hard to imagine you're only 11 kilometers from Suva.

The park (tel. 332-0211) is open daily 0900–1600, and there's a F$5 pp entry fee (under age 14 F$1, under age two free) to cover maintenance and management. Security has improved since a police post was set up opposite Raintree Lodge, but you must still keep an eye on your gear if you go swimming in the pools (valuables can be left at the park office). Colo-i-Suva is easily accessible on the Sawani or Serea buses (F$.90), which leave from Lane No. 3 at Suva Bus Station every hour (Sunday every two hours). A 22-seater minibus (F$1.60) also operates and is much faster than the regular buses. It picks up passengers from a different part of Suva Bus Station—ask the drivers of the Nausori minibuses parked on the corner closest to the market. The last bus back to Suva leaves at about 1800. A taxi will be F$8. Make a circle trip of it by catching a bus from the park on to Nausori, rather than returning directly to Suva. And try to come on a dry day, as it's even rainier than Suva and the creeks are prone to flooding.

Also consider spending the night at Raintree Lodge, 50 meters from the entrance to the park (see Accommodations for details). Lunch and drinks can be ordered at the lodge's attractive restaurant/bar (tel. 332-0562), which overlooks a small lake.

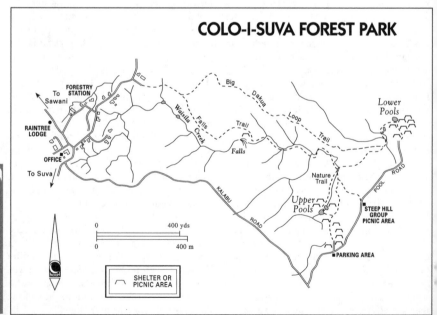

COLO-I-SUVA FOREST PARK

Sports and Recreation

Hiking

For a bird's-eye view of Suva and the entire surrounding area, spend a morning climbing to the volcanic plug atop **Mt. Korobaba** (429 m), the highest peak around. Take a Shore bus to the cement factory beyond the Tradewinds Hotel at Lami, then follow the dirt road past the factory up into the foothills. After about 45 minutes on the main track, you'll come to a fork just after a sharp descent. Keep left and cross a small stream. Soon after, the track divides again. Go up on the right and look for a trail straight up to the right where the tracks rejoin. It's a 10-minute scramble to the summit from here. A guide would be helpful.

There's a far more challenging climb to the top of **Joske's Thumb,** a volcanic plug 15 kilometers west of Suva. Take a bus to Naikorokoro Road, then walk inland 30 minutes to where the road turns sharply right and crosses a bridge. Follow the track straight ahead and continue up the river till you reach a small village. It's necessary to request permission of the villagers to proceed and to hire a guide. From the village to the Thumb will take just less than three hours. The last bit is extremely steep, and ropes may be necessary. It even took Sir Edmund Hillary two tries to climb the Thumb.

Scuba Diving

Beqa Divers (75 Marine Dr.; tel. 336-1088, www.beqadivers.com), near the Lami Shopping Center, is the country's oldest dive shop (established as Scubahire by Dave and Lorraine Evans in 1970). Their four-day PADI certification course (F$800) employs Fiji's only purpose-built diver-training pool on their Lami premises. You'll need to show a medical certificate proving you're fit for diving. Beqa Divers arranges full-day diving trips to the Beqa Lagoon from their Pacific Harbor base for F$143, including two tanks, weight belt, backpack, and lunch. Other equipment can be rented. Beqa Divers will also take snorkelers out on their full-day dive trips for F$66 pp, snorkeling gear and lunch included. When things are slow, they may offer a "special" reduced rate for the all-day scuba trip, if you ask. All diving is out of Pacific Harbor—the Suva office only takes bookings, does certification courses, and sells equipment.

Dive Center Ltd. (4 Matua St., Walu Bay; tel. 330-0599, fax 330-2639), opposite Budget Rent-a-Car, fills scuba tanks but doesn't rent equipment or offer diving.

Other Recreation

Surfers should call Matthew Light (tel. 999-8830), who runs a shuttle out to Sandspit Lighthouse where there's good surfing on a southwest swell at high tide (F$25 pp round-trip).

At the 18-hole, par-72 **Fiji Golf Club** (15 Rifle Range Rd., Vatuwaqa; tel. 338-2872) the course record is 65. Greens fees are F$15/20 for nine/18 holes, club hire F$20 for a full set, plus pull trolley hire at F$5. Call ahead to ask if any competitions are scheduled, as the course may be

© DAVID STANLEY

Suva Lawn Bowling Club

SUVA AND VICINITY

closed to the public at those times. Don't carry large amounts of cash or valuables with you around the course.

The **Olympic Swimming Pool** (224 Victoria Parade) charges F$1.65 admission. It's open Monday–Friday 1000–1800, Saturday 0800–1800 (Apr.–Sept.), or Monday–Friday 0900–1900, Saturday 0700–1900 (Oct.–Mar.). Lockers are available.

The **Suva Lawn Tennis Club** (tel. 331-1726; closed Sun.), Cakobau Road opposite the Fiji Museum, charges F$5 an hour to use their courts

during the day or F$6.50 from 1800–2100. You can order lunch and drinks here.

The Fijians are a very muscular, keenly athletic people who send champion teams far and wide in the Pacific. You can see rugby (Apr.–Sept.) and soccer (Mar.–Oct.) on Saturday afternoons at 1400 at the **National Stadium** near the University of the South Pacific. Rugby and soccer are also played at Albert Park on Saturday, and you could also see a cricket game here (mid-Oct.–Easter). Soccer is also played on Sunday (but rugby is only on Saturday).

Accommodations

Suva offers a wide variety of places to stay, and the low-budget accommodations can be neatly divided into two groups. The places on the south side of the downtown area near Albert Park are mostly decent and provide communal cooking facilities to bona fide travelers. However, some of those northeast of downtown are dicey and cater mostly to "short-time" guests; few of these bother providing cooking facilities. Many of the medium-priced hotels and self-catering apartments are along Gordon Street and its continuation, MacGregor Road. If you want to spend some time in Suva to take advantage of the city's good facilities and varied activities, look for something with cooking facilities and weekly rates.

Some of the medium-priced hotels along Gordon Street offer specials when things are slow. You might save money by calling a few of the places listed below to inquire about the day's "local rate," then take a taxi to the place of your choice. When things are slow, the receptionist may also agree to upgrade you to deluxe at no additional charge, provided you agree to stay for a few nights. Of course, these deals don't apply to overseas bookings.

SOUTH SUVA

Under US$25

The 42-room **South Seas Private Hotel** (6 Williamson Rd.; tel. 331-2296, fax 330-8646, www.fiji4less.com), one block east of Albert

Park, really conveys the flavor in its name. The building originally housed workers involved in laying the first telecommunications cable across the Pacific, and until 1983 it served as a girl's hostel. Things changed when backpackers took over the dormitories (and break-ins through the floorboards by amorous young men came to an end). Today, you can get a bed in a five-bed dorm for F$13.50, a fan-cooled room with shared bath at F$22/32 single/double, or a better room with private bath at F$45 double. The owners have decided to keep their costs down by not paying commissions to the Nadi travel agencies—the only reason they aren't promoted by these outfits. You won't find the "Feejee Experience" crowd here either. Instead, you'll receive a F$1 discount if you have a youth hostel, VIP, or Nomads card. This quiet hotel has a pleasant veranda and a large communal kitchen. For a refundable F$10 deposit, you may borrow a plate, mug, knife, fork, and spoon, but there's a longstanding shortage of pots and pans. It's possible to leave excess luggage at the South Seas for free while you're off visiting other islands, but lock your bag securely. The staff changes money at bank rates. It's worth it to catch a taxi here from the market the first time (F$2).

Travel Inn (19 Gorrie St.; tel. 330-4254, www.fiji4less.com), a two-story building opposite the Fiji Red Cross, is owned by the same company as the South Seas Private Hotel. There are

DOWNTOWN SUVA

Walu Bay

Suva

Harbor

KINGS WHARF

PRINCES WHARF

To Nadi

ELIZA ST.

FOSTER RD.

MAY ST.

EDINBURGH

DR.

To Nausori Airport

BALI HAI NIGHTCLUB

CARPENTERS SHIPPING

WILLIAMS & GOSLING

RICHARDS AVE.

RENOWN RD.

RD.

ROWELL RD.

HARRIS

JELLICOE

ESCOTT

LAUTOKA BUSES

SUVA FLEA MARKET

CARRIERS

BUS STATION

USHER

MARKET

NADI TAXIS

ROBERTSON

STRUAN ST.

NINA ST.

TOP VIEW HOTEL

CAPRICORN HOTEL

MOTEL CAPITOL

SAF'S HOTEL

TROPIC TOWERS MOTEL

HARBOR LIGHT INN

COLONIAL LODGE

ROBERTSON RD.

RD.

ANNANDALE APARTMENTS

RD.

OCEANVIEW HOTEL

DAVEY

ST. FORT RD.

WAIMANU

BREWSTER

STEWART ST.

MOTEL 6

WAIMANU RD.

NEW HAVEN MOTEL

COLONIAL WAR MEMORIAL HOSPITAL

BROWN ST.

SUVA PRIVATE HOSPITAL

BREWSTER ST.

PATTERSON BROTHERS

★ CENTENARY CHURCH

SCOTT ST.

HARBOR TERMINAL

MINIBUS STATION

VILLAGE 6 CINEMAS

VISITORS BUREAU

EDWARD ST.

THOMSON

POST OFFICE

HANDICRAFT MARKET

CENTRAL ST.

STINSON

YWCA

THE TRIANGLE

Sukuna Park

POLICE STATION

AIR NEW ZEALAND

RESERVE BANK ★

PRATT ST.

JOSKE ST.

MARKS ST.

CUMMING ST.

RENWICK RD.

GREIG ST.

ELLERY ST.

RAOJIBHAI RD.

PATEL ST.

Nubukalou

KINGS HOTEL

KOREA HOUSE

UPTOWN MOTEL

FIJI INDIAN CULTURAL CENTER

PACIFIC CONCERNS RESOURCE CENTER

TOORAK RD.

SUVA ST.

HIGH ST.

GANGARAM'S LAUNDRY

SPRING ST.

TOURIST MOTOR INN

DUDLEY MEMORIAL CHURCH

SHIRDI SAI MANDIR

AMY ST.

HUON ST.

JAME MOSQUE

JOHNSON ST.

EDEN ST.

DOWNTOWN BOULEVARD CENTER

CATHOLIC CATHEDRAL

FINTEL BUILDING

CITY HALL

MURRAY ST.

FOSTER ST.

TOWN HOUSE HOTEL

SUNSET MOTEL

GORDON ST.

BUTT ST.

GREENPEACE

OLYMPIC POOL

CIVIC TOWER

CITY LIBRARY

MACARTHUR ST.

SARITA FLATS

SUKUNA HOUSE

ANGLICAN CATHEDRAL

HERCULES ST.

SELBORNE ST.

TOWER ST.

HOLLAND ST.

LAXMI NARAYAN TEMPLE

HOLLAND ST.

Cree

DISRAELI RD.

KNOLLYS ST.

NATIONAL ARCHIVES

SOUTHERN CROSS HOTEL

KIMBERLY ST.

ELIXIR MOTEL

GOODENOUGH ST.

U.S. EMBASSY

WOMEN'S CRISIS CENTER

TANOA PLAZA

MALCOLM ST.

GORDON ST.

THURSTON ST.

DESVOUEX RD.

BERRY ST.

FNPF PLACE

NATIVE LAND TRUST BOARD

CARNARVON ST.

MCGREGOR ST.

TUVALU HIGH COMMISSION

GLADSTONE RD.

TRAVEL INN

GORRIE ST.

MARION ST.

PENDER ST.

SUVA APARTMENTS

PENDER COURT

HOLIDAY INN SUVA

VICTORIA PARADE

GOVERNMENT BUILDINGS ★

BRITISH HIGH COMMISSION

GLADSTONE ST.

SOUTHERN CROSS RD.

MITCHELL ST.

SUVA MOTOR INN

WILLIAMSON RD.

ALLIANCE FRANÇAISE

NORMANBY

PENINSULA HOTEL

MACGREGOR RD.

GRAND PACIFIC HOTEL

Albert Park

SOUTH SEAS PRIVATE HOTEL

0   200 yds

0   200 m

16 fan-cooled rooms with shared bath at F$23/33 single/double, all with access to communal cooking facilities (shortage of utensils), and four self-contained apartments for F$45 triple daily (F$13 extra for a fourth person). A small discount is offered to youth hostel, VIP, and Nomads cardholders. There are plenty of blankets and good locks on the doors. Visitors from other Pacific islands often stay here, as this is one of Suva's better buys.

Pender Court (31 Pender St.; tel. 331-4992), has 13 rooms beginning at F$35 single or double. There are also six one-bedroom studios for F$45. It's sometimes a little noisy, and maybe sleazy.

The high-rise **YWCA** (tel. 330-4829, fax 330-3004) on Sukuna Park has two singles and one double available for female foreign visitors only at F$10 pp.

US$25–50

Several apartment hotels on the hill behind the Central Police Station are worth a try. The congenial **Town House Apartment Hotel** (3 Forster St.; tel. 330-0055, fax 330-3446) is a five-story building with panoramic views from the rooftop bar (happy hour 1700–1900). The 28 air-conditioned units with cooking facilities and fridge are good value at F$48/60/72 single/double/triple and up.

Nearby and under the same ownership is the four-story **Sunset Apartment Motel** (tel. 330-1799, fax 330-3446), at the corner of Gordon and Murray Streets. Avoid the four rooms without cooking facilities that go for F$42/48 single/double, and instead ask for one of the 10 two-bedroom apartments with kitchens and fridge at F$50/65, or the deluxe apartment at F$70/90. The two-bedroom apartments cost F$11 per additional person. Some of the cheaper rooms are noisy and have uncomfortably soft beds. Sunset has a 12-bed dorm, which at F$9 pp is a bit cheaper than the one at the South Seas Private Hotel. The central location is great, but Sunset's dorm is three times as big as the one at the South Seas, and cooking facilities are not provided. Security could be a problem here, as the dorm door is left open all day.

The Town House reception also handles bookings at nearby **Sarita Flats** (39 Gordon St.; tel. 330-0084), where a bed-sitting room apartment with cooking facilities will be F$80 single or double (extra adult F$12). This two-story building lacks the balconies and good views of the Town House, but it is well maintained.

The **Southern Cross Hotel** (63 Gordon St.; tel. 331-4233, fax 331-1819) is a high-rise concrete building. The 32 air-conditioned rooms accommodating up to three people start at F$95 for a standard room on the fourth floor, or F$135 for the deluxe rooms on the second, third, and fifth floors. The hotel restaurant on the sixth floor serves Korean dishes.

Four-story **Elixir Motel Apartments** (tel. 330-3288, fax 330-3383, plantworld@connect.com.fj), on the corner of Gordon and Malcolm Streets, has 15 two-bedroom apartments with cooking facilities and private bath at F$63 without air-conditioning for up to three people, or F$74 with air-conditioning. Weekly rates are 10 percent lower.

Twenty self-catering units owned by the National Olympic Committee are available at **Suva Apartments** (17 Bau St.; tel. 330-4280, fax 330-1647, fasanoc@fasanoc.org.fj), a few blocks east of Pender Court. The 10 fan-cooled units in this new four-story building are F$40/55/70 single/double/triple, while the 10 air-conditioned apartments are F$50/65/80. Ten percent is taken off on weekly rentals. By staying here, you help support organized sports in Fiji!

Duncan Apartments (9 Duncan Rd.; tel. 330-0377, fax 330-8716) has 15 self-catering air-conditioned flats with TV at F$60/350/800 a day/week/month for up to three people (add about F$100 to the monthly rate for gas, water, and electricity). This well-kept two-story complex is in a nice residential area east of Albert Park.

Anyone with any sort of business at the University of the South Pacific should consider staying at **USP Lodges** (tel. 321-2005, fax 331-4827, usplodges@usp.ac.fj). The accommodations here are in two clusters. The Upper Campus Lodge, overlooking the Botanical Garden on the main campus, has six small flats with TV and cooking facilities at F$54/64 single/double (or F$360/430 a week). Four rooms with shared bath in an older wooden building here are F$39/45. Down beside Laucala Bay near the School of Marine Studies is Marine Lodge with 20 self-contained rooms at F$44 single, and five self-catering units with TV at F$59/69 single/double. The reception for Marine Lodge is at Upper Campus Lodge. For a longer stay, ask about Waqavuka Flats near Upper Campus Lodge, which offers monthly rates of F$475/750. Rooms in both sections of USP Lodges are often occupied by students on a semi-permanent basis, so it's best to call ahead to check availability.

US$50–100

The 10-story **Tanoa Plaza Hotel** (tel. 331-2300, fax 330-1300, www.tanoahotels.com), formerly known as the Berjaya Hotel, at the corner of Malcolm and Gordon Streets, is the tallest hotel in Fiji. The 60 air-conditioned rooms with fridge and TV all face the harbor. It's F$179 single or double (or F$410 for one of four penthouse suites). The local "corporate rate" is F$143. Completely renovated in 2003, the Tanoa Plaza has a business center and conference facilities for groups of up to 200 people, plus a swimming pool behind the building.

The **Suva Motor Inn** (tel. 331-3973, fax 330-0381, suvamotorinn@connect.com.fj), a three-story complex near Albert Park, corner of Mitchell and Gorrie Streets, has 36 air-conditioned studio apartments with kitchenette at F$103 single or double, F$118 triple (10 percent discount by the week). The nine two-bedroom apartments capable of accommodating five persons are F$173 for the first two, plus F$10 for each extra person. A courtyard swimming pool with waterslide and cascade faces the restaurant/bar. This building (erected in 1996 by the Hexagon Group of Hotels) is well worth considering by families who want a bit of comfort.

The **Peninsula International Hotel** (tel. 331-3711, fax 331-4473, peninsula@connect.com.fj), at the corner of MacGregor Road and Pender Street, is a stylish four-floor building with a swimming pool. The 32 standard air-conditioned rooms are F$90/110 single/double, while the eight suites with kitchenettes run F$100/115.

In 2000, another eight deluxe rooms were added, costing F$110/125.

US$100–150

Suva's largest hotel is the **Holiday Inn Suva** (tel. 330-1600, fax 330-0251, sales@holidayinn suva.com.fj), on the waterfront opposite the Government Buildings. Formerly a Travelodge, the Holiday Inn is a big American-style place with 130 air-conditioned rooms with fridge and TV beginning at F$205 single or double. The newly renovated "superior" rooms are F$320 (the standard rooms are rather musty). The swimming pool behind the two-story buildings compensates for the lack of a beach and the view of Viti Levu from here is splendid. A UTC tour desk is at the hotel, and there's a brasserie-style restaurant, bar, lounge, and three conference rooms.

NORTH SUVA

Under US$25

The four-story **Top View Motel** (58 Robertson Rd.; tel. 331-2612, fax 330-2101), a six-minute walk up the hill from the market bus station, has 12 rooms with shared bath and ceiling fans at F$20 single or double, and 13 with private bath at F$30/35 single/double. It's basic but okay for one night.

Certainly the nicest budget place in this area is **Colonial Lodge** (19 Anand St.; tel. 330-0655, coloniallodge@connect.com.fj). This old wooden house on a side street near town has three fan-cooled rooms with shared bath at F$38/48 single/double. The large open dormitory downstairs is F$20 pp, or you can camp in the garden for F$15 pp. All rates include a cooked breakfast; dinner is good value at F$6. The large sitting room and terrace upstairs are pleasant, but Colonial Lodge is sometimes noisy due to a loud television, excited children, and barking dogs.

An alley at the end of Anand Street leads straight up to **Annandale Apartments** (265 Waimanu Rd.; tel. 331-1054), opposite the Oceanview Hotel. The 12 spacious two-bedroom apartments are F$45/315/900 a day/week/month for up to three or four people. A fridge, kitchen, sitting room, and balcony are provided in each, but it's all a bit scruffy (you only get what you pay for). Washing machines and dryers are available downstairs.

The colorful, 44-room **Oceanview Hotel** (270 Waimanu Rd.; tel. 331-2129), has two singles at F$15, 33 doubles at F$25, and nine four-person family rooms at F$35. All rooms have shared bath. They usually try to put foreigners in the rear block rooms (No. 10 is the best of those), but some of the "local" rooms in the old wooden building closer to the main street are actually nicer. The Oceanview has a pleasant hillside location, and it's one of the only "lowlife" hotels in this area with any atmosphere.

Three raunchy establishments just down Robertson Road from the Oceanview cater mostly to short time clients. The 15-room **Harbor Light Inn** (124 Robertson Rd.; tel. 330-5495) is cheap at F$20 single or double, but it's used mostly for one purpose. Also of ill repute is the 23-room **Motel Capitol** (91 Robertson Rd.; tel. 331-3246), with seven rooms with shared bath at F$20 single or double, and 16 with private bath at F$25–30.

The same crowd uses **Saf's Apartment Hotel** (100 Robertson Rd.; Safique Mohd, tel. 330-1849), between the Crossroad and Capitol. The 40 bare rooms with bath in this three-story concrete building are F$25 single or double downstairs, F$35 upstairs, or F$45 with TV and cooking facilities (F$10 extra for air-conditioning). A bed in the six-bed dorm is F$7 pp.

Just up Waimanu Road from the Oceanview is the seedy, 14-room **New Haven Motel** (tel. 331-5220), another one to avoid. It's F$30 single or double a night upstairs, or F$10 an hour downstairs.

Up the hill is the two-story **Outrigger Hotel** (349 Waimanu Rd.; tel. 331-4944), near the hospital. The 20 air-conditioned rooms with bath and fridge are F$48 single or double. Most of the rooms have a good view of Suva Harbor. There's a pizza restaurant on the roof (daily 1600–2200; pizzas F$6–14). Unfortunately, feedback about the Outrigger is mixed (and it has no connection with the Hawaiian Outrigger chain).

Back down near the center of town, the **Kings Suva Hotel** (tel. 330-4411, beater@connect.com.fj) on Waimanu Road is rough, with four rowdy bars and a dubious clientele. The 20 noisy rooms with shared bath are F$20 single or double, while the five with private bath cost F$25.

The **Uptown Motel** (55 Toorak Rd.; tel./fax 330-6094), has 12 spacious self-contained rooms with balcony, phone, fridge, sofa, table and chairs, and coffee-making facilities at F$35 single or double with fan, F$45 with air-conditioning. One room has been converted into a six-bunk dorm at F$20 a bed. It's convenient to the shopping district.

The 23 units at the **Tourist Motor Inn** (98 Amy St.; tel. 331-5745), several blocks east of Waimanu Road, are F$25/30 single/double with fan. This three-story building painted pink and cream is seldom full. It can be rather noisy with shouts and laughter echoing through the halls.

Lami Lodge (tel. 336-2240, fax 331-2875, volau@connect.com.fj), on Queens Road next to Beqa Divers at Lami, has three singles (F$25), two doubles (F$45), and one 12-bed dorm (F$15 pp) in two wooden houses between the highway and the lagoon. Camping in their front yard is F$5 pp. You can cook your own food and there's a lounge.

Raintree Lodge (Tom Davis, tel. 332-0562, fax 332-0113, www.raintreelodge.com), near the entrance to Colo-i-Suva Forest Park, 11 kilometers north of Suva, caters well to both ends of the market. Their 20-bed split-level dormitory (F$18 pp) shares toilet, cooking, and bathing facilities with the thirteen double rooms at F$50. Camping is F$10 pp. More upscale are the four lodges or bungalows in another section just up the hill. These cost F$110 single or double, and are quite luxurious with a sitting room, TV, fridge, private bath, and deck overlooking a small lake (but no cooking facilities). If you'll be using the cooking facilities in the dorm, bring groceries from Suva, as there's no store here. Raintree's large thatched restaurant/bar overlooks a former rock quarry, which has been converted into a lovely lake teeming with tiny tilapia fish. It's possible to borrow a bamboo raft and paddle out to the center of the lake for swimming. Aside from its easy access to the forest park, the lodge can be used as a base for visiting Suva (the last bus back is at 1900 daily). Bus connections are covered in the Colo-i-Suva Forest Park listing above. A taxi from Suva will cost F$8 (if arriving by air at Nausori, a taxi will be F$12). Call ahead, as Raintree Lodge does fill up some nights. The whole complex is a model for ecotourism in Fiji.

US$25–50

Up in the Waimanu Road area, the **Capricorn Apartment Hotel** (7 St. Fort St.; tel. 330-3732, fax 330-3069, www.capricorn-hotels-fiji.com)has 34 spacious air-conditioned units with cooking facilities, fridge, and TV beginning at F$94 single or double, plus tax. A room upstairs is F$11 more, a one-bedroom flat another F$22. The three- and four-story apartment blocks edge the swimming pool, and there are good views of the harbor from the individual balconies.

Tropic Towers Apartment Motel (86 Robertson Rd.; tel. 330-4470, fax 330-4169, tropic towers@connect.com.fj), has 34 air-conditioned apartments with cooking facilities, fridge, and TV in a four-story building starting at F$51/62 single/double. Ask about the 13 "budget" units in the annex, which are F$34 single or double with shared bath. Washing machines (F$9) and a swimming pool are available for guests. Both Tropic Towers and the Capricorn are good choices for families.

Motel 6 (1 Walu St.; tel. 330-7477, fax 330-7133), off Waimanu Road, is one of Suva's best deals. Of the 16 clean, comfortable air-conditioned rooms in the main building, the eight with fridge only are F$55 single or double, while those with a balcony, cooking facilities, and a separate bedroom are F$88. Nine self-catering units facing the car park are F$99. All have a regular TV, but only the deluxe rooms have Sky TV. There's a swimming pool and some of the balconies have an excellent view of Walu Bay.

Nanette's Homestay (56 Extension St.; Nanette MacAdam, tel. 331-6316, fax 331-6902, www.nanetteshomestay.com), off Waimanu Road just past the entrance to the Outpatients Department at Colonial War Memorial Hospital, is a modern bed and breakfast run by an Australian-Fijian couple. The four upstairs rooms (F$75 single or double) share a kitchen and lounge area. Downstairs are three self-catering apartments (F$110). All rooms have private bath, air-conditioning, and breakfast included in the price. It's an excellent value.

US$50–100

The **Raffles Tradewinds Hotel** (tel. 336-2450, fax 336-1464, www.rafflestradewinds.com), at Lami on the Bay of Islands seven kilometers west of Suva, includes a 500-seat convention center, waterside swimming pool, and oceanfront seafood restaurant. The 109 rooms in this tasteful two-story building are F$113/144 double/triple standard or F$174/206 deluxe with private bath, fridge, and air-conditioning (reduced walk-in "local rates" are often available). Internet access is F$.30 a minute. Many cruising yachts anchor here, and the location is the most picturesque of any Suva hotel. Although far from the center, bus service into Suva is good.

Food

Fast Food

Familiar, easy eating is available in the American-style food courts in the **Downtown Boulevard Center** (weekdays 0730–1800, Sat. 0730–1700), on Ellery Street; the **Harbor Center** (Mon.–Sat. 0700–1900), along Nubukulou Creek between Scott and Thomson Streets; and **Dolphins Food Court** (tel. 330-7440; daily 0900–2100) at FNPF Place, Victoria Parade and Loftus Street.

One of the few places serving a regular cooked breakfast (F$6.50) is the **Palm Court Bistro** (tel. 330-4662; Mon.–Fri. 0700–1630, Sat. 0700–1430), in the Queensland Insurance Arcade behind Air New Zealand on Victoria Parade. Their burgers and sandwiches are good at lunchtime.

The **Headworks Café** (tel. 330-9449; weekdays 0800–1900, Sat. 0900–1700), upstairs from The Triangle, Renwick Road opposite the Westpac

DOWNTOWN SUVA RESTAURANTS AND BARS

PRINCES WHARF

FOOD STALLS

MARKET

ROBERTSON RD.

USHER

NINA ST.

STEWART ST.

Suva

Harbor

CLUB 2000 ▼

SCOTT ST.

ST.

Nubukalou

MARKS ST.

PARADE

EDWARD ST.

HARBOR CENTER ▼

FRIENDS BAR & NIGHTCLUB ▼

CURRY HOUSE ▼

CUMMING

GOVINDA RESTAURANT ▼

KIM'S CAFE ▼

PUBLIC TOILET ▪

THOMSON

PIER ST.

SICHUAN PAVILION ▼

DONALD'S KITCHEN ▼

CHEQUERS NIGHTSPOT ▼

HANDICRAFT MARKET RESTAURANT ▼

CHEF'S THE CORNER ▼

■ PUBLIC TOILET

RD.

STINSON

CENTRAL ST.

HEADWORKS COFFEE BAR ▼

RENWICK

ELLERY ST.

GREIG ST.

Creek

JJ'S ON THE PARK ▼

METAL OX BAR & GRILL ▼

LANTERN PALACE ▼

TIKO'S FLOATING RESTAURANT ▼

PUBLIC TOILET ▪

HARE KRISHNA RESTAURANT ▼

ST.

DOWNTOWN BOULEVARD CENTER ▪

Sukuna Park

PALM COURT BISTRO ▼

VANUA ARCADE ▼

JOSKE ST.

PRATT ST.

SINGH'S CURRY HOUSE ▼

GORDON

MURRAY ST.

ROOFTOP GARDEN BAR ▼

ST.

PARADE

PHOENIX RESTAURANT ▼

BUTT ST.

FORSTER ST.

TOWER

PEKING RESTAURANT ▼

MING PALACE ▼

BAD DOG CAFE ▼

ZEN RESTAURANT ▼

DA KYUNG KOREAN RESTAURANT ▼

O'REILLY'S PUB ▼

THE MERCHANTS CLUB ▼

HERCULES ST.

SELBORNE ST.

SIGNALS NIGHT CLUB ▼

MACARTHUR ST.

PURPLE HAZE ▼

BOJANGLES ▼

BIRDLAND JAZZ CLUB ▼

VICTORIA ST.

FONG LEE RESTAURANT ▼

HOLLAND ST.

MALCOLM ST.

DESVOUEX RD.

TRAPS BAR ▼

KIMBERLY ST.

GOODENOUGH

GORDON ST.

N

| 0 | 100 yds |
| 0 | 100 m |

DOLPHINS FOOD COURT ▼

DAIKOKU RESTAURANT ▼

OLD MILL COTTAGE CAFE ▼

CARNARVON

LOFTUS ST.

THURSTON ST.

GORRIE ST.

GOLDEN DRAGON ▼

SHOOTERS TAVERN ▼

THE BARN ▼

GLADSTONE RD.

Bank, serves coffee and cakes on a nice outdoor terrace with a view of downtown.

Jackson Takeaway (tel. 330-3986; Mon.–Sat. 0700–1800, Sun. 0900–1700), in the old town hall next to the Ming Palace Restaurant on Victoria Parade, serves Chinese lunches at F$3 or fish and chips at F$2. It's also good for a quick cup of coffee.

Shooters Tavern (54 Carnarvon St.; tel. 995-1954; Mon.–Sat. 0730–1500) has a pleasant outdoor terrace serving breakfast or lunch for F$5. There's a regular menu priced F$5–15 in addition to the blackboard specials.

An inexpensive snack bar (tel. 330-1443; Mon.–Sat. 0800–1600) with concrete outdoor picnic tables is at the back side of the **Handicraft Market** facing the harbor. Dishes like chop suey, chow mein, fried rice, long soup, and rump steak cost F$3–5 and the portions are gargantuan. This place is really packed with locals around lunchtime—the best deal in town.

Low-budget snacks are also served at **Donald's Kitchen** (103 Cumming St.; tel. 331-5587). One block over on Marks Street are cheaper Chinese snack bars, such as **Kim's Café** (128 Marks St.; tel. 331-3252) where you can get a toasted egg sandwich and coffee for about F$1.50. Kim's has been there for ages. There are scores more cheap milk bars around Suva, and you'll find them for yourself as you stroll around town.

Fijian

A popular place to sample Fijian food is the **Old Mill Cottage Café** (49 Carnarvon St.; tel. 331-2134; Mon.–Sat. 0700–1700), located on the street behind the Dolphins Food Court. Government employees from nearby offices and staff from the adjacent U.S. Embassy descend on this place at lunchtime for the inexpensive curried freshwater mussels, curried chicken livers, fresh seaweed in coconut milk, taro leaves creamed in coconut milk, and fish cooked in coconut milk. It's also very good for breakfast.

Also try the food stalls between the market and bus station, on the back side of the bus station closer to the harbor. The best deal here is the fish in *lolo* (coconut milk) served at two open kiosks with red tiles on the walls for F$3 a plate.

Ask for Emi Whippy, who is famous for her food. You have to eat standing at a counter using a spoon and your hands, but there are taps between the kiosks where you can wash up. Arrive before 1300, as they sell out fast!

Indian

The **Hare Krishna Vegetarian Restaurant** (tel. 331-4154; closed Sun.), at the corner of Pratt and Joske Streets, serves ice cream (12 flavors), sweets, and snacks downstairs, main meals upstairs (available Mon.–Fri. 1100–1400). If you want the all-you-can-eat vegetarian *thali* (F$7.50), just sit down upstairs, and they'll bring it to you. No smoking or alcohol is allowed.

A cheaper Indian place is the very popular **Curry House** (87 Cumming St.; tel. 331-3756; Mon.–Fri. 0900–1745, Sat. 0900–1430). Their special vegetarian *thali* (F$3.30) is a good lunch, and they also have meat curries from F$5. Try the takeaway *rotis*.

Govinda Vegetarian Restaurant (93 Cumming St.; Mon.–Fri. 0800–1700, Sat. 0900–1400) has a combination *thali* for F$6.50, plus sweets, ice cream, milkshakes, and masala tea.

Singh's Curry House (tel. 359-1019; Mon.–Sat. 0930–2130, Sun. 1030–2000), Gordon Street off Victoria Parade, serves spicy South Indian dishes in the F$3–8 range. Choose from the warmer on the counter.

Suva's only upscale Indian restaurant is **Ashiyana** (tel. 331-3000; Tues.–Sat. 1130–1430, 1800–2200, Sun. 1800–2130), in the old town hall next to the Ming Palace Restaurant on Victoria Parade. Their hot and spicy dishes are prepared in a tandoor clay oven by a chef from India.

Asian

Not many Indian restaurants in Suva are open evenings or on Sunday, so this is when you should turn to Suva's many excellent, inexpensive Asian restaurants. Most serve beer, while the Indian restaurants are usually "dry."

Two good-value Chinese places are adjacent to one another on Pratt Street near Hare Krishna. Dishes in the glass-covered steam table at the **Lantern Palace Cafeteria** are F$4, while those at the **Guang Wha Restaurant** next door start at

vegetable vendors at Suva's bustling main market

F$3. The Guang Wha is more likely to be open on holidays, and nothing on their regular menu is more than F$8. The **Lantern Palace Restaurant** (tel. 331-4633; Mon.–Sat. 1130–1400 and 1700–2100) between these two offers individually prepared dishes priced F$6–16.

The **Sichuan Pavilion Restaurant** (6 Thomson St.; tel. 331-5194; Mon.–Sat. 1100–1400 and 1700–2200, Sun. 1730–2300), upstairs in the old Garrick Hotel building, is perhaps Suva's finest Asian restaurant. Employees of the Chinese Embassy frequent it for the spicy-hot Chinese dishes (though they're not as hot as Szechuan food elsewhere). Almost everything is good, so avoid the lamb. Entrees average F$8–13. Weather permitting, sit outside on the balcony and watch all Suva go by.

The **Phoenix Restaurant** (155 Victoria Parade; tel. 331-1889) has inexpensive Chinese dishes like red pork with fried rice (F$5) in their steam table. Big bottles of beer are sold. They're also open on Sundays 1100–2100.

The popular **Peking Restaurant** (195 Victoria Parade; tel. 331-2714; daily 1130–2200) is only a bit more expensive than the down-market Chinese places, but the meals are individually prepared (averaging F$5–10).

Suva's most imposing Chinese restaurant by far is the 300-seat **Ming Palace** (tel. 331-5546; Mon.–Sat. 1130–1430 and 1800–2200, Sun. 1800–2200) in the old town hall next to the public library on Victoria Parade. Weekdays 1130–1430, there's a lunch buffet for F$9 (dinner entrées are F$9–18).

Fong Lee Seafood Restaurant (293 Victoria Parade; tel. 330-4233; Mon.–Sat. 1130–1400 and 1800–2200, Sun. 1800–2200) is more expensive than the places just mentioned, but the food is said to be the tastiest in Suva (notice the many affluent local Chinese having dinner there).

For upscale Japanese food, it's **Daikoku** (FNPF Place, 359 Victoria Parade; tel. 330-8968; Mon.–Sat. 1200–1400 and 1800–2200). The *teppan-yaki* dishes (F$10–25) are artistically prepared right at your table.

The **Zen Restaurant** (tel. 330-6314; weekdays 1130–1430 and 1630–2130, Sat. 1130–1430), in Pacific House, Butt and Gordon Streets, has lunch specials at F$7. Dinner will cost about F$16, and photos of their dishes are in the menu.

The **Da Kyung Korean Restaurant** (43 Gordon St.; tel. 359-1224; Mon.–Sat. 1000–2200, Sun. 1600–2200) also has a nifty photographic menu depicting dishes like bulgogy (F$11), steak barbecue (F$15), and vegetarian tofu soup (F$11). A variety of side dishes are included with each order. The pleasant open dining room is in an old colonial house.

The more prosaic **Korea House Restaurant** (178 Waimanu Rd.; tel. 331-1711; daily 1200–1500 and 1800–2200), at Brewster, offers Korean dishes (F$9–15), Chinese dishes (F$6–9), *bulgogy* (F$10), and *bibimbab* (F$9).

International Cuisine

Elegant **Tiko's Floating Restaurant** (tel. 331-3626; weekdays 1200–1400 and 1800–2200, Sat. 1800–2200) is housed in the MV *Lycianda,* an ex-Blue Lagoon cruise ship launched at Suva in 1970 and now anchored off Stinson Parade behind Sukuna Park. Their steaks and seafood are good. A real mountain of crabs will run F$31. A bar called "Tingles" downstairs is open Friday and Saturday 1700–0100. It's a romantic spot, and you can feel the boat rock gently in the waves.

The **Metal Ox Bar & Grill** (tel. 331-4330; weekdays 1100–1400 and 1800–2230, weekends 1800–2230), in Regal Lane around behind the Qantas and Air Pacific offices, allows you to sit at a table with a view of Suva Harbor and consume steaks of 250, 300, or 400 grams priced from F$19–27. Fancier dishes on the main menu cater to other tastes.

The Nadi tourist-caterer Chef's has opened branches in Suva. **Chef's The Corner** (Mon.–Sat. 0800–2130), Thomson and Pier Streets beside Jack's Handicrafts, serves coffee and snacks to trendy youths who wish to be seen here. Upstairs, tourists and the affluent consume meat and seafood at **Chef's The Restaurant** (tel. 330-8325). The casual lunches (F$10–22) are from 1100–1400, while candlelit dinners (F$28–38) run from 1800–2200.

JJ's On The Park (tel. 330-5005; daily 1130–2200), in the YWCA Building on Sukuna Park, is a casual restaurant of quality, with daily specials listed on blackboards. If you don't want any of the main courses (F$11–32), order a couple of appetizers (F$7–14), such as the sashimi (F$7/10 small/large) or the calamari rings (F$12). Otherwise, there are hamburgers (F$11), catch of the day (F$18.50), and lobster (F$32). One reader recommended the chicken. You'll like the gentile atmosphere and harbor views. Coup master George Speight once owned a small stake in JJ's, and you never know who you'll meet at JJ's classic long wooden bar (which stays open until 0200).

Entertainment and Events

In 1996, **Village Six Cinemas** (tel. 330-6006) opened on Scott Street, next to Nubukalou Creek, giving you a choice of six top Hollywood films several times a day. Regular admission is F$5, reduced to F$4 on Tuesday. The air-conditioning is a relief on a hot day.

The best time to be in Suva is in August during the **Hibiscus Festival,** which fills Albert Park with stalls, games, and carnival revelers.

Nightclubs

There are numerous nightclubs in Suva, all of which have F$3–5 cover charges on weekends and require neat dress. Nothing much happens until after 2200, and women shouldn't enter these places alone. Late at night, it's wise to take a taxi back to your hotel. Suva is still a very safe city, but nasty, violent robberies do occur.

The Barn (54 Carnarvon St.; tel. 330-7845; Tues.–Thurs. 1900–0100, Fri. 1800–0100, Sat. 1930–0100) is a popular country-and-western club with live entertainment and a cover charge from 2100. The crowd here is a bit older than in some of the other clubs.

The **Golden Dragon** (379 Victoria Parade; tel. 331-1018; Sat. 1830–0100, Sun.–Fri. 1700–0100) is frequented by university students and islanders from other parts of the Pacific (such as Samoa and Tonga).

Signals Night Club (255 Victoria Parade; tel. 331-3590; daily 1800–0100), opposite the Suva City Library, is popular among Asian seamen (F$3 cover charge after 2000). Gay travelers will feel comfortable here.

Bourbon Bluez (tel. 331-3927), beside Air Nauru across the street from O'Reilly's Pub, caters to an older, Fijian crowd.

Birdland R&B Club (6 Carnarvon St.; tel. 330-3833; daily from 1800), up and around the corner from O'Reilly's Pub, has outstanding live jazz from 2000 on Sunday. On other nights, there's recorded music. It's a late-night place where people come after they've been to the other clubs.

Bojangles Night Club (tel. 330-3776; Mon.–Sat. from 1800), adjacent to Birdland, is a disco where Fijian students come to dance (cover charge after 2200).

Purple Haze Night Club (tel. 330-3092; Wed.–Sun. from 1930), Butt and MacArthur streets (above The Merchants Club), just up the hill from O'Reilly's Pub, is a predominately Indo-Fijian disco. It's one of the few places in town where you'll see mostly straight men dancing with each other!

Liquids Night Club (tel. 330-0679; closed Sun.), upstairs in the Harbor Center (access from beside Wishbone outside on the Nubukalou Creek side of the building), is crowded with local sports teams on weekends.

Be aware that the places north of Nubukalou Creek are considerably rougher than those just mentioned. **Friends Bar and Niteclub** (34 Cumming St., Mon.–Sat 1700–0100) has live music Tuesday and Wednesday (happy hour 1700–2000). Security is tight.

Club 2000 (tel. 330-9754), in the former Metropole Hotel building upstairs, at Usher and Scott streets near the market, supplies cheap mugs of beer, and it's safe enough during the day. At night, you'd better know what you're doing. It's loud, hot, and dirty—great. The outside terrace to the right as you come in is quieter than the bar on the left.

Wildest of all is the **Bali Hai Night Club** (194 Rodwell Rd.; tel. 331-7164), located north of the bus station, with dances Thursday–Saturday nights. The middle floor is okay, but the top floor is very rough.

Bars

O'Reilly's Pub (5 MacArthur St.; tel. 331-2884), just off Victoria Parade, has a happy hour daily 1600–2000. It's a nice relaxed way to kick off a night on the town, and the big sports screen and canned music are tops.

The whimsically named **Bad Dog Cafe** (tel. 331-2968; Mon.–Wed. 1100–2300, Thurs.–Sat. 1100–0100, Sun. 1700–2300), next door to O'Reilly's, is a trendy wine bar serving margaritas, sangria, and 25 different brands of imported beers. At happy hour 1700–1900, you can order a jug of sangria for F$11 or get F$2 off the mixed drinks. The regular menu features Thai food, steaks, and fish for F$9–14, pizza F$12, appetizers F$5–8, and the food has a reputation for being among Suva's best. For F$6 corkage, you may BYO bottle of wine from the nearby Victoria Wines shop. A back door from Bad Dog leads into O'Reilly's.

A block up from O'Reilly's at MacArthur is **The Merchants Club** (15 Butt St.; tel. 330-4256; Mon. and Tues. 1600–2130, Wed. and Thurs. 1600–2230, Fri. 1600–2330, Sat. 1100–2230, Sun. 1100–1830). Properly dressed overseas visitors are welcome in this classic South Seas bar with a largely male clientele.

Next to the Shell service station, **Traps Bar** (305 Victoria Parade; tel. 331-2922; weekdays 1700–0100, weekends 1800–0100) is a group-y Suva social scene with a happy hour until 2000 (drunks and youths under 18 are unwelcome here). There's live music from 2200 on Tuesday, *the* night to be there. If you can only visit one Suva bar, pick this one.

Shooters Tavern (54 Carnarvon St.; tel. 995-1954), next to The Barn, has a happy hour Monday–Saturday 1730–2000. They play harder rock music than the others, and the atmosphere is somewhere between O'Reilly's and Traps. Shooters is a youth hangout where you might even bump into high school kids.

The bar at the **Suva Lawn Bowling Club** (tel. 330-2394; daily 0900–2200), facing the lagoon opposite Thurston Botanical Gardens and just off Albert Park, is a very convenient place to down a large bottle of Fiji Bitter—the perfect place for a cold one after visiting the museum. You can sit and watch the bowling, or see the sun set over Viti Levu.

Those in search of more subdued drinking should try the **Piano Bar** in the lobby at the Holiday Inn (tel. 330-1600), which often presents rather good jazz singers, or the **Rooftop Garden Bar** at the Town House Apartment Hotel (tel. 330-0055) which has a happy hour 1700–1900.

Shopping

The **Government Handicraft Center** (tel. 331-5869; Mon.–Fri. 0800–1630, Sat. 0800–1230) behind Ratu Sukuna House, MacArthur and Carnarvon Streets, is a low-pressure place to familiarize yourself with what is authentic. **Jack's Handicrafts** (tel. 330-8893, www.jacksfiji.com), Renwick Road and Pier Street, has Fijian crafts, postcards, and other tourist goods with prices clearly marked.

The large **Curio and Handicraft Market** (Mon.–Sat. 0800–1700) on the waterfront behind the post office is a good place to haggle over crafts, so long as you know what is really Fijian (avoid masks and "tikis"). Unfortunately, many of the vendors are rather aggressive, and it's not possible to shop around in peace. Never come here on the day when a cruise ship is in port—prices shoot up. And watch out for the annoying "sword sellers" (see the Dangers and Annoyances section in the Introduction chapter for more information), as they could accost you anywhere in Suva. (Strangers who greet you on the street in Suva almost always want something from you.)

Cumming Street is Suva's busiest shopping street. Expect to obtain a 10–40 percent discount at the "duty-free" shops by bargaining, but *shop around* before you buy. Be especially wary when purchasing gold jewelry, as it might be fake. Commission agents may try to show you around and get you a "good price." If the deal seems too good to be true, it probably is.

The **Suva Flea Market** on Rodwell Road opposite the bus station features a large selection of island clothing and many good little places to eat. You won't be hassled here.

For more upmarket apparel, examine the fashionable hand-printed clothing and beachwear at **Sogo Fiji** (tel. 331-5007), on Cumming Street and on Victoria Parade next to Air New Zealand. You could come out looking like a real South Seas character at a reasonable price.

Bob's Hook Line & Sinker (tel./fax 330-1013), on Thomson Street in an outside corner of the Harbor Center, sells snorkeling and fishing gear.

J.R. White & Co. (tel. 330-2325), in the mall behind Air New Zealand, has all kinds of sporting equipment (but not camping gear or backpacks). They can repair worn-out zippers.

Wai Tui Surf (tel. 330-0287), Parade Arcade, Victoria Parade opposite McDonald's, sells surfing paraphernalia, including stylish bathing suits and trendy beachwear.

The **Philatelic Bureau** (tel. 321-8377, www.stampsfiji.com), next to the General Post Office, sells the stamps of Niue, Pitcairn, Papua New Guinea, Samoa, Solomon Islands, Tonga, Tuvalu, and Vanuatu, as well as those of Fiji.

Fuji Film in the Vanua Arcade, opposite Sukuna Park on Victoria Parade, does one-hour photo finishing.

Information

The **Fiji Visitors Bureau** (tel. 330-2433; Mon.–Fri. 0800–1630, Sat. 0800–1200) is on Thomson Street across from the General Post Office. They have a good supply of brochures and can answer most questions. Ask for a copy of the free Jasons map of Fiji and *Fiji What's On.*

The **South Pacific Tourism Organization** (FNPF Plaza, 343–359 Victoria Parade, 3rd Fl.; tel. 330-4177, fax 330-1995, www.spto.org), at Loftus Street, provides information on the entire South Pacific.

The **Bureau of Statistics** (tel. 331-5822, fax 330-3656, www.statsfiji.gov.fj), on the 8th floor of the Ratu Sukuna House at Victoria Parade and MacArthur Street, has many interesting technical publications on the country and a library where you may browse.

The **Maps and Plans Shop** (tel. 321-1395; Mon.–Fri. 0800–1300 and 1400–1530) of the Lands and Survey Department on the ground floor within the Government Buildings, sells excellent topographical maps of Fiji.

Carpenters Shipping (tel. 331-2244, www.carpship.com.fj), on Edinburgh Road across from the BP service station, sells British navigational charts of Fiji at a whopping F$81 each (buy these overseas). The **Fiji Hydrographic Office** (tel. 331-5457; Mon.–Fri. 0800–1300 and 1400–1600), top floor, Freeston Road, Walu Bay, sells navigational charts of the Yasawas, Kadavu, eastern Vanua Levu, and the Lau Group at F$23 a sheet (all other areas are covered by the British charts).

Bookstores

The **Dominion Book Center** (tel. 330-4334), Dominion House Arcade behind the Fiji Visitors Bureau, has some books on Fiji.

The **Fiji Museum** shop also sells a few excellent books at reasonable prices.

Suva's number-one bookstore is the **USP Book Center** (tel. 321-2500, fax 330-3265; Mon.–Thurs. 0800–1700, Fri. 0800–1630, Sat. 0830–1300, www.uspbookcentre.com), next to the ANZ Bank branch at the main Laucala Bay university campus. Not only do they have one of the finest Pacific sections in the region, but they stock the publications of several dozen occasional publishers affiliated with the university, and you can turn up some truly intriguing items. Also visit the Book Display Room in the **Institute of Pacific Studies** building (tel. 321-2332), not far from the Book Center. They sell assorted books by local authors, published by the IPS itself.

The Government Bookstore (Mon.–Thurs. 0900–1630, Fri. 0900–1530, Sat. 0900–1300), Harbor Terminal, corner of Usher and Scott Streets (enter through one of the shops), sells Fijian dictionaries and grammar books.

The **New Coconut Frond** (tel. 331-1963), at the back of the Suva Flea Market on Rodwell Road, has a large stock of used paperbacks.

Libraries

The **Suva City Library** (196 Victoria Parade; tel. 331-3433, ext. 241; Mon., Tues., Thurs., Fri. 0930–1800, Wed. 1200–1800, Sat. 0900–1300) allows visitors to take out four books upon payment of a refundable F$20 deposit.

The **National Archives of Fiji** (25 Carnarvon St.; tel. 330-4144; Mon.–Fri. 0800–1300 and 1400–1600) has an air-conditioned library upstairs with a large collection of local newspapers.

The excellent **Fiji Museum Library** (tel. 331-5944; Mon.–Fri. 0830–1300 and 1400–1600) is directly behind the main museum in a separate building. They charge F$1 to use the facilities.

The library at the Laucala Campus of the **University of the South Pacific** (tel. 321-2322) is open Monday–Friday 0800–1600 year-round. During semesters, they also are open Saturday, Sunday afternoon, and in the evening. You'll find a reading room with international newspapers downstairs. Tourists can request a free one-day visitors card to visit the Pacific Collection upstairs once only. Otherwise, it's possible to buy a two-week visitors card for F$11, which allows access to the Pacific Collection during that time. Prior to entry, bags must be left in a cloakroom behind and below the library.

The **Alliance Française** (14 MacGregor Road; tel. 331-3802, fax 331-3803) has an excellent selection of French books, magazines, and newspapers. You're welcome to peruse materials in the reading room Mon.–Fri. 0900–1800. Ask about their video and film evenings.

Ecology Groups

The **Greenpeace Pacific Campaign** (tel. 331-2861, fax 331-2784; Mon.–Fri. 0830–1700) is above the Ming Palace Restaurant in the old town hall on Victoria Parade.

The **Pacific Concerns Resource Center** (83 Amy St.; tel. 330-4649, fax 330-4755, www.pcrc.org.fj) has a library open to the public Monday, Tuesday, Thursday, and Friday 0900–1300 and 1400–1630, Wednesday 0900–1300. A large collection of periodicals on Pacific environmental and social issues can be accessed here, and some books are for sale. The Center is the directing body of the Nuclear-Free and Independent Pacific (NFIP) movement, a regional grass-roots coalition.

The **National Trust for Fiji** (3 Ma'afu St.; tel. 330-1807, fax 330-5092) manages several nature reserves and historic sites around Fiji. Their neighbor, the **World Wide Fund for Nature** (4 Ma'afu St.; tel. 331-5533, fax 331-5410, www.wwfpacific.org.fj) assists various projects for the support of wildlife and wild habitats.

Travel Agents

Hunts Travel (tel. 331-5288, fax 330-2212), upstairs from the Dominion House arcade behind the Fiji Visitors Bureau, is the place to pick up air tickets. They often know more about Air Pacific flights than the Air Pacific employees themselves!

Rosie The Travel Service (46 Gordon St.; tel. 331-4436), near Sarita Flats, books tours and accommodations all around Fiji. The **UTC** tour desk (tel. 331-2287) in the lobby of the Holiday Inn Hotel does the same.

Nina and Oro at **Rainbow-way Travel Services** (tel. 330-6613, fax 330-6593, rain boway1@connect.com.fj), which is located in the back section of the second floor of the Honson Building on Thomson Street (opposite the Fiji Visitors Bureau), can arrange stays on Rotuma at F$40 pp a night including meals. They can also organize stays at villages in the interior and Tailevu.

Airline Offices

Reconfirm your onward flight reservations at your airline's Suva office: **Air Fiji** (185 Victoria Parade; tel. 331-3666), which also represents Air Vanuatu and Polynesian Airlines; **Air Nauru** (Ratu Sukuna House, 249 Victoria Parade; tel. 331-2377); **Air New Zealand** (Queensland Insurance Center, 9 Victoria Parade; tel. 331-3100); **Air Pacific** (tel. 330-4388) in the Colonial Building on Victoria Parade; **Qantas Airways** (tel. 331-3888) in the Colonial Building on Victoria Parade; **Royal Tongan Airlines** (6 Ellery St., upstairs; tel. 330-9877); **Solomon Airlines** (Global Air Service, 3 Ellery St.; tel. 331-5889); and **Sun Air** (tel. 330-8979), in Parade Arcade on Victoria Parade opposite McDonald's. While you're there, check your seat assignment.

Services

Money

Rates at the banks vary slightly, and you might get a dollar or two more on a large exchange by checking the Westpac Bank, ANZ Bank, and Bank of Hawaii before signing your checks (and remember the F$5 commission deducted at the ANZ Bank). All of them have branches on Victoria Parade near The Triangle. The **ANZ Bank** (51 Renwick Rd.) has a special exchange office open weekdays 0900–1700, Saturday 0900–1300.

The ANZ Bank has Visa/MasterCard ATMs at their Victoria Parade and Renwick Road branches, outside Village Six Cinemas, at the food court in Downtown Boulevard Center on Ellery Street, at the ANZ Bank branch in Lami, and at 14 other locations around Suva.

Lotus Foreign Exchange (103 Cumming St.; tel. 331-7755), off Renwick Road, gives a better rate than the banks for traveler's checks without commission.

Money Exchange (tel. 330-3566; Mon.–Fri. 0830–1700, Sat. 0830–1300), Thomson and Pier streets opposite the Fiji Visitors Bureau, is similar.

Thomas Cook Travel (tel. 330-1603; Mon.–Fri. 0900–1600, Sat. 0930–1200), on Victoria Parade in the center of town, changes foreign currency at competitive rates, and sells the banknotes of neighboring countries like New Caledonia, Samoa, Solomon Islands, Tonga, and Vanuatu—convenient if you're headed for any of them.

If you need a quick infusion of funds, **Global Transfers Ltd.** (tel. 331-4812, weekdays 0800–1645, Sat. 0800–1345), Victoria Parade at Gordon Street, is the Western Union agent. Money can be sent to you here from almost anywhere in world through the Western Union network.

On Sunday and holidays, changing money is a problem (try your hotel if you get stuck).

Telecommunications

Fintel, the **Fiji International Telecommunications** office (158 Victoria Parade; tel. 331-2933, fax 330-1025, www.fintel.com.fj) is open Monday–Saturday 0800–2000 for long-distance calls and telegrams.

Telecom Fiji (tel. 330-3300, www.tfl.com.fj) operates a telephone center at Downtown Boulevard Center in the mall off Ellery Street.

The public fax at Suva General Post Office on Edward Street is fax 330-2666, should you need to receive a fax from anyone. Otherwise have your fax sent via Fintel at fax 330-1025.

Internet Access

Several places around Suva offer Internet access at F$.08 a minute, including the **Alpha Computer Center** (181 Victoria Parade; tel. 330-0211; Mon.–Fri. 0800–2000, Sat. 0800–1700, Sun. 1000–1600), between Gordon and MacArthur Streets, and, opposite Sukuna Park, the upstairs **Cyber Zone** (107 Victoria Parade; tel. 331-6967). The noisy cyber games being played by kids are a drawback at Cyber Zone.

At last report, the cheapest Internet access in Suva was F$.05 a minute, available at **Lamtec Services** (tel. 992-6719; weekdays 0730–1930,

Sat. 0730–1800) on the third floor of the Honson Building on Thomson Street (across the street from the Fiji Visitors Bureau). You may have to wait a while for a computer.

Connect Internet (10 Thomson St.; tel. 330-0777; weekdays 0800–1900, Sat. 0900–1700, www.connect.com.fj), across the street from Thomas Cook, provides Internet access in airconditioned comfort at F$5 an hour.

The Republic of Cappuccino (tel. 330-0333; Mon.–Fri. 0700–2300, Sat. 0800–2300, Sun. 0900–1900), in Dolphins Food Court at FNPF Place, Victoria Parade and Loftus Street, is Suva's original Internet café. Aside from Internet access at F$.15 a minute, they serve a variety of teas and coffees (F$2–3).

Immigration

The **Immigration Office** (tel. 331-2622; Mon.–Fri. 0830–1230, 1400–1500) for extensions of stay, etc., is in the Civic Tower behind the library on Victoria Parade.

Yachts must report to the **Customs and Excise Boarding Office** (tel. 330-2322; weekdays 0800–1300 and 1400–1600) in the Ports Authority Tower on Kings Wharf.

Consulates

The following countries have diplomatic missions in Suva:

• Australia: 10 Reservoir Rd., off Princes Rd., Samabula; tel. 338-2219, www.austhighcomm.org.fj

• China: 147 Queen Elizabeth Dr., Suva Point; tel. 330-0215

• Chile: Asgar & Co. Optometrists, Queensland Insurance Building behind Air New Zealand, Victoria Parade; tel. 330-0433

• European Union: Development Bank Center, 360 Victoria Parade, 4th Fl.; tel. 331-3633

• Federated States of Micronesia: 37 Loftus St.; tel. 330-4566

• Finland: 42 Gorrie St.; tel. 331-3188

• France: Dominion House, 7th Fl., Scott St.; tel. 331-2233

• Germany: 30 Deovji St., Tamavua Heights; tel. 332-2405

• Japan: Dominion House, 2nd Fl., Scott St.; tel. 330-4633

• Kiribati: 36 Gordon St.; tel. 338-0599

• Korea: Vanua House, Victoria Parade; tel. 330-0977

• Malaysia: Pacific House, 5th Fl., Butt and MacArthur Sts.; tel. 331-2166

• Marshall Islands: 41 Borron Rd., Samabula; tel. 338-7899

• Nauru: Ratu Sukuna House, 7th Fl., Victoria Parade and MacArthur St.; tel. 331-3566

• Netherlands: Cromptons, Queensland Insurance Building behind Air New Zealand, Victoria Parade; tel. 330-1499

• New Zealand: Reserve Bank Building, 10th Fl., Pratt St.; tel. 331-1422

• Papua New Guinea: Credit House, 3rd Fl., Gordon and Malcolm Sts.; tel. 330-4244

• Pakistan: 12 Leka St.; tel. 338-4981

• Sweden: 42 Gorrie St.; tel. 331-3188

• Taiwan: Pacific House, 6th Fl., Butt and MacArthur Sts. tel. 331-5922

• Tuvalu: 16 Gorrie St.; tel. 330-1355, fax 330-8479

• United Kingdom: 47 Gladstone Rd.; tel. 331-1033, fax 330-1406

• U.S.A.: 31 Loftus St.; tel. 331-4466, fax 330-0081, www.amembassy-fiji.gov

The Suva City Council has asked the U.S. embassy to relocate away from downtown Suva. The street in front of the heavily guarded embassy was closed in 1999 after threats were received, creating traffic and security problems for the city.

Everyone other than New Zealanders requires a visa to visit Australia, and these are available at the Australian High Commission weekdays 0830–1200. To get there, it's probably easier to go by taxi, then return to town by bus. Canada and Italy have consuls at Nadi.

Launderettes
Gangaram's Laundry (126 Toorak Rd.; tel. 330-2269; Mon.–Fri. 0730–1800, Sat. 0730–1400) offers same-day cleaning services.

Public Toilets
Free public toilets are just outside the Handicraft Market on the side of the building facing the harbor; in the Thurston Botanical Gardens; in Downtown Boulevard Center on Ellery Street; on the food court level at the Harbor Center; beside Nubukalou Creek off Renwick Road; and between the vegetable market and the bus station.

The public toilets in Sukuna Park (Mon.–Sat. 0800–1535) cost F$.65 or you can also have a shower here for F$1.10.

Yachting Facilities
The **Royal Suva Yacht Club** (tel. 330-4201, fax 330-4433, VHF channel 16, rsyc@connect.com.fj), on Foster Road between Suva and Lami, offers visiting yachts such amenities as mooring privileges, warm showers, laundry facilities, restaurant, bar, email, and the full use of club services by the whole crew at F$39 a week (F$20 for solo mariners). There have been reports of thefts from boats anchored here, so watch out. Many yachts anchor off the Raffles Tradewinds Hotel on the Bay of Islands, a recognized hurricane anchorage.

Health

Suva's **Colonial War Memorial Hospital** (tel. 331-3444), about a kilometer northeast of the center, is available 24 hours a day for emergencies. You can see a doctor in the Outpatients Department on Extension Street off Waimanu Rd. weekdays 0800–1600 for a F$20 nonresident fee, but you'll have to line up, as there will be many locals waiting for free service. Built in 1914, this hospital may be an interesting sight-seeing attraction, but if you actually need medical attention, you're better off seeing a private doctor.

Suva Private Hospital (120 Amy St.; tel. 330-3404, fax 330-3456, healthcare@connect.com.fj), at Brewster, which opened in 2001, offers state-of-the-art facilities. The medical center here is open 24 hours a day (F$20/50 to see a general practitioner/specialist) and provides service vastly superior to Colonial War Memorial for the same

price (if you're a foreigner). There's an excellent pharmacy here. The **Fiji Recompression Chamber Facility** (tel. 330-5154 or 885-0630, recompression@connect.com.fj), donated by the Cousteau Society in 1992, is also here, but it's only open for emergencies—you must call ahead.

The **Downtown Boulevard Medical Center** (tel. 331-3355; Mon.–Fri. 0830–1700, Sat. 0830–1130), in the mall off Ellery Street, has several foreign doctors (one female) on their roster, and a good pharmacy (tel. 330-3770) is nearby.

Two dentists are **Dr. David M. Charya** (The Dental Center, 59 Cumming St.; tel. 330-2160) and **Dr. Abdul S. Haroon** (Epworth House, Suite 12; tel. 331-3870), off Nina Street (just down the hall from Patterson Brothers).

The **Fiji Women's Crisis Center** (88 Gordon St.; tel. 331-3300 answered 24 hours, www.fiji women.com), opposite the Tanoa Plaza Hotel, offers free and confidential counseling for women and children. Their office is open Monday–Friday 0830–1630, Saturday 0900–1200.

Transportation

Although nearly all international flights arrive at Nadi, Suva is Fiji's main domestic transportation hub. Interisland shipping crowds the harbor, and if you can't find a ship going exactly your way, Air Fiji and Sun Air fly to all the major Fiji islands, while Air Pacific serves Australia and New Zealand, and Air Fiji goes to Tonga and Tuvalu—all from Nausori Airport. Make the rounds of the shipping offices listed below, then head over to Walu Bay to check the information. Compare the price of a cabin and deck passage, and ask if meals are included.

Keep in mind that all of the ferry departure times mentioned in this book are only indications of what was true in the past. It's essential to check with the company office for current departure times during the week you wish to travel. Quite a few ships leave Suva on Saturday, but none depart on Sunday. Readers have questioned safety standards on these ships, some of which seem to be nearing the end of their working lives—use them at your own risk.

A solid block of buses awaits your patronage at the market bus station near the harbor, with continuous local service, and frequent long-distance departures to Nadi and Lautoka. Many of the points of interest around Suva are accessible on foot, but if you wander too far, jump on any bus headed in the right direction, and you'll wind up back in the market. Taxis are also easy to find and relatively cheap.

Suva's bus station can be a little confusing, as there are numerous companies, and timetables

are not posted. Most drivers know where a certain bus will park, so just ask. For information on bus services around Viti Levu and domestic flights from Nausori Airport, see the Getting Around section in the Exploring the Islands section. Shipping services from Suva are covered below.

Ferries to Ovalau Island

The Suva to Levuka service is operated by **Patterson Brothers Shipping** (tel. 331-5644, fax 330-1652, patterson@connect.com.fj), Suite 1, 1st floor, Epworth Arcade off Nina Street. Patterson's "Sea-Road" bus leaves from the bus station opposite the Suva Flea Market Monday–Saturday at 1400 (F$24). At Natovi (67 km), it drives onto the *Princess Ashika,* an old Japanese ferry, for Buresala on Ovalau, then continues to Levuka, where it should arrive around 1745. For the return journey, you leave the Patterson Brothers office in Levuka Monday–Saturday at 0500, arriving in Suva at 0800. Bus tickets must be purchased in advance at the office, and on Saturdays and public holidays, reservations should be made at least a day ahead. These trips should take four or five hours right through, but can be late if the ferry connection is delayed. This is most likely to happen on the afternoon trip to Levuka, making it wise to fly to Ovalau (F$52) and return to Suva on the boat.

On Tuesday, Thursday, Friday, and Saturday, the 50-passenger boat *Viro* operates to Levuka

ISA LEI (THE FIJIAN SONG OF FAREWELL)

Isa, isa vulagi lasa dina,
Nomu lako, au na rarawa kina?
Cava beka, ko a mai cakava,
Nomu lako, au na sega ni lasa.

Isa, isa, you are my only treasure,
Must you leave me, so lonely and forsaken?
As the roses will miss the sun at dawning,
Every moment, my heart for you is yearning.

Isa lei, na noqu rarawa,
Ni ko sana vodo e na mataka.
Bau nanuma, na nodatou lasa,
Mai Suva nanuma tikoga.

Isa lei, the purple shadows falling,
Sad the morrow will dawn upon my sorrow.
Oh! Forget not, when you are far away,
Precious moments beside Suva Bay.

Vanua rogo, na nomuni vanua,
Kena ca, ni levu tu na ua.
Lomaqu voli, me'u bau butuka,
Tovolea, ke balavu na bula.

Isa lei, my heart was filled with pleasure,
From the moment, I heard your tender greeting.
'Mid the sunshine, we spent the hours together,
Now so swiftly those happy hours are fleeting.

Isa lei, na noqu rarawa,
Ni ko sana vodo e na mataka.
Bau nanuma, na nodatou lasa,
Mai Suva nanuma tikoga.

Isa lei, the purple shadows fall,
Sad the morrow will dawn upon my sorrow.
Oh! Forget not, when you are far away,
Precious moments beside Suva Bay.

Domoni dina, na nomu yanuyanu,
Kena kau, wale na salusalu,
Mocelolo, bua, na kukuwalu,
Lagakali, baba na rosidamu.

O'er the ocean your island home is calling,
Happy country where roses bloom in splendor,
Oh, I would but journey there beside you,
Then forever my heart would sing in rapture.

Isa lei, na noqu rarawa,
Ni ko sana vodo e na mataka.
Bau nanuma, na nodatou lasa,
Mai Suva nanuma tikoga.

Isa lei, the purple shadows fall,
Sad the morrow will dawn upon my sorrow.
Oh! Forget not, when you are far away,
Precious moments beside Suva Bay.

(F$16). The connecting carrier leaves from opposite the Suva Flea Market at 0800. Call **Turtle Island Transport** (tel. 339-4996 or 992-1297) for information.

Ships to Northern Fiji

Patterson Brothers Shipping (tel. 331-5644, patterson@connect.com.fj), Suite 1, 1st floor, Epworth Arcade off Nina Street, takes reservations for the Suva-Natovi-Nabouwalu-Labasa "Sea-Road" ferry/bus combination, which departs the bus station opposite the Suva Flea Market Monday, Wednesday, and Friday at 0530. Fares from Suva are F$48 to Nabouwalu or F$54 right through to Labasa, an interesting 10-hour trip. Forthcoming departures are listed on a blackboard in Patterson's Suva office, and the schedule varies slightly each week. Patterson Brothers also has offices in Labasa, Lautoka, and Levuka.

Taina's Travel Services (tel. 330-5889, fax 330-6189), upstairs in Epworth House opposite Patterson Brothers, handles bookings on the 65-meter MV *Adi Savusavu*, a former Swedish Scarlett Line ferry once used on the Landskrona-Copenhagen run. Now operated by **Beachcomber Cruises,** this ferry generally leaves Walu Bay, Suva, northbound for Savusavu and Taveuni Tuesday at 1000, Thursday at noon, and Saturday at 1800. Fares from Suva are F$42/62 economy/first class to Savusavu or F$47/67 to Taveuni. A bus connection from Savusavu to Labasa is an extra F$6. The air-conditioned first-class lounge contains 30 airline-style seats, plus six long tables with chairs. If you're fast, it's possible to rent a mattress in first class at F$5 pp for the trip. Downstairs in economy are another 246 padded seats and space in which to spread a mat. Ask when lunch and dinner will be served in first class, as they're good value. The *Adi Savusavu* also carries 12 cars and 15 trucks. Beachcomber Cruises' main office is on Freeston Road, Walu Bay.

Consort Shipping Line (tel. 331-3344 or 330-2877, fax 330-3389, consortship@connect.com.fj), in the Dominion House arcade on Thomson Street, operates the MV *Spirit of Fiji Islands* or "Sofi," an old Greek ferry with 182 airline-style seats in two video rooms, plus numerous long wooden benches outside on deck. First class consists of 20 four-berth cabins. The ship leaves Suva on Wednesday at 1000 and Saturday at 1800 for Koro (nine hours, F$35), Savusavu (14 hours, F$42/77), and Taveuni (23 hours, F$47/87 deck/cabin). The snack bar on board sells basic meals, but you're better off taking along your own food. Consort Shipping's main office is on Matua Street, Walu Bay.

Ships to Kadavu and Rotuma

Kadavu Shipping Co. (tel. 331-1766, fax 331-2987), in the Ports Authority office building hidden between hangers Nos. 11 and 12, Rona Street, Walu Bay, runs the MV *Bulou-ni-ceva* to Kadavu twice a week. The boat leaves Suva Monday and Thursday at midnight, with the Monday trip going to Matana and Vunisea and not calling at Jona's, Albert's, or Matava. The Thursday boat reaches Kavala Bay near Albert's Place around 1400. Saturday around 1000 they pick up passengers to return to Suva, arriving at 1700. Fares are F$47/66/90 deck/cabin/lounge, but only the cabin and lounge fares include meals. The cabins have four bunks, the lounge two beds, and deck passengers can stretch out on long benches on the middle deck when it isn't crowded. Once a

month, this ship sails to Rotuma, a two-day journey costing F$100/170/190 deck/cabin/lounge. The *Bulou-ni-ceva* is a former Chinese riverboat now owned by Kadavu Province (the entire crew is from Kadavu).

Western Shipping (tel. 331-4467), in a yellow container on Muaiwalu Wharf, operates the *Cagi Mai Ba* to Kadavu twice a week, usually leaving for Vunisea Monday at midnight and Kavala Bay Thursday at midnight (F$47 on deck, F$48 in an air-conditioned lounge, and F$57 in a 10-bed salon). The monthly trip to Rotuma is F$98/118/148 deck/lounge/salon.

Khans Shipping (tel. 330-8786), hanger No. 16 at the end of Rona Street, operates the *Cagidonu* to Kadavu and Rotuma on an irregular schedule. The *Degei II* goes to Lomaiviti and Lau occasionally.

Ships to Other Islands

Salia Basaga Shipping (tel. 330-3403) runs the MV *Tunatuki II* to the Lau Group twice a month. This large metal trading ship styles itself the "inter island trail blazer." There are two four-bunk cabins, and the fare to Lakeba or Vanua Balavu is F$82/113 deck/cabin one-way, meals included. A four to five-day round-trip to Cicia, Vanua Balavu, Tuvuca, Nayau, Lakeba, and Oneata will cost F$180/250 deck/cabin including meals. Their office is in a green container on Muaiwalu Wharf.

The **Kabua Development Corporation** (tel. 330-2258), near Consort Shipping on Matua Street near Muaiwalu Wharf, runs the *Taikabara* to Lakeba and the other islands of southern Lau every fortnight (F$68 deck or F$79 in one of two two-berth cabins).

Patterson Brothers Shipping, mentioned above, operates the car ferry *Island Navigator* to Gau (F$60), Moala (F$75), Lakeba (F$85), and Vanua Balavu (F$85) every week or two. They also handle the small wooden copra boat *Adi Lomai* to Lomaiviti, Lau, and Rotuma. Other small boats, such as the *Cagidonu* and *Taikabara,* run from Suva to Lau every week or two. Ask the crews of vessels tied up at Muaiwalu Jetty, Walu Bay, for passage to Nairai, Gau, Koro, Lau, etc. Don't believe the first person who tells you there's no boat going where you want—*keep trying.*

Food is usually included in the price, and on the outward journey it will probably be okay, but on the return don't expect much more than rice and tea. If you're planning a long voyage by interisland ship, a big bundle of kava roots to captain and crew as a token of appreciation for their hospitality works wonders.

Ships to Other Countries

The Wednesday issue of *The Fiji Times* carries a special section on international shipping, though most are container ships that don't accept passengers. Most shipping is headed for Tonga and Samoa—there's not much going westward, and actually getting on any of the ships mentioned below requires considerable persistence. Ships from neighboring countries sometimes come to Suva for repairs, and they carry passengers back on their return. It's often easier to sign on as crew on a yacht, and they'll probably be heading west. Try both yacht anchorages in Suva: Put up a notice, ask around, etc.

Williams & Gosling Ltd. Ships Agency (189 Rodwell Rd.; tel. 331-2633, fax 330-7358, www.wgfiji.com.fj), near the market bus station, handles the monthly departure of the *Nivaga II* or *Manu Folau* to Funafuti, but the dates are variable. Fares in Australian dollars are A$234 one-way in a four-person cabin, A$166 in an eight-person cabin, and A$58 deck. Meals will be another A$57.50 cabin-class or A$15 deck. Unless you have an onward plane ticket from Funafuti, you'll be required to pay for a round-trip. Williams & Gosling will only know about a week beforehand approximately when the ship may sail. After reaching Funafuti, the ship cruises the Tuvalu Group.

Williams & Gosling also books passengers on the Kiribati Shipping Services vessel *Nei Matangare,* which leaves Suva for Funafuti and Tarawa occasionally. The three-day trip to Funafuti costs A$95/190 deck/cabin one-way; otherwise the seven-day journey, Suva-Tarawa with a day at Funafuti, is A$184/368, meals included. Unless you have a ticket to leave Tuvalu or Kiribati, you're required to purchase a round-trip fare,

and no refund will be given until you can show an air ticket. Deck passengers sleep at the back of the ship and often get wet at night.

Pacific Agencies (tel. 331-5444, fax 330-2754), on Robertson Road between Rodwell Road and Nina Street, knows about Pacific Forum Line container ships from Suva to Apia, Pago Pago, and Nuku'alofa, such as the Samoan government-owned *Forum Samoa* (every two weeks) and the *Forum Fiji.* This office doesn't sell passenger tickets, so just ask when these ships will be in port, then go and talk to the captain, who is the only one who can decide if you'll be able to go.

Carpenters Shipping (tel. 331-2244, fax 330-1572, www.carpship.com.fj) on Edinburgh Road is an agent for the monthly **Bank Line** service to Lautoka, Port Vila, Luganville, Honiara, Papua New Guinea, and on to the United Kingdom. Again, they cannot sell you a passenger ticket and will only tell you when the ship is due in port and where it's headed. It's up to you to make arrangements personally with the captain, and the fare will be higher than airfare. Most passengers book months in advance.

Long-Distance Taxis and Minibuses

Minibuses to Nadi and Lautoka (F$12 to either) park at the **Stinson Parade Mini Bus Station** on the waterfront behind Village Six Cinemas. Service is throughout the day until 1930. The regular buses at the bus station are slower and safer, and you see more.

Long-distance taxis to Nadi and Lautoka park outside Foodland, corner of Robertson Road and Struan Street near the market. To Nadi, it's F$15 pp or F$60 for the whole car. For an extra F$40 or so, you should be able to negotiate a slower trip with stops along the way. Write out a list of the places you might like to stop, and show it to the driver beforehand, so he can't demand more money later on.

Taxis

Taxi meters are set at level one daily 0600–2200 with F$1 charged at flag-fall and about F$.50 a kilometer. From 2200 to 0600, the flag-fall is F$1.50 plus F$.50 a kilometer. Always ask the driver to use the meter. Fares average F$2 in the city center or F$3 to the suburbs. To hire a taxi for a city tour might cost about F$15 an hour.

Nausori Taxi (tel. 330-4178 or 331-2185), based at the taxi kiosk in the parking lot at the Holiday Inn, offers a shuttle service from Suva to Nausori Airport at F$3 pp. Trips are scheduled at 0545, 0845, 0945, 1100, 1330, and 1445 weekdays, and perhaps also on weekends, but only if bookings have been made. Thus it's important to reserve the day before if you want to be sure of getting this fare.

Car Rentals

Car rentals are available in Suva from **Avis** (tel. 331-3833, www.avis.com.fj), on Foster Road, Walu Bay, **Budget** (123 Foster Rd., Walu Bay; tel. 331-5899, www.budget.com.fj), **Central** (295 Victoria Parade; tel. 331-1866, www.central-rent-car.com.fj), **Dove** (tel. 331-1755), Brewster Street near Korea House, and **Thrifty** (46 Gordon St.; tel. 331-4436, www.rosiefiji.com).

Tours

For information on day trips from Suva offered by **Wilderness Ethnic Adventure Fiji** (tel. 331-5730, fax 331-5450, www.wildernessfiji.com.fj), turn to the Navua section in this book. Wilderness also runs two-hour city sightseeing tours (adults F$49, children under 13 years F$33). These trips can be booked through the UTC tour desk at the Holiday Inn or through Rosie Tours on Gordon Street.

Nausori and Beyond

NAUSORI

In 1881, the Rewa River town of Nausori, 19 kilometers northeast of Suva, was chosen as the site of Fiji's first large sugar mill, which operated until 1959. In those early days, it was incorrectly believed that sugar cane grew better on the wetter eastern side of the island. Today, cane is grown only on the drier, sunnier western sides of Viti Levu and Vanua Levu. The old sugar mill is now a rice mill and storage depot, as the Rewa Valley has become a major rice-producing area. Chicken feed is also milled here.

Nausori is Fiji's fifth-largest town and the headquarters of Central Division and Rewa Province. There are several banks in Nausori. The Rewa is Fiji's largest river, and the nine-span **Rewa River Bridge** here was erected in 1937. Long lines of vehicles crawl across this narrow bridge throughout the day, with a policeman directing traffic at the Nausori end right next to the bustling market. Construction of a new bridge was delayed for several years by sanctions imposed on Fiji after the May 2000 coup, but in 2003 tenders were finally taken (€12.2 million in overseas assistance for the bridge has been budgeted by the European Union).

The town is better known for its large international airport three kilometers southeast, built as a fighter strip to defend Fiji's capital during World War II. The population of 22,000 is predominantly Indo-Fijian. In mid-2000, the interior regions upriver from Nausori were scenes of terror as indigenous Fijian nationalists carried out ethnic-cleansing operations against Indo-Fijians living in isolated farmhouses. Some 300 people from Baulevu village alone were evacuated to refugee camps.

The **Syria Monument** (1983), at the end of the Rewa bridge, commemorates the wreck of the iron sailing ship *Syria* on Nasilai Point in May 1884. Of the 439 indentured Indian laborers aboard ship at the time, 57 were drowned. The monument tells the story of the rescue of the others.

Accommodations and Food

The only place to stay is **Riverside Accommodations** (tel. 995-0484), near the Nausori Club down the alley behind Big Bear furniture store in the vicinity of the Shell service station on Kings Road. The three rooms with shared bath are F$35 single or double. A pleasant sitting room is provided in this colonial-style wooden

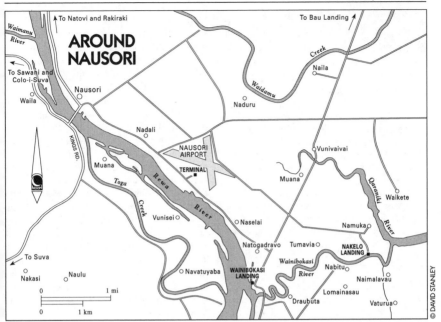

© DAVID STANLEY

house with a veranda and lovely garden on the river. Don't be put off by the House Full sign you may see outside, as this probably only applies to a separate section used by the locals for "short times." The rooms for foreigners are in the next building.

Krishna Milk Bar (3 Ross St.; tel. 347-7825; closed Sun.), down from the Westpac Bank and on the right, is Nausori's only vegetarian restaurant. You can get a vegetarian *thali* meal (F$3), *samosas,* and flavored masala tea.

The **Whistling Duck Pub,** around the corner from Krishna Milk Bar, and **KB's Bar and Night Club** (Fri. and Sat. 1900–0300, F$5 admission), opposite the bus station, are worth a look. Also try the **Nausori Club** (tel. 347-8287), on the river behind Big Bear.

Transportation
Local buses to the airport (F$.50) and Suva (F$1.40) are fairly frequent, with the last bus to Suva at 2200. A taxi to the airport will be F$3. You can catch Sunbeam Transport express buses from Nausori to Lautoka at 0635, 0715,

0855, 1240, 1405, and 1745 (246 km, 5.5 hours, F$12).

EAST OF NAUSORI
Rewa Delta
Take a bus from Nausori to Nakelo Landing to explore the heavily populated Rewa River Delta. Many outboards leave from Nakelo to take villagers to their riverside homes, and passenger fares are about F$1 for short trips. Larger boats leave Nakelo sporadically for Levuka, Gau, and Koro, but finding one would be pure chance. Some also depart from nearby Wainibokasi Landing. At **Nailili** in the delta, French Catholic missionaries built St. Joseph's Church (1905) of solid limestone with stained-glass windows.

Bau Island
Bau, a tiny, eight-hectare island just east of Viti Levu, has a special place in Fiji's history as this was the seat of High Chief Cakobau, who used European cannons and muskets to subdue most of western Fiji in the 1850s. At its pinnacle,

TANOA—CANNIBAL KING OF BAU

Tanoa was about 65 years old in 1840 when the U.S. Exploring Expedition, under Lt. Charles Wilkes, toured Fiji. His rise to power threw the island into several years of strife, as Tanoa had to do away with virtually every minor chief who challenged his right to rule. With long colorful pennants hung from the mast and thousands of *Cypraea ovula* shells decorating the hull, his 30-meter outrigger canoe was the fastest in the region. One of Tanoa's favorite sports was overtaking and ramming smaller canoes at sea. The survivors were then fair game for whoever could catch and keep them. At feasts where most nobles were expected to provide a pig, Tanoa always furnished a human body.

Bau had a population of 3,000, hundreds of war canoes guarded its waters, and more than 20 temples stood on the island's central plain. After the Battle of Verata on Viti Levu in 1839, Cakobau and his father Tanoa presented 260 bodies of men, women, and children to their closest friends and allied chiefs for gastronomical purposes. Fifteen years after this slaughter, Cakobau converted to Christianity and prohibited cannibalism on Bau. In 1867, he became a sovereign, crowned by European traders and planters desiring a stable government in Fiji to protect their interests.

The great stone slabs that form docks and seawalls around much of the island once accommodated Bau's fleet of war canoes. The graves of the Cakobau family and many of the old chiefs lie on the hilltop behind the school. The large, sturdy stone church located near the provincial offices was the first Christian church in Fiji. Inside its nearly one-meter-thick walls, just in front of the altar, is the old sacrificial stone once used for human sacrifices, today the baptismal font. Now painted white, this font was once known as King Cakobau's "skull crusher," and it's said that a thousand brains were splattered against it. Across from the church are huge ancient trees and the thatched Council

House on the site of the onetime temple of the war god Cagawalu. The family of the late Sir George Cakobau, governor-general of Fiji from 1973–83, has a large traditional-style home on the island. You can see everything on the island in an hour or so.

To get to Bau, take the Bau bus (five daily, F$.80) from Nausori to Bau Landing, where there are outboards to cross over to the island. Be aware that Bau is not considered a tourist attraction, and from time to time visitors are prevented from going to the island. It's important to get someone to invite you across, which they'll do willingly if you show a genuine interest in Fijian history. Like most Fijians, the inhabitants of Bau are friendly people. Bring a big bundle of *waka* for the *turaga-ni-koro,* and ask permission very politely to be shown around. There could be some confusion about who's to receive the *sevusevu,* however, as everyone on Bau is a chief! The more respectful your dress and demeanor, the better your chances of success. If you're told to contact the Ministry of Fijian Affairs in Suva, just depart gracefully, as that's only their way of saying no. After all, it's up to them.

Viwa Island

Before Cakobau adopted Christianity in 1854, Methodist missionaries working for this effect resided on Viwa Island, just across the water from Bau. Here the first Fijian New Testament was printed in 1847; Rev. John Hunt, who did the translation, lies buried in the graveyard beside the church that bears his name.

Viwa is a good alternative if you aren't invited to visit Bau itself. To reach the island, hire an outboard at Bau Landing. If you're lucky, you'll be able to join some locals who are going. A single Fijian village stands on the island.

Toberua Island

Created in 1968, **Toberua Island Resort** (tel. 347-2777 or 330-2356, fax 347-2888, www.to berua.com), on a tiny reef island off the east tip of Viti Levu, was one of Fiji's first luxury outer-island resorts. The 15 thatched *bure* are designed in the purest Fijian style, yet it's all

Fiji's longest bridge crosses the Rewa River at Nausori.

very luxurious, and the small size means peace and quiet. The tariff is F$490/540 single/double, plus F$110 for the three-meal plan (five-night minimum stay). Discounts are available for children under 16 sharing with adults. Babysitters are F$30 a day or F$20 an evening. Toberua is outside eastern Viti Levu's wet belt, so it doesn't get a lot of rain as does nearby Suva, and weather permitting, meals are served outdoors. There are no mosquitoes.

Don't expect tennis courts or a golf course at Toberua, though believe it or not, there's tropical golfing on the reef at low tide! (Nine holes from 90–180 m, course par 32, clubs and balls provided free.) Sportfishing is F$90 an hour and scuba diving F$88/450 for one/six tanks. Massage is F$55 an hour. All other activities are free, including snorkeling, sailing, windsurfing, and boat trips to a bird sanctuary or mangrove forest. A swimming pool is provided. Launch transfers from Nakelo Landing to Toberua are F$38 per person each way.

NORTHWEST OF NAUSORI

Vunidawa

If you have a few days to spare, consider exploring the untouristed river country northwest of Nausori. The main center of Naitasiri Province is Vunidawa on the Wainimala River, a big village with four stores, a hospital, a post office, a police station, two schools, and a provincial office. There are five buses a day, except Sunday, from Suva to Vunidawa, but no bus connection to Korovou or Monasavu.

Go for a swim in the river or borrow a horse to ride around the countryside. Stroll two kilometers down the road to Waidawara, where there's a free hourly punt near the point where the Wainibuka and Wainimala rivers unite to form the mighty Rewa River. Take a whole day to hike up to Nairukuruku and Navuniyasi and back.

River-Running

There's an exciting bamboo raft *(bilibili)* trip through the Waiqa Gorge between Naitauvoli and Naivucini, two villages on the Cross-Island Highway west of Vunidawa. Two men with long poles guide each raft through the frothing rapids as the seated visitor views towering boulders enveloped in jungle. For the two-hour ride, an individual *bilibili* will have to be constructed for you. (There's no way to get a used *bilibili* back up to Naitauvoli.)

Raft trips cost about F$50 pp, and unless you've rented a car, it will probably be necessary to spend the night at Naitauvoli. If you do stay overnight, a *sevusevu* and monetary contribution to your hosts are expected in addition to the F$50 fee. No trips are made on Sunday, so don't arrive on a Saturday. One Tacirua Transport bus a day departs Suva for Naivucini at 1455 (except Sunday); once there you'd have to look for a carrier on to Naitauvoli.

THE TRANS–VITI LEVU TREK

Experienced hikers can consider doing the rugged two-day trek from the Cross-Island Highway to Wainimakutu, up and down jungle river valleys through the rainforest. It will take a strong, fast

crossing Waisomo Creek on the Trans–Viti Levu Trek

hiker about three hours to get from Balea on the highway to Nasava, then another four over the ridge to Wainimakutu. The Trans-Viti Levu Trek passes through several large Fijian villages and gives you a good cross section of village life.

On this traditional route, you'll meet people going down the track on horseback or on foot. Since you must cross the rivers innumerable times, this trek is probably impossible for visitors during the rainy season (Dec.–Apr.), although the locals still manage to do it. If it's been raining, sections of the trail become a quagmire, stirred up by horses' hooves. Hiking boots aren't much use here; you'd be better off with shorts and an old pair of running shoes in which to wade across the rivers. There are many refreshing places to swim along the way. Some of the villages have small trade stores, but you're better off carrying your own food, and pack some *yaqona* for formal presentations as well.

But remember, you aren't the first to undertake this walk; the villagers have played host to trekkers many times, and some previous hikers have not shown much consideration to local residents along the track. Unless you have been specifically invited, do not presume automatic hospitality. If a villager provides food or a service, be prepared to offer adequate payment. This applies equally to the Sigatoka River Trek, described later.

The Route

Bus service on the Cross-Island Highway from Suva to Nadarivatu was interrupted in 1993 by Hurricane Keno, which destroyed the bridge at Lutu just beyond **Balea,** the Trans-Viti Levu trailhead. Though the bridge has since been repaired, Tacirua Transport buses now go only as far as Lutu, leaving Suva's market bus station Mon.–Sat. at 1300, Sun. at 0930 (F$5.40). The Lutu bus could drop you at Balea, otherwise large carrier trucks to Lutu (F$6–8 pp) park near Foodtown, corner of Robertson Road and Struan Street near Suva Market, and most depart around midday.

From Balea, walk down to the Wainimala River, which must be crossed three times before you reach the bank opposite Sawanikula. These crossings can be dangerous and almost impossible in the rainy season, in which case it's better to stop and wait for some local people who might help you across. From Sawanikula, it's not far to **Korovou,** a fairly large village with a clinic and two stores. Between Korovou and **Nasava,** you cross the Wainimala River 14 times, but it's easier because you're farther upstream. Try to reach Nasava on the first day. If you sleep at Korovou, you'll need an early start and a brisk pace to get to the first village south of the divide before nightfall on the second day.

From Nasava, follow the course of the Waisomo Creek up through a small gorge and past a waterfall. You zigzag back and forth across the creek all the way up almost to the divide. After a steep incline, you cross to the south coast watershed. There's a clearing among the bamboo groves on top where you could camp, but there's no water. Before **Wainimakutu** (Nasau), the scenery gets better as you enter a wide valley with Mt. Naitaradamu (1,152 m) behind you and the jagged outline of the unscaled Korobasabasaga Range to your left. Wainimakutu is a large village with two stores and carriers to

Suva. Begin your trek early in the week in order to avoid getting stuck here on a weekend.

Namosi

The carrier from Wainimakutu to Suva goes via Namosi, spectacularly situated below massive Mt. Voma (927 m), with sheer stone cliffs on all sides. You can climb Mt. Voma in a day from Namosi for a sweeping view of much of Viti Levu. It's steep, but not too difficult. Allow at least four hours up and down (guides can be hired at Namosi village). Visit the old Catholic church at Namosi.

There are low-grade copper deposits estimated at 500,000 tons at the foot of the Korobasabasaga Range, which Rupert Brooke called the "Gateway to Hell," 14 kilometers north of Namosi by road. No mining has begun, due to depressed world prices of copper and high production costs, though feasibility studies continue. A 1979 study indicated that an investment of F$1 billion would be required.

Northern Viti Levu

Northern Viti Levu has far more spectacular landscapes than the southern side of the island, and if you can only travel one way by road between Suva and Nadi, you're better off taking the northern route. Kings Road is now paved from Suva north to Korovou, then again from Dama to Lautoka, but between Korovou and Dama is a 62-kilometer gravel stretch. (Roadwork from the Dama end may have extended the pavement 13 kilometers or so by the time you get there, but at the present rate it will be decades before the asphalt reaches Korovou.) If driving, check your fuel before heading this way. Since Kings Road follows the **Wainibuka River** from Wailotua village almost all the way to Viti Levu Bay, you get a

good glimpse of the island's lush interior, and the north coast west of Rakiraki is breathtaking. In years gone by, the Fijians would use bamboo rafts to transport bundles of bananas down the Wainibuka to markets in Vunidawa and Nausori, and the road is still called the "Banana Highway." These days, many visitors stop for a sojourn on Nananu-i-Ra Island near Rakiraki, and intrepid hikers occasionally trek south down the Sigatoka River from the hill station of Nadarivatu. The rugged north coast is known as the Sunshine Coast for its relatively dry climate.

NORTHERN VITI LEVU HIGHLIGHTS

Wainibuka River: bamboo rafting, Banana Highway (p. 212)
Nananu-i-Ra Island: beaches, diving, small resorts (p. 215)
Emperor Gold Mine: history, spectacles, mine tours (p. 220)
Navala: most picturesque village, river trips (p. 223)
Nadarivatu: hill station, mountain climbing, hiking (p. 224)

Northeastern Viti Levu

Korovou and the Tailevu Coast

A good paved highway runs 31 kilometers north from Nausori to Korovou, a small town of about 350 souls on the east side of Viti Levu. Korovou is at the junction of Kings Road and the road to Natovi, terminus of the Ovalau and Vanua Levu ferries, and this crossroads position makes it an important stop for buses plying the northern route around the island. Sunbeam Transport express buses leave Korovou for Lautoka at 0720, 0800, 0940, 1325, 1500, and 1830 (215 km, five hours), with local westbound buses departing at 0920 and 0950 (7.5 hours). (Be aware that because *korovou* means "new village," there are many places called that in Fiji—don't mix them up.)

Korovou is the headquarters of Tailevu Province, and the district officer's office is in Waimaro House on the south side of town. The Seventh-Day Adventist Church operates Fulton College, a large Bible college just south of Korovou. Coup master George Speight hails from near Korovou, and a rather unpleasant atmosphere hangs over the town.

The dilapidated **Tailevu Hotel** (Warrick Williams, tel. 343-0028, fax 343-0244), on a hill overlooking the Waibula River just across the bridge from Korovou, has three double rooms in an old building at F$45 double, or F$55 for a four-person family room. Better are the six new air-conditioned units in a long block facing an

unfinished swimming pool at F$60 double. Two basic single rooms in a nearby cottage are F$25 (or F$15 if you request the "backpackers rate"). This rustic colonial-style hotel features a large bar and restaurant, and a disco opens on Friday and Saturday nights.

North of Korovou is Natovi, terminus of ferry services from Vanua Levu and Ovalau. The **Natalei Eco-Lodge** (tel. 881-1168) at Nataleira village, up the coast beyond Natovi, offers dormitory

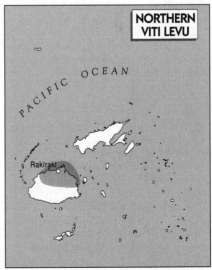

NORTHERN VITI LEVU

PACIFIC OCEAN

Rakiraki

© DAVID STANLEY

accommodations at F$35 pp and *bure* at F$100 double, meals included. Buses to Nataleira leave Suva bus station weekdays at 1330, 1430, and 1630 (F$4). Horseback riding, hiking, waterfall visits, snorkeling, and cultural activities can be arranged. Natalei Eco-Lodge makes an ideal base from which to climb **Mt. Tova** (647 m) for its sweeping view of the entire Tailevu area. The trail begins at Silana village, a couple of kilometers northwest of Nataleira.

Kings Road to Viti Levu Bay

The large dairy farms along the highway west of Korovou were set up after World War I. **Dorothy's Waterfall** on the Waimaro River, a kilometer east of Dakuivuna village, is 10 kilometers west of Korovou. It's a nice picnic spot if you have your own transportation.

At Wailotua No. 1, 20 kilometers west of Korovou, is a large **snake cave** (admission F$5) right beside the village and easily accessible from the road. One stalactite in the cave is shaped like a six-headed snake. "Feejee Experience" groups are taken *bilibili* rafting on the Wainibuka River here. At Dama, the paved road starts again and continues 45 kilometers northwest to Rakiraki. (As you drive along this road, you may be flagged down by Fijians emphatically inviting you to visit their village. At the end of the tour, you'll be asked to sign the visitors book and make a financial contribution. If you decide to stop, don't bother trying to present anyone with kava roots, as hard cash is all they're after.)

The old Catholic Church of St. Francis Xavier at **Naiserelagi,** on a hilltop above Navunibitu Catholic School, on Kings Road about 25 kilometers southeast of Rakiraki, was beautifully decorated with frescoes by Jean Charlot in 1962–1963. Typical Fijian motifs, such as the *tabua, tanoa,* and *yaqona,* blend together in the powerful composition behind the altar. Father Pierre Chanel, who was martyred in 1841 on Futuna Island between Fiji and Samoa, appears on the left holding the weapon that killed him, a war club. Christ and the Madonna are portrayed in black. Charlot had previously collaborated with the famous Mexican muralist

Diego Rivera, and his work (restored in 1998) is definitely worth stopping to see. Flying Prince Transport (tel. 669-4346) runs buses from Vaileka to Naiserelagi at 0845, 1130, 1200, 1330, 1430, 1545, 1630, and 1730 (F$2), otherwise all the local Suva buses stop there. A taxi from Vaileka might cost F$22 one-way or F$30 round-trip with waiting time. At **Nanukuloa** village just north of here is the headquarters of Ra Province.

Near Ellington Wharf

Adventure Water Sports (Warren Francis, tel. 669-3333, fax 669-3366, www.safarilodge.com.fj) on Ellington Wharf offers catamaran cruises (from F$55 pp), two-hour snorkeling tours (F$25/30 pp to the inner/outer reef), kayak tours (F$149 a full day), game fishing (F$115/195 pp for two/four hours), and windsurfing lessons (F$60/110 beginner/advanced an hour, plus F$40/85 board hire). A minimum of two persons is required for most trips. You can also rent windsurfers, snorkeling gear, and Hobie cats. Their shop serves basic meals at F$4–5 or coffee for F$1. You can use the phone here to call the island at F$1 a call or check your email at F$.18 a minute. Boat transfers to Nananu-i-Ra can be arranged.

The **Make It Happen Store** (tel. 927-9678 or 991-7684), opposite Adventure Water Sports, can arrange half-day treks to the top of Uluisupani (540 m), the highest peak behind Ellington Wharf, via Navolau II village, at F$30 pp.

The upscale **Wananavu Beach Resort** (John Gray, tel. 669-4433, fax 669-4499, www.wananavu.com), on a point facing Nananu-i-Ra Island, three kilometers off Kings Road, is near Viti Levu's northernmost tip. There are 15 air-conditioned bungalows costing F$300–365 single or double—reasonable value for the quality. No cooking facilities are provided, but each room does have a fridge. Adjacent to the resort are three two-bedroom villas with kitchens renting for F$372 for up to four persons. Local rate discounts are possible. The three-meal plan is F$85 pp. The resort has a swimming pool, tennis court, and small brown beach. The Nananu-i-Ra dive shops offer scuba diving from the Wananavu,

Ellington Wharf near Rakiraki is used by both car ferries plying to Vanua Levu and outboards bound for nearby Nananu-i-Ra.

and a variety of other water sports are available. Daily snorkeling trips are organized to different sites, and a picnic lunch on the beach is included in the F$28 pp charge.

NANANU-I-RA ISLAND

This small 355-hectare island, three kilometers off the northernmost tip of Viti Levu, is a good place to spend some quality time amid tranquility and beauty. The climate is dry and sunny, and there are great beaches, reefs, snorkeling, walks, sunsets, and moonrises over the water—only roads are missing. Seven or eight separate white sandy beaches lie scattered around the island, and it's big enough that you won't feel confined. In the early 19th century, Nananu-i-Ra's original Fijian inhabitants were wiped out by disease and tribal warfare, and an heir sold the island to the Europeans, whose descendants now operate small family-style resorts and a 219-hectare plantation on the island.

The northern two-thirds of Nananu-i-Ra Island, including all of the land around Nananu Island Lodge, is owned by Mrs. Louise Harper of Southern California, who bought it for a mere US$200,000 in 1966 (she also owns a sizable chunk of Proctor & Gamble back in the States). Today, Harper's cattle graze beneath coconuts on the Harper Plantation.

To hike right around Nananu-i-Ra on the beach takes about four hours of steady going, or all day if you stop for picnicking and snorkeling. The thickest section of mangroves is between Nananu Island Lodge and the Bamboo Beach Resort, on the west side of the island, and this stretch should be covered at low tide. However you do it, at some point you'll probably have to take off your shoes and wade through water just over your ankles or scramble over slippery rocks. The entire coastline is public, but only as far as two meters above the high tide line. Avoid becoming stranded by high tide.

Scuba Diving

Ra Divers (Elizabeth and Graham Burnett, tel. 669-4511, fax 669-4611, www.radivers.com) has been operating on Nananu-i-Ra for more than a decade. They offer scuba diving at F$85/150/650 for one/two/10 tanks, plus F$15

windsurfers off Nananu-i-Ra's Mile Long Beach

for gear. Night diving is F$100. Snorkelers can go along for F$25 (mask and snorkel supplied). Ra Diver's resort course costs F$160; full four-day PADI or NAUI certification is F$600 if you're alone or F$525 pp for two or more. They pick up clients regularly from all of the resorts. Ra Divers tends to stay close to Nananu-i-Ra, and the diving here is only spectacular if you observe the small details—there's not the profuse marinelife or huge reefs you'll find elsewhere. The underwater photographer will like it.

An American named Dan Grenier runs a more upscale dive operation called **Crystal Divers** (tel. 669-4747, fax 669-4877, www.crystaldivers.com) at the south end of Nananu-i-Ra. Many of Dan's clients book from overseas via his website, paying F$150/190 for two tank dives to the fringing/outer reef, plus F$40 a day for gear (if required). Third tanks are F$80. Dan prefers to work with experienced divers and usually doesn't have time for certification courses unless a group is interested. His 12-meter jet boat, *Crystal Explorer*, allows him to offer live-aboard-quality diving from a land-based location. He frequents extraordinary

Bligh Water sites, and he's constantly searching for new locations. Crystal Divers closes for annual leave in January and February.

Accommodations

Accommodation prices on Nananu-i-Ra have crept up in recent years, and the number of beds is limited. With the island's growing popularity, it's best to call ahead to one of the resorts and arrange to be picked up at Ellington Wharf. None of the innkeepers will accept additional guests when they're fully booked, and camping is often not allowed. There's no public telephone at Ellington Wharf, but the staff of Adventure Water Sports on the wharf will make local calls for you at F$1 each.

If you want an individual room or *bure*, make 100 percent sure one is available, otherwise you could end up spending a few nights in the dormitory waiting for one to become free. All the budget places have cooking facilities, and a few also serve snacks and meals. MacDonald's, Betham's, and Nananu Island Lodge have minimarkets with a reasonable selection of groceries (including beer). Bring enough cash, as only the Bamboo Beach Resort accepts credit cards.

Nananu Island Lodge (tel./fax 669-4290, www.nananu-island-lodge.com), formerly known as Kontiki Island Lodge, has been upgraded since a change of ownership in 2001. It's at the unspoiled north end of the island, with the long deserted beach facing One Bay just a 20-minute walk away. Hike up onto the hill behind the lodge for the view. They offer three modern self-catering bungalows, each capable of sleeping four at F$110/125/140 double/triple/quad, plus tax. If you want more privacy, ask for one of the four rooms in the two thatched duplex *bure* and two rooms in another building, which are F$54 double. The two dorms each have six beds at F$20 pp. Camping is F$10 pp. There's no hot water. All guests have access to a fridge and cooking facilities, and a small shop is on the premises. Otherwise, you can order meals. The "Feejee Experience" people stay here, so reservations are essential. On Saturday night, they're always full.

At the other end of Nananu-i-Ra, a one-hour walk along the beach at low tide, are several other inexpensive places to stay, all offering cooking fa-

© DAVID STANLEY

cilities. They're less crowded than Nananu Island Lodge and perhaps preferable for a restful holiday. They almost always have a few free beds in the dorms, but advance bookings are recommended.

MacDonald's Nananu Beach Cottages (tel. 669-4633, fax 669-4302) offers two attractive beach houses and one garden house, all with bath and fridge, at F$80 single or double, plus F$9 per additional person to four maximum. A duplex is F$70 for each of the two units, while a larger two-story house accommodating up to six is F$175. The four-bunk dorm is F$20 pp. All units have access to cooking facilities, and a three-meal package is available at F$33 pp. Mabel MacDonald's Beachside Café serves excellent grilled cheese sandwiches (F$5) and pizzas (F$15–20), as well as selling groceries. Dinner (F$10–16) must be ordered by 1500. A Fijian *lovo* feast (F$15/25 for vegetarians/carnivores) is arranged once a week. It's peaceful and attractive, with excellent snorkeling (lots of parrot fish) from the long private wharf off their beach. Ryan MacDonald takes guests on a snorkeling trip to the outer reef at F$25 pp (minimum of four). A two-person kayak is F$12.50/25 a half/full day. The atmosphere at MacDonald's is excellent.

Right next to MacDonald's and facing the same white beach is friendly **Betham's Beach Cottages** (Peggy and Oscar Betham, tel./fax 669-4132, www.bethams.com.fj). They have four units in two cement-block duplex houses, each sleeping up to six, at F$90 single or double, F$100 triple. The one wooden beachfront bungalow costs the same. Two mixed dormitories, one with eight beds and another with six, are F$20 pp. There's no hot water, but cooking facilities and a fridge are provided. The electric generator is switched off at 2200. A paperback lending library is at your service. Betham's impressive grocery store also sells alcohol, and their well-stocked beachfront bar serves dinner at F$12–20, though the food is better at MacDonald's. A snorkeling trip is F$15, plus F$10 for gear.

Sharing the same high sandy beach with the above is **Charley's Place** (Charley and Louise Anthony, tel. 669-4676). Each of the two houses on the hillside has a three-bed dorm (F$20 pp) in the same area as the kitchen and one double room with shared bath (F$45). You can watch the sunrise on one side of the hill and the sunset on the other. Charley's also rents another house at F$70 double.

Just a few minutes walk across the peninsula via a 200-meter right-of-way next to Charley's is **Morrison's Beach Cottage** (Phyl and John Morrison, tel./fax 669-4516, tipple@connect.com.fj), on Long Beach on the east side of the island. The two-bedroom bungalow is F$85/95/105 double/triple/quad, the five-bed dorm F$20 pp. Two people can reserve the entire dorm for themselves at F$75. Both units are fully screened and have cooking facilities, fridge, and private bath (no meals served). It's cleaner and quieter than some of the other places. John's a retired engineer from the Emperor Gold Mine who loves to go fishing, and he'll gladly take you out in his boat at F$40/65 a half/full day, plus fuel. He also rents paddleboats at F$10/15 a half/full day, snorkeling gear at F$10/15. Morrison's closes for holidays in January and February.

At the high end of the price spectrum, the **Bamboo Beach Resort** (tel. 669-4444, fax 669-4404), formerly known as Mokusigas Island Resort, is owned by the same people who run the Marlin Bay Resort on Beqa Island. Completely rebuilt in 2003, the 20 bungalows with fridge and outdoor shower are F$370 single or double, with another F$110 pp payable for the meal plan (no cooking facilities). Scuba divers are the target market, and Dan Grenier of Crystal Divers manages the diving operation. To create a diving attraction, the 33-meter *Papuan Explorer* was scuttled in 22 meters of water, 150 meters off the 189-meter Bamboo Beach jetty, which curves out into the sheltered lagoon. Only a skimpy little beach facing a mudflat is on the west side of the property, but there's a mile-long picture-postcard beach over the hill on the other side of the island. All the resort facilities, including the restaurant, bar, and dive shop, are strictly for houseguests only.

Getting There

Boat transfers from Ellington Wharf to Nananu-i-Ra are about F$20 pp return (20 minutes), though the resorts may levy a surcharge for one person alone. Check prices when you call to make your accommodation booking. The Nadi Downtown Motel arranges minibus rides from Nadi direct to Ellington Wharf, which cost anywhere from F$25–45 pp depending on how many people are going, though it's cheaper to take an express bus from Lautoka to Vaileka, then a taxi to the landing at F$10 for the car. Otherwise, all of the express buses will drop you on the highway, a two-kilometer walk from Ellington Wharf. Coming from Nadi, you will have to change buses in Lautoka.

Patterson Brothers operates a vehicular ferry between Ellington Wharf and Nabouwalu a few times a week, a great shortcut to/from Vanua Levu (F$39 one-way). The ferry leaves Ellington Wharf at 0700, departing Nabouwalu for the return at 1130. There's a connecting bus to/from Labasa at Nabouwalu (112 km). Often you'll be allowed to spend the night on the boat at Ellington Wharf. Patterson's best customers are large trucks carrying pine logs from Vanua Levu to the mills of Lautoka. The schedule changes all the time, and the only way to find out which days they'll be going that week is to call Patterson's Lautoka office at tel. 666-1173.

RAKIRAKI

This part of northern Viti Levu is known as Rakiraki, but the main town is called **Vaileka** (population 5,000). The Penang Sugar Mill was erected here in 1881. The mill is about a kilometer from the main business section of Vaileka, beyond the golf course. The sugar is loaded aboard ships at Ellington Wharf, connected to the mill by an 11-kilometer cane railway. There are three banks and a large produce market in Vaileka, but most visitors simply pass through on their way to/from Nananu-i-Ra Island.

Right beside Kings Road, just 100 meters west of the turnoff to Vaileka, is the grave of **Ratu Udreudre,** the cannibal king of this region, who is alleged to have consumed 872 corpses. A rocky hill named **Uluinavatu** (stone head), a few kilometers west of Vaileka, is reputed to be the jumping-off point for the disembodied spirits of the ancient Fijians. A fortified village and temple once stood on its summit. Uluinavatu's triangular shape is said to represent a man, while a similar-looking small island offshore resembles a woman with flowing hair.

The **Nakauvadra Range,** towering south of Rakiraki, is the traditional home of the Fijian serpent-god Degei, who is said to dwell in a cave on the summit of Mt. Uluda (866 m). This "cave" is little more than a cleft in the rock. To climb the Nakauvadra Range, which the local Fijians look upon as their primeval homeland, permission must be obtained from the chief of Vatukacevaceva village, who will provide guides. A *sevusevu* must be presented.

Accommodations and Food

The **Rakiraki Hotel** (tel. 669-4101, fax 669-4545, www.tanoahotels.com), on Kings Road a couple of kilometers north of Vaileka, has 36 air-conditioned rooms with fridge and private bath at F$99 single or double, F$123 triple in the new blocks, and 10 rather musty fan-cooled rooms at F$35/48 single/double in the old wing. Reduced rates are sometimes offered on the air-conditioned rooms. The reception area, restaurant, and old wooden wing occupy the core of the original hotel, which dates back to 1945; the two-story accommodations blocks were added much later. Extensive gardens surround the hotel, and the Rakiraki's outdoor bowling green draws middle-aged lawn-bowling enthusiasts from Australia and New Zealand. Those folks like old-fashioned "colonial" touches, such as the typed daily menu featuring British-Indian curry dishes, and gin and tonic in the afternoon. The manager can arrange for you to play at the nearby nine-hole golf course owned by the Fiji Sugar Corporation (greens fees are F$20, and you must bring your own clubs). The Tui Ra (or king of Ra) lives in the village across the highway from the hotel. Only the local or "stage" buses will drop you off on Kings Road right in front of the hotel (the express buses will take you to Vaileka). A taxi from Vaileka will be F$2.50.

A number of restaurants near the bus station at Vaileka serve basic Chinese meals. At F$6.50 and up per plate, **Gafoor & Sons** (tel. 669-4225) is the most expensive as the Sunbeam express buses

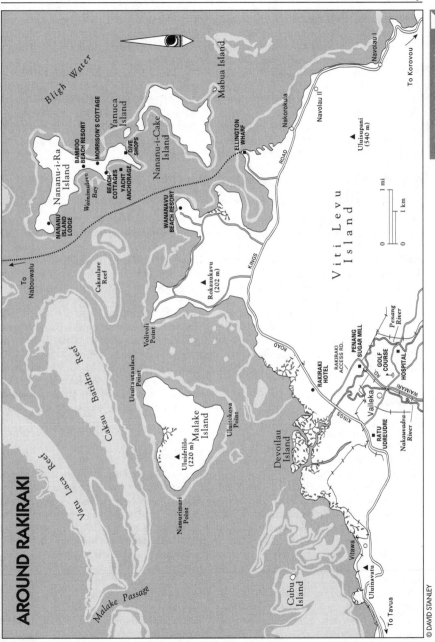

AROUND RAKIRAKI

© DAVID STANLEY

stop there. **Rakiraki Lodge** (tel. 669-4336) on the west side of the square serves some excellent curry meals for F$4.50 from a glass-covered warmer at the rear counter. The **Cosmopolitan Club** (tel. 669-4330), two blocks from Vaileka bus station, is the local drinking place.

Transportation
A taxi from Vaileka to Ellington Wharf, where outboard motorboats from the Nananu-i-Ra resorts pick up guests, will run F$10. Otherwise

take a local bus east on Kings Road to the turnoff and walk two kilometers down to the wharf. All buses from Lautoka and Suva stop at this turnoff.

Sunbeam Transport has express buses from Vaileka to Lautoka (108 km) at 1010, 1035, 1230, 1605, 1730, and 2105, and to Suva at 0830, 0900, 1100, 1440, and 1850. Flying Prince buses to Suva (157 km, F$9) leave Vaileka at 0745, 0845, and 1230. More frequent local buses also operate.

Northwestern Viti Levu

West of Rakiraki, Kings Road passes the government-run Yaqara Cattle Ranch, where Fijian cowboys keep 5,500 head of cattle and 200 horses on a 7,000-hectare spread enclosed by an 80-kilometer fence. In 1996, an ultramodern artesian water bottling plant owned by Canadian businessman David Gilmour opened here, and plastic bottles of Fiji Water are now the country's fastest growing export. In 2003, an Australian company leased 5,000 hectares of land around Yaqara, with the intention of creating a Studio City for foreign film producers.

TAVUA

Tavua (population 2,500), an important junction on the north coast, is useful mostly as a base for visiting the gold mine at Vatukoula. Of the three banks in Tavua, the ANZ Bank has a Visa/MasterCard ATM.

The two-story **Tavua Hotel** (tel. 668-0522), a wooden colonial-style building on a hill, is only a five-minute walk from the bus stop. Fully renovated in 2002, the 11 air-conditioned rooms with bath are now reasonable value at F$45/68 single/double. The five-bed dormitory is F$18 pp. Meals are F$10 here. This hotel looks like it's going to be noisy due to the large bar downstairs, but all is silent after the bar and restaurant close at 2100. It's a good base from which to explore Vatukoula or break a trip across northern Viti Levu.

Roy's Wine & Dine (Michael Roy, tel. 668-

1474; Mon.–Sat. 0700–1800), on Leka Street near the post office, serves a fish-and-chips lunch for less than F$2. Socialize at the **Tavua Farmers Club** (tel. 668-0236) on Kings Road toward Ba, or the more elitist **Tavua Club** (tel. 668-0265) on Nasivi Street.

Transportation
Sunbeam Transport has express buses from Tavua to Suva (198 km) at 0725, 0750, 1000, 1340, and 1750, and to Lautoka (67 km) at 1105, 1130, 1320, 1655, 1825, and 2200. Local buses from Tavua to Vaileka (41 km), Vatukoula (8 km), or Lautoka are frequent, but the bus service from Tavua to Nadrau via Nadarivatu has been suspended.

VATUKOULA

In 1932, an old Australian prospector named Bill Borthwick discovered gold at Vatukoula, eight kilometers south of Tavua. Two years later, Borthwick and his partner, Peter Costello, sold their stake to an Australian company, and in 1935 the **Emperor Gold Mine** opened. In 1977, there was a major industrial action at the mine, and the government had to step in to prevent it from closing. In 1983, the Western Mining Corporation of Australia bought a 20 percent share and took over management. Western modernized the facilities and greatly increased production, but after another bitter strike in 1991, they sold out, and the mine is now operated by the Emperor Gold Mining Company once again. The 700 miners who walked out in 1991 have been replaced by other workers who belong to a more amenable union.

The ore comes up from the underground area, through the Smith Shaft near "Top Gate." It's washed, crushed, and roasted, then fed into a flotation process and the foundry, where gold and silver are separated from the ore. Counting both underground operations and an open pit, the mine presently extracts 130,000 ounces of gold annually from 600,000 metric tons of ore. A ton of silver is also produced each year, and waste rock is crushed into gravel and sold. Since 1935, the Emperor has produced five million ounces of gold worth more than a billion U.S. dollars at today's prices. Proven recoverable ore reserves at Vatukoula are sufficient for another 20 years of

mining, with another 3.5 million ounces awaiting extraction underground. In 1999, the Smith Shaft was deepened to allow easier access to high-grade ores, followed by work on the Cayzer Shaft in 2000 and the Philips Shaft in 2002.

The Emperor is Fiji's largest private employer, and Vatukoula is a typical company town of 10,000 inhabitants, with education and social services under the jurisdiction of the mine. The 2,500 miners employed here, most of them indigenous Fijians, live in World War II-style Quonset huts in racially segregated ghettos. In contrast, tradespeople and supervisors, usually Rotumans and part-Fijians, enjoy much better living conditions, and senior staff and management live in colonial-style comfort. Women are forbidden by law from working underground.

To arrange a guided tour of the mine, you

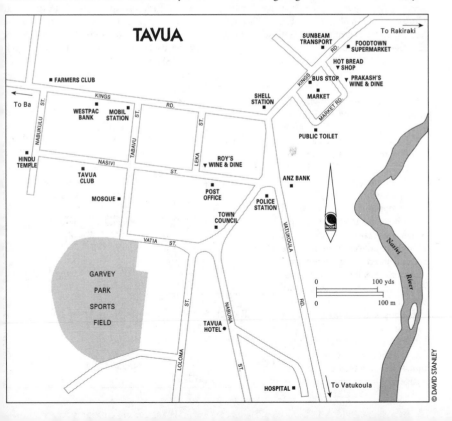

© DAVID STANLEY

must contact the public relations officer at Emperor Gold Mining Co. Ltd. (tel. 668-0477, ext. 201, fax 668-0779, www.emperor.com.au), at least 24 hours in advance. Surface tours cost F$30 per group of between one and 30 persons, plus F$1 per additional person for groups of more than 30 (underground tours not offered). The tour office is behind the Credit Union, 100 meters from "Bottom Gate." Rosie The Travel Service in Nadi runs gold-mine tours (F$55 pp without lunch).

From Tavua, minibuses (F$.70) marked "Loloma" go to Bottom Gate every half hour, while those marked "Korowere" go to Top Gate. Even if you don't get off, it's worth making the round-trip to see the varying classes of company housing, to catch a glimpse of the nine-hole golf course and open pit, and to enjoy the lovely scenery. Cold beer is available at the **Bowling Club** (tel. 668-0719; Mon.–Fri. 1600–2300, Sat. 0830–2300) near Bottom Gate, where meals are served upon request.

BA

The large Indo-Fijian town of Ba (population 15,000) on the Ba River is seldom visited by tourists. As the attractive mosque in the center of town suggests, nearly half of Fiji's Muslims live in Ba Province. Small fishing boats depart from behind the Shell service station opposite the mosque, and it's fairly easy to arrange to go along on all-night trips. A wide belt of mangroves covers much of the river's delta. Ba's original town site was on the low hill where the post office is today, and the newer lower town is often subjected to flooding. Ba is well known in Fiji for the large Rarawai Sugar Mill, built by the Colonial Sugar Refining Co. in 1886. In 2002, the transnational company Nestlé established a large food-processing plant at Ba.

The **Ba Hotel** (110 Bank St.; tel. 667-4000, fax 667-0559) has 13 air-conditioned rooms with bath at F$57/67 single/double—very pleasant with a swimming pool, bar, and restaurant.

Of the many places along Main Street serving Indian and Chinese meals, your best choice is probably **Chand's Restaurant** (tel. 667-0822; daily 0800–2100), just across the bridge from the mosque. Their upstairs dining room serves an Indian vegetarian *thali* for F$6.50, other meals F$4–11. Chand's fast-food center downstairs serves quick lunches from the warmer on the counter at F$3. It's great for a hot cup of tea, coffee, or milo. **Jolly Good** (tel. 667-1885; daily 0900–2100), across Main Street from the bus station and toward town, is clean and pleasant with main dishes from F$4.

The **Town Square Cinema** (tel. 667-4048), on Tabua Park just up the hill from the hotel, shows mostly Indian films. For drinks, it's the **Farmers Club** (tel. 667-5511), on Bank Street near the Ba Hotel, or the **Central Club** (tel. 667-4348) on Tabua Park.

The ANZ and Westpac banks on Bank Street

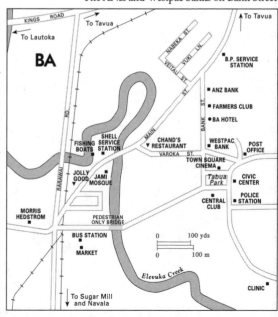

both have Visa/MasterCard ATMs outside facing the street. Otherwise try Money Exchange (tel. 667-0766; Mon.–Fri. 0800–1700, Sat. 0830–1300), around the corner on Main Street.

Important express buses leaving Ba daily are the regular Sunbeam Transport buses to Suva via Tavua at 0655, 0715, 0915, 1300, and 1715 (227 km, five hours), and the one Pacific Transport bus to Suva via Sigatoka at 0615 (259 km, six hours, F$13.35). Local buses to Tavua (29 km, F$1.60) and Lautoka (38 km, F$2) are frequent. Buses to Navala are at 1200 and 1715 daily, except Sunday (F$2.25).

Vatia Point

Noted photographer Jim Siers operates a sportfishing lodge at Vatia Point between Ba and Tavua. **Angler's Paradise** (tel. 668-1612 or 651-2105, www.fijifishing.com) has a three-room guesthouse (F$154 plus tax pp a day for room and board), a couple of fast fishing boats (F$1,163 plus tax a day for up to four anglers), and good giant trevally fishing! Fishing rods, reels, and lures are available for hire, or bring your own. Fishing trips to the Yasawa Islands are easily arranged.

© DAVID STANLEY

Jame Mosque is a landmark in Ba. Half of Fiji's Muslim population live in this province.

Into the Interior

Although Navala receives white-water rafters and sightseers, and regular tours from Nadi visit the Nausori Highlands, the rest of central Viti Levu is seldom visited. The dirt roads are too rough for ordinary rental vehicles, and facilities for tourists don't exist. Yet Fiji's highest mountains and deepest valleys are there, and some spectacular hiking possibilities await self-sufficient backpackers. Nadarivatu is the still undiscovered jewel of central Viti Levu.

NAUSORI HIGHLANDS

A rough unpaved road runs 25 kilometers southeast from Ba to Navala, a large traditional village on the sloping right bank of the Ba River. It then climbs another 20 kilometers south to Bukuya village in the Nausori Highlands, from whence other gravel roads continue south into the Sigatoka Valley and 40 kilometers due west to Nadi. The Nadi road passes Vaturu Dam, which supplies Nadi with fresh water. Gold strikes near Vaturu may herald a mining future for this area, if the water catchment can be protected. The forests here were logged out in the 1970s, but the open scenery of the highlands still makes a visit well worthwhile.

Navala is the last fully thatched village on Viti Levu, its *bure* standing picturesquely above the Ba River against the surrounding hills, and the villagers have made a conscious decision to keep it that way. When water levels are right, white-water rafters shoot the rapids through the scenic Ba River Gorge near here, and guided hiking or horseback riding can also be arranged. Sightseers are welcome but one must pay a F$15

a country road in the Nausori Highlands

© DON PITCHER

pp admission/photography fee toward village development. Access is fairly easy on the two buses a day that arrive from Ba, but they only depart Navala to return to Ba at 0600 and 0800, so you must stay for the night. **Bulou's Lodge** (tel. 666-6644, ext. 2116), one kilometer past Navala, provides accommodations at F$45 pp including meals. To hire a taxi from Ba to Navala will cost F$30 one-way or F$45 round-trip, with an hour of waiting time. By rental vehicle, you'll probably need a 4WD. During the rainy season, the Navala road can be flooded and impassable.

Bukuya, in the center of western Viti Levu's highland plateau, is far less traditional than Navala, and some of the only thatched *bure* in the village are those used by visitors on hiking/village stay tours organized by backpacker travel agencies in Nadi. The Tui Magodro, or high chief of the region, resides in Bukuya. During the Colo War of 1876, Bukuya was a center of resistance to colonial rule.

The easiest way to experience this area is on a day trip from Nadi. For example, Rosie The

Travel Service (tel. 670-2726), opposite the Nadi Handicraft Market and at numerous other locations, operates full-day hiking tours to the Nausori Highlands daily, except Sunday, at F$69 including lunch, tax, and a souvenir *sulu.* **Victory Tours** (tel. 670-0243) in downtown Nadi offers day tours to a waterfall in the Nausori Highlands at F$95 pp including lunch. Tours to Navala are also offered.

NADARIVATU AND BEYOND

An important forestry station is at Nadarivatu, a small settlement above Tavua. Its 900-meter altitude means a cool climate and fantastic panorama of the north coast from the ridge. Beside the road, right in front of the Forestry Training Center is **The Stone Bowl,** official source of the Sigatoka River, and a five-minute walk from the Center is the **Governor-General's Swimming Pool** where a small creek has been dammed. Go up the creek a short distance to the main pool, though it's dry much of the year, and the area has not been maintained. The trail to the fire tower atop **Mt. Lomalagi** (Mt. Heaven) begins nearby, a one-hour hike each way. The tower itself has collapsed and is no longer climbable, but the forest is lovely, and you may see and hear many native birds. Pine forests cover the land.

In its heyday, Nadarivatu was a summer retreat for expatriates from the nearby Emperor Gold Mine at Vatukoula, and the mine still has two 14-bed guesthouses at Nadarivatu which can be rented at F$33 for a whole house. To reserve, call the mine office in Vatukoula (tel. 668-0477, ext. 201 or 406, fax 668-0779), which will inform the caretaker of your arrival. You can cook, but bring groceries with you. Visitors with tents are allowed to camp at the Forestry Training Center. Ask permission at the Ministry of Forests office as soon as you arrive. Some canned foods are available at the canteen opposite the mine guesthouse, but bring food from Tavua. Cabin crackers are handy.

Only carriers operate between Tavua and Nadarivatu, leaving Tavua in the early afternoon and Nadarivatu in the morning—a spectacular

1.5 hour ride (F$3). Ask the market women in Tavua where and when to catch the trucks. They often originate/terminate in Nadrau village, where you might also be able to stay (take along a *sevusevu* if you're thinking of this). It's also possible to hitch.

Mount Victoria

The two great rivers of Fiji, the Rewa and the Sigatoka, originate on the slopes of Mt. Victoria (Tomaniivi), highest mountain in the country (1,323 m). The trail up the mountain begins near the bridge at Navai, 10 kilometers southeast of Nadarivatu. Turn right up the hillside a few hundred meters down the jeep track, then climb up through native bush on the main path all the way to the top. Beware of misleading signboards. There are three small streams to cross; no water after the third. On your way back down, stop for a swim in the largest stream. There's a flat area on top where you could camp—if you're willing to take your chances with Buli, the devil king of the mountain. Local guides (F$20) are available and advisable, but permission to climb the mountain is not required, as this a nature reserve under the Forestry Department. Allow about six hours for the round-trip. Bright red epiphytic orchids *(Dendrobium mohlianum)* are sometimes in full bloom, and if you're very lucky, you might spot the rare red-throated lorikeet or pink-billed parrot finch. Mount Victoria is on the divide between the wet and dry sides of Viti Levu, and from the summit you should be able to distinguish the contrasting vegetation of these zones.

Monasavu Hydroelectric Project

The largest development project ever undertaken in Fiji, this massive F$230 million scheme at Monasavu, on the Nadrau Plateau near the center of Viti Levu, took 1,500 men six years to complete. An earthen dam, 82 meters high, was built across the Nanuku River to supply water to the four 20-megawatt generating turbines at the Wailoa Power Station on the Wailoa River, 625 meters below. The dam forms a lake 17 kilometers long, and the water drops through a 5.4-kilometer tunnel at a 45-degree angle, one of the steepest engineered dips in the world. Over-

head transmission lines carry power from Wailoa to Suva and Lautoka. At present, Monasavu is filling 95 percent of Viti Levu's needs, representing an annual savings of F$22 million on imported diesel oil.

The Cross-Island Highway that passes the site was built to serve the dam project. Bus service ended when the project was completed and the construction camps closed in 1985. At the present time, buses go only from Tavua to Nadrau and from Suva to Naivucini, although occasional carriers go farther. In 1998, there were tense scenes near the dam as landowners set up roadblocks to press claims for land flooded in the early 1980s. In July 2000, during the hostage crisis at Fiji's parliament, landowners occupied the dam and cut off power to much of Viti Levu for almost a month. At last report, lawyers for the landowners were demanding F$52.8 million in compensation from the Fiji Electricity Authority.

THE SIGATOKA RIVER TREK

One of the most rewarding trips available on Viti Levu is the three-day hike south across the center of the island from Nadarivatu to Korolevu on the Sigatoka River. Northbound, the way is much harder to find. Many superb campsites can be found along the trail, and luckily this trek isn't included in the Australian guidebooks, so the area isn't overrun by tourists. Have a generous bundle of *waka* ready in case you're invited to stay overnight in a village. (Kava for presentations on subsequent days can be purchased at villages along the way.) Set out from Nadarivatu early in the week, so you won't suffer the embarrassment of arriving in a village on a Sunday. Excellent topographical maps of the entire route can be purchased at the Lands and Survey Department in Suva.

Follow the dirt road south from Nadarivatu to **Nagatagata,** where you should fill your canteen, as the trail ahead is rigorous and there's no water to be found. From Nagatagata, walk south about one hour. When you reach the electric high-power line, where the road turns right and begins to descend toward Koro, look for the well-worn footpath ahead. The trail winds along the ridge, and you can see as far as Ba. The primeval forests that once covered this part of Fiji were destroyed long ago by the slash-and-burn agricultural techniques of the Fijians.

When you reach the pine trees, the path divides, with Nanoko to the right and Nubutautau down to the left. During the rainy season, it's better to turn right and head to Nanoko, where you may be able to find a carrier to Bukuya or all the way to Nadi. If you do decide to make for Nanoko, beware of a very roundabout loop road on the left. Another option is to skip all of the above by taking a carrier from Tavua to Nadrau, from whence your hike would then begin.

Rev. Thomas Baker, the last missionary to be clubbed and devoured in Fiji (in 1867), met his fate at **Nubutautau.** Jack London wrote a story, "The Whale Tooth," about the death of the missionary, and the ax that brought about Reverend Baker's demise is still kept in the village (other Baker artifacts are in the Fiji Museum). You should be able to stay in the community center in Nubutautau. In 2003, Baker's descendents traveled to Nubutautau from Australia for a *matanigasau* ceremony during which the villagers apologized for this old crime, and a curse which had hung over the village for 136 years was lifted. The Nubutautau-Korolevu section of the trek involves 22 crossings of the Sigatoka River, which is easy enough in the dry season (cut a bamboo staff for balance), but almost impossible in the wet (Dec.–Apr.). Hiking boots will be useless in the river, so wear a pair of old running shoes.

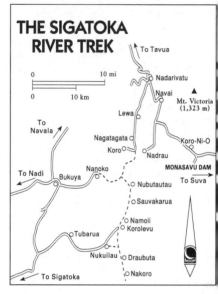

THE SIGATOKA RIVER TREK

It's a fantastic trip down the river to **Korolevu** if you can make it. The Korolevu villagers can call large eels up from a nearby pool with a certain chant. A few hours' walk away are the pottery villages, Draubuta and Nakoro, where traditional, long Fijian pots are still made. From Korolevu, you can take a carrier to Tubarua, where there are five buses a day to Sigatoka. A carrier leaves Korolevu direct to Sigatoka very early every morning except Sunday (F$7), departing Sigatoka for the return at about 1400 (if you want to do this trip in reverse).

Lautoka and Vicinity

Fiji's second city, Lautoka (population 45,000), is the focus of the country's sugar and timber industries, a major port, and the Western Division and Ba Province headquarters. It's a likable place with a row of towering royal palms along the main street. Although Lautoka grew up around the Fijian village of Namoli, the temples and mosques standing prominently in the center of town reflect the large Indo-Fijian population. In recent years, things have changed somewhat, with many Indo-Fijians abandoning Fiji as indigenous Fijians move in to take their place, and Lautoka's population is now almost evenly bal-

anced between the groups. Yet in the countryside, Indo-Fijians still comprise a large majority.

The **Lautoka Sugar Mill,** one of the largest in the Southern Hemisphere, was founded in 1903. It's busiest June–Dec., with trains and trucks constantly depositing loads of cane to be fed into the crushers. Mill tours are not offered, but you can get a good view of the operation from the main gate on the south side of the complex. South Pacific Distilleries on Navutu Road south of the mill is a government-owned plant that bottles rum, whiskey, vodka, and gin under a variety of labels, and molasses from the sugar mill, of course,

© DAVID STANLEY

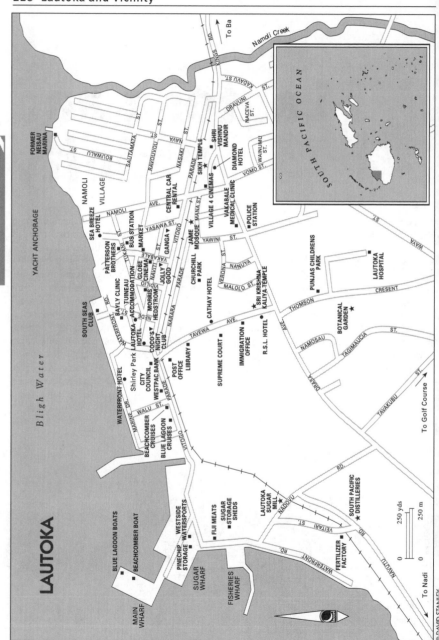

LAUTOKA

SOUTH PACIFIC OCEAN

Namoli Creek

To Ba

KINGS RD.

Bligh Water

YACHT ANCHORAGE

FORMER NEISAU MARINA

BOUWALU ST.
SALTAMATA ST.
RAVOUVOU ST.
NASAKI ST.
NAVA ST.
TADAVU ST.
DRAVUNI ST.
NACEVA ST.
WAINUNU ST.
VOMO ST.

SEA BREEZE HOTEL
NAMOLI VILLAGE
NAMOLI AVE.
PATTERSON BROTHERS
BUS STATION
MARKET
YASAWA ST.
VITOGO PARADE
GANGA ST.
JOLLY GOOD
MANA ST.
YAWINI ST.
VERONA ST.
NANUYA ST.
MALOLO ST.

SHRI VISHNU MANDIR ★
SIKH TEMPLE ★
CENTRAL CAR RENTAL
VILLAGE 4 CINEMAS ■
DIAMOND HOTEL ■
VAKABALE MEDICAL CLINIC ■
POLICE STATION ■

GLOBE CINEMA
TUINEAU BAYLY CLINIC
LAUTOKA ACCOMMODATION
MORRIS HEDSTROM
TUVANI ST.
VIDILIA ST.
NAVITI ST.
YAKABALE ST.
NEDE ST.
NARARA ST.
JAME MOSQUE
CHURCHILL PARK

SOUTH SEAS CLUB ■
WATERFRONT RD.

WATERFRONT HOTEL ■
SHIRLEY PARK
CITY COUNCIL ■
WESTPAC BANK ■
COCO'S ▼
JOLLY NIGHT CLUB ■
CATHAY HOTEL ■
SRI KRISHNA KALIYA TEMPLE ★
PUNJAS CHILDRENS PARK ■
LAUTOKA HOSPITAL ■

POST OFFICE ■
LIBRARY ■
SUPREME COURT ■
IMMIGRATION OFFICE ■
R.S.L. HOTEL ●
TAVEWA AVE.
THOMSON AVE.
VERONA ST.
CRESENT

BOTANICAL GARDEN ★
NAMOSAU ST.
TAGIMAUCIA ST.
DRASA ST.
ST.
NAVA ST.
MATA ST.

MARINE DR.
WATERFRONT PARADE
BEACHCOMBER CRUISES ■
BLUE LAGOON CRUISES ■
WALU ST.
VITOGO PARADE
TAVAKUBU RD.
To Golf Course

BLUE LAGOON BOATS ■
BEACHCOMBER BOAT ■
MAIN WHARF
PINECHIP STORAGE ■
WESTSIDE WATERSPORTS ■
FIJI MEATS ■
SUGAR STORAGE SHEDS
SUGAR WHARF
FISHERIES WHARF
LAUTOKA SUGAR MILL ★
NADOVU ST.
VEITARI ST.
WATERFRONT RD.
FERTILIZER FACTORY ■
SOUTH PACIFIC DISTILLERIES ★
NADOVU RD.
To Nadi

0   250 yds
0   250 m

LAUTOKA AND VICINITY HIGHLIGHTS

Lautoka Sugar Mill: picturesque scene, cane railway (p. 227)

Jame Mosque: photogenic, symbolic of the region (p. 229)

Sri Krishna Kaliya Temple: ceremonies, feasts, architecture (p. 229, 233)

Botanical Garden: plants, birds, quiet benches (p. 230)

Koroyanitu National Heritage Park: spectacular hiking and climbing (p. 234)

is the distillery's main raw material. The fertilizer factory, across the highway from the distillery, uses mill mud from the sugar-making process. To the north, just beyond the conveyor belts used to load raw sugar onto the ships, is a veritable mountain of pine chips ready for export to Japan, where they are used to make paper.

This is the main base for Blue Lagoon cruises to the Yasawa Islands, yet because Lautoka doesn't depend on tourism, you get a truer picture of ordinary life than you would in Nadi, and the city has a rambunctious nightlife. There's some shopping, but mainly this is just a pleasant place to wander around on foot.

SIGHTS

Begin at Lautoka's big, colorful **market,** next to the bus station, which is busiest on Saturday (open Mon.–Fri. 0700–1730, Sat. 0530–1600). From here, walk south on Yasawa Street to the photogenic **Jame Mosque,** a prominent symbol of Lautoka's large Indo-Fijian population. Five times a day, local male Muslims direct prayers toward a small niche known as a *mihrab,* where the prayers fuse and fly to the Kaaba in Mecca, and thence to Allah. You can visit the mosque outside prayer times if you're conservatively dressed and willing to remove your shoes. During the crushing season (June–Nov.), narrow-gauge trains rattle past the mosque along a line parallel to Vitogo Parade, bringing cane to Lautoka's large sugar mill.

Follow the line east to the **Sikh Temple,** rebuilt after a smaller temple was burned by arson in 1989. To enter, you must wash your hands and cover your head (kerchiefs are provided at the door), and cigarettes and liquor are forbidden inside the compound. The teachings of the 10 Sikh gurus are contained in the Granth, a holy book prominently displayed in the temple. Sikhism began in the 16th century in the Punjab region of northwest India as a reformed branch of Hinduism much influenced by Islam: For example, Sikhs reject the caste system and idolatry. The Sikhs are easily recognized by their beards and turbans.

Follow your map west along Drasa Avenue to the **Sri Krishna Kaliya Temple** on Tavewa Avenue, the most prominent Krishna temple in the South Pacific (open daily until 1900). The images on the right inside are Radha and Krishna, while the central figure is Krishna dancing on the snake Kaliya to show his mastery over the

© DAVID STANLEY

The Sunday afternoon festival and feast at Lautoka's Hare Krishna temple, the largest in the South Pacific, is worth attending.

reptile. The story goes that Krishna chastised Kaliya and exiled him to the island of Ramanik Deep, which Indo-Fijians believe to be Fiji. (Curiously, the indigenous Fijian people have also long believed in a serpent-god, named Degei, who lived in a cave in the Nakauvadra Range.) The two figures on the left are incarnations of Krishna and Balarama. At the front of the temple is a representation of His Divine Grace A. C. Bhaktivedanta Swami Prabhupada, founder of the International Society for Krishna Consciousness (ISKCON). Interestingly, Fiji has the highest percentage of Hare Krishnas in the population of any country in the world. The temple gift shop (tel. 666-4112; daily 0900–1630) sells stimulating books, compact discs, cassettes, and posters, and it's possible to rent videos. On Sunday, there's a lecture at 1100, *arti* or prayer *(puja)* at 1200, and a vegetarian feast at 1300, and visitors are welcome to attend.

Opposite the hospital, half a kilometer south on Thomson Crescent, is the entrance to Lautoka's **botanical garden** (weekdays 0800–1800, weekends 1000–1800; admission free). It's a pleasant shady spot with a varied array of plants. Birds are surprisingly numerous in the gardens, and picnic tables are provided. **Punjas Children's Park** (admission free), across the street from the gardens, is perfect if you're with the kids, and it has a snack bar.

SPORTS AND RECREATION

There aren't any dive shops in Lautoka although **Westside Watersports** (tel. 661-1462, www.fiji-dive.com) has an office on Wharf Road that handles bookings for their Tavewa Island operation.

The **Lautoka Golf Club** (tel. 666-1384), a nine-hole, par-69 course, charges F$10 greens fees plus F$20 club rentals. A taxi from the market should cost about F$3–4.

All day Saturday, you can catch exciting rugby (Apr.–Sept.) or soccer (Sept.–May) games at the stadium in Churchill Park. Ask about league games.

ACCOMMODATIONS
Under US$25

A good choice is the clean, quiet, three-story **Sea Breeze Hotel** (5 Bekana Lane; tel. 666-0717, fax 666-6080), on the waterfront near the bus station. They have 26 rooms with private bath from F$33/37 single/double (air-conditioned rooms F$40/45, seaview F$45/49). A good breakfast is F$8 extra. The pleasant lounge has a color TV, and a swimming pool overlooks the lagoon.

Tuineau Accommodation (tel. 666-0351), above Harry's Printery on Nede Street, occupies the top two floors of a three-story building (entrance from the side alley—no sign). The 11 basic rooms with shared bath are F$25 single or double, or F$9 pp in a 10-bed dorm. It's rather grim, but cheap.

To be closer to the action, stay at the 38-room **Lautoka Hotel** (2 Naviti St.; tel. 666-0388, fax 666-0201, ltkhotel@connect.com.fj), which has a nice swimming pool. Room prices vary from F$30 single or double for a spacious fan-cooled room with shared bath to F$49 single or double with air-conditioning and private bath, or F$62 with TV and fridge. It's F$15 pp in the six-bed dorm. The new rooms are good, but those above the reception in the old building are subjected to a nocturnal rock beat from nearby discos most nights.

Better are the 40 rooms at the friendly **Cathay Hotel** (tel. 666-0566, fax 666-0136, www.fiji4less.com) on Tavewa Avenue, which features a swimming pool, TV room, and bar. The charge is F$35/44 single/double with fan and private bath, F$46/55 with air-conditioning. Some of the rooms in less desirable locations have been divided into dormitories, with 3–6 beds or bunks. Each dorm has its own toilet and shower at F$12/18 pp fan/air-conditioned (F$1 discount for youth hostel, VIP, or Nomads cardholders). The dorms here are the best deal in the city; otherwise, take one of the superior air-conditioned rooms upstairs. The Cathay offers free luggage storage for guests, and the notice board at the reception often has useful information on travel to Fijian villages and the outer islands. The hotel bar upstairs is pleasant. The only reason you won't hear a lot of hype about this place at Nadi Airport is because the owners refuse to pay commissions to the Nadi travel agents.

The **R.S.L. Hotel** (tel. 665-1679), on Tavewa Avenue opposite the Sri Krishna Kaliya Temple, has six clean rooms with bath at F$50 single or double. Owned by the Fiji Ex-Servicemen League, there's a large public bar on the premises.

The 14-room **Diamond Hotel** (tel. 666-6721), on Nacula Street, charges F$25/29 single/double for a room with fan. The new manager is trying to upgrade the place, but they still have water problems.

US$25–50

Lautoka's top hotel is the **Waterfront Hotel** (tel. 666-4777, fax 666-5870, www.tanoahotels.com), a two-story building erected in 1987 on Marine Drive. The 47 waterbed-equipped air-conditioned rooms are F$88 single or double, F$107 triple (children under 12 are free if no extra bed is required). There's a swimming pool. The Waterfront's Fins Restaurant serves a dinner mains from F$18–28.

The **Bekana Garden Island Resort** (Kim Waters, tel. 651-1600, fax 651-0628, bekanaislandfiji@connect.com.fj), on the long low island opposite the Lautoka waterfront, has four deluxe beachfront *bure* at F$350 single or double, plus two one-bedroom units at F$265. Low-budget travelers are catered for with six thatched *bure* at F$95/108 single/double and a 12-bed dormitory at F$53 pp. Continental breakfast and lunch are included in the Fijian *bure* and dorm rates, but not with the deluxe *bure*. Camping is F$18 pp. The beach here is poor, but it's fun to borrow a kayak and paddle through the nearby mangroves. Windsurfers, fishing lines, and snorkeling gear are also loaned free, and transfers from Lautoka's Neisau Marina are provided at no cost. A dozen free moorings are available for cruising yachties.

Saweni Beach Apartment Hotel (tel. 666-1777, fax 666-6001, www.fiji4less.com), a kilometer off the main highway south of Lautoka, offers two rows of flats, each with six self-catering apartments with fan and hot water at

© DAVID STANLEY

Saweni Beach

F$70/85 poolside/oceanview for up to three persons. A renovated four-bedroom "beach house" (www.fiji-beach-house.com) with full kitchen, air-conditioned bedrooms, living room, and TV is F$300 for up to four, then F$50 per additional person to a maximum of eight. Four dormitories in the annex, with two beds each, are F$13 pp, or you can pitch your own tent here at F$10 pp and still use the dorm's communal kitchen. Guests unwind by the pool. Bird-watchers can observe waders on the flats behind the hotel. The so-so beach comes alive on weekends, when local picnickers arrive from Lautoka. During the season, more than a dozen yachts are generally anchored offshore, and the crews often come ashore here for curry dinners. A bus runs right to the hotel from bay No. 14 at Lautoka Bus Station six times a day. Otherwise any of the local Nadi buses will drop you off a 10-minute walk away (a taxi from Lautoka is F$7 for the 18 km).

FOOD

Chandu's Restaurant (tel. 666-5877; Mon.–Sat. 0700–2100, Sun. 0800–1830), Tukani Street on the ocean side of the bus station, serves cheap meals like fish and chips (F$2.50) or meat and rice (F$3) to the drivers of the taxis parked outside.

Jolly Good Fast Food (tel. 666-9980; daily 0800–2200), at Vakabale and Naviti Streets opposite the market, is a great place to sit and read a newspaper over a Coke. Their best dishes are listed on the "made on order" menu on the wall beside the cashier. Beef and pork are not offered, so have fish, chicken, mutton, or prawns instead—the portions are large. Eating outside in their covered garden is fun, and the only drawback is the lack of beer.

Yangs Restaurant (27 Naviti St.; tel. 666-1446; Mon.–Sat. 0700–1900) is an excellent breakfast or lunch place with inexpensive Chinese specialties.

Morris Hedstrom (tel. 666-2999; Mon.–Sat. 0730–1930, Sun. 0800–1300), Vidilio and Tukani Streets, is Lautoka's largest supermarket. At the back of the store is a food court which offers fish or chicken and chips, hot pies, ice cream, and breakfast specials. It's clean and only a bit more expensive than the market places.

More trendy is the **Chilli Tree Café** (tel. 665-1824; weekdays 0900–1800, Sat. 0800–1700, Sun. 1000–1400, www.chillitreecafe.com), corner of Nede and Tukani Streets. They serve a good, filling breakfast for F$8.50, plus cakes and specially brewed coffee. You can "build your own" salad and sandwich from the menu.

The **Pizza Inn** (2 Naviti St.; tel. 666-4592) in the Lautoka Hotel serves pizzas for F$6–22.

Also try the **Dynasty Restaurant** (10 Mana St.; tel. 665-2413; daily 1200–1430 and 1800–2130), down the road from Village 4 Cinemas. Their menu lists fried rice (F$5–9), chow mein (F$5–12), sweet and sour dishes (F$8–13), vegetable stir-fry (F$6.50), fish (F$8–23), lobster (F$28), and Indian curries (F$11).

Indian

The unpretentious **Hot Snax Shop** (56 Naviti St.; tel. 666-1306; Mon.–Fri. 0830–1800, Sat. 0830–1600), opposite Yangs, may be the number one place in Fiji to sample South Indian dishes, such as *masala dosai,* a rice pancake with coconut chutney that makes a nice light lunch, or *samosas, iddili,* puri, and *palau.* The deep-fried puri are great for breakfast, and you can also get ice cream. This spot is recommended.

The **Ganga Vegetarian Restaurant** (tel. 666-2990; Mon.–Fri. 0700–1800, Sat. 0700–1700), on the corner of Naviti and Yasawa Streets near the market, has a vegetarian *thali* plate lunch for F$4.75.

For spicy curries (F$5–10) and authentic tandoori dishes (F$6–8), try **Dharshan's Indian Restaurant** (tel. 664-5566; Mon.–Sat. 1000–2200, Sun. 1100–1500 and 1800–2200), 42 Vitogo Parade beside the Jame Mosque. If you're not sure what to order, ask for a *thali* (plate meal) consisting of several vegetarian (F$5.50) or non-vegetarian (F$7.50) specialties, accompanied by rice or roti. Dharshan's is air-conditioned, the staff is in uniform, the decor is nice, and you can get meat dishes and beer.

ENTERTAINMENT

Lautoka has a flashy new mega-theater called **Village 4 Cinemas** (25 Namoli Ave.; tel. 666-3555). It costs about F$4 to view a film on one of their four screens. Your only other choice is **Globe Cinema** (tel. 666-1444), opposite the market, which usually shows Indian films.

The **Hunter's Inn** (tel. 666-0388; Mon.–Wed. 1700–0100, Thurs.–Sat. 1600–0100), next to the Lautoka Hotel, is often the venue of special functions advertised on placards outside, though it's rather rough and dark. During the day, the same place is called **City Pub** (Thurs.–Sat. 1200–1600). Also at the Lautoka Hotel is the **Ashiqi Nite Club** (Thurs.–Sat. 2000–0100), which caters to the city's Indo-Fijian residents, whereas Hunter's Inn is patronized mostly by indigenous Fijians.

Rougher than these are **The Zone Nite Club** (tel. 666-1199; Wed.–Sat. 1900–0100), upstairs in a building almost opposite the Chilli Tree

Café on Naviti Street, and **Bollywood Nite Club,** above Ganga Vegetarian Restaurant.

A safer place to go is **Coco's** (151 Vitogo Parade; tel. 666-8989; Mon.–Sat. 1700–0100). Happy hour is 1700–2000, and a live rock band plays on Friday and Saturday from 2200. Admission is free until 2100 daily (F$5 cover charge Friday and Saturday after 2100).

The **South Seas Club** (tel. 666-0784), on Nede Street, is a predominately male drinking place where you'll be welcome.

Sunday Puja

The big event of the week is the Sunday *puja* (prayer) at the **Sri Krishna Kaliya Temple** (5 Tavewa Ave.; tel. 666-4112). The noon service is followed by a vegetarian feast at 1300, and visitors may join in the singing and dancing, if they wish. Take off your shoes and sit on the white marble floor, men on one side, women on the other. Bells ring, drums are beaten, conch shells blown, and stories from the Vedas, Srimad Bhagavatam, and Ramayana are acted out as everyone chants, *"Hare Krsna, Hare Krsna, Krsna Krsna, Hare Hare, Hare Rama, Hare Rama, Rama, Rama, Hare, Hare."* It's a real celebration of joy and a most moving experience. At one point, children will circulate with small trays covered with burning candles, on which it is customary to place a donation; you may also drop a small bill in the yellow box in the center of the temple. You'll be readily invited to join the vegetarian feast later, and no more money will be asked of you.

INFORMATION AND SERVICES
Information

Caroline Tawake at **Tawake Travel Center** (159 Vitogo Parade; tel. 651-2148, tawakestravels @yahoo.com), in back of Tawake's Craft Designs near the Colonial National Bank, takes bookings for most of the Yasawa backpacker resorts.

The people staffing the tour desks at the Lautoka and Cathay hotels can also organize any sort of Yasawa Islands trip.

Rosie World Travel (157 Vitogo Parade; tel. 666-0311), next to the Colonial Bank, is a more traditional travel agent.

The **Lautoka City Bookshop** (19 Yasawa St.; tel. 666-1715) sells used books.

The **Western Regional Library** (tel. 666-0091) on Tavewa Avenue is open Monday–Friday 1000–1700, Saturday 0900–1200.

Services

There's a Westpac Bank branch on Vitogo Parade, a little west of the post office beyond the Shell station. The ANZ Bank on Vitogo Parade diagonally opposite the post office, and on Naviti Street near the market, has Visa/MasterCard ATMs. Other ANZ Bank ATMs are found next to Rajendra Prasad Foodtown on Yasawa Street opposite the bus station and at Village 4 Cinemas.

Money Exchange (161 Vitogo Parade; tel. 665-1941; Mon.–Fri. 0830–1700, Sat. 0830–1300), just up from the ANZ Bank, changes traveler's checks without commission and buys/sells the banknotes of other Pacific countries.

The public fax number at Lautoka Post Office is fax 666-4666.

Cyberzone Netcafe (tel. 665-1675; Mon.–Sat. 0800–1800, Sun. 1000–1700), next to Tavake Travel Center just down the alley beside Money Exchange near the ANZ Bank on Vitogo Parade, provides Internet access at F$.10 a minute or F$5 an hour (F$4 an hour on weekends).

Compuland Cyberlink (tel. 666-6457; weekdays 0800–1900, Sat. 0800–1700, Sun. 1000–1600), upstairs at 145 Vitogo Parade, charges identical rates and is air-conditioned!

The **Immigration Department** (tel. 666-1706) is on the ground floor of Rogorogoivuda House on Tavewa Avenue almost opposite the Sri Krishna Kaliya Temple. Customs is in an adjacent building.

Free public toilets are next to Bay No. 1A, on the back side of the bus station facing the market, in Shirley Park between the Waterfront Hotel and Lautoka City Council, and at the botanical gardens.

Yachting Facilities

The **Neisau Marina Complex,** at the end of Bouwalu Street, fell on hard times after a hurricane twisted their wharf. At last report, it was half abandoned, although some yachts still anchor there.

The **Vuda Point Marina** (tel. 666-8214, fax 666-8215, vudamarina@connect.com.fj) is between Lautoka and Nadi, three kilometers down Vuda Road off Viseisei Back Road. Here yachts moor Mediterranean-style in a well-protected oval anchorage blasted through the reef. The excellent facilities include a yacht club, chandlery, workshop, general store (daily 0730–1900), inexpensive café (daily 0700–1500, until 2100 Tues., Thurs., and Sat.), fuel depot, laundry, showers, and sail repair shop.

Health

The emergency room at the **Lautoka Hospital** (tel. 666-0399), off Thomson Crescent south of the center, is open 24 hours a day.

Otherwise there's the **Bayly Clinic** (4 Nede St.; tel. 666-4598; Mon.–Fri. 0800–1300 and 1400–1630, Sat. 0800–1300). You can see a dentist (Dr. Mrs. Suruj Naidu) and an eye doctor, as well as general practitioners here.

Dr. Suresh Chandra's dental office (tel. 666-0999; Mon.–Fri. 0800–1700, Sat. 0800–1200) is opposite Village 4 Cinemas on Namoli Avenue.

The **Vakabale Medical Center** (Dr. Mukesh C. Bhagat, 47 Drasa Ave.; tel. 665-2955 or 995-2369; weekdays 0830–1700, Sat. 0830–1300), charges F$15 for consultations. You'll receive good service at this convenient suburban office.

TRANSPORTATION

Sun Air (27 Vidilio St.; tel. 666-4753) has an office in Lautoka.

Patterson Brothers (15 Tukani St.; tel. 666-1173), upstairs and opposite the bus station, runs a bus/ferry/bus service between Lautoka, Ellington Wharf, Nabouwalu, and Labasa (F$60), departing Lautoka a couple of times a week at around 0500. Call or visit their office for the current schedule.

Beachcomber Cruises (tel. 666-1500), Walu Street at Vitogo Parade toward the main wharf, books cruises to **Beachcomber Island** (F$69 pp including lunch, reductions for children), de-

parting Lautoka daily except Tuesday and Thursday at 1030—a great way to spend a day.

The **Awesome Adventures** (tel. 675-0499) ferry, *Yasawa Flyer,* leaves Lautoka for the Yasawa Islands daily at 0800, although most passengers board at Nadi.

Buses, carriers, taxis—everything leaves from the bus stand beside the market. **Pacific Transport** (tel. 666-0499) has express buses to Suva daily at 0630, 0700, 1210, 1550, and 1730 (221 km, five hours, F$11.60) via Sigatoka (Queens Road). Five other "stage" buses also operate daily along this route (six hours). The daily **Sunset Express** leaves for Suva via Sigatoka at 0900, 1330, and 1515 (four hours, F$10). **Sunbeam Transport** (tel. 666-2822) has expresses to Suva via Tavua (Kings Road) at 0615, 0630, 0815, 1215, and 1630 (265 km, six hours, F$13.90), plus two local buses on the same route (nine hours). Sunbeam also has buses to Suva via Sigatoka at 1010, 1110, and 1240. The northern route is more scenic than the southern, although some Sunbeam buses play insipid videos that detract from the ride. Local buses to Nadi (33 km, F$1.90) and Ba (38 km, F$2) depart every half hour or so.

Collective taxis to Suva (F$15 per seat) park on Tukani Street behind the bus station. Pick one that's almost full if you're in a hurry.

Car rentals are available in Lautoka from **Central** (75 Vitogo Parade; tel. 666-4511).

KOROYANITU NATIONAL HERITAGE PARK

With help from New Zealand, an ecotourism reserve has been created between Abaca (am-BA-tha) and Navilawa villages in the Mount Evans Range, 15 kilometers east of Lautoka. Koroyanitu National Heritage Park takes its name from the range's highest peak, 1,195-meter Koroyanitu, and is intended to preserve Fiji's only unlogged tropical montane forest and cloud forest by creating a small tourism business for the local villagers. The village carrier used to transport visitors also carries the local kids to and from school, the women earn money by staffing the office or arranging room and board, and the men get jobs as drivers, guides, and

canefields and grasslands around the Mount Evans Range near Lautoka

wardens. By visiting Koroyanitu, you not only get to see some of Fiji's top sights but support this worthy undertaking.

Four waterfalls are close to the village, and Batilamu, with sweeping views of the western side of Viti Levu and the Yasawas, is nearby. More ambitious hikes to higher peaks beckon. The landscape of wide green valleys set against steep slopes is superb. Doves and pigeons abound in the forests, and you'll also find honeyeaters, Polynesian starlings, Fijian warblers, yellow-breasted musk parrots, golden whistlers, fantailed cuckoos, and wood swallows. It's an outstanding opportunity to see this spectacular area. The park entry fee is F$5 pp.

Sights

You can swim in the pools at **Vereni Falls,** a five-minute walk from the park lodge. Picnic shelters are provided. From the viewpoint above the falls, it's 15 minutes up the Navuratu Track to **Kokobula Scenic Outlook,** with its 360 degree view of the park and coast. The trail continues across the open grassland to **Savuione Falls,**

passing an old village site en route (guide required). From Savuione, there's a trail through the secondary forest directly back to the park lodge (watch for pigeons and doves). You can do all of this in just over two hours if you keep going and don't lose your way.

The finest hike here is to **Mount Batilamu** along a trail which begins at the visitor center in Abaca village. You'll pass large kauri trees *(makadre)* and get a terrific view from on top. This part of the range is also known as the "Sleeping Giant," because that's how it appears from Nadi. Allow half a day to return from Abaca to Batilamu.

The Batilamu Track continues across the range to **Navilawa** village, from which a six-kilometer road runs south to Korobebe village, where there's regular bus service to/from Nadi. Trekkers often spend the night in Fiji's highest *bure* on Batilamu, although fewer than 100 people a year actually do this walk. An even more ambitious trek is northeast to **Nalotawa** via the site of Navuga, where the Abaca people lived, until their village was destroyed by a landslide in the 1930s.

To explore the various archaeological sites of this area and to learn more about the environment and culture, you should hire a guide (F$5–20, depending on how far you want to go).

Accommodations

The **Nase Forest Lodge,** 400 meters from Abaca village, has two six-bunk rooms at F$25 pp (or F$80 for the whole room). Camping is F$10 pp. Children under 15 are half price, and all prices include the park entry fee. Good cooking facilities are provided, but take food, as there's no shop. Meals can be ordered at F$5/7/10 for breakfast/lunch/dinner. Otherwise, you can stay with a family in Abaca or Navilawa villages at F$30 pp including meals.

For information, call Abaca village at tel. 666-6644 (wait for two beeps, then dial 1234). The receptionist at the Cathay Hotel in Lautoka should also be able to help you. (On Sunday, avoid entering the village during the church service 1000–1200. Village etiquette should be observed at all times.)

Getting There

The closest public bus stop to the park is Abaca Junction on the Tavakuba bus route, but it's 10 kilometers from Abaca village. An official village carrier to the park leaves the Cathay Hotel in Lautoka around 0900, charging F$10 pp (F$20 if only one person). It returns to Lautoka in the afternoon.

At Nadi Airport, contact **Tourist Transport Fiji** (tel. 672-0455, fax 672-0184, www.batila mutrek.com), next to the washrooms in the international arrivals area, which books a three-day Mount Batilamu Trek package at F$300 pp. Their day trek to Abaca is F$75 pp from Nadi. During the rainy season, floods can close the road to Abaca and the trekking possibilities may also be limited.

The Yasawa Islands

The Yasawas are a chain of 16 large volcanic islands and dozens of smaller ones, stretching 80 kilometers in a north-northeast direction, roughly 35 kilometers off the west coast of Viti Levu. In the lee of Viti Levu, the Yasawas are dry and sunny, with beautiful, isolated beaches, cliffs, bays, and reefs. The waters are crystal clear and almost totally shark-free. The group was romanticized in two movies about a pair of child castaways who eventually fall in love on a de-serted isle. The original 1949 version of *The Blue Lagoon* starred Jean Simmons, while the 1980 remake featured Brooke Shields. (A 1991 sequel *Return to the Blue Lagoon* with Milla Jovovich was filmed on Taveuni.)

It was from the north end of the Yasawas that two canoe-loads of cannibals sallied forth and gave chase to Capt. William Bligh and his 18 companions in 1789, less than a week after the famous mutiny. More than two centuries later,

YASAWA ISLANDS HIGHLIGHTS

Vatuvula Peak, Wayasewa: great hike, superb view (p. 242)

Waya Island: beaches, hiking, villages, small resorts (p. 243)

Tavewa and the Blue Lagoon: swimming, snorkeling, natural beauty (p. 246)

Long Beach, Nacula: long white beach, snorkeling, resort (p. 248)

Sawa-i-Lau cave: swimming, boating, legends (p. 251)

increasing numbers of ferries and mini–cruise ships ply the islands, but there are still no motorized land vehicles or roads. The $1,000-a-day crowd is whisked straight to Turtle Island by seaplane, while most backpackers arrive from Nadi on a high-speed catamaran.

Super-exclusive Turtle Island Resort and the backpacker camps on Tavewa Island have coexisted for decades, but only since 2000 have the Yasawans themselves recognized the money-making potential of tourism. Now a bumper crop of low-budget "resorts" is bursting forth, up and down the chain, as the villagers rush to cash in. The **Nacula Tikina Tourism Association** (tel. 672-2921, www.fijibudget.com) coordinates the development of locally owned backpacker resorts on the central islands around the Blue Lagoon. Thankfully, the resorts associated with the scheme have committed to a code of conduct to preserve and protect the natural environment. Some of the backpacker resorts are better than others, but shared bathrooms, a lack of electricity, water shortages, and variable food are to be expected. What you pay for is the superb natural beauty of this region.

Resort Booking Tips

At Nadi Airport, the **Turtle Island Resort office** (tel. 672-2921, nacula@hotmail.com), on the left in the arrivals concourse, should be able to provide information about the Yasawa Islands resorts. Other booking agents at Nadi Airport include **Island Travel Tours** (Louise Blake, tel. 672-4033 or 672-5930, www.travellingfiji.com), in office No. 14 upstairs from arrivals, **Western Travel Services** (tel. 672-4440), in office No. 4, **Sunset Tours** (Poni Natadra, tel. 672-0266), and **Rabua's Travel Agency** (Ulaiasi "Rambo" Rabua, tel. 672-1377 or 672-3234) in office No. 23. Caroline Tawake at **Tawake Travel & Tourist Information Center** (159 Vitogo Parade, Lautoka; tel. 651-2148, tawakestravels@yahoo.com), can book any of the Yasawa places. Resort-specific booking offices are mentioned in the listings which follow.

Only book your first two nights if you wish to allow yourself the flexibility of moving elsewhere after arrival or bargaining for a lower rate. The Nadi travel agents take 30 percent commission, so you can often get a better deal by booking direct over the phone. Most of the Yasawa backpacker resorts have radio telephones accessed via tel. 666-6644. Dial this number, then key in the extension after hearing two beeps. Only one party can speak at a time over these connections.

The rates quoted in this chapter usually include all meals and taxes (only Oarsman's and Safe Landing resorts on Nacula Island sometimes quote rates with meals and tax additional). Virtually all of the resorts have mixed dormitories, where you pay per person and *bure* are intended for two persons. Singles who don't wish to sleep in the dormitory are at a disadvantage as many resorts charge the same single or double for their *bure,* even though they only have to feed one person instead of two. The Yasawas backpacker resorts are ideal for campers, as virtually all have unlimited tent space and reservations are unnecessary. Campers with their own tents pay slightly less than people in the dorm.

One shouldn't expect gourmet cuisine at any of the backpacker resorts, and at times the meals can be pretty basic. A vegetarian meal is often the same thing with the meat removed. At times, it seems like the numerous vegetarian requests have resulted in plates of cabbage and rice being served to one and all! You should ask other travelers for their opinion of the food at the places where they stayed—just keep in mind that the person's standards and expectations may be different from yours, as impressions vary considerably. All too often, what you pay for isn't what you get.

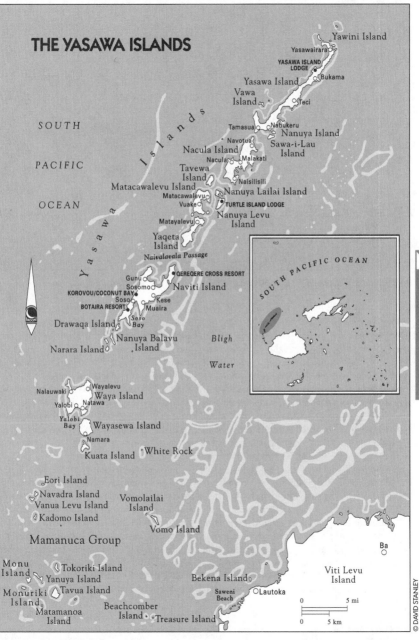

THE YASAWA ISLANDS

Yawini Island
Yasawairara
YASAWA ISLAND LODGE
Bukama
Yasawa Island
Vawa Island
Teci

SOUTH

Tamasua
Nabukeru
Navotua
Nanuya Island
Sawa-i-Lau Island

PACIFIC

Nacula Island
Nacula
Malakati

Tavewa Island
Naisilisili

Matacawalevu Island
Matacawalevu

OCEAN

Nanuya Lailai Island

Vuake
TURTLE ISLAND LODGE
Matayalevu
Nanuya Levu Island

Yaqeta Island

Naivalavala Passage

Yasawa Islands

Gunu
QEREQERE CROSS RESORT
Sosomo
Naviti Island
KOROVOU/COCONUT BAY
Soso
Kese
BOTAIRA RESORT
Muaira
Soso Bay

Drawaqa Island
Narara Island
Nanuya Balavu Island
Bligh
Water

SOUTH PACIFIC OCEAN

Nalauwaki
Wayalevu
Wayalevu
Waya Island
Yalobi
Natawa
Yalobi Bay
Wayasewa Island
Namara
Kuata Island
White Rock

Eori Island
Navadra Island
Vanua Levu Island
Kadomo Island
Vomolailai Island

Mamanuca Group

Vomo Island

Ba

Monu Island
Tokoriki Island
Yanuya Island
Monuriki Island
Tavua Island
Matamanoa Island
Beachcomber Island
Bekena Island
Saweni Beach
Lautoka
Viti Levu Island

Treasure Island

0   5 mi
0   5 km

© DAVID STANLEY

THE YASAWA ISLANDS

Bure such as these await backpackers traveling to the Yasawa Group.

Money

Don't expect to be able to use your credit card in the Yasawas (although Oarsman's and Safe Landing resorts on Nacula accept *only* credit cards). Changing foreign currency is also usually not possible. Thus it's important to bring along sufficient Fijian currency in cash. Even if you've prepaid all your food, accommodations, and interisland transportation, you'll still need a minimum of F$20 pp extra per day to cover alcohol drinks, bottled water, excursions, equipment rentals, etc. The more optional activities you plan to book, the more cash you'll need. Failure to budget for your expenses accurately may force you to return to Nadi early or miss out on some activities.

Prices continue to creep up in the Yasawas, and on a visit of a week or less, you'll spend at least F$100 pp a day on transportation, food, and dormitory accommodations alone. On stays of more than a week, the transportation component falls exponentially and long-stay discounts kick in.

Getting There

Turtle Airways (tel. 672-1888, www.turtleair ways.com) offers reduced F$119 one-way fares to backpackers headed for the low-budget resorts in the Yasawas. These discounted flights are based on availability, but if they have four backpacker bookings, they'll schedule a special service. Ask at the Turtle Island Resort office at Nadi Airport. It only takes 30 minutes by air from Turtle's Nadi base at Wailoaloa Beach to go all the way to the seaplane landing area off Nacula Island. The emerald lagoons and colorful reefs are truly dazzling when seen from above.

The vast majority of visitors arrive on the fast 25-meter catamaran *Yasawa Flyer* operated by **Awesome Adventures** (tel. 675-0499, fax 675-0501, www.awesomefiji.com), a subsidiary of South Sea Cruises. The *Yasawa Flyer* zips up and down the Yasawa Chain daily, leaving Nadi's Port Denarau at 0915 and arriving at Beachcomber Island at 1000, Kuata at 1045, Waya at 1115, Naviti at 1215, and Nacula at 1315. The return trip leaves Nacula at 1330, with stops at Naviti at 1420, Waya at 1550, Kuata at 1600, Beachcomber Island at 1645, and reaching Port Denarau at 1730. Fares from Nadi are F$70 one-way to Kuata or Waya, F$80 to Naviti, and F$90 to

Nacula or Tavewa, bus transfers in Nadi included. Interisland fares within the Yasawas vary between F$25 from Kuata to Octopus Resort, F$40 from Waya to Naviti, or F$50 from Kuata to Nacula. The *Yasawa Flyer* is actually based in Lautoka, and you can begin or end your journey there for the same price, if you want.

Awesome Adventures offers a "Bula Pass" which includes one round-trip transfer between Nadi and Nacula on the *Yasawa Flyer*, with unlimited stops at Kuata, Wayalailai, Waya, Naviti, or anywhere else along their route (the only limitations are that only one trip back to Nadi is included, and the pass cannot be used between Beachcomber Island and Nadi at all). The Bula Pass costs F$235/350/399 for seven/14/21 days, and it's worth considering if you plan to make a stop or two on the way to Nacula. The 21-day pass includes a one-night Wanna Taki Cruise. Though there are 150 seats on the ferry, reservations are sometimes necessary. Each individual sector can be booked at the time you buy your pass, thus it's a good idea to work out an itinerary in advance. Reservations can also be made by phone 24 hours in advance. Awesome Adventures sells optional accommodations packages along with the pass, but these carry heavy cancellation penalties if not used exactly as specified, and you'll have no control over where you stay. Skip the "Full Monty" package which includes all sorts of add-ons you can purchase for the same price once you're there.

The "yellow boat" is the safest and most comfortable way to go. Awesome Adventures doesn't have an office of their own at Nadi Airport, but any travel agency in Fiji can book their services. There are no refunds on unused tickets. Outboards from the backpacker resorts pick up passengers from the *Yasawa Flyer's* rear deck and transfer them to the beach. Some resorts do this for free, while others will charge you F$5–10 pp each way to go ashore (none of the islands has a wharf). Know where your backpack is at *Yasawa Flyer* stops, as cases of people grabbing the wrong pack in the rush to disembark do occur.

Yasawa Island Eco Tours (tel. 672-1658, fax 672-5208, yiet@connect.com.fj), next to Rik's Café in Martintar (Nadi), operates the 20-meter catamaran *Tamusua Explorer* to the Yasawas every Tuesday, Thursday, and Saturday, departing Lautoka at 0800. It's basically intended as a day cruise to the Sawa-i-Lau Cave, costing F$189 round-trip including lunch. However, they also drop passengers on Nacula or Tavewa at F$89 pp one-way including Nadi hotel pickups (or F$70 if you book direct and find your own way to the wharf).

Some of the Yasawa backpacker camps have boats of their own (costing around F$70/120 one-way/round-trip from Lautoka), and when booking with them, it's best to avoid prepaying your return boat fare. Safety can be an issue on some of the smaller resort and village boats, which often carry more passengers than life jackets (if any). One traveler reported that the local boat he was on ran out of gas a kilometer short of Lautoka and ended up drifting in high seas, until it bumped into a container ship which was able to radio for help. Cases of local boats being lost at sea are not unknown. There are few government controls over the village boats, and they aren't that much cheaper than the perfectly safe *Yasawa Flyer*.

However you go, it's risky to schedule a return to Nadi on the same day you must catch an international flight, as adverse weather conditions can lead to the cancellation of all boat trips. This does happen at times, and even allowing two days leeway won't be sufficient if a hurricane warning has been issued.

KUATA ISLAND

Kuata is the *Yasawa Flyer's* first stop in the Yasawa Islands. Like neighboring Wayasewa and Waya, it's a scenically spectacular island, though without any Fijian villages. You can climb to the island's summit (171 m) for the view. With a buddy, you could also snorkel across the open channel to Wayasewa in half an hour, although this activity involves obvious risks, and we cannot recommend it.

The **Kuata Island Resort** (tel. 666-6644, ext. 3233), on a nice beach on the side of the island facing Wayasewa, accommodates up to 52 guests at F$40 pp in a 15-bed dorm or F$110 double in a thatched *bure* with private bath.

Three average meals are included. There's no electricity, and the food and accommodations aren't overwhelming, but the location is great. An optimum snorkeling area is just across the point on the southwest side of Kuata. Look for the cave near the seagull rocks at the point itself.

WAYASEWA ISLAND

Wayalailai Resort (tel. 666-9715 or 666-1572, www.bbr.ca/wayalailai), formerly known as Dive Trek Wayasewa, is spectacularly situated on the south side of Wayasewa opposite Kuata Island. It's directly below Wayasewa's highest peak, Vatuvula (349 m), with Viti Levu clearly visible behind Vomo Island to the east. Photos don't do this place justice.

The resort is built on two terraces, one 10 meters above the beach and the other 10 meters above that. The lower terrace has the double, duplex, and dormitory *bure,* while the upper accommodates the restaurant/bar and the former village schoolhouse of Namara village, now partitioned into 14 tiny double rooms. Simple rooms with shared bath and open ceiling in the school building are F$50 pp (a good option for singles), while the five individual *bure* with private bath and a small porch are F$120 double. One duplex *bure* with four beds on each side serves as an eight-bed dormitory or *bure-bau* at F$45 pp. The camping space nearby is F$35 pp. The minimum stay is three nights. Upon arrival, ask the staff to change the sheets if they haven't already done so.

Three meals are included in all rates. Wednesday and Sunday evenings, a *lovo* is prepared. An electric generator is used in the evening, and there's no shortage of water. Informal musical entertainment occurs nightly, and because this resort is collectively owned by the village, the staff is like one big happy family.

There's lots to see and do at Wayalailai, with hiking and scuba diving the main activities. Aside from scuba and snorkeling trips, the resort's dive shop offers a PADI open-water certification course. For groups of six or more, there are snorkeling trips to a reef halfway to Vomo.

The most popular hike is to the top of **Vatuvula Peak,** the fantastic volcanic plug hanging directly over the resort. The well-trodden path

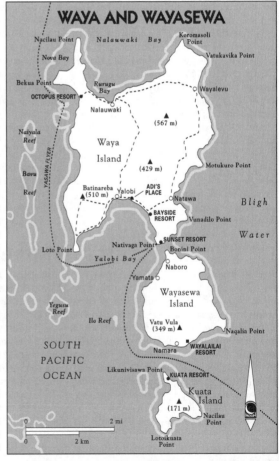

WAYA AND WAYASEWA

circles the mountain and comes up the back, taking about 1.5 hours total excluding stops (a guide really isn't necessary). From the top of Vatuvula, you get a sweeping view of the west side of Viti Levu, the Mamanucas, and the southern half of the Yasawa chain—one of the scenic highlights of the South Pacific. From Vatuvula, you can trek northwest across the grassy uplands to another rock with a good view of Yalobi Bay (also known as Alacrity Bay).

Transfers from Lautoka on Wayalailai's own boat depart Monday–Saturday at 1300 (1.5 hours, F$55 pp each way). The boat leaves Wayalailai to return to Lautoka Monday–Saturday at 0900. In both directions, the boat fare includes bus transfers to/from Nadi/Lautoka hotels. You can also get there on the Awesome Adventures shuttle from Nadi at F$70 one-way. Passengers on the *Yasawa Flyer* are picked up by a boat from Wayalailai at Kuata. Rabua's Travel Agency (tel. 672-1377 or 672-3234, wayalailai@connect.com.fj), in office No. 23 upstairs at Nadi Airport, takes Wayalailai bookings.

WAYA ISLAND

The high island clearly visible to the northwest of Lautoka is Waya, closest of the larger Yasawas to Viti Levu and just 60 kilometers away. At 579 meters, it's also the highest island in the chain. Waya is an excellent choice for the hyperactive traveler, as the hiking possibilities are unlimited. The beaches are very nice, and it's a great place to experience unspoiled Fijian culture. So if you can live with a few rough edges, Waya is *the* place to go.

Four Fijian villages are sprinkled around Waya: Nalauwaki, Natawa, Wayalevu, and Yalobi. The rocky mass of Batinareba (510 m) towers over the west side of Yalobi Bay, and in a morning or afternoon you can scramble up the mountain's rocky slope from the west end of the beach at Yalobi. Go through the forested saddle on the south side of the highest peak, and follow the grassy ridge on the far side all the way down to Loto Point. Many wild goats are seen along the way. An easier hike from Yalobi leads southeast from the school to the sandbar over to Wayasewa.

© DAVID STANLEY

Waya's Batinareba mountain can be climbed from Yalobi village in half a day.

One of the most memorable walks in the South Pacific involves spending two hours on a well-used trail from Yalobi to Nalauwaki village. Octopus Resort is just a 10-minute walk west over a low ridge, and from there it's possible to hike back to Yalobi down Waya's west coast and across Loto Point in another two or three hours. Due to rocky headlands lapped by the sea, you can only go down the west coast at low tide, thus one must set out from Yalobi at high tide and from Octopus at low tide. It's a great way to fill a day.

Accommodations

The **Sunset Resort** (tel. 666-6644, ext. 6383) is right next to the sandbar that links Waya to Wayasewa. The three *bure* are F$90/140 single/double, the 20-bed dorm F$45 pp, and camping space F$30 pp, meals included. Scuba diving is available at F$70/130 for one/two tanks, plus F$25 for gear, and there's good snorkeling right offshore anytime. At low tide it's possible to cross to Wayasewa without removing your shoes, and two villages, Naboro and Yamata, are nearby.

It's even possible to hike over the mountains to the Wayalailai Resort in about three hours. However, the vast majority of guests headed for the three backpacker places in this area, Sunset, Bayside, and Adi's, arrive on the *Yasawa Flyer* which stops nearby.

A 30-minute walk northwest toward Yalobi village is the **Bayside Resort** (tel. 666-6644, ext. 6383), run by a guy named Manasa, the brother of Adi Sayaba of Adi's Place. Count on paying about F$100 double to stay in a simple *bure* here, or F$40 pp in a 14-bed dorm (all prices include meals).

Adi's Place (tel. 665-0573), at Yalobi village on the south side of Waya, is a small family-operated resort in existence since 1981. Although primitive, it still makes a good hiking base, with prices designed to attract and hold those on the barest of budgets. The accommodations consist of one eight-bunk dorm at F$35 pp, a solid European-style house with three double rooms with shared bath at F$40 pp, and camping space at F$25 pp. Lighting is by kerosene lamp. The rates include three meals of variable quality. The beach looks good from shore, but it's hard to swim here due to the corals (don't leave valuables unattended on this beach). It's all a little messy and shouldn't be your first choice.

On a high white-sand beach in Likuliku Bay on northwestern Waya is **Octopus Resort** (Nick Woods, tel. 666-6442 or 666-6337, fax 666-6210, www.octopusresort.com), one of the nicest budget resorts in the South Pacific. The 17 comfortable *bure* with private bath are F$135/155/185 garden/oceanview/beachfront single or double. Otherwise it's F$60 pp in a clean 13-bed dorm, or F$100 double to sleep in one of Octopus's four safari tents. If you bring your own tent, it's also F$50 pp. A good lunch and dinner are included in all rates (the menu rotates every 21 days, so there's some variety). The minimum stay is two nights. Drinks are served at their large restaurant/bar, and a generator provides electricity. Octopus has its own dive shop, which also gives PADI certification courses. The snorkeling here is best at high tide (beware of receiving coral cuts at low tide). The Awesome Adventures ferry *Yasawa Flyer* from Nadi calls here, and Octopus has its own launch from Lautoka's Fisheries Wharf daily at 1000. Both charge F$70 each way, and the *Yasawa Flyer* is a smoother ride. Some readers have reported confusion over their reservations and bills at Octopus.

NAVITI ISLAND

Naviti, at 33 square kilometers, is the largest of the Yasawas. All of Naviti's villages are on the east coast, including Soso, residence of one of the group's highest chiefs. Soso's church houses fine wood carvings, and on the hillside above the village are two caves containing the bones of ancestors. Yawesa, the secondary boarding school on Naviti, is a village in itself. The Awesome Adventures shuttle from Nadi (F$80 one-way) cruises right up the west side of Naviti, where most of the resorts are found.

Natuvalo Bay

Three backpacker resorts, Coconut Bay, Korovou, and White Sandy Beach, share a beach on Natuvalo Bay directly across Naviti from Kese village. From the beach, a huge mango tree is visible atop the ridge to the southeast. A shady, well-trodden path leaves the beach 20 meters before the first rocky headland south of Coconut Bay Resort and climbs to the tree, a 40-minute walk. Go south along the ridge a few hundred meters to a grassy hill with great views as far as Wayasewa. The trail continues to Kese village. Do this hike right after breakfast while it's still relatively cool.

A much easier walk is to Honeymoon Point, the peninsula overlooking the north end of Natuvalo Bay. The trail begins next to White Sandy Beach Resort Dive Center and takes only 15 minutes. You'll have a view of the entire west side of Naviti, plus the long low island of Viwa at the 1100 clock position on the horizon, far to the west.

The **White Sandy Beach Dive Center** on Natuvalo Bay does one-tank dives at F$70–80 depending on the site, two-tank dives F$130–160. An introductory dive is F$75. Snorkeling trips to a plane wreck in three meters of water are F$20, while snorkeling with manta rays is F$16. A boat trip around the island, including both of these

looking down at Natuvalo Bay, site of several backpacker resorts on Naviti Island

sites is F$30 (minimum of eight persons). Snorkeling gear is for rent at F$6/10 a half/full day. Only Fijian currency in cash is accepted.

Accommodations

The **Botaira Resort** (tel. 666-2266), on the southwest side of Naviti, has seven upscale *bure* with bath tubs at F$350/425 double/triple. The two 10-bed dorms are F$90 pp. All prices include meals, tax, and some sporting activities. The travel agents at Nadi Airport should be able to discount these rack rates by a third.

On Natuvalo Bay, a few kilometers north of the Botaira Beach Resort is the **Coconut Bay Resort** (Milika and Veretariki Buli, tel. 666-6644, ext. 1300, coconutbay@yahoo.com). The 10 duplex units with private bath are F$150 for up to three persons or F$200 for four (you can reduce this to F$110 double, if you book direct by phone). The two large 20-bed dorms are F$46 pp, camping F$35 pp. The meals are served in an enclosed building with no view, but the food is good, with a buffet dinner nightly. Water shortages happen here. A snorkeling trip is F$10 pp.

The **Korovou Eco-Tour Resort** (Eta and Siairo Seutinaviti, tel. 666-6644, ext. 2244, korovoultk@connect.com.fj), a few minutes on foot from the Coconut Bay Resort, has four older duplex *bure* and two thatched *bure* at F$120 double, plus four newer *bure* with private bath at F$150/183 double/triple. The 24-bed dorm is F$46 pp, camping F$35 pp. All prices include meals. Korovou's *bure* are more private than those at Coconut Bay, and a generator provides electricity in the evening. In 2003, a spacious new restaurant with a large deck right above the beach was constructed at Korovou. Activities include snorkeling with manta rays and an evening fire dancing show.

The **White Sandy Beach Dive Resort,** run by Peter and Sulu Seutinaviti on the beach next to Korovou, has two neat little bungalows with tin roofs at F$110 double including meals. The dorm is F$45 pp. All three resorts just mentioned include afternoon tea in their prices and provide free transfers from the ferry to shore. Drinking water is scarce, and you'll be expected to buy bottled water. The swimming on Natuvalo Bay is only good at high tide.

Qereqere Cross Resort (tel. 666-6644, ext. 6558), at the northeast end of Naviti, is less accessible, as the *Yasawa Flyer* doesn't stop right in front of the resort, and you must arrange to be picked up off the northwest coast (F$20 pp transfer fee). Turtle Airways can bring you directly here. The 12 thatched *bure* with private bath are F$75 double, plus F$20 pp for meals. Dorm beds are F$35 pp, plus meals. Horseback riding and scuba diving are offered.

TAVEWA ISLAND

Tavewa is much smaller and lower than Waya and twice as far from Nadi, yet it's also strikingly beautiful, with excellent bathing in the warm waters off a picture-postcard beach on the south-east side, as well as a good fringing reef with super snorkeling. Tall grass covers the hilly interior of this two-kilometer-long island. Tavewa is in the middle of the Yasawas, and from the summit, you can behold the long chain of islands stretching out on each side, with Viti Levu in the background. The summit offers the best view of the adjacent **Blue Lagoon,** and the sunsets can be splendid.

There's no chief here, as this is freehold land. In the late 19th century, an Irishman named William Doughty married a woman from Nacula who was given Tavewa as her dowry. A decade or two later, a Scot named William Bruce married

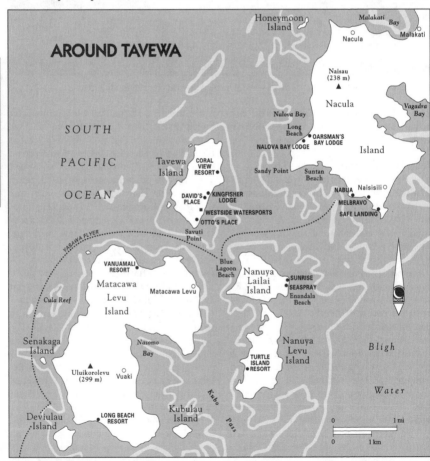

AROUND TAVEWA

Honeymoon Island

Malakati Bay

Nacula

Malakati

SOUTH

PACIFIC

OCEAN

Naisau (238 m) ▲

Nacula

Nulova Bay

Vagadra Bay

Tavewa Island

CORAL VIEW RESORT

Long Beach

OARSMAN'S BAY LODGE

NALOVA BAY LODGE

Island

DAVID'S PLACE

KINGFISHER LODGE

Sandy Point

Suntan Beach

NABUA

Naisisili

WESTSIDE WATERSPORTS

MELBRAVO

OTTO'S PLACE

SAFE LANDING

Savuti Point

YASAWA FLYER

Blue Lagoon Beach

VANUAMALI RESORT

Nanuya Lailai Island

SUNRISE

SEASPRAY

Enandala Beach

Matacawa Levu Island

Matacawa Levu

Cula Reef

Senakaga Island

Nasomo Bay

Nanuya Levu Island

Bligh

Uluikorolevu (299 m) ▲

Vuaki

TURTLE ISLAND RESORT

Water

Deviulau Island

LONG BEACH RESORT

Kubulau Island

Kubo Pass

0   1 mi

0   1 km

into the Doughty family, and some time thereafter, beachcombers called Murray and Campbell arrived on the scene and did the same, with the result that today some 50 Doughtys, Bruces, Murrays, and Campbells comprise the population of Tavewa. William Doughty himself died in 1926 at the ripe age of 77.

The islanders are friendly and welcoming; in fact, accommodating visitors is their main source of income. Coral View, David's, and Otto's have been operating since the 1980s, long before the current crop of backpacker resorts appeared on Naviti, Nacula, and Nanuya Lailai, and their experience shows (better food, accommodations, and tours). Most of their guests are backpackers who usually stay six nights, and most are sorry to leave. It's idyllic, but bring along mosquito coils, toilet paper, a flashlight (torch), bottled water, and a *sulu* to cover up. Be prepared for water shortages.

Sports and Recreation

Westside Watersports (tel./fax 661-1462, www.fiji-dive.com) has a dive center on the beach between David's and Otto's where the price gets cheaper the more diving you do (F$95/155 for one/two dives, subsequent dives F$55 each). Open-water scuba certification is F$565. Credit cards are accepted for diving. Their two dive boats, *Absolute II* and *Aftershock,* go out at 0900 and 1330, and which side of the island you'll dive on depends upon the wind. Aside from the spectacular underwater topography, encounters with sea turtles, reef sharks, and eagle rays are fairly common. You can also rent snorkeling gear (F$5) from Westside.

Accommodations

Coral View Resort (Don Bruce, tel. 666-2648 or 651-0730, coral@connect.com.fj), nestling in a cozy valley on a secluded beach with high hills on each side, is one of the nicest low-budget places to stay in Fiji. It has 14 thatched *bure* with shared bath at F$85/95 single/double, two hotel-style rooms with private bath at F$150 double, and one four-bunk and two eight-bunk dorms at F$40 pp. Camping with your own tent is F$30 pp. Mosquito nets are supplied.

© DAVID STANLEY

bure at Coral View Resort on Tavewa Island

Included are three decent meals and one free organized activity a day. Coral View's beach isn't that great, but boat trips to Honeymoon Island and Blue Lagoon Beach are only F$5 (minimum of five). The boat trip to the Sawa-i-Lau caves requires a minimum of five people willing to pay F$35 pp to operate. Snorkeling gear is F$5 extra. Trolling is F$30 pp (minimum of two). Although there are lots of organized activities, Coral View is also a place where people come to relax and socialize, and most guests tend to be under 35. You'll be touched when the genuinely friendly staff gathers to sing **Isa Lei,** the Fijian song of farewell, when the time comes for you to go. Transfers to/from the *Yasawa Flyer* are free.

Kingfisher Lodge (Joe Doughty, tel. 665-2830 or 666-6644, ext. 2288), next to David's Place, offers one self-contained beach bungalow at F$130/160 single/double including meals. Plastic canoes are for rent at F$5 an hour. Westside Watersports (tel. 666-1462) handles bookings here.

David's Place (David Doughty and Fi Liutaki, tel. 665-2820, davidsplaceresort@yahoo.com) stands in a coconut grove near a small church on the island's longest beach. There are 14 thatched *bure* with shared bath at F$80/110 single/double, one larger bungalow with private bath at F$100/150, a five-bed dorm at F$50 pp, and an eight-bed dorm at F$45 pp. Camping is F$35 pp with your own tent. The minimum stay is two nights. David's *bure* are larger and more comfortable than those at Coral View, though the communal toilets and showers are inadequate when the place is full. Three meals are included in the price, with the Thursday *lovo* and Saturday barbecue as part of the regular meal plan (opinions about the food vary). David's takes credit cards. At David's, you don't get the free trips provided at Coral View (beach visits are F$10 each), and the optional tours cost F$35 for the cave trip or to visit Naisisili village (minimum of seven). If you're a fun-loving backpacker, you'll like the holiday-camp atmosphere here, though David's does cater to all ages. Bookings can be made through David's Travel Service (tel. 672-1820), office No. 31 upstairs in the arrivals concourse at Nadi Airport.

Otto's Place (Otto and Fanny Doughty, tel. 666-6481), on spacious grounds near the south end of the island, caters to a more mature clientele less interested in activities and partying. They have two large bungalows with toilet, shower, and sink at F$90 single or double, F$105 triple. Two thatched *bure* with private bath cost the same. The single 10-bed dormitory is F$40 pp. Camping is not allowed. Add F$40 pp to all rates for three good meals. The generator is on until 2300, but the light is dim. The *bure* are nicely scattered through the plantation, but they don't overlook the beach. Credit cards are accepted. Yachties anchored at the nearby Blue Lagoon are welcome to order dinner here (F$20 pp), so long as 24 hours notice is given. From 1500–1630, afternoon tea is served to both guests and nonguests at Aunty Fanny's Tea House, costing F$3 for tea with some of the richest banana or chocolate cake in Fiji. It's an island institution. Ice cream is also available. You can book Otto's Place through Westside Watersports (tel. 661-1462) in Lautoka, which can also arrange transfers on their own boat at F$80 pp each way.

Getting There

Most visitors arrive from Nadi on the Awesome Adventures catamaran *Yasawa Flyer* at F$90 one-way. An island hop from Tavewa to Naviti or Waya on the catamaran is F$50. Outboard transfers from Tavewa to Nacula or Nanuya Lailai are F$10 pp each way. Turtle Airways (tel. 672-1888) offers special "backpacker rates" on seaplane transfers from Nadi to Tavewa.

NACULA ISLAND

Ten-kilometer-long Nacula, between Tavewa and Yasawa islands, is the third largest in the chain. From its contorted coastline rise hills like Naisau (238 m) and Korobeka (258 m). Of the four villages, Naisisili and Nacula are the most important, and the Tui Drola, or chief of the middle Yasawas, resides on the island. Some of Fiji's best snorkeling is available just off the high white sands of **Long Beach,** in the southwest corner of Nacula opposite Tavewa. Since 2000, several small resorts have been built on Nacula. Meals are included in most of the rates quoted below, but be aware that water-taxi transfers to/from the *Yasawa Flyer* cost F$5–10 pp.

On a good beach on the southeast side of Nacula is **Nabua Lodge** (Sailasa Ratu, tel. 666-9173 or 666-6644, ext. 6369) with six thatched *bure,* four with shared bath at F$89 double and two with private bath at F$120. The five-bed dorm is F$45 pp, camping F$35 pp. Great sunsets can be seen from the hill just above the lodge, and you can hike along the ridge right to the center of the island (take water).

Melbravo Lodge (Laite Nasau, tel. 665-0616 or 666-6644, ext. 7472), right next to Nabua Lodge, has six thatched *bure,* two with private bath at F$120 double and four with shared bath at F$88 including meals. The eight-bed dorm is F$44 pp. If you call direct rather than booking through a Nadi travel agent, these prices are reduced to F$100/70/30. There's electricity in the dining area, but none in the rooms. The food can be monotonous and the portions small, but drinking water is supplied free. Activities here include a Sawa-i-Lau cave tour (F$30, minimum of six persons), Blue Lagoon snorkeling (F$10), village entertainment (F$10), and snorkeling gear rental (F$3). Both Melbravo and Nabua Lodge charge F$5 pp for the transfer from the *Yasawa Flyer*.

Safe Landing Resort (Tevita and Kara Volavola, tel. 672-2921) is on a white-sand beach tucked between two dark headlands, on the next bay over from Melbravo. The five well-constructed Fijian *bure* with shared bath are F$117 double, while the six duplex units with bath are F$179. The six-bunk dorm is F$64 pp, camping F$59 pp. The meals are good and include a lot of fish. It's a nice spot with good swimming at high tide, though the beach at Oarsman's Bay Lodge is much better. Profits from Safe Landing go to community projects in nearby Naisisili village.

Oarsman's Bay Lodge (Ratu Epeli Vuetibau, tel. 672-2921) is on fabulous **Long Beach**, at the southwest end of Nacula. There's a 13-bed dormitory above the restaurant/bar at F$73 pp, six high-quality, self-contained bungalows with solar panels at F$190 double, and two large family bungalows sleeping six at F$428. Camping with your own tent costs F$61 pp. Paddleboats, kayaks, and snorkeling gear are loaned free. These rates include meals and tax, but Oarsman's often quotes prices for accommodations only, so assume that's what is happening if you're told a lower price. Most of the staff hail from Nacula village on the north side of the island, and resort profits go to village projects. If you're staying at Safe Landing or one of its neighbors and wish to visit Oarsman's for the day, it takes a bit more than an hour to walk, utilizing a shortcut trail across the island to/from Suntan Beach. It's only easy to walk there along the beach at low tide—at high tide, you'll need to wade part of the way.

Oarsman's and Safe Landing have many things in common. Both were built in 2000 with interest-free loans provided by the owner of Turtle Island Resort. To ensure that the loans are repaid, both resorts are now managed by Turtle Island, and bookings are controlled by the Turtle Island office (tel. 672-2921 or 672-2780, nacula@hotmail.com) at Nadi Airport. To further control finances, all accounts must be paid by credit card (cash not accepted anywhere, not even at the bar). The transfer fees from the *Ya-sawa Flyer* are F$10 pp each way at both, and both resorts operate on "Bula Time" (one hour ahead of Fiji time) to give guests an extra hour of daylight. Oarsman's and Safe Landing are run as businesses rather than as family operations, and a high percentage of the guests tend to be middle-aged tourists (rather than young backpackers) who "discovered" these places on the Internet. Compared to the rest of the Yasawa backpacker resorts, Oarsman's and Safe Landing are rather expensive, yet compared to Mamanuca resorts like Malolo, Castaway, and Matamanoa, they're dirt cheap. So this is your chance to stay at a trendy—even pretentious—tourist resort at something approaching backpacker rates! Needless to say, bookings are tight, and you should reserve as far ahead as possible.

Adjacent to Oarsman's is **Nalova Bay Lodge,** with four *bure* of similar quality to those at Oarsman's. It started out much like its neighbor, but the Waqa family fell out with the Turtle Island people, and financing for Nalova Bay Lodge was abruptly terminated. The family is now attempting to finish the resort from their own resources. If they succeed, it will probably be a better buy than Oarsman's Bay.

AROUND THE BLUE LAGOON
Nanuya Lailai Island

Nanuya Lailai, between Tavewa and Nanuya Levu islands, is best known for Blue Lagoon Beach on the island's west side. The snorkeling here is about the finest in the area, and this beach is often visited by cruise-ship passengers. Many yachts anchor just offshore. You can tell the fish have been fed at the Blue Lagoon from the way they swim straight at you. Unfortunately, much of the coral is now dead.

Since 2000, the island's seven families, related to the Naisisili people on Nacula, have established five small backpacker resorts along Enandala Beach on Nanuya Lailai's east side. Expect water shortages (bring bottled water), a lack of electricity (this could change), and no credit cards accepted (all prices include meals). Transfers from the *Yasawa Flyer* to Nanuya Lailai are F$10 pp each way. It's only a 10-minute walk across the island from the backpacker camps to Blue Lagoon Beach. To avoid conflicts with powerful tour operators, your hosts may ask you to stay away from groups of cruise-ship passengers swimming in the Blue Lagoon—the beach is long enough for everyone.

Sunrise Lagoon Resort (Poasa Naivalu, tel. 666-6644, ext. 9484), at the north end of Enandala Beach, charges F$102 double in six thatched *bure* with shared bath and F$150 in one garden *bure* with private bath. Both the seven-bed family beach *bure* and a 14-bed dorm are F$46 pp. At last report, Sunrise Lagoon was the only resort on Nanuya Lailai with electricity, but opinions about the quality of the food and accommodations here vary considerably. This place is well promoted by the Nadi travel agents, so there are usually lots of guests.

On a long stretch of beach next door to Sunset Lagoon is the more spacious **Seaspray Lodge** (Daniel Bokini, tel. 666-8962) with eight simple *bure* with shared bath at F$95 double, plus an eight-bed dorm at F$45 pp. Lighting is by kerosene lamp, but the outdoor eating area is nice and the food okay. Sadly, we've heard reports of petty theft from the dorm at Seaspray.

Al's Place (Amelia and Alosio Bogileka, tel. 666-6644, ext. 9484) has six *bure* with shared bath on a low hill behind Seaspray. The poor location means it shouldn't be your first choice.

The **Gold Coast Inn** (Philomena Saucoko, tel. 666-6644, ext. 9484), on the beach right next to Seaspray, has five *bure* with shared bath at F$88 double, and two *bure* with private bath at F$120. It's worth considering.

At the south end of the strip is **Kimi's Place** (tel. 666-6644, ext. 9484) with two basic thatched *bure* with shared bath at F$45 pp. It's more of a place to buy souvenirs or to have afternoon tea and cakes (F$3) than a resort. At low tide, you can easily walk across the sandbar behind Kim's Place to Nanuya Levu Island, though you'll be most unwelcome there.

Nanuya Levu Island

In 1972, an eccentric American millionaire named Richard Evanson bought 200-hectare Nanuya Levu Island in the middle of the Yasawa Group for US$300,000. He still lives there, and his **Turtle Island Resort** (tel. 672-2921 or 666-3889, fax 672-0007, www.turtlefiji.com) has gained a reputation as one of the South Pacific's ultimate hideaways. Only 14 fan-cooled, two-room *bure* grace Turtle, and Evanson swears that there will never be more.

Turtle is Tavewa at 25 times the price. The 28 guests pay F$2,850 per couple per night (or F$3,450 in a grand *bure*), but that includes all meals, drinks, and activities (12.5 percent tax is extra). You'll find the fridge in your cottage well stocked with beer, wine, soft drinks, and champagne, refilled daily, with no extra bill to pay when you leave. Sports such as sailing, snorkeling, scuba diving, canoeing, windsurfing, deep-sea fishing, horseback riding, guided hiking, and moonlight cruising are all included in the tariff. Resort staff will even do your laundry at no additional charge (only Lomi Lomi massage costs extra).

If you want to spend the day on any of the dozen secluded beaches, just ask, and you'll be dropped off. Later, someone will be back with lunch and a cooler of wine or champagne (or anything else you'd care to order over the walkie-talkie). Otherwise, use the beach a few steps from your door. Meals are served at remote and romantic dine-out locations, or taken at the community table; every evening Richard hosts a small dinner party. He's turned down many offers to develop the island with hundreds more units or to sell out for a multimillion-dollar price. That's not Richard's style, and he's quite specific about who he *doesn't* want to come: "Trendies, jetsetters, obnoxious imbibers, and plastic people won't get much out of my place. Also, opinionated, loud, critical grouches and anti-socials should give us a miss."

Of course, all this luxury and romance has a price. Aside from the per diem, it's another F$1,380 per couple for round-trip seaplane transportation to the island from Nadi. There's also a six-night minimum stay, but as nearly half the guests are repeaters, that doesn't seem to be an impediment. Actress Julia Roberts was a recent visitor. (Turtle Island is off-limits to anyone other than hotel guests.) Turtle's success may be measured by its many imitators, including Vatulele Island Resort, Lalati Resort, the Wakaya Club, Nukubati Island Resort, Qamea Beach Resort, Katafanga Island Resort, and the Yasawa Island Resort.

Turtle Island has also set the standard for environmentally conscious resort development. Aside from planting tens of thousands of trees and providing a safe haven for birds, Evanson has preserved the island's mangroves, cleverly erecting a boardwalk to turn what others might have considered an eyesore into a major attraction. A model of sustainability, the resort grows 90 percent of its own herbs and vegetables in an organic garden, gets honey from its own apiary, uses solar water heaters and wind-powered generators, and makes its own furniture from local timber. And some of Evanson's guests do more than sun themselves. Every year since 1991, a group of California eye specialists has briefly converted Turtle Island into an unlikely clinic for dozens of Fijian villagers requiring eye surgery or just a recycled pair of prescription glasses, all for free. Nearly 160 local Fijians have jobs here, all to serve 28 guests!

Recently, Evanson began an innovative program to save the endangered green and hawksbill turtles of the Yasawas. The resort now purchases all live turtles brought in by hunters, and auctions them to resort guests, with all profits going to the staff fund. The names of the new "owners" are painted on the shells, and the reptiles are released. Although the paint does no harm to the turtles, it renders their shells worthless in the turtle-shell market, thereby prolonging the animals' lives.

Evanson has a reputation in Fiji, and some former Fijian employees have complained about being paid low wages, fed vegetarian food, and subjected to authoritarian discipline. Contemporary Captain Bligh or not, Richard certainly is a character. During the 2000 coup turmoil, Turtle Island was briefly occupied by villagers from Naisisili on nearby Nacula. They claimed that the island had been wrongfully given away by a Fijian chief in 1868 and that it still belonged to them. Over many bowls of kava, Evanson and the villagers came to an understanding, and Turtle Island is again as safe as safe can be. In true Hollywood fashion, some of the interlopers have now established backpacker resorts of their own on

CAPTAIN WILLIAM BLIGH

In 1789, after being cast adrift by the mutineers on his HMS *Bounty*, Captain Bligh and 18 others in a seven-meter longboat were chased by two Fijian war canoes through what is now called Bligh Water. His men pulled the oars desperately, headed for open sea, and managed to escape the cannibals. They later arrived in Timor, finishing the most celebrated open-boat journey of all time. Captain Bligh did some incredible charting of Fijian waters along the way.

neighboring islands—all with Richard's blessing and full support! And so life continues on these legendary isles.

Matacawa Levu Island

Matacawa Levu, west of Nanuya Levu, is less developed touristically, although this is changing fast. **Long Beach Resort** (tel. 666-6644, ext. 3032) stands on the long white beach on Matacawa Levu's south side. A mattress on the mat-covered floor of the eight-bed dorm costs F$55 pp with meals, but unfortunately we've received complaints about the primitive conditions and poor food here. At low tide, you can walk across to nearby Deviulau Island and good snorkeling is available. Passengers are transferred from the *Yasawa Flyer* at the south end of Matacawa Levu at F$5 pp each way. Ask about the newer **Vanuamali Resort** opposite Tavewa on the north side of Matacawa Levu.

SAWA-I-LAU ISLAND

On Sawa-i-Lau is a large limestone **cave** illuminated by a crevice at the top. There's a clear, deep pool in the cave where you can swim, and an underwater opening leads back into a smaller, darker cave (bring a light). A Fijian legend tells how a young chief once hid his love in this cave when her family wished to marry her off to another. Each day, he brought her food until they could both escape to safety on another island. In the 1980 film *The Blue Lagoon*, Brooke Shields runs away to this very cave. Many cruise ships stop at the cave, and the backpacker resorts on Tavewa and Nacula also run tours. Yachties should present a *sevusevu* to the chief of Nabukeru village, just west of the cave, to visit.

YASAWA ISLAND

The Tui Yasawa, highest chief of the group, resides at Yasawairara village at the north end of Yasawa, northernmost island of the Yasawa group.

For many years, the Fiji government had a policy that the Yasawas were "closed" to land-based tourism development, and it was only after the 1987 coups that approval was granted for the construction of **Yasawa Island Resort** (Garth and Denise Downey, tel. 666-3364 or 672-2266, fax 666-5044 or 672-4456, www.yasawa.com). This exclusive Australian-owned resort opened in 1991 on a creamy white beach on Yasawa's upper west side. Most of the resort's employees come from Bukama village, which owns the land.

The accommodations consist of four air-conditioned duplexes at F$1,500 double, 10 one-bedroom deluxes at F$1,700, and a honeymoon unit at F$2,400. All meals are included, but, unlike at most other resorts in this category, alcoholic drinks are *not*. Scuba diving (www.diveyasawa.com), game fishing, and massage also cost extra. The resort often grants a 10 percent discount for off-season, last-minute bookings made in person at their Nadi airport office. The only swimming pool in the Yasawa Islands is here. Guests arrive on a chartered flight (F$620 pp return), which lands on the resort's private airstrip. Children under 12 are only admitted in January.

Kadavu

This big, 50-by-13-kilometer island 100 kilometers south of Suva is the third largest in Fiji (450 square km). A mountainous, varied island with waterfalls plummeting from the rounded rainforested hilltops, Kadavu is outstanding for its vistas, beaches, and reefs. The three hilly sections of Kadavu are joined by two low isthmuses, with the sea biting so deeply into the island that on a map its shape resembles that of a wasp. Just northeast of the main island is smaller Ono Island and the fabulous Astrolabe Reef, stretching halfway to Suva. A process is now underway to have Ono's fringing reefs declared a marine conservation area.

The **birdlife** is rich with some species of honeyeaters, fantails, and velvet fruit doves found only here. The famous red-and-green Kadavu musk parrots are readily seen and heard. But Kadavu really stands out for what it lacks. There are not only no mongoose, but also no mynahs, or bulbuls, or cane toads. Few islands of this size anywhere in the Pacific have as much endemic biodiversity left as Kadavu.

In the 1870s, steamers bound for New Zealand and Australia would call at the onetime whaling station at Galoa Harbor to pick up passengers and goods, and Kadavu was considered as a possible site for a new capital of Fiji. Instead, Suva was chosen, and Kadavu was left to lead its sleepy village life; only in the past two decades has the outside world made a comeback with the arrival of roads, planes, and just less than a dozen small resorts, many of them on the channel between Kadavu and Ono. Some 10,000 indigenous Fijians live in 60 remote villages scattered around Kadavu.

SIGHTS

The airstrip and wharf are each a 10-minute walk, in different directions, from the post office and hospital in the small government station of **Vunisea,** the largest of Kadavu's villages and headquarters of Kadavu Province. Vunisea is strategically located on a narrow, hilly isthmus where Galoa Harbor and Namalata Bay almost cut Kadavu in two.

Just two kilometers south of the airstrip by road and a 10-minute hike inland is **Waikana Falls.** Cool spring water flows over a 10-meter-high rocky cliff between two deep pools, the perfect place for a refreshing swim on a hot day. A good beach is at **Muani** village, eight kilometers south of Vunisea by road.

The women of **Namuana** village just west of the airstrip can summon **giant turtles** up from

the sea by singing traditional chants to the *vu* (ancestral spirits) Raunidalice and Tinadi Caboga. On a bluff 60 meters above the sea the garlanded women begin their song, and in 15 minutes a large turtle will appear. This turtle, and sometimes its mates, will swim up and down slowly offshore just below the overhanging rocks. The calling of turtles is performed for a fee of F$400 per group.

West of Vunisea

A road crosses the mountains from Namuana to **Tavuki** village, seat of the Tui Tavuki, paramount chief of Kadavu. The provincial office is also at Tavuki. A couple of hours west on foot is the **Yawe District,** where large pine tracts have been established. In the villages of Nalotu, Yakita, and Naqalotu at Yawe, traditional Fijian **pottery** is still made. Without a potter's wheel or kiln, the

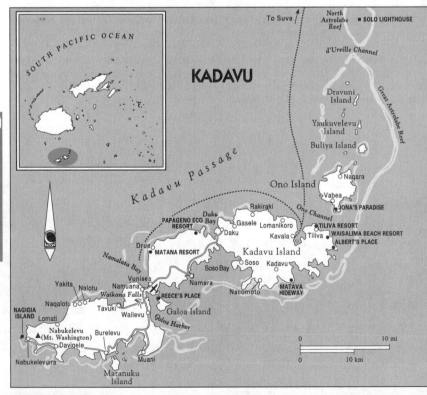

KADAVU HIGHLIGHTS

birdlife: Kadavu musk parrots and many other species (p. 253)

The Great Astrolabe Reef: scuba divers' paradise, marinelife (p. 255)

East Kadavu: small resorts, beaches, diving (p. 255, 258)

Ono Island: beaches, snorkeling, diving (p. 257)

women shape the pots with a paddle and fire them in an open fire. Sap from the mangroves provides a glaze.

Another road runs along the south coast from Vunisea to **Nabukelevuira** at the west end of Kadavu. There's good surfing at Cape Washington in this area, and a deluxe surf camp on Denham Island just off the cape caters to the needs of surfers. The abrupt, extinct cone of **Nabukelevu**, or Mt. Washington (838 m), dominates the west end of Kadavu. Petrels nest in holes on the north side of the mountain. This dormant volcano erupted as recently as 2,000 years ago.

The Great Astrolabe Reef

The Great Astrolabe Reef stretches unbroken for 30 kilometers along the east side of the small islands north of Kadavu. One kilometer wide, the reef is unbelievably rich in coral and marinelife, and because it's so far from shore, it still hasn't been fished out. The reef surrounds a lagoon containing 10 islands, the largest of which is 30-square-kilometer Ono. The reef was named by French explorer Dumont d'Urville, who almost lost his ship, the *Astrolabe,* here in 1827.

There are frequent openings on the west side of the reef, and the lagoon is never more than 20 meters deep, which makes it a favorite of scuba divers and yachties. The Astrolabe also features a vertical drop-off of 10 meters on the inside and 1,800 meters on the outside, with visibility up to 75 meters. The underwater caves and walls here must be seen to be believed. However, the reef is exposed to unbroken waves generated by the southeast trade winds, and diving conditions are often dependent on the weather. Surfing is possible at Vesi Passage (boat required).

Many possibilities exist for ocean kayaking in the protected waters around Ono Channel, and there are several inexpensive resorts at which to stay. Kayak rentals are available and several companies mentioned in the Exploring the Islands chapter offer kayaking tours to Kadavu.

ACCOMMODATIONS

Under US$25

Reece's Place (Humphrey and Edward Reece, tel. 333-6097), on Galoa Island just off the northwest corner of Kadavu, was the first to accommodate visitors to Kadavu. It's a 15-minute walk from the airstrip to the dock, then a short launch ride to Galoa itself (F$12 pp return). To stay in a *bure* or European-style house here is F$25/40 single/double, or pay F$12 pp in the dormitory. Pitch your tent for F$6 pp. Three meals are another F$24 pp, and add 12.5 percent tax to all charges. There are longstanding water problems here, and the electric generator is seldom used at night. The view of Galoa Harbor from Reece's Place is nice, but snorkeling in the murky water off their so-so beach is a waste of time. For a fee, they'll take you out to the Galoa Barrier Reef, where the snorkeling is vastly superior. Scuba diving may be offered—call to ask. There's good anchorage for yachts just off Reece's Place.

Bai's Place (tel. 338-2566 or 996-9308), just a few minutes walk from Reece's Place on Galoa Island's Vunuku Beach, provides accommodations in three traditional *bure* and a large house at F$35 pp with shared bath, all meals included. Transfers from Kadavu are F$8 pp each way. There's no electricity, and it's even more basic than Reece's Place, though congenial. The owner Bai Whippy once worked as a divemaster at Pacific Harbor, and he arranges diving at F$35 per tank.

One of the best value places to stay is **Albert's Place** (Bruce O'Connor, tel. 333-6086), a family operation at Lagalevu at the **east end of Kadavu**. Each of the five *bure* has a double and a single bed, coconut mats on the floor, and kerosene lighting at F$16/30 single/double, or F$12 pp in a three-bed dorm. Camping is F$10. The units share rustic flush toilets and cold showers, and mosquito nets and coils are

backpacker accommodations at Albert's Place at Kadavu's east end

supplied (bring repellent anyway). Meals cost another F$25 pp for all three, and you'll receive generous portions. The snorkeling off Albert's beach is fine, though the swimming is only good at high tide (Jona's on Ono has a far superior beach). Scuba with **Naiqoro Divers** (run by Bruce O'Connor) is F$65/110 for one/two-tank boat dives including equipment. A four-day package with eight dives is F$400. A reef trip for snorkeling is F$10 pp, surfing trips F$15, fishing trips F$10, kayaking F$5, and the two/three-waterfall trip F$20/35. Ask Elizabeth to give you her garden tour, where she explains which herbs she uses in her cooking and which are medicinal. The cheapest way to get there from Suva is by boat on the *Bulou-ni-Ceva,* which will bring you directly to Kavala Bay (a good three hours west of Albert's on foot). A boat pickup from Kavala Bay will cost F$30 per trip; otherwise, they'll pick you up at Vunisea Airport at F$60 for the first two persons or F$30 pp for three or more for the two-hour boat ride (these prices are fixed, so don't bother bargaining).

US$25–50

Manueli and Tamalesi Vuruya run **Biana Accommodation** (tel. 333-6010), on a hill overlooking Namalata Bay near the wharf at Vunisea. The three rooms with cold showers are F$40/60 single/double including breakfast, plus F$5 each for lunch or dinner. They ask that you call ahead before coming.

The **Waisalima Beach Resort** (tel./fax 331-6281, www.waisalimafiji.com) faces a golden two-kilometer beach with a lovely panorama on the north side of Kadavu, between Albert's and Kavala Bay. The three *bure* with shared bath are F$50/65 single/double, while the three with private bath are F$130/150. *Bure* guests pay F$47 pp extra for three meals, while those staying in the six-bed dorm are charged F$60 pp including meals. It's a bit overpriced compared to Jona's and Albert's, and rather basic for the price, though they do have a permanent electricity supply. Campers can pitch their tents at the end of the property, a few hundred meters down the beach and across a small bridge, at F$8/12 single/double. Two-tank dives are F$120, plus F$25 for gear. A four-day open-water certification course will cost F$500. Kayaks are for rent at F$15 a day. Waisalima is a one-hour walk from Albert's. Their launch will pick you up at Kavala wharf for F$15 pp (more than two hours walk). From Vunisea airport they charge F$50 pp each way with a two-person minimum.

Jona's Paradise Resort (tel. 330-7058, fax 330-9696, www.jonasparadise.com) is at Vabea on the southern tip of **Ono Island** opposite Kadavu. The accommodations are good with two deluxe *bure* (private bath) at F$105 pp, three standard *bure* (shared bath) at F$95 pp, two four-bed dorm *bure* at F$70 pp, and camping space at F$53 pp. Children under 12 sharing with their parents are 50 percent off. All prices include three tasty meals, but bring a few snack foods with you, as the portions are sometimes skimpy. Jona's generator is unreliable, and the lights can go off as early at 2140. Surprisingly, there are no trails leading away from the resort to local villages. This small, family-style resort has a steep, non-tidal white-sand beach which is always right for swimming and very safe for the kids (no currents or big waves). The snorkeling is great (hundreds of clownfish in crystal-clear water), and the gorgeous Great Astrolabe Reef is only a five-minute boat ride away. Jonas is the closest Kadavu-area resort to the top dive sites. Turtles, sharks, and big fish are seen on most channel dives, and the fish and coral on the reefs are first rate too. Australian Russell Thornley (married to Albert O'Connor's daughter) runs the dive operation, charging F$130 for a two-tank dive including gear. A "discover scuba" course for novices costs F$120 pp including three dives and gear. The high-speed one-hour boat trip from Vunisea Airport costs F$55 pp each way. The 200-horsepower engine on their custom-built eight-meter aluminum dive boat allows the scuba staff to make regular trips to Suva, and they'll happily bring you back with them from the Tradewinds Marina at F$100 pp (call ahead to find out when this might be possible).

US$50–100

Not to be confused with the more expensive Matana Resort is **Matava, The Astrolabe Hideaway** (tel. 333-6098 or 330-5222, fax 333-6099, www.matava.com), a 30-minute walk east of Kadavu village and almost opposite tiny Waya Island on the southeast side of the island. Opened in 1996, this is one of the most ecoconscious resorts in Fiji. The managers, Jeanie from New York and Richard and Adrian from the United Kingdom, have installed solar electricity and water heating, an organic vegetable garden, and a spring water system. There's no beach in front of Matava, but the snorkeling in the marine reserve off Waya is fine. There are three thatched oceanview *bure* with private bath and solar lighting at F$120 single or double, three waterfront *bure* with private bath at F$100, two waterfront *bure* with shared bath at F$55, and one four-bed dormitory at F$18 pp. The meal plan is F$50 pp, and you eat at communal tables, which is fun. A local village store is a 20-minute walk away. Most guests come to scuba dive on the nearby Great Astrolabe Reef, which costs F$60/115/540 for one/two/10 tanks, plus F$25 for equipment. The manta dive is exceptional. PADI open-water certification is F$550. Surfing trips are F$35 (own board). Kayaks and canoes are for rent. Snorkeling trips are F$15 pp, plus F$10 for gear (if required). Game fishing is F$100 an hour plus fuel. Boat transfers from the airport are F$30 pp each way. It's rustic and remote, but just fine for the diehard diver.

US$150 and up

In April 2000, a surfing camp called **Nagigia Island** (tel. 331-5774, www.fijisurf.com) opened on tiny Denham Island off Cape Washington at the west end of Kadavu. The seven neat little bungalows perched on a limestone cliff are F$154 pp if you're willing to share a double or F$200 single. A dorm bed is F$114. Reductions are offered after one week. The meal plan is F$54 pp extra, unlimited surf transfers F$28 a day, and boat transfers to Vunisea Airport F$58 pp each way. Scuba diving and fishing also cost extra. There's good swimming directly below the units and at nearby sandy beaches. The traditional surfing season is Apr.–Nov., but this resort has excellent surf during the other months as well, due to its outer reefs' curving 270 degrees. For surfing

Shoppers from outlying villages headed for Kadavu's market land on this beach near Vunisea. The hiking trails of Kadavu vie with untouched beaches such as this one in "downtown" Vunisea.

details and advice on transporting your boards, consult their website.

The **Matana Beach Resort** (tel. 331-1780, fax 330-3860, www.matanabeachresort.com) at Drue, six kilometers north of Vunisea, caters mostly to scuba divers who have booked from abroad with Dive Kadavu (www.divekadavu.com). The two oceanview *bure* on the hillside and six larger beachfront units are F$275/475/660/800 single/double/triple/quad (local rate discounts often available). All rates include three meals of variable quality (three-night minimum stay). Windsurfers, kayaks, and paddleboards are free. The morning two-tank boat dive is F$165 without gear. The snorkeling off Matana's golden beach is good, and the Namalata Reef is straight out from the resort (the east end of the Great Astrolabe Reef is an hour away). Boat transfers from Vunisea airport are free. The feedback has been mixed.

The **Papageno Eco Resort** (tel. 330-3355, fax 330-3533, www.papagenoecoresort.com) is on the north side of Kadavu, 15 kilometers east of Vunisea and accessible only by boat. The four

colonial-style cottages are F$300/600/750 single/double/triple including meals, airport transfers, and tax. The main house on this 140-hectare property is used as the resort's dining room. Scuba diving and combined village-wildlife trips can be arranged. Papageno offers a two-week marine-biology course that costs F$2,000 pp including room and board, instruction, and materials. They also have a Kadavu Shining Parrot conservation project for which they accept long-term (minimum three months) volunteers who pay to work on the project.

Kadavu's newest place is the **Tiliva Resort** (tel./fax 331-5127, www.tilivaresortfiji.com), near Tiliva village between Kavala Bay and Waisalima on **east Kadavu**, faces a golden beach with a nice view of Ono. Opened in late 2002, it's run by an ex-British soldier named Kemu Yabaki and his wife Barbara. They have one honeymoon beachfront bungalow at F$500 double, and five spacious fan-cooled twin bungalows at F$250/400 single/double. All meals in the modern restaurant/bar overlooking the resort are included. There's 24-hour electricity. Scuba diving is F$55/30/70 for boat/shore/night dives and sportfishing can be arranged. Airport transfers are included in the rates (minimum stay three nights).

OTHER PRACTICALITIES

Vunisea has no restaurants, but a coffee shop at the airstrip opens for flights, and six small general stores sell canned goods. Vunisea Market opens Monday–Saturday 0800–1600 with cooked meals, hot coffee, and stacks of fruit available. A woman at the market sells roti, pies, and juice.

The small National Bank agency at the post office in Vunisea doesn't deal in foreign currency, so change enough money before coming (and don't leave it unattended in your room or tent).

Occasional carriers ply the rugged, muddy roads of west Kadavu, but there are no buses.

GETTING THERE

Air Fiji arrives from Suva once a day (F$81), and **Sun Air** has daily flights from Nadi (F$104). Be sure to reconfirm your return flight immediately upon arrival. Boat pickups by the resorts on east Kadavu and Ono should be prearranged. The speedboats to east Kadavu are often without safety equipment or roofs, and in rough weather everything could get wet. Have sunblock and a hat ready if it's sunny, rain gear if it's not, as it's a one- to two-hour ride to east Kadavu or Ono. There's no road from Vunisea to east Kadavu.

Ships like the *Bulou-ni-Ceva* and *Cagi Mai Ba* ply between Suva and Kadavu twice a week, calling at villages along the north coast. These vessels are only of interest to low-budget travelers headed for Waisalima or Albert's who can disembark at Kavala Bay. Take seasickness precautions before boarding. For details, turn to Transportation in the Suva chapter.

KADAVU

The Lomaiviti Group

The Lomaiviti (or central Fiji) Group lies in the Koro Sea near the heart of the archipelago, east of Viti Levu and south of Vanua Levu. Of its nine main volcanic islands, Gau, Koro, and Ovalau are among the largest in Fiji. Lomaiviti's climate is moderate, neither as wet and humid as Suva, nor as dry and hot as Nadi. The population is mostly Fijian and engaged in subsistence agriculture and copra making.

The old capital island, Ovalau, is by far the best-known and most visited island of the group, and several small islands south of Ovalau on the way to Suva bear backpacker resorts. Naigani also has a tourist resort of its own, but Koro and Gau are seldom visited, due to a lack of facilities for visitors. Ferries ply the Koro Sea to Ovalau, while onward ferries run to Vanua Levu a couple of times a week.

Ovalau Island

Ovalau, a large volcanic island just east of Viti Levu, is the main island of the Lomaiviti Group. Almost encircled by high peaks, the Lovoni Valley in the center of Ovalau is actually the island's volcanic crater and about the only flat land. The crater's rim is pierced by the Bureta River, which escapes through a gap to the southeast. The highest peak is 626-meter Nadelaiovalau (meaning, the top of Ovalau), behind Levuka. Luckily, Ovalau lacks the magnificent beaches found elsewhere in Fiji, which has kept the package-tour crowd away, and upscale scuba divers have better places to go, so it's still one of the most peaceful, pleasant, picturesque, and historic areas to visit in the South Pacific.

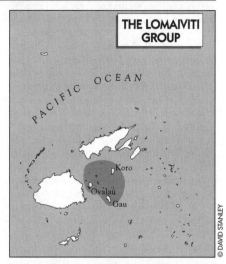

THE LOMAIVITI GROUP

© DAVID STANLEY

LEVUKA

The town of Levuka on Ovalau's east side was Fiji's capital until the shift to Suva in 1882. Founded as a whaling settlement in 1830, Levuka became the main center for European traders in Fiji, and a British consul was appointed in 1857. The cotton boom of the 1860s brought new settlers, and Levuka quickly grew into a boisterous town, with more than 50 hotels and taverns along Beach Street. Escaped convicts and debtors fleeing creditors in Australia swelled the throng, until it was said that a ship could find the reef passage into Levuka by following the empty gin bottles floating out on the tide. The honest traders felt the need for a stable government, so in 1871 Levuka became the capital of Cakobau's Kingdom of Fiji. The disorders continued, with extremist elements forming a "Ku Klux Klan," defiant of any form of Fijian authority.

On October 10, 1874, a semblance of decorum came as Fiji was annexed by Great Britain, and a municipal council was formed in 1877. British rule soon put a damper on the wild side of the blackbirding. Ovalau's central location seemed ideal for trade, and sailing boats from Lau or Vanua Levu could easily enter the port on the southeast trade winds. Yet the lush green hills that rise behind the town were to be its downfall,

LOMAIVITI GROUP HIGHLIGHTS

Levuka Community Center: exhibits, books, tours (p. 263)
Beach Street, Levuka: most picturesque street in Fiji (p. 263)
The Peak, Ovalau: picturesque hill, challenging hike (p. 263)
Leleuvia Island: beach, snorkeling, diving, small resort (p. 271)
Wakaya Island: exclusive resort, diving (p. 274)

as colonial planners saw that there was no room for the expansion of their capital, and in August 1882, Gov. Sir Arthur Gordon moved his staff to Suva. Hurricanes in 1888 and 1895 destroyed much of early Levuka, with the north end of town around the present Anglican church almost flattened, and many of Levuka's devastated buildings were not replaced.

Levuka remained the collection center for the Fiji copra trade right up until 1957, and the town seemed doomed when that industry, too, moved to a new mill in Suva. But with the

THE LOMAIVITI GROUP

establishment of a fishing industry in 1964, Levuka revived, and today it is a minor educational center, the headquarters of Lomaiviti Province, and a low-key tourist center. Thanks to the tuna cannery, there's a public electricity supply.

It's rather shocking that Levuka still hasn't been approved by UNESCO as a World Heritage Site, because Levuka is to Fiji what Lahaina is to Hawaii, a slice of living history. Each year, another century-old building is lost due to the lack of an internationally sanctioned conservation program. In 2003, the historic Mavida Guesthouse burned to the ground, followed in February 2004 by the supermarket, bank, and Air Fiji office on Beach Street. It doesn't take much imagination to see how the rest of Levuka's old wooden buildings are similarly threatened.

Yet the false-fronted buildings and covered sidewalks that survive along Beach Street still give this somnolent town of 4,000 mostly Fijian or part-Fijian inhabitants a 19th-century, Wild West feel. From the waterfront, let your eyes follow the horizon from left to right to view the islands of Makogai, Koro, Wakaya, Nairai, Batiki, and Gau respectively. Levuka is a perfect base for excursions into the mountains, along the winding coast, or out to the barrier reef a kilometer offshore.

It's customary to say "Good morning," *"Bula,"* or simply "Hello" to people you meet while strolling around Levuka, especially on the backstreets, and the locals have been rather put off by tourists who failed to do so. This is one of the little adverse effects of tourism, and a very unnecessary one at that.

SIGHTS

Levuka

Near Levuka Wharf is the old Morris Hedstrom general store, erected by Percy Morris and Maynard Hedstrom in 1880s, great-granddaddy of

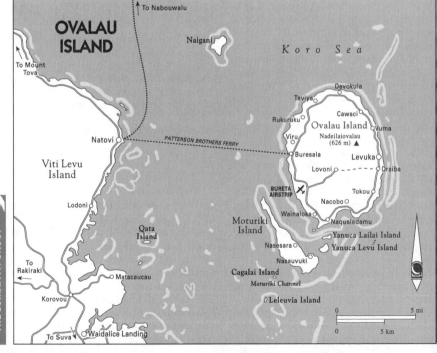

today's Pacific-wide Morris Hedstrom chain. The store closed when the lease expired in 1979, and the building was turned over to the National Trust for Fiji. In 1981, the facility reopened as the **Levuka Community Center** (tel. 344-0356; weekdays 0800–1630, Sat. 0800–1300) with a museum and library, where cannibal forks vie with war clubs and clay pots for your attention. The many old photos of the town in the museum are fascinating, and a few relics of the mystery ship *Joyita* are on display. The Community Center receives no outside funding, and your F$2 admission fee helps keep this place going. Right next door, Ovalau Watersports can arrange a number of tours, including a historical walking tour and village visits.

Stroll north on **Beach Street** along Levuka's sleepy waterfront past a long row of wooden storefronts that haven't changed much in a century. The sea wall opposite was constructed by the Royal Engineers in 1874. Just beyond the wall is the **Church of the Sacred Heart,** erected by French Marist priests who arrived in 1858. The church's square clock tower was added in 1898 to commemorate the first priest, Father Breheret. The green neon light on the stone tower lines up with another green light farther up the hill to guide mariners into port. The tower's French clock strikes the hour twice, with a minute interval in between. Go through the gate behind the church to the formidable **Marist Convent School** (1892), originally a girls' school operated by the sisters and still a primary school.

Totogo Lane leads north from the convent to a small bridge over Totogo Creek and the **Ovalau Club** (1904), adjoining the old **Town Hall** (1898), also known as Queen Victoria Memorial Hall. Next to the town hall is the gutted shell of the **Masonic Lodge building,** erected in 1913. The Little Polynesia chapter of the Masonic Order was formed here in 1875. In July 2000, the lodge was burned down by a frenzied mob from Lovoni, which had been told by superstitious preachers that it was a center of devil worship.

Follow Garner Jones Road west up the creek to the **Levuka Public School** (1881), the birthplace of Fiji's present public educational system.

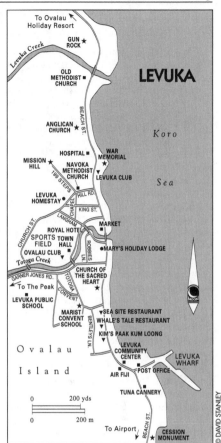

Before World War I, the only Fijians allowed to attend this school were the sons of chiefs. Other Levuka firsts include Fiji's first newspaper (1869), first Masonic Lodge (1875), first bank (1876), and first municipal council (1877).

Continue straight up Garner Jones Road for about 15 minutes, past the lovely colonial-era houses, and you'll eventually reach a locked gate at the entrance to the town's water catchment. A trail on the right just before the gate leads down to a **pool** in the river below the catchment where you can swim. Overhead, you may see swallows that live in a cave just upstream. The path to **The Peak,** the picturesque green hill that's visible from much of Levuka, branches off to the left

THE LOMAIVITI GROUP

THE RIDDLE OF THE JOYITA

One of the strangest episodes in recent Pacific history is indirectly related to Levuka. On November 10, 1955, the crew of the trading ship *Tuvalu* sighted the drifting, half-sunken shape of the 70-ton MV *Joyita,* which had left Apia on October 3, bound for Fakaofo in the Tokelau Islands north of Samoa, carrying seven Europeans and 18 Polynesians. The *Joyita* had been chartered by Tokelau's district officer to take badly needed supplies to the atolls and pick up their copra, which was rotting on the beach. When the vessel was reported overdue, a fruitless aerial search began, which only ended with the chance discovery by the *Tuvalu* some 150 kilometers north of Fiji. There was no sign of the 25 persons aboard, and sacks of flour, rice, and sugar had been removed from the ship.

Also missing were 40 drums of kerosene, seven cases of aluminum strips, and the three life rafts.

The ghost ship was towed to Fiji and beached. Investigators found that the engines had been flooded due to a broken pipe in the saltwater cooling system, the rudder was jammed, and the radio equipment wrecked. The navigation lights and galley stove were switched on. The *Joyita* hadn't sunk, because the holds were lined with eight centimeters of cork. Though several books and countless newspaper and magazine articles have been written about the *Joyita* mystery, no one has learned what really happened, and none of the missing persons has been seen again. Some relics of the *Joyita* can be seen in the Levuka Community Center.

---

between a large steel water tank and the gate at the end of the main trail. It takes about an hour to scale The Peak through the dense bush, and an experienced guide will be required (arranged through the Royal Hotel at F$6/8 single/double). At the end of the challenging hike, you'll have a view of much of the island's east side.

As you come back down the hill, turn left onto Church Street, and follow it around past the sports field (once a Fijian village site) to **Navoka Methodist Church** (1862). From beside this church, 199 concrete steps ascend **Mission Hill** to Delana Methodist High School, which affords fine views. The original mission school formed here by Rev. John Binner in 1852 was the first of its kind in Fiji. A stairway leads down through the high school to the hospital.

North of Levuka

On a low hill farther north along the waterfront is the **European War Memorial,** which recalls British residents of Levuka who died in World War I. Before Fiji was ceded to Britain, the Cakobau government headquarters was situated on this hill. The 1870s cottage on the hilltop across the street from the monument is called **Sailors Home** for the steamship *Sailors Home,* which worked the England-to-China route in the 1850s. The **Holy Redeemer Anglican**

Church (1902) farther north has period stained-glass windows.

Follow the coastal road north from Levuka to a second bridge, where you'll see the **old Methodist church** (1869) on the left. Ratu Seru Cakobau worshiped here, and in the small cemetery behind the church is the grave of the first U.S. consul to Fiji, John Brown Williams (1810–1860). For the story of Williams's activities, see the History and Government section in the Introduction chapter. Levuka Creek here marks the town's northern boundary. In the compound across the bridge and beneath a large *dilo* tree is the tomb of an old king of Levuka. The large house in front of the tree is the residence of the present Tui Levuka, customary chief of this area (ask permission before entering the compound).

Directly above this house is **Gun Rock,** which was used as a target by the captain of the HMS *Havanah* in 1849. The intention, of course, was to demonstrate to Cakobau the efficacy of a ship's cannon, so that he might be more considerate to resident Europeans. In 1874, Commodore Goodenough pumped a few more rounds into the hill to entertain a group of Fijian chiefs, and the scars can still be seen. Long before that, the early Fijians had a fort atop the Rock to defend themselves against the Lovoni hill tribes. Ask permission of the Tui Levuka (the "Roko") or a member of his

THE TUNNELS OF LEVUKA

Early on Monday, July 10, 2000, toward the end of the hostage crisis in Suva, a mob from the mountain village of Lovoni sacked and burned Levuka's historic Masonic Lodge. They had first attempted to storm Queen's Wharf, but when the soldiers on duty there fired warning shots, the mob turned its attention to the lodge. Senior members of the Methodist Church in Levuka had been telling their parishioners for years that the lodge was a center of immorality and devil worship. Rumors also abounded of secret tunnels beneath the building that led to the Royal Hotel, or to Nasova House near the Cession Monument south of town. A few true believers were even convinced that a tunnel existed through the core of the earth to Scotland, the headquarters of the Masonic movement!

Frustrated at the wharf and unable to take over the nearby police station, the Lovoni people broke the lodge's windows and poured in gasoline; the lodge was soon set alight. An hysterical throng of 300 cheered and shouted, "Out with the devil!" as the building burned, and it's alleged that the *talatala* (head priest) of the local Methodist Church observed the entire event in ecstasy from Mission Hill. Some looting took place, and among the ob-

Levuka's Masonic Lodge ablaze

jects taken by the mob were ceremonial swords and a human skull, a Masonic symbol of equality and mortality. What was never found was any trace of a tunnel, nor any of the ghostly British masons thought to use the passageway to attend secret rites.

All of this happened in support of a demand for amnesty by the George Speight terrorists in Fiji's parliament, and the mob was disciplined by an agitator, who made sure that none of Levuka's shops or other historic monuments were looted (only a few windows had been broken). The same group also invaded Levuka's tuna cannery and occupied it for several days. Later, when the army and police regained control of the town, some 120 people were identified as participants in the sacking of the lodge, most of them eventually discharged by the courts. In recent years, membership in the Masonic order has declined steadily around Fiji, and the Levuka lodge often had difficulty achieving the required quorum of eight persons at their monthly meetings. The lodge will not be rebuilt, but the building's shell will probably be left standing as a monument to the folly of mankind. The last sacking of Levuka by the Lovoni folk had been in 1855, and few residents ever dreamed it could happen again.

household to climb Gun Rock for a splendid view of Levuka. If a small boy leads you up and down, it wouldn't be out of place to give him something for his trouble.

Continue north on the road, around a bend and past the ruin of a large concrete building, and you'll reach a cluster of government housing on the site of a cricket field where the Duke of York (later King George V) played in 1878.

There's a beautiful deep pool and waterfall behind **Waitovu** village, about two kilometers north of Levuka. You may swim here, but please don't skinny-dip; this is offensive to the local people and has led to confrontations in the past. Also, avoid arriving on a Sunday.

At Cawaci, a 30-minute walk beyond the Ovalau Holiday Resort, is a small white **mausoleum** (1922) high up on a point, with the tombs of Fiji's first and second Catholic bishops, Bishop Julien Vidal and Bishop Charles Joseph Nicholas. The large coral stone church (1893) of **St. John's College** is nearby. This is the original seat of the Catholic Church in Fiji, and the sons of the Fijian chiefs were educated here from 1894 onwards. The French-style church's walls are three meters thick around the buttresses.

South of Levuka

The **Pacific Fishing Company** tuna cannery (tel. 344-0055, fax 344-0400) is just south of Queen's Wharf. A Japanese cold-storage facility opened here in 1964, followed by the cannery in 1975. After sustaining losses for four years, the Japanese company involved in the joint venture pulled out in 1986, turning the facility over to the government, which now owns the cannery. Major improvements to the wharf, freezer, storage, and other facilities were completed in 1992. The plant is supplied by Taiwanese fishing boats. In 2002, a seven-year agreement was signed with the U.S. seafood company Bumble Bee to supply tuna loins to a cannery in San Diego, California, now Pafco's largest market. Nearly 1,000 residents of Ovalau (85 percent of them women) have jobs directly related to tuna canning, and the government has heavily subsidized the operation.

A little farther along is the **Cession Monument,** where the Deed of Cession, which made Fiji a British colony, was signed by Chief Cakobau in 1874. The traditional *bure* on the other side of the road was used by Prince Charles during his 1970 visit to officiate at Fiji's independence. It's now the venue of provincial council meetings. A nearby European-style bungalow is **Nasova House** (1869), the former Government House or residence of the governor and now the Levuka Town Council building.

One of Fiji's most rewarding hikes begins at Draiba village, a kilometer south of the Cession Monument. A road to the right, around the first bend and just after a small bridge, marks the start of the 4.5-hour hike through enchanting forests and across clear streams to **Lovoni** village. Go straight back on this side road until you see an overgrown metal scrap yard on your right, near the end of the road. Walk through the middle of the scrap yard and around to the right past two huge mango trees. The unmarked Lovoni trail begins at the foot of the hill, just beyond the trees.

The Lovoni trail is no longer used by the locals and requires attentiveness to follow, so consider Epi's Midland Tour if you're not an experienced hiker. Be sure to reach Lovoni before 1500 to be able to catch the last carrier back to Levuka. In 1855, the fierce Lovoni tribe, the Ovalau, burned Levuka, and they continued to threaten the town right up until 1871, when they were finally captured during a truce and sold to European

The provincial council meeting place at Levuka is built to resemble a traditional Fijian chief's *bure*.

planters as laborers. In 1875, the British government allowed the survivors to return to their valley, where their descendants live today. In July 2000, a Lovoni mob again ran amok through Levuka during the George Speight coup attempt.

If you forgo this hike and continue on the main road, you'll soon come to the old **Town Cemetery,** a little south of Draiba. Many of the graves here date back to the early colonial period. A few kilometers farther along is the **Devil's Thumb,** a dramatic volcanic plug towering above **Tokou** village, one of the scenic highlights of Fiji. Catholic missionaries set up a printing press at Tokou in 1889 to produce gospel lessons in Fijian, and in the center of the village is a sculpture of a lion made by one of the early priests. It's five kilometers back to Levuka.

Wainaloka village on the southwest side of Ovalau is inhabited by descendants of Solomon Islanders from the Lau Lagoon region who were blackbirded to Fiji more than a century ago.

SPORTS AND RECREATION

Ovalau Watersports (tel. 344-0166, www.owl fiji.com), across the street from the Westpac Bank, is run by Nobi and Andrea Dehm with help from Ned Fisher, all of whom worked as divemasters at Leleuvia Island Resort for many years. They offer diving around Levuka at 0900 daily at F$140/600 for two/10 tanks including gear (minimum of two divers). An open-water certification course is F$480 (taught in English or German). They also take out snorkelers at F$35 pp—just show up at their dive shop around 0845. You'll visit the two sites used by the divers that day. Nobi and Ned also rent bicycles at F$5/10/15 an hour/half day/full day. Andrea can help you arrange any land tours you may require.

Inn's Boutique Fashion Wear (tel. 344-0374 or 344-0059), below Kim's Paak Kum Loong Restaurant, rents bicycles at F$3/10/15 an hour/half day/full day.

At high tide, the river mouth near the Royal Hotel is a popular swimming hole for the local kids (and some tourists). The rest of the day, some locals cool off by just sitting in the water fully dressed.

ACCOMMODATIONS

Levuka

There are a couple of budget places to stay around Levuka (but thankfully, no luxury resorts). **Mary's Holiday Lodge** (tel. 344-0013), formerly known as the Old Capitol Inn, on Beach Street, occupies a large wooden house on the waterfront. The 12 basic fan-cooled rooms with shared bath are F$20/30 single/double, or F$12 pp in a three-bed dorm. A cooked breakfast is included, while dinner (order by 1400) is F$6. A cool breeze blowing in from the east helps keep the mosquitoes away.

For the full Somerset Maugham flavor, stay at the 15-room **Royal Hotel** (tel. 344-0024, fax 344-0174, www.royallevuka.com) on Robbies Lane. Originally built in 1852 and rebuilt in 1913 by Capt. David Robbie after a fire in the 1890s, this is Fiji's oldest hotel, run by the Ashley family since 1927. The platform on the roof is a widow's watch, where wives would watch for the overdue return of their husband's ships. In the lounge, ceiling fans revolve above the rattan sofas and potted plants, and upstairs the 15 fan-cooled rooms with private bath are pleasant, with much-needed mosquito nets provided. Each room in the main building is in a different style, including six singles (F$21), six doubles (F$29), and three triples (F$39). The section between the hotel and Beach Street contains five cottages, of which only the three closer to the ocean have kitchens (all cost F$80 double). The garden section beside the main building includes the Captain Robbie duplex with two air-conditioned apartments (F$90), the Captain Kaad cottage with two air-conditioned rooms (F$58 double), and the Captain Volk house with four budget rooms with shared bath at F$11 pp in shared three-bed rooms. Communal cooking facilities are available in this dorm. Checkout time is 1000, but you can arrange to stay until 1500 by paying another 50 percent of the daily rate (no credit cards accepted). The restaurant serves breakfast at F$4.50–6.50 and dinner (order before 1500) at F$7.50. The service is slow and the food rather bland. The bar, beer garden, snooker tables, dart boards, swimming pool, gym, and videos (at 2000) are strictly

Levuka's Royal Hotel is the oldest operating hotel in Fiji.

for guests only. The anachronistic prices and colonial atmosphere make the Royal about the best value in Fiji.

The more upscale **Levuka Homestay** (John and Marilyn Milesi, tel. 344-0777, www.levuka homestay.com), on Church Street behind the Royal Hotel, has four rooms with bath at F$118/133 single/double, including breakfast and tax. The three lower air-conditioned rooms in this custom-built house, which climbs the hillside on five levels, are preferable to the fourth room tucked away directly below the owners' apartment.

The folks at Ovalau Watersports (tel. 344-0166, www.owlfiji.com) rent the **Levuka Holiday Cottage** in front of Gun Rock, a 15-minute walk north of Levuka. This self-catering bungalow (F$70/420 double a day/week) is ideal for couples who want to melt into the local scene for a while.

Around the Island

The **Ovalau Holiday Resort** (tel. 344-0329) is opposite a rocky beach at Vuma, four kilometers north of Levuka (taxi F$5). The five two-room bungalows with kitchen and fridge are F$35/66/86 single/double/triple. There's also a four-bed dorm, which costs F$12.50 pp. If you plan to use the cooking facilities, make sure your groceries are protected from mice. Given sufficient advance notice, the resort's restaurant does some fine cooking. Their Bula Beach Bar, in a converted whaler's cottage, adjoins the swimming pool, and the snorkeling off their beach is okay. It's a nice place for an afternoon at the beach, even if you prefer to stay in Levuka.

Bobo's Farm (Karin and Bobo Ahtack, tel. 344-0166 or 993-3632), near Rukuruku, provides accommodations for four people in two rooms at F$25 pp, plus F$6/6/10 for breakfast/lunch/dinner (real Fijian food). It's a great place to relax. You can book this homestay through Ovalau Watersports.

FOOD

Coffee in the Garden (tel. 344-0471; Mon.–Sat. 0800–1800), on the waterfront in Patterson Gardens between the Levuka Community Center and the power plant, is the perfect place for a breakfast of tea and muffins, or a coffee anytime.

Kim's Paak Kum Loong Restaurant (tel. 344-0059; Mon.–Sat. 0700–2100, Sun.

1200–1400 and 1800–2100), upstairs in a building near Court's Furniture Store, is Levuka's most popular restaurant. A full breakfast is F$8. Lunch from the glass warmers near the door is F$3.50, while the dinner menu includes Chinese dishes for F$5–10 (meals ordered from the menu are individually prepared). On the dinner menu are several Fijian dishes (F$7–9) and six vegetarian choices for less than F$5. Sundays from 1800, there's a buffet (F$13.50), which includes salad and ice cream. Beer is available. If you can get a table, dine on their breezy front terrace with a view of the waterfront.

The **Whale's Tale Restaurant** (Liza Ditrich, tel. 344-0235; Mon.–Sat. 1130–1500 and 1700–2100) on Beach Street is a favorite for its real home cooking at medium prices. Buttered pasta for lunch costs F$8.80, and the three-course dinner special, with a choice from among three main plates, is F$16.90. They're licensed, so you can get a beer with your meal, and their specially percolated coffee (F$2.75) is the best in town. They also sell bags of pounded kava (F$1).

The **Sea Site Restaurant** (tel. 344-0553), a bit north of Whale's Tale, is basic, but decent for ice cream.

Emily Cafe (tel. 344-0382), between the Sea Site and the Church of the Sacred Heart, is a good place for coffee and cakes during the day. Daily from 1800–2100, the locale becomes **Ovalau Pizza,** with pizzas from F$6–16.

ENTERTAINMENT

Despite the Members Only sign, you're welcome to enter the **Ovalau Club** (tel. 344-0507; Mon.–Thurs. 1600–2230, Fri. 1400–midnight, Sat. 1000–midnight, Sun. 1000–2100), just across Totoga Creek from the police station, said to be the oldest membership club in the South Pacific. You'll meet genuine South Seas characters here, and the place is brimming with atmosphere. The original billiard table is still in use. Ask the bartender to show you the framed letter from Count Felix von Luckner, the World War I German sea wolf. Von Luckner left the letter and some money at the unoccupied residence of a trader on Katafaga Island in the Lau Group, from which he took some provisions. In the letter, Count von Luckner identifies himself as Max Pemberton, an English writer on a sporting cruise through the Pacific.

The **Levuka Club** (tel. 344-0272) on Beach Street is a good place for sunsets, especially from the picnic tables in their nice backyard beside the water.

INFORMATION AND SERVICES

Metuisela Tabaki at the Levuka Community Center (tel. 344-0356) may have information on the offshore island resorts and various land tours around Ovalau. You can borrow up to three books from the Community Center library for a F$2.50 fee (plus a refundable F$10 deposit).

Liza at the Whale's Tale Restaurant (tel. 344-0235) will be happy to give you her frank opinion of the offshore resorts—invaluable when planning a trip. Andrea at Ovalau Watersports is also very helpful.

The Westpac Bank (with an ATM) and Colonial National Bank on Beach Street change traveler's checks.

Ovalau Watersports provides Internet access at F$.20 a minute (F$1 minimum). The Royal Hotel also charges F$.20 a minute for Internet access.

Public toilets are available across the street from the Colonial National Bank and behind the post office. Ovalau Watersports does laundry at F$10 a load, while the Royal Hotel charges F$7 a bag.

Levuka's new sub-divisional hospital (tel. 344-0088) is on the north side of town. In 2000, F$3.6 million were spent rebuilding this facility.

TRANSPORTATION

Air Fiji (tel. 344-0139) has two flights a day between Bureta Airport and Suva (F$52). The minibus from Levuka to the airstrip is F$4 pp. A taxi to the airport will run F$20.

Inquire at **Patterson Brothers Shipping** (tel. 344-0125), beside the market on Beach Street, about the direct ferry from Ovalau to Nabouwalu, Vanua Levu, via Natovi. The connecting bus departs Levuka Monday–Saturday at about 0500. At Nabouwalu, there's an onward bus to Labasa, but bookings must be made in advance (F$55 straight through).

The bus/ferry/bus service between Suva and Levuka was discussed previously under Transportation in the Suva chapter. It should take just less than five hours right through, and costing F$24. The Patterson Brothers combination involves an express bus from Levuka to Buresala, departing daily except Sunday at 0500, a 45-minute ferry ride from Buresala to Natovi, then the same bus on to Suva (change at Korovou for Lautoka). Bicycles are carried free on the ferry. Advance bookings are required on the Patterson Brothers bus/ferry/bus service. In the opposite direction, the bus to Natovi leaves Suva at 1400, and the ferry is often late. Thus it's a good idea to fly from Suva to Levuka, returning to Suva by bus.

Metuisela Tabaki at the Levuka Community Center (tel. 344-0356) sells tickets for the 50-passenger boat *Viro* from Levuka to Suva (F$16). The connecting carrier to the landing leaves Levuka at 0800 on Tuesday, Thursday, Friday, and Saturday. Also ask about the "Bureta boat," whose carrier picks up passengers in front of the Community Center at 0730 Monday, Wednesday, Friday, and Saturday.

Both taxis and carriers park across the street from the Church of the Sacred Heart in Levuka. Due to steep hills on the northwest side of Ovalau, there isn't a bus right around the island. Carriers leave Levuka for Taviya (F$1.50) or Rukuruku (F$2) villages Monday–Saturday at 0730, 1130, and 1700 along a beautiful, hilly road. During the school holidays, only the 1200 trip may operate. Occasional carriers to Bureta (F$1.50), Lovoni (F$2), and Viru (F$2) park across the street from Kim's Paak Kum Loong Restaurant. To Lovoni, they leave Levuka at 0630, 1100, and 1700, Saturday at 1100 only. There's no service on Sunday.

A truck direct to Rukuruku leaves Levuka at 1200 on Tuesday, Thursday, and Saturday, and it's possible to do a round-trip for F$4, as the carrier returns immediately to Levuka. Monday–Saturday, you can have a day at the beach at Rukuruku by taking the 0730 carrier to Taviya,

then walking the remaining kilometer to Rukuruku (from the top of the hill, turn right down the side road to the beach). A vanilla plantation and beautiful verdant mountains cradle Rukuruku on the island side. Return to Levuka on the 1500 carrier from Taviya (check all this with the driver).

Tours

Epi's Midland Tour (tel. 923-6011) is a guided hike to Lovoni that departs Levuka Monday–Saturday at about 1000 (F$30 pp including lunch). You hike over and return by truck (or you can just go both ways by truck if you don't wish to walk). The route is steep, and rugged footwear is essential. At Lovoni, you may go for a swim in the river or ask to meet the village chief. Epi is an enthusiastic guy very knowledgeable about forest plants, and there have been very good reports about his tour. His reservations book is at Ovalau Watersports. This tour is recommended.

Ovalau Watersports (tel. 344-0146; weekdays 0800–1600, Sat. 0800–1300, www.owl fiji.com), beside the Levuka Community Center, arranges a variety of tours. The 1.5-hour historical town walking tour with Henry Sahai (tel. 344-0096), who has lived here since 1919, is good value at F$8 pp (at 0900 and 1400 daily). He's still very fit and quite a character (if there's only one of you, no problem). The "tea and talanoa" program with Duncan Crichton (tel. 344-0481) or Bubu Kara allows you to meet local residents in their own homes for tea and conversation (F$15 pp). Ovalau Watersports also organizes village visits at F$30 pp including a *lovo* lunch (minimum of five). You can even stay in a village at F$25 pp including breakfast and participate in activities like fishing, trolling, canoeing, rafting, and snorkeling at additional cost.

If you wish to organize your own tour, it costs F$85 for the vehicle to hire a taxi or 15-person carrier right around the island. (A taxi tour to Cawaci with stops along the way should cost F$20 for a four-passenger car.)

Islands off Ovalau

Caqalai Island

Caqalai (THANG-ga-lai) is owned by the Methodist Church of Fiji, which operates a small backpacker resort (tel. 343-0366) on this palm-fringed isle. The 12 simple *bure* are F$40 pp, the three-bed dorm F$30 pp, and camping space F$25 pp, three meals included. A communal fridge is provided. You must take your own alcohol, as none is sold on the island. It's primitive but adequate, and the island and people are great. Dress up for Sunday service in the village church, and enjoy the *lovo* that afternoon. There's good snorkeling all around the island, and you can wade to Snake Island, where banded sea snakes congregate. With nearby Leleuvia Island Resort showing signs of age, Caqalai has increased in popularity. Information is available at the Royal Hotel (boat from Ovalau/Viti Levu F$20/25 pp each way). The Royal Hotel also arranges day trips to Caqalai Monday–Saturday at 1000 (F$50 pp, minimum of two). Those already staying on Caqalai can make shopping trips to Levuka at a reduced rate.

A California reader sent us this:

Caqalai is not for every tourist. It's very small, taking about 10 minutes to walk around, and has simple unhygienic facilities. The one outhouse-style toilet must be flushed with buckets of seawater. Bathing is accomplished in a small shed with brackish water hand-pumped into buckets. Electricity is generated only during dinner hours, if the generator works (it did briefly on only one of my three nights there). On the positive side, the people are wonderfully friendly hosts, with music and kava in the evenings, but there is little to do. The snorkeling is fairly good in the vicinity (bring your own gear). I think Caqalai might appeal to people who have not spent much time on islands, who would enjoy a rough Gilligan's Island experience.

Leleuvia Island

Leleuvia is a lovely isolated 17-hectare reef island with nothing but coconut trees, fine sandy beaches, and a ramshackle assortment of tourist huts scattered around. The small backpacker resort (tel. 330-1584, www.owlfiji.com/leleuvia.htm), originally built in the 1980s, is now run by Epenisa Cakobau, a member of the indigenous Fijian nobility from Bau Island. Unfortunately, the resort has gone downhill in recent years, but the island's attractions—the beach, snorkeling, and diving—are as good as ever and still worth it.

Accommodations, including three basic meals, run F$30 pp in the dorm, F$35 pp in a thatched hut, F$42 pp in a wooden bungalow, or F$24 pp if you camp. Water is in short supply on Leleuvia, and bathing is with a bucket of brackish water. You should watch your gear here.

A few activities are laid on, such as reef trips by boat and scuba diving, and on Sunday they'll even take you to church! For a nominal amount, they'll drop you off on one-tree "Honeymoon Island." Leleuvia's diving concession, **Nautilus Dive,** offers scuba diving at F$75/130 for one/two tanks. The resident instructor—a German named Thomas—has taught diving to quite a few guests. This isn't surprising, because at F$390, Nautilus' PADI open-water certification course is one of the least expensive in Fiji (this price only applies if several people are taking lessons at the same time). Many backpackers learn to dive at Leleuvia before going to Taveuni, where such courses are F$250 more expensive. The snorkeling here is also excellent, though the sea is sometimes cold.

Getting there from Levuka costs F$25 pp each way (two-person minimum) from Levuka. Book through Ovalau Watersports. To arrange a transfer from Suva (F$40 pp), call the island direct for instructions. The resort may arrange your taxi from Suva to Waidalice Landing between Nausori and Korovou, where you'll transfer to the Leleuvia boat.

Moturiki Island

In 2002, a 2,600-year-old female skeleton was discovered on the southeast coast of Moturiki Island. The burial style and fragments of Lapita pottery found nearby suggest a connection with Santa Cruz in the Solomon Islands dating back as far as 3,170 years.

Small outboards to Moturiki Island depart Naqueledamu Landing on Ovalau most afternoons. The finest beaches are on the east side of Moturiki. Camping is officially discouraged, but possible.

Naigani Island

Naigani, 11 kilometers off Viti Levu, is a lush tropical island near Ovalau at the west end of the Lomaiviti Group. It's just the right size for exploring on foot, with pristine beaches and only one Fijian village in the southwest corner.

Naigani Island Resort (tel. 330-0925 or 331-2069, www.naigani.com) offers 12 comfortable two-bedroom fan-cooled villas at F$320 for up to five people. Three of the villas have double rooms attached, which go for F$185 double by themselves. The meal plans are F$45/65 pp for two/three meals (no cooking facilities). Children under 13 are charged half price for meals and transfers. There's a swimming pool with water slide. Some non-motorized water sports are free, but fishing

trips are charged extra. Scuba diving to sites like Nursery and Swim Through costs F$95/110 for one/two tanks, plus F$20 for gear. At high tide, when the sea is calm, some of Fiji's best snorkeling is here. The friendly staff organizes many activities for families with children. The daily minibus/launch connection from Suva at 1030 is F$70 pp round-trip. From Levuka, call them up and arrange to be collected by the speedboat at Taviya village on the northwest side of Ovalau (accessible by carrier) at F$35 pp round-trip.

Yanuca Lailai Island

It was on tiny Yanuca Lailai Island, just off the south end of Ovalau, that the first 463 indentured Indian laborers to arrive in Fiji landed from the ship *Leonidas* on May 14, 1879. To avoid the introduction of cholera or smallpox into Fiji, the immigrants spent two months in quarantine on Yanuca Lailai. Later, Nukulau Island off Suva became Fiji's main quarantine station.

It's possible to stay on Yanuca Lailai at **Lost Island Resort.** *Bure* accommodations are F$30 pp, camping F$15 pp. Meals are extra. Current information should be available from Mr. Tavaki (tel. 344-0356) at the Levuka Community Center. Expect to pay F$15 pp each way for the boat over. A day trip from Levuka will be F$30 pp (1000–1600).

Other Islands of the Lomaiviti Group

Batiki Island

Batiki has a large interior lagoon of brackish water flanked by mudflats. A broad barrier reef surrounds Batiki. Four Fijian villages are on Batiki, and you can walk around the island in four hours. Waisea Veremaibau of Yavu village, on the north side of the island, has accommodated guests in past. Fine baskets are made on Batiki. Due to hazardous reefs, there's no safe anchorage for ships.

Gau Island

Gau is the fifth-largest island in Fiji, with 16 villages and 13 settlements. There's a barrier reef on the west coast, but only a fringing reef on the

east. A hot-spring swimming pool is close to the Public Works Department depot at **Waikama.** From Waikama, hike along the beach and over the hills to **Somosomo** village. If you lose the way, look for the creek at the head of the bay, and work your way up it until you encounter the trail. There's a bathing pool in Somosomo with emerald-green water.

A road runs from Somosomo to **Sawaieke** village, where the Takalaigau, high chief of Gau, resides. The remnants of one of the only surviving pagan temples *(bure kalou)* in Fiji is beside the road at the junction in Sawaieke. The high stone mound is still impressive.

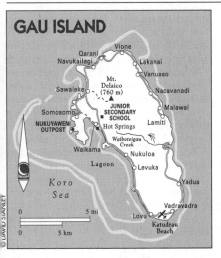

GAU ISLAND

Vione
Qarani
Navukailagi
Lekanai
Vanuaso
Mt.
Delaico
(760 m)
Sawaieke
Nacavanadi
JUNIOR
SECONDARY
SCHOOL
Malawai
Somosomo
NUKUYAWENI
OUTPOST
Hot Springs
Lamiti
Waiboteigau
Creek
Waikama
Nukuloa
Lagoon
Levuka
Koro
Sea
Yadua
Vadravadra
Lovu
Katudrau
Beach

0   5 mi
0   5 km

© DAVID STANLEY

It's possible to climb **Delaico** (760 m), highest on the island, from Sawaieke in three or four hours. The first hour is the hardest. From the summit is a sweeping view. The Fiji petrel, a rare seabird of the albatross family, lays its eggs underground on Gau's jungle-clad peaks. Only two specimens have ever been taken: one by the survey ship *Herald* in 1855, and a second by local writer Dick Watling in 1984.

The co-op and government station (hospital, post office, etc.) are at **Qarani** at the north end of Gau. Two ships a week arrive here from Suva on an irregular schedule, but there is no wharf, so they anchor offshore. The wharf at **Waikama** is used only for government boats.

There are a number of waterfalls on the east coast, the most impressive are behind **Lekanai** and up Waiboteigau Creek, both an hour's walk off the main road. The "weather stone" is on the beach, a five-minute walk south of **Yadua** village. Bad weather is certain if you step on it or hit it with another stone.

No guesthouses are on Gau. The airstrip is on Katudrau Beach at the south end of Gau. The three weekly flights to/from Suva on Air Fiji are F$64 each way.

A designer resort called the **Nukuyaweni Outpost** (Kevin Wunrow, tel. 344-0880, www.bay ofangels.com) is slowly being built on a point a couple of kilometers southwest of Somosomo. Conceived as a sort of artists' hideaway, it will have four upscale cottages, each with an outdoor bathing grotto. Aside from the swimming pool, guests will be able to enjoy the great snorkeling off the 500-meter beach. There's extraordinary diving in Nigali Passage, just 15 minutes away by boat (large schools of big fish and manta rays).

Koro Island

Koro is an eight-by-16-kilometer island shaped like a shark's tooth. A ridge traverses the island from northeast to southwest, reaching 561 meters near the center. High jungle-clad hillsides drop sharply to the coast. The top beach is along the south coast, between Mundu and the lighthouse at Muanivanua Point. Among Koro's 14 large Fijian villages is **Nasau,** the government center, with post office, hospital, and schools.

The road to **Vatulele** village on the north coast climbs from Nasau to the high plateau at the center of the island. The coconut trees and mangoes of the coast are replaced by great tree ferns and thick rainforest.

The track south between Nacamaki and Tua Tua runs along a golden palm-fringed beach. There's a cooperative store at **Nagaidamu** where you can buy *yaqona* and supplies. Koro kava is Fiji's finest. A 30-minute hike up a steep trail from the co-op brings you to a waterfall and an idyllic swimming hole. Keep left if you're on your own (taking a guide would be preferable).

The **Dere Bay Resort** (tel. 330-2631, fax 331-2306, www.derebayresort.com), on a long white beach at the northwestern tip of Koro, opened in October 2000. The three spacious bungalows are F$200 pp including meals (children under 16 half price). There's also a three-bedroom house which rents at the same rate. The *Captain Dan* takes divers out from Dere Bay's dive shop. Sea kayaks are also available. Transfers from the airport/harbor are F$30/20 pp each way.

Koro has an unusual inclined **airstrip** on the east side of the island near Namacu village. You land uphill, take off downhill. Air Fiji can bring you here from Suva once a week (F$92), and several carriers meet the flight.

The weekly **Consort Shipping Line** ferry,

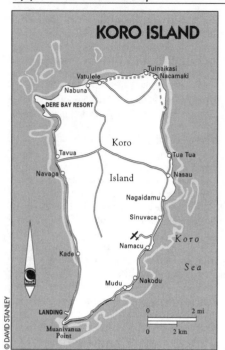

KORO ISLAND

Vatulele
Tuinaikasi
Nacamaki
Nabuna
● DERE BAY RESORT

Koro

Tavua
Navaga
Tua Tua
Island
Nasau

Nagaidamu

Sinuvaca

Koro

Namacu

Kade
Sea

Mudu
Nakodu

LANDING

Muanivanua
Point

0   2 mi
0   2 km

© DAVID STANLEY

Spirit of Fiji Islands, plies between Suva and Savusavu/Taveuni and ties up to the wharf near Muanivanua Point. The ship calls northbound in the middle of the night on Wednesdays and Sundays; the southbound trips stop at Koro late Monday and Thursday nights. The fare to/from Suva is F$35 deck one-way.

Makogai Island

Makogai shares a figure-eight-shaped barrier reef with neighboring Wakaya. The anchorage is in Dalice Bay on the northwest side of the island. From 1911 to 1969, this was a leper colony staffed by Catholic nuns, and many of the old hospital buildings still stand. Over the years, some 4,500 patients were sheltered here, including many from various other Pacific island groups.

Among the 1,241 souls interred in the patients' cemetery on the hill is Mother Marie Agnes, the "kindly tyrant" who ran the facility for 34 years. Both the British and French governments honored her with their highest decorations, and upon re-

tiring at the age of 80, she commented that "the next medal will be given in heaven." Also buried here is Maria Filomena, a Fijian sister who had worked at the colony from its inception. After contracting leprosy in 1925, she joined her patients and continued serving them for another 30 years. Only in 1948 was an effective treatment for leprosy introduced, allowing the colony to be phased out over the next two decades.

Today, Makogai is owned by the Department of Agriculture, which runs an experimental sheep farm here, with some 2,000 animals. A new breed intended as a source of mutton and bearing little wool was obtained by crossing British and Caribbean sheep.

Nairai Island

Seven Fijian villages are found on this 336-meter-high island between Koro and Gau. The inhabitants are known for their woven handicrafts. Hazardous reefs stretch out in three directions, and in 1808 the brigantine *Eliza* was wrecked here. Among the survivors was Charles Savage, who served as a mercenary for the chiefs of Bau for five years, until he fell into the clutches of Vanua Levu cannibals.

Wakaya Island

A high cliff on the west coast of Wakaya is known as Chieftain's Leap, for a young chief who threw himself over the edge to avoid capture by his foes. In those days, a hill fort sat at Wakaya's highest point, so that local warriors could scan the horizon for unfriendly cannibals. Chief Cakobau sold Wakaya to Europeans in 1840, and it has since had many owners. In 1862, David Whippy set up Fiji's first sugar mill on Wakaya.

The German raider Count Felix von Luckner was captured on Wakaya during World War I. His ship, the *Seeadler,* had foundered on a reef at Maupihaa in the Society Islands on August 2, 1917. The 105 survivors (prisoners included) camped on Maupihaa, while on August 23, von Luckner and five men set out in an open boat to capture a schooner and continue the war. On September 21, 1917, they found a suitable ship at Wakaya. Their plan was to go aboard pretending to be passengers and capture it, but a

It's unlikely you'll meet another tourist on this deserted beach north of Tua Tua, Koro Island.

British officer and four Indian soldiers happened upon the scene. Not wishing to go against the rules of chivalry and fight in civilian clothes, the count gave himself up and was interned at Auckland as a prisoner of war. He later wrote a book, *The Sea Devil,* about his experiences.

In 1973, Canadian industrialist David Harrison Gilmour bought the island for US$3 million, and in 1990 he and wife Jill opened **The Wakaya Club** (tel. 344-8128, fax 344-8406, www.wakaya.com), with nine spacious cottages starting at F$3,200 double plus tax, all-inclusive (five-night minimum stay). Children under 16 are not accommodated. The service is excellent, the snorkeling superb, and there's scuba diving, a nine-hole golf course, a swimming pool,

and an airstrip for charter flights (F$1,660 round-trip per couple from Nadi). Only game fishing and massage cost extra. As you might expect at these prices (Fiji's highest!), it's all very tasteful and elegant—just ask Pierce Brosnan, Carol Burnett, Russell Crowe, Tom Cruise, Céline Dion, Bill Gates, Nicole Kidman, Michelle Pfeiffer, or Burt Reynolds. It's a sort of country club for the rich and famous, rather than a trendy social scene. This is one of the only places in Fiji where it's possible to swim discretely nude. Profits from the resort are used to fund public health and education throughout Fiji. A third of Wakaya has been subdivided into 100 parcels, which are available as homesites; red deer imported from New Caledonia run wild across the rest.

THE LOMAIVITI GROUP

Vanua Levu

Though only half as big as Viti Levu, 5,587-square-kilometer Vanua Levu (Great Land) has much to offer. The transport is good, scenery varied, and people warm and hospitable. Far fewer visitors reach this part of Fiji than heavily promoted Nadi, the Coral Coast, and the Yasawas. Fijian villages are numerous all the way around the island—here you'll be able to experience real Fijian life, so it's well worth making the effort to visit Fiji's second-largest island.

The drier northwest side of Vanua Levu features sugar cane fields and pine forests, while on the damper southeast side, copra plantations predominate, with a little cocoa around Natewa Bay. Toward the southeast, the scenery is more a bucolic beauty of coconut groves dipping down toward the sea. Majestic bays cut into the island's south side, and one of the world's longest barrier reefs flanks the north coast. There are some superb locations here just waiting to be discovered, both above and below the waterline.

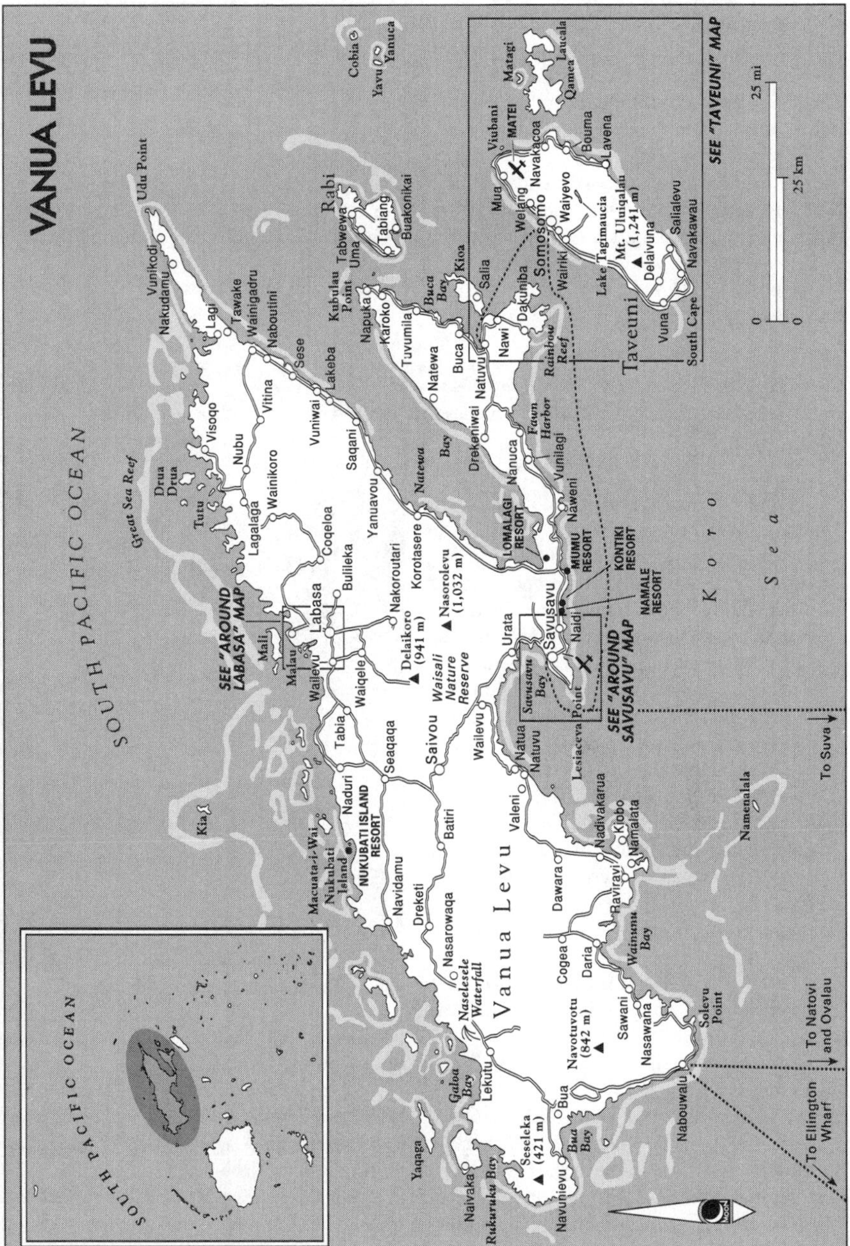

VANUA LEVU

VANUA LEVU

SOUTH PACIFIC OCEAN

SOUTH PACIFIC OCEAN

Koro Sea

SEE "TAVEUNI" MAP

SEE "AROUND LABASA" MAP

SEE "AROUND SAVUSAVU" MAP

Great Sea Reef

Uda Point
Vunikodi
Nakudamu
Lagi
Tawake
Wainigadru
Naboutini
Rabi
Cobia
Yavu
Yanuca
Matagi
Visoqo
Vitina
Sese
Lakeba
Uma
Tabiang
Buakonikai
Vuniwai
Kuhulau Point
Tabwewa
Viubani
MATEI
Navakacoa
Mua
Welang
Nubu
Wainikoro
Coqeloa
Saqani
Napuka
Karoko
Tuvumila
Salia
Kioa
Somosomo
Bouma
Lavena
Waiyevo
Waiqoro
Drua Drua
Turu
Lagalaga
Yanuavou
Natewa
Buca Bay
Buca
Natuvu
Nawi
Dakuniba
Wainikeli
Lake Tagimaucia
Mt. Uluigalau (1,241 m)
Delaivuna
Salialevu
Navakakawu
Nakoroutari
Koroiasere
Natewa Bay
Drekeniwai
Nanuca
Rainbow Reef
Taveuni
Bulileka
Malau
Mali
Labasa
Waiqele
Wailevu
Tabia
Delaikoro (941 m)
Nasorolevu (1,032 m)
Waisali Nature Reserve
Fawn Harbor
Vunilagi
Naweni
LOMALAGI RESORT
Vuna
South Cape
Seaqaqa
Saivou
Wailevu
Urata
Savusavu
Naidi
MUMU RESORT
KONTIKI RESORT
NAMALE RESORT
Naduri
Batiri
Waileu
Natua
Natuvu
Savusavu Bay
Lesiaceva Point
To Suva
NUKUBATI ISLAND RESORT
Macuata-i-Wai
Nukubati Island
Navidamu
Nasarowaqa
Dreketi
Valeni
Nadivakarua
Kobo
Namalata
Kia
Cogea
Daria
Ravirayi
Wainunu Bay
Solevu Point
To Natovi and Ovalau
Naselesele Waterfall
Navotuvotu (842 m)
Dawara
Sawani
Nasawaia
Naboowalu
Namenalala
Gidoa Bay
Lekutu
Bua
Seseleka (421 m)
Bua Bay
Navuhieyu
Naiyaka
Rukuruku Bay
Yaqaga
Navotuvotu (842 m)
Vanua Levu

To Ellington Wharf

25 mi
25 km

© DAVID STANLEY

Indo-Fijians live in the large market town of Labasa and in the surrounding cane-growing area; most of the rest of Vanua Levu is Fijian. Together Vanua Levu, Taveuni, and adjacent islands form Fiji's Northern Division (often called simply "the north"), which is subdivided into three provinces: The west end of Vanua Levu is Bua Province; most of the north side of Vanua Levu is Macuata Province; and the southeast side of Vanua Levu and Taveuni make up Cakaudrove Province. You won't regret touring this area.

VANUA LEVU HIGHLIGHTS

Snake Temple, Labasa: the rock that is growing (p. 281)

Natewa Bay: South Pacific's largest bay, scenic bus ride (p. 285)

Savusavu: yachting paradise, picturesque location (p. 286)

Namenalala Island: nature reserve, snorkeling, diving (p. 293)

Rabi Island: Micronesian people and way of life (p. 295)

Western Vanua Levu

Nabouwalu

The ferry from Viti Levu ties up to a wharf in this friendly little government station (the headquarters of Bua Province), near the southern tip of Vanua Levu. The view from the wharf is picturesque, with Seseleka (421 m) and, in good weather, Yadua Island visible to the northwest. Nabouwalu has a high-technology 24-hour electricity supply system based on windmills and solar panels, installed in early 1998. Most of the 600 residents of this area are indigenous Fijians.

Shlomo Trading (tel. 883-6087) runs a guesthouse behind their restaurant next to the store at the end of the wharf. The three very basic rooms with shared facilities are F$25 pp, breakfast included. Three small stores nearby sell groceries. Fijian women in the small market on the corner of the coastal and wharf roads serve a good lunch of fish in *lolo* (coconut milk) for F$3.

The lovely **Government Resthouse,** near the police station on the hillside above the wharf at Nabouwalu, has two rooms with shared cooking facilities at F$15 pp. Try to make advance reservations with the district officer of Bua, in Nabouwalu (tel. 883-6027; weekdays 0800–1700). Upon arrival, check in at the administrative offices in the new provincial headquarters, a kilometer up the road from the post office. If you already have a booking, you can check in with the caretaker at the Resthouse itself Saturdays from 0800–1200, but

rustic suspension bridge at Bua village

it's not possible to check in on Saturday afternoons, Sundays, or after 1700.

The large Patterson Brothers car ferry sails from Natovi on Viti Levu to Nabouwalu at about 0800 several times a week (four hours, F$38), returning from Nabouwalu to Natovi at 1230. At Natovi, there are immediate bus connections to/from Suva, and the boat continues to Ovalau Island, where it spends the night. Other days, there's a direct Patterson Brothers ferry from

Nabouwalu to Ellington Wharf near Rakiraki at 1030 (F$39), where there are connections to Nananu-i-Ra Island and Lautoka. Getting a car onto the ferry without reservations can be difficult, as more than a dozen logging trucks are often lined up waiting to go. The schedule often varies due to mechanical problems with Patterson's decrepit fleet. Patterson Brothers runs an express bus between Nabouwalu and Labasa for ferry passengers only (must be booked in conjunction with a ferry ticket). This bus takes only four hours to cover the 137 kilometers to Labasa, compared to the six hours required by the four regular buses, which make numerous detours and stops.

East of Nabouwalu

There's a 141-kilometer road along the south coast of Vanua Levu from Nabouwalu to Savusavu, but eastbound-only carriers reach as far as Daria, while westbound buses go as far as Kiobo beyond the former Mount Kasi Gold Mine (Kubulau bus). The gap is covered by occasional carrier trucks. At Cogea, five kilometers north of Daria, are some small hot springs the local people use for bathing.

The **Mount Kasi Gold Mine** near Dawara, in the hills above the west end of Savusavu Bay, 70 kilometers from Savusavu, produced 60,000 ounces of gold between 1932 and 1946. Beginning in 1979, several companies did exploratory work in the area in hope of reviving the mine, and in 1996 it was recommissioned by Pacific Island Gold, which began extracting about 40,000 ounces a year from the mine. In 1998, the mine was forced to close again, and the 170 workers were laid off due to low gold prices on the world market. During the 1970s, bauxite was mined in this area.

The Road to Labasa

The twisting, tiring north coast bus ride from Nabouwalu to Labasa takes you past Fijian villages, rice paddies, and cane fields. The early sandalwood traders put in at **Bua Bay.** At Bua village on Bua Bay is a large suspension bridge. Dry open countryside stretches west of Bua to Seseleka (421 m). Much of this part of the island has been reforested with pine.

Farther east, the road passes a major rice-growing area and runs along the **Dreketi River,** Vanua Levu's largest. A rice mill at Dreketi and citrus project at Batiri are features of this area. The pavement begins at Dreketi but older sections, beyond the junction with the road from Savusavu, are in bad shape. In the Seaqaqa settlement area between Batiri and Labasa, about 60 square kilometers of native land were cleared and planted with sugar cane and pine during the 1970s.

THE CRESTED IGUANA

In 1979, a new species of lizard, the crested iguana (*Brachylophus vitiensis*), was discovered on uninhabited Yaduatabu Island, a tiny 70-hectare dot in Bligh Water off the west end of Vanua Levu. These iguanas are similar to those of the Galapagos Islands, and they may have arrived thousands of years ago on floating rafts of vegetation. The same species was later found on some islands in the Yasawa and Mamanuca groups.

Both sexes are shiny emerald green with white stripes, and the animals turn black when alarmed. The females have longer tails, growing up to 90 centimeters long. Both sexes have a yellow snout. They're not to be confused with the more common banded iguana found elsewhere in Fiji, the male of which is also green with white stripes, while the female is totally green.

Yaduatabu is separated from neighboring Yadua Island by only 200 meters of shallow water, and upon discovery the iguanas were threatened by a large colony of feral goats that was consuming their habitat. Fortunately, the National Trust for Fiji took over management of the island, created an iguana sanctuary with an honorary warden from the Fijian village on Yadua, and eliminated the goats.

About 6,000 lizards are present, basking in the sun in the canopy during the day and coming down to the lower branches at night. It's possible to visit Yaduatabu by taking the ferry to Nabouwalu, then hiring a local boat to Yadua, where guides can be arranged. Prior permission must be obtained from the National Trust for Fiji office in Suva.

VANUA LEVU

Nukubati Island

The luxury-category **Nukubati Island Resort** (tel. 881-3901, fax 881-3914, www.nukubati.com) sits on tiny Nukubati Island, one kilometer off the north shore of Vanua Levu, 40 kilometers west of Labasa. The seven oversized fan-cooled bungalows are F$1,260–1,560 double plus 12.5 percent tax, with a five-night minimum stay. Children are not allowed. Meals (emphasis on seafood, especially lob-ster), drinks, and activities are included, but sportfishing and scuba diving (certified divers only) are extra. Round-trip seaplane transfers from Nadi are F$700 pp. This is the closest resort to the Great Sea Reef, fifth-longest barrier reef in the world. And while other reefs around Fiji have been seriously damaged by coral bleaching, this area is less affected. No swimming pool is provided, but the beach consists of white coral sand.

Labasa and Vicinity

Labasa is a busy Indian market town that services Vanua Levu's major cane-growing area. It's Fiji's fourth-largest town, with 25,000 inhabitants, four banks, and the Northern Division and Macuata Province headquarters. Vanua Levu's only sugar mill is here. Labasa was built on a delta where the shallow Labasa and Oawa rivers enter the sea; maritime transport is limited to small boats. Large ships must anchor off Malau,

11 kilometers north, where Labasa's sugar harvest is loaded. Labasa's lack of an adequate port has hindered development.

Other than providing a good base from which to explore the surrounding countryside, as well as a good choice of places to spend the night, Labasa has little to interest the average tourist. That's its main attraction: Since few visitors come, there's adventure in the air, good

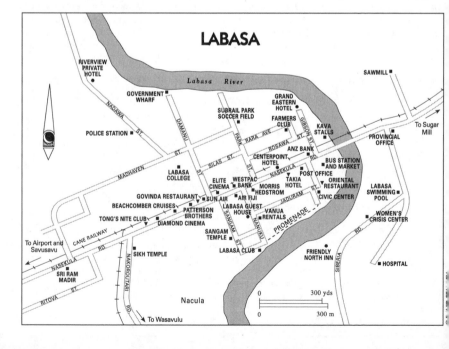

food in the restaurants, and fun places to drink for males (a bit rowdy for females). It's not beautiful, but it is real, and the bus ride that brings you here is great.

An Austrian reader sent us this:

> *After reading your remarks, I headed straight for Labasa upon arrival in Fiji and ended up spending a month there, moving back and forth between Sikhs in town, Indian sugar cane farmers in the surroundings, and Fijian villagers in the interior. It was there where I got introduced into both Indo-Fijian and Fijian culture, where I experienced a genuinely Fijian yaqona ceremony and a meke, got treated to both a Sikh and a Hindu wedding, made lots of friends, and saw people living up to the image of the "friendly north." Even though almost all of Fiji was superb, those weeks remain special.*

SIGHTS

Labasa has an attractive riverside setting, with one long main street lined with shops and restaurants. The park along the riverside near the Labasa Club is quite pleasant.

The **Labasa Sugar Mill,** beside the Oawa River two kilometers east of town, opened in 1894. At the height of the crushing season (May—Dec.), there's usually a long line of trucks, tractors, and trains waiting to unload cane at the mill—a picturesque sight. From the road here, you get a view of **Three Sisters Hill** to the right.

Around Labasa

The **Snake Temple** (Naag Mandir) at Nagigi, 12 kilometers northeast of Labasa, contains a large rock shaped like a cobra that Hindu devotees swear is growing. Frequent buses pass Naag Mandir.

On your way back to Labasa from Nagigi, ask to be dropped at Bulileka Road, just before the sugar mill. Here you can easily pick up a yellow-and-blue bus to the **hanging bridge,** a suspension footbridge at Bulileka, six kilometers east of Labasa. Get off the Bulileka bus at Boca Urata where it turns around. The hanging bridge is 150 meters down the road from that point (ask). Cross the bridge, and continue through the fields a few hundred meters to the paved road, where you can catch another bus back to Labasa. The main reason for coming is to see this picturesque valley, so you may wish to walk part of the way back.

The **Waiqele hot springs,** located 14 kilometers southwest of town, are near a Hindu temple called Shiu Mandir, about four kilometers beyond Labasa airport (green-and-yellow Waiqele bus). Again, the only reason to come is to see a bit of the countryside.

You can get a view of much of Vanua Levu from the telecommunications tower atop **Delaikoro** (941 m), 25 kilometers south of Labasa, farther down the same road past the airport. Only a 4WD vehicle can make it to the top.

Farther afield is the **Floating Island** in a circular lake at Kurukuru, between Wainikoro and Nubu, 44 kilometers northeast of Labasa (accessible on the Dogotuki, Kurukuru, and Lagalaga buses). It's a 45-minute walk from the turnoff at Lagalaga to Kurukuru. North of Labasa, the pavement ends at Coqeloa.

If you're a surfer, ask about hiring a boat out to the **Great Sea Reef** north of Kia Island, 40 kilometers northwest of Labasa.

SPORTS AND RECREATION

The **Municipal Swimming Pool** (tel. 881-6387; daily 0900–1800), just before the hospital, is the place to cool off. Admission is F$1.10. A snack bar adjoins the pool, and the Friendly North Inn's nice open bar is only a short walk away.

ACCOMMODATIONS
Under US$25
The 10-room **Riverview Private Hotel** (tel. 881-1367) is in a quiet two-story concrete building on Namara Street beyond the police station. The four fan-cooled rooms with shared bath are F$25/30 single/double, while another four with private bath are F$30/40. There are also two deluxe air-conditioned rooms with TV,

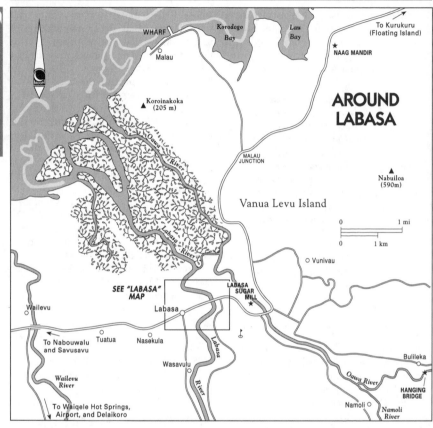

fridge, and hot plate at F$48. The best deal is the breezy five-bed dormitory with a terrace overlooking the river at F$15 pp (one of the nicest dorms in Fiji). Communal cooking facilities are available. There's a very pleasant riverside bar here. The friendly manager Pardip Singh will do his best to make you feel at home. The gate closes at 2200.

The **Labasa Guest House** (tel. 881-2155), on Nanuku Street, has eight fan-cooled rooms at F$24/30 single/double. Some rooms have a toilet and shower, while others don't, but the price of all is the same (the two back rooms are the best). You can put your own padlock on your door. Communal cooking facilities are provided. There's a laundry room in which to do washing by hand.

The doors are locked at 2200, and you'll hear a lot of dog and rooster noise through the night.

The four-story **Takia Hotel** (10 Nasekula Rd.; tel. 881-1655, fax 881-3527), next to the post office, has seven fan-cooled rooms at F$35/45 single/double, 26 air-conditioned rooms at F$66/70, and one family suite at F$90/100, all with private bath. The fan rooms are along the corridor between the disco and the bar, and will only appeal to party animals (free admission to the disco for hotel guests).

A better medium-priced place is the **Friendly North Inn** (tel. 881-1555, fax 881-6429, countdown@connect.com.fj) on Siberia Road opposite the hospital, about a kilometer from the bus station (F$2 by taxi). They have four rooms with fan

VIDI VIDI

Vidi vidi is a game similar to billiards, except that the ball is propelled by a flick of the finger, rather than the tap of a cue. Two or four players position themselves around a rectangular "cram board," with holes in the four corners. The eight or nine brown balls are placed in the center of the board, and the players try to knock them into the holes by using a striker ball. The red "king ball" must go in last, and if a player knocks it in prematurely, all the balls he had previously sunk must come out and be knocked in again. Originally played in India, vidi vidi was brought to Fiji by Indian immigrants.

at F$35/45 single/double, eight air-conditioned rooms with TV and fridge at F$45/55, two with fan and cooking facilities at F$55 single or double, and two more with air-conditioning and cooking facilities at F$65. Opened in 1996, it's just a short walk from the municipal swimming pool, and the Inn's large open-air bar is a very pleasant place for a beer.

US$25–50

The **Centerpoint Hotel** (24 Nasekula Rd.; tel. 881-1057, fax 881-5057, centerp@connect.com.fj) has one fan-cooled room at F$45/55 single/double and 10 air-conditioned rooms at F$55/63. One free breakfast is included with each room (F$6.50 for a second person's breakfast). The upstairs hotel restaurant is not recommended.

The splendid **Grand Eastern Hotel** (tel. 881-1022, fax 881-4011, grest@connect.com.fj) on Gibson Street overlooking the river, just a few minutes' walk from the bus station, reopened in late 1997 after a complete renovation by Hexagon Hotels, and it is now one of Fiji's top hotels. The 10 standard rooms with terraces in the wing facing the river are F$72 single or double, while the larger deluxe rooms facing the swimming pool are F$98. There are also four suites upstairs in the main two-story building, each capable of accommodating a family of up to five at F$123 double plus F$25 per additional person (children under 12 free). All rooms have air-condi-

tioning, fridge, and private bath. Despite modernization, the Grand Eastern's atmospheric dining room and bar retain much of the colonial flavor of the original hotel.

FOOD

The **Oriental Restaurant & Bar** (Mon.–Sat. 1000–1500 and 1830–2200, Sun. 1830–2200), next to the bus station, is surprisingly reasonable with Chinese dishes at F$4–7, grilled dishes at F$5–15, vegetarian dishes at F$2–7, curries at F$3–10, and lobster at F$10–27. Cold bottles of "long-neck" Fiji Bitter are served. Thankfully, there's no smoking inside, only out on the balcony.

Simple Fijian, Chinese, and Indian meals are available for less than F$4 at many places along Nasekula Road, including the **Wun Wah Cafe** (tel. 881-1653), across from the post office, **Joe's Restaurant** (tel. 881-1766; Mon.–Sat. 0730–2130, Sun. 1100–1500 and 1800–2130), and the **Golden Terrace Restaurant** (tel. 881-8378) below the Centerpoint Hotel, a few doors down.

The **Kwong Tung Restaurant** (18 Nasekula Rd.; tel. 881-1980; Mon.–Sat. 0730–1930, Sun. 1100–1500), opposite the Takia Hotel, is hugely popular from breakfast and lunch, with large crowds of locals (no beer served).

The **Govinda Restaurant** (tel. 881-1364; Mon.–Sat. 0730–1800), on Nasekula Road next to Sun Air, offers a choice of four tasty vegetarian thali (plate meals) priced F$2–7 (the F$4 thali includes three curries, dhal, chutney, two roti, and palau rice).

Breakfast is hard to order in Labasa, although several places along the main street will serve buttered cakes and coffee.

ENTERTAINMENT

Elite Cinema (tel. 881-1260) has films in English and Hindi, and there are shows at 1300 and 2000. **Diamond Cinema** (tel. 881-1471) is often used for special events, including local variety shows.

This is a predominantly Indo-Fijian town, so most of the nightlife is male-oriented. The **Labasa Club** (tel. 881-1304) and the **Farmers**

Club (tel. 881-1633) both serve cheap beer in a congenial atmosphere. Couples will feel more comfortable at the Labasa Club than at the Farmers, and there are two large snooker tables inside and a nice terrace out back facing the river (both open daily 1000–2200).

The **Bounty Nightclub** (tel. 881-1655; Wed.–Sat. 2100–0100) at the Takia is accessible via an orange stairway on the side of the building. A much rougher place frequented mostly by indigenous Fijians is **Tong's Nite Club** (tel. 925-4918; Wed.–Sat. 2000–0100), 66 Nasekula Road near Diamond Cinema.

Indian **firewalking** takes place once a year, sometime between June–Oct. at Agnimela Mandir, the Firewalkers Temple at Vunivau, five kilometers northeast of Labasa.

OTHER PRACTICALITIES
Information and Services
There's a **public library** (tel. 881-2617; Mon.–Fri. 0900–1300 and 1400–1700, Sat. 0900–1200) in the Civic Center near Labasa Bus Station.

The **ANZ Bank** is opposite the bus station, and the Westpac Bank is farther west on Nasekula Road. Both provide ATMs outside their offices.

The public fax number at Labasa Post Office is fax 881-3666.

You can check your email at the **Govinda Internet Café** (tel. 881-1364) in the back of the restaurant of the same name on Nasekula Road.

Public toilets are behind the market.

Health
The **Northern District Hospital** (tel. 881-1444), northeast of the river, is open 24 hours a day for emergencies.

Less serious medical problems should be taken to a private doctor, such as Dr. Pardeep Singh (tel. 881-3824; weekdays 0800–1300 and 1400–1600, Sat. 0800–1200), on Reddy Place next to the Civic Center. A private dentist, Dr. Ashwin Kumar Lal (tel. 881-4077), is on Jaduram Street near the Labasa Guest House.

The **Labasa Women's Crisis Center** (tel. 881-4609; weekdays 0830–1430, www.fiji women.com), in Bayly House on Siberia Road near the Municipal Swimming Pool, offers free and confidential counseling for women.

Nasekula Drug Store (tel. 881-1178) is on Nasekula Road opposite the post office.

TRANSPORTATION
By Air
Air Fiji (tel. 881-1188), on Nasekula Road opposite the Westpac Bank, has service five times a day between Labasa and Suva (F$139). **Sun Air** (tel. 881-1454; Mon.–Fri. 0800–1700, Sat. 0800–1200), at Northern Travel on the corner of Nasekula Road and Damanu Street, flies to Nadi (F$175) and Suva (F$147) twice daily, and to Taveuni (F$75) twice a week. Most flights to Nadi are via Suva. Check signs outside their office for special reduced fares.

To get to the airport, 10 kilometers southwest of Labasa, take a taxi (F$8) or the green-and-yellow Waiqele bus. Sun Air has a bus based at the airport that brings arriving passengers into town free of charge, but departing passengers must sometimes find their own way from Labasa to the airport. Air Fiji's bus takes passengers to/from the airport at F$.85 pp (free for Air Fiji passengers).

By Boat
Patterson Brothers Shipping (tel. 881-2444; Mon.–Fri. 0830–1330 and 1430–1630, Sat. 0830–1200) has an office near Sun Air on Nasekula Road where you can book your bus/ferry/bus ticket through to Suva via Nabouwalu and Natovi (10 hours, F$54). This bus leaves Labasa at 0600 several times a week, and passengers arrive in Suva at 1830. There's also a direct bus/boat/bus connection from Labasa to Lautoka (F$60) via Ellington Wharf (near Nananu-i-Ra Island) several times a week, and another service straight through to Levuka.

Beachcomber Cruises (tel. 881-7788; Mon.–Fri. 0800–1700, Sat. 0800–1300), near Patterson Brothers on Nasekula Road, books passage on the car ferry MV *Adi Savusavu.* Their through bus/boat ticket to Suva via Savusavu is F$49/70 economy/first-class (or F$6 less for the boat only).

The bus station at Labasa on Vanua Levu is always buzzing with activity.

Consort Shipping Line (tel. 881-1144, fax 881-4411) has an office behind Sun Air on Damanu Street where you can book passage on the *Spirit of Fiji Islands* from Savusavu to Suva and Taveuni.

The Wun Wah Cafe (tel. 881-1653), across from the post office, books the **Raja Ferry Services** (tel. 881-8587) bus/boat to Taveuni, departing weekdays at 0530 (seven hours, F$20).

To be dropped off on Kia Island on the Great Sea Reef, negotiate with the fishing boats tied up near the Labasa Club. Village boats from Kia and Udu Point sometimes unload at the Government Wharf on the other side of town.

By Road

There are three regular buses a day (at 0630, 1030, and 1400) to Nabouwalu (210 km, F$8), a dusty, tiring six-hour trip. Another five buses a day (at 0700, 0800, 0930, 1230, and 1615) run from Labasa to Savusavu (94 km, three hours, F$6), a very beautiful ride on an excellent paved highway over the Waisali Saddle between the Korotini and Valili mountains and along the palm-studded coast. Take the early bus before clouds obscure the views.

Rental cars are available from **Vanua Rentals** (tel. 881-3512, fax 881-3754), in the Mobil service station on the corner of Nanuku and Jadaram Streets. Their cars start at F$125 a day, insurance included (F$1,500 deductible). **Budget Rent A Car** (tel. 881-1999) is at Niranjans Mazda dealership on Zoing Place up Ivi Street from opposite the Jame Mosque west of town. Obtaining gasoline outside the two main towns is difficult, so tank up.

NATEWA BAY AND UDU POINT

Natewa Bay is the largest bay in the South Pacific, almost dissecting the island of Vanua Levu. It's an area seldom visited by tourists, although a daily bus service between Labasa and Savusavu makes it easily accessible. The sea kayaking is often good along this coast.

A unique feature of Natewa Bay is the "dolphin-calling" trips, during which a Fijian boatman "calls" dolphins, by using traditional magic. It's said to work every time when the bay is flat and calm, and that two pods totaling as many as 100 dolphins can be seen!

At Udu Point, Vanua Levu's northeasternmost tip, a Meridian Wall was built in 1999 just west of Vunikodi village to mark the spot where the 180-degree longitudinal meridian and international date line cut across the island. Both sunset and sunrise can be observed from the wall.

M

VANUA LEVU

FIJI'S FINEST BUS RIDE

The scenic seven-hour bus ride between Labasa and Savusavu via Natewa Bay is like a trip through two distinct countries. For the first few hours, you're among sugar fields or dry barren hills, and the bus passengers around you will be mostly Indo-Fijian. Then you climb through a thickly forested area with few farms, and as the road drops again, extensive coconut plantations begin to appear. You look over your shoulder and notice that most of the bus passengers are now indigenous Fijians. Then comes the spectacular ride down Natewa Bay, climbing over lush headlands or roaring along the beach. Your first glimpse of Savusavu Bay as the bus lumbers slowly over the hill beyond the airport is a thrilling culmination to this fascinating trip.

Accommodations

Don and Seta Chute operate the **Udurara Resort** (no phone) at Udu Point. Until Hurricane Ami devastated the area in January 2003, they had six *bure,* but four were destroyed. Back-

packers now stay in the remaining two at F$50 pp including meals. The Chutes have an electric generator, but one should not expect to find luxuries in this remote location. To get there, you must "charge" (charter) hire a boat from Wainigadru, where the Natewa Bay buses call. This will cost F$50 if it's a 15-horsepower outboard (one-hour trip) or F$80 for a 40-horsepower boat (35-minute trip). If you're lucky, you'll find a "returning boat" (one that is planning to make the trip anyway) from Wainigadru to Udu Point, in which case you will only need to pay F$13 pp. For information on staying at the Udurara Resort, speak to Mr. Pat Chute (tel. 881-6749) who owns Valu City, the shop closest to the river behind the Oriental Restaurant at Labasa.

Transportation

A Vishnu Holdings (tel. 885-0276) bus between Labasa and Savusavu takes the roundabout route via Natewa Bay, departing both ends at 0900 every morning (seven hours, F$11.50). Other Natewa Bay buses from Savusavu may finish their runs at Yanuavou or Wainigadru.

Savusavu and Vicinity

Savusavu is a picturesque little town opposite Nawi Island on Savusavu Bay. The view from here across to the mountains of southwestern Vanua Levu and down the coast toward Nabouwalu is superlatively lovely. In the 1860s, Europeans arrived to establish coconut plantations. They mixed with the Fijians, and even though the copra business went bust in the 1930s, their descendants and the Fijian villagers still supply copra to a coconut-oil mill, eight kilometers west of Savusavu, giving this side of Vanua Levu a pleasant agricultural air. In 2000, the first pearl farms were established on the far side of Nawi Island, and this is an industry that is bound to grow. Savusavu's urban population of 5,000 is almost evenly split between Indo-Fijians and indigenous Fijians, with many part-Fijians here too. One of Fiji's largest white expatriate communities is also present.

Savusavu is Vanua Levu's main port, and cruising yachts often rock at anchor offshore, sheltered from the open waters of Savusavu Bay by Nawi Island. The surrounding mountains and reefs also make Savusavu a well-protected hurricane refuge. The diving possibilities of this area were recognized by Jean-Michel Cousteau in 1990, when he selected Savusavu as the base for his Project Ocean Search. Access to good snorkeling is difficult, however, as the finest beaches are under the control of the top-end resorts and much other shore access is over extremely sharp karst. Although much smaller than Labasa, Savusavu is the administrative center of Cakaudrove Province and has three banks. In recent years, tourism has taken off around Savusavu, with new resorts springing up, though the town is far from spoiled.

SIGHTS

The one main street through Savusavu consists of a motley collection of Indian and Chinese shops, parked taxis, loitering locals, and a clutch of tourists. The **market** in the center of town always bustles but is biggest early Saturday morning. Notice the kava dens behind the market. Nearby, the **Handicraft Center** (tel. 888-3095; weekdays 0730–1700, Sat. 0730–1400), behind the Savusavu Town Council opposite the ANZ Bank, displays numerous grotesque masks with a few good objects mixed in.

The **Copra Shed Marina** is like a small museum, with map displays and historical photos, information boards, fancy boutiques, and many of Savusavu's tourist services. In front of the marina is a stone dated to 1880, which is said to be from Fiji's first copra mill. To the west is Savusavu's second yachting center, the **Waitui Marina,** run by Curly Carswell of Eco Divers. A wonderful scenic viewpoint (and romantic spot to watch a sunset) is on the hill just above and west of the Hot Springs Hotel, above the Waitui Marina.

Visit the small **hot springs** boiling out among fractured coral below and behind the Hot Springs Hotel. Residents use the springs to cook native vegetables; bathing is not possible. These and smaller hot springs along the shore of Savusavu Bay, across the street from Consort Shipping near the main wharf, remind one that the whole area was once a caldera.

For a good circle trip, take a taxi from Savusavu past the airport to **Nukubalavu** village (six km, F$7), at the end of road along the south side of the peninsula. From here you can walk west along the beach to the Cousteau Fiji Islands Resort on **Lesiaceva Point** in about an hour at low tide. Try to avoid cutting through the resort at the end of the hike, as the Cousteau management disapproves (all beaches in Fiji are public up to two meters above the high-tide mark). From Lesiaceva, it's six kilometers by road back to Savusavu.

For some mountain hiking, ask one of the Labasa buses to drop you at the entrance to the **Waisali Nature Reserve,** established by the National Trust for Fiji in 1991, about 40 kilometers

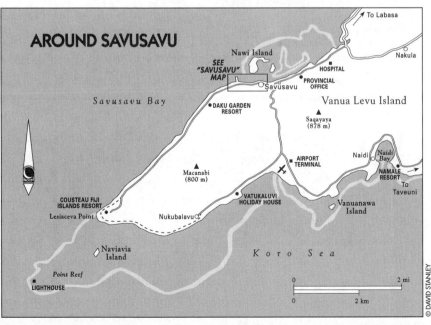

northwest of Savusavu. This 116-hectare reserve protects one of Vanua Levu's last unexploited tropical rainforests, with native species such as the *dakua, yaka,* and *kuasi* well represented. Some of Fiji's few remaining giant kauri trees are here. A nature trail leads to viewpoints offering sweeping views.

SPORTS AND RECREATION

Eco Divers (Curly Carswell, tel. 885-0122 or 885-0345, fax 885-0344, channel 16 or 80, www.ecodivers-tours.com), behind the BP service station opposite the Waitui Marina, offers scuba diving, snorkeling, sailing, village visits, rainforest tours, and guided hiking. They charge F$146 for a two-tank boat dive (plus F$22 for gear), or F$557 including the manual for a PADI open-water certification course. Snorkeling from the boat is F$25 pp for two people (two hours). Eco Divers and the Cousteau Fiji Islands Resort use 21 of the same buoyed dive sites off southern Vanua Levu. Ocean-kayak rental is F$30/40 a day for a single/double kayak, a catamaran F$15 an hour, mountain bikes F$15/25 for four/eight hours.

Savusavu Game Fishing (tel. 885-0195), based at the Hot Springs Hotel, has a fast game-fishing boat for hire at F$400/600 a half/full day for the boat. Two or three people can go for that price. You'll be trawling for trevally, tuna, sailfish, marlin, or wahoo (they recommend "tag and release" for billfish).

ACCOMMODATIONS

Under US$25

The **Copra Shed Marina Apartments** (tel. 885-0457, coprashed@connect.com.fj), above the Captain's Café in the Copra Shed Marina, has two apartments for rent. One is F$45 for up to three persons with the shower downstairs; the other is F$75 accommodating four with private bath. Both have cooking facilities.

Hidden Paradise Guest House (Graham and Elenoa Weatherall, tel. 885-0106), just beyond Morris Hedstrom, has six rather hot wooden rooms at F$15 pp with fan and shared bath (F$20 pp with air-conditioning), including a good self-service breakfast. Cooking and washing facilities are provided, and it's clean and friendly—don't be put off by the plain exterior. The restaurant here is inexpensive and good.

David Manohar Lal's six-room **Budget Holiday House** (tel. 885-0149), also known as "David's Place," is just behind the Hot Springs Hotel. Five rooms with shared bath cost F$25/30 double/triple, and one four-person family room is F$30. The seven-bed dorm is F$15 pp, while camping is F$9/15 single/double. Stay more than a week, and you'll get 10 percent off and free laundry service. The shortage of blankets and sheets is a drawback. All rates include a cooked breakfast, and there's a well-equipped kitchen. David's a delightful character to meet and also a strict Seventh-Day Adventist, so no alcoholic beverages are allowed on the premises. A

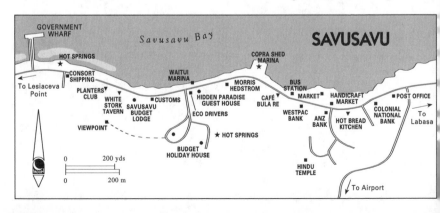

cacophony of dogs, roosters, and the neighbor's kids will bid you good morning. It's often used by people from Eco Divers.

Savusavu Budget Lodge (tel. 885-3127, fax 885-3157), a two-story concrete building on the main street, has eight standard rooms with bath at F$17/30 single/double and five air-conditioned rooms at F$45 single or double, breakfast included. Their restaurant (daily 0800–2300) serves meals in the F$3.50–5 range. Though this place was recently renovated, it shouldn't be your first choice.

US$25–50

The **Hot Springs Hotel** (Lorna Eden, tel. 885-0195, fax 885-0430, hotspringshotel@connect.com.fj), on the hillside overlooking Savusavu Bay, is named for the nearby thermal springs and steam vents. There are 48 rooms, all with balconies offering splendid views. Fan rooms on the second floor are F$80 single or double, while the air-conditioned rooms on the third and fourth floors are F$125. The four ground-floor rooms each have three dorm beds at F$25 pp including breakfast. No beach is nearby, but the swimming pool terrace is pleasant. Many sporting activities can be arranged. This former Travelodge is a convenient, medium-priced choice, and the hotel bar is open daily, including Sunday. Catch the sunset here.

The **Vatukaluvi Holiday House** (tel. 885-0397, coprashed@connect.com.fj), on the south side of the peninsula, one kilometer west of Savusavu airport, accommodates four people at F$100 for the whole breezy house (or a reduced rate for two weeks). Cooking facilities and fridge are provided, and there's good snorkeling off the beach. Ask for Geoff Taylor, vice-commodore of the Savusavu Yacht Club, at the Copra Shed Marina. A taxi to Vatukaluvi will cost F$4 from the airport, F$6 from Savusavu.

US$50–100

Until recently the **Daku Resort** (Robin Irwin, tel. 885-0046, fax 885-0334, www.dakuresort.com), one km west of the ferry landing, was called Beachcomber's Driftwood Village and was run by the Beachcomber Island crowd from Lautoka.

Beachcomber couldn't make a go of it, and in 2004 this "upscale budget" property was re-launched. The four tin-roofed garden *bure* with fan and fridge (but no cooking) on the nicely landscaped grounds just below the pool go for F$95 single or double, while two larger family bungalows above the restaurant rent for F$110. If you want a kitchen, there's a cottage (F$110) and villa (F$135) on the hill. A self-catering, two-bedroom "beach house" next to the entrance is F$150. Included in all rates is tax and a "Planter's Breakfast" served in the large restaurant next to the swimming pool (dinner here is F$15 but lunch is not available). A mediocre beach just across the dusty road has some snorkeling possibilities though the visibility isn't the best (and don't leave valuables unattended). Airport transfers are F$5 pp each way.

US$150 and up

In 1994, oceanographer Jean-Michel Cousteau, son of the famous Jacques Cousteau, purchased a hotel on Lesiaceva Point, six kilometers southwest of Savusavu. The **Jean-Michel Cousteau Fiji Islands Resort** (tel. 885-0188, fax 885-0340, www.fijiresort.com) stylishly re-creates a Fijian village with 25 authentic-looking thatched *bure*. Garden accommodations, airport transfers, and all meals begin at F$875 double, plus 12.5 percent tax. In line with the ecotourism theme, all rooms have fans but no air-conditioning, telephones, or cooking facilities. Bring insect repellent. The restaurant is built like a towering pagan temple, and nonguests wishing to dine there *must* reserve (it's pricey, and the food could be better). Children under 13 eat and sleep free when sharing with their parents, and the resort's Bula Camp (operating from 0900–2100) is designed to help those aged 3–9 learn while having fun. This resort also caters to the romantic-couples market with spa and massage treatments (beginning at F$120), private island picnics (F$88 per couple), and pier dining by candlelight (F$62 for the set-up). Free activities include sailing, kayaking, glass-bottom boat trips, tennis, yoga, water aerobics in the freshwater pool, videos, slide shows, tours and evenings with the on-site marine biologist or cultural host, rainforest trips, and visits to a local Fijian village. In addition, the outstanding on-site dive operation, "L'Aventure Cousteau," offers scuba diving (F$135/230 for one/two tanks plus tax and gear), PADI/TDI scuba instruction (F$905 plus tax for full certification), and underwater-photography courses (F$300 plus tax). Cousteau himself is in residence occasionally, and he joins guests on the morning dive when he's in the mood. There's good snorkeling off their beach (ask about Split Rock), though the resort's large Private Property signs warn nonguests to keep out. A taxi from Savusavu will run F$6.

FOOD

Italian Pizza (tel. 925-9604; daily 1130–2100), below Savusavu Budget Lodge, is run by a Neapolitan named Alberto and his local wife Ana. They serve 14 varieties of real Italian pizza priced F$7–20.

The breakfast buffet (F$3.50, or F$5 including eggs) at the **Seaview Restaurant** (tel. 885-0106; daily 0700–1000), at Hidden Paradise Guest House near the Waitui Marina, is outstanding value. Monday to Saturday from 0900–1600, you can get an excellent curry lunch here for F$3.50.

The **Captain's Café** (tel. 885-0511; open Mon.–Fri. 0830–2030, Sat. 0900–2100, Sun. 1100–2030) at the Copra Shed Marina is a yachtie hangout. Breakfast is F$6–9, pizzas F$7–24, dinner F$10–15. In the evening, the outdoor seating on the wharf is nice, but the food is nothing special.

The trendy **Bula Re Restaurant** (tel. 885-0307; Mon.–Sat. 0900–2100, Sun. 1700–2200), opposite the bus station, is the place to be seen by other tourists. They offer breakfast (F$5–8), crepes (F$6–8.50), lunch specials (F$6–9), ice cream with coffee (less than F$5), Chinese dishes (F$6–10), and a wide range of dinner dishes for less than F$20. The food is "absolutely okay."

The **Country Kitchen** (tel. 885-0829; daily 0600–1800), near the Westpac Bank opposite the bus station, offers large servings of curries, chop suey, and fried rice at F$3.50. **Charans**

Food Center (tel. 885-0448; Mon.–Sat. 0700–1800, Sun. 0700–1600) nearby is more crowded and not as good.

The spacious **Chong Pong Restaurant** (tel. 885-0588), above a supermarket opposite Savusavu Market, serves local chicken, pork, beef, mutton, seafood, and vegetarian meals at F$4–8. You can even order a beer!

The **Mereia Bros. Restaurant** (tel. 885-0375; weekdays 0700–2000, Sat. 0700–1600), opposite the Hot Bread Kitchen east of the ANZ Bank, serves generous Chinese meals at F$4–6.

Savusavu's best Chinese restaurant, however, is the **Wing Yuen Restaurant** (tel. 885-0108), near the Colonial National Bank. Most of their chicken, beef, pork, seafood, fried rice, and chow mein plates are F$6–10. Don't be deceived by the shabby exterior or surly staff: The food is good, and alcohol is available.

If that's not enough, **Fong's Café** (tel. 885-0066; weekdays 0700–1700, Sat. 0700–1400), between the Colonial National Bank and the post office, has chicken, beef, and fish dishes priced F$4–6.

ENTERTAINMENT

Drinkers can repair to the **Planters Club** (tel. 885-0233; Mon.–Thurs. 1000–2200, Fri. and Sat. 1000–2300, Sun. 1000–2000) toward the wharf—this place never runs out of Fiji Bitter. The weekend dances at the club are local events. Despite the Members Only sign, visitors are welcome. It's a vintage colonial club.

The **White Stork Tavern,** next to the Planters Club, is a rough public bar open Monday–Saturday 1130–2100.

The bar at the **Copra Shed Marina** (daily 1100–2200) is rather hidden in the northeast corner of the building—ask. Happy hour is Wednesday and Friday 1730–1830.

The bar at the **Waitui Marina** (tel. 885-0122; daily 1130–2200, until midnight Tues., Thurs., and Sat.) organizes a *lovo* or curry night on Thursdays and a barbecue on Saturdays (both F$8). Book before 1000 at Eco Divers across the street.

The beer on tap at the **Hot Springs Hotel** (tel. 885-0195) is produced in their own microbrewery at the bottom of the hill below the hotel. Savusavu Draft comes in bitter, lager, and ale varieties.

OTHER PRACTICALITIES

Information and Services

A shop in the Copra Shed Marina sells nautical charts.

The ANZ Bank (with an ATM), Colonial National Bank, and Westpac Bank all have branches in Savusavu.

Internet access is available for F$.35 a minute at **Savusavu Real Estate** (tel. 885-0929; Mon.–Fri. 0800–1700, Sat. 0830–1200, savusavurealest@connect.com.fj) in the Copra Shed Marina.

DHL Express Internet (tel. 885-0801; weekdays 0900–1600), at Plantation Real Estate next to Morris Hedstrom, also charges F$.35 a minute and is less crowded.

At the **Bula Re Restaurant** (tel. 885-0307), opposite the bus station, you can use a computer to check email for a mere F$.30 a minute.

Free public toilets are behind the Town Council office opposite the ANZ Bank.

Yachting Facilities

The **Copra Shed Marina** (tel. 885-0457, fax 885-0989, coprashed@connect.com.fj) near the bus station allows visiting yachts to moor alongside at F$10 a day. Anchorage and use of the facilities by the whole crew is F$6 a day. You can have your laundry done for F$7 (wash and dry).

The **Waitui Marina** (tel. 885-0122) offers similar services. In fact, Waitui's owner, Curly Carswell of Eco Divers, will probably come out to meet you in his boat and will guide you to the anchorage, provided he gets wind of your arrival over channels 16 or 80. Curly's a great source of local information, and he's quite a character.

Yachts can clear Fiji customs in Savusavu. Arriving yachts should contact the Copra Shed Marina over VHF 16. The customs office (tel. 885-0727; weekdays 0800–1300 and 1400–1600), where yachties must report after the quarantine check, is next to Savusavu Budget Lodge west of the Waitui Marina. After clearing quarantine and customs controls, yachties can proceed to the Immigration Department, across the street from the Waitui Marina. If you check in after 1630 or on weekends

Savusavu has one of Fiji's favorite yacht anchorages just offshore. Pearl farms have recently been established on the far side of Nawi, the long island behind the boats.

or holidays, there's an additional charge on top of the usual quarantine fee.

Health

The **District Hospital** (tel. 885-0444; open 0830–1600) is two kilometers east of Savusavu on the road to Labasa (taxi F$2).

Dr. Joeli Taoi's **Savusavu Private Health Center** (tel. 885-0721; Mon.–Thurs. 0830–1600, Friday 0830–1400) is between the Colonial National Bank and the post office.

TRANSPORTATION

By Air

Air Fiji (tel. 885-0538), at the Copra Shed Marina, flies into Savusavu twice daily from Suva (F$111) and Taveuni (F$74). **Sun Air** (tel. 885-0141), in the Copra Shed Marina, has flights to Savusavu twice daily from Nadi (F$159) and Taveuni (F$75). The airstrip is beside the main highway, three kilometers east of town. Local buses to Savusavu pass the airport about once an hour, or take a taxi for F$4.

By Boat

Consort Shipping Line Ltd. (tel. 885-0443, fax 885-0442), beside the Planters Club, runs the large car ferry MV *Spirit of Fiji Islands* from Suva to Savusavu (14 hours, F$42/77 deck/cabin). The ferry leaves Savusavu southbound Monday and Thursday at 1900, calling at Koro on the way to Suva. Wednesday at midnight and Sunday at 0900, the "Sofi" leaves Savusavu for Taveuni (F$22 deck). These schedules often change.

Beachcomber Cruises (tel. 885-0266, fax 885-0499), at the Copra Shed Marina, runs the 65-meter car ferry MV *Adi Savusavu* from Savusavu direct to Suva Wednesday, Friday, and Sunday at 1900 (F$43/64 economy/first-class). It leaves Savusavu for Taveuni Wednesday and Friday at 0100 and Sunday at 0600 (F$22/42).

Charans Food Center (tel. 885-8587), next to the Westpac Bank opposite the bus station, sells tickets on the **Raja Ferry Services** bus/boat to Taveuni, departing weekdays at 0830 (F$15).

If you're interested in getting aboard a cruising yacht as unpaid crew, put up a notice advertising yourself at both yacht clubs and ask around.

By Road

Regular buses leave Savusavu for Labasa at 0730, 0930, 1300, 1430, and 1530, Sunday at 0930, 1300, and 1530 only (92 km, three hours, F$6). This ride over the Waisali Saddle is one of the most scenic in Fiji.

Otherwise, there's the seven-hour bus ride from Savusavu to Labasa via Natewa Bay (F$11.50), more than twice as long but even more intriguing. It departs each end at 0900 daily.

The Kubulau bus to Kiobo, west of Savusavu toward Nabouwalu, departs weekdays at 0900 and 1500, Saturday at 1400.

Buses along the Hibiscus Highway from Savusavu to Buca Bay and Napuka leave at 1030 and 1430 daily except Sunday (three hours, F$6.30). Shorter runs to villages like Naweni are more frequent.

Buses leave Savusavu for Lesiaceva Point at 0730, 1200, 1400, and 1600 (F$.70). For more information on buses headed south or east of Savusavu, call Vishnu Holdings at tel. 885-0276.

Numerous taxis congregate at Savusavu market; they're quite affordable for short trips in the vicinity.

Tours

Eco Divers (tel. 885-0122, www.ecodivers-tours.com), opposite the Waitui Marina, offers a variety of day tours, including a village tour (F$25), plantation tour (F$25), and a Waisali Reserve tour (F$40). They only need two participants to run a tour.

Trip 'N Tour Travel (tel. 885-3154, fax 885-0344), in the Copra Shed Marina, also arranges local sightseeing tours at F$25–90 (minimum of two persons) depending on what's offered. Trip 'N Tour also represents Budget Rent a Car with 4WD vehicles starting at F$122 a day, plus F$22 insurance.

Cruises to Koro or the Lau Group on the three-masted schooner *Tui Tai* (discussed in the Getting There section in the Exploring the Islands chapter) can be booked at **Tui Tai Adventure Cruises** (tel. 885-3032, fax 885-3026, www.tuitai.com) in the Copra Shed Marina. They also offer a day cruise around Savusavu Bay Tuesdays from 1000–1600 at F$99 pp including lunch and kayaking on the Nasekawa River.

SeaHawk Charters (tel. 885-0787, seahawk @connect.com.fj) offers a five-hour yacht cruise on Savusavu Bay at F$85 pp including lunch (minimum of two). The two-hour sunset cruise is F$50 pp (two-person minimum). The 16-meter yacht *SeaHawk* can be chartered at reasonable rates. Eco Divers takes SeaHawk bookings.

NAMENALALA ISLAND

Moody's Namena (tel. 881-3764, fax 881-2366, www.moodysnamenafiji.com), on a narrow high island southwest of Savusavu in the Koro Sea, is one of Fiji's top hideaways. Hosts Tom and Joan Moody ran a similar operation in Panama's San Blas Islands for 15 years, until June 1981, when they were attacked by Cuna Indians who shot Tom in the leg and tried to burn the resort. The media reported at the time that the Indians had been scandalized by hotel guests who smoked marijuana and cavorted naked on the beach, but Joan claims it was all part of a ploy to evict foreigners from San Blas to cover up drug-running activities.

In 1984, after a long search for a replacement, the couple leased Namenalala from the Fiji government, which needed a caretaker to protect the uninhabited island from poachers. Their present resort occupies less than 10 percent of Namenalala's 45 hectares, leaving the rest as a nesting ground to great flocks of red-footed boobies, banded rails, and Polynesian starlings. Giant clams proliferate in the surrounding waters within the 24-kilometer **Namena Barrier Reef**, and Nov.– Mar., hawksbill turtles haul themselves up onto the island's golden sands to lay their eggs (Namenalala is the last important nesting site for hawksbills left in Fiji). The corals along the nearby drop-offs are fabulous, and large pelagic fish glide in from the Koro Sea. Sea snakes abound. The Moodys have fought long and hard to protect Namenalala's fragile reefs from live-aboards that sometimes use them for high-impact night diving.

Each of the Moody's six bamboo-and-wood hexagonal-shaped *bure* are perched on clifftops, allowing panoramic views, while still well tucked away in the lush vegetation to ensure maximum privacy. Illuminated by romantic gas lighting, each features a private hardwood terrace with 270-degree views. Alternative energy is used as much as possible to maintain the atmosphere (though a diesel generator used to do the laundry and recharge batteries).

The cost to stay here is F$498/708 single/double plus tax, including all meals (five-night minimum stay). The food is excellent, thanks to Joan's firm hand in the kitchen and Tom's island-grown produce. (One reader found the food too "American" and would have preferred more fresh fish.) The ice water on the tables and in the *bure* is a nice touch, but they don't sell liquor, so bring your own. In the evening, it's very quiet. Namenalala is in a rain shadow, so insects are not a problem.

This resort is perfect for bird-watching, fishing, and snorkeling, and scuba diving is available at F$169 plus tax for two tanks (certification card required). The soft corals at Namenalala are among the finest in the world, and the diversity of species is greater than on the Barrier Reef. If you want a holiday that combines unsullied nature with interesting characters and a certain elegance, you won't go wrong here. The remoteness is reflected in the price of getting there. Pacific Island Seaplanes charges F$2,400 round-trip per couple for transfers from Nadi. Transfers from Savusavu in an 11-meter Searov boat are F$250 pp each way. Moody's closes in March and April every year.

Buca Bay and Rabi

ALONG THE HIBISCUS HIGHWAY

This lovely coastal highway runs 75 kilometers east from Savusavu to Natuvu on Buca Bay, then up the east coast of Vanua Levu to the Catholic mission station of **Napuka** at the end of the peninsula. In 2001, the first 20 kilometers or so east of Savusavu was paved.

Old frame mansions from the heyday of the 19th-century planters and 21st-century homes of newly-arrived foreigners can be spotted among the palms, and offshore you'll see tiny flowerpot islands where the sea has undercut the coral rock. Buca Bay is a recognized "hurricane hole," where ships can find shelter during storms. Former Prime Minister Rabuka hails from **Drekeniwai** village on Natewa Bay.

Buses to Savusavu leave Buca Bay at 0800 and 1600 (75 km, three hours, F$5). The ferry *Raja* leaves Natuvu for Taveuni weekdays at 1100 (F$7). It's a beautiful boat trip, but can be rough if the wind is up.

Accommodations

The most pretentious place around Savusavu is the **Namale Fiji Resort** (Anthony Robbins, tel. 885-0435, fax 885-0400, www.namalefiji.com) on a white-sand beach nine kilometers east of Savusavu. The superb food, great entertainment, and refined atmosphere amid exotic landscapes and refreshing beaches make this one of Fiji's most exclusive resorts. The 13 thatched *bure* begin at F$1,580 single or double, and rise to F$2,180 for the honeymoon *bure* with a private wading pool on its deck (add 12.5 percent tax to these nightly rates). Included are gourmet meals and drinks, airport transfers, and all activities other than scuba diving. Private seminars in a 60-seat conference center are now Namale's stock in trade. It caters only to in-house guests—there's no provision for sightseers who would like to stop in for lunch. Children under 12 are also banned.

The **Koro Sun Resort** (tel. 885-0262, fax 885-0352, www.korosunresort.com) is 14 kilo-

meters east of Savusavu on the Hibiscus Highway. The 13 tasteful hillside and garden bungalows start at F$454/555 single/double, plus 12.5 percent tax. Three of the two-bedroom bungalows are F$566/667, while another with two bathrooms is F$647/748. Included are meals, but not drinks. Set in a well-kept coconut grove, the Koro Sun has many interesting caves, pools, trails, falls, ponds, and lakes nearby to explore. The resort's own "Rainforest Spa" offers massage and body treatments. Scuba diving is available at Koro Sun's private marina (F$190 plus tax for two tanks), including underwater weddings! A dive site known as Dream House (a deep-water pinnacle) is right at Koro Sun's front door. The snorkeling is fine as well, but the nearest swimmable beach is a kilometer away. There are two swimming pools, a waterslide, two tennis courts, sportfishing, sea kayaking, mountain biking and many other activities (nonmotorized sports are included). The nine-hole golf course is pitted with crab holes and gets swampy after rains, but it's picturesque. It's too hilly for golf carts to be used.

Vanua Levu's only real backpacker camp, **Mumu Resort** (Rosie Edris, tel. 885-0416), 17 kilometers east of Savusavu, occupies land on the site of the spiritual home of Radini Mumu, a legendary queen of Fiji. The nine *bure* are F$45 single or double, the four bunkhouse rooms F$40 single or double, and the four-person "dream house" F$130. There's also a six-bed dorm at F$17 pp, and you can camp for F$8 pp. Communal cooking and bathing facilities are available, and Mumu's kitchen serves tasty Fijian and European dishes. Mumu is surrounded by the Koro Sea on three sides, and two small uninhabited islands nearby are easily accessible. Although the scenery is good, the snorkeling is poor; it's a very long swim over a shallow flat before reaching a snorkelable area. There's no hot water, and one must be aware of their dogs. A taxi here from Savusavu should be F$15, a bus about F$1.

Ms. Collin McKenny from Seattle owns and operates the upscale **Lomalagi Resort** (tel. 881-6098, fax 881-6099, www.lomalagi.com) on

Natewa Bay, three kilometers west of Nasinu village. It's three kilometers off the Hibiscus Highway up unpaved Salt Lake Road, about 25 kilometers from Savusavu airport. The six deluxe self-catering villas start at F$800 double including tax, airport transfers, laundry, and meals (children under 12 not admitted, three-night minimum stay). For an additional F$170 per couple per day, all drinks can be added to the package. The villas are well spaced along the hillside above 500 meters of beach, and each has an excellent view. Two artificial waterfalls drop into the S-shaped saltwater swimming pool. Kayaks, mountain bikes, and snorkeling gear are loaned free. Beatle George Harrison is well remembered at Lomalagi for an evening of song he shared with local villagers during his stay. Nonguests are welcome to stop by for drinks, but call ahead to say you're coming if you'd like to order a meal.

Hannibal's Eco-Adventure Resort (tel./fax: 885-3131, www.hannibalsresort.com), at Fawn Harbor 62 kilometers east of Savusavu, has five *bure* at F$600 double plus 12.5 percent tax. Included are all meals (but not drinks), airport transfers, and nonmotorized activities such as kayaking. Sportfishing, scuba diving, and sailing charters are extra. The electricity comes from solar panels, water is recycled into their organic garden, and wastes are composted.

Vanaira Bay

Dolphin Bay Divers Retreat (tel. 888-0531 or 992-0531, www.dolphinbaydivers.com) is on Vanaira Bay at the far east end of Vanua Levu, directly across Somosomo Strait from Taveuni. It's run by a German woman named Viola Koch, who formerly managed Susie's Plantation on Taveuni. The accommodations are in two Fijian *bure* at F$50 single or double and three large safari tents at F$35, plus F$30 pp for all meals. It's an electricity-free hideaway with snorkeling and hiking possibilities. Dive kayaks are for rent at F$10/50 an hour/day. The resident PADI diving instructor, Roland, offers boat dives at F$130/350/550 for two/six/10 tanks including gear. Shore dives are F$50, and Dolphin Bay offers night dives at F$75. Dolphin Bay is the only dive resort right on the famous Rainbow Reef.

Their four-day scuba certification course (taught in English or German) costs F$500 if you're alone or F$480 pp if there are two of you. Boat transfers from the Korean Wharf on Taveuni are F$20 per group each way. The regular supply boat often goes to Taveuni on Friday afternoon, and they may take you for free if they're going anyway, so call ahead. It's also possible to be picked up at Buca Bay (F$25 pp each way) if you're coming from Savusavu.

KIOA ISLAND

The Taveuni ferry passes between Vanua Levu and Kioa, home to some 300 Polynesians from Vaitupu Island, Tuvalu (the former Ellice Islands). Captain Owen of the ship *Packet* obtained Kioa from the Tui Cakau in 1853, and since then it was operated as a coconut plantation. In 1946, it was purchased by the Ellice Islanders, who were facing overpopulation on their home island.

The people live at **Salia** on the southeast side of Kioa. The women make baskets for sale to tourists in Savusavu, while the men go fishing alone in small outrigger canoes. If you visit, try the coconut toddy *(kaleve)* or the more potent fermented toddy *(kamanging)*. There are no facilities for tourists on Kioa.

RABI ISLAND

In 1855, at the request of the Tui Cakau on Taveuni, a Tongan army conquered some Fijian rebels on Rabi. Upon the Tongans' departure a few years later, a local chief sold Rabi to Europeans to cover outstanding debts, and until World War II, the Australian firm Lever Brothers ran a coconut plantation here. In 1940, the British government began searching for an island to purchase as a resettlement area for the Micronesian inhabitants of Ocean Island (Banaba) in the Gilbert Islands (presently part of Kiribati), whose home island was being ravaged by phosphate mining. At first, Wakaya Island in the Lomaiviti Group was considered, but the outbreak of war and the occupation of Ocean Island by the Japanese intervened. Back in Fiji, British officials

THE BANABANS

The people of Rabi Island, between Vanua Levu and Taveuni in northern Fiji, are from Banaba, a tiny, six-square-kilometer raised atoll 450 kilometers southwest of Tarawa in the Micronesian Gilbert Islands. Like Nauru, Banaba was once rich in phosphates, but from 1900 through 1979, the deposits were exploited by British, Australian, and New Zealand interests in what is perhaps the best example of a corporate/colonial rip-off in the history of the Pacific islands.

After the Sydney-based Pacific Islands Company discovered phosphates on Nauru and Banaba in 1899, a company official, Albert Ellis, was sent to Banaba in May 1900 to obtain control of the resource. In due course, "King" Temate and the other chiefs signed an agreement granting Ellis's firm exclusive rights to exploit the phosphate deposits on Banaba for 999 years in exchange for £50 a year. Of course, the guileless Micronesian islanders had no idea what the scheme was all about.

As Ellis rushed to have mining equipment and moorings put in place, a British naval vessel arrived on September 28, 1901, to raise the British flag, joining Banaba to the Gilbert and Ellice Islands Protectorate. The British government reduced the term of the lease to a more realistic 99 years, and the Pacific Phosphate Company was formed in 1902.

Things ran smoothly until 1909, when the islanders refused to lease any additional land to the company, after 15 percent of Banaba had been stripped of both phosphates and food trees. The British government arranged a somewhat better deal in 1913, but in 1916 it changed the protectorate into a colony so the Banabans could not withhold their land again. After World War I, the company was renamed the British Phosphate Commission (BPC), and in 1928 the resident commissioner, Sir Arthur Grimble, signed an order expropriating the rest of the land, against the Banabans' wishes. The islanders continued to receive their tiny royalty right up until World War II.

On December 10, 1941, with a Japanese invasion deemed imminent, the order was given to blow up the mining infrastructure on Banaba, and on February 28, 1942, a French destroyer evacuated company employees from the island. In August, some 500 Japanese troops and 50 laborers landed on Banaba and began erecting fortifications. The six Europeans they captured eventually perished as a result of ill treatment, and all but 150 of the 2,413 local mine laborers and their families were eventually deported to Tarawa, Nauru, and Kosrae. As a warning, the Japanese beheaded three locals and used another three to test an electrified anti-invasion fence.

Meanwhile the BPC decided to take advantage of this situation to rid itself of the island's original inhabitants once and for all, to avoid any future interference in mining operations. In March 1942, the commission purchased Rabi Island off Vanua Levu in Fiji for £25,000 as an alternative homeland for the Banabans. In late September 1945, the British returned to Banaba, with Albert Ellis the first to step ashore. Only surrendering Japanese troops were found on Banaba; the local villages had been destroyed.

Two months later, an emaciated and wild-eyed Gilbertese man named Kabunare Koura emerged from three months in hiding and told his story to a military court:

We were assembled together and told that the war was over and the Japanese would

*soon be leaving. Our rifles were taken
away. We were put in groups, our names
taken, then marched to the edge of the
cliffs where our hands were tied and we
were blindfolded and told to squat. Then
we were shot.*

Kabunare either lost his balance or fainted, and fell
over the cliff before he was hit. In the sea, he came
to the surface and kicked his way to some rocks,
where he severed the string that tied his hands.
He crawled into a cave and watched the Japanese
pile up the bodies of his companions and toss
them into the sea. He stayed in the cave two nights
and, after he thought it was safe, made his way
inland, where he survived on coconuts until he
was sure the Japanese had left. Kabunare said he
thought the Japanese had executed the others to
destroy any evidence of their cruelties and atroci-
ties on Banaba. After a postwar trial on Guadal-
canal, the Japanese commander of Banaba, Suzuki
Naoomi, was hanged for his crimes.

As peace returned, the British implemented
their plan to resettle all 2,000 surviving Banabans
on Rabi, which seemed a better place for them
than their mined-out homeland. The first group arrived on Rabi on December 14, 1945, and in time
they adapted to their mountainous new home and
traded much of their original Micronesian culture
for that of the Fijians. There, they and their descendants live today.

During the 1960s, the Banabans saw the much
better deal Nauru was getting from the BPC.
Mainly through the efforts of Hammer De-
Roburt and the "Geelong Boys," who had been
trapped in Australia during the war and thus received an excellent education and understanding of the white people's ways, the Nauruan
leadership was able to hold its own against colonial bullying. Meanwhile, the Banabans were
simply forgotten on Rabi.

In 1966, Mr. Tebuke Rotan, a Banaban
Methodist minister, journeyed to London on behalf of his people to demand reparations from the
British for laying waste to their island. After some
50 visits to the Foreign and Commonwealth offices, he was offered £80,000 compensation, which
he rejected. In 1971, the Banabans sued for damages in the British High Court. After lengthy litigation, the British government in 1977 offered
the Banabans an ex gratia payment of A$10 mil-
lion, in exchange for a pledge that there would
be no further legal action.

In 1975, the Banabans asked that Banaba be
separated from the rest of Kiribati and joined to
Fiji, their present country of citizenship.
Gilbertese politicians, anxious to protect their
fisheries zone and wary of the dismemberment
of the country, lobbied against this, and the
British rejected the proposal. The free entry of
Banabans to Banaba was guaranteed in the Kiribati constitution, however. In 1979, Kiribati
obtained independence from Britain and mining on Banaba ended the same year. Finally, in
1981, the Banabans accepted the A$10 million
compensation money, plus interest, from the
British, though they refused to withdraw their
claim to Banaba. (Much of the money "disappeared" between 1989 and 1991, during a period of corruption in the Rabi Council of
Leaders.) The present Kiribati government re-
jects all further claims from the Banabans, as-
serting that they should be settled with the
British. The British are simply trying to forget
the whole thing.

On weekdays the local ferry *Raja* links Vanua Levu to Taveuni.

decided Rabi Island would be a better home-land for the Banabans than Wakaya, and in March 1942, they purchased Rabi from Lever Brothers using £25,000 of phosphate royalties deposited in the Banaban Provident Fund.

Meanwhile, the Japanese had deported the Banabans to Kosrae in the Caroline Islands to serve as laborers, and it was not until December 1945 that the survivors could be brought to Rabi, where their 4,500 descendants live today. Contemporary Banabans are citizens of Fiji and live among Lever Brothers' former coconut plantations in the northwest corner of the island. The nine-member Rabi Island Council administers the island.

Rabi lives according to a different set of rules than the rest of Fiji; in fact, about all they have in common are their monetary, postal, and educational systems, kava drinking (a Fijian implant), and Methodism. The local language is Gilbertese, and the social order is that of the Gilbert Islands. Most people live in hurricane-proof concrete-block houses devoid of furniture, with personal possessions kept in suitcases and trunks. The cooking is done outside in thatched huts. The islanders fish with handlines from outrigger canoes.

Alcoholic beverages are not allowed on Rabi, so take something else as gifts. On Friday nights, the local *maneaba* (community hall) in Tabwewa village rocks to a disco beat, and dancing alternates with sitting around the omnipresent kava bowl, but on Sunday virtually everything grinds to a halt. Another charming feature: Adultery is a legally punishable offense on Rabi.

The island reaches a height of 472 meters and is well wooded. The former Lever Brothers headquarters is at Tabwewa, while the disused airstrip is near Tabiang at Rabi's southwest tip. Rabi's other two villages are Uma and Buakonikai. At Nuku, between Uma and Tabwewa, is a post office, Telecom office, clinic, handicraft shop, and general store. The hill behind the Catholic mission at Nuku affords a fine view. Enjoy another fine view from the Methodist church center at Buakonikai.

Accommodations

Up on the hillside above the post office at Nuku is the four-room **Rabi Island Council Guest House.** This colonial-style structure is the former Lever Brothers manager's residence, and it is little changed since the 1940s, except for the extension now housing the dining area and lounge. View superb sunsets from the porch. One of the rooms is reserved for island officials; the rest are used mostly by contract workers. Other guests pay F$50 pp a night, which includes three meals. The facilities are shared (no hot water), and the electric generator operates 1800–2200 only—just enough time to watch a video (the library next to the courthouse rents *Go Tell It to the Judge,* a documentary about the Banaban struggle for compensation).

Considering the limited accommodations and the remoteness of Rabi, it's important to call the **Rabi Island Council** (tel. 881-2913, ext. 30) for guesthouse bookings and other information before setting out. Foreign currency cannot be changed on Rabi, and even Fijian bills larger than F$10 may be hard to break. Insect repellent is not sold locally.

Transportation

To get to Rabi, catch the daily Napuka bus at 1030 from Savusavu to Karoko. A chartered speedboat from Karoko to the wharf at Nuku on the northwest side of Rabi costs F$60 each way, less if people off the Napuka bus are going over anyway. The ferries *Raja* from Taveuni and *Adi Savusavu* from Suva visit Rabi occasionally.

Motorized transport on Rabi consists of two or three island-council trucks plying the single 23-kilometer road from Tabwewa to Buakonikai weekdays and Saturday mornings (less than F$1 each way).

Taveuni

Long, green, coconut-covered Taveuni is Fiji's fourth-largest island. It's 42 kilometers long, 15 kilometers wide, and 442 square kilometers in area. Only eight kilometers across the Somosomo Strait from Vanua Levu's southeast tip, Taveuni is known as the Garden Island of Fiji because of the abundance of its flora. About 60 percent of the land is tropical rainforest, and virtually all of Fiji's coffee is grown here. Its surrounding reefs and those off nearby Vanua Levu are some of the world's top dive sites. The strong tidal currents in the strait nurture the corals, but can make diving a tricky business for the unprepared.

Because Taveuni is free of the mongoose, there are many wild chickens, *kula* lorikeets, red-breasted musk parrots, honeyeaters, silktails, fern-tails, goshawks, and orange-breasted doves, making this a special place for bird-watchers. Here you'll still find the jungle fowl, banded rail, and purple swamp hen, all extinct on Viti Levu and Vanua Levu. The Fiji flying fox and mastiff bat are also seen only here. The Taveuni longhorn beetle is the largest beetle in Australasia.

The island's 16-kilometer-long, 1,000-meter-high volcanic spine causes the prevailing trade winds to dump colossal amounts of rainfall on the island's southeast side, as well as considerable quantities on the northwest side. Southwestern Taveuni is much drier. At 1,241 meters, Uluiqalau in southern Taveuni is the second-highest peak in Fiji, and Des Voeux Peak (1,195 m) in central Taveuni is the highest point in the

TAVEUNI

SOUTH PACIFIC OCEAN

Laucala Island

Matagi Island
MATAGI ISLAND RESORT
Qamea Island
Niubavu
Vatosogosogo
Dreketi
Kocoma

QAMEA BEACH RESORT
Pagai
Tasman Strait

Viubani Island
Naselesele
Naselesele Point
MATEI
Mua
Qeleni
Navakacoa
Waitabu
Vidawa
Koroturaga (864 m)
TAVORO FOREST PARK
Bouma National Heritage Park
Lavena
Lavena Point
Ravilevo Coast

Welagi
Lamini
Naqara
SOMOSOMO
Somosomo
Lovonivonu
Lake Tagimaucia

PRINCE CHARLES BEACH

Waiyevo
Wairiki
GARDEN ISLAND RESORT
Korolevu Island
Des Voeux Peak (1,195 m)
Taveuni Island
Ravilevu Nature Reserve

Somosomo Strait

Mt. Uluiqalau (1,241 m)

Salialevu

DOLPHIN BAY DIVERS RETREAT
Vanaira Bay
Naucunilawe (814 m)
Naqarawalu
Delaivuna
Navakawau

Kioa Island
Saliao
Bucca Bay

SOQULU PLANTATION

MATAMAIQI BLOWHOLE

Vanua Levu Island
Buca
Natuvu
Dakuniba
Vagai
Nawii

NOK'S DIVE CENTER
SUSIE'S PLANTATION
VATUWIRI FARM RESORT
VUNA LAGOON LODGE
Kanacea
Vuna
Vuna Lagoon
South Cape

Rainbow Reef

To Savusavu and Suva

Nukum Passage

5 mi
5 km

© DAVID STANLEY

TAVEUNI

country accessible by road. The European discoverer of Fiji, Abel Tasman, sighted this ridge on the night of February 5, 1643. Vuna in southwestern Taveuni is presently dormant, but it's considered Fiji's most active volcano, having erupted within the past 350 years. The almost inaccessible southeast coast features plummeting waterfalls, soaring cliffs, and crashing surf. The 12,000 inhabitants live on the island's gently sloping northwest side. Indigenous Fijians make up the bulk of the population, but Indo-Fijians run many of the shops, hotels, buses, and taxis.

The deep, rich volcanic soil nurtures indigenous floral species, such as *Medinilla spectabilis,* which hang in clusters like red sleigh bells, and the rare *tagimaucia (Medinilla waterhousei),* a climbing plant with red-and-white flower clusters 30 centimeters long. *Tagimaucia* grows only around Taveuni's 900-meter-high crater lake and on Vanua Levu. It cannot be transplanted and blossoms only Oct.–Jan. The story goes that a young woman was fleeing from her father, who wanted to force her to marry a crotchety old man. As she lay crying beside the lake, her tears turned to flowers. Her father took pity on her when he heard this and allowed her to marry her young lover.

Taveuni is a popular destination for scuba divers, and the nature reserves of northeastern Taveuni make it an ideal ecotourism destination. In 1991, the producers of the film *Return to the Blue Lagoon* chose Taveuni for their remake of the story of two adolescents on a desert isle. This is a beautiful, scenic, and friendly island on which to hang out, so be sure to allow yourself enough time there.

Getting There

Matei Airstrip at the north tip of Taveuni is served twice daily by **Air Fiji** (tel. 888-0062) from Nadi (F$183), Suva (F$138), and Savusavu (F$74), and by **Sun Air** (tel. 888-0461) from Nadi (F$183) and Savusavu (F$75). Sun Air also arrives from Labasa (F$75) three times a week. Flights to/from Taveuni are often heavily booked, so reconfirm to avoid being bumped. You get superb views of Taveuni from the plane: Sit on the right side going up, the left side coming back. Krishna

---

TAVEUNI HIGHLIGHTS

Rainbow Reef: famous scuba-diving venue, soft corals (p. 303)
Bouma Falls: three waterfalls, hiking (p. 308)
Waitabu Marine Park: nature reserve for snorkelers (p. 309)
Lavena Coastal Walk: hiking, swimming, village life (p. 309)
Lake Tagimaucia: challenging hike, rare birds and flowers (p. 311)

Brothers (tel. 888-0504) in Naqara is the agent for Air Fiji. Sun Air has an office at the airport, and the Garden Island Hotel also takes bookings.

Consort Shipping operates the twice-weekly *Spirit of Fiji Islands* service from Taveuni to Suva via Koro and Savusavu (23 hours, F$47/87 deck/cabin). Taveuni to Savusavu is F$22. This ferry departs Taveuni southbound Monday and Thursday at noon, having left Suva northbound Wednesday at 1100 and Saturday at 1800. The Consort agent is the First Light Inn (tel. 888-0339; weekdays 0800–1300 and 1400–1700, Sat. 0800–1300) in Waiyevo, and it's F$10 cheaper to purchase your ticket there, rather than on the ferry itself.

The **Beachcomber Cruises** car ferry, *Adi Savusavu,* departs Taveuni for Savusavu and Suva Wednesday, Friday, and Sunday around noon. It takes five hours to reach Savusavu, and after a three-hour stop, it continues to Suva, where it arrives Thursday, Saturday, and Monday mornings (F$48/68 economy/first-class). The agent is Ian Simpson (tel. 888-0187 or 888-0261) at the fish market opposite the Garden Island Resort (F$2 discount on advance ticket sales here).

The small passenger boat MV *Raja* departs Taveuni for Natuvu weekdays at 0900 (two hours, F$7). Through boat/bus tickets with a bus connection at Natuvu are available to Savusavu (four hours, F$15) and Labasa (six hours, F$20). The *Raja* also does trips to Rabi whenever there's cargo. Information on the *Raja* is available at an upstairs office (tel. 888-0134) opposite Kaba's Supermarket in Naqara.

If you arrive by boat at Taveuni, you could

disembark at one of three places. The large ferries from Suva tie up at an old wharf a kilometer north of Waiyevo or at a new wharf just south of the Garden Island Hotel. There's a third wharf called the "Korean Wharf" at Lovonivonu village, a kilometer north of the old Waiyevo wharf, midway between Waiyevo and Naqara. This wharf is usually used by the Vanua Levu ferries and other smaller cargo boats.

Getting Around

Monday–Saturday at 0900, 1100, and 1645, **Pacific Transport** (tel. 888-0278) buses leave Waiyevo and Naqara northbound to Bouma (F$2.95) and southbound to Vuna (F$2.75). Buses to Lavena (F$3.35) are more complicated. On Tuesdays and Thursdays, the 0900, 1100, and 1645 Bouma buses continue to Lavena, but on Saturdays, only the 1100 and 1645 buses do so. Other days, only the 1645 bus goes to Lavena. Both the northbound and southbound 1645 buses stop and spend the night at their turnaround points, Lavena and Navakawau, heading back to Naqara the next morning at 0600 (at 0730 on Sun.). Sunday service is infrequent, although there are buses to Lavena and Vuna at around 1600. Check the current schedule carefully as soon as you arrive, and beware of buses leaving a bit early. The buses begin their journeys at the Pacific Transport garage at Naqara, but they all go to Waiyevo hospital to pick up passengers before heading north or south.

The sporadic bus service and rather expensive taxi fares make getting around rather inconvenient. Taveuni's minibus taxis don't run along set routes, picking up passengers at fixed rates as they do on other islands, but only operate on an individual charter basis. The taxi fare from the wharf to Naqara is reasonable at F$3, but from the airport to Naqara, it's expensive at F$15. In general, the taxi fare will be about 10 times the corresponding bus fare. Save money by using the buses for long rides and taxis for shorter hops. Hitchhiking also works fine (drivers often expect you to give them the equivalent of bus fare).

You could hire a minibus taxi and driver for the day. Write out a list of everything you want to see, then negotiate a price with a driver. The Garden Island Resort minibus is F$110 to Bouma or F$140 to Lavena for up to five people (six persons and up is F$25/30 pp to Bouma/Lavena). To the Matamaiqi Blowhole in southern Taveuni, it's F$100.

Mr. Nand Lal (tel. 888-0705) operates a regular shuttle service to Bouma National Heritage Park at F$40/60 round-trip from Matei to Bouma/Lavena for up to five people including waiting time. Call him up, or ask at Lal's Restaurant in Matei.

Garden State General Merchants, beside the BP service station opposite Kaba's Motel in Naqara, represents **Budget Rent a Car** (tel. 888-0291) with Suzuki jeeps at F$210 a day all inclusive, reduced to F$150 after bargaining.

Northern Taveuni

The bulk of Taveuni's tourist facilities, including accommodations, restaurants, and dive shops, are within walking distance of the airport at Matei. It's an ideal area in which to stay if you're arriving by air, although boat passengers and those planning to use public transportation for sightseeing may find central Taveuni more convenient. When selecting a place to stay, be aware that the beach east of Matei Point is little more than a broad mud flat at low tide and that the best places for swimming are west of the airport in the vicinity of Beverly's Campground.

SPORTS AND RECREATION

Taveuni and its surrounding waters have earned a reputation as one of Fiji's top diving areas. The fabulous 32-kilometer **Rainbow Reef** off the south coast of eastern Vanua Levu abounds in turtles, fish, overhangs, crevices, and soft corals, all in 5–10 meters of water. Favorite dive sites here include Annie's Bommie, Blue Ribbon Eel Reef, Cabbage Patch, Coral Garden, Jack's Place, Jerry's Jelly, Orgasm, Pot Luck, The Ledge, The Zoo, and White Sandy Gully. At the Great White Wall,

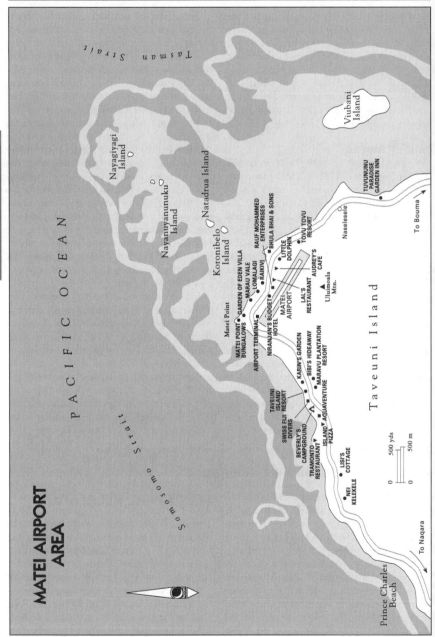

MATEI AIRPORT AREA

Taveuni Island

PACIFIC OCEAN

Tasman Strait

Somosomo Strait

Viubani Island

Nayagiyagi Island

Nayanyanunuku Island

Natadrua Island

Koronibelo Island

TUVUNUNU PARADISE GARDEN INN

To Bouma

Naselesele

RAUF MOHAMMED ENTERPRISES

BHULA BHAI & SONS

LITTLE DOLPHIN

TOVU TOVU RESORT

AUDREY'S CAFE

Uluimoala Mtn.

LAL'S RESTAURANT

MATEI AIRPORT

RAIKIVI

LOMALAGI

MARAU VALE

GARDEN OF EDEN VILLA

MATEI POINT BUNGALOWS

Matei Point

AIRPORT TERMINAL

NIRANJAN'S BUDGET HOTEL

KARIN'S GARDEN

BIBI'S HIDEAWAY

MARAVU PLANTATION RESORT

TAVEUNI ISLAND RESORT

SWISS FIJI DIVERS

BEVERLY'S CAMPGROUND

ISLAND AQUAVENTURE

TRAMONTO RESTAURANT

PIZZA

LISI'S COTTAGE

NEI KELEKELE

Prince Charles Beach

To Naqara

0   500 yds
0   500 m

women and children taking it easy in a village on northern Taveuni

a tunnel in the reef leads past sea fans to a magnificent drop-off and a wall covered in awesome white soft coral. Unfortunately, the hard corals on the Rainbow Reef have been heavily impacted by coral bleaching. The soft corals are still okay, and the White Wall is as spectacular as ever. Beware of strong currents in the Somosomo Strait.

Snorkelers should be aware that shark attacks are not unknown on northern Taveuni. Never snorkel alone out to the edge of the reef anywhere around Matei. This is less of a problem elsewhere around the island, although one should always seek local advice. Northern Taveuni is one of the few places in Fiji where sharks are a problem.

Aquaventure (tel./fax 888-0381, www.aquaventure.org), run by Tania de Hoon, has its base on the beach a 20-minute walk south of Matei Airport. Trips start at 0800 and 1300, costing F$140 for two tanks, plus F$30 for gear (F$620 for 10 dives). Aquaventure offers an introductory scuba dive for F$140. Tania also books guided snorkeling tours to the Waitabu Marine

Park (F$50 pp all inclusive, minimum of four), an excellent option if you're a bit nervous about snorkeling here on your own.

A few minutes walk north of Aquaventure is **Swiss Fiji Divers** (tel. 888-0586, fax 888-2587, www.swissfijidivers.com), between the beaches of the Taveuni Island Resort and Maravu Plantation. Divemasters Dominique Egerter and Evi Antonietti charge F$180 for a two-tank dive, plus F$20 for rental gear. For those staying longer, they have five-day packages for F$830 or ten days for F$1,400. Their five- to six-day PADI open-water course is F$760, and many other specialized dive courses are offered. A "discover diving" experience is F$160. This is Taveuni's newest dive shop, and their equipment is first rate. They guarantee a ratio of not less than one guide for every three divers. From 0900–1700, you can check your email here at F$.25 a minute.

Way back in 1976, Ric and Do Cammick's **Dive Taveuni** (tel. 888-0445, fax 888-0466, www.divetaveuni.com) pioneered scuba diving in this area, discovering and naming most of the sites now regularly visited by divers. These days, they cater exclusively to small groups that have prebooked stays at the Taveuni Island Resort from abroad. Nonguests need not apply.

Matei Game Fishing (Geoffry Amos, tel. 888-0371 or 888-2667), opposite Rauf Mohammed Enterprises at Matei, does game-fishing trips on his boat, the *Lucky Strike*. It's F$570/900 for a half/full day for up to four people.

Island Pizza (Ken Madden, tel. 888-2888), adjacent to Aquaventure, rents single/double fiberglass kayaks at F$10/14 an hour. Half-day snorkeling trips are F$30 pp (minimum of four), while full-day boat trips to Qamea/Yanuca islands are F$150/200 for the boat (four persons). Fishing trips are also possible.

ACCOMMODATIONS

Places to stay are scattered all around Taveuni, with the main cluster within walking distance of Matei Airport. There are several good places to eat out in this vicinity, so avoid booking with hotels that try to force you to prepay for all your meals. Also beware of misleading resort websites or the glowing reports of travel agents and glossy magazine writers who came on freebie trips. For some reason, a good many of the complaints we receive regarding tourist accommodations in Fiji relate to places on northern Taveuni and its adjacent islands.

Taveuni still doesn't have a public electricity supply, but most of the places to stay have their own generators, which typically run 1800–2100 only.

Under US$25

Beverly's Campground (tel. 888-0684) is on a good beach a bit more than one kilometer south of the airport. Run by Bill Madden, it's a peaceful, shady place, adjacent to Maravu Plantation's beach. It's F$8 pp in your own tent, or F$10 pp to sleep in a set tent. The toilet and shower block is nearby. Cooking facilities are available, but bring groceries (Bill provides free fresh fruit from his garden daily). The kitchen shelter by the beach is a nice place to sit and swap traveler's tales with the other guests, and the clean white beach is just seconds from your tent.

A few hundred meters south is **Lisi's Accommodation** (tel. 888-0194), in a small village across the highway from a white-sand beach. It's F$8 pp to camp or F$15/25 single/double in a clean four-room bungalow with shared cooking and bathing facilities. Your friendly hosts Mary and Lote Tuisago serve excellent Fijian meals at F$6/8 for breakfast/dinner. Horseback riding (F$10 an hour) can be arranged here.

US$25–50

Tuvununu Paradise Garden Inn (tel. 888-0465, taveuni@paradisefiji.com), 700 meters east of Naselesele village in northern Taveuni, offers eight rooms in a large wooden building overlooking Viubani Island at F$55/75 single/double, or F$24 pp in the backpacker dorm. Camping is F$9 pp. The tidal flat in front of the inn is beautiful, but not ideal for swimming. The Tuvununu has been closed for several years and is in need of major renovations before it can reopen.

The Petersen family runs the **Tovu Tovu Resort** (tel. 888-0560, fax 888-0722, tovutovu@con

nect.com.fj) at Matei just east of Bhula Bhai & Sons Supermarket. It's across the road from a shallow beach with murky water, and guests often walk the two kilometers to Beverly's Campground to swim. The two front *bure* capable of sleeping three are self-catering at F$75 single or double. Just behind are another two *bure* with private bath but no cooking at F$65. A larger self-catering bungalow sleeping four is F$85. The three-meal plan is F$35 pp, and the restaurant terrace is a nice place to sit and socialize.

Little Dolphin (tel. 888-0130), opposite Bhula Bhai & Sons Supermarket, less than a kilometer east of the airport, has an airy, two-story cottage with cooking facilities called the "treehouse." At F$80/90 single/double a night, it's good value, and the view from the porch is great. Little Dolphin is run by an Australian named Scott, who is a mine of information. He has a three-person outrigger canoe and a double kayak; he rents either of them to guests at F$30 a day (F$40 a day to non-guests).

Niranjan's Budget Hotel (tel. 888-0406) is just a five-minute walk east of the airport. The four rooms in the main building, each with two beds and fan, go for F$44/55 single/double. The electric generator is on 1800–2200. Niranjan himself is very hospitable guy.

Bibi's Hideaway (tel. 888-0443), about 600 meters south of the airport, has some of the gracious atmosphere of neighboring properties, but without the sky-high prices. A variety of accommodations is available. The film crew making *Return to the Blue Lagoon* stayed here for three months, and with the extra income, the owners built a honeymoon *bure* with a picture window, which is F$80 double. Nearby is a two-room house at F$50 per room or F$80 for the whole house. A small cottage is F$60 double, while a mini-*bure* with two single beds is F$25 pp. There's also a larger family unit accommodating eight at F$100. All five units have access to cooking facilities and fridge. Bibi's is located on lush, spacious grounds, and James, Victor, and Pauline Bibi will make you feel right at home. It's an excellent medium-priced choice, if you don't mind being a bit away from the beach.

US$50–100

Audrey of **Audrey's Café** (tel. 888-0039), half a kilometer east of the airport, has a cute cottage with tile floors that she rents at F$125 (children not admitted).

Directly opposite the airport terminal is the **Garden of Eden Villa** (Peter Madden, tel. 888-2344), a large two-bedroom house with cooking facilities at F$100 double or F$120 for four if you book direct. Set on a bluff above the sea, this place was once a favorite retreat of Fiji's former president Ratu Mara.

Matei Point Bungalows (tel. 888-0422), right on the point at the end of the driveway opposite the airport access road, has three self-catering villas at F$140 double, plus F$20 per additional person.

Karin's Garden (tel./fax 888-0511), almost opposite Bibi's Hideaway 650 meters south of the airport, overlooks the same coast as the over-priced Taveuni Island Resort next door. The two screened rooms with fan in a large self-catering bungalow are each F$115 single or double. It's nice, but the beds are a bit soft. Don't stay here unless you like dogs.

US$100–150

A retired American tour operator named Bob Goddess (tel. 888-0522, www.fiji-rental-accommodations.com) rents three beachfront houses near Matei Airport. **Sere-ni-Ika,** a six-minute walk east of the terminal, has three bedrooms at F$415 per group. **Lomalagi,** two houses west of Sere-ni-Ika, has two bedrooms at F$265 for both. A hundred meters west toward the terminal is **Marau Vale,** a two-bedroom house in a large garden costing F$455. Bob offers low-season and long-stay discounts. It's all very nice, although the beach in front of these houses is a mud flat at low tide.

US$150 and up

About 600 meters south of the airport are two of Taveuni's most exclusive properties. **Maravu Plantation Resort** (Angela and Jochen Kiess, tel. 888-0555, fax 888-0600, www.maravu.net) is a village-style resort on a 20-hectare copra-making plantation. Maravu consists of five "planters" *bure*

at F$420/640 single/double and five "honeymoon" *bure* at F$480/760. The four "honeymoon suites," each with a private spa and sundeck, are F$880 double. Included are meals, transfers, taxes, horseback riding, bicycles, and some other activities. Two children under 14 can stay free, paying only for their meals (F$60 per day per child). When space is available, you might get the local walk-in rate of F$198/396 single/double all inclusive. On the landscaped grounds are an elegant bar, spa, and swimming pool. The resort often arranges a *meke* to go with dinner (F$60 for non-guests) on Wednesday or Thursday. If you're not staying there, you must reserve meals in advance. Maravu's wine menu is way overpriced.

Almost across the street from Maravu Plantation is the **Taveuni Island Resort** (tel. 888-0441, fax 888-0466, www.taveuniislandresort.com), run by the Cammick family. This resort started out in the 1970s as a low-budget scuba camp known as Ric's Place, but today it's patronized by an eclectic mix of divers, anglers, honeymooners, and "romantic couples" who arrive on prepaid package tours. The eight *bure* range in price from F$1,156–1,520 single or double, including meals, transfers, and tax. In addition, the cliff-top honeymoon *bure* with private staff is F$2,400 double all inclusive. Unlike Maravu, which encourages visits by families, children under 15 are not accepted here. The open terrace dining area and swimming pool added in 1997 merge scenically with the sea on the horizon. Be aware that only registered house guests are welcome on the property (a sign on the gate says Beware of the Dogs).

OTHER PRACTICALITIES
Food

The nicest place to eat out around Matei is the **Vunibokoi Restaurant** (tel. 888-0560) at the Tovu Tovu Resort, east of Bhula Bhai & Sons Supermarket. From 1800–2000, upscale dinners (F$13–17) prepared by Mareta are served on a terrace overlooking the sea. The Friday-night *lovo* buffet here is F$17.50. Reservations are recommended.

Audrey's Island Cafe & Pastries (tel. 888-0039; daily 1000–1800), run by a charming

Yaqona (kava) drying on a corrugated iron rack in a village on northern Taveuni

The **Matei Restaurant** (tel. 888-0406), at Niranjan's Budget Hotel just east of the airport terminal, can prepare an excellent curry buffet dinner (F$15 pp), provided you order before 1700.

The snack bar at Matei Airport (open only at flight times) sells tasty curry *rotis*. They're kept under the counter, so ask. The two supermarkets in this area also sell roti packets at F$.70.

Island Pizza (Ken Madden, tel. 888-2888; daily 1000–2130), on the beach next to Aquaventure, has pizzas priced F$17/20 regular/large.

The **Tramonto Restaurant** (Peter Madden, tel. 888-2224; Mon.–Thurs. 1100–1400 and 1800–2100, Fri. 1100–2100), on a hilltop at the southwest end of the Matei tourist strip, serves lunch/dinner at about F$7.50/15.50. When available, lobster is F$20. The portions tend to be small here. If you can get a group of at least six persons together, the Tramonto lays out an excellent smorgasbord dinner at F$20 pp. There's a superb view of the beach and Somosomo Strait from their open terrace.

American woman at Matei, serves afternoon tea (F$7 pp) to guests who also enjoy the great view from her terrace, and Audrey has various homemade goodies to take away.

Lal's Restaurant (tel. 888-0705; daily 1100–2030), just east of the airport, serves spicy boneless chicken, lamb, fish, and vegetarian Indian curry dishes at F$10 a serving.

Groceries

Those staying at Matei will appreciate the well-stocked **Bhula Bhai & Sons Supermarket** (tel. 888-0369; Mon.–Sat. 0730–1800, Sun. 0800–1000) at the Matei Postal Agency between the airport and Naselesele village. A second grocery store, **Rauf Mohammed Enterprises** (tel. 888-0431; Mon.–Sat. 0630–1900, Sun. 0700–1100 and 1500–2000), is between Bhula Bhai and the airport. Public telephones are outside both stores.

Eastern Taveuni

Bouma National Heritage Park

This important nature reserve between Bouma and Lavena in northeastern Taveuni has been developed with New Zealand aid money. In 1990, an agreement was signed with the communities of Waitabu, Vidawa, Korovou, and Lavena putting this area in trust for 99 years, and the Tavoro Forest Park at Bouma was established a year later. The Lavena Coastal Walk, Vidawa Rainforest Hike, and Waitabu Marine Park are other features of the park, and the various admission fees and tour charges are used for local community projects, to provide local residents with an immediate practical reason for preserving their natural environment.

There are three lovely **waterfalls** just south of Bouma (admission F$8). From the information kiosk on the main road, it's an easy 10-minute walk up a broad path along the river's right bank to the lower falls, which plunge 20

The first pool at Bouma National Heritage Park is an easy walk from the main road.

guides introduce the birdlife, flora, and archaeological sites of the area to visitors. You scramble over volcanic ridges offering spectacular views and explore old village sites with their temple platforms and ring ditches still clearly visible. Your guide brings it all to life with tales of the old ways of his people. A picnic lunch is served by a spring-fed stream deep in the interior. The trek ends at **Bouma Falls,** where hikers are rewarded with a refreshing swim. The F$60 pp cost (F$40 for children) includes park entry fees and transportation from anywhere on northern Taveuni (call 888-0390 to book).

Similar is the **Waitabu Marine Park,** where a lagoon area two kilometers before Bouma has been declared a "no fishing" sanctuary for fish and snorkelers. The F$50 pp tour price also includes snorkeling gear, transportation, and food. Book five-hour snorkeling tours here through the dive shop Aquaventure (tel. 888-0381) south of Matei Airport. Reductions for children are available. The departure time varies according to tide and weather conditions. These tours are good value, and you'll be supporting a worthy cause.

Bouma is accessible by public bus. If you depart Waiyevo or Naqara on the 0900 bus, you'll have about two hours to see the falls and have a quick swim before catching another bus back to Waiyevo. On Tuesdays and Thursdays, this second bus does a round-trip to Lavena, six kilometers south, and it's worth jumping on for the ride, even if you don't intend to get off at Lavena. Other days, the second bus only goes as far as Bouma. Verify the time of the return bus with the driver of the 0900 bus.

meters into a deep pool. You can swim here, and change rooms, toilets, picnic tables, and a barbecue are provided. A well-constructed trail leads up to a second falls in about 30 minutes, passing a spectacular viewpoint overlooking Qamea Island and Taveuni's northeast coast. You must cross the river once, but a rope is provided for balance. Anyone in good physical shape can reach this second falls with ease, and there's also a pool for swimming. The muddy, slippery trail up to the third and highest falls involves two river crossings with nothing to hold onto, and it would be unpleasant in the rain. This trail does cut through the most beautiful portion of the rainforest with the richest birdlife, and these upper falls are perhaps the most impressive of the three, as the river plunges over a black basalt cliff, which you can climb and use as a diving platform into the deep pool. The water here is very sweet.

A new activity in this area is the six-hour **Vidawa Rainforest Hike,** during which local

Lavena

The **Lavena Coastal Walk** officially opened in 1993. You pay your F$8 admission fee (separate from the F$8 fee charged at Bouma) at the Lavena Lodge Visitor Center, right at the end of the road at Lavena. Guides are available at F$18. From the Visitor Center, you can hike the five kilometers down the Ravilevo Coast to **Wainibau Falls** in about 1.5 hours. You'll pass Naba village, where the descendants of blackbirded Solomon Islanders live to this day, and a suspension bridge over the Wainisairi River, which drains Lake Tagimaucia in Taveuni's interior. The last 15 minutes is a scramble up a creek bed, which can be very slippery as you wade along. Two falls here plunge into the same deep basalt pool, and during the rainy season you must actually swim a short distance to see the second pool. Diving into either pool is excellent fun. Be on guard, however, as flash flooding often occurs. Keep to the left near the base of the falls. Several lovely beaches and places to stop are along the trail (allow four hours there and back from Lavena with plenty of stops).

If you also want to see **Savulevu Yavonu Falls,** which plummet off a cliff directly into the sea, you must hire a boat at F$75 for up to three people or F$25 pp for up to six. Intrepid ocean kayakers sometimes paddle down this back side of Taveuni, past countless cliffs and waterfalls. The steep forested area south of Wainibau Stream forms part of the Ravilevu Nature Reserve.

It's not possible to visit Lavena as a day trip by public bus (taxis charge F$60 round-trip to bring you here). Buses depart Lavena for Naqara Monday–Saturday at 0600, Tuesday and Thursday also at 1400, and Sunday at 0730—beware of their leaving a bit early.

Accommodations

At Bouma, visitors can camp by the river behind the park information kiosk (tel. 888-0390) at F$10 per head. Toilets and showers are provided. Meals can be ordered, or you can cook your own in a communal kitchen.

Lavena Lodge, next to Lavena village at the end of the bus route, is a pleasant European-style building with running water and lantern lighting. The four rooms (two doubles and two three-bed dorms) are F$15 pp. Sinks are provided in the rooms, but the bath is shared. Good cooking facilities are provided, and you can eat at a picnic table on a hill overlooking the beach or on the lodge's terrace. Dinner can be ordered for F$10. A village store is opposite the lodge, and two other small trade stores are nearby (however, it's best to bring groceries with you). Mosquito coils are essential (the flies are a nuisance too). An excellent golden beach is right in front of the lodge, and at Ucuna Point, a five-minute walk away, is a picnic area where you can spend an afternoon (be careful with the currents if you snorkel). It's a great place to hang out for a few days—the film *Return to the Blue Lagoon* was filmed here. To book, call Lavena via radio telephone at 811-6801 (answered 0800–0900 and 1400–1500 only).

Central Taveuni

Taveuni's police station, hospital, and government offices are on a hilltop at **Waiyevo,** above the Garden Island Resort. On the coast below are the island's post office and largest hotel.

The 180th degree of longitude passes through a point marked by a display called **Taveuni's Time Line** at Waiyevo, 500 meters up the road from the shops near the Garden Island Resort. It's said that one early Taveuni trader overcame the objections of missionaries to his doing business on Sunday by claiming the international date line ran through his property. According to him, when it was Sunday at the front door, it was already Monday around back. Similarly, European planters got their native laborers to work seven days a week by having Sunday at one end of the plantation, and

Monday at the other. An 1879 ordinance ended this by placing all of Fiji west of the date line, so you're no longer able to stand here with one foot in the past and the other in the present. Despite this, it's still the most accessible place in the world that is crossed by the 180th meridian.

To get to the **Waitavala Sliding Rocks,** walk north from the Garden Island Resort about five minutes on the main road, then turn right onto the side road leading to Waitavala Estates. Take the first road to the right up the hill, and when you see a large metal building on top of a hill, turn left and go a short distance down a road through a coconut plantation to a clearing on the right. The trail up the river to the sliding rocks begins here. The waterslide in the river is especially fast after heavy rains, yet the local kids go down standing up! Admission is free.

At **Wairiki,** a kilometer south of Waiyevo, are a few stores and the picturesque Catholic mission, with a large stone church containing interesting sculptures and stained glass. There are no pews: The congregation sits on the floor Fijian-style. From Wairiki Secondary School, you can hike up a tractor track to the large **concrete cross** on a hill behind the mission (30 minutes each way). You'll be rewarded with a sweeping view of much of western Taveuni and across Somosomo Strait. A famous 19th-century naval battle occurred here when Taveuni warriors turned back a large Tongan invasion force, with much of the fighting done from canoes. The defeated Tongans ended up in Fijian ovens, and the French priest who gave valuable counsel to the Fijian chief was repaid with laborers to build his mission.

A jeep road from Wairiki climbs to the telecommunications station on **Des Voeux Peak.** This is an all-day trip on foot, with a view of Lake Tagimaucia as a reward (clouds permitting). The lake itself is not accessible from here. This peak is one of Taveuni's best bird-watching venues, and the rare monkey-faced fruit bat *(Pteralopex acrodonta)* survives only in the mist forest around the summit. Unless you hire a jeep to the viewpoint, it will take four arduous hours to hike the eight kilometers up and another two to walk back down.

AROUND SOMOSOMO

Somosomo, four kilometers north of Waiyevo, is the chiefly village of Cakaudrove and the seat of the Tui Cakau, Taveuni's "king"; the late Ratu Sir Penaia Ganilau, last governor-general and first president of Fiji, hailed from here. The two distinct parts of the village are divided by a small stream where women wash their clothes. The southern portion called **Naqara** is the island's commercial center, with several large Indo-Fijian stores, the island's bank, and a couple of places to stay. Pacific Transport has its bus terminus here.

Somosomo, to the north of Naqara, is the chiefly quarter, with the personal residence of the Tui Cakau on the hill directly above the bridge (no entry). Beside the main road below is the large hall built for the 1986 meeting of the Great Council of Chiefs. Missionary William Cross, one of the creators of today's system of written Fijian, who died at Somosomo in 1843, is buried in the attractive new church next to the meeting hall. There's even electric street lighting in this part of town!

The challenging trail up to lovely **Lake Tagimaucia,** 823 meters high in the mountainous interior, begins at the south end of Naqara. The first half is the hardest. You'll need between six hours and a full day to do a round-trip, and a guide (F$20) will be necessary, as there are many trails to choose from. You must wade for a half hour through knee-deep mud in the crater to reach the lake's edge. Much of the lake's surface is covered with floating vegetation, and the water is only five meters deep. From Oct.–Jan., you have a chance of seeing the rare red-and-white *tagimaucia* flower blossoming near the lake.

SPORTS AND RECREATION

Aqua-Trek Taveuni (tel. 888-0544, fax 888-0288, www.aquatrekdiving.com), at the Garden Island Resort, does daily two-tank dives at F$165 plus gear (no one-tank dives). PADI scuba certification costs F$660, or take a one-tank "discover scuba course" at F$148). You'll find cheaper dive shops, but Aqua-Trek's facilities are first rate. This is the closest dive shop to the famous Rainbow Reef.

The dive shop at the Garden Island Resort rents kayaks at F$15/50 an hour/half day. In good weather, Korolevu Island opposite the resort would make a great destination.

ACCOMMODATIONS
Under US$25

The original budget hotel on Taveuni was **Kaba's Motel & Guest House** (tel. 888-0233, fax 888-0202, kaba@connect.com.fj) at Naqara, which charges F$25/35/40 single/double/twin in one of four double rooms with shared facilities in the guesthouse. The cooking facilities are very good. The newer motel section is F$45/55/60 for one of the six larger units with kitchenette, fridge, fan, and private bath. The water is solar-heated, so cold showers are de rigueur in overcast weather (ask for a discount in that case). Kaba's Supermarket is just up the street. No check-ins are accepted after 1800. Naqara is a convenient place to stay for catching buses, but at night there's nothing much to do other than watch the BBC on TV.

A friendly Indo-Fijian family runs **Kool's Accommodation** (tel. 888-0395), opposite Kaba's Supermarket at Naqara. The six rooms in two long blocks facing the eating area are F$15 pp, and cooking facilities are provided (but no fridge).

Sunset Accommodation (Baiya Kondaiya, tel. 888-0229), on a busy corner near the Korean Wharf at Lovonivonu, has two rooms with shared bath in the main house at F$15/25 single/double. A separate bungalow with kitchen and bath is F$40 for up to three. They prepare tasty Indian meals (F$5) upon request.

For information on the **Dolphin Bay Divers Retreat** (tel. 888-0531 or 992-0531, www.dolphinbaydivers.com), on Vanua Levu but most easily accessible from Taveuni, turn to Buca Bay and Rabi in the Vanua Levu chapter.

US$25–50

The **First Light Inn** (tel. 888-0339, fax 888-0387, firstlight@connect.com.fj), near the Garden Island Resort at Waiyevo, was built in late 1999, just in time for the millennium celebrations. This large, two-story concrete building has 20 rooms with bath and TV at F$52/60 fan/air-conditioned for up to three people. Communal cooking facilities are provided. Local contract workers sometimes book rooms here on the weekends to watch the football games on TV and have fun, so be prepared.

US$50–100

The **Garden Island Resort** (tel. 888-0286, fax 888-0288, garden@connect.com.fj) is by the sea at Waiyevo, three kilometers south of Naqara. Formerly known as the Castaway, this was Taveuni's premier (and only) hotel when it was built by the Travelodge chain in the 1960s. In 1996, the scuba operator Aqua Trek USA purchased the property. The 28 air-conditioned rooms in an attractive two-story building are F$154/194 single/double, or F$35 pp in the two four-bed dorms. The buffet meal plan is F$80 pp, and eating by the pool is fun (dinner reservations before 1700 required). The food won't win any awards, but the house band is pretty good! There's no beach, but the Garden Island offers evening entertainment, a swimming pool, excursions, and water sports. Snorkeling trips (F$10 pp, plus F$11 for snorkeling gear, if required) are arranged to Korolevu Island at 1000 and 1400, and a large dive shop is on the premises. Airport transfers are F$30 pp roundtrip (unless you're alone, a taxi will be cheaper). The Garden Island is an okay place to hang out—better value than the high-end places around Matei.

OTHER PRACTICALITIES

Food

Frank Fong's **Waci-Pokee Restaurant** (tel. 888-0036; Mon.–Fri. 0700–2000, Sat. 0700–1400), below the First Light Inn in Waiyevo, serves tasty Chinese and local meals for about F$5. You can eat outside in the thatched **Cannibal Cafe** directly behind the Waci-Pokee, a nice terrace overlooking Vanua Levu. A piece of chocolate cake is less than a dollar, but their slogan is "we'd love to have you for dinner." Order dinner beforehand, if possible.

Several unpretentious places in the fish market opposite the Garden Island Resort serve cheap picnic-table meals. Of these, the **Makuluva Restaurant** (tel. 994-5394; Sun.–Thurs. 0800–1630 and 1800–2000, Fri. 0800–1630) serves a good fish lunch/dinner for F$5/10. You must order dinner before 1600.

Dinner mains at the restaurant of the **Garden Island Resort** (tel. 888-0286) will set you back F$23. The hotel organizes a *meke* and *lovo* (F$35 pp) if enough paying guests are present to make it worth their while.

Jack's Restaurant (tel. 888-0173; daily 0700–2000), diagonally opposite the bus station in Naqara, serves mediocre curries in the F$4 range. For breakfast, order an egg sandwich with coffee for F$2. Verify prices while ordering.

Groceries

The variety of goods available at **Kaba's Supermarket** (tel. 888-0088) in Naqara is surprising, and a cluster of other small shops is adjacent. The **Morris Hedstrom** supermarket (tel. 888-0053) is a bit north in Somosomo. Small grocery stores also exist at Wairiki and Waiyevo.

Shopping

Ross Handicrafts (tel. 888-0972), below the First Light Inn in Waiyevo, has a typical selection of Fijian handicrafts.

Services

Traveler's checks can be changed at the Colonial National Bank (weekdays 0900–1600) in Naqara. The bank doesn't give cash advances on credit cards. In a pinch, supermarkets on Taveuni may agree to do it, but you'll pay a 10 percent surcharge.

Taveuni's main post office is below the First Light Inn at Waiyevo.

Card phones are at Matei Airport, at Bhula Bhai & Sons Supermarket and Rauf Mohammed Enterprises in Matei, at Krishna Brothers Store in Naqara, at the fish market in Waiyevo, and at several other locations.

Garden State General Merchants (tel. 888-0291), beside the BP service station opposite Kaba's Motel in Naqara, provides Internet access at F$.40 a minute.

The island's hospital (tel. 888-0444) at Waiyevo received a F$2.4 million upgrade in 2003.

Southern Taveuni

The southern end of Taveuni is one of the island's most beautiful areas, but transportation is spotty, with bus service from Naqara Monday–Saturday at 0900, 1100, and 1645 only. Since the 1645 bus spends the night at Vuna and doesn't return to Naqara until the next morning, the only way to really see southern Taveuni is to also spend the night there. If this isn't possible, the round-trip bus rides, which leave Naqara at 0900 and 1100, are still worth doing.

The bus from Naqara runs south along the coast to Susie's Plantation Resort, where it turns inland to Delaivuna. There it turns around and returns to the coast, which it follows southeast to Navakawau via South Cape. On the way back, it cuts directly across some hills to Kanacea and continues up the coast without going to Delaivuna again. Southeast of Kanacea, there is very little traffic.

A hike around southern Taveuni provides an interesting day out for anyone staying at Susie's Plantation Resort. From Susie's, a road climbs east over the island to **Delaivuna,** where the bus turns around at a gate. The large Private Property sign here is mainly intended to ward off miscreants who create problems for the plantation owners by leaving open cattle gates. Visitors with enough sense to close the gates behind themselves may proceed.

You hike one hour down through the coconut plantation to a junction with two gates, just before a small bridge over a (usually) dry stream. If you continue walking 30 minutes down the road straight ahead across the bridge, you'll reach **Salialevu,** site of the Bilyard Sugar Mill (1874–1896), one of Fiji's first. In the 1860s, European planters tried growing cotton on Taveuni, turning to sugar when the cotton market collapsed. Later, copra was found to be more profitable. A tall chimney, boilers, and other equipment remain below the school at Salialevu.

After a look around, return to the two gates at the bridge and follow the other dirt road southwest for an hour through the coconut plantation to **Navakawau** village at the southeast end of the island. Some of Fiji's only Australian magpies (large black-and-white birds) inhabit this plantation.

Just east of South Cape as you come from Navakawau is the **Matamaiqi Blowhole,** where waves, driven by trade winds, crash into the unprotected black volcanic rocks, sending geysers of sea spray soaring skyward, especially on a southern swell. The viewpoint is just off the main road.

At **Vuna,** lava flows have formed pools beside the ocean, which fill up with fresh water at low tide and are used for washing and bathing.

SPORTS AND RECREATION

Nok's Dive Center (tel. 888-0246, fax 888-0072), at Kris Backplace north of Susie's Plantation Resort, offers diving at F$75/130 for one/two dives, plus F$20 a day for gear. Night dives are F$80. Snorkelers can go along in the boat for F$15, although some dive sites are not really suitable for snorkeling (ask). They dive on both the Vuna and Rainbow reefs.

One of the only stretches of paved road on southern Taveuni is at **Soqulu Plantation** or "Taveuni Estates" (tel. 888-0044), about eight kilometers south of Waiyevo. This upscale residential development features an attractive nine-hole golf course (greens fees F$20) by the sea, tennis courts, dive shop (tel. 888-0063, www.taveunidive.com), and a bowling green. Visitors are sometimes accommodated in a 120-year-old plantation house a four-minute walk from the golf course.

ACCOMMODATIONS

Under US$25

Susie's Plantation Resort (Susie Leonard, tel. 888-0125, www.susiesplantation.com), just north of Vuna Point at the south end of Taveuni, offers peace and quiet amid picturesque bucolic surroundings. The two rooms with shared bath in the main house are F$25–30 single or double depending on size, while the one suite with private bath is F$35. The three seaside *bure* with bath rent for F$40–50 double, plus F$10 per additional person to four maximum. Dorm beds are F$15 each, or pay F$10 pp to camp. Meals in the restaurant (housed in the oldest missionary building on the island) are F$6/10 for continental/full breakfast, F$5–8 for lunch, or F$16 for dinner. Otherwise, you can cook your own food in a common kitchen for a F$2 charge (but not in the *bure* or rooms), and Kutty's Grocery Store is a 10-minute walk up the road to Delaivuna. At sundown, the Sunset Boys serenade you from behind the kava bowl. Nok's Dive Center offers daily trips to the Great White Wall and Rainbow Reef. Even

The Sunset Boys serenade guests each evening at Susie's Plantation Resort on southern Taveuni.

if you're not a diver, you'll enjoy snorkeling off their rocky beach. Horseback riding (F$35 for a half day) and bird-watching tours can be arranged at this atmospheric resort on spacious landscaped grounds.

Vuna Lagoon Lodge (tel. 888-0627), on the Vuna Lagoon near Vuna village, a kilometer south of Vatuwiri Farm, consists of two European-style houses just back from a black lava coastline highlighted by small golden beaches. The two rooms with shared bath are F$30 single or double, the two with private bath F$50, and the two dorms with three or four beds are F$15 pp. Cooking facilities are provided (two tiny stores are in the village), or you can order meals. Namoli Beach, a 10-minute walk away, is good for swimming and snorkeling (better at low tide, as the current picks up appreciably when the tide comes in). The friendly propri-

etor, Adi Salote Samanunu, is a daughter of the chief of Vuna.

US$50–100
The **Vatuwiri Farm Resort** (tel. 888-0316) at Vuna Point, two kilometers south of Susie's Plantation, offers the possibility of staying on an authentic working farm, established in 1871 by James Valentine Tarte. The family's history was the subject of a 1988 novel titled *Fiji* by Daryl Tarte. Today, the Tartes produce beef, vanilla, cocoa, pigs, and copra, and rent two small cottages to tourists for F$120 double a night. Good meals can be ordered at additional cost. The rocky coast here is fine for snorkeling, and horseback riding (F$40) is available. The Tarte family is congenial, and this is perhaps your best chance to stay on a real working farm in Fiji. You can fax them at 888-0314, but call first to ask them to turn their machine on.

Islands off Taveuni

Qamea Island
Qamea (ngga-ME-a) Island, just three kilometers east of Taveuni, is the 12th-largest island in Fiji. It's 10 kilometers long, with lots of lovely bays, lush green hills, and secluded white-sand beaches. Land crabs *(lairo)* are gathered in abundance here during their migration to the sea, at the beginning of the breeding season in late November or early December. The birdlife is also rich, due to the absence of the mongoose.

In 2001, Dr. Patrick D. Nunn of the University of the South Pacific conducted excavations of settlement sites on Qamea and surrounding islands, and he discovered *lapita*-era remains dating back 2600–3000 years. Vatusogosogo, one of six villages on Qamea, is inhabited by descendants of blackbirded Solomon islanders. Outboards from villages on Qamea land near Navakacoa village on the northeast side of Taveuni. The best time to try for a ride over is Thursday or Friday afternoons.

The upscale **Qamea Beach Resort** (tel. 888-0220, fax 888-0092, www.qamea.com), on the west side of Qamea, has 11 air-conditioned *bure* at F$1,180 double, and one split-level honeymoon villa at F$1,450 (children under 13 not

accepted). Substantial meals, airport transfers, and tax are included. All units have a ceiling fan, mini-fridge, giant outdoor showers, lawn furniture, and hammock-equipped front deck. Meals are served in a tall central dining room and lounge designed like a *burekalou* (temple), and a trio sings around dinnertime. Drink prices are astronomical, so bring along a duty-free bottle. The new owners, Ron and Bryce, go out of their way to assist physically challenged guests, although Qamea is not fully wheelchair-accessible. The swimming off Qamea's 400 meters of fine white sands is good, with lava pools emerging at low tide, and there's also a small freshwater swimming pool. Activities such as snorkeling, sailing, windsurfing, village tours, and hiking are included in the basic price, but tours to Taveuni and Laucala, fishing, and scuba diving are extra. Unfortunately, we've received mixed feedback about the dive shop. A waterfront spa (one-hour massage F$70, facial F$95) was added in 2002.

Matangi Island
Matangi is a tiny horseshoe-shaped volcanic island just north of Qamea, its sunken crater forming a

lovely palm-fringed bay. The island is privately owned by the Douglas family, which has been producing copra on Matangi for five generations and still does. In 1988, they diversified into the hotel business.

Matangi Island Resort (Noel Douglas, tel. 888-0260, fax 888-0274, www.matangiisland.com), 10 kilometers northeast of Taveuni, markets itself as a honeymoon destination by advertising in the U.S. bridal magazines. It tries to do the same as far as scuba diving goes, but the prime dive sites in the Somosomo Strait are a long way from this resort. Matangi's three tree-house *bure* are intended for the recently wed (F$1,100 double). Other guests are accommodated in the neat thatched *bure* scattered among the coconut palms below Matangi's high jungly interior. The seven "deluxe" *bure* are F$490/620 single/double, while the two standards and one duplex are F$370/620. Family *bure* are F$1,120/1,350 standard/deluxe. Prices include meals, snacks, laundry, some excursions, and tax, but return boat transfers from Taveuni are F$124 pp extra. Scuba diving with Tropical Dive (tel./fax 888-0776, www.matangidive.com) is F$195 plus gear for two tanks. Reader feedback on Matangi Island has been mixed.

Laucala Island

Laucala Island, which shares a barrier reef with Qamea, was depopulated and sold to Europeans in the mid-19th century by the chief of Taveuni, after the inhabitants sided with Tongan chief Enele Ma'afu in a local war. In 1972, the late billionaire businessman and New York publisher Malcolm Forbes bought 12-square-kilometer Laucala from the Australian company Morris Hedstrom for US$1 million. He then spent additional millions on an airstrip, wharf, and roads, and on replacing the thatched *bure* of the 300 Fijian inhabitants with 40 red-roofed houses with electricity and indoor plumbing. Forbes died in 1990 and is buried on the island. His former private residence stands atop a hill overlooking the native village, the inhabitants of which make copra. In 1984, Forbes opened a small resort called "Fiji Forbes" on Laucala. During the turbulence following the Speight coup attempt in mid 2000, Laucala Island was invaded by thugs with scores to settle, and the resort managers were beaten and held for 24 hours. Although peace has now returned to the island, the resort has closed. In 2003, the island was sold to Dietrich Mateschitz, the Austrian founder of the energy-drink producer Red Bull, for US$10 million. Tourists from Qamea visit occasionally to snorkel in Laucala's tidal pools.

The Lau Group and Rotuma

The Lau Group is by far the most remote region of Fiji, its 57 islands scattered over a vast area of ocean between Viti Levu and Tonga. Roughly half of them are inhabited. Though all are relatively small, they vary from volcanic islands to uplifted atolls to some combination of the two. Tongan influence has always been strong in Lau, and due to Polynesian mixing, the people have a somewhat lighter skin color than other Fijians. The westward migrations continue today: More than 40,000 Lauans live on Viti Levu, and less than 13,000 live on their home islands. Historically the chiefs of Lau have always had a political influence on Fiji far out of proportion to their economic or geographical importance.

Vanua Balavu (52 square km) and Lakeba (54 square km) are the largest and most important islands of the group. These are also the only islands with organized budget accommodations, and Vanua Balavu is the more rewarding of the two. Once accessible only after a long sea voyage on infrequent copra-collecting ships, four islands in Lau—Lakeba, Vanua Balavu, Moala, and Cicia—now have regular air service from Suva. Occasional private ships also circulate through Lau, usually calling at five or six islands on a single trip. No banks are to be found in Lau, and it's important to bring sufficient Fijian currency.

Rotuma is on the opposite side of the country from Lau, 600 kilometers north of Viti Levu.

This isolated 5-by-14-kilometer volcanic island is surrounded on all sides by more than 322 kilometers of open sea. There's a saying in Fiji that if you can find Rotuma on a map, then it's a fairly good map. Rotuma's climate is damper and hotter than other parts of Fiji. The Rotumans are a Polynesian people linked to Melanesian Fiji by historical and geographical chance.

Few of these islands are prepared for tourism, so it really helps to know someone. But contrary to what is written in some guidebooks, individual tourists *do not* require a special permit or invitation to visit Lau or Rotuma—you just get on a plane and go. (Cruising yachties do need a permit.) Since the best selection of places to stay is on Vanua Balavu in Northern Lau, that's the logical place to head first. Words like pristine, untouched, and idyllic all seem to have been invented for Lau and Rotuma, and the unconditional friendliness of the local people is renowned. This is one area where you don't need to worry about bumping into a McDonald's!

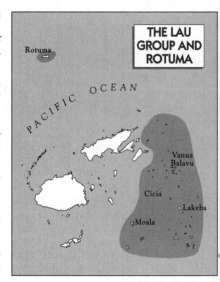

Northern Lau

VANUA BALAVU ISLAND

The name means the "long land." The southern portion of this unusual, seahorse-shaped island is mostly volcanic, while the north is uplifted coral. This unspoiled environment of palm-fringed beaches backed by long grassy hillsides and sheer limestone cliffs is a wonderful area to explore. Varied vistas and scenic views are on all sides. To the east is a 130-kilometer barrier reef enclosing a 37-by-16-kilometer lagoon. The Bay of Islands at the northwest end of Vanua Balavu is a recognized hurricane shelter. The villages of Vanua Balavu are impeccably clean, the grass cut and manicured. Large mats are made on the island, and strips of pandanus can be seen drying in front of many houses.

In 1840, Commodore Wilkes of the U.S. Exploring Expedition named Vanua Balavu and its adjacent islands enclosed by the same barrier reef the "Exploring Isles." In the days of sail, Lomaloma, the largest settlement, was an important Pacific port. The early trading company Hennings Brothers had its headquarters here. The great Tongan warlord Enele Ma'afu conquered northern Lau from the chiefs of Vanua Levu in 1855 and made Lomaloma the base for his bid to dominate Fiji. A small monument flanked by two cannons on the waterfront near the wharf recalls the event. Fiji's first public botanical garden was laid out here more than a century ago, but nothing remains of it. History has passed Lomaloma by. Today, it's only a big sleepy village, with a hospital and a couple of general stores. Some 400 Tongans live in Sawana, the south portion of Lomaloma village, and many of the houses have the round ends characteristic of Lau. Fiji's first prime minister and later president, Ratu Sir Kamisese Mara, was born in Sawana.

Sights

Copra is the main export, and there's a small coconut-oil mill at **Lomaloma.** A road runs inland from Lomaloma, up and across the island to

LAU GROUP AND ROTUMA HIGHLIGHTS

Lomaloma, Vanua Balavu Island: remote location, small resort (p. 318)

Katafanga Island: new upscale resort (p. 321)

limestone caves, Lakeba: numerous, seldom visited caves (p. 323)

Sisilo Hill, Rotuma: historic relics, burials of kings (p. 326)

Dakuilomaloma. From the small communications station on a grassy hilltop midway, there's an excellent view.

Follow the road south from Lomaloma three kilometers to **Narocivo** village, then continue two kilometers beyond to the narrow passage that separates Vanua Balavu and Malata islands. At low tide, you can easily wade across to **Namalata** village. Alternatively, work your way around to the west side of Vanua Balavu, where there are isolated tropical beaches. There's good snorkeling in this passage.

A guide can show you **hot springs** and **burial caves** among the high limestone outcrops between Narocivo and Namalata. This can be easily arranged at Nakama, the tiny collection of houses closest to the cliffs, upon payment of F$5 pp or F$10 per group (bargain if more is asked). Small bats inhabit some of the caves.

Rent a boat to take you over to the **Raviravi Lagoon** on Susui Island, the favorite picnic spot near Lomaloma for the locals. The beach and snorkeling are good, and there's a lake where sea turtles are kept.

Events

A most unusual event occurs from time to time at Masomo Bay, west of **Mavana** village, usually around Christmas. For a couple of days, the Mavana villagers, clad only in skirts of *drauniqai* leaves, enter the waters and stir up the muddy bottom by swimming around clutching logs. No one understands exactly why, and magic is thought to be involved, but this activity stuns the *yawa*, or mullet fish, that inhabit the bay, rendering them easy prey for waiting spears. Peni,

the *bete* (priest) of Mavana, controls the ritual. No photos are allowed. A Fijian legend tells how the *yawa* were originally brought to Masomo by a Tongan princess.

Accommodations

Moana's Guesthouse (tel. 889-5006, www.moanasguesthouses.com) in Sawana village is run by Tevita and Carolyn Fotofili, with the help of daughter Moana. They offer a three-bed dorm and double room in an oval-ended Tongan-style house in the village, plus another room in an adjacent house. In 2000, the eager-to-please Fotofilis built three traditional-style Tongan *bure* on the beach about a kilometer away. Either way, it's F$50 pp including all meals and snacks (children under 12 half price). The food is outstanding and plentiful, with lots of fresh fruit. Some very good snorkeling is available, although it takes a bit of effort to get to it. A motorboat is for hire for use on trips around Vanua Balavu or even to nearby islands like Kanacea and Mago. There's also a Fijian outrigger sailing canoe and horseback riding.

LAU GROUP AND ROTUMA

© DAVID STANLEY

Simple island accommodations are available at Moana's Guesthouse.

If you enjoy peace and solitude and aren't too worried about amenities, this is the place.

If Moana's is full, try Mr. Poasa Delailomaloma (tel. 889-5060) and his brother Laveti's guest house in the middle of Lomaloma village, a short walk away. They charge F$45 pp including meals. Both Poasa's and Moana's make perfect bases from which to explore the island, and you get a feel for village life while retaining a degree of privacy. It's a true Fiji experience.

You can also stay at Joe and Hélène Tuwai's **Nawanawa Estate** (tel. 811-6833), a kilometer from Daliconi village near the airport on the northwest side of the island. They meet all flights (transfers F$30 pp round-trip) and can accommodate 10 persons in their own home on the estate. In the unlikely event that they were full, something else could be arranged. The Tuwais charge F$55/100 single/double including three meals (children under 10 F$25). You'll share their attractive colonial-style home, with solar electricity (no generator noise). Aside from hiking, snorkeling, and fishing, you can ask to be dropped on a deserted island for a small charge. If you have a tent, you can camp there all by yourself for a small fee. Boat trips to the pris-

tine Bay of Islands for caving and snorkeling are also possible (F$10 an hour plus fuel). All three places just mentioned accept cash only (take insect repellent and sunscreen too).

Getting There

Air Fiji flies to Vanua Balavu twice a week from Suva (F$130). The flights are heavily booked, so reserve your return journey before leaving Suva. Even then, if it has been raining too hard, the soggy airstrip may be closed. You can hitch a ride from the airstrip to Lomaloma with the Air Fiji agent for F$1.50. After checking in at the airstrip for departure, you'll probably have time to scramble up the nearby hill for a good view of the island. Boat service from Suva on the *Tunatuki II* is only once every two weeks (F$82/113 deck/cabin).

Several carriers a day run from Lomaloma north to Mualevu, and some continue on to Mavana.

OTHER ISLANDS OF NORTHERN LAU

After setting himself up at Lomaloma on Vanua Balavu in 1855, Chief Ma'afu encouraged the establishment of European copra and cotton plantations, and several islands are freehold land to this day. **Kanacea,** to the west of Vanua Balavu, was sold to a European by the Tui Cakau in 1863, and the Kanacea people now reside on Taveuni. **Mago** (20 square km), a copra estate formerly owned by English planter Jim Barron, was purchased by the Tokyu Corporation of Japan in 1985 for F$6 million.

Naitauba is a circular island about 186 meters high, with high cliffs on the north coast. Originally owned by Hennings Brothers, in 1983 it was purchased from TV star Raymond Burr by the California spiritual group Johannine Daist Communion for US$2.1 million. Johannine Daist holds four-to-eight-week meditation retreats on Naitauba for longtime members of the communion. The communion's founder and teacher, Baba Da Free John, the former Franklin Albert Jones, who attained enlightenment in Hollywood in 1970, resides on the island.

There's a single Fijian village and a gorgeous white-sand beach on **Yacata Island.** Right next to Yacata and sharing the same lagoon is 260-hectare Kaimbu Island, where a small adults-only luxury resort opened in 1987. In 2004, **Kaimbu Island Resort** (Nigel Douglas, tel. 888-0333, fax 888-0334, kaimbu@connect.com.fj) was closed for renovations. In the past, the three spacious octagonal guest cottages have cost F$2,250 per couple per night, including meals, drinks, snorkeling, sailing, windsurfing, sportfishing, and scuba diving (minimum stay seven nights). The only thing lacking was a swimming pool. Kaimbu catered to folks in search of personalized service and total privacy at any price. The chartered flight from Suva or Taveuni to Kaimbu's central airstrip cost another F$2,225 per couple roundtrip, and a 12.5 percent government tax had to be added to all rates. If this sounds interesting, check to see if they've reopened.

Vatu Vara to the south, with its soaring interior plateau, golden beaches, and azure lagoon, is privately owned and unoccupied much of the time. The circular, 314-meter-high central limestone terrace, which makes the island look like a hat when viewed from the sea, gives it its other name, Hat Island. There is reputed to be buried treasure on Vatu Vara.

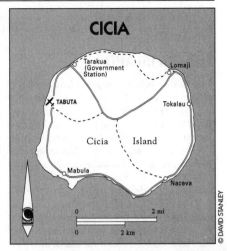

CICIA

Tarakua (Government Station) — Lomaji — TABUTA — Tokalau — Cicia Island — Mabula — Naceva

0 — 2 mi
0 — 2 km

© DAVID STANLEY

Katafanga to the southeast of Vanua Balavu was at one time owned by Harold Gatty, the famous Australian aviator who founded Fiji Airways (later Air Pacific) in 1951. In 2004, the super deluxe **Katafanga Island Resort** (tel. 330-7333, www.katafanga.com) opened on this 1.5-kilometer-long private island. The main complex with the dining pavilion and spa is on a coral cliff, while the 20 air-conditioned villas with individual Jacuzzis and dipping pools are along a white lagoon beach. Rates start at F$2,900 double including meals, drinks, activities, and spa treatments, plus F$800 pp return airfare from Suva and 12.5 percent tax (five-night minimum stay). Children under 17 are only accepted on certain dates. Scuba diving is available at additional cost. A nine-hole golf course separates Katafaga's airstrip from the rest of the resort.

Cicia, between Northern and Southern Lau, receives Air Fiji flights from Suva (F$121) once a week. Five Fijian villages are found on Cicia, and much of the 34-square-kilometer island is covered by coconut plantations. Fiji's only black-and-white Australian magpies have been introduced to Cicia and Taveuni.

Wailagi Lala, northernmost of the Lau Group, is a coral atoll bearing a lighthouse, which beckons to ships entering Nanuku Passage, the northwest gateway to Fiji.

Southern Lau

LAKEBA ISLAND

Lakeba is a rounded volcanic island reaching a height of 215 meters. The fertile red soils of the rolling interior hills have been planted with pine, but the low coastal plain, with eight villages and all of the people, is covered with coconuts. To the east is a wide lagoon enclosed by a barrier reef. In the olden days, the population lived on Delai Kedekede, an interior hilltop well suited for defense.

The original capital of Lakeba was Nasaqalau on the north coast, and the present inhabitants of Nasaqalau retain strong Tongan influence. When the Nayau clan conquered the island, their paramount chief, the Tui Nayau, became ruler of all of Southern Lau from his seat at Tubou. From the 1970s to the 1990s, Ratu Sir Kamisese Mara, the current Tui Nayau, served as prime minister and later as president of Fiji.

Sights

A 29-kilometer road runs all the way around Lakeba. From the Catholic church, you get a good view of **Tubou,** an attractive village and one of the largest in Fiji, with a hospital, wharf, several stores, and the Lau provincial headquarters. Tubou was originally situated at Korovusa just inland, where the foundations of former houses can still be seen. Farther inland on the same road is the forestry station and a nursery.

The Tongan chief Enele Ma'afu (died 1881) is buried on a stepped platform behind the Provincial Office near Tubou's wharf. In 1847, Ma'afu arrived in Fiji with a small Tongan army, ostensibly to advance the spread of Christianity, and by 1855 he dominated eastern Fiji from his base at Vanua Balavu. In 1869, Ma'afu united the group into the Lau Confederation and took the title Tui Lau. Two years later, he accepted the supremacy of Cakobau's Kingdom of Fiji, and in 1874 he signed the cession to Britain. Alongside Ma'afu is the grave of Ratu Sir Lala Sukuna (1888–1958), an important figure in the development of indigenous-Fijian self-government.

the tombs of Ma'afu and Ratu Sukuna at Tubou, Lakeba Island

David Cargill and William Cross, the first Methodist missionaries to arrive in Fiji, landed on the beach just opposite the burial place on October 12, 1835. Here they invented the present system of written Fijian.

The number one beach near Tubou is **Nukuselal,** which you can reach by walking east along the coastal road as far as the Public Works Department workshops. Turn right onto the track which runs along the west side of the compound to Nukuselal Beach.

Many forestry roads have been built throughout the interior of Lakeba. You can walk across the island from Tubou to Yadrana in a couple of hours, enjoying excellent views along the way. A radio station operates on solar energy near the center of the island. **Aiwa Island,** which can be seen to the southeast, is owned by the Tui Nayau and is inhabited only by flocks of wild goats.

Nasaqalau and Vicinity

The finest **limestone caves** on the island are near the coast on the northwest side of Lakeba, 2.5 kilometers southwest of Nasaqalau. **Oso Nabukete** is the largest; the entrance is behind a raised limestone terrace. You walk through two chambers before reaching a small, circular opening about one meter in diameter, which leads into a third chamber. The story goes that women attempting to hide during pregnancy are unable to pass through this opening, thus giving the cave its name, the "Tight Fit to the Pregnant" Cave.

Nearby is a smaller cave, **Qara Bulo** (Hidden Cave), which one must crawl into. Warriors used it as a refuge and hiding place in former times. The old village of Nasaqalau was located on top of the high cliffs behind the caves at Ulu-ni-koro. The whole area is owned by the Nautoqumu clan of Nasaqalau, and they will arrange for a guide to show you around for a fee. Take a flashlight and some newspapers to spread over the openings to protect your clothing.

Each October or November, the Nasaqalau people perform a shark-calling ritual. A month before the ritual, a priest *(bete)* plants a post with a piece of tapa tied to it in the reef. He then keeps watch to ensure that no one comes near the area, while performing a daily kava ceremony. When the appointed day arrives, the caller wades out up to his neck and repeats a chant. Not long after, a large school of sharks led by a white shark arrives and circles the caller. He leads them to

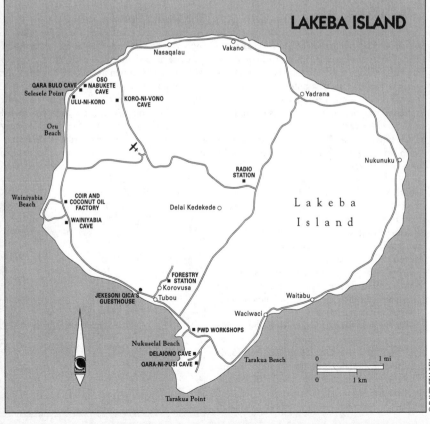

LAKEBA ISLAND

LAU GROUP AND ROTUMA

Nasaqalau   Vakano

QARA BULO CAVE   OSO NABUKETE CAVE
Selesele Point
ULU-NI-KORO   KORO-NI-VONO CAVE

Yadrana

Oru Beach

Nukunuku

RADIO STATION

Wainiyabia Beach

COIR AND COCONUT OIL FACTORY

Delai Kedekede

L a k e b a
I s l a n d

WAINIYABIA CAVE

FORESTRY STATION
Korovusa
JEKESONI QICA'S GUESTHOUSE   Tubou

Waitabu

Waciwaci

PWD WORKSHOPS

Nukuselal Beach
DELAIONO CAVE
QARA-NI-PUSI CAVE

Tarakua Beach

0   1 mi
0   1 km

MOON

Tarakua Point

© DAVID STANLEY

shallow water, where all but the white shark are formally killed and eaten.

Accommodations

Jekesoni Qica's Guesthouse (tel. 882-3035) in Tubou offers rooms with shared bath at F$40 pp for room and board. The locals at Tubou concoct a potent homebrew *(uburu)* from cassava—ask Jack where you can get some.

Getting There

Air Fiji flies to Lakeba three times a week from Suva (F$131). A bus connects the airstrip to Tubou, and buses run around the island four times daily on weekdays, three times daily on weekends.

OTHER ISLANDS OF SOUTHERN LAU

Unlike the islands of northern Lau, many of which are freehold and owned by outsiders, the isles of southern Lau are communally owned by the Fijian inhabitants. This is by far the most remote corner of Fiji. In a pool on **Vanua Vatu** are red prawns similar to those of Vatulele and Vanua Levu. Here the locals can summon the prawns with a certain chant.

Oneata is famous for its mosquitoes and tapa cloth. In 1830, two Tahitian teachers from the London Missionary Society arrived on Oneata and were adopted by a local chief who had previously visited Tonga and Tahiti. The men spent the rest of their lives on the island, and there's a monument to them at Dakuloa village.

Moce is known for its tapa cloth, which is also made on Namuka, Vatoa, and Ono-i-Lau. **Komo** is famous for its handsome women and dances *(meke)*, which are performed whenever a ship arrives. Moce, Komo, and Olorua are unique in that they are volcanic islands without uplifted limestone terraces.

The **Yagasa Cluster** is owned by the people of Moce, who visit it occasionally to make copra. Fiji's finest *tanoa* are carved from *vesi* (ironwood) at **Kabara,** the largest island in southern Lau. The surfing is also said to be good at Kabara, if you can get there.

Fulaga is known for its wood carvings; large outrigger canoes are still built on Fulaga, as well as on **Ogea.** More than 100 tiny islands in the Fulaga lagoon have been undercut into incredible mushroom shapes. The water around them is tinged with striking colors by the dissolved limestone, and there are numerous beaches. Yachts can enter this lagoon through a narrow pass.

Ono-i-Lau, far to the south, is closer to Tonga than to the main islands of Fiji. It consists of three small volcanic islands, remnants of a single crater, in an oval lagoon. A few tiny coral islets sit on the barrier reef. The people of Ono-i-Lau make the best *magi magi* (sennit rope) and *tabu kaisi* mats in the country. Only high chiefs may sit on these mats. Ono-i-Lau formerly had air service from Suva, but this has been suspended, and the only access now is by ship.

The Moala Group

Structurally, geographically, and historically, the high volcanic islands of Moala, Totoya, and Matuku have more to do with Viti Levu than with the rest of Lau. In the mid-19th century, the Tongan warlord Enele Ma'afu conquered the islands, and today they're still administered as part of the Lau Group. All three islands have varied scenery, with dark green rainforests above grassy slopes, good anchorage, many villages, and abundant food. Their unexplored nature yet relative proximity to Suva by boat make them an ideal escape for adventurers. No tourist facilities of any kind exist in the Moala Group.

Triangular **Moala** is an intriguing 68-square-kilometer island, the ninth-largest in Fiji. Two small crater lakes on the summit of Delai Moala (467 m) are covered with matted sedges, which will support a person's weight. Though the main island is volcanic, an extensive system of reefs flanks the shores. Ships call at the small government station of Naroi, also the site of an airstrip that receives **Air Fiji** flights twice a week from Suva (F$118).

Totoya is a horseshoe-shaped high island en-closing a deep bay on the south. The bay, actually the island's sunken crater, can only be entered through a narrow channel known as the Gullet, and the southeast trade winds send high waves across the reefs at the mouth of the bay, making this a dangerous place. Better anchorage is found off the southwest arm of the island. Five Fijian villages are found on Totoya, while neighboring **Matuku** has seven. The anchorage in a submerged crater on the west side of Matuku is one of the finest in Fiji.

Rotuma

According to legend, Rotuma was formed by Raho, a Samoan folk hero who dumped two basketfuls of earth here to create the twin islands, joined by the Motusa Isthmus. Tongans from Niuafo'ou conquered Rotuma in the 17th century and ruled from Noa'tau until they were overthrown.

The first recorded European visit was by Captain Edwards of HMS *Pandora* in 1791, while he was searching for the *Bounty* mutineers. Tongan Wesleyan missionaries introduced Christianity in 1842, followed in 1847 by Marist Roman Catholics. Their followers fought pitched battles in the religious wars of 1871 and 1878, with the Wesleyans emerging victorious. Tiring of strife, the chiefs asked Britain to annex the island in 1879. Cession officially took place in 1881, and Rotuma has been part of Fiji ever since. European traders ran the copra trade from their settlement at Motusa, until local cooperatives took over.

On Rotuma today, the administration is in the hands of a district officer responsible to the district commissioner at Levuka. Most decisions of the 15-member Rotuma island council pertain to local concerns. The island remains remote from the rest of Fiji, and a desire for independence is felt among some Rotumans. Some 2,800 Rotumans presently inhabit the island, and another 4,700 live in Suva and Naitasiri. The light-skinned Polynesian Rotumans are easily distinguished from Fijians. The women weave fine white mats. Fiji's juiciest oranges are grown here, and Rotuma kava is noted for its strength. Most visitors to Rotuma are relatives or friends of local residents, and the number of foreign tourists arriving here is negligible.

SIGHTS

Ships arrive at a wharf on the edge of the reef, connected to Oinafa Point by a 200-meter coral causeway, which acts as a breakwater. There's a lovely white beach at **Oinafa.** The airstrip is to

M.G.L. DOMENY DE RIENZI

18th-century transfer of authority on Rotuma Island

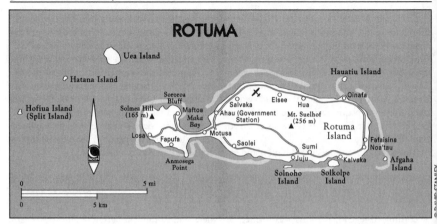

the west, between Oinafa and Ahau, the government station. At **Sisilo** near Noa'tau, visit a hill with large stone slabs and old cannons scattered about, marking the burial place of the kings of yore. Look for the fine stained-glass windows in the Catholic church at **Sumi** on the south coast. Inland near the center of the island is Mt. Suelhof (256 m), the highest peak; climb it for the view.

Maftoa, across the Motusa Isthmus, has a graveyard with huge stones brought here long ago. It's said that four men could go into a trance and carry the stones with their fingers. **Sororoa Bluff,** (218 m) above Maftoa, can be climbed, though the view is obstructed by vegetation. Deserted **Vaioa Beach,** on the west side of Sororoa Bluff, is one of the finest in the Pacific. A kilometer southwest of Vaioa Beach is **Solmea Hill** (165 m), with an inactive crater on its north slope. On the coast at the northwest corner of Rotuma is a natural **stone bridge** over the water. A cave with a swimmable freshwater pool is at **Fapufa** on the south coast.

Hatana, a tiny islet off the west end of Rotuma, is said to be the final resting place of Raho, the demigod who created Rotuma. A pair of volcanic rocks before a stone altar surrounded by a coral ring are said to be the King and Queen stones. Today, Hatana is a refuge for seabirds. **Hofiua,** or Split Island, looks like it was cut in two with a knife; a circular boulder bridges the gap.

Visitors are expected to request permission before visiting sites like Sisilo or the cave at Fap-ufa. Inquire at Ahau about who to ask (permission will always be given unless something peculiar has come up), but it is a courtesy expected by the Rotumans and will avoid unpleasant misunderstandings.

PRACTICALITIES
Accommodations
Though the airport opened as far back as 1982, places to stay on Rotuma are few. Many Rotumans live in Suva, however, and if you have a Rotuman friend he/she may be willing to send word to his/her family to expect you. Ask your friend what you should take along as a gift. It's appropriate to make a financial contribution to your host family soon after you arrive, in order to compensate them for your stay (F$40 a day per couple is the minimum you should offer). When deciding on the amount, bear in mind that groceries purchased in the small stores around Rotuma cost about double what they would on Viti Levu. Rainbow-way Travel Services (tel. 330-6613, fax 330-6593, rainboway1@connect.com.fj) in Suva arranges stays on Rotuma.

The only official place to stay is **Mojito's Barfly** (tel. 889-1144) across the street from Motusa Primary School. The four rooms with shared bath in two Polynesian-style houses are used to accommodate government workers, who pay F$65 pp including meals and laundry, or F$30 pp without meals (no cooking facilities provided). Despite the name, the bar no longer functions here.

There's no bank on Rotuma, so be sure to change enough money to cover all local expenditures before leaving Suva. In emergencies, you might be able to have someone wire money to you via Western Union, care of the Post Shop at Ahau.

Getting There

Air Fiji flies from Suva to Rotuma weekly (F$339 one-way). Ships like the *Bulou-ni-ceva* and *Cagi Mai Ba* operate from Suva to Rotuma once a month (two days, F$100/170/190 deck/cabin/ lounge each way). Turn to Transportation in the Suva chapter for more information.

Be aware that transportation to and from Rotuma, either by boat or plane, can be erratic, and you should be as flexible as possible. It's not uncommon for the boat from Suva to be delayed two weeks with engine trouble, and the plane has also been known not to go on schedule, or flights can be cancelled.

LAU GROUP AND ROTUMA

Resources

Glossary

A$: Australian dollars

adi: the female equivalent of *ratu*

archipelago: a group of islands

ATM: automated teller machine

atoll: a low-lying, ring-shaped coral reef enclosing a lagoon

balabala: tree fern

balawa: pandanus, screw pine

balolo: in Fijian, a reef worm *(Eunice viridis)*

bark cloth: *see* tapa

barrier reef: a coral reef separated from the adjacent shore by a lagoon

bêche-de-mer: sea cucumber; an edible sea slug

beka: flying fox

bete: a traditional priest of the old religion

bilibili: a bamboo raft

bilo: a kava-drinking cup made from a coconut shell

blackbirder: A 19th-century European recruiter of island labor, mostly ni-Vanuatu and Solomon Islanders taken to work on plantations in Queensland and Fiji

Bose vaka-Turaga: Great Council of Chiefs

Bose vaka-Yasana: Provincial Council

breadfruit: a large, round fruit with starchy flesh, often baked in the *lovo*

bula **shirt:** a colorful Fijian aloha shirt

buli: Fijian administrative officer in charge of a *tikina;* subordinate of the *roko tui*

bure: a Fijian house

BYO: Bring Your Own (an Australian term used to refer to restaurants that allow you to bring your own alcoholic beverages)

C: Celsius

caldera: a wide crater formed through the collapse or explosion of a volcano

cassava: manioc; the starchy edible root of the tapioca plant

CDW: collision damage waiver

chain: an archaic unit of length equivalent to 20 meters

ciguatera: a form of fish poisoning caused by microscopic algae

code share: a system whereby two or more airlines own seats on a single flight

coir: coconut-husk sennit used to make rope, etc.

confirmation: A confirmed reservation exists when a supplier acknowledges, either orally or in writing, that a booking has been accepted.

copra: dried coconut meat used in the manufacturing of coconut oil, cosmetics, soap, and margarine

coral: a hard, calcareous substance of various shapes, composed of the skeletons of tiny marine animals called polyps

coral bank: a coral formation more than 150 meters long

coral bleaching: the expulsion of symbiotic algae by corals

coral head: a coral formation a few meters across

coral patch: a coral formation up to 150 meters long

cyclone: Also known as a hurricane (in the Caribbean) or typhoon (in Japan). A tropical storm that rotates around a center of low atmospheric pressure, it becomes a cyclone when its winds reach force 12 or 64 knots. At sea, the air will be filled with foam and driving spray, and the water surface will be completely white with 14-meter-high waves. In the Northern Hemisphere, cyclones spin counterclockwise, while south of the equator they move clockwise. The winds of cyclonic storms are deflected toward a low-pressure area at the center, although the "eye" of the cyclone may be calm.

dalo: *see* taro

Degei: the greatest of the pre-Christian Fijian gods

desiccated coconut: the shredded meat of dehydrated fresh coconut

direct flight: a through flight with one or more stops, but no change of aircraft, as opposed to a nonstop flight

drua: an ancient Fijian double canoe

dugong: a large plant-eating marine mammal; called a manatee in the Caribbean

EEZ: Exclusive Economic Zone; a 200-nautical-mile offshore belt of an island nation or seacoast state that controls the mineral exploitation and fishing rights

endemic: native to a particular area and existing only there

expatriate: a person residing in a country other than his/her own; in the South Pacific, such persons are also called "Europeans" if their skin is white, or simply "expats."

F$: Fiji dollars

FAD: fish aggregation device

fissure: a narrow crack or chasm of some length and depth

FIT: foreign independent travel; a custom-designed, prepaid tour composed of many individualized arrangements

fringing reef: a reef along the shore of an island

GPS: Global Positioning System, the space-age successor of the sextant

guano: manure of seabirds, used as a fertilizer

guyot: a submerged atoll, the coral of which couldn't keep up with rising water levels

hurricane: *see* cyclone

ika: fish

ivi: the Polynesian chestnut tree *(Inocarpus edulis)*

jug: a cross between a ceramic kettle and a pitcher, used to heat water for tea or coffee in Australian-style hotels

kai: freshwater mussel

kaisi: a commoner

kava: a Polynesian word for the drink known in the Fijian language as *yaqona* and in English slang as "grog." This traditional beverage is made by squeezing a mixture of the grated root of the pepper shrub *(Piper methysticum)* and cold water through a strainer of hibiscus-bark fiber.

kerekere: asking or borrowing something from a member of one's own group

kph: kilometers per hour

knot: about three kilometers per hour

kokoda: chopped raw fish and sea urchins marinated with onions and lemon

km: kilometer

koro: village

kumala: sweet potato *(Ipomoea batatas)*

kumi: stenciled tapa cloth

lagoon: an expanse of water bounded by a reef

lali: a hollow-log drum hit with a stick

lapita **pottery:** pottery made by the ancient Polynesians from 1600–500 B.C.

LDS: Latter-day Saints; the Mormons

leeward: downwind; the shore (or side) sheltered from the wind; as opposed to windward

live-aboard: a tour boat with cabin accommodation for scuba divers

LMS: London Missionary Society; a Protestant group that spread Christianity from Tahiti (1797) across the Pacific

lolo: coconut cream

lovo: an underground, earthen oven (called an *umu* in the Polynesian languages); after A.D. 500, the Polynesians had lost the art of making pottery, so they were compelled to bake their food rather than boil it.

magiti: feast

mahimahi: dorado, Pacific dolphin fish (no relation to the mammal)

mana: authority, prestige, virtue, "face," psychic power, a positive force

mangrove: a tropical shrub with branches that send down roots forming dense thickets along tidal shores

manioc: cassava, tapioca, a starchy root crop

masa kesa: freehand painted tapa

masi: see tapa

mata ni vanua: an orator who speaks for a high chief

mataqali: a landowning extended family

matrilineal: a system of tracing descent through the mother's familial line

meke: traditional song and dance

Melanesia: the high island groups of the western Pacific (Fiji, New Caledonia, Vanuatu, Solomon Islands, Papua New Guinea); from *melas* (black)

Micronesia: chains of high and low islands mostly north of the Equator (Carolines, Gilberts, Marianas, Marshalls); from *micro* (small)

mm: millimeters

MV: motor vessel

mynah: an Indian starling-like bird *(Gracula)*

NAUI: National Association of Underwater Instructors

NGO: nongovernmental organization

NFIP: Nuclear-Free and Independent Pacific movement

N.Z.: New Zealand

overbooking: the practice of confirming more seats, cabins, or rooms than are actually available to insure against no-shows

Pacific rim: the continental landmasses and large countries around the fringe of the Pacific

PADI: Professional Association of Dive Instructors (also Put Another Dollar In, or Pay And Dive Immediately)

palusami: a Samoan specialty of coconut cream wrapped in taro leaves and baked

pandanus: screw pine with slender stem and prop roots. The sword-shaped leaves are used for plaiting mats and hats.

parasailing: a sport in which participants are carried aloft by a parachute pulled behind a speedboat

pass: a channel through a barrier reef, usually with an outward flow of water

passage: an inside passage between an island and a barrier reef

patrilineal: a system of tracing descent through the father's familial line

pawpaw: papaya

pelagic: relating to the open sea, away from land

Polynesia: divided into Western Polynesia (Tonga and Samoa) and Eastern Polynesia (French Polynesia, Cook Islands, Hawaii, Easter Island, and New Zealand); from *poly* (many)

pp: per person

punt: a flat-bottomed boat

Quonset hut: a prefabricated, semicircular, metal shelter popular during World War II; also called a Nissan hut

rain shadow: the dry side of a mountain, sheltered from the windward side

rara: a grassy village square

ratu: a title for Fijian chiefs, prefixed to their names

reef: a coral ridge near the ocean surface

roko tui: senior Fijian administrative officer

roti: a flat Indian bread

sailing: the fine art of getting wet and becoming ill while slowly going nowhere at great expense

salusalu: garland, lei

scuba: self-contained underwater breathing apparatus

SDA: Seventh-Day Adventist

self-catering: *see* self-contained

self-contained: a room with private facilities (a toilet and shower not shared with other guests); the brochure term "en suite" means the same thing; as opposed to a "self-catering" unit with cooking facilities

sennit: braided coconut-fiber rope

sevusevu: a formal presentation of *yaqona*

shifting cultivation: a method of farming involving the rotation of fields instead of crops

shoal: a shallow sandbar or mud bank

shoulder season: a travel period between high/peak and low/off-peak seasons

SPARTECA: South Pacific Regional Trade and Economic Cooperation Agreement; an agreement that allows certain manufactured goods from Pacific countries duty-free entry to Australia and New Zealand

SPREP: South Pacific Regional Environment Program

subduction: the action of one tectonic plate wedging under another

subsidence: geological sinking or settling

sulu: a wraparound skirt or loincloth similar to a sarong

symbiosis: a mutually advantageous relationship between unlike organisms

tabu: taboo, forbidden, sacred, set apart, a negative force

tabua: a whale's tooth, a ceremonial object

takia: a small sailing canoe

talanoa: to chat or tell stories

tanoa: a special wide wooden bowl in which *yaqona* (kava) is mixed; used in ceremonies in Fiji, Tonga, and Samoa

tapa: a cloth made from the pounded bark of the paper mulberry tree *(Broussonetia papyrifera)*. It's soaked and beaten with a mallet to flatten and intertwine the fibers, then painted with geometric designs; called *siapo* in Samoan, *masi* in Fijian

tapu: *see* tabu

taro: a starchy elephant-eared tuber *(Colocasia esculenta)*, a staple food of the Pacific islanders; called *dalo* in Fijian

tavioka: tapioca, cassava, manioc, arrowroot

teitei: a garden

tel.: telephone

tiki: a humanlike sculpture used in the old days for religious rites and sorcery

tikina: a group of Fijian villages administered by a *buli*

timeshare: part ownership of a residential unit with the right to occupy the premises for a certain period each year, in exchange for payment of an annual maintenance fee

TNC: transnational corporation (also referred to as a multinational corporation)

trade wind: a steady wind blowing toward the equator from either northeast or southeast

trench: the section at the bottom of the ocean where one tectonic plate wedges under another

tridacna clam: eaten everywhere in the Pacific, its size varies between 10 centimeters and one meter

tropical storm: a cyclonic storm with winds of 35–64 knots

tsunami: a fast-moving wave caused by an undersea earthquake; sometimes erroneously called a tidal wave

tui: king

turaga: chief

turaga-ni-koro: village herald or mayor

U.S.: United States

US$: U.S. dollars

vakaviti: in the Fijian way

vale lailai: toilet

vanua: land, region

vigia: a mark on a nautical chart indicating a dangerous rock or shoal

VSO: Volunteer Service Overseas, the British equivalent of the Peace Corps

4WD: four-wheel drive

waka: a bundle of whole kava roots

windward: the point or side from which the wind blows, as opposed to leeward

yam: the starchy, tuberous root of a climbing plant

yaqona: *see* kava

yasana: an administrative province

zories: rubber shower sandals, thongs, flip-flops

Basic Fijian

Although most people in Fiji speak English fluently, mother tongues include Fijian, Hindi, and other Pacific languages. Knowledge of a few words of Fijian, especially slang words, will make your stay more exciting and enriching. Fijian has no pure *b, c,* or *d* sounds, as they are known in English. When the first missionaries arrived, they invented a system of spelling, with one letter for each Fijian sound. The reader should be aware that the sound "mb" is written *b,* "nd" is *d,* "ng" is *g,* "ngg" is *q,* and "th" is *c.*

Au lako mai Kenada. I come from Canada.
Au ni lako mai vei? Where do you come from?
Au sa lako ki vei? Where are you going?

bula: a Fijian greeting

Daru lako! Let's go!
dua: one
dua oo: said by males when they meet a chief or enter a Fijian *bure*
dua tale: once more

io: yes

kaivalagi: foreigner
kana: eat
kauta mai: bring
kauta tani: take away
Kocei na yacamu? What's your name?
koro: village

lailai: small
lako mai: come
lako tani: go
levu: big, much
lima: five
Loloma yani: Please pass along my regards.

magimagi: coconut rope fiber
magiti: feast
maleka: delicious

marama: madam
mataqali: a clan lineage
moce: goodbye

Na cava oqo? What is this?
ni sa bula: Hello, how are you? (can also say *sa bula* or *bula vinaka;* the answer is *an sa bula vinaka*)
ni sa moce: good night
ni sa yadra: good morning

qara: cave

rua: two

sa vinaka: it's okay
sega: no, none
sega na leqa: you're welcome
sota tale: see you again

talatala: reverend
tolu: three
tulou: excuse me
turaga: sir, Mr.

uro: a provocative greeting for the opposite sex

va: four
vaka lailai: a little, small
vaka levu: a lot, great
vaka malua: slowly
vaka totolo: fast
vale: house
vale lailai: toilet
vanua: land, custom, people
vinaka: thank you
vinaka vakalevu: thank you very much
vu: an ancestral spirit

wai: water

yadra: good morning
yalo vinaka: please
yaqona: kava, grog

Basic Hindi

aao: come
accha: good
bhaahut julum: very beautiful (slang)
chota: small (male)
choti: small (female)
dhanyabaad: thank you
ek aur: one more
haan: yes
hum jauo: I go (slang)
jalebi: an Indian sweet
jao: go
kab: when
kahaan: where
Kahaan jata hai?: Where are you going?
Kaise hai? How are you?

khana: food
Kitna? How much?
kya: what
laao: bring
maaf kijye ga: excuse me
nahi: no
namaste: hello, goodbye
pani: water
rait: okay
ram ram: same as *namaste*
roti: a flat Indian bread
seedhe jauo: go straight
Theek bhai: I'm fine
Yeh kia hai?: What's this?
yihaan: here

Suggested Reading

Description and Travel

Brunes, Evangeline. *Traveling the South Pacific Without Reservations*. Mechanicsville, Va.: Penrith Publications, 2001. A timid grandmother's account of eight months on the road in Fiji, the Samoas, and Cook Islands.

Geraghty, Craig, Glen, and Paul. *Children of the Sun*. Gympie, Australia: Glen Craig Publishing, 1996. This photo book available at the Fiji Visitors Bureau office in Suva is like one big Fiji family picture album in glorious color.

Gravelle, Kim. *Romancing the Islands*. Suva: Graphics Pacific, 1997. In these 42 stories, ex-American, now-Fiji resident Kim Gravelle shares a quarter century of adventures in the region. A delightfully sympathetic look at the islands and their characters.

Sahadeo, Muneshwar, et al. *Holy Torture in Fiji*. Suva: Institute of Pacific Studies, 1974. Rituals involving knives, oil, and fire; covers resistance to pain, the function of the ordeals, and other manifestations of religious devotion by Indo-Fijians.

Stephenson, Dr. Elsie. *Fiji's Past on Picture Postcards*. Suva: Fiji Museum, 1997. Some 275 old postcards of Fiji from the Caines Jannif collection.

Theroux, Paul. *The Happy Isles of Oceania: Paddling the Pacific*. London: Hamish Hamilton, 1992. The author of classic accounts of railway journeys sets out with kayak and tent to tour the Pacific.

Traditional Handicrafts of Fiji. Suva: Institute of Pacific Studies, 1997. The significance and history of Fijian handicrafts.

Wright, Ronald. *On Fiji Islands*. New York: Penguin Books, 1986. Wright relates his travels to Fijian history and tradition in a most pleasing and informative way.

Geography

Derrick, R. A. *The Fiji Islands: Geographical Handbook*. Suva: Government Printing Office, 1965. Derrick's earlier *History of Fiji* (1946) was a trailblazing work.

Donnelly, Quanchi, and Kerr. *Fiji in the Pacific: A History and Geography of Fiji*. Australia: Jacaranda Wiley, 1994. A high school text on the country.

Nunn, Patrick D. *Oceanic Islands*. Cambridge, Mass.: Blackwell, 1994. A basic text on island formation, coral reefs, and sea-level change.

Nunn, Patrick D. *Pacific Island Landscapes*. Suva: Institute of Pacific Studies, 1998. A leading geographer demystifies the geology and geomorphology of Fiji, Samoa, and Tonga, with emphasis on the origin of the islands.

Natural Science

Allen, Gerald R., and Roger Steene. *Indo-Pacific Coral Reef Field Guide*. El Cajon, Calif.: Odyssey Publishing, 1998. Essential for identifying the creatures of the reefs.

Harrison, Peter. *Seabirds of the World*. Princeton, N.J.: Princeton University Press, 1996. An ideal field guide to carry aboard a yacht or ship.

Lebot, Vincent, Lamont Lindstrom, and Mark Marlin. *Kava—the Pacific Drug*. New Haven, Conn.: Yale University Press, 1993. A thorough examination of kava and its many uses.

Randall, John E., Gerald Robert Allen, and Roger C. Steene. *Fishes of the Great Barrier Reef and Coral Sea*. Honolulu: University of Hawaii Press, 1997. An identification guide for amateur diver and specialist alike.

Ryan, Paddy. *Fiji's Natural Heritage*. Auckland: Exisle Publishing, 2000. With 500 photos and 288 pages of text, this is probably the most comprehensive popular book on any Pacific island ecosystem. It's so good, that every school in Fiji was given a copy by the New Zealand Ministry of Foreign Affairs, and the Seacology Foundation paid to have it translated into Fijian.

Ryan, Paddy. *The Snorkeler's Guide to the Coral Reef*. Honolulu: University of Hawaii Press, 1994. An introduction to the wonders of the Indo-Pacific reefs. The author spent 10 years in Fiji and knows the country well.

Veron, J. E. N. *Corals of Australia and the Indo-Pacific*. Honolulu: University of Hawaii Press, 1993. An authoritative, illustrated work.

Watling, Dick. *A Guide to the Birds of Fiji & Western Polynesia*. Suva: Environmental Consultants, 2001. The guide has detailed species accounts for the 173 species with confirmed records in the region, and notes a further 22 species with unconfirmed records. Copies can be ordered through www.pacificbirds.com.

Watling, Dick. *Mai Veikau: Tales of Fijian Wildlife*. Suva: Fiji Times, 1986. A wealth of easily digested information on Fiji's flora and fauna. Copies are available in Fiji bookstores.

Whistler, W. Arthur. *Flowers of the Pacific Island Seashore*. Honolulu: University of Hawaii Press, 1993. A guide to the littoral plants of Hawaii, Tahiti, Samoa, Tonga, Cook Islands, Fiji, and Micronesia.

History

Clunie, Fergus. *Yalo i Viti*. Suva: Fiji Museum, 1986. An illustrated catalog of the museum's collection, with lots of intriguing background information provided.

Denoon, Donald, et al. *The Cambridge History of the Pacific Islanders*. Australia: Cambridge University Press, 1997. A team of scholars examines the history of the inhabitants of Oceania, from first colonization to the nuclear era. While acknowledging the great diversity of Pacific peoples, cultures, and experiences, the book looks for common patterns and related themes, presenting them in an insightful and innovative way.

Derrick, R. A. *A History of Fiji*. Suva: Government Press, 1946. This classic work, by a former director of the Fiji Museum, deals with the period up to 1874 only. It was reprinted in 1974 and is currently available at bookstores in Fiji.

Ewins, Rory. *Colour, Class and Custom: The Literature of the 1987 Fiji Coup*. 2nd ed., 1998. Available online at http://speedysnail.com/pacific/fiji_coup.

Howard, Michael C. *Fiji: Race and Politics in an Island State*. Vancouver: University of British Columbia Press, 1991. Perhaps the best scholarly study of the background and root causes of the first two Fiji coups.

Howe, K. R. *Nature, Culture, and History*. Honolulu: University of Hawaii Press, 2000. A wide range of contemporary Pacific issues are examined in this timely book.

Kirch, Patrick Vinton. *On the Road of the Winds*. Berkeley, Calif.: University of California Press, 2000. This archaeological history of the Pacific islands before European contact is easily the most important of its kind in two decades.

Lal, Brij V. *Broken Waves: A History of the Fiji Islands in the 20th Century.* Honolulu: University of Hawaii Press, 1992. Lal is a penetrating writer who uses language accessible to the layperson.

Mara, Ratu Sir Kamisese. *The Pacific Way: A Memoir.* Honolulu: University of Hawaii Press, 1997. Personal observations and reminiscences by the man who did so much to shape modern Fiji.

McEvedy, Colin. *The Penguin Historical Atlas of the Pacific.* New York: Penguin USA, 1998. Through stories and maps, McEvedy brings Pacific history into sharp focus—a truly unique book.

Ravuvu, Asesela. *The Facade of Democracy: Fijian Struggles for Political Control 1830–1987.* Suva: Institute of Pacific Studies, 1991. European politics, colonial rule, the Indian threat, multiculturalism, and cultural insensitivity—factors in the 1987 coups as seen by a Fijian nationalist.

Sharpham, John, *Rabuka of Fiji: The Authorized Biography of Major General Sitiveni Rabuka.* Rockhampton, Australia: Central Queensland University Press, 2000. In this volume, Rabuka claims that Ratu Sir Kamisese Mara had prior knowledge of his 1987 coup and approved, a claim denied by Mara himself.

Thomson, Peter. *Kava in the Blood.* Auckland: Tandem Press, 1999. Thomson served as permanent secretary to Fiji's governor-general at the time of the 1987 Rabuka coups. His behind-the-scenes account helps one understand the complicated political situation in Fiji.

Tubanavau-Salabula, Losena, Josua Namoce, and Nic Maclellan, eds. *Kirisimasi.* Suva: Pacific Concerns Resource Center, 1999. The story of the Fijian troops who served in Britain's dirty nuclear-testing program on Christmas Island in 1957–1958.

Wallis, Mary. *Life in Feejee: Five Years Among the Cannibals.* First published in 1851, this book is the memoir of a New England sea captain's wife in Fiji. It's a charming, if rather gruesome, firsthand account of early European contact with Fiji and has some fascinating details of Fijian customs. You'll find ample mention of Cakobau, who hadn't yet converted to Christianity. Reprinted by the Fiji Museum, Suva, in 1983, but again out of print. A rare South Seas classic!

Wallis, Mary. *The Fiji and New Caledonia Journals of Mary Wallis, 1851–1853.* Suva: Institute of Pacific Studies, 1994. This reprint of the sequel to *Life in Feejee* offers many insights, and the editor, David Routledge, has added numerous notes.

Waterhouse, Joseph. *The King and People of Fiji.* Honolulu: University of Hawaii Press, 1997. The Rev. Joseph Waterhouse witnessed Fijian life at the earliest stages of the 19th century. His work offers an excellent insight into the traditional Fijian way of life.

Social Science

Colpani, Satya. *Beyond the Black Waters: A Memoir of Sir Sathi Narain.* Suva: Institute of Pacific Studies, 1996. Having migrated from southern India with his family, Sir Sathi Narain (1919–1989) became a leader in the construction industry and an influential figure in the country's life.

Norton, Robert. *Race and Politics in Fiji.* St. Lucia, Australia: University of Queensland Press, 1990. A revised edition of the 1977 classic. Norton emphasizes the flexibility of Fijian culture, which was able to absorb the impact of two military coups without any loss of life.

Ravuvu, Asesela. *Development or Dependence: The Pattern of Change in a Fijian Village.* Suva: Institute of Pacific Studies, 1988. Highlights the unforeseen negative impacts of development in a Fijian village.

Roth, G. Kingsley. *Fijian Way of Life*. 2nd ed. Melbourne: Oxford University Press, 1973. A standard reference on Fijian culture.

Language and Literature

Capell, A. *A New Fijian Dictionary*. Suva: Government Printer, 1991. A Fijian-English dictionary invaluable for anyone interested in learning the language. Scholars have a generally low opinion of this work, which contains hundreds of errors, but it's still a handy reference. Also see C. Maxwell Churchward's *A New Fijian Grammar*.

Griffen, Arlene, ed. *With Heart and Nerve and Sinew: Post-coup Writing from Fiji*. Suva: Marama Club, 1997. An eclectic collection of responses to the first coups and life in Fiji thereafter.

Hereniko, Vilsoni, and Teresia Teaiwa. *Last Virgin in Paradise*. Suva: Institute of Pacific Studies, 1993. The Rotuman Hereniko has written a number of plays, including *Don't Cry Mama* (1977), *A Child for Iva* (1987), and *The Monster* (1989).

Kikau, Eci. *The Wisdom of Fiji*. Suva: Institute of Pacific Studies, 1981. This extensive collection of Fijian proverbs opens a window to understanding Fijian society, culture, and philosophy.

London, Jack. *South Sea Tales*. New York: Random House (Modern Library Classics), 2002. Stories based on London's visit to Tahiti, Samoa, Fiji, and the Solomon Islands in the early 20th century.

Lynch, John. *Pacific Languages: An Introduction*. Honolulu: University of Hawaii Press, 1998. The grammatical features of the Oceanic, Papuan, and Australian languages.

Tarte, Daryl. *Islands of the Frigate Bird*. Suva: Institute of Pacific Studies, 1999. A novel about the struggle for survival of Central Pacific peoples.

Veramu, Joseph C. *Moving Through the Streets*. Suva: Institute of Pacific Studies, 1994. A fast-moving novel providing insights into the lifestyles, pressures, and temptations of teenagers in Suva. Veramu has also written a collection of short stories called *The Black Messiah* (1989).

Wendt, Albert, ed. *Nuanua: Pacific Writing in English Since 1980*. Honolulu, University of Hawaii Press, 1995. This worthwhile anthology of contemporary Pacific literature includes works by 10 Fijian writers including Prem Banfal, Sudesh Mishra, Satendra Nandan, and Som Prakash.

Reference Books

Crocombe, Ron. *The South Pacific*. Suva: University of the South Pacific, 2001. Parameters, patterns, perceptions, property, power, and prospects in the 28 nations and territories of Oceania.

Douglas, Ngaire and Norman Douglas, eds. *Pacific Islands Yearbook*. Suva: Fiji Times, 1994. First published in 1932, this is the 17th edition of the original sourcebook on the islands. Although the realities of modern publishing have led to the demise of both the *Yearbook* and its cousin, *Pacific Islands Monthly*, this final edition remains an indispensable reference work for students of the region.

Gorman, G.E., and J.J. Mills. *Fiji: World Bibliographical Series, Volume 173*. Oxford: Clio Press, 1994. Critical reviews of 673 of the most important books about Fiji.

Lal, Brig V., and Kate Fortune, eds. *The Pacific Islands: An Encyclopedia*. Honolulu: University of Hawaii Press, 2000. This important book combines the writings of 200 acknowledged experts on the physical environment, peoples, history, politics, economics, society, and culture of the South Pacific. The accompanying CD-ROM provides a wealth of maps, graphs, photos, biographies, and more.

Booksellers and Publishers

Some of the books listed above are out of print and not available at bookstores. Major research libraries should have a few; otherwise, check the specialized antiquarian booksellers or regional publishers listed below for hard-to-find books on Fiji. Sources of detailed topographical maps or navigational charts are provided in the following section. Many titles can be ordered online through www.southpacific.org/books.html.

Bibliophile, 24A Glenmore Rd., Paddington, Sydney, NSW 2021, Australia (tel. 02/9331-1411, fax 02/9361-3371, www.biblio phile.com.au). An antiquarian bookstore specializing in books about Oceania. View their extensive catalog online.

Book Bin, 228 S.W. Third St., Corvallis, OR 97333, U.S.A. (tel. 541/752-0045, fax 541/754-4115, www.bookbin.com). Their searchable catalog of books on the Pacific Islands lists hundreds of rare books, including some from the Institute of Pacific Studies in Suva.

Books of Yesteryear, P.O. Box 257, Newport, NSW 2106, Australia (tel./fax 02/9918-0545, www.abebooks.com/home/booksofyesteryear). Another source of old, fine, and rare books on the Pacific.

Books Pasifika, P.O. Box 68–446, Newtown, Auckland 1, New Zealand (tel. 09/303-2349, fax 09/377-9528, www.ak.planet.gen.nz/pasi fika/Pasifika.html). Besides being a major publisher, Pasifika Press is one of New Zealand's best sources of mail-order books on Oceania, including those of the Institute of Pacific Studies.

Institute of Pacific Studies, University of the South Pacific, P.O. Box 1168, Suva, Fiji Islands (fax 330-1594, www.usp.ac.fj/ips). Their catalog, *Books from the Pacific Islands,* lists numerous books about the islands written by the Pacific islanders themselves. Some are rather dry academic publications of interest only to specialists, so order carefully. For Internet access to the catalog, see the University Book Centre listing below.

Pacific Island Books, 2802 East 132nd Circle, Thornton, CA 80241, U.S.A. (tel. 303/920-8338, www.pacificislandbooks.com). One of the best U.S. sources of books about Fiji. They stock many titles published by the Institute of Pacific Studies.

Serendipity Books, P.O. Box 340, Nedlands, WA 6009, Australia (tel. 08/9382-2246, fax 08/9388-2728, http://members.iinet.net.au /~serendip). The largest stocks of antiquarian, secondhand, and out-of-print books on the Pacific in Western Australia.

University Book Centre, University of the South Pacific, P.O. Box 1168, Suva, Fiji Islands (fax 330-3265, www.uspbookcentre.com). An excellent source of books written and produced in the South Pacific itself.

University of Hawaii Press, 2840 Kolowalu St., Honolulu, HI 96822-1888, U.S.A. (tel. 808/956-8255, www.uhpress.hawaii.edu). Their *Hawaii and the Pacific* catalog is well worth requesting if you're trying to build a Pacific library.

Maps

Bier, James A. *Reference Map of Oceania.* Honolulu: University of Hawaii Press, 1995. A fully indexed map of the Pacific Islands with 51 detailed inset maps of individual islands. Useful details such as time zones are included.

Bluewater Books & Charts, 1481 S.E. 17th St., Fort Lauderdale, FL 33316, U.S.A. (tel. 954/763-6533 or 800/942-2583, fax 954/522-2278, www.bluewaterweb.com). An outstanding source of navigational charts and cruising guides to the Pacific.

Fiji Hydrographic Office, P.O. Box 362, Suva, Fiji Islands (tel. 331-5457). Produces navigational charts of the Yasawas, Kadavu, eastern Vanua Levu, and the Lau Group. Their U.S. agent is Captains Nautical Supplies, 2500 15th Ave. West, Seattle, WA 98119, U.S.A. (tel. 800/448-2278, fax 206/281-4921, www.captainsnautical.com).

International Maps. Hema Maps Pty. Ltd., P.O. Box 4365, Eight Mile Plains, QLD 4113, Australia (tel. 07/3340-0000, fax 07/3340-0099, www.hemamaps.com.au). Maps of the Pacific, Fiji, Solomon Islands, Vanuatu, and Samoa.

Lands and Surveys Department. Plan and Map Sales, P.O. Box 2222, Government Buildings, Suva, Fiji Islands (tel. 321-1395, fax 330-9331). The main publisher of topographical maps of Fiji with a 1:50,000 series covering most of the country. Some of these maps are online at www.fiji.gov.fj/fijifacts/maps/index.shtml.

Periodicals

Commodores' Bulletin. Seven Seas Cruising Assn., 1525 South Andrews Ave., Suite 217, Fort Lauderdale, FL 33316, U.S.A. (tel. 954/463-2431, fax 954/463-7183, www.ssca.org; US$57 a year worldwide by airmail). This monthly bulletin is chock-full of useful information for anyone wishing to tour the Pacific by sailing boat. All Pacific yachties and friends should be Seven Seas members!

The Contemporary Pacific. University of Hawaii Press, 2840 Kolowalu St., Honolulu, HI 96822, U.S.A. (www.uhpress.hawaii.edu, published twice a year, US$35 a year). Publishes a good mix of articles of interest to both scholars and general readers; the country-by-country "Political Review" in each number is a concise summary of events during the preceding year. The "Dialogue" section offers informed comment on the more controversial issues in the region, while recent publications on the islands are examined through book reviews. Those interested in current topics in Pacific island affairs should check recent volumes for background information.

Islands Business. P.O. Box 12718, Suva, Fiji Islands (tel. 330-3108, fax 330-1423, www.pacificislands.cc; annual airmailed subscription A$35 to Australia, NZ$55 to New Zealand, US$45 to North America, US$55 to Europe). A monthly newsmagazine, with in-depth coverage of political and economic trends around the Pacific. It even has a "Whispers" gossip section, which is an essential weather vane for anyone doing business in the region. Travel and aviation news gets some prominence.

Pacific Magazine. P.O. Box 913, Honolulu, HI 96808, U.S.A. (www.pacificislands.cc; US$15 a year). This monthly newsmagazine, published in Hawaii since 1976, will keep you up to date on what's happening in the South Pacific and Micronesia.

Pacific News Bulletin. Pacific Concerns Resource Center, 83 Amy St., Toorak, Private Mail Bag, Suva, Fiji Islands (fax 330-4755, www.pcrc.org.fj: US$15 a year in the South Pacific, US$20 in North America and Asia, US$30 elsewhere). A 16-page monthly newsletter with up-to-date information on nuclear, independence, environmental, and political questions.

The Review. P.O. Box 12095, Suva, Fiji Islands (fax 330-2852, www.fijilive.com). A fortnightly news magazine with excellent coverage of business and politics in Fiji.

Surfer Travel Reports. P.O. Box 1028, Dana Point, CA 92629, U.S.A. (www.surfermag.com

/travel/pacific). Each month, this newsletter provides a detailed analysis of surfing conditions at a different destination (the last report on Fiji was issue 7#12). Back issues on specific countries are available at US$7 each. This is your best source of surfing information by far.

Undercurrent. 125 East Sir Francis Drake Blvd., Suite 200, Larkspur, CA 94939-9809, U.S.A. (tel. 800/326-1896 or 415/461-5906, www.undercurrent.org, US$78 a year). A monthly consumer-protection-oriented newsletter for serious scuba divers. Unlike virtually every other diving publication, *Undercurrent* accepts no advertising or free trips, which allows its writers to tell it as it is.

Discography

Bula Fiji Bula. New York: Arc Music, 2001. Music of the Fiji Islands, including the famous *Isa Lei.* This recording and those which follow can be ordered through www.south pacific.org/music.html.

Fanshawe, David, ed. *Exotic Voices and Rhythms of the South Seas.* New York: Arc Music, 1994. Cook Island drum dancing, a Fijian *tralala meke,* a Samoan *fiafia,* a Vanuatu string band, and Solomon Islands panpipes selected from 1,200 hours of tapes in the Fanshawe Pacific Collection.

Fanshawe, David, ed. *Spirit of Melanesia.* United Kingdom: Saydisc Records, 1998. An an-

thology of the music of the five countries of Melanesia, with seven tracks from Fiji. Recorded in 1978, 1983, and 1994.

Fanshawe, David, ed. *South Pacific: Island Music.* New York: Nonesuch Records, 2003. Originally released in 1981, this recording takes you from Tahiti to the Cook Islands, Tonga, Samoa, Fiji, Kiribati, and the Solomon Islands.

Linkels, Ad, and Lucia Linkels, eds. *Rabi.* The Netherlands: Pan Records, 2000. Music from Rabi, the new home of the exiled Banabans of Ocean Island, recorded on Rabi in 1997 and 1998.

Linkels, Ad, and Lucia Linkels, eds. *Tautoga.* The Netherlands: Pan Records, 1999. The songs and dances of Rotuma, Fiji, recorded on the island in 1996. It's believed the *tautoga* dance arrived from Tonga in the 18th century.

Linkels, Ad, and Lucia Linkels, eds. *Viti Levu.* The Netherlands: Pan Records, 2000. This unique recording provides 20 examples of real Fijian music, from *Isa Lei* to Bula rock, plus four Indo-Fijian pieces. Recorded between 1986 and 1998, it's the best of its kind on the market.

Magic of the South Seas. New York: Arc Music, 2000. An anthology of music from Tahiti, the Marquesas Islands, Tonga, and Fiji.

Internet Resources

Top 20 Fiji Websites

Backpacking Fiji
www.fijibudget.com

An umbrella website for more than a dozen backpacker resorts and dive shops in the central Yasawas.

Come Meet the Banabans
www.banaban.com

Learn everything you ever wanted to know about the Banabans of Rabi and Ocean Island.

David Robie's Café Pacific
www.asiapac.org.fj/cafepacific

This journalism website is brimming with links to provocative articles and analysis not found elsewhere.

Dive Fiji
www.divefiji.com

Provides loads of specific information on scuba diving all around Fiji, with handy maps, photos, and links.

Fiji Accommodation and Travel
www.fiji.travelmaxia.com

This Travelmaxia site documents dozens of upscale resorts and hotels, with details on specials and packages, plus maps, photos, and online forms. It's surprisingly precise and up to date.

Fiji A to Z
www.fijiatoz.com

This "small guide" to Fiji presents information about the country in a pleasing alphabetical format.

Fiji Beaches
www.fijibeaches.com

Numerous interactive maps lead to photos and travel information on Fiji's best beaches and islands.

Fiji for Less
www.fiji4less.com

An introduction to Fiji's largest budget hotel chain, with properties in Suva, Lautoka, and on the Coral Coast.

Fiji Government Online
www.fiji.gov.fj

This crisply clear, dynamic site is well worth visiting to taste the image local politicians and bureaucrats try to present to the world. You can listen to Fiji's national anthem, peruse recent news briefs, and consult topographical maps. The press releases are often edifying.

Fiji Islands Backpackers Guide
http://fiji-backpacking.com

A well-organized website full of budget-saving ideas, background on Fiji and the Fijians, accommodations listings, information on transportation and activities, and even a Fijian language section.

Fiji Island Travel
www.fiji-island.com

Interactive travel maps show the locations of resorts all around Fiji, with pictures of beaches and scenery to help you plan your vacation.

Fiji Meteorological Service
www.met.gov.fj

Everything you ever wanted to know about Fiji's weather, including a daily Fiji weather bulletin and regional forecasts for eight other Pacific countries.

Fiji Visitors Bureau
www.bulafiji.com

This site is used by Fiji's national tourist office to disseminate information about accommodations, activities, transportation, events, and the like. Precise, factual information is provided about most tourist facilities.

Ovalau Watersports
www.owlfiji.com

This Ovalau-based company can take you diving with sharks and manta rays in the Koro Sea. Aside from describing their dive sites, the site provides an introduction to historic Levuka, Fiji's first capital.

Radio Fiji News
www.radiofiji.org

Come here to hear the latest news, weather, or sports report in English, Fijian, or Hindi.

Rivers Fiji
www.riversfiji.com

Provides extensive information on whitewater rafting and kayaking on southern Viti Levu.

Rob Kay's Fiji Guide
www.fijiguide.com

An online travel guide covering subjects like accommodations, recreation, natural history, and facts about Fiji. The site's bulletin board allows you to ask questions and share experiences.

Rotuma Website
www2.hawaii.edu/oceanic/rotuma/os/hanua.html

Every niche relating to Rotuma is here, including history, culture, language, maps, population, politics, news, photos, humor, proverbs, recipes, art, and music.

Savusavu Fiji
www.savusavufiji.com

The pleasant design conveys the atmosphere of Savusavu, the way Fiji used to be. The photos, fast facts, and links introduce you to the accommodations, diving, sailing, fishing, transport, and tours of the town.

Subsurface Fiji
www.fijidiving.com

Subsurface operates the diving and sportfishing concessions at 10 Mamanuca resorts, and their site will appeal to anyone with an interest in the area, not only scuba divers.

Index

A

Abaca: 235–236

accessories and toiletries: 81–82

acclimatization: 76–77

accommodations: general information 59–61; categories 61–62; Coral Coast 153, 155; Kadavu 255–259; Korolevu 163–167; Korotogo 160–161; Koroyanitu National Heritage Park 236; Labasa 281–283; Lakeba Island 324; Lautoka 230–231; Lavena 310; Levuka 267–268; Mamanuca Group 140–150; Mana Island 148; Nadi 119–127; Nananu-i-Ra Island 216–217; Natewa Bay 286; Nausori 206–207; Naviti Island 245–246; Pacific Harbor 170–171; price ranges 61; Rabi Island 298–299; Rakiraki 218, 220; reservations 61, 238; Rotuma 326–327; Savusavu 288–290, 294–295; Sigatoka 157–158; Suva 186–191; Tailevu Coast 213–214; Taveuni 305–307, 311–312, 314–315; Tavewa Island 247–248; Turtle Island 238; Vanua Balavu Island 319–320; Viseisei village 136–137; Waya Island 243–244

agriculture: 33–35, 156

AIDS/HIV: 76–77

Air Nauru: 94, 199

Air New Zealand: 88–92, 199

Air Pacific: 85, 88, 91–93, 199

air travel: general information 85–95, 107–108; air fares 85–88; airlines 88–94, 130–131, 199; airport codes 90; airports 113–114, 302; air routes 86, 89, 108; booking tips 85–87; Kadavu 259; Labasa 284; Lakeba Island 324; Levuka 269; Nadi 132, 135; Rotuma 327; Savusavu 292; Suva 202; Taveuni 302; Vanua Balavu Island 320; Yasawa Group 240

Aiwa Island: 322

Albert Park: 180

alcoholic beverages: general information 66–67; Lautoka 227, 229; Rabi Island 298; safety issues 76; Savusavu 288

amphibians: 15

animals: 12–16

arachnids: 16

artesian water: 35

arts and crafts: *see* handicrafts

ATMs: general information 70, 113; Labasa 284; Lautoka 233; Levuka 269; Nadi 131; Sigatoka 159; Suva 199

automobiles: *see* car travel; rental cars

B

Ba: 222–223; map 222

Baba, Tupeni: 26

backpacking: general information 60; Levuka 271; Mana Island 147–148; Naviti Island 244–246; Tavewa Island 238, 247; Yasawa Group 250, 251

baggage: *see* luggage

Bainimarama, Voreqe: 27–29, 32

Baker, Thomas: 19, 226

Balea: 210

balolo: 47

Banabans: 296–297

Birds/Bird-Watching

general information: 14–15

Bouma National Heritage Park: 308–309

Colo-i-Suva Forest Park: 184

Gau Island: 272–273

Hatana: 326

Kadavu: 253

Koroyanitu National Heritage Park: 235

Kula Eco Park: 159

Mount Lomalagi: 224

mynah birds: 14–15

Namenalala Island: 293

Navakawau: 313

Qamea Island: 315

Taveuni: 5

Vidawa Rainforest Hike: 309

Waisali Nature Reserve: 287–288

Index

banks: general information 70, 113–114; Labasa 284; Lautoka 233; Levuka 269; Nadi 131; Savusavu 291; Sigatoka 159; Suva 199; Taveuni 313
bars: 196–197
Batiki Island: 272
bats: 12, 300
Bau Island: 18–19, 43, 207–208
Bavadra, Timoci: 22–24, 135–136, 180
Beachcomber Island: 143–144
beachcombers: 18
Beach Street (Levuka): 263
bêche-de-mer: 14, 18
beer: 66
Beqa Island: 175–176; map 176
Biausevu Falls: 163
bicycling: 55, 95, 267
Big W, The: 139
Bilyard Sugar Mill: 313
blackbirding: 20, 41, 261
Bligh, William: 16–17, 251
Blue Lagoon: 237, 251
Blue Lagoon: 246
boating: *see* ships; yachting
Bole, Filipe: 23
booking tips (air travel): 85–87
bookstores: 198, 233
botanical gardens: *see* gardens
Bouma Falls: 309
Bouma National Heritage Park: 51–52, 308–309
Bounty, HMS: 17, 181, 251
Bounty Island: 144
British rule: 18–22, 295–298
British six-inch guns: 136, 138
Bua Bay: 279
Buca Bay: 294–299
Bukuya: 224
Bulileka: 281
bure: 39, 64, 135
Bureta River: 261
burial caves (Namalata): 319
Bushart, Martin: 18
bus travel: general information 110; Korotogo 162; Labasa 285; Lautoka 234; Levuka 270; Nadi 132–133; Nananu-i-Ra Island 218; Natewa Bay 286; Nausori 207; Pacific Harbor 171; Rabi Island 299; Rakiraki 220; Savusavu 292; Sigatoka 159; Suva 202, 205; Taveuni 303; tours 100–101; Viti Levu 151–152

C

Cakobau, Ratu Seru: 18–20, 207–208, 264
Cakobau, Ratu Sir George: 21, 208
calling cards: 71–72; *see also* telephone service
camping/campgrounds: 62–63, 80–81
cannibalism: 16, 18–19, 208, 218
Cape Washington: 255
Caqalai Island: 271
Cargill, David: 19, 43, 322
Carnegie, Andrew: 180
car travel: 111–113; *see also* rental cars
cassava: 66–67
Castaway: 149
Castaway Island: 145
Catholic cathedral: 180
Catholic Church of St. Francis Xavier: 214
caves: burial caves (Namalata) 319; Great Astrolabe Reef 255; Lakeba Island 323; Rotuma 326; Sawa-i-Lau Island 251–252; Tailevu Coast 214; Vatulele Island 174
Cawaci: 265
centipedes: 16
Cession Monument: 266
Chaudhry, Mahendra: 26–29, 31
Chinese population: 40–41
Christianity: *see* missionaries; religion
Church of the Sacred Heart: 263
Cicia: 321; map 321
cinema: *see* movies
Circus, The: 140
City Library (Suva): 180, 198
climate: 8–11
clothing: 80–81
Cloudbreak: 117, 143
coconut palm: 11, 67
coconut plantation: 313, 321
Colo-i-Suva Forest Park: 51–52, 184; map 184
concrete cross (Wairiki): 311
condoms: 76–77
conduct: 47–48
cone shells: 14
consulates: 69, 132, 200–201
Cook, James: 16
copra: general information 34–35; Levuka 261; Mago 321; Savusavu 286; Taveuni 313; Vanua Balavu Island 318
Copra Shed Marina: 287, 290–291
Coral Coast: 152–167
Coral Reef Adventure: 98
cotton: 19

Cousteau, Jean-Michel: 286, 289–290
credit cards: 70
crested iguana: 279
cricket: 56
crime: 48, 79
cross section, Gau Island: 2
Cross, William: 19, 43, 311, 322
cruises/charters: general information 101–103;
    Labasa 284; Lautoka 234; Nadi 132,
    134–135; Savusavu 292–293; *see also* yachting
Cultural Center (Pacific Harbor): 168
Cumming Street: 180
currency: 70, 82, 199–200
customs: 44–47, 63–65
Customs and Excise Boarding Office: 200
cyclones: *see* hurricanes

D

dakua: 11
Dakuilomaloma: 319
dancing: 56–57
Darwin, Charles: 5
Darwin's Theory of Atoll Formation: 5
dehydration: 76
Delaico: 273
Delaikoro: 281
Delaivuna: 313
dengue fever: 79
Denham, H.M.: 18
Des Voeux Peak: 300, 311
Devil's Thumb: 267
diarrhea: 78, 81
diplomatic offices: 69
directory assistance: 72
distilleries: 227, 229
dolphin-calling: 285
Dorothy's Waterfall: 214
Doughty, William: 246–247
Draiba: 266
Drekeniwai: 294
Dreketi River: 279
dress code: 48, 64
drinking water: 35, 77
driver's license: 111
Dudley, Hannah: 181
Dumont d'Urville, J.: 18, 255

E

economic aid: 37
economic issues: 36

ecotourism: 38
education: 41
Edwards, Captain: 325
eels: 14
electric current: 84
Ellington Wharf: 214–215
email: 73, 291
embassies: 69
Emperor Gold Mine: 220–222
entertainment: 56–57, 128–129
equipment, camping: 80–81
ethnic groups: 39–41
etiquette: 64
European exploration and settlement: 16–21
European War Memorial: 264
Evanson, Richard: 250–251
exchange rates: 70

F

Fapufa: 326
fauna: 12–16
faxes: 73, 200
ferries: Labasa 284–285; Lautoka 234; Levuka
    270; Nananu-i-Ra Island 218; Savusavu 292;
    Suva 202–203; Taveuni 302–303; Vanua
    Levu 278–279
festivals: 57, 195
Field, Michael: 30–31
Fijian language: 334
Fijian people: 39
Fijian Princess: 155
Fijian Resort: 153, 155
Fijian Song of Farewell (Isa Lei): 203
Fiji Bitter beer: 66
Fiji Museum: 181
Fiji Trade and Investment Bureau: 69
Fiji Visitors Bureau: 68, 130, 178, 198
film, photographic: 83, 197
Fintel Building: 180, 200
fire-walking: Beqa Island 175; Coral Coast 153;
    Fijian fire-walking 44, 56, 153, 163, 175; In-
    dian fire-walking 44, 284; Korolevu 163, 167;
    lovo feasts 67; Yanuca Island 175
first-aid: 78
fish drives: 47
fish/fishing: general information 12–13, 35; fish
    spearing event 319; Levuka 261, 266; Ma-
    manuca Group 139–140; Pacific Harbor 169;
    Savusavu 288; Taveuni 305; Vatulele Island 174
flightseeing: 135

Floating Island: 281
flora: 11–12, 302
food: general information 66–67; Korotogo
    161–162; Labasa 283; Lautoka 232; Levuka
    268–269; Nadi 127–128; Nausori 207; Pacific
    Harbor 171; Rakiraki 218, 220; Savusavu
    290; Sigatoka 158–159; Suva 191–195; Tave-
    uni 307–308, 312–313
Forbes, Malcolm: 316
foreign trade: 37
forests: 11–12, 35
freighters: 104–105
Frigate Passage: 153, 169, 175
Fulaga: 324

G
Ganilau, Epeli: 25
Ganilau, Ratu Sir Penaia: 21, 22–24, 311
gardens: 136, 181, 230
garment industry: 36
Garrick Hotel: 178
gas stations: 112
Gates, Anthony: 30
Gau Island: 2, 272–273; map 273
geckos: 15
gender issues: 42
geography: 2–11, 32
Gilbertese: 298
glossary: 330–333
gold mining: 21, 35, 220–222, 279
golf: general information 55; Coral Coast 155;
    Lautoka 230; Nadi 119; Pacific Harbor 169;
    Suva 185
Gordon, Sir Arthur: 20, 261
Gotham City: 139
government: 32–33
Government Buildings: 180
Governor-General's Swimming Pool: 224
Grand Pacific Hotel: 180–181
gratuities: *see* tipping
Great Astrolabe Reef: 5, 255
Great Britain: *see* British rule
Great Sea Reef: 5, 280, 281
greenhouse effect: 8
Greenpeace: 199
groceries: 308, 313
Gun Rock: 264–265

H
handicrafts: general information 57–58; Nadi
    129; Nairai Island 274; Sigatoka 159; Suva
    197; Taveuni 313; Vatukarasa 162
hanging bridge (Labasa): 281
Hatana: 326
health issues: 41, 76–79
helicopter tours: 135
hepatitis A: 78–79
hepatitis B: 77, 79
Hibiscus Festival: 195
Hibiscus Highway: 294–295
Hindi: 335
history: 16–32
HIV: *see* AIDS/HIV
Hofiua: 326
holidays: 57
Holy Redeemer Anglican Church: 264
horseback riding: 119, 152, 160, 214, 250
hospitals: general information 75; Labasa 284;
    Lautoka 234; Levuka 269; Nadi 132;
    Savusavu 292; Sigatoka 159; Suva 201–202;
    Taveuni 313
hotels: *see* accommodations
hot springs: 272, 281, 287, 319
Hunt, John: 208
hurricanes: 8–9, 11, 57, 106

IJ
iguanas: 15, 279
Iloilo, Ratu Josefa: 28–32, 135
immigration office: 132, 200, 233
immunizations: 69, 79
independence movements: 22–32
Indian food: 66
Indian immigrants: 20, 22, 39–40, 272
Indo-Fijian people: 39–40
industries: 33–36
infectious diseases: 41, 76–79
insect bites: 78
insects: 16
Institute of Pacific Studies: 183, 198
insurance: 75–76, 112
International Bula Marathon: 57
international date line: 84
International Society for Krishna Consciousness:
    230
Internet access: general information 73; air travel
    87; Labasa 284; Lautoka 233; Levuka 269;
    Nadi 131–132; Savusavu 291; Suva 200; Tave-
    uni 313
Internet resources: 343–344

Hiking/Climbing

general information: 55
Beqa Island: 175–176
Biausevu Falls: 163
Blue Lagoon: 246
Bouma National Heritage Park: 51–52, 308–309
Delaico: 273
Gau Island: 272–273
Gun Rock: 264–265
Joske's Thumb: 182, 185
Koro Island: 273–274
Koroyanitu National Heritage Park: 51, 234–236
Lake Tagimaucia: 311
Lavena Coastal Walk: 309
Levuka: 263–264, 266–267
Lovoni: 266–267
Moala Group: 324–325
Mount Batilamu: 235
Mount Korobaba: 185
Mount Lomalagi: 224
Mount Tova: 214
Mount Victoria: 225
Nabukelevu: 255
Nagaidamu: 273

Naigani: 272
Nakauvadra Range: 218
Nananu-i-Ra Island: 215
Nanuya Levu Island: 250
Navuga: 235
organized tours: 100
Peak, The (Levuka): 263–264
Rotuma: 326
Savuione Falls: 235
Sigatoka River Trek: 225–226
Sigatoka Sand Dunes: 51, 153, 155
Sororoa Bluff: 326
Suva: 185
Tailevu Coast: 214
Taveuni: 308–311, 313
Tavewa Island: 246–248
Trans–Viti Levu Trek: 209–211
Vatulele Island: 174
Vatuvula Peak: 242–243
Vidawa Rainforest Hike: 309
Wainibau Falls: 309–310
Waisali Nature Reserve: 287–288
Waya Island: 243–244
Wayasewa Island: 242–243

Isa Lei: 203
itinerary suggestions: 51
Jame Mosque: 229
jellyfish: 14
Joske's Thumb: 182, 185
Joyita: 264

K
Kabara: 324
Kadavu: 5, 253–259; map 254
Kaimbu Island: 321
Ka Levu Cultural Center: 155
Kamikamica, Josevata: 25
Kanacea: 321
Katafaga: 321
kauri tree: 11
kava: 16, 35, 45–47, 64, 298
kayaking: general information 55, 109; airline regulations 95; Kadavu 255; Pacific Harbor 173; Taveuni 305, 310
Kioa Island: 295

Kokobula Scenic Outlook: 235
Komo: 324
Korobasabasaga Range: 211
Koro Island: 273–274; map 274
Korolamalama Cave: 174
Korolevu: 162–167, 226; map 164–165
Korotogo: 159–162
Korovou: 211, 213–214
Koroyanitu National Heritage Park: 51, 234–236
Kuata Island: 241–242
Kula Eco Park: 159
Kulukulu: 156

L
Labasa: 280–285; maps 280, 282
Labasa Sugar Mill: 281
Lakeba Island: 322–324; map 323
Lake Tagimaucia: 311
Lal, Brij: 25
land: 2–11
land rights: 41–42

language: 43
Laucala Island: 316
Lau Group: 5, 317–325
launderettes: 132, 201, 269
Lautoka: 227–236; map 228
Lautoka Sugar Mill: 227
Lavena: 309–310
Lavena Coastal Walk: 309
Lekanai: 273
Leleuvia Island: 271
leper colony: 274
Lesiaceva Point: 287
Lever Brothers: 295, 298
Levuka: 261–270; map 263
Levuka Community Center: 263
Levuka Public School: 263
libraries: 198–199, 233, 284
limestone caves: 323
literacy: 41
lizards: 15
Lomaiviti Group: 260–275
Lomaloma: 318
London Missionary Society: 19, 324
Long Beach: 248
lovo: 67
Lovoni: 265, 266
Lovoni Valley: 261
Luckner, Felix von: 269, 274–275
luggage: 80, 95, 113

M
Ma'afu, Enele: 19–20, 316, 318, 322
Maftoa: 326
magazines: 74
Mago: 321
mahogany: 35, 52, 184
mail: *see* post offices
Makogai Island: 274
Malaqereqere Villas: 155
Malolo Barrier Reef: 139–140
Malolo Island: 142
Malololailai Island: 140–142
Mamanuca Group: 117, 139–150; map 140
mammals: 12, 300
Mana Island: 146–148
mangroves: 12, 215
Manilal, D. M.: 20
manufacturing: 36
maps: 198
Mara, Ratu Sir Kamisese: 22–28, 30, 318, 322

Marist Convent School: 263
maritime coordinates: 104–105
Marketplace of Fiji: 168
Masonic Lodge (Levuka): 263, 265
Matacawa Levu Island: 251
Matamaiqi Blowhole: 313
Matamanoa Island: 149
Matangi Island: 315–316
Matei Airstrip: 302
Mateschitz, Dietrich: 316
Matuku: 325
Mau: 173
Mavana: 319
measurement system: 84
medical care: general information 75; Labasa
    284; Lautoka 234; Nadi 132; Savusavu 292;
    Sigatoka 159; Suva 201–202
medications: 81–82
meke: 56–57, 67, 324
Melanesians: 39
Meridian Wall: 285
Methodist Church (Levuka): 264
metric system: 84
Micronesians: 41
military coups: 22–23, 27–29
military service: 37
mining industry: 21, 35–36, 220–222, 279,
    296–297
missionaries: conversion efforts 42–43; Lakeba
    Island 322; last missionary 226; Lau Group
    324; Levuka 267; London Missionary Society
    19, 324; Methodists 19, 20, 208; Rotuma
    325; Taveuni 311
Mission Hill (Levuka): 264
Moala: 325; map 324
Moala Group: 324–325
Moce: 324
Momi Battery Historic Park: 117, 138
Monasavu Hydroelectric Project: 225
money: 70–71, 82, 199–200, 233, 240
mongoose: 12
Monuriki Island: 117, 149
mosquitoes: 79, 324
motels: *see* accommodations
Moturiki Island: 272
Mount Batilamu: 235
Mount Kasi Gold Mine: 279
Mount Korobaba: 185
Mount Lomalagi: 224
Mount Naitaradamu: 211

Mount Suelhof: 326
Mount Tova: 214
Mount Victoria: 225
Mount Voma: 211
Mount Washington: 255
movies: 56, 195, 232, 283
Muani: 254
municipal market (Suva): 178
Musket Cove: 141
mynah birds: 14–15

N
Nabouwalu: 278–279
Nabukelevu: 255
Nabukelevuira: 255
Nacamaki: 12
Nacula: 248
Nacula Island: 248–249
Nadarivatu: 224–225
Nadelaiovalau: 261
Nadi: 9, 116–135; maps 118, 119
Nadi International Airport: 113–114
Nadi Market: 116, 117
Nagaidamu: 273
Nagatagata: 225
Naigani Island: 272
Naililili: 207
Nairai Island: 274
Naiserelagi: 214
Naisisili: 248
Naitauba: 321
Nakauvadra Range: 218
Nalauwaki: 243
Nalotawa: 235
Namalata: 319
Namena Barrier Reef: 293
Namenalala Island: 293
Namosi: 211
Namotu Island: 139, 143
Namuamua: 171
Namuana: 12, 254
Nananu-i-Ra Island: 215–218
Nanukuloa: 214
Nanuya Lailai Island: 249–250
Nanuya Levu Island: 250–251
Napuka: 294
Naqara: 311
Narocivo: 319
Nasaqalau: 322, 323–324
Nasau: 273

Nasava: 211
Nasova House: 266
Natadola Beach: 152–153
Natawa: 243
Natewa Bay: 285–286
National Stadium: 186
National Trust of Fiji: 51–52, 155, 199, 279, 287
Native Land Trust Board: 180
nature tours: 100
Natuvalo Bay: 244–245
Nausori: 206–207; map 207
Nausori Airport: 114
Nausori Highlands: 223–224
Navakawau: 313
Navala: 223–224
Navilawa: 235
Navini Island: 145
Naviti Island: 244–246
Navoka Methodist Church: 264
Navola Falls: 164
Navua: 171–173
Navua River: 171–172
Navua River Gorge: 153, 172
Navuga: 235
Navula Reef: 139
newspapers: 74
nightclubs: general information 56; Labasa 283–284; Lautoka 232–233; Nadi 129; Savusavu 290; Suva 195–196
Noa'tau: 326
Nubukalou Creek: 178
Nubutautau: 226
nuclear testing: 21
Nukubalavu: 287
Nukubati Island: 280
Nukulau: 182–183
Nukuselal Beach: 322

O
ocean currents: 9
Oceania Center for Arts and Culture: 183
ocean kayaking: *see* kayaking
Ogea: 324
Oinafa: 325
Oneata: 324
Ono-i-Lau: 324
organized tours: bus tours 100–101; cruises/charters 101–103, 134–135; helicopter tours 135; hiking 100; kayaking 99;

Korotogo 162; Levuka 270; Nadi 133–135; nature tours 100; packaged tours 95–98; river tours 172–173; Savusavu 292–293; scuba diving/snorkeling 98–99; seniors 101; surfing 99–100; Suva 206; Yasawa Group 240–241
Oso Nabukete Cave: 323
Ovalau Club: 263, 269
Ovalau Island: 261–270; map 262
overbooking: 94–95

P

Pacific Concerns Resource Center: 199
Pacific Fishing Company: 266
Pacific Harbor: 167–173; map 168
Pacific Theological College: 182
packing tips: 80–83
parks: 51–52
Parliament of Fiji: 182
passports: 69, 82
Peak, The: 263–264
Penang Sugar Mill: 218
Perry Mason's Orchid Garden: 136
philately: 197
photography: 83, 197
Plantation Island: 140–141
plants: 11–12, 302
political divisions: 31, 32
political unrest: 22–32
Polynesian Airlines: 93–94
Polynesians: 16, 39, 41
population statistics: 32
post offices: 71, 113, 131, 313
pottery making: 58, 159, 226, 254–255
poverty: 41
precipitation: 8–11
Presidential Palace: 182
price ranges (accommodations): 61
prickly heat: 78, 81
Pritchard, W.T.: 18
pronunciation guide: 43
puja, Sunday: 233
Punjas Children's Park: 230

QR

Qamea Island: 309, 315
Qara Bulo Cave: 323
Qarani: 273
Qarase, Laisenia: 28–32
Queen Victoria Memorial Hall: 180
Rabi Island: 295, 298–299

Rabuka, Sitiveni: 22–26, 29, 180
racial issues: 41
radio stations: 74–75
rain: 8–11, 57
Rainbow Reef: 303, 305
rainforests: 273, 288, 300, 309, 324
Rakiraki: 218–220; map 219
Rarawai Sugar Mill: 222
Raviravi Lagoon: 319
reading resources: 336–342
recompression facilities: 75, 202
red prawns: 174, 324
Reeves, Sir Paul: 25
regional airlines: 92–94
religion: 24, 40, 42–43
rental cars: general information 111–113; Korotogo 162; Labasa 285; Sigatoka 159; Suva 206; Taveuni 303
reptiles: 15
reservations (accommodations): 61, 238
Reserve Bank of Fiji: 180
reserves: 51–52
residence permits: 69
resorts: *see* accommodations
resources: 329–344
Rewa Delta: 207

Reefs

general information: 5–8, 52
Blue Lagoon: 246
climate change effects: 8
conservation: 6–7
coral types: 4, 6
Gau Island: 2, 272–273
Great Astrolabe Reef: 5, 255
Great Sea Reef: 5, 280, 281
Leleuvia Island: 271
Malolo Barrier Reef: 139–140
Namena Barrier Reef: 293
Namenalala Island: 293
Navula Reef: 139
Nukubati Island: 280
Rainbow Reef: 303, 305
sealife habitat: 12–13
South Mana Reef: 140
Taveuni: 5, 300–316
Tavewa Island: 246–248

Rewa River Bridge: 206
rice: 34
river tours: 172–173, 209
Robinson Crusoe Island: 153
Rotuma: 317–318, 325–327; map 326
Royal Suva Yacht Club: 183, 201
rugby: 56, 186, 230
running: 57

S

safety issues: car travel 111–113; crime 48, 79; dehydration 76; drinking water 77; health issues 76–78; money 71; scuba diving/snorkeling 13–14, 53, 305; sealife 13–14; women travelers 79, 111
sailing: see yachting
Sailors Home: 264
St. John's College: 265
St. Joseph's Church (Naililili): 207
salato: 11
Salia: 295
Salialevu: 313
sandalwood: 17–18

Savage, Charles: 18, 274
Savua, Isikia: 31
Savuione Falls: 235
Savulevu Yavonu Falls: 310
Savusavu: 286–293; maps 287, 288
Sawaieke: 272
Sawa-I-Lau Island: 251–252
Sawana: 318
scorpions: 16
sea cucumbers: 14, 18
sealife: 12–14
seaplanes: 174
Seashell Cove: 138–139
seasickness: 76–77
sea snakes: 15, 271
seasons: 8–9, 57, 86–87, 106
sea turtles: 15, 58, 155, 247, 254; see also turtles
sea urchins: 14
self-guided tours: 134
Seniloli, Ratu Jope: 28–29, 31
seniors: 101
Seseleka: 278, 279
Shangri-La's Fijian Resort: 153, 155

Scuba Diving/Snorkeling

general information: 52–54
Beqa Island: 175–176
Blue Lagoon: 246
Caqalai Island: 271
Coral Coast: 153, 155
Frigate Passage: 153, 169, 175
Gau Island: 272–273
Great Astrolabe Reef: 255
health issues: 76
Kadavu: 255–259
Korolevu: 162–167
Korotogo: 160
Kuata Island: 241–242
Leleuvia Island: 271
Levuka: 267
Malololailai Island: 141
Mamanuca Group: 139–150
Matangi Island: 316
Nadi: 117, 138–139
Naigani Island: 272
Nananu-i-Ra Island: 215–216
Nanuya Lailai Island: 249–250

Nanuya Levu Island: 250
Natuvalo Bay: 244–245
Nukubati Island: 280
organized tours: 98–99, 102
Pacific Harbor: 169
Rainbow Reef: 303, 305
recompression facilities: 75, 202
safety issues: 13–14, 53, 305
Savusavu: 286–293
Sulfur Passage: 169
Suva: 185
Tailevu Coast: 214–215
Taveuni: 300–305
Tavewa Island: 246–248
Vanaira Bay: 295
Vanua Balavu Island: 320
Vatulele Island: 174
Wakaya Island: 274–275
Waya Island: 243–244
Wayasewa Island: 242–243
Yanuca Island: 175

shark-calling ritual: 323–324
sharks: 13–14, 139–140, 247, 305, 323–324
ships: general information 104–105, 108–109; Labasa 284–285; Levuka 269–270; Rotuma 327; Savusavu 292; Suva 203–205; Taveuni 302–303
shopping: general information 59; Nadi 129–130; Sigatoka 159; Suva 197; Taveuni 313; *see also* handicrafts
Sigatoka: 156–159; maps 154, 157
Sigatoka River Trek: 225–226; map 226
Sigatoka Sand Dunes: 51, 153, 155
sightseeing highlights: Fiji 49–52; Kadavu 254–255; Labasa 281; Lakeba Island 322; Lau Group 318–319; Lautoka 229–230; Levuka 262–267; Lomaiviti Group 261; Nadi 116, 117; northern Viti Levu 213; Pacific Harbor 168; Rotuma 325–326; Savusavu 287–288; southern Viti Levu 153; Suva 178–184; Taveuni 302; top ten sights 50; Vanua Levu 278
Sikh Temple: 229
Sisilo: 326
skinks: 15
skydiving: 119
Smith, Charles Kingsford: 180
snake cave: 214
Snake Island: 271
snakes: 15
Snake Temple: 281
soccer: 56, 186
social conditions: 41
Solmea Hill: 326
Somosomo (Gau Island): 272
Somosomo (Taveuni): 311
Sonaisali Island Resort: 137–138
Sororoa Bluff: 326
South Mana Reef: 140
South Pacific Distilleries: 227, 229
South Sea Island: 145
souvenirs: 59
Speight, George: 27–32, 182–183
Sri Krishna Kaliya Temple: 229–230, 233
Sri Siva Subrahmaniya Swami Temple: 116, 117
stalactites: 214
stamps, commemorative: 197
starfish: 14
stingray spearing: 47
Stone Bowl, The: 224
stone bridge (Rotuma): 326

Surfing

general information: 54
airline regulations for surfboards: 95
Beqa Island: 175–176
Frigate Passage: 153, 169, 175
Great Astrolabe Reef: 255
Great Sea Reef: 280, 281
Kabara: 324
Kadavu: 255
Korolevu: 164–166
Kulukulu: 156
Mamanuca Group: 139, 142–145
Nadi: 117, 138
Natadola Beach: 152
organized tours: 99–100
Pacific Harbor: 169
Sulfur Passage: 169
surfboard storage at airports: 113
Suva: 185
Tavarua Island: 142–143
Yanuca Island: 174–175

---

stonefish: 14
student fares: 87–88
sugarcane: 12
sugar industry: general information 33–34; Ba 222; Indian immigrants 20–21; Lautoka 227, 229; Nausori 206; Rakiraki 218; sugar mill process 34; Taveuni 313; Vanua Levu 280–281
Sukuna Park: 180
Sukuna, Ratu Sir Lala: 22, 322
Sulfur Passage: 169
Sumi: 326
sunburn: 77–78
Sunday *puja*: 233
Supermarket: 139
Susui Island: 319
Suva: 9, 177–206; maps 179, 187, 192
Suva Cemetery: 183
Suva Point: 182
Suva Prison: 183
Suvavou: 183
swimming pools: 186, 272, 281
Syria Monument: 206

T

tabua: 46–47
Tabua, Inoke: 22
Tailevu Coast: 213–214
tanoa: 45–47, 57, 324
Tanoa, Chief: 208
tapa cloth: 58, 174, 324
taro: 66–67
Tasman, Abel: 16, 302
Taukei movement: 22–23, 27
Tavarua Island: 142–143
Taveuni: 5, 300–316; map 301, 304
Taveuni's Time Line: 310
Tavewa Island: 246–248; map 246
Tavua: 220; map 221
Tavuki: 254
Tavuni Hill Fort: 153
taxes: 24, 59, 71, 114
taxis: general information 110–111; Lautoka 234; Levuka 270; Savusavu 292; Suva 205–206; Taveuni 303
team sports: 56
telephone service: 71–73, 200, 313
television: 74
temperature: 8–10
tennis: 186
Three Sisters Hill: 281
Thurston Botanical Gardens: 181
Thurston, John: 20
timber industry: 35
time: 84
tipping: 71, 111
Toberua Island: 208–209
toilets: Labasa 284; Lautoka 233; Levuka 269; Nadi 132; Savusavu 291; Suva 201
Tokoriki Island: 149–150
Tokou: 267
Tonga: 19, 41
Tora, Apisai: 22, 23, 27
Totoya: 325
tourism industry: 37–39
tourist information: general information 68; Lautoka 233; Levuka 269; Nadi 130; Suva 198; Yasawa Group 238
tours: *see* organized tours
Town Cemetery (Levuka): 267
Town Hall (Levuka): 263
trade winds: 9, 106
traditional foods: 66–67
trains: 152, 155, 229

transportation: *see specific types*
Trans-Viti Levu Trek: 209–211
travel agencies: 68, 130, 199
traveler's checks: 70–71, 82, 199
travel insurance: 75–76
travel tips: 48
Treasure Island: 145–146
Triangle, The: 180
Trunk Radio System (TRS): 72
Tubou: 322
Tuivaga, Timoci: 31
Tunnels of Levuka: 265
Turtle Island: 238, 250–251
turtles: general information 15, 58; Kadavu 254; Namotu Island 139; Sigatoka Sand Dunes 155; Tavewa Island 247; turtle calling 12, 254
Twain, Mark: 18

UV

Udreudre, Ratu: 218
Udu Point: 285
Uluinavatu: 218
Uluiqalau: 300
University of the South Pacific: 183, 198
vaccinations: 69, 79
Vaileka: 218
Vaioa Beach: 326
Vakatora, Tomasi: 25
valuables: 79, 82
value-added tax (VAT): 24, 59, 71
Vanaira Bay: 295
Vanua Balavu Island: 318–320; map 319
Vanua Levu: 5, 276–299; map 277
Vanua Vatu: 324
Vatia Point: 223
Vatukarasa: 162
Vatukoula: 220–222
Vatulele: 273
Vatulele Island: 174
Vatu Vara: 321
Vatuvula Peak: 242–243
vegetation: 11–12
Vereni Falls: 235
Vidawa Rainforest Hike: 309
videotapes: 84
vidi vidi: 283
village stays: 63–65
visas: 69
Viseisei village: 135–137

Viti Levu: 5, 151–176, 212–226; *see also* Lautoka; Nadi; Suva
Viwa Island: 208
volcanism: 2, 5; *see also specific place*
voltage: 84
Vomo Island: 150
Vuna: 314
Vunidawa: 209
Vunisea: 254

W

Wadigi Island: 146
Waikama: 272
Waikana Falls: 254
Wailagi Lala: 321
Wainaloka: 267
Wainibau Falls: 309–310
Wainibuku River: 212–213
Wainimakutu: 211
Wainimala River: 209–211
Waiqa Gorge: 209
Waiqele hot springs: 281
Wairiki: 311
Waisali Nature Reserve: 287–288
Waitabu Marine Park: 309
Waitavala Sliding Rocks: 310–311
Waitovu: 265
Waiyevo: 310
Wakaya Island: 274–275
waterfalls: Bouma National Heritage Park 308–310; Gau Island 273; Kadavu 254; Korolevu 163, 164; Koroyanitu National Heritage Park 235; Pacific Harbor 172–173; Suva 184; Tailevu Coast 214
Waya Island: 243–244; map 242
Wayalevu: 243

Wayasewa Island: 242–243; map 242
weather: 8–11, 106
weaving: 58
Whippy, David: 18, 274
white-water rafting: 55, 173
wildflowers: 302
Wilkes, Charles: 18, 208, 318
Williams, John Brown: 18, 182, 264
winds: *see* trade winds
windsurfing: 54–55, 156, 174, 250
wood carvings: 57, 324
World War II: British six-inch guns 136, 138; historical background 21; Mamanuca Group 140; Rabi Island 295–298; Suva 180; Viseisei village 136
World Wide Fund for Nature: 199

XYZ

Yacata Island: 321
yachting: general information 55, 105–107; Lautoka 233–234; Malololailai Island 141–142; permits 69; ports of entry 69; quarantine checks 291–292; Savusavu 287, 291–292; Suva 200, 201; tours 102–103
Yadua: 273
Yaduatabu Island: 279
Yagasa Cluster: 324
Yalobi: 243
Yanuca Island: 174–175
Yanuca Lailai Island: 272
yaqona: see kava
Yaqona ceremony: 45–47
Yasawa Group: 5, 237–252; map 239
Yasawa Island: 252
yavirau: 47
Yawe District: 254

Acknowledgments

The nationalities of those listed below are identified by the following signs which follow their names: au (Australia), ca (Canada), dk (Denmark), fj (Fiji), nl (Netherlands), nz (New Zealand), and us (United States).

The antique engravings by M. G. L. Domeny de Rienzi are from the classic three-volume work *Océanie ou Cinquième Partie du Monde* (Paris: Firmin Didot Frères, 1836).

Special thanks Dr. Patrick D. Nunn (fj) of the University of the South Pacific for reading and correcting parts of the main introduction, to Dulcie Wong (ca) and Barbara Gaston (us) for updating airfares, to Alan Howard (us) and Kim Birkedahl (dk) for information on Rotuma, to Carolyn Fotofili (fj) for updating Vanua Balavu, and to Wouter Adamse (nl) for a detailed report on his trip.

Thanks to all of the following readers who took the trouble to write us letters about their trips: Susan Bejeckian (us), Andrew Brown (fj), Ed Candela (us), Les Charters (nz), Larry J. Cohen (au), Tony Cottrell (fj), Nancy Daniels (us), Steve Evers (us), Warren Francis (fj), Bob Goddess (us), Chris Godfrey (ca), Scott Graham (fj), Merrill Hartman (us), Bob Hirsch (us), Suein Hwang (us), Carole Jacobs (us), Lindsay Johnson (us), Stacey King (au), Viola Koch (fj), Steve Maurer (us), Melissa McCoy (us), Rich McIntyre (us), Jibralta Merrill (us), Paul and Cheryl Negro (fj), Erica Noorlander (nl), Pat O'Connell (us), Ivan Pisoni (fj), Brian Rutherford (au), Helen Sykes (fj), and Sara Tatro (us).

All of their comments have been incorporated into the volume you're now holding. To have your own name included here in the next edition, write: David Stanley, *Moon Handbooks Fiji*, Avalon Travel Publishing, 1400 65th St., Suite 250, Emeryville, CA 94608, U.S.A., atpfeedback@avalonpub.com.

Hotel keepers, tour operators, and divemasters are also encouraged to send us current information about their businesses. If you don't agree with what we've written, please tell us why—there's never any charge or obligation for a listing.

From the Author

While out researching my books, I find it cheaper to pay my own way, and you can rest assured that nothing in this book is designed to repay freebies from hotels, restaurants, tour operators, or airlines. I prefer to arrive unexpected and uninvited, and to experience things as they really are. On the road, I seldom identify myself to anyone. The essential difference between this book and the myriad travel brochures free for the taking at travel agencies and resorts throughout Fiji is that this book represents you, the traveler, while the brochures represent the travel industry. The companies and organizations included herein are there for informational purposes only, and a mention in no way implies an endorsement.

*S*tay in touch ...

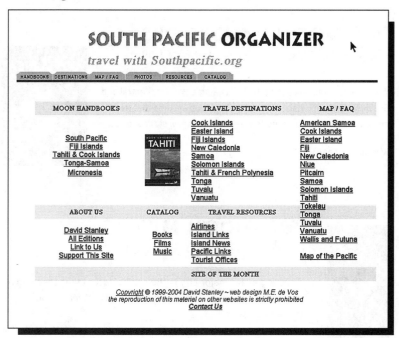

Southpacific.org takes you beyond Fiji to Tahiti and French Polynesia, the Cook Islands, Tonga, Samoa, Niue, New Caledonia, the Solomons, and everything in between.

Guidebook writer David Stanley's personal website provides mini-guides to South Pacific destinations, island maps, listings of films, music, and books, FAQs, and links to numerous other travel sites.

www.southpacific.org

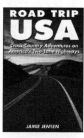

U.S.~Metric Conversion

1 inch	=	2.54 centimeters (cm)
1 foot	=	.304 meters (m)
1 yard	=	0.914 meters
1 mile	=	1.6093 kilometers (km)
1 km	=	.6214 miles
1 fathom	=	1.8288 m
1 chain	=	20.1168 m
1 furlong	=	201.168 m
1 acre	=	.4047 hectares
1 sq km	=	100 hectares
1 sq mile	=	2.59 square km
1 ounce	=	28.35 grams
1 pound	=	.4536 kilograms
1 short ton	=	.90718 metric ton
1 short ton	=	2000 pounds
1 long ton	=	1.016 metric tons
1 long ton	=	2240 pounds
1 metric ton	=	1000 kilograms
1 quart	=	.94635 liters
1 US gallon	=	3.7854 liters
1 Imperial gallon	=	4.5459 liters
1 nautical mile	=	1.852 km

To compute Celsius temperatures, subtract 32 from Fahrenheit and divide by 1.8. To go the other way, multiply Celsius by 1.8 and add 32.

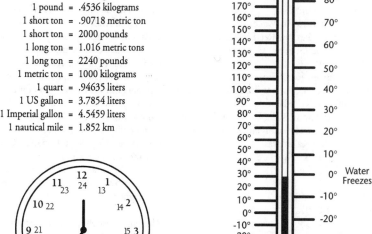

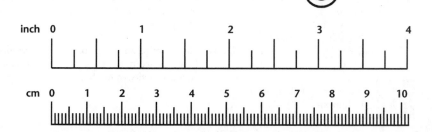

Keeping Current

Although we strive to produce the most up-to-date guidebook humanly possible, change is unavoidable. Between the time this book goes to print and the moment you read it, a handful of the businesses noted in these pages will undoubtedly change prices, move, or even close their doors forever. Other worthy attractions will open for the first time. If you have a favorite gem you'd like to see included in the next edition, or see anything that needs updating, clarification, or correction, please drop us a line. Send your comments via email to atpfeedback@avalonpub.com, or use the address below.

Moon Handbooks Fiji
Avalon Travel Publishing
1400 65th Street, Suite 250
Emeryville, CA 94608, USA
www.moon.com

Editor: Grace Fujimoto
Series Manager: Kevin McLain
Copy Editor: Matthew Reed Baker
Production and Graphics Coordinator:
    Justin Marler
Cover Designer: Kari Gim
Interior Designers: Amber Pirker, Alvaro
    Villanueva, Kelly Pendragon
Map Editor: Naomi Adler Dancis, Olivia Solís
Cartographers: Mike Morgenfeld, Suzanne
    Service, Kat Kalamaras
Proofreader: Erika Howsare
Indexer: Judy Hunt

ISBN: 1-56691-497-3
ISSN: 1534-049X

Printing History
1st Edition—1985
7th Edition—September 2004
5 4 3 2 1

Text and maps © 2004 by David Stanley.
All rights reserved.

Some photos and illustrations are used by permission and are the property of the original copyright owners.

Avalon Travel Publishing
An Imprint of
Avalon Publishing Group, Inc.

AVALON
publishing group incorporated

Front cover photo: © Ron Dahlquist/pacific
    stock.com
Table of contents photos: © David Stanley

Printed in USA by Malloy

No subscription fees or payments in services have been received from any of the tourism operators included in this book.